Selecting Plants
PACIFIC NORTHWEST GARDENS

Joe Seals

"Right plant, right place." ~~ Beth Chatto (along with many others in many other ways).

"Define the place and then find a plant to fit that place." ~~ Joe Seals

ISBN: 9798596468861

First Edition. Revised with corrections, updates, June 2022

Printed in the United States of America

Acknowledgements

Shout out to my "crew" (my PNW gardener-advisors): Cherry Adair, Erin Albers, Karin Duval, Erica Browne Grivas, Lars Holmberg, Aida Mengistu, Tiffany O'Brien, Sandy George Rankin, Jessica Roach, Aline So, and Ann Wiggins. They lent their invaluable insight about the content of this book.

All photos and illustrations used for this book are copyright-, license-, and royalty-free downloads.

INTRO

The plants collected in this book are appropriate to the Pacific Northwest, west of the Cascades, from southwest British Columbia through western Washington and western Oregon, not including the higher mountain regions (Coast Ranges and Olympic Mountains). This is generally referred to as USDA Zone 8b (higher areas or areas farther from water may be 8a; while areas around Portland and south may have become Zone 9 with the changing climate) and as ***Sunset Western Garden Book*** Zones 5 (coastal and around the Sound) and 6 (Oregon's Willamette Valley and surrounds). Almost all will also grow in Sunset's Zone 4 with the exception of the marginally hardy "Tropicalesque" plants (in the "Styles & Themes" section).

The purpose of this collection is twofold.

First and foremost, it is to provide a methodology for finding the best plant for the place. This is the concept of ***"right plant, right place."*** The most successful gardens and landscapes are based on the process of defining the environment (the "place") first and then finding the "plant" or "plants" which fit that defined environment.

Second, it is to illustrate the great wealth of plant material which we PNW'ers use and can use in our gardens and landscapes. At the risk of overwhelming the reader, I've tried to be comprehensive in the offerings here (and yet I know I'm still missing a great many plants). This is to break the "gardener's block" of frustratingly throwing up one's hands when faced with the common situations of "too shady, too wet" or "flowers in summer and then nothing the rest of the year." Hence why I show several plants for each situation and, when the situation is complex (such as sandy soil which is dry which needs a spring blooming plant), the overlap of lists will provide at least one or two or 100 plant candidates. "Expanding horizons" and all that.

I've consciously chosen a succinct breadth of selection over conciseness. This breadth has run to nearly 500 pages. Hence why no photos (aside from the token bits of art at the beginning of each major section), nor excessive symbols/codes/keys, nor annotations, nor sub-lists within sub-lists. Otherwise this book would have to be four times this size and even then, I would have to be frustratingly discriminating about which photos and notes are selected. A plant encyclopedia this is not. This is an old-school process, the forerunner to today's on-line "databases" and "apps."

Another reason for the expansive lists is to make sure that something is available. Retail garden centers and mail-order nurseries can carry only so many plants. And all of them run out of product on a regular basis. It's nice to have a Plan B, and maybe a Plan C, D, E, F, etc.

Speaking of availability, the list of sources on the last pages includes suppliers which, as a whole and combined with retail stores, offer up pretty much everything in these lists. In fact, a hefty chunk of the lists were compiled from the catalogs of these listed companies.

There are several ways to use this list of lists. The best way to get to the plant or plants which will fit a particular situation is to create a list of priorities and work down the line of those priorities, in order of their importance, going from a list which addresses the first of one's priorities and subsequently visiting lists which address the other priorities.

The very general criteria which should be considered in plant selection are, in no particular order of importance:

- Basic type (tree, shrub, perennial, etc.)
- Native or not
- Size (height and/or spread)
- Sun/shade
- Soil type
- Bloom time
- Pests/problems
- Ornamental features
- Design style

Of course, your only criteria may be that you need a tree and that leaves four longish lists: "Choice Native Trees," "Medium to Large Trees," "Small to Medium Flowering Trees," and "Non-Flowering Small Trees." If you want, you can throw in "Smallest Trees (Actually Tallest Shrubs)." For some gardeners, it might be easier to go to the more discriminating, "short cut" lists such as "An English Cottage Style Garden" or "Rock Garden Plants" (certainly not for "trees").

From whichever angle you take, you will probably be left with several choices. That's a good thing. The very last section of this book offers instructions for effectively and efficiently finding accurate photos and info on the internet to help boil down the choices.

With all the preceding said, may I suggest the reader first peruse the entire book, from start to finish, to get an overview of exactly what's available and to see how many "angles" there are to look at plant selection and landscape design.

For those who like the idea of hardcopy gardening reference books in hand, there is one recommendation for a book which comes as close as possible to offering up everything you need to know: *"The Sunset Western Garden Book."*

Plants in this book are listed by their *botanical names* first (with the exception of "ORNAMEDIBLES"). For lots of good reasons but I won't get into that. Bottom line, if you want to find more information about any plant including good photos, it's much better to use the botanical name than the common name. The botanical names herein are *italicized*, as per scientific custom, while the common names, which follow the botanical name, are ALL CAPS.

Speaking of botanical names, I've done my best to use the most up-to-date nomenclature for all species listed. There's still a handful in here where the scientific naming is in flux. As far as common names go, I've had to make up quite a few, simply because many plants have no common names (one of the "good reasons" as mentioned above).

Some abbreviations used throughout:

ssp. = *subspecies*, a population within a species but differing from the defined population, compounded by a geographical gap. Not to be confused with *"spp."* which is the abbreviation for the plural of species; this latter indication has been spelled out, as needed, to avoid confusion.

var. = *variety*, a variation occurring in nature throughout the geographic range of the species. The term "variety" as used by almost every gardener, by the way, should more accurately be indicated as *"cultivar"* (short for cultivated variety).

f. = an uncommonly used abbreviation, both in real life and in this list. It stands for *"form"* (technically "forma"), a rank one step down from variety which occurs sporadically within any population and is further reproduced only by nursery growers.

This book is divided into eight basic sections with each section divided into chapters, each chapter being a list and sometimes divided into sub-lists. The sections, based on your approach to selection, are:

1. PNW Native Plants — starting with the idea that you want native plants for your landscape.

2. Basic Plants — you want a basic plant type such as a tree, a shrub, a perennial, and so on.

3. Site Specific — you have defined environmental conditions to consider.

4. A Calendar of Bloom — you want something which blooms at a given time of year. Includes a calendar for sowing flower seeds.

5. Problem Areas, Plant Problems — you have a problem or potential problem which may limit or influence selection.

6. Special Gardens, Special Plants — you wish to create a particular kind of garden or want a particularly talented plant.

7. Ornamental Features — you want a specific look in a plant, such as bloom color, foliage color or texture, bark, berries, etc.

8. Styles & Themes — you want an overall look or "message" to your landscape.

Additionally there are two last sections to help you make a final decision:

9. Sources — mail-order companies for seeds, plants, bulbs.

10. How to Find Plant Photos & Information — step by step to researching plants.

Plus an **Index** to provide you with another, more honed way to search for plants.

A CALENDAR OF BLOOM 139

PROBLEM AREAS, PLANT PROBLEMS 175

SPECIAL GARDENS, SPECIAL PLANTS   221

ORNAMENTAL FEATURES   279

PNW NATIVE PLANTS

In a sense, these are the best fit for the "place." The species and their selections within these first lists are the "choice" native plants — the ones which perform well, maintain a pleasing habit, and/or bloom (if such is their nature) as freely as cultivated garden plants. Some of these are nice enough to be used as "specimen plants" (a single individual meant to be the focus of a landscape view). There are no hybrids here aside from "natural hybrids." The named selections ("cultivars") were originally taken from plants in the wild. To be fair, I have included a handful of iconic native plants — madrone, for instance — which aren't necessarily the easiest of garden plants; but they do have a unique beauty despite their intolerance of cultivation.

Keep in mind that just because it is "native" doesn't mean that it is perfect for any spot in your garden. Just as with any ornamental plant, natives have their specific needs. Many natives are riparian species, hence they require wet conditions. Many are dryland species (yes, there are dry spots in the PNW), hence they are the ones that will best fit the drier areas of the garden.

Native plants, the term used for the purposes of this book, indicates those plants which have evolved in this bioregion (within the political boundaries of southwest British Columbia, Washington, and Oregon) with the other native plants since the last glacial period. Although this book is intended for gardens west of the Cascades and not including any mountain gardens, some of the native plants here are from mountainous regions, as well as from the warmer, drier eastern part of our states.

NATIVE TREES

EVERGREEN CONIFERS

Abies amabilis	PACIFIC SILVER FIR
Abies grandis	GRAND FIR
Selection: 'Johnsonii' (narrow)	
Abies lasiocarpa var. *lasiocarpa*	MT. HOOD SUBALPINE FIR
Abies procera	NOBLE FIR

   Selections: 'Glauca' (bluish foliage),
   'Sherwoodi' (yellowish foliage).

Callitropsis (Chamaecyparis, Cupressus) nootkatensis	ALASKA YELLOW-CEDAR

   Selections: 'Glauca' (blue foliage, smaller habit),
   'Pendula (exaggerated weepiness),
   'Van den Akker' (extremely narrow).

Calocedrus decurrens	INCENSE-CEDAR
Chamaecyparis lawsoniana	PORT ORFORD CEDAR

   Selections: 'Alumii' (to about 50 feet high, narrow conical-upright, needles blue-green
   to gray-blue, bears few cones),
   'Dik's Weeping' (extremely narrow, branches drooping). Buy on CFI rootstock.

Juniperus occidentalis var. *occidentalis*	WESTERN JUNIPER
Picea breweriana	BREWER'S WEEPING SPRUCE
Picea sitchensis	SITKA SPRUCE
Pinus contorta ssp. *contorta*	SHORE PINE
Pinus contorta ssp. *latifolia*	LODGEPOLE PINE
Pinus contorta ssp. *murrayana*	TAMARACK PINE
Pinus monticola	WESTERN WHITE PINE
Selection: 'Pendula' (weeping branches, needs to be staked)	
Pseudotsuga menziesii	DOUGLAS-FIR

   Selections: var. *glauca* (naturally-occurring form with bluish-green needles, more
   compact with branches that are upright than the species; more drought-tolerant),
   'Blue' (very blue needles),
   'Fastigiata' (distinctly upright, forming a spire),
   'Graceful Grace' (weeping form with gracefully-drooping, lax branches).

Thuja plicata	WESTERN RED-CEDAR

   Selections: 'Excelsa' (50 x 20 feet),
   'Green Giant' (most likely a hybrid; fast-growing, reaching 50-feet tall x 10 feet wide),
   'Hogan' (compact, dense narrow habit),
   'Virescens' (slightly narrower habit than species)

Tsuga heterophylla	WESTERN HEMLOCK
Selection: 'Iron Springs' (slow-growing, broad upright)	
Tsuga mertensiana	MOUNTAIN HEMLOCK

BROAD-LEAVED EVERGREENS

Arbutus menziesii — MADRONE
Chrysolepis chrysophylla — GOLDEN CHINQUAPIN
Notholithocarpus densiflorus — TANBARK OAK
Quercus chrysolepis — CANYON LIVE OAK
Quercus garryana — GARRY OAK
Rhododendron macrophyllum (a tree with age) — PACIFIC RHODODENDRON
   A handful of vegetatively-propagated selections are available
Umbellularia californica — OREGON MYRTLE, CALIFORNIA BAY LAUREL

DECIDUOUS

Acer circinatum — VINE MAPLE
   Selections (tree-scale): 'Monroe' (cut-leaf),
   'Pacific Fire' (fiery bark, autumn color),
   plus several dwarf forms that are anything but tree-like.
Acer glabrum var. *douglasii* — DOUGLAS' MAPLE
Acer macrophyllum — BIG-LEAF MAPLE
   Selections: 'Rubrum' ("Bigleaf Rubrum;" red leaves),
   'Seattle Sentinel' (unusually upright),
   'Kimballiae' (very deeply cut leaves; much slower growing than the species).
Alnus rhombifolia — WHITE ALDER
Amelanchier alnifolia — WESTERN SERVICEBERRY, JUNEBERRY, SASKATOON
   Selection: 'Altaglow' (columnar to narrow conical, over 20 feet, bright autumn foliage);
   selected from a wild plant and is tree form.
Betula papyrifera — PAPER BIRCH
   Selection: 'Snowy' (handsome white bark and purported resistance to borers).
Fraxinus latifolia — OREGON ASH
Larix occidentalis (a deciduous conifer) — WESTERN LARCH
Quercus kelloggii — KELLOGG BLACK OAK
Rhamnus (Frangula) purshiana — CASCARA

NATIVE SHRUBS

Abies amabilis   PACIFIC SILVER FIR
  Selections: 'Compacta' (very dwarf, very slow);
  'Spreading Star' (3 feet high and spreading)
Abies procera   NOBLE FIR
  Selections: 'Blaue Hexe' (dwarf, blue foliage),
  'Glauca Prostrata' (low-spreading, blue foliage),
  'Jeddeloh' (very dwarf, blue foliage)
Acer circinatum   VINE MAPLE
  Selections (shrub-scale): 'Baby Buttons' (2x2, dense),
  'Bort's Broom' (4', bronze to red foliage),
  'Burgundy Jewel' (6', burgundy red foliage),
  'Del's Dwarf' (6', bronze-orange leaves, fall color),
  'Ki Setsudoe' (12' multi, coppery-orange, more deeply cut leaves),
  'Little Gem' (3', dense rounded, small leaves),
  'Pacific Sprite' (6x2, dense, upright, golden fall color),
  'Sunglow' (6', foliage apricot/peach changing to lime-chartreuse-yellow)
Amelanchier alnifolia   WESTERN SERVICEBERRY, JUNEBERRY, SASKATOON
  Selections: 'Regent' (compact shrub, vigorous, sweet fruit),
  'Thiessen' (oval to round shape, to about 15 feet tall; largest fruit)
Arctostaphylos columbiana   HAIRY MANZANITA
Arctostaphylos x *media*   MEDIA MANZANITA
  Selections: 'Lolo' (small shrub to 18 inches tall with wider spread, burnished red stems, pink
       flowers winter-spring),
  'Martha Ewan' (deep green foliage, vigorous, mounding habit)
Arctostaphylos uva-ursi   KINNIKINNICK
  Selections: 'Massachusetts' (disease resistant, smaller leaves than the species),
  'Point Reyes' (deep-green foliage color, more heat and drought tolerant),
  'Vancouver Jade' (larger, glossier leaves, more vigorous; foliage develops wine
  color in the fall)
Ceanothus thyrsiflorus   BLUE BLOSSOM
  Selections: 'El Dorado' (upright 8 feet, variegated foliage), many more
Cercis occidentalis   WESTERN REDBUD
Chamaecyparis lawsoniana   PORT ORFORD CEDAR
  Many good selections on CF1 rootstock
Cornus sericea (C. stolonifera) including ssp. *occidentalis*   RED-TWIG DOGWOOD
  Selections: 'Baileyi' (bright red stems, clumping instead of spreading habit),
  'Cardinal' (bright red stems in winter, fairly disease resistant, 10-feet tall and wide),
  'Flamiramia' (golden-yellow stems),
  'Isanti' (6', dense growth),
  'Silver and Gold' (stems are yellow, variegated leaves)
Fraxinus latifolia   OREGON ASH
Frangula (Rhamnus) purshiana   CASCARA
Garrya elliptica   COAST SILK TASSEL
Gaultheria shallon   SALAL
  Selection: 'Cascade Sunrise' (bright orange-red new growth),
Holodiscus discolor   OCEAN SPRAY

Juniperus communis   COMMON JUNIPER
   Native natural varieties include *depressa, kellyi, saxatilis (jackii);* all prostrate.
Larix occidentalis (a deciduous conifer)
   Shrubby selection: 'Bollinger'   BOLLINGER WESTERN LARCH
Lonicera ciliosa (vine)   ORANGE HONEYSUCKLE
Mahonia aquifolium   OREGON-GRAPE
   Selections: 'Apollo' (1.5 feet x 5 feet+), 'Compacta' (2-3 feet high, liberally spreading),
   'Golden Abundance' (golden foliage, sun tolerant), 'Mayhan Strain' (2.5-3.5 feet),
   'Orange Flame' (5 feet, new leaves bronzy-orange, then glossy green, wine red in winter).
Mahonia nervosa   CASCADE OREGON-GRAPE
Mahonia piperiana   PIPER'S OREGON-GRAPE
Monardella villosa ssp. *franciscana*   COYOTE MINT
   Selection: 'Russian River' (more vigorous than species)
Notholithocarpus densiflorus var. *echinoides*   SHRUB TANOAK
Oplopanax horridus   DEVIL'S CLUB
Paxistima (Pachystima) myrsinites   OREGON BOXWOOD
Penstemon serrulatus   COAST PENSTEMON
Philadelphus lewisii   PACIFIC MOCK ORANGE
   Selection: 'Goose Creek' (double-flowered form).
Physocarpus capitatus   PACIFIC NINEBARK
   Selection: 'Tilden Park' (2 to 3 feet tall, and wide-spreading).
Picea sitchensis   SITKA SPRUCE
   Selection: 'Papoose' (slow-growing compact dwarf, blue-green foliage).
Pinus monticola   WESTERN WHITE PINE
   Selection: 'Nana' (2x2, compact)
Quercus garryana var. *breweri*   BREWER'S OAK
Quercus vacciniifolia   HUCKLEBERRY OAK
Rhododendron macrophyllum   PACIFIC RHODODENDRON
   A handful of vegetatively-propagated selections are available
Rhododendron occidentale   WESTERN AZALEA
   Selections: 'Leonard Frisbee' (4 x 4 feet, flowers light red with an orange-yellow flare),
   'Rouge River Belle' (flowers white with pink markings, yellow blotch),
   'Stagecoach Frills' (flowers white, strong yellow blotch, frilled margins)
Rhododendron 'Oregon Queen' (natural hybrid of *R. macrophyllum* X *R. occidentale*)
                                                       AZALEODENDRON
Rhus glabra   SMOOTH SUMAC
   Selection: 'Laciniata' (cut-leaf form)
Ribes aureum   GOLDEN CURRANT
Ribes sanguineum   RED-FLOWERING CURRANT
   Selections: 'Elk River Red' (red flowers; 8 to 10 × 7 feet),
   'Heart's Delight' (long racemes of deep rosy pink; 6 feet or more),
   'King Edward VII' (pinkish-red flowers, more compact than the type, 7 × 7 feet),
   'Pokey's Pink' (light pink flowers, 6-8 × 6 feet)
   'Spring Showers' (pink flowers, blooms a little later than 'Elk River Red', 6-8 × 6 feet),
   'White Icicle' (white flowers, blooms early, compact, 6-8 × 6 feet)
Sambucus racemosa   RED ELDERBERRY
   Sambucus racemosa var. *arborescens* (more treelike),
   Sambucus racemosa var. *racemosa* (red berries), var. *melanocarpa* (black berries),
Sorbus sitchensis   SITKA MOUNTAIN-ASH

Spiraea betulifolia   WHITE SPIREA
     Selections: 'Tor' (dark green leaves, white flowers),
     'Glow Girl' (yellow-chartreuse foliage, white flowers),
     'Pink Sparkler' (blue-green leaves, pink flowers).
Spiraea splendens (S. densiflora)   ROSE MEADOWSWEET
Symphoricarpos albus   COMMON SNOWBERRY
Symphoricarpos mollis var. *hesperius*   CREEPING SNOWBERRY
Taxus brevifolia 'Nana'   DWARF PACIFIC YEW
Tsuga heterophylla   WESTERN HEMLOCK
     Selections: 'Thorsen's Weeping' (dwarf, low-spreading or, if staked, 5 feet tall, pendulous).
Tsuga mertensiana   MOUNTAIN HEMLOCK
     Selections: 'Bump's Blue' (small pyramidal shape, bluish foliage),
     'Elizabeth' (low-growing, spreading),
     'Glacier Peak' (compact growth, blue foliage)
Vaccinium ovatum   EVERGREEN HUCKLEBERRY
     Selections: 'Cascade Sunburst' (multi-colored variegation),
     'Scarlet Ovation' (intensely-colored new growth),
     'St. Andrews' (dwarf), 'Thunderbird' (fruitful).
Viburnum ellipticum   WESTERN WAYFARING TREE
Viburnum trilobum (V. opulus var. *americanum)*   AMERICAN CRANBERRYBUSH
     Selections: 'Compactum' (5 to 6 feet high and wide; fall color is yellow).

EDIBLE NATIVES FOR GARDEN, LANDSCAPE

I was hesitant to include this list. First, because I didn't want to encourage wild foraging — a practice that can sometimes reduce important food supplies for our wildlife, and misidentification can lead to health issues. Secondly, because taste is subjective and many of these vary in taste from plant to plant and tongue to tongue.

Amelanchier alnifolia   WESTERN SERVICEBERRY, JUNEBERRY, SASKATOON
Claytonia perfoliata   MINER'S LETTUCE
Corylus cornuta var. *californica*   HAZELNUT, FILBERT
Gaultheria shallon   SALAL
Mahonia aquifolium   OREGON-GRAPE
Malus fusca (tart)   PACIFIC CRABAPPLE
Ribes aureum var. *aureum*   GOLDEN CURRANT
Rubus leucodermis   BLACK RASPBERRY
Rubus parviflorus   THIMBLEBERRY
Rubus spectabilis (strong grower)   SALMONBERRY
Rubus ursinus   TRAILING BLACKBERRY
Sambucus nigra ssp. *caerulea*   BLUE ELDERBERRY
Vaccinium membranaceum   BLACK HUCKLEBERRY
Vaccinium ovalifolium   OVAL-LEAFED BLUEBERRY
Vaccinium ovatum   EVERGREEN HUCKLEBERRY
Vaccinium parvifolium (sour)   RED HUCKLEBERRY
Viburnum edule   HIGHBUSH CRANBERRY

NATIVE PLANTS
FOR GROUNDCOVER USE

Arctostaphylos x media   HYBRID MANZANITA
Arctostaphylos nevadensis   PINE-MAT MANZANITA
Arctostaphylos uva-ursi   KINNIKINNICK
    Selections: 'Massachusetts' (1 x 6, small leaves, tolerates wetness better than others),
    'Point Reyes' (compact, more heat and drought tolerant than others)
    'San Bruno Mountain' (1 x 6, vigorous, large-leaved, showy fruit)
Asarum caudatum   WILD GINGER
Asarum hartwegii   MARBLED WILD GINGER
Campanula rotundifolia   COMMON HAREBELL
Carex inops (C. pensylvanica)   CREEPING SEDGE
Carex obnupta   SLOUGH SEDGE
Carex pansa   DUNE SEDGE, MEADOW SEDGE
Carex praegracilis   FIELD SEDGE
Carex tumulicola   FOOTHILL SEDGE
Ceanothus prostratus   MAHALA MAT
Ceanothus pumilus   DWARF CARPET
Clinopodium (Micromeria, Satureja) douglasii   YERBA BUENA
Coptis asplenifolia   FERN-LEAF GOLDTHREAD
Erigeron glaucus   SEASIDE DAISY
Fragaria chiloensis   BEACH STRAWBERRY
Fragaria vesca ssp. *californica*   WOODLAND STRAWBERRY
Gaultheria ovatifolia   WESTERN TEABERRY
Gaultheria shallon   SALAL
    Selection: 'Cascade Sunrise' (bright orange-red new growth),
Juniperus communis   COMMON JUNIPER
Linnaea borealis   TWINFLOWER
Luetkea pectinata   PARTRIDGE-FOOT
Mahonia nervosa   CASCADE OREGON GRAPE
Mahonia repens   CREEPING BARBERRY
Maianthemum dilatatum   FALSE LILY-OF-THE-VALLEY
Oxalis oregana   REDWOOD SORREL
Sedum oreganum   OREGON STONECROP
Sedum oregonense   CREAMY-FLOWERED STONECROP
Sedum spathulifolium   BROAD-LEAF STONECROP
    Selections: 'Blood Red' (foliage heavily tinted with red),
    'Cape Blanco' (powdery white foliage),
    'Carnea' (gray foliage that turns deep red-maroon in winter),
    'Moon Glow' (dusky blue foliage),
    'Purpureum' (purple-tinged foliage)
Symphyotrichum (Aster) chilense 'Point Saint George'   TRAILING PACIFIC ASTER
Vancouveria hexandra   INSIDE-OUT FLOWER
Vancouveria chrysantha   SISKIYOU INSIDE-OUT FLOWER
Viola adunca   EARLY BLUE VIOLET
Whipplea modesta   WHIPPLEVINE, MODESTY VINE

NATIVE PERENNIALS

Actaea (Cimicifuga) elata	TALL BUGBANE
Adiantum aleuticum (A. pedatum)	MAIDENHAIR FERN

    Selections: 'Imbricatum' (compact dwarf), 'Subpumilum' (dwarf)

Aquilegia formosa	WESTERN COLUMBINE
Aconitum columbianum	COLUMBIAN MONKSHOOD
Adelinia (Cynoglossum) grande	GRAND HOUND'S TONGUE
Agastache occidentalis	WESTERN GIANT-HYSSOP
Androsace (Douglasia) laevigata	SMOOTH DOUGLASIA
Anemone multifida	PACIFIC ANEMONE, CUT-LEAF ANEMONE

    Selection: *A. m.* var. *saxicola* "Rubra" (Red Windflower)

Aruncus dioicus var. *acuminatus*	SYLVAN GOATSBEARD
Asarum marmoratum	MARBLED WILD GINGER
Athyrium filix-femina	LADY FERN

    Selections: 'Corymbiferum' (crested frond tips),
    'Frizelliae' (skinny fronds, condensed "beaded" foliage),
    'Howardii' (extra cut-leaf),
    'Plumosum Axminster' (full, fluffy foliage),
    'Prichardii Cristatum' (crinkly-crested foliage)

Balsamorhiza deltoidea	DELTOID BALSAMROOT, PUGET BALSAMROOT
Balsamorhiza incana	HOARY BALSAMROOT
Blechnum (Struthiopteris) spicant	DEER FERN
Calypso bulbosa	FAIRY SLIPPERS
Calystegia sepium ssp. *angulata*	HEDGE BINDWEED
Campanula rotundifolia	COMMON HAREBELL, BLUEBELLS
Clematis columbiana	ROCK CLEMATIS
Clematis hirsutissima var. *hirsutissima*	DOUGLAS CLEMATIS, HAIRY CLEMATIS
Chamaenerion (Epilobium) angustifolium	FIREWEED
Corydalis scouleri	SCOULER'S CORYDALIS
Cypripedium montanum	MOUNTAIN LADY'S-SLIPPERS
Darmera peltata 'Nana'	DWARF UMBRELLA PLANT
Delphinium nuttallii	NUTTALL'S LARKSPUR
Delphinium trolliifolium	COLUMBIAN LARKSPUR
Deschampsia caespitosa	TUFTED HAIRGRASS

    Selections: 'Gold Dew' (compact habit, buff-golden seed heads),
    'Northern Lights' (white variegated leaves with a pink blush during cool weather),
    'Bronze Veil' (larger than species, floriferous), 'Petite Fountain' (petite and neat)

Dicentra formosa	WESTERN BLEEDING HEART

    Selections *with white and green flowers*: 'Langtrees' (bluish-green leaves,
    'Pearl Drops'), 'Margaret Fish' (bluish-gray-green), 'Quicksilver' (bluish-gray-green)
    Selections with *pink and red flowers*: 'Bacchanal' (deep red flowers), 'Coldham' (deep
    burgundy), 'Luxuriant' (red flowers), 'Zestful' (deep rose-pink)

Dodecatheon austrofrigidum	FRIGID SHOOTING STAR
Dodecatheon cusickii	CUSICK'S SHOOTING-STAR
Dryopteris expansa (D. austriaca)	SHIELD FERN
Eriogonum latifolium	COAST BUCKWHEAT
Eriogonum ovalifolium	OVAL-LEAF BUCKWHEAT

Eriogonum umbellatum	SULPHUR BUCKWHEAT
Eriophyllum lanatum var. *integrifolium*	OREGON SUNSHINE
Eriophyllum lanatum var. *lanatum;* var. *leucophyllum*	WOOLLY SUNFLOWER
Erythranthe (Mimulus) guttatus	YELLOW MONKEYFLOWER
Erythranthe (Mimulus) lewisii	PINK MONKEYFLOWER
Eutrochium maculatum	JOE-PYE-WEED
Festuca idahoensis	IDAHO FESCUE

Selections: 'Joseph' (gray-blue-green, upright form; seed form),
'Little Bald Hills' (blue-gray, compact form), 'Muse Meadow' (blue, very small form),
'Stony Creek' (chalky blue, most sun tolerant), 'Warren Peak' (the bluest)

Fragaria chiloensis	BEACH STRAWBERRY
Gaillardia aristata	BLANKET FLOWER
Gymnocarpium dryopteris	WESTERN OAK FERN
Helenium autumnale	SNEEZEWEEDS
Helianthella uniflora var. *douglasii*	LITTLE SUNFLOWER
Iris douglasiana	DOUGLAS IRIS
Iris missouriensis	ROCKY MOUNTAIN IRIS
Iris tenax	OREGON IRIS, TOUGH-LEAF IRIS
Iris tenuis	CLACKAMAS IRIS
Juncus effusus	COMMON RUSH

Selections: 'Spiralis' (spiraled stalks),
'Big Twister' (giant version of previous)

Juncus patens	SPREADING RUSH

Selections: 'Elk Blue', 'Occidental Blue' (both blue-ish)

Lathyrus japonicus	BEACH PEA
Lewisia cotyledon	LEWISIA
Linnaea borealis	TWINFLOWER
Luina hypoleuca	SILVERBACK LUINA
Lupinus albicaulis	SICKLE-KEEL LUPINE
Lupinus latifolius	BROADLEAF LUPINE
Lupinus polyphyllus	BROADLEAF LUPINE
Lupinus sulphureus ssp. *kincaidii*	KINCAID'S LUPINE
Mertensia ciliata	FRINGED BLUEBELLS
Mertensia paniculata	TALL BLUEBELLS
Mertensia umbratilis	SHADE BLUEBELLS
Monardella odoratissima	MOUNTAIN COYOTE MINT, MOUNTAIN PENNYROYAL
Monardella purpurea	SISKIYOU MONARDELLA
Monardella sheltonii	SHELTON'S MONARDELLA
Olsynium (Sisyrinchium) douglasii var. *douglasii*	DOUGLAS' BLUE-EYED GRASS
Opuntia fragilis	BRITTLE PRICKLYPEAR
Oxalis oregana	REDWOOD SORREL
Pedicularis groenlandica	ELEPHANT-HEAD LOUSEWORT
Penstemon azureus	AZURE PENSTEMON
Penstemon cardwellii	CARDWELL'S PENSTEMON
Penstemon davidsonii	DAVIDSON'S PENSTEMON
Penstemon eatonii	FIRECRACKER PENSTEMON
Penstemon eriantherus var. *argillosus*	JOHN DAY FUZZY-TONGUE PENSTEMON
Penstemon euglaucus	GLAUCUS PENSTEMON
Penstemon gairdneri var. *gairdneri*	GAIRDNER'S BEARDTONGUE

Penstemon glandulosus var. *chelanensis*	CHELAN PENSTEMON
Penstemon newberryi	NEWBERRY'S PENSTEMON
Penstemon newberryi var. *berryi*	BERRY'S PENSTEMON
Penstemon parvulus	SMALL AZURE BEARDTONGUE
Penstemon procerus var. *procerus*	PINCUSHION BEARDTONGUE
Penstemon richardsonii var. *curtiflorus*	CURVED-CUT-LEAF BEARDTONGUE
Penstemon rupicola	ROCK PENSTEMON
Penstemon speciosus	ROYAL PENSTEMON
Phacelia sericea	SILKY PHACELIA
Phlox diffusa	SPREADING PHLOX
Polemonium elegans	ELEGANT JACOB'S LADDER, ELEGANT SKY PILOT
Polystichum munitum var. *munitum*	WESTERN SWORD FERN
Prosartes (Disporum) hookeri	HOOKER'S FAIRY BELLS
Salvia dorrii	PURPLE SAGE, DORR'S SAGE, MINT SAGE
Sanguisorba officinalis	GREAT BURNETT
Sedum oreganum	OREGON STONECROP
Sedum oregonense	CREAMY-FLOWERED STONECROP
Sedum spathulifolium	BROAD-LEAF STONECROP

Selections: 'Blood Red' (foliage heavily tinted with red),
'Cape Blanco' (powdery white foliage),
'Carnea' (gray foliage that turns deep red-maroon in winter),
'Moon Glow' (dusky blue foliage), 'Purpureum' (purple-tinged foliage)

Sidalcea campestris	MEADOW CHECKER MALLOW
Sidalcea cusickii	CUSICK'S CHECKER MALLOW
Sidalcea hendersonii	HENDERSON'S CHECKER-MALLOW
Sidalcea oregana	OREGON CHECKER-MALLOW
Silene acaulis	MOSS CAMPION
Sisyrinchium californicum	GOLDEN-EYED GRASS
Sisyrinchium idahoense	IDAHO BLUE-EYED GRASS
Solidago simplex ssp. *simplex* var. *nana*	DWARF GOLDENROD
Stenanthium occidentale	WESTERN FEATHERBELLS
Symphyotrichum (Aster) bracteolatum (S. eatonii)	OREGON ASTER
Symphyotrichum (Aster) jessicae	JESSICA'S ASTER
Symphyotrichum (Aster) laeve	SMOOTH ASTER

Selection: 'Bluebird' (larger flowers/clusters; 3 feet)

Symphyotrichum (Aster) lateriflorum	CALICO ASTER

Selection: 'Prince' (dark foliage, flowers with deep pink centers)

Symphyotrichum (Aster) subspicatum	DOUGLAS' ASTER
Synthyris (Veronica) cordata	HEART-LEAF SNOW QUEEN
Synthyris (Veronica) missurica ssp. *stellata*	COLUMBIA KITTEN-TAILS
Synthyris (Veronica) reniformis	SPRING QUEEN
Synthyris (Veronica) schizantha	FRINGED KITTEN-TAILS
Tellima grandiflora	FRAGRANT FRINGECUP
Thermopsis montana	MOUNTAIN GOLD-BANNER
Trautvetteria caroliniensis	FALSE BUGBANE
Viola adunca	EARLY BLUE VIOLET
Viola glabella	YELLOW STREAM VIOLET
Wyethia angustifolia	NARROWLEAF WYETHIA
Xerophyllum tenax	BEAR GRASS, INDIAN BASKET GRASS

NATIVE BULBS

Allium acuminatum	HOOKER'S ONION
Allium amplectens 'Graceful Beauty'	SLIM-LEAF ONION
Allium campanulatum	SIERRA ONION
Allium cernuum	NODDING ONION
Allium douglasii	DOUGLAS' ONION
Allium falcifolium	SICKLE-LEAF ONION
Allium geyeri var. *geyeri*	GEYER'S ONION
Allium lemmonii	LEMMON'S ONION
Allium nevii	NEVIUS' ONION
Bloomeria (Triteleia) crocea	GOLDEN STARS
Brodiaea coronaria	HARVEST BRODIAEA
Brodiaea elegans ssp. *hooveri*	HARVEST LILY
Brodiaea rosea	INDIAN VALLEY BRODIAEA
Calochortus coxii	COX'S MARIPOSA LILY
Calochortus elegans var. *elegans*	ELEGANT CAT'S EAR
Calochortus lyallii	LYALL'S STAR TULIP
Calochortus macrocarpus var. *macrocarpus*	SAGEBRUSH MARIPOSA LILY
Calochortus subalpinus	CASCADE MARIPOSA LILY
Calochortus tolmiei	TOLMIE'S CAT'S EAR
Calochortus umpquaensis	UMPQUA MARIPOSA LILY
Calochortus uniflorus	LARGE-FLOWERED STAR-TULIP
Camassia cusickii	CUSICK'S CAMAS

   Selection: 'Zwanenburg' (dark blue)

Camassia howellii	HOWELL'S CAMAS
Camassia leichtlinii	GREAT CAMAS

   C. leichtlinii var. *suksdorfii* (dark violet-blue)
   Selections: 'Blue Danube' (deep dusky lilac blue),
   'Blue Heaven' (pure sky blue),
   'Sacajawea' (cream flowers, variegated leaves),
   'Semiplena' (double-flowered form).

Camassia quamash	CAMAS

   C. quamash var. *maxima* ("Puget Blue"; very full flower stems),
   Selection: 'Blue Melody' (rich, dusky violet-blue)

Chlorogalum pomeridianum	WAVYLEAF SOAP PLANT
Dichelostemma capitatum ssp. *capitatum*	BLUEDICKS
Dichelostemma congestum	OOKOW, FIELD CLUSTER LILY, HARVEST LILY
Dichelostemma ida-maia	FIRECRACKER FLOWER
Dichelostemma x venustum	SNAKE-LILY
Erythronium elegans	COAST RANGE FAWN-LILY
Erythronium grandiflorum	YELLOW AVALANCHE-LILY, GLACIER LILY
Erythronium hendersonii	HENDERSON'S FAWN-LILY
Erythronium howellii	HOWELL'S FAWN-LILY
Erythronium klamathense	KLAMATH FAWN-LILY
Erythronium montanum	AVALANCHE-LILY
Erythronium oregonum ssp. oregonum	GIANT FAWN-LILY
Erythronium quinaultense	OLYMPIC FAWN-LILY, QUINAULT TROUT-LILY

Erythronium revolutum	MAHOGANY FAWN-LILY, COAST FAWN-LILY
Fritillaria affinis (F. lanceolata)	CHOCOLATE LILY
Fritillaria atropurpurea	SPOTTED FRITILLARY, SPOTTED MOUNTAIN BELLS
Fritillaria camschatcensis	INDIAN RICE
Fritillaria x gentneri	GENTNER'S FRITILLARY
Fritillaria glauca	SISKIYOU FRITILLARY
Fritillaria pudica	YELLOW BELLS
Fritillaria recurva	SCARLET FRITILLARY
Lilium bolanderi	BOLANDER'S LILY
Lilium columbianum	TIGER LILY
Lilium occidentale	WESTERN TIGER LILY
Lilium pardalinum ssp. *vollmeri*	LEOPARD LILY
Lilium washingtonianum	WASHINGTON'S LILY
Lilium washingtonianum ssp. *purpurascens*	PURPLE FLOWERED WASHINGTON LILY
Lloydia serotina	ALP LILY
Narthecium californicum	CALIFORNIA BOG ASPHODEL
Trillium albidum	GIANT WHITE WAKEROBIN
Trillium kurabayashii	GIANT PURPLE WAKEROBIN
Trillium ovatum	WESTERN WHITE TRILLIUM, WAKE ROBIN

Selections: several double-flowered forms exist.

Trillium parviflorum	SMALL-FLOWERED TRILLIUM
Triteleia bridgesii	BRIDGES' TRITELEIA
Triteleia grandiflora	LARGE-FLOWERED TRIPLET-LILY, WILD HYACINTH
Triteleia (Brodiaea) hyacinthina	WHITE TRIPLET-LILY
Triteleia ixioides	PRETTYFACE
Veratrum viride	INDIAN HELLEBORE

A PNW "MEADOW"

These are the plants native to various types of "meadows" throughout the PNW. They can be used to create that large sweep of herbaceous flowers (with some grasses) for that "wildflower" look so many want from a package of seed. Those marked ** are native to the lowland prairies on the west side of the Cascades.

Achillea millefolium	COMMON YARROW
Allium acuminatum	TAPER-TIP ONION
Allium cernuum	NODDING ONION **
Anaphalis margaritacea	PEARLY EVERLASTING
Aquilegia flavescens	GOLDEN COLUMBINE
Aquilegia formosa	RED COLUMBINE
Armeria maritima	SEA THRIFT **
Asclepias speciosa	SHOWY BUTTERFLYWEED
Balsamorhiza deltoidea	PUGET BALSAMROOT **
Brodiaea coronaria	CROWN BRODIAEA **
Brodiaea elegans	ELEGANT BRODIAEA
Camassia leichtlinii	GREAT CAMAS **
Camassia quamash	CAMASS **
Campanula rotundifolia	HAREBELLS
Carex densa	DENSE SEDGE **
Carex inops ssp. *inops*	LONG-STOLON SEDGE **
Carex tumulicola	FOOTHILL SEDGE **
Castilleja hispida	HARSH PAINTBRUSH **
Castilleja levisecta	GOLDEN PAINTBRUSH **
Chamaenerion (Epilobium, Chamaerion) angustifolium	FIREWEED
Delphinium menziesii	MENZIES LARKSPUR **
Delphinium nuttallii	NUTTALL'S LARKSPUR **
Deschampsia caespitosa	TUFTED HAIRGRASS **
Dodecatheon pulchellum	FEW-FLOWER SHOOTING STAR
Dodocatheon hendersonii	HENDERSON'S SHOOTING STAR **
Erigeron speciosus	SHOWY FLEABANE
Eriophyllum lanatum var. *lanatum;* var. *leucophyllum*	WOOLLY SUNFLOWER **
Festuca roemeri	ROEMER'S FESCUE
Fritillaria affinis	CHOCOLATE LILY **
Fritillaria pudica	YELLOW BELLS
Gaillardia aristata	BLANKET FLOWER
Geum trifolium	PRAIRIE SMOKE
Grindelia integrifolia	COASTAL GUMWEED
Helianthus bolanderi	BOLANDER'S SUNFLOWER
Ipomopsis aggregata	SKYROCKET, SCARLET GILIA
Iris douglasii	DOUGLAS IRIS **
Iris tenax	OREGON IRIS, TOUGH-LEAF IRIS **
Linum lewisii	WILD BLUE FLAX
Lithophragma pariflorurn	WOODLAND PRAIRIE STAR
Lomatium nudicaule	BARE-STEM BISCUITROOT **
Lomatium utriculatum	SPRING GOLD **
Lotus pinnatus	MEADOW BIRD'S-FOOT TREFOIL **

Luetkea pectinata	PARTRIDGE-FOOT
Lupinus albicaulis	SICKLE-KEEL LUPINE **
Lupinus latifolius	BROAD-LEAFED LUPINE
Lupinus lepidus var. *lepidus*	PRAIRIE LUPINE **
Lupinus polyphyllus	LARGE LEAVED LUPINE **
Lupinus sulphureus ssp. *kincaidii*	KINCAID'S LUPINE **
Microseris laciniata	CUT-LEAF SILVER-PUFFS **
Monarda fistulosa 'Claire Grace'	WILD BERGAMOT
Olsynium (Sisyrinchium) douglasii	DOUGLAS' BLUE-EYED-GRASS
Pedicularis groenlandica	ELEPHANT-HEAD LOUSEWORT
Penstemon confertus	YELLOW PENSTEMON
Penstemon euglaucus	GLAUCUS PENSTEMON
Penstemon ovatus	BROAD-LEAF PENSTEMON
Penstemon serrulatus	CASCADE PENSTEMON
Perideridia gairdneri	GAIRDNER'S YAMPAH **
Polemonium carneum	GREAT POLEMONIUM **
Potentilla gracilis	GRACEFUL CINQUEFOIL
Ranunculus occidentalis	WESTERN BUTTERCUP
Rudbeckia occidentalis	GREEN WIZARD
Sedum oreganum	OREGON STONECROP **
Sedum spathulifolium	BROADLEAF STONECROP **
Sidalcea campestris	MEADOW CHECKER MALLOW
Sidalcea hendersonii	HENDERSON'S CHECKER-MALLOW
Sidalcea malviflora var. *virgata*	ROSE CHECKERBLOOM **
Sidalcea oregana	OREGON CHECKER MALLOW
Sisyrinchium idahoense	IDAHO BLUE-EYED GRASS **
Solidago missouriensis	MISSOURI GOLDENROD **
Solidago simplex var. *simplex* (*S. spathulata*)	STICKY GOLDENROD **
Symphyotrichum (Aster) subspicatus (*S. douglasii*)	DOUGLAS' ASTER
Thalictrum occidentale	WESTERN MEADOWRUE
Thermopsis montana	MOUNTAIN GOLD-BANNER
Triteleia grandiflora	HOWELL'S TRITELEIA **
Triteleia (Brodiaea) hyacinthina	WHITE TRIPLET-LILY **
Veratrum californicum	CALIFORNIA WILD HELLEBORE **
Veratrum viride	AMERICAN WILD HELLEBORE **
Viola adunca	EARLY BLUE VIOLET **
Wyethia angustifolia	NARROW-LEAF MULE'S EARS

Plus see "PRAIRIE ANNUALS" next page

PRAIRIE ANNUALS**

These are the flowers most associated with the term "wildflowers," the ones offering up the familiar large masses of color from spring into summer.

Clarkia amoena ssp. *lindleyi*	FAREWELL-TO-SPRING
Clarkia purpurea ssp. *quadrivulnera*	WINE CUPS CLARKIA, FOUR-SPOT
Collinsia grandiflora	LARGE-FLOWERED BLUE-EYED MARY
Collinsia parviflora	SMALL-FLOWERED BLUE-EYED MARY
Collomia grandiflora	LARGE-FLOWERED COLLOMIA
Crocidium multicaule	GOLD-STAR, SPRING-GOLD
Gilia capitata	QUEEN ANNE'S THIMBLES
Leptosiphon bicolor	BABY-STARS
Limnanthes douglasii	DOUGLAS' MEADOWFOAM
Lupinus bicolor ssp. *bicolor*	FIELD LUPINE
Lupinus polycarpus	SMALL-FLOWERED LUPINE
Microsteris gracilis	SLENDER PHLOX
Nuttallanthus texanus	BLUE TOADFLAX
Phacelia linearis	THREAD-LEAF PHACELIA
Rhinanthus minor (a hemi-parasite on grasses)	LITTLE YELLOW RATTLE
Trifolium microcephalum	PINK CLOVER
Trifolium willldenowii	SAND CLOVER
Triodanis perfoliata	VENUS'-LOOKING-GLASS
Valeriana (Plectritis) congesta ssp. *congesta*	SEA-BLUSH

** = actual western PNW prairie (meadow) inhabitant

"What a lonely place it would be to have a world without a wildflower!" ~~ Roland R Kemler

PNW NATIVES FOR A ROCK GARDEN

Generally smallish, low-growing, dense plants suitable for gardens of rock with excellent drainage especially on a slope.

* = true PNW "alpines" (inhabitants of high mountain areas [Cascade Range and Olympic Mountains]; some occupy seep areas so they need moisture; others grow in well-drained rocky areas, such as talus and scree, and prefer drier conditions).

Achillea millefolium	COMMON YARROW
Allium acuminatum	HOOKER'S ONION
Allium amplectens	SLIM-LEAF ONION
Allium cernuum	NODDING ONION
Allium crenulatum	SCALLOPED ONION
Allium douglasii	DOUGLAS' ONION
Allium falcifolium	SICKLE-LEAF ONION
Allium geyeri var. *geyeri*	GEYER'S ONION
Allium lemmonii	LEMMON'S ONION
Allium nevii	NEVIUS' ONION
Allium robinsonii	ROBINSON'S ONION
Allium siskiyouense	SISKIYOU ONION
Allium tolmiei var. *tolmiei*	TOLMIE'S ONION
Androsace (Douglasia) laevigata*	SMOOTH DOUGLASIA
Anemone drummondii*	WINDFLOWER
Anemone occidentalis*	WESTERN PASQUE FLOWER
Antennaria alpina*	ALPINE PUSSYTOES
Antennaria lanata*	WOOLLY PUSSYTOES
Antennaria rosea	PINK PUSSYTOES
Aquilegia flavescens	YELLOW COLUMBINE
Arabis aculeolata	WALDO ROCKCRESS
Arabis nuttallii*	NUTTALL'S ROCKCRESS
Arctostaphylos uva-ursi*	KINNIKINNICK
Armeria maritima	SEA PINK
Arnica rydbergii*	RYDBERG'S ARNICA
Artemisia trifurcata*	FORKED WORMWOOD
Asarum marmoratum	MARBLED WILD GINGER
Asplenium trichomanes	SPLEENWORT
Balsamorhiza incana	HOARY BALSAMROOT
Bistorta bistortoides*	WESTERN BISTORT
Bloomeria (Triteleia) crocea	GOLDEN STARS
Boechera lyallii*	RISING SUNCRESS, JEWELED SUNCRESS
Brodiaea coronaria	HARVEST BRODIAEA
Brodiaea elegans ssp. *hooveri*	HARVEST LILY
Calochortus coxii	COX'S MARIPOSA LILY
Calochortus elegans var. *elegans*	ELEGANT CAT'S EAR
Calochortus eurycarpus	BIGPOD MARIPOSA LILY
Calochortus howellii	HOWELL'S MARIPOSA LILY
Calochortus macrocarpus var. *macrocarpus*	SAGEBRUSH MARIPOSA LILY

Calochortus tolmiei	TOLMIE'S CAT'S EAR
Calochortus umpquaensis ssp. *umpquaensis*	UMPQUA MARIPOSA LILY
Calochortus uniflorus	LARGE-FLOWERED STAR-TULIP
*Caltha leptosepala**	WHITE MARSH MARIGOLD
*Campanula rotundifolia**	BLUEBELL BELLFLOWER
*Carex spectabilis**	SHOWY SEDGE
*Cassiope mertensiana**	WHITE MOUNTAIN HEATHER, WESTERN MOSS HEATHER
*Cistanthe (Spraguea) umbellata**	MOUNT HOOD PUSSY-PAWS
Claytonia megarhiza	FELLFIELD SPRING BEAUTY
Clematis columbiana	ROCK CLEMATIS
Clematis hirsutissima var. *hirsutissima*	DOUGLAS CLEMATIS, HAIRY CLEMATIS
*Collomia debilis**	ALPINE COLLOMIA
Convolvulus soldanella	BEACH MORNING GLORY
Cryptogramma cascadensis	CASCADE PARSLEY FERN
Dichelostemma capitatum ssp. *capitatum*	BLUEDICKS
Dichelostemma congestum	OOKOW, FIELD CLUSTER LILY, HARVEST LILY
Dichelostemma ida-maia	FIRECRACKER FLOWER
Dodecatheon austrofrigidum	FRIGID SHOOTING STAR
Dodecatheon hendersonii	SHOOTING STAR, MOSQUITO BILL
Dodocatheon pulchellum	PRETTY SHOOTING STAR
*Draba lonchocarpa**	LANCE-POD DRABA
*Dryas drummondii**	MOUNTAIN AVENS
*Elmera racemosa**	YELLOW CORAL-BELLS
*Empetrum nigrum**	CROWBERRY
*Erigeron aureus**	ALPINE YELLOW FLEABANE
Erigeron compositus var. *discoideus**	CUT-LEAF ALPINE FLEABANE
Erigeron glacialis var. *glacialis*	SUBALPINE DAISY
Eriogonum marifolium	MARUM-LEAF BUCKWHEAT
Eriogonum ovalifolium var. *nivale**	CUSHION BUCKWHEAT
Eriogonum ternatum	TERNATE BUCKWHEAT
Eriogonum umbellatum var. *majus*	SUB-ALPINE BUCKWHEAT
Eriophyllum lanatum varieties	OREGON SUNSHINE, WOOLLY SUNFLOWER
Erythronium grandiflorum	YELLOW AVALANCHE-LILY
Erythronium montanum	WHITE AVALANCHE-LILY
Erythronium revolutum	PINK FAWN-LILY
Frasera speciosa	MONUMENT PLANT
Fritillaria glauca	SISKIYOU FRITILLARY
Geum triflorum	PRAIRIE SMOKE, OLD-MAN'S WHISKERS
*Hedysarum occidentale**	WESTERN SWEET-VETCH
Heuchera cylindrica	ROUND-LEAF ALUM ROOT
Heuchera micrantha	SMALL- FLOWERED ALUMROOT
Horkelia fusca	DUSKY HORKELIA
Hulsea nana	DWARF ALPINE-GOLD, DWARF HULSEA
Iris chrysophylla	YELLOW-LEAF IRIS
Iris purdyi	PURDY'S IRIS
Iris tenuis	CLACKAMAS IRIS
*Juncus drummondii**	DRUMMOND'S RUSH
*Juniperus communis**	COMMON JUNIPER
Kalmiopsis leachiana	KALMIOPSIS

Leptosiphon nuttallii	NUTTALL'S LINANTHUS
Lewisia columbiana var. *columbiana*	COLUMBIAN LEWISIA
Lewisia cotyledon	SISKIYOU LEWISIA
Lewisiopsis tweedyi	TWEEDY'S LEWISIA
Linanthus nuttallii	NUTTALL'S LINANTHUS
*Lomatium martindalei (L. angustatum)**	CASCADE DESERT PARSLEY
*Luetkea pectinata**	PARTRIDGE-FOOT
Luina hypoleuca	SILVERBACK LUINA
*Lupinus lepidus**	PACIFIC LUPINE
*Lupinus lyallii**	ALPINE LUPINE
*Luzula glabrata**	SMOOTH WOODRUSH
Mertensia longiflora	SAGEBRUSH BLUEBELLS
*Mertensia paniculata**	TALL BLUEBELLS
Minuartia (Arabis) obtusiloba	ALPINE SANDWORT
Monardella odoratissima	MOUNTAIN PENNYROYAL
Myosotis alpestris (M. asiaticus)	ALPINE FORGET-ME-NOT
Myriopteris (Cheilanthes) gracillima	LACE LIP FERN
Olsynium (Sisyrinchium) douglasii	DOUGLAS' BLUE-EYED-GRASS
*Oreostemma (Aster) alpigenum**	TUNDRA ASTER
Oxalis oregana	REDWOOD SORREL
*Oxytropis campestris**	FIELD LOCOWEED
Penstemon azureus var. *azureus*	AZURE PENSTEMON
Penstemon barrettiae	BARRETT'S BEARDTONGUE
Penstemon cardwellii	CARDWELL'S PENSTEMON
*Penstemon davidsonii**	DAVIDSON'S BEARDTONGUE
Penstemon fruticosus	SHRUBBY PENSTEMON
Penstemon newberryi var. *berryi*	BERRY'S MOUNTAIN PRIDE
Penstemon procerus var. *tolmiei**	TOLMIE'S PENSTEMON
Penstemon richardsonii	RICHARDSON'S BEARDTONGUE
Penstemon rupicola	ROCK PENSTEMON
Phacelia sericea	SILKY PHACELIA
*Phlox diffusa**	SPREADING PHLOX
*Phyllodoce glanduliflora**	YELLOW MOUNTAIN-HEATH
Phyllodoce x intermedia	HYBRID MOUNTAIN-HEATH
Polemonium carneum	SALMON POLEMONIUM
*Polemonium elegans**	ELEGANT SKY PILOT
Polemonium pulcherrimum	SHOWY JACOB'S-LADDER
Polypodium amorpha	IRREGULAR POLYPODY
Polystichum lemmonii	LEMMON'S HOLLYFERN, LEMMON'S SWORD FERN
Polystichum lonchitis	MOUNTAIN HOLLY FERN
*Potentilla diversifolia**	MOUNTAIN MEADOW CINQUEFOIL
*Potentilla flabellifolia**	HIGH MOUNTAIN CINQUEFOIL
*Potentilla nivea**	SNOW CINQUEFOIL
*Ranunculus eschscholtzii**	ESCHSCHOLTZ'S BUTTERCUP
Rhodiola integrifolia ssp. *integrifolia*	WESTERN ROSEROOT
Romanzoffia sitchensis	SITKA MIST-MAIDEN
*Salix nivalis**	DWARF SNOW WILLOW
*Sanguisorba stipulata**	SITKA BURNET
*Saxifraga bronchialis**	YELLOW-DOT SAXIFRAGE

Saxifraga caespitosa	TUFTED SAXIFRAGE
Saxifraga occidentalis	WESTERN SAXIFRAGE
*Saxifraga oppositifolia**	PURPLE MOUNTAIN SAXIFRAGE
*Sedum divergens**	SPREADING STONECROP
Sedum lanceolatum	LANCE-LEAVED STONECROP
Sedum obtusatum	SIERRAN STONECROP
Sedum oreganum	OREGON STONECROP
Sedum spathulifolium	BROAD-LEAVED STONECROP
*Silene acaulis**	MOSS CAMPION
*Silene hookeri**	HOOKER'S INDIAN-PINK
*Silene suksdorfii**	SUKSDORF'S CATCHFLY
Sisyrinchium bellum	WESTERN BLUE-EYED GRASS
Sisyrinchium californicum	GOLDEN-EYED GRASS
Sisyrinchium hitchcockii	HITCHCOCK'S BLUE-EYED-GRASS
Sisyrinchium idahoense	BLUE-EYED GRASS
Solidago simplex ssp. *simplex* var. *nana*	DWARF GOLDENROD
Solidago simplex ssp. *simplex* var. *spathulata**	DUNE GOLDENROD
Synthyris (Veronica) pinnatifida var. *lanuginosa**	OLYMPIC CUT-LEAF SYNTHYRIS
Synthyris (Veronica) reniformis	SPRING QUEEN, KITTEN TAILS
Triteleia bridgesii	BRIDGES' TRITELEIA
Triteleia grandiflora	LARGE-FLOWERED TRIPLET-LILY, WILD HYACINTH
Triteleia hendersonii	HENDERSON'S TRITELEIA
Triteleia (Brodiaea) hyacinthina	WHITE TRIPLET-LILY
Triteleia ixioides	PRETTYFACE
Vaccinium deliciosum	CASCADE BLUEBERRY
Vaccinium scoparium	GROUSE WHORTLEBERRY
*Vahlodea (Deschampsia) atropurpurea**	MOUNTAIN HAIRGRASS
*Veronica cusickii**	CUSICK'S SPEEDWELL
*Veronica wormskjoldii**	AMERICAN ALPINE SPEEDWELL
Viola adunca	EARLY BLUE VIOLET, SAND VIOLET
Viola glabella	STREAM VIOLET, YELLOW WOOD VIOLET
Viola langsdorfii	ALASKA VIOLET
Viola trinervata	SAGEBRUSH VIOLET

Throughout the rest of the chapters and listings, look for the symbol ❖ which indicates a native plant.

BASIC PLANTS

The concept of "right plant, right place" includes space, of course. That is, given the measurements of a selected site, it is a good idea to plant that which will eventually fill that site and no more.

When gardeners decide they need a plant for a space, it is most often in terms of plant types: tree, shrub, perennial/bulb, etc. In a sense, these are general interpretations of size. Trees for big spaces, shrubs for smaller spaces and so on. Hence why this chapter breaks it down by type and then breaks down those types even further by relative size.

Look for the symbol ❖ which indicates a native plant.

MEDIUM TO LARGE TREES

Trees are the "bones" of a landscape. A landscape plan, when it comes time to designate plants, usually starts with tree choice. A landscape, when it comes time to actually plant, starts with the planting of trees. The rest of the plan and the landscape itself flows from the trees.

Trees serve a purpose. Actually several purposes and it's wise to decide what those purposes are before selecting a tree. "I want a tree" or "I want a beautiful tree" aren't enough to make the best choice. Trees can be used to frame a house (versus hiding a house), to help direct a visitor's eyes to a designated location (e.g., the entrance to the house), to add privacy, to save on energy bills (deciduous trees block sun in the hot summer and let sun through in the cold winter), and to provide food and shelter for wildlife. They can help set the mood for a particular style of landscape. With their foliage, they can help make a landscape look larger (with fine foliage) or smaller (with large foliage). Those with flowers can herald spring or summer or even brighten things up in winter; those with fall foliage can brighten the sometimes dreary prospect of the coming winter or simply make the gardener feel good with nostalgia. There's beauty in their form, their leaf, their flower, their fruit, their bark.

Included here are some natives along with non-natives. These Medium to Large Trees are in the range of 50 to 100 feet and more. This scale matches that of large properties and large homes.

Abies amabilis	PACIFIC SILVER FIR ❖
Abies concolor	WHITE FIR ❖
Abies grandis	GRAND FIR ❖
Acer negundo 'Flamingo'	FLAMINGO BOXELDER
Acer tegmentosum	MANCHURIAN SNAKE-BARK MAPLE
Alnus rhombifolia	WHITE ALDER ❖
Arbutus menziesii	MADRONE ❖
Betula nigra 'Heritage'	HERITAGE RIVER BIRCH
Calocedrus decurrens	INCENSE-CEDAR ❖
Calocedrus macrolepis	CHINESE INCENSE-CEDAR, YUNNAN CYPRESS
Carpinus betulus	HORNBEAM
Cedrus atlantica 'Glauca'	BLUE ATLANTIC CEDAR
Cedrus deodara	DEODAR CEDAR
Cercidiphyllum japonicum	KATSURA
Chamaecyparis lawsoniana	PORT ORFORD-CEDAR ❖
Chrysolepis chrysophylla	GOLDEN CHINQUAPIN ❖
Cornus 'Eddie's White Wonder'	EDDIE'S WHITE WONDER DOGWOOD
Cornus × *rutgersensis* 'Starlight'	STARLIGHT FLOWERING DOGWOOD
Cryptomeria japonica	SUGI, JAPANESE PLUME CEDAR
Cunninghamia lanceolata	CHINESE FIR
Eucryphia moorei	PINKWOOD, PLUMWOOD, EASTERN LEATHERWOOD
Eucryphia x *nymansensis* 'Nymansay'	NYMAN'S EUCRYPHIA
Fagus sylvatica Purple forms	PURPLE BEECH
Fitzroya cupressoides	PATAGONIAN CYPRESS
Fraxinus ornus	BOUQUET ASH
Ginkgo biloba	GINKGO
Gymnocladus dioica	KENTUCKY COFFEE TREE
Hesperocyparis (Cupressus) bakeri	BAKER CYPRESS

Juniperus occidentalis var. *occidentalis*	WESTERN JUNIPER ❖
Lagarostrobos (Dacrydium) franklinii	HUON PINE
Liriodendron tulipifera 'Aureomarginatum'	VARIEGATED TULIP TREE
Magnolia x brooklynensis 'Lois', 'Yellow Bird'	YELLOW MAGNOLIA
Magnolia campbellii	CAMPBELL'S MAGNOLIA
Magnolia 'Galaxy'	GALAXY MAGNOLIA
Magnolia sprengeri 'Diva'	SPRENGER'S MAGNOLIA
Metasequoia glyptostroboides	DAWN REDWOOD
Nothofagus antarctica	ANTARCTIC BEECH
Nothofagus solandri var. *cliffortioides*	MOUNTAIN BEECH
Notholithocarpus densiflorus	TANBARK OAK ❖
Nyssa sylvatica	BLACK GUM, BLACK TUPELO
Picea breweriana	BREWER'S WEEPING SPRUCE ❖
Picea omorika	SERBIAN SPRUCE
Picea sitchensis	SITKA SPRUCE ❖
Pinus bhutanica	BHUTAN WHITE PINE
Pinus contorta var. *contorta*	SHORE PINE ❖
Pinus densiflora	JAPANESE RED PINE
Pinus parviflora	JAPANESE WHITE PINE
Pinus thunbergii	JAPANESE BLACK PINE
Pinus wallichiana	HIMALAYAN PINE
Pseudotsuga menziesii	DOUGLAS-FIR ❖
Quercus acutissima	SAWTOOTH OAK
Quercus chrysolepis	CANYON LIVE OAK ❖
Quercus coccinea	SCARLET OAK
Quercus frainetto	HUNGARIAN OAK
Quercus garryana	GARRY OAK, OREGON WHITE OAK ❖
Quercus hypoleucoides	SILVERLEAF OAK
Quercus palustris	PIN OAK
Quercus phellos	WILLOW OAK
Sassafras tzumu	CHINESE SASSAFRAS, CHA MU
Sequoiadendron giganteum	BIG TREE, INTERIOR REDWOOD
Sorbus alnifolia	KOREAN MOUNTAIN ASH
Stewartia pseudocamellia	JAPANESE STEWARTIA
Styphnolobium (Sophora) japonicum	JAPANESE PAGODA TREE
Taiwania cryptomerioides	TAIWAN CEDAR
Thuja plicata	WESTERN RED-CEDAR ❖
Ulmus davidiana var. *japonica (U. propinqua)* 'Emerald Sunshine'	
	EMERALD SUNSHINE ELM
Ulmus pumila	SIBERIAN ELM
Xanthocyparis vietnamensis	VIETNAMESE GOLDEN CYPRESS
Zelkova serrata	KEAKI

"The best time to plant a tree was 20 years ago. The second best time is now." ~~ Chinese proverb

SMALL TO MEDIUM FLOWERING TREES

These are more in scale with smaller properties, albeit probably not the smallest properties. Some are used as understory; some requiring a bit of training to be "tree"-like.

Aesculus x carnea 'Briotii'	RED HORSE CHESTNUT
Amelanchier x grandiflora	SERVICEBERRY
Catalpa ovata	CHINESE CATALPA
Cercis canadensis especially 'Little Woody', 'The Rising Sun', 'Sparkling Wine'	
	EASTERN REDBUD
Cercis siliquastrum	LOVE TREE
Chionanthus retusus	CHINESE FRINGE TREE
Cladrastis kentukea	YELLOWWOOD
Cornus controversa 'Variegata'	WEDDING CAKE TREE
Cornus x elwinortonii 'Hyperion'	HYPERION DOGWOOD
Cornus x elwinortonii 'Rosy Teacups'	ROSY TEACUPS DOGWOOD
Cornus x elwinortonii 'Venus'	VENUS DOGWOOD
Cornus hongkongensis	HONG KONG DOGWOOD
Cornus kousa 'Heart Throb'	PINK FLOWERING KOUSA DOGWOOD
Cornus kousa 'Satomi'	RED FLOWERING KOUSA DOGWOOD
Cornus kousa var. *chinensis* 'Milky Way'	MILKY WAY DOGWOOD
Cornus kousa 'Wolf Eyes'	VARIEGATED KOREAN DOGWOOD
Cornus mas	CORNELIAN CHERRY
Cotinus obovatus	AMERICAN SMOKE TREE
Crinodendron patagua	
	CHILEAN LILY-OF-THE-VALLEY TREE, EVERGREEN SNOWBELL
Davidia involucrata 'Sonoma'	DOVE TREE, HANDKERCHIEF TREE
Diospyros kaki	JAPANESE PERSIMMON
Drimys winteri	WINTER'S BARK
Embothrium coccineum	CHILEAN FIRE TREE
Eucryphia glutinosa	NIRRHE
Eucryphia x intermedia 'Rostrevor'	BRUSHBUSH
X *Gordlinia grandiflora* 'Sweet Tea'	MOUNTAIN GORDLINIA
Halesia tetraptera	SILVER-BELLS
Hoheria angustifolia	NARROW-LEAVED LACEBARK
Koelreuteria paniculata	GOLDEN RAIN TREE
Lagerstroemia hybrids 'Arapaho', 'Natchez'	HYBRID CRAPE MYRTLE
Lagerstroemia indica 'Dynamite', 'Red Rocket'	CRAPE MYRTLE
Lyonothamnus floribundus ssp. *asplenifolius*	ISLAND IRONWOOD
Maackia amurensis	AMUR MAACKIA
Magnolia denudata	YULAN
Magnolia foveolata X *M. laevifolia*	FIGLAR'S HYBRID MAGNOLIA
Magnolia 'Heaven Scent'	HEAVEN SCENT MAGNOLIA
Magnolia insignis	RED LOTUS TREE
Magnolia x kewensis 'Wada's Memory'	WADA'S MEMORY MAGNOLIA
Magnolia kobus	KOBUSHI
Magnolia laevifolia (*Michelia yunnanensis*)	YUNNAN MAGNOLIA
Magnolia x loebneri 'Leonard Messel'	PINK LOBNER MAGNOLIA

Magnolia x loebneri 'Merrill'	MERRILL MAGNOLIA
Magnolia x soulangeana 'Rustica Rubra'	RUSTICA RUBRA SAUCER MAGNOLIA
Magnolia wilsonii	WILSON'S MAGNOLIA
Magnolia 'Vulcan'	VULCAN MAGNOLIA
Malus 'Golden Raindrops'	GOLDEN RAINDROPS CRABAPPLE
Malus 'Royal Raindrops'	ROYAL RAINDROPS CRABAPPLE
Melliodendron xylocarpum	CHINESE PARASOL
Oxydendrum arboreum	SOURWOOD
Parrotiopsis jacquemontiana	HATAB, POHU
Polyspora (Gordonia) longicarpa	POLYSPORA
Poliothyrsis sinensis	CHINESE PEARLBLOOM
Prunus 'Gyoiko', 'Pink Perfection', 'Tai-Haku'	FLOWERING CHERRIES
Pterostyrax corymbosa	LITTLE EPAULETTE TREE
Pterostyrax hispidus	EPAULETTE TREE
Rehderodendron macrocarpum	CHINESE REHDERODENDRON
Sorbus pseudohupehensis 'Pink Pagoda'	PINK PAGODA ROWAN
Sorbus verrucosa var. *subulata*	VIETNAM MOUNTAIN ASH
Staphylea holocarpa (including 'Rosea')	CHINESE BLADDERNUT
Stewartia monadelpha	ORANGE-BARK STEWARTIA
Stewartia monadelpha 'Black Dog'	BLACK-STEM STEWARTIA
Stewartia rostrata	BEAKED STEWARTIA
Stewartia 'Scarlet Sentinel'	SCARLET SENTINEL STEWARTIA
Stewartia serrata	SAWTOOTH STEWARTIA
Styrax japonicus 'Pink Chimes', 'Snow Crown', 'Snowcone'	SNOWBELL
Syringa reticulata	TREE LILAC
Tetradium (Evodia) daniellii	KOREAN EVODIA

NON-FLOWERING SMALL TREES

Abies concolor 'Candicans'	CANDICANS WHITE FIR
Abies koreana	KOREAN FIR
Abies nebrodensis	SICILIAN FIR
Acer buergerianum	TRIDENT MAPLE
Acer campestre	HEDGE MAPLE
Acer caudatifolium (A. kawakamii)	KAWAKAMI MAPLE
Acer circinatum cultivars	VINE MAPLE ❖
Acer ginnala	AMUR MAPLE
Acer glabrum var. *douglasii*	DOUGLAS MAPLE ❖
Acer griseum	PAPER-BARK MAPLE
Acer japonicum 'Aconitifolium'	FERN-LEAF FULLMOON MAPLE
Acer laevigatum 'Hóng Lóng'	RED DRAGON EVERGREEN CHINESE MAPLE
Acer palmatum	JAPANESE MAPLE
Acer pseudosieboldianum	KOREAN MAPLE
Acer tataricum	TATARIAN MAPLE
Acer triflorum	ROUGH-BARK MAPLE
Acer truncatum	SHANTUNG MAPLE
Asimina triloba	PAW-PAW
Betula nigra 'Little King'	LITTLE KING RIVER BIRCH
Carpinus caroliniana	AMERICAN HORNBEAM
Cryptomeria japonica 'Sekkan-sugi'	GOLDEN JAPANESE CEDAR
Cryptomeria japonica 'Spiralis'	GRANNY'S RINGLETS
Cunninghamia lanceolata var. *glauca*	BLUE CHINA FIR
Dendropanax trifidus	IVY TREE
Emmenopterys henryi (will produce showy flowers after many years)	EMMENOPTERYS
Fokienia (Chamaecyparis) hodginsii	FUJIAN CYPRESS
Frangula (Rhamnus) purshiana (insignificant flowers)	CASCARA, FALSE-BUCKTHORN ❖
Hesperocyparis (Cupressus) pygmaea	PIGMY CYPRESS
Juniperus maritima	SEASIDE JUNIPER ❖
Laurus nobilis (tiny, non-showy flowers)	GRECIAN LAUREL, BAY LAUREL
Nothaphoebe cavaleriei	NOTHAPHOEBE
Ostrya virginiana	HOP HORNBEAM
Parrotia persica	PERSIAN IRONWOOD
Parrotia subaequalis	CHINESE IRONWOOD
Peumus boldus	BOLDO
Picea glauca 'Densata'	BLACK HILLS SPRUCE
Picea orientalis 'Skylands'	SKYLANDS ORIENTAL SPRUCE
Pinus densiflora 'Umbraculifera'	TANYOSHO PINE
Podocarpus chingianus	BLUE YEW
Quercus hypoleucoides	SILVERLEAF OAK
Quercus myrsinifolia	CHINESE EVERGREEN OAK
Taxus brevifolia	PACIFIC YEW ❖
Trochodendron aralioides	WHEEL TREE
Ulmus parvifolia	LACE-BARK ELM, CHINESE ELM
Xanthocyparis vietnamensis	VIETNAM CYPRESS

NATURALLY-NARROW TREES

For accent, for screening in narrow places, or for height where there is no width for planting typical trees. Mostly evergreen but a few extra-special deciduous species.

Acer ginnala 'Beethoven'	BEETHOVEN AMUR MAPLE
Acer palmatum 'Tsukasa Silhouette'	T. S. JAPANESE MAPLE
Acer palmatum 'Twombly's Red Sentinel'	T. R. S. JAPANESE MAPLE
Acer x *freemanii* 'Armstrong'	ARMSTRONG MAPLE
Athrotaxis cupressoides	TASMANIAN CEDAR, PENCIL PINE
Betula platyphylla 'Fargo'	DAKOTA PINNACLE BIRCH
Callitropsis (Chamaecyparis, Cupressus, Xanthocyparis) nootkatensis 'Green Arrow'	
	ALASKA YELLOW-CEDAR
Carpinus betulus 'Frans Fontaine'	FRANZ FONTAINE EUROPEAN HORNBEAM
Cedrus atlantica 'Fastigiata'	COLUMNAR ATLAS CEDAR
Chamaecyparis lawsoniana 'Alumii'	ALUMII PORT ORFORD CEDAR
Chamaecyparis lawsoniana 'Columnaris'	COLUMNAR LAWSON CYPRESS
Chamaecyparis lawsoniana 'Oregon Blue'	OREGON BLUE LAWSON CYPRESS
Cryptomeria japonica 'Rasen'	RASEN JAPANESE CEDAR
Chionanthus retusus 'Tokyo Tower'	CHINESE FRINGETREE
Cupressus sempervirens	ITALIAN CYPRESS
Cupressus torulosa	HIMALAYAN CYPRESS
Embothrium coccineum	CHILEAN FIRE-TREE
Fagus sylvatica 'Dawyck Purple'	DAWYCK PURPLE BEECH
Fitzroya cupressoides	PATAGONIAN CYPRESS
Ginkgo biloba 'Goldspire'	GOLDSPIRE GINKGO
Juniperus chinensis 'Robusta', Spartan'	UPRIGHT CHINESE JUNIPER
Juniperus communis 'Hibernica'	HIBERNICA JUNIPER
Juniperus scopulorum 'Blue Arrow', 'Wichita Blue'	ROCKY MOUNTAIN JUNIPER
Juniperus virginiana 'Skyrocket'	SKYROCKET CEDAR/JUNIPER
Magnolia grandiflora 'Teddy Bear'	TEDDY BEAR MAGNOLIA
Parrotia persica 'Ruby Vase', 'Vanessa'	UPRIGHT PERSIAN IRONWOOD
Picea abies 'Cupressina'	COLUMNAR NORWAY SPRUCE
Picea breweriana	BREWER'S SPRUCE ❖
Picea omorika	SERBIAN SPRUCE
Picea pungens 'Fastigiata'	COLUMNAR BLUE SPRUCE
Pinus cembra 'Columnaris'	COLUMNAR SWISS STONE PINE
Pinus nigra 'Arnold Sentinel'	COLUMNAR AUSTRIAN PINE
Pinus strobus 'Fastigiata'	UPRIGHT WHITE PINE
Pinus sylvestris 'Fastigiata'	UPRIGHT SCOTS PINE
Quercus 'Crimson Spire'	CRIMSON SPIRE OAK
Sciadopitys verticillata 'Joe Kozey'	COLUMNAR JAPANESE UMBRELLA PINE
Taxodium distichum 'Skyward'	SKYWARD BALD CYPRESS
Taxus baccata 'Fastigiata'	UPRIGHT IRISH YEW
Thuja occidentalis 'Brandon', 'Degroot's Spire', 'Fastigiata', 'Nigra'	
	NORTHERN WHITE-CEDAR
Thuja plicata 'Forever Goldy'	FOREVER GOLDY GOLDEN ARBORVITAE
Thuja 'Smaragd'	EMERALD GREEN ARBORVITAE
Trachycarpus fortunei	CHINESE WINDMILL PALM

SEMI-DWARF CONIFERS

Although this general category of plants is considered "trees," by definition ("trees are 20 feet or more tall"), they are on the scale of shrubs. Their size fits average landscapes nicely. About 8 to 15 feet tall. Good for screening, specimen plant

Abies koreana 'Silver Show'	SILVER SHOW KOREAN FIR
Abies koreana 'Horstmann's Silberlocke'	SILVER LOCK KOREAN FIR
Calocedrus decurrens 'Maupin Glow'	MAUPIN GLOW INCENSE CEDAR ❖
Cedrus atlantica 'Aurea'	GOLDEN ATLAS CEDAR
Cedrus deodara 'Albospica'	WHITE-TIPPED DEODAR CEDAR
Cephalotaxus fortunei	CHINESE PLUM-YEW, FORTUNE'S YEW PLUM
Cephalotaxus harringtonia	COW-TAIL PINE, PLUM YEW
Chamaecyparis lawsoniana 'Imbricata Pendula'	WEEPING LAWSON CYPRESS ❖
Chamaecyparis lawsoniana 'Wisselii'	WISSEL'S LAWSON CYPRESS ❖
Chamaecyparis obtusa 'Aurea'	GOLDEN HINOKI CYPRESS
Chamaecyparis obtusa 'Confucius'	CONFUCIUS HINOKI CYPRESS
Chamaecyparis obtusa 'Filicoides Compacta'	FERN-SPRAY HINOKI CYPRESS
Chamaecyparis obtusa 'Gracilis'	HINOKI CYPRESS
Chamaecyparis obtusa 'Graciosa'	HINOKI CYPRESS
Chamaecyparis obtusa 'Templehof'	TEMPLEHOF HINOKI FALSE-CYPRESS
Chamaecyparis pisifera 'Boulevard'	BOULEVARD FALSE-CYPRESS
Chamaecyparis pisifera 'Plumosa'	SOFT SAWARA CYPRESS
Chamaecyparis pisifera 'Squarrosa'	BUSHY SAWARA CYPRESS
Chamaecyparis thyoides 'Ericoides'	ERICOIDES WHITE CEDAR
Chamaecyparis thyoides 'Glauca Pendula'	WEEPING WHITE CEDAR
Cryptomeria japonica 'Black Dragon'	BLACK DRAGON JAPANESE CEDAR
Cryptomeria japonica 'Elegans Compacta'	DWARF JAPANESE PLUME CEDAR
Cryptomeria japonica 'Spiralis'	GRANNY'S RINGLETS
Ginkgo biloba 'Jehosephat' (deciduous)	SEMI-DWARF GINKGO
Juniperus (lots, particularly cultivars of *J. scopulorum*)	JUNIPERS
Larix kaempferi 'Diana' (deciduous)	CONTORTED JAPANESE LARCH
Larix kaempferi 'Jacobsen's Pyramid' (")	JACOBSEN'S PYRAMID JAPANESE LARCH
Metasequoia glyptostroboides 'Miss Grace'	MISS GRACE DAWN REDWOOD
Picea omorika 'Pendula Bruns'	DWARF WEEPING SERBIAN SPRUCE
Pinus aristata, P. longaeva	BRISTLECONE PINE
Pinus contorta var. *latifolia* 'Chief Joseph'	GOLDEN LODGEPOLE PINE ❖
Pinus contorta var. *latifolia* 'Taylor's Sunburst'	T. B. LODGEPOLE PINE ❖
Pinus densiflora 'Golden Ghost'	GOLDEN GHOST JAPANESE RED PINE
Pinus nigra 'Oregon Green'	OREGON GREEN AUSTRIAN PINE
Pinus strobus 'Louie'	LOUIE (EASTERN) WHITE PINE
Pinus thunbergii 'Thunderhead'	COMPACT JAPANESE BLACK PINE
Sequoiadendron giganteum 'French Beauty'	FRENCH BEAUTY GIANT REDWOOD
Thuja occidentalis 'Yellow Ribbon'	YELLOW RIBBON ARBORVITAE
Thuja plicata 'Can-Can'	SEMI-DWARF WESTERN RED CEDAR ❖
Tsuga canadensis 'Summer Snow'	SUMMER SNOW HEMLOCK
Widdringtonia nodiflora	BERG CYPRESS

SMALLEST TREES (ACTUALLY TALLEST SHRUBS)

At 12 to 20 feet tall, they can be considered "trees" in many gardens. Left on their own, they produce bushy growth from ground to top but they can be left as a minimally-pruned multi-trunked small tree (with a little "limbing up" and thinning out) or can be pruned more adventurously to a "standard" (single bole; more tree-like). Some may take their time getting there.

Acer circinatum cultivars	VINE MAPLE ❖
Amelanchier alnifolia	WESTERN SERVICEBERRY, JUNEBERRY, SASKATOON ❖
Arbutus unedo	STRAWBERRY TREE
Arctostaphylos columbiana	HAIRY MANZANITA ❖
Arctostaphylos manzanita 'St. Helen'	ST. HELENS MANZANITA ❖
Argyrocytisus battandieri	MOROCCAN PINEAPPLE BROOM
Azara microphylla	SMALL-LEAVED AZARA
Azara serrata	TOOTHED LEAVED AZARA
Ceanothus 'Ray Hartman'	RAY HARTMAN CEANOTHUS
Ceanothus thyrsiflorus 'Oregon Mist'	OREGON MIST CEANOTHUS
Ceanothus thyrsiflorus 'Rogue Sky'	COAST BLUE BLOSSOM
Cercis chinensis	CHINESE REDBUD
Cercis occidentalis	WESTERN REDBUD
Chrysolepis sempervirens	BUSH CHINQUAPIN ❖
Cinnamomum checkiangense	HARDY CINNAMON LAUREL
Clerodendrum trichotomum	HARLEQUIN GLORYBOWER
Clethra barbinervis	JAPANESE CLETHRA
Cotinus coggygria 'Royal Purple' (and other similar cultivars)	PURPLE SMOKEBUSH
Cotinus 'Grace'	HYBRID SMOKEBUSH
Crinodendron hookerianum	CHILEAN LANTERN TREE
Disanthus ovatifolius	VIETNAMESE HAZEL
Eucryphia glutinosa	NIRRHE
Eucryphia milliganii	DWARF LEATHERWOOD
Exochorda racemosa	COMMON PEARL-BUSH
Feijoa (Acca) sellowiana	PINEAPPLE GUAVA
Hamamelis x intermedia	HYBRID WITCH-HAZEL
Heptacodium miconioides	SEVEN-SON FLOWER
Heptapleurum (Schefflera) taiwanianum	HARDY SCHEFFLERA
Hydrangea paniculata 'Grandiflora'	PEE-GEE HYDRANGEA
Itea ilicifolia	HOLLY-LEAVED SWEET SPIRE
Kalmia latifolia 'Fresca', 'Olympic Fire'	MOUNTAIN LAUREL
Juniperus squamata 'Meyeri'	MEYER'S JUNIPER
Leptospermum lanigerum	WOOLLY TEA TREE
Lindera erythrocarpa	RED-BERRY SPICEBUSH
Linnaea (Dipelta) yunnanensis	YUNNAN HONEYSUCKLE
Luma apiculata (hardy form)	CHILEAN GUAVA
Magnolia 'Butterflies'	BUTTERFLIES MAGNOLIA
Magnolia compressa var. *langyuense*	DWARF ASIAN MAGNOLIA
Magnolia sapaensis	MOUNTAIN MAGNOLIA
Magnolia sieboldii	OYAMA MAGNOLIA
Metapanax (Nothopanax) delavayi	DELAVAY FALSE GINSENG
Osmanthus x fortunei 'San Jose'	FORTUNE'S TREE OLIVE

Osmanthus fragrans	FRAGRANT TEA-OLIVE
Pittosporum tenuifolium	KOHUHU, TAWHIWI
Pseudocydonia sinensis	CHINESE QUINCE
Rhododendron arboreum (eventually quite tall)	TREE RHODODENDRON
Rhododendron auriculatum	RHODODENDRON
Rhododendron falconeri	KORLINGA
Rhododendron fortunei	FORTUNE'S RHODODENDRON
Rhododendron Loderi Group	LODERI HYBRID RHODODENDRON
Rhododendron macrophyllum	PACIFIC OR COAST RHODODENDRON ❖
Rhododendron 'Polar Bear'	POLAR BEAR RHODODENDRON
Rhododendron protistum giganteum	GIANT RHODODENDRON
Sambucus nigra 'Black Beauty', 'Black Lace'	PURPLE CUT-LEAF ELDERBERRY
Sambucus nigra f. *laciniata*	CUT-LEAF ELDERBERRY
Sorbus sitchensis	SITKA MOUNTAIN-ASH ❖
Stachyurus praecox	STACHYURUS
Stranvaesia (Photinia) davidiana	CHINESE PHOTINIA
Styrax obassia	FRAGRANT SNOWBELL
Sycopsis sinensis	CHINESE FIG-HAZEL
Syringa tomentella	FUZZY LILAC
Tasmannia (Drimys) lanceolata	MOUNTAIN PEPPER
Trochodendron aralioides	WHEEL TREE
Viburnum arbicolon 'Honey Tree'	HONEY TREE VIBURNUM
Viburnum suspensum	SANDANKWA
Vitex agnus-castus	CHASTE TREE

TREES FOR CREATING SHADE

Generally with crowns well above the ground and with proportionately greater horizontal dimensions than the average tree.

LARGE TREES

Alnus rhombifolia	WHITE ALDER ❖
Chamaecyparis lawsoniana	PORT ORFORD-CEDAR ❖
Chrysolepis chrysophylla	GOLDEN CHINQUAPIN ❖
Ginkgo biloba 'Autumn Gold'	AUTUMN GOLD GINKGO
Gymnocladus dioicus	KENTUCKY COFFEETREE
Laurus 'Saratoga'	SWEET BAY
Notholithocarpus densiflorus	TANBARK OAK ❖
Pseudotsuga menziesii	DOUGLAS-FIR ❖
Quercus cerris	TURKEY OAK
Tilia cordata 'Greenspire', 'Shamrock'	LITTLE-LEAF LINDEN
Ulmus 'Patriot'	PATRIOT ELM

SMALL TO MEDIUM TREES
(Some requiring training to be "tree"-like)

Acer buergerianum	TRIDENT MAPLE
Acer davidii	DAVID'S MAPLE
Acer glabrum var. *douglasii*	DOUGLAS MAPLE ❖
Acer griseum	PAPERBARK MAPLE
Acer tataricum var. *ginnala*	AMUR MAPLE
Cercis canadensis	REDBUD
Cercis siliquastrum	LOVE TREE
Betula nigra 'Heritage'	RIVER BIRCH
Frangula (Rhamnus) purshiana	CASCARA, FALSE-BUCKTHORN ❖
Halesia tetraptera	CAROLINA SILVERBELL
Maackia amurensis	AMUR MAACKIA
Parrotia subaequalis	CHINESE IRONWOOD
Stewartia pseudocamellia	JAPANESE STEWARTIA
Styrax japonicus	JAPANESE SNOWBELL

TREES FOR SCREENING/BACKGROUND

<u>CONIFERS</u> *10 ft to 40 ft in height at maturity*

Abies concolor 'Blue Cloak'	BLUE CLOAK WHITE FIR
Cephalotaxus harringtonia 'Fastigiata'	UPRIGHT JAPANESE PLUM YEW
Chamaecyparis obtusa 'Aurea'	GOLDEN HINOKI CYPRESS
Chamaecyparis obtusa 'Gracilis'	HINOKI CYPRESS
Cryptomeria japonica Elegans Group	PLUMOSE JAPANESE CEDAR
Cryptomeria japonica 'Sekkan-sugi'	GOLDEN JAPANESE CEDAR
Cryptomeria japonica 'Yoshino'	YOSHINO JAPANESE CEDAR
Cupressus torulosa	HIMALAYAN CYPRESS
Juniperus chinensis 'Kaizuka'	HOLLYWOOD JUNIPER
Picea orientalis 'Skylands'	GOLDEN CAUCASIAN SPRUCE
Pinus densiflora 'Umbraculifera'	TANYOSHO PINE
Pinus flexilis 'Vanderwolf's Pyramid'	LIMBER PINE
Pinus thunbergii 'Thunderhead'	COMPACT JAPANESE BLACK PINE
Pseudotsuga menziesii 'Graceful Grace'	WEEPING DOUGLAS-FIR
Taxodium ascendens (T. distichum var. *imbricatum)* 'Nutans'	POND CYPRESS
Thuja plicata 'Excelsa'	WESTERN RED-CEDAR
Thujopsis dolabrata	HIBA CEDAR
Tsuga diversifolia	NORTHERN JAPANESE HEMLOCK
Tsuga mertensiana	MOUNTAIN HEMLOCK

See also "SEMI-DWARF CONIFERS"

<u>BROADLEAF EVERGREENS</u> *10 ft to 20 ft (or more) at maturity*

Arbutus unedo	STRAWBERRY TREE
Azara microphylla	BOX-LEAF AZARA
Ilex x *altaclarensis* 'Lawsoniana'	LAWSON'S HIGHCLERE HOLLY
Laurus nobilis	GRECIAN BAY LAUREL
Magnolia grandiflora 'Edith Bogue'	SOUTHERN MAGNOLIA
Magnolia virginiana	SWEET BAY MAGNOLIA
Morella (Myrica) californica	PACIFIC WAX MYRTLE ❖
Pittosporum tenuifolium	KOHUHU
Quercus hypoleucoides	SILVER-LEAF OAK
Quercus myrsinifolia	CHINESE EVERGREEN OAK
Rhododendron macrophyllum	PACIFIC RHODODENDRON ❖
Trochodendron aralioides	WHEEL TREE
Umbellularia californica	CALIFORNIA BAY LAUREL ❖

See also "SMALLEST TREES"

GROVE TREES

Contrary to popular practice, it's okay to plant trees of any one species with spacing less than what's recommended. These trees are at their best and look more natural when planted close together. To create a whole "forest", develop several contiguous mini-groves, each with its own species, within the whole.

Acer buergerianum	TRIDENT MAPLE
Acer griseum	PAPERBARK MAPLE
Acer negundo	BOXELDER
Acer tataricum ginnala	AMUR MAPLE
Alnus cordata	ITALIAN ALDER
Alnus glutinosa 'Laciniata'	CUT-LEAF ALDER
Alnus rhombifolia	WHITE ALDER ❖
Arbutus x reyorum 'Marina'	MARINA STRAWBERRY TREE
Calocedrus decurrens	INCENSE CEDAR
Castanea sativa	CHESTNUT
Cedrus deodara	DEODAR CEDAR
Cercis canadensis	REDBUD
X Chitalpa tashkentensis	CHITALPA
Cinnamomum japonicum	JAPANESE CINNAMON
Feijoa (Acca) sellowiana	PINEAPPLE GUAVA
Fraxinus angustifolia 'Raywood'	RAYWOOD ASH
Ginkgo biloba	GINKGO
Hesperocyparis (Cupressus) arizonica var. *glabra*	SMOOTH ARIZONA CYPRESS
Hesperocyparis (Cupressus) forbesii	TECATE CYPRESS
Koelreuteria paniculata	GOLDEN RAIN TREE
Lagerstroemia hybrids 'Arapaho', 'Natchez'	HYBRID CRAPE MYRTLE
Lagerstroemia indica 'Dynamite', 'Red Rocket'	CRAPE MYRTLE
Laurus 'Saratoga'	SARATOGA LAUREL
Liriodendron tulipifera	TULIP TREE
Lyonothamnus floribundus ssp. *asplenifolius*	ISLAND IRONWOOD
Metasequoia glyptostroboides	DAWN REDWOOD
Notholithocarpus densiflora	TANBARK OAK
Perkinsiodendron (Halesia, Rehderodendron) macgregorii	CHINESE SILVERBELLS
Pinus muricata	BISHOP PINE
Pinus thunbergii	JAPANESE BLACK PINE
Pistacia chinensis	CHINESE PISTACHE
Prunus caroliniana	CAROLINA CHERRY
Quercus garryana	OREGON WHITE OAK
Sequoia sempervirens	COAST REDWOOD
Sequoiadendron giganteum	BIG TREE, GIANT REDWOOD
Trachycarpus fortunei	WINDMILL PALM
Umbellularia californica	CALIFORNIA BAY LAUREL
Zelkova serrata	KEAKI

SHRUBS

The simplest definition of a shrub (bush) is an upright woody plant bearing multiple stems and foliage from near the ground up. This is unlike typical trees which bear a single stem (the trunk or bole) with an upper crown of foliage. Shrubs generally provide the secondary foundation of the garden, after trees. Their most common use is for seasonal color but they are superb as background, screening, and transitionally "tying down" the vertical expanse of a structure (house, shed, garage, wall, fence) to the earth. A traditional use, "foundation planting," has its drawbacks.

LARGE SHRUBS, SHRUBBY "TREES" *(8 to 16 feet tall)*

Amelanchier alnifolia	WESTERN SERVICEBERRY, JUNEBERRY, SASKATOON ❖
Arbutus unedo	STRAWBERRY TREE
Arctostaphylos densiflora 'Howard McMinn'	MANZANITA
Berberis x *ottawensis* 'Royal Cloak'	PURPLE-LEAF JAPANESE BARBERRY
Berberis julianae	WINTERGREEN BARBERRY
Camellia japonica	CAMELLIA
Camellia reticulata	FOREST CAMELLIA
Camellia x *williamsii*	HYBRID CAMELLIA
Cephalotaxus fortunei	CHINESE PLUM-YEW, FORTUNE'S YEW PLUM,
Clethra fargesii	SWEET PEPPERBUSH
Cornus alba	RED-TWIG DOGWOOD
Cornus sericea 'Baileyi'	RED-OSIER DOGWOOD
Cotinus coggygria 'Royal Purple' (and other purple cultivars)	PURPLE SMOKEBUSH
Cotinus 'Grace'	PURPLE SMOKEBUSH
Disanthus cercidifolius	REDBUD HAZEL
Disanthus ovatifolius	VIETNAMESE HAZEL
Elaeagnus x *submacrophylla* (*E.* x *ebbingei*)	HYBRID ELAEAGNUS
Elaeagnus pungens 'Maculata'	GOLDEN ELAEAGNUS
Eucryphia milliganii	DWARF LEATHERWOOD
Exochorda racemosa	COMMON PEARL-BUSH
Garrya elliptica	SILK-TASSEL
Grevillea 'Audrey' (sold as 'Poorinda Constance')	AUDREY GREVILLEA
Grevillea 'Canberra Gem'	SPIDER FLOWER
Grevillea miqueliana var. *moroka*	ROUND-LEAF GREVILLEA
Grevillea victoriae	ROYAL GREVILLEA
Hamamelis x *intermedia*	HYBRID WITCH-HAZEL
Hamamelis mollis	CHINESE WITCH-HAZEL
Hibiscus syriacus	ROSE-OF-SHARON
Holodiscus discolor	OCEANSPRAY, CREAMBUSH ❖
Hydrangea aspera 'Macrophylla'	BIG-LEAF CHINESE HYDRANGEA
Hydrangea aspera Villosa Group	ROUGH-LEAF HYDRANGEA
Hydrangea paniculata 'Grandiflora'	PANICLE HYDRANGEA
Indigofera pendula	WEEPING INDIGO
Leptospermum minutifolium	SMALL-LEAVED TEA TREE
Lindera obtusiloba	JAPANESE SPICEBUSH
Linnaea (Dipelta) yunnanensis	YUNNAN HONEYSUCKLE
Lomatia myricoides	RIVER LOMATIA

Lonicera ferdinandii (L. versicaria)	KOREAN HONEYSUCKLE
Morella (Myrica) californica	PACIFIC WAX MYRTLE ❖
Myrceugenia parvifolia	PATAGÜILLA
Notholithocarpus densiflorus var. *echinoides*	SHRUB TANOAK ❖
Osmanthus heterophyllus	PURPLE-LEAF FALSE HOLLY
Philadelphus lewisii	WESTERN MOCK ORANGE ❖
Physocarpus capitatus	PACIFIC OR WESTERN NINEBARK ❖
Physocarpus opulifolius	NINEBARK
Prostanthera lasianthus	VICTORIAN CHRISTMAS BUSH
Pyracantha 'Mohave'	FIRETHORN
Rhaphithamnus spinosus	PRICKLY MYRTLE
Rhododendron macrophyllum	PACIFIC OR COAST RHODODENDRON ❖
Rhododendron occidentale	WESTERN AZALEA ❖
Sambucus nigra 'Black Beauty', 'Black Lace'	PURPLE CUT-LEAF ELDERBERRY
Sambucus nigra f. *laciniata*	CUT-LEAF BLACK ELDER
Sorbus sitchensis	SITKA MOUNTAIN-ASH ❖
Stachyurus praecox	STACHYURUS
Vaccinium ovatum	EVERGREEN HUCKLEBERRY ❖
Vaccinium parvifolium	RED HUCKLEBERRY, RED BILBERRY ❖
Viburnum edule	HIGHBUSH CRANBERRY ❖
Viburnum ellipticum	OREGON VIBURNUM, WESTERN WAYFARING TREE ❖
Viburnum plicatum f. *tomentosum* 'Mariesii'	DOUBLEFILE VIBURNUM
Vitex 'Flip Side'	FLIP SIDE CHASTE TREE

MEDIUM SHRUBS *(5 to 8 feet tall)*

Arctostaphylos canescens var. *sonomensis*	SONOMA MANZANITA
Arctostaphylos columbiana	BRISTLY OR HAIRY MANZANITA ❖
Arctostaphylos glandulosa ssp. *glandulosa* 'Demeter'	DEMETER OREGON MANZANITA
Berberis × gladwynensis 'William Penn'	WILLIAM PENN BARBERRY
Berberis darwinii	DARWIN'S BARBERRY
Callianthe megapotamica hybrids	BRAZILIAN BELL FLOWER
Carpenteria californica cultivars	BUSH ANEMONE
Ceanothus × delileanus 'Gloire de Versailles'	HARDY HYBRID CEANOTHUS
Ceanothus 'Skylark' ('Victoria')	VICTORIA CALIFORNIA LILAC
Ceanothus thyrsiflorus 'Dark Star'	DARK STAR CALIFORNIA LILAC
Ceanothus thyrsiflorus 'Julia Phelps'	JULIA PHELPS CALIFORNIA LILAC
Chrysojasminum (Jasminum) fruticans	COMMON YELLOW JASMINE
Chrysolepis chrysophylla var. *minor*	BUSH CHINQUAPIN ❖
Cistus × ladanifer 'Blanche'	LARGE WHITE ROCKROSE
Cistus × pagei	FRAGRANT ROCKROSE
Corylopsis spicata	SPIKE WINTERHAZEL
Cotinus coggygria 'Winecraft Black'	BLACK SMOKE TREE
Deutzia scabra 'Flore-pleno'	DOUBLE-FLOWERED FUZZY DEUTZIA
Enkianthus campanulatus	ENKIANTHUS
Exochorda × macrantha 'The Bride'	THE BRIDE PEARL-BUSH
Fabiana imbricata 'Violacea'	CHILEAN HEATHER

Fothergilla gardenii	DWARF WITCH ALDER
Frangula (Rhamnus) californica	COFFEEBERRY ❖
Grevillea australis	SOUTHERN GREVILLEA
Grevillea 'Poorinda Leanne' ('Poorinda Queen')	LEANNE GREVILLEA
Grevillea rivularis	CARRINGTON FALLS GREVILLEA
Hydrangea macrophylla 'Mariesii'	LACE-CAP HYDRANGEA
Hydrangea paniculata 'Beeguile'	BEEGUILE PANICLED HYDRANGEA
Hydrangea quercifolia 'Snow Queen'	OAKLEAF HYDRANGEA
Hydrangea serrata 'Beni-gaku'	MOUNTAIN HYDRANGEA
Hydrangea serrata 'Preziosa'	MOP-HEAD HYDRANGEA
Hypericum x *inodorum*	SANGRIA ST. JOHN'S WORT
Kalmia latifolia	MOUNTAIN LAUREL
Leptospermum sericeum	SILVER TEA TREE
Leycesteria crocothyrsos	YELLOW HIMALAYAN HONEYSUCKLE
Mahonia aquifolium	OREGON-GRAPE ❖
Mahonia x *media* cultivars	HYBRID MAHONIA
Olearia moschata	INCENSE PLANT
Olearia x *oleifolia* 'Waikariensis'	HARDY DAISY-ON-A-STICK
Osmanthus x *burkwoodii*	BURKWOOD'S SWEET OLIVE
Osmanthus delavayi	SWEET OLIVE
Osmanthus heterophyllus 'Goshiki'	VARIEGATED FALSE HOLLY
Paeonia delavayi (includes the yellow forms called *P. lutea*)	DELAVAY'S TREE PEONY
Paeonia rockii and hybrids	ROCK'S TREE PEONY
Philadelphus 'Belle Etoile'	MOCK ORANGE
Philadelphus coronarius 'Aureus'	GOLDEN MOCK ORANGE
Philadelphus madrensis	DESERT MOUNTAIN MOCK ORANGE
Pieris 'Brouwer's Beauty'	LILY-OF-THE-VALLEY SHRUB
Pieris japonica	LILY-OF-THE-VALLEY SHRUB, ANDROMEDA
Ribes aureum	GOLDEN CURRANT ❖
Ribes sanguineum	RED CURRANT ❖
Salvia rosmarinus (*Rosmarinus officinalis*)	ROSEMARY
Symphoricarpos albus	COMMON SNOWBERRY ❖
Syringa pubescens ssp. *patula* 'Miss Kim'	DWARF KOREAN LILAC
Viburnum x *bodnantense* 'Dawn'	PINK DAWN VIBURNUM
Viburnum plicatum var. *tomentosum* 'Pink Sensation'	PINK SENSATION VIBURNUM
Weigela florida	WEIGELA

SMALL SHRUBS *(1 to 5 feet tall)*

Arctostaphylos x *media*	HYBRID MANZANITA ❖
Baeckea gunniana	HEATHMYRTLE
Berberis buxifolia 'Nana'	DWARF BOX-LEAF BARBERRY
Berberis (?triacanthophora) 'Cally Rose'	CALLY ROSE BARBERRY
Berberis x *stenophylla* 'Corallina Compacta'	MINIATURE HEDGE BARBERRY
Berberis thunbergii f. *atropurpurea*	PURPLE-LEAF JAPANESE BARBERRY
Berberis verruculosa	WARTY BARBERRY
Berberis wilsoniae	WILSON'S BARBERRY
Brachyglottis monroi	MONRO'S DAISY BUSH

Brachyglottis 'Otari Cloud'	OTARI CLOUD DAISY BUSH
Calluna vulgaris	HEATHER
Camellia hiemalis 'Aglaia'	HIEMALIS CAMELLIA
Camellia sasanqua 'Chansonette', 'Dream Quilt', 'Jewel Box', 'October Magic Carpet', 'Reverend Ida', 'Sarrel', 'Showa No Sakae', 'Tanya', 'Twinkle Twinkle', 'Winter's Rose'	SASANQUA CAMELLIA
Caryopteris incana	BLUEBEARD
Caryopteris x clandonensis	BLUEBEARD
Chaenomeles speciosa 'Contorta'	CONTORTED FLOWERING QUINCE
Choisya ternata	MEXICAN MOCK ORANGE
Chrysojasminum (Jasminum) floridum	SHOWY JASMINE
Chrysojasminum (Jasminum) parkeri	DWARF JASMINE
Cistus x bornetianus 'Jester'	JESTER ROCKROSE
Cistus x canescens 'Albus'	WHITE ROCKROSE
Cistus x crispatus 'Warley Rose'	WARLEY ROSE ROCKROSE
Cistus x dansereaui 'Jenkyn Place'	JENKYN PLACE ROCKROSE
Cistus x florentinus 'Tramontane'	SPOTTED ROCKROSE
Cistus x heterocalyx 'Chelsea Bonnet'	CHELSEA BONNET ROCKROSE
Cistus x obtusifolius	COMPACT WHITE ROCKROSE
Cistus 'Snowfire'	SNOWFIRE ROCKROSE
Cotoneaster adpressus 'Little Gem'	COMPACT COTONEASTER
Cotoneaster dammeri	BEARBERRY COTONEASTER
Cotoneaster salicifolius 'Repens'	SPREADING WILLOW-LEAF COTONEASTER
Cotoneaster hodjingensis (C. glaucophyllus)	GRAY-LEAF COTONEASTER
Daphne x burkwoodii 'Carol Mackie'	VARIEGATED HYBRID DAPHNE
Daphne x medfordensis 'Lawrence Crocker'	DWARF DAPHNE
Daphne x transatlantica	HYBRID DAPHNE
Daphne odora 'Aureomarginata'	VARIEGATED WINTER DAPHNE
Daphne tangutica	DAPHNE
Dasiphora (Potentilla) fruticosa (ss)	SHRUBBY CINQUEFOIL ❖
Deutzia gracilis 'Chardonnay Pearls', 'Nikko'	DWARF DEUTZIA
Deutzia setchuenensis var. *corymbiflora*	CHINESE SNOW FLOWER
Erica x darleyensis (ss)	DARLEY DALE HEATH
Erica terminalis	CORSICAN HEATH, UPRIGHT HEATH
Elsholtzia stauntonii (ss)	CHINESE MINT SHRUB
Forsythia x intermedia 'Fiesta'	VARIEGATED FORSYTHIA
Fuchsia 'Lord Byron' (ss)	HARDY FUCHSIA
Grevillea juniperina cultivars	JUNIPER-LEAF GREVILLEA
Hebe 'Blue Mist'	BLUE MIST HEBE
Hebe 'Emerald Gem'	HEBE
Hebe 'Hinerua'	HEBE
Hebe cupressoides	HEBE
Hebe pinguifolia 'Sutherlandii'	BLUE-LEAF HEBE
Hebe topiaria	HEBE
Helichrysum splendidum (ss)	CAPE GOLD
Hydrangea arborescens 'Annabelle'	SMOOTH HYDRANGEA
Hydrangea involucrata	BRACTED HYDRANGEA
Hydrangea macrophylla	MOP-HEAD HYDRANGEA

Hydrangea quercifolia 'Munchkin'	DWARF OAK-LEAF HYDRANGEA
Hydrangea serrata 'Little Geisha'	MOUNTAIN HYDRANGEA
Hypericum olympicum f. *uniflorum* 'Citrinum'	CITRINUM ST. JOHN'S WORT
Ilex crenata 'Dwarf Pagoda'	DWARF JAPANESE HOLLY
Ilex crenata 'Green Island'	JAPANESE HOLLY
Kalmia latifolia 'Elf'	DWARF MOUNTAIN LAUREL
Kalmia latifolia 'Minuet'	MOUNTAIN LAUREL
Kerria japonica 'Picta'	JAPANESE KERRIA
Leptodermis oblonga	HIMALAYAN LILAC
Leptospermum namadgiensis	ALPINE TEA TREE
Leptospermum rupestre 'Highland Pink'	HIGHLAND PINK TEA TREE
Leucothoe fontanesiana 'Zeblid'	DROOPING LAUREL
Linnaea (Abelia) x *grandiflora*	GLOSSY ABELIA
Lonicera pileata	BOX-LEAF HONEYSUCKLE
Mahonia piperiana	PIPER'S OREGON-GRAPE
Melaleuca (Callistemon) viridiflorus 'Xera Compact'	
	COMPACT MOUNTAIN BOTTLEBRUSH
Myrteola nummularia	CRANBERRY-MYRTLE
Paeonia Itoh hybrids	INTERSECTIONAL TREE PEONY
Paeonia x *suffruticosa* hybrids	TREE PEONY
Penstemon fruticosus (ss)	SHRUBBY PENSTEMON, BUSH PENSTEMON ❖
Phlomis italica (ss)	BALEARIC ISLAND-SAGE
Pieris japonica 'Cavatine', 'Little Heath'	DWARF LILY-OF-THE-VALLEY SHRUB
Prostanthera cuneata	ALPINE MINT BUSH
Rhodanthemum (Chrysanthemum) hosmariense (ss)	MOROCCAN DAISY
Rhododendron glaucophyllum	ROSY RHODODENDRON
Ribes laurifolium	EVERGREEN CURRANT
Ruscus x *microglossus*	GROUNDCOVER BUTCHERS BROOM
Salix nakamurana var. *yezoalpina*	CREEPING ALPINE WILLOW
Salix purpurea 'Nana'	DWARF PURPLE OSIER
Sarcococca confusa	SWEETBOX
Sarcococca hookeriana	SWEETBOX
Spiraea betulifolia 'Tor'	BIRCH-LEAF SPIREA
Spiraea splendens (*S. densiflora*)	SUBALPINE OR MOUNTAIN SPIREA ❖
Spiraea japonica	JAPANESE SPIRAEA
Spiraea thunbergii	THUNBERG'S SPIREA, BRIDALWREATH SPIREA
Symphoricarpos mollis	CREEPING SNOWBERRY ❖
Viburnum cassinoides 'Lil' Ditty'	DWARF BLUE HAW
Viburnum davidii	DAVID'S VIBURNUM
Viburnum farreri 'Nanum'	DWARF FRAGRANT VIBURNUM
Viburnum opulus 'Nanum'	DWARF SNOWBALL
Vitex agnus-castus 'Blue Puffball'	CHASTE TREE

(ss) = technically a "subshrub" (or even more technically, a *"chamaephyte"*). Often called "dwarf-shrubs" or "woody perennials," they are, in a sense, something in-between. They're more like perennials which develop a woodiness or corkiness to the lower parts of their stems during droughty conditions. Most popular species and hybrids of *Lavandula* actually fall here but their popularity with the name "perennials" has made me decide, at least for now, to keep that in that category.

DWARF CONIFERS

Distinctively shrub-like.

Abies balsamea 'Nana', 'Piccolo'	DWARF BALSAM FIR
Abies koreana 'Gait'	DWARF KOREAN FIR
Cephalotaxus harringtonia 'Duke Gardens'	DWARF PLUM YEW
Chamaecyparis obtusa many dwarf cultivars	DWARF HINOKI CYPRESS
Chamaecyparis pisifera many dwarf cultivars	DWARF SAWARA CYPRESS
Chamaecyparis thyoides many dwarf cultivars	DWARF ATLANTIC CEDAR
Cryptomeria japonica dwarf cultivars	DWARF PLUME CEDAR
Ginkgo biloba 'Mariken'	DWARF GINKGO
Juniperus communis selections	COMMON JUNIPER
Juniperus squamata cultivars	FLAKY JUNIPER
Larix kaempferi 'Haverbeck'	DWARF JAPANESE LARCH
Metasequoia glyptostroboides 'North Light'	DWARF VARIEGATED DAWN REDWOOD
Picea abies dwarf cultivars	DWARF NORWAY SPRUCE
Picea engelmannii 'Bush's Lace'	BUSH'S LACE SPRUCE ❖
Picea engelmannii 'Missy'	MISSY DWARF SPRUCE ❖
Picea glauca dwarf cultivars	DWARF WHITE SPRUCE
Picea mariana 'Nana'	DWARF BLACK SPRUCE
Picea orientalis 'Bergman's Gem'	BERGMAN'S GEM ORIENTAL SPRUCE
Picea pungens dwarf cultivars	DWARF COLORADO SPRUCE
Pinus cembra 'Blue Mound'	BLUE MOUND SWISS STONE PINE
Pinus heldreichii 'Compact Gem'	COMPACT BOSNIAN PINE
Pinus mugo dwarf cultivars	MUGO PINE
Pinus strobus 'Pincushion'	DWARF EASTERN WHITE PINE
Podocarpus alpinus 'Blue Gem'	ALPINE PLUM YEW
Sciadopitys verticillata 'Picola'	DWARF JAPANESE UMBRELLA PINE
Thuja occidentalis 'Teddy'	TEDDY WHITE CEDAR
Thuja orientalis dwarf cultivars	DWARF ORIENTAL ARBORVITAE
Thuja plicata 'Stoneham Gold'	DWARF WESTER RED-CEDAR ❖
Thujopsis dolabrata 'Nana'	DWARF HIBA ARBORVITAE
Tsuga canadensis dwarf cultivars	DWARF HEMLOCK
Tsuga diversifolia 'Loowit'	DWARF NORTHERN JAPANESE HEMLOCK
Tsuga mertensiana 'Bump's Blue'	BUMP'S BLUE DWARF MOUNTAIN HEMLOCK ❖
Tsuga sieboldii 'Greenball'	DWARF JAPANESE HEMLOCK

NATURALLY-NARROW/UPRIGHT SHRUBS

Sometimes the landscape has a vertical space (height) that needs to be filled but doesn't have the horizontal space to accommodate the spread. Often for the sake of screening and privacy. There are trees which fill such a space (see "NATURALLY-NARROW TREES") but they may be too large. Then there are these.

Acer circinatum 'Pacific Sprite'	PACIFIC SPRITE VINE MAPLE
Berberis thunbergii 'Gold Pillar'	BERBERIS
Buxus sempervirens 'Dee Runk'	DEE RUNK BOXWOOD
Buxus sempervirens 'Graham Blandy'	GRAHAM BLANDY BOXWOOD
Camellia sasanqua "October Magic" series	UPRIGHT SUN CAMELLIA
Cephalotaxus harringtonia 'Fastigiata'	COLUMNAR JAPANESE PLUM YEW
Chamaecyparis lawsoniana 'Chilworth Silver'	SILVER BLUE LAWSON'S CYPRESS
Chamaecyparis lawsoniana 'Grayswood Feather'	FEATHER LAWSON CYPRESS
Cupressus sempervirens 'Tiny Tower'	TINY TOWER CYPRESS
Eucryphia lucida 'Spring Glow'	SPRING GLOW TASMANIAN LEATHERWOOD
Euonymus japonicus 'Aureo-marginatus', 'Chollipo', 'Greenspire'	EUONYMUS
Frangula alnus (*Rhamnus frangula*) 'Fine Line Improved'	FERNLEAF BUCKTHORN
Hibiscus syriacus 'Purple Pillar'	ROSE OF SHARON
Ilex x *aquipernyi* 'Meschick'	DRAGON LADY HOLLY
Ilex x *attenuata* 'Foster'	FOSTER HOLLY
Ilex 'Carolina Sentinel'	CAROLINA SENTINEL HOLLY
Ilex 'Centennial Girl'	CENTENNIAL GIRL HOLLY
Ilex cornuta 'Fineline'	FINELINE HOLLY
Ilex cornuta 'Needlepoint'	NEEDLEPOINT HOLLY
Ilex crenata 'Mariesii'	JAPANESE HOLLY
Ilex crenata 'Patti O'	PATTI O HOLLY
Ilex crenata 'Sky Pencil'	SKY PENCIL HOLLY
Ilex 'Mary Nell'	MARY NELL HOLLY
Ilex x *meserveae* 'Castle Spire' *(female)*	BLUE HOLLY
Ilex x *meserveae* 'Castle Wall' *(male)*	BLUE HOLLY
Ilex 'National'	NATIONAL HOLLY
Ilex 'Nellie R. Stevens'	NELLIE STEVENS HOLLY
Juniperus chinensis 'Robusta Green'	ROBUSTA GREEN JUNIPER
Juniperus chinensis 'Spartan'	SPARTAN JUNIPER
Juniperus communis 'Hibernica'	HIBERNICA JUNIPER
Juniperus communis 'Little Spire'	LITTLE SPIRE JUNIPER
Juniperus scopulorum 'Moonglow'	MOONGLOW JUNIPER
Olearia paniculata	AKIRAHO
Podocarpus macrophyllus 'Maki'	DWARF YEW PINE
Sambucus nigra 'Black Tower'	BLACK TOWER ELDERBERRY
Sambucus nigra 'Golden Tower'	GOLDEN TOWER ELDERBERRY
Taxus cuspidata 'Minuet' (not *Taxus baccata*)	MINUET JAPANESE YEW
Taxus x *media* 'Hicksii'	ANGLO-JAPANESE YEW
Taxus x *media* 'Stonehenge'	STONEHENGE ANGLO-JAPANESE YEW

DISEASE-RESISTANT ROSES

Note that roses found resistant in one location may be susceptible in another location due to the presence of different fungal strains. Also, resistant roses may become susceptible after a few years due to changes in the local fungal population.

COLOR CODES

ab	apricot/ apricot blend	**dr**	dark red	**lp**	light pink
m	mauve/ mauve blend	**mr**	medium red	**ob**	orange/ orange blend
or	orange red	**r**	russet	**w**	white/ white blend
dp	deep pink	**dy**	deep yellow	**ly**	light yellow
mp	medium pink	**my**	medium yellow	**op**	orange pink
pb	pink blend	**rb**	red blend	**yb**	yellow blend

*Varieties marked with an '**F**' have medium fragrance; those marked with '**VF**' are very fragrant.*

HYBRID TEAS & GRANDIFLORAS

'Electron'	(dp)	'New Day'	(my)
'Firefighter'	(dr) **F**	'New Zealand'	(lp) **VF**
'Gemini'	(pb)	'Polarstern'	(w)
'Helmut Schmidt'	(my)	'Princess Margaret'	(mp)
'Just Joey'	(ob)	'Silver Jubilee'	(pb)
'Keep Sake'	(pb)	'Sugar Moon'	(w) **VF**
'Las Vegas'	(ob)	'Tournament of Roses'	(mp)
'Lasting Love'	(dr) **VF**	'Voodoo'	(ob)
'Love'	(rb)		

FLORIBUNDAS

'Betty Boop'	(rb)	'Play Girl'	(mp)
'Bolero'	(w) **VF**	'Regensberg'	(pb)
'Europeana'	(dr)	'Sarabande'	(r)
'Impatient'	(or)	'Sexy Rexy'	(mp)
'Julia Child'	(my) **VF**	'Showbiz'	(mr)
'Lava Flow'	(dr)	'Sparkle & Shine'	(my)
'Liverpool Echo'	(ob)	'Trumpeter'	(or)
'Livin' Easy'	(ob)	'Violet's Pride'	(m) **F**
'Matangi'	(rb)	'Viva'	(dr)
'Playboy'	(rb)		

CLIMBERS/RAMBLERS/PILLARS

'Autumn Sunset'	(ob) **VF**	'Dortmund'	(mr)
'Candy Land'	(pb) **F**	'Dublin Bay'	(mr)
'Constance Spry'	(lp) **F**	'Royal Sunset'	(ab)
'Darlow's Enigma' (rambler) (w) **F**		'Sally Holmes Cl.'	(w) **F**

MODERN SHRUBS ("LANDSCAPE ROSES")

'Alfred Sisley'	(pb)	'Kaleidoscope'	(ob)
'Appleblossom Rose' ('Noamel') (mp)		'Knock Out'	(rb)
'Apricot Drift'	(ab)	'Lemon Drift'	(ly)
'Baby Love'	(my)	'Lemon Fizz'	(dy)
'Carefree Celebration'	(op)	'Milwaukee's Calatrava'	(w)
'Carefree Delight'	(lp)	'Morden Sunrise'	(yb)
'Carefree Spirit'	(rb)	'Pillow Fight'	(w)
'Carefree Sunshine'	(my)	'Radway Sunrise'	(ob) **F**
'Coral Drift'	(ob)	'Rainbow Happy Trails'	(pb)
'Fire Meidiland'	(dr)	'Sally Holmes'	(lp)
'Gourmet Popcorn'	(w)	'Sea Foam'	(w)
'Happy Chappy'	(ob)	'Sevillana'	(dr)
'Home Run'	(mr)	'White Out'	(w)

ENGLISH SHRUBS

'Benjamin Britten'	(mr) **F**	'Lady Emma Hamilton'	(ob) **F**
'Boscobel'	(pb) **F**	'Mary Rose'	(mp) **F**
'Carding Mill'	(ab) **F**	'Munstead Wood'	(dr) **F**
'Charlotte'	(my)	'Princess Anne'	(dp) **F**
'Crown Princess Margareta' (ob)		'Queen of Sweden'	(mp) **F**
'Emily Bronte'	(pb) **F**	'Sceptr'd Isle'	(pb) **F**
'Gentle Hermione'	(mp) **F**	'Strawberry Hill'	(pb) **F**
'Golden Celebration'	(ob) **F**	'Susan Williams-Ellis'	(w) **F**
'Grace'	(ob) **F**	'Sweet Juliet'	(pb) **F**
'Harlow Carr'	(dp) **F**	'The Mayflower'	(mp)
'Heritage'	(ly)	'Wollerton Old Hall'	(ly) **F**
'James Galway'	(mp) **F**		

»» More ...

SPECIES AND OLD ROSES

Rosa gallica var. *officinalis*   APOTHECARY ROSE (dp) **VF**
Rosa gallica var. *officinalis* 'Versicolor'   ROSA MUNDI (dp+w) **VF**
Rosa glauca   RED-STEM ROSE (mp) **F**
Rosa x *odorata* 'Mutabilis'   BUTTERFLY ROSE (op) **F**
Rosa primula   INCENSE ROSE (ly) **F**
Rosa rugosa   BEACH ROSE (w, lp, dp, mr)
Rosa sericea ssp. *omeiensis* f. *pteracantha*   WINGED ROSE (w)

ROSA RUGOSA HYBRIDS

'Belle Poitevine' (mp/pb) **VF**   'Robusta' (dr) **F**
'Blanc Double de Coubert' (w) **VF**   'Rosalina' (mp) **F**
'Buffalo Gal' (dp) **VF**   'Roseraie de l'Haÿ' (dr) **VF**
'Charles Albanel' (dp/m) **F**   'Rugelda' (yb) **F**
'Frau Dagmar Hastrup' (lp) **VF**   'Souvenir de Philemon Cochet' (w) **VF**
'Hansa' (dp) **F**   'Sarah Van Fleet' (mp) **F**
'Jens Munk' (mp) **VF**   'Thérèse Bugnet' (dp) **F**
'Linda Campbell' (dr)   'Topaz Jewel' (ly) **VF**
'Mrs. Doreen Pike' (mp) **VF**   'Wildberry Breeze' (mp) **VF**
'Purple Pavement' (m) **VF**

OLD GARDEN ROSE HYBRIDS (OGRs)

'Adélaide d'Orléans' (w)   'Francis E. Lester' (w+lp) **VF**
'Ballerina' (mp+w) **F**   'Ghislaine de Feligonde' (ob) **F**
'Charles de Mills' (dp) **VF**   'Golden Wings' (my) **F**
'Duchesse de Montebello' (lp) **F**   'Madame Alfred Carrière' (lp) **VF**
'Fairy' (mp)   'Marchesa Boccella' (lp-mp) **F**
'Félicité Perpétue' (w/lp) **F**   'Reine des Violettes' (dr+m) **F**

"Won't you come into the garden? I would like my roses to see you."
~~ Richard Brinsley Sheridan

SHRUBS FOR SCREENING/BACKGROUND

Those shrubs which are intended for use as screening (blocking a bad view or providing privacy) must be strong growers and must be dense. Evergreen plants provide privacy all year. Deciduous plants allow light to come in during the coldest months and work for "screening" when the view doesn't need serious blocking.

CONIFERS *5 ft to 10 ft in height at maturity*

Abies concolor 'Blue Cloak'	BLUE CLOAK WHITE FIR
Juniperus communis 'Gold Cone'	GOLD CONE JUNIPER ❖
Picea glauca 'Sander's Blue'	SANDER'S BLUE SPRUCE
Picea orientalis 'Aureospicata'	GOLDEN ORIENTAL SPRUCE
Picea pungens 'Montgomery'	MONTGOMERY BLUE SPRUCE
Pinus parviflora 'Ogon Janome'	DRAGON'S EYE WHITE PINE
Pinus strobus 'Louie'	LOUIE EASTERN WHITE PINE
Taxus x *media* 'Hatfieldii'	ANGLO-JAPANESE YEW
Thuja 'Emerald Green'	EMERALD GREEN ARBORVITAE
Tsuga canadensis 'Moon Frost'	MOON FROST HEMLOCK

BROADLEAF EVERGREENS *5 ft to 10 ft at maturity*

Arbutus unedo 'Compacta'	COMPACT STRAWBERRY TREE
Arctostaphylos columbiana	BRISTLY OR HAIRY MANZANITA ❖
Arctostaphylos densiflora 'Howard McMinn'	MANZANITA
Arctostaphylos manzanita 'St. Helena'	ST. HELENA MANZANITA
Aucuba japonica	JAPANESE LAUREL
Berberis julianae	WINTERGREEN BARBERRY
Berberis x *ottawensis* 'Auricoma'	RED HEDGE BARBERRY
Berberis x *stenophylla*	HEDGE BARBERRY
Buxus sempervirens 'Dee Runk'	DEE RUNK BOXWOOD
Buxus sempervirens 'Fastigiata'	FASTIGIATED BOXWOOD
Ceanothus thyrsiflorus many cultivars	BLUE BLOSSOM
Choisya ternata 'Sundance'	SUNDANCE MEXICAN ORANGE
Elaeagnus x *submacrophylla* (*E.* x *ebbingei*)	HYBRID ELAEAGNUS
Escallonia bifida	ESCALLONIA
Escallonia x *langleyensis* 'Pride of Donard'	PRIDE OF DONARD ESCALLONIA
Fargesia dracocephala	DRAGON'S HEAD BAMBOO
Fargesia murielae	UMBRELLA BAMBOO
Fatsia japonica	FATSIA
Feijoa (Acca) sellowiana	PINEAPPLE GUAVA
Frangula (Rhamnus) californica 'Eve Case'	COFFEEBERRY ❖
Garrya fremontii	FREMONT SILK-TASSEL ❖
Grevillea 'Audrey' (sold as 'Poorinda Constance')	AUDREY GREVILLEA
Grevillea victoriae	ROYAL GREVILLEA
Ilex x *meserveae* 'Blue Girl'	BLUE GIRL MESERVE HOLLY
Ilex x *meserveae* 'Castle Spire' *(female)*	BLUE HOLLY

Ilex x *meserveae* 'Castle Wall' *(male)*	BLUE HOLLY
Leptospermum lanigerum	WOOLLY TEA TREE
Leptospermum sericeum	SILVER TEA TREE
Notholithocarpus densiflorus var. *echinoides*	SHRUB TANOAK ❖
Olearia moschata	INCENSE PLANT
Olearia paniculata	AKIRAHO
Osmanthus x burkwoodii	BURKWOOD'S OSMANTHUS
Osmanthus delavayi	DELAVAY OSMANTHUS
Osmanthus heterophyllus	HOLLY-LEAF OLIVE
Pieris japonica	LILY-OF-THE-VALLEY SHRUB, ANDROMEDA
Pieris formosa var. *forrestii*	CHINESE PIERIS, HIMALAYAN PIERIS
Rhaphithamnus spinosus	PRICKLY MYRTLE
Rhododendron, especially 'Roseum Elegans', 'Catawbiense Boursault', 'Arthur Bedford', 'Horizon Monarch', 'Lem's Monarch', 'Loderi King George', 'Loderi Venus', 'Mrs. G. W. Leak'	RHODODENDRON
Tasmannia (Drimys) lanceolata	MOUNTAIN PEPPER
Ternstroemia gymnanthera	JAPANESE TERNSTROEMIA
Vaccinium ovatum	EVERGREEN HUCKLEBERRY ❖
Viburnum x *pragense*	PRAGUE VIBURNUM
Viburnum suspensum	SANDANKWA VIBURNUM
Viburnum tinus	LAURUSTINUS

BROADLEAF EVERGREENS *10 ft to 20 ft at maturity*

Arbutus unedo	STRAWBERRY TREE
Azara microphylla	BOX-LEAF AZARA
Camellia japonica	CAMELLIA
Ceanothus thyrsiflorus 'Zanzibar'	BLUE BLOSSOM
Cercocarpus ledifolius	CURLLEAF MOUNTAIN-MAHOGANY ❖
Chusquea culeou	CHILEAN BAMBOO
Crinodendron hookerianum	CHILEAN LANTERN TREE
Garrya elliptica	SILK-TASSEL ❖
X *Hibanobambusa tranquillans* 'Shiroshima'	SHIROSHIMA BAMBOO
Himalayacalamus planatus (H. asper)	MALINGE NAGALO BAMBOO
Ilex x *altaclarensis* 'Lawsoniana'	LAWSONIANA HIGH CLERE HOLLY
Ilex × *attenuata* 'Foster #2'	FOSTER'S #2 HOLLY
Ilex latifolia	LUSTER-LEAF HOLLY
Ilex x *meserveae*	HYBRID HOLLY
Itea ilicifolia	HOLLY-LEAF SWEETSPIRE
Laurus nobilis	GRECIAN BAY LAUREL
Morella (Myrica) californica	PACIFIC WAX MYRTLE ❖
Myrceugenia parvifolia	PATAGÜILLA
Olearia macrodonta	DAISY BUSH, NEW ZEALAND HOLLY
Osmanthus × fortunei	FORTUNE'S OSMANTHUS
Phillyrea latifolia	MOCK PRIVET
Prostanthera lasianthus	VICTORIAN CHRISTMAS BUSH
Quillaja saponaria	SOAP-BARK TREE

Rhododendron macrophyllum	PACIFIC RHODODENDRON ❖
Stranvaesia (Photinia) davidiana	CHINESE PHOTINIA
Thamnocalamus crassinodus	TIBETAN BAMBOO
Viburnum x *burkwoodii*	BURKWOOD VIBURNUM
Viburnum cinnamomifolium	CINNAMON VIBURNUM
Viburnum odoratissimum var. *awabuki*	AWABUKI SWEET VIBURNUM

BROADLEAF DECIDUOUS *5 ft to 10 ft at maturity*

Aronia arbutifolia 'Brilliantissima'	BRILLIANT RED CHOKEBERRY
Callicarpa bodinieri	BODINIER'S BEAUTYBERRY
Ceanothus x *delileanus* 'Gloire de Versailles'	HARDY HYBRID CEANOTHUS
Cornus alba 'Elegantissima'	VARIEGATED DOGWOOD
Cornus sericea	RED TWIG DOGWOOD ❖
Enkianthus campanulatus	RED-VEIN ENKIANTHUS
Forsythia x *intermedia*	BORDER FORSYTHIA
Hibiscus syriacus	ROSE OF SHARON
Hydrangea quercifolia	OAKLEAF HYDRANGEA
Philadelphus virginalis 'Natchez'	NATCHEZ MOCK ORANGE
Ribes sanguineum	RED FLOWERING CURRANT ❖
Viburnum trilobum	AMERICAN CRANBERRY BUSH ❖

BROADLEAF DECIDUOUS *over 10 ft at maturity*

Acer campestre	HEDGE MAPLE
Carpinus betulus 'Frans Fontaine'	EUROPEAN HORNBEAM
Corylus avellana	EUROPEAN FILBERT
Cotinus coggygria	SMOKE TREE
Fagus sylvatica 'Purple Fountain'	EUROPEAN PURPLE BEECH
Magnolia liliiflora	LILY MAGNOLIA
Magnolia stellata 'Royal Star'	STAR MAGNOLIA
Malus sargentii	CRABAPPLE
Physocarpus capitatus	PACIFIC OR WESTERN NINEBARK ❖
Staphylea trifolia	AMERICAN BLADDERNUT
Syringa vulgaris	COMMON LILAC

NON-INVASIVE BUTTERFLY BUSHES

Buddleja davidii, for decades the most commonly planted "butterfly bush," became an invasive species, not only annoying gardeners with its promiscuous reseeding but assaulting the biodiversity of our natural ecosystems, as well. Yet still loved for its ability to attract our flying jewels, both butterflies and hummingbirds (and it does a pretty good job making moths happy, too). Fortunately, other species and several hybrids bear the same enticing talent without the "invasive" repercussions.

Buddleja alternifolia	ALTERNATE-LEAVED BUTTERFLY BUSH
Buddleja asiatica	DOG-TAIL
Buddleja colvilei	TREE BUDDLEJA
Buddleja crispa	HIMALAYAN BUTTERFLY BUSH
Buddleja curviflora	LAVENDER BUTTERFLY BUSH
Buddleja fallowiana	SUMMER LILAC
Buddleja globosa	CHILEAN ORANGE BALL TREE
Buddleja japonica	JAPANESE BUTTERFLY BUSH
Buddleja knappii	LILAC BUTTERFLY BUSH
Buddleja lindleyana	WEEPING BUTTERFLY BUSH
Buddleja loricata	POPCORN BUDDLEJA
Buddleja macrostachya	LONG-SPIKED BUTTERFLY BUSH
Buddleja marrubiifolia	WOOLLY BUTTERFLY BUSH
Buddleja nivea ssp. *yunnanensis*	SNOWY BUTTERFLY BUSH
Buddleja salviifolia	SAGE WOOD

Interspecific Hybrid cultivars/groups

Buddleja 'Asian Moon'	ASIAN MOON BUTTERFLY BUSH
Buddleja "Flutterby Grande"	HYBRID BUTTERFLY BUSH
Buddleja x 'Lochinich'	LOCHINICH BUTTERFLY BUSH
Buddleja 'Miss Molly'	MISS MOLLY BUTTERFLY BUSH
Buddleja 'Morning Mist' ('Silver Anniversary')	MORNING MIST BUTTERFLY BUSH
Buddleja 'Orange Sceptre'	ORANGE SCEPTRE BUTTERFLY BUSH
Buddleja x pikei 'Hever'	HEVER BUTTERFLY BUSH
Buddleja x weyeriana (many cultivars)	HYBRID BUTTERFLY BUSH

Extra special

Rostrinucula dependens	WEEPING ROSTRINICULA

With butterfly bush-like flowers and similar butterfly-attracting qualities

VINES

When it comes to use in the landscape, the most important factor in vine selection is size; no other plant types are as misused as vines where space is a key factor.

Second in importance, as far as gardeners are concerned, are the mechanisms and processes which vines use for climbing. They "climb" by **tendrils** (sometimes specialized), by **clinging**, by **twining**, or by simply **scrambling**. The support upon which you want to put the vine now plays a role in selection.

Tendril climbers have slender, coiling structures. Tendrils usually won't grab onto anything much larger than ½-inch wide. Tendrils cling to smaller objects better than do twiners; they are happy with wire netting on your fence or a twig on a host plant. Hence, these vines are excellent choices for latticework supports such as chain-link fences and lath trellises. These vines are also great growing over large shrubs or even over larger vines. With *Clematis*, the tendrils are leafy rather than stringy structures. Indicated with a **"Te"** after the common name.

Clinging vines climb with either disk-like adhesive tips — called holdfasts — that attach themselves to any surface (these are another kind of specialized tendril) or small aerial rootlets along the stems, rootlets that can squeeze themselves into even the tiniest crevices of a rough-textured surface. Clinging vines are a good choice when you need to cover a wide wall, especially of stone, block, or brick. Vines with aerial roots will not, however, climb up metal or glass. Indicated with a "C" after the common name.

Twiners, technically called "bines") twist their entire stems around a support as they grow. Because of this habit, these vines grow best on poles or fences; they won't grow on a wall by themselves. Some of these types, almost always the annual types or deciduous herbaceous types, are light enough to be happy on small structures. Others demand a hefty structure. Interestingly, some twining vines grow with their stems circling in a counterclockwise fashion; wisteria is a common example. Others circle their stems clockwise; honeysuckle for example. Do not try to train a vine to grow opposite to its natural habit. Depending on the ultimate size and vigor of the vine, you should provide something at least 1-inch in diameter and no more than about 4 inches in diameter. If you find a need for a trellis, it's usually best to build one yourself, in some custom fashion; the tiny trellises found at retail outlets almost never do the job satisfactorily. Indicated with a **"Tw"** after the common name.

Scramblers, also called clambering vines or scandent vines, have no means of attachment. They merely scramble or trail over surrounding vegetation, debris, or bare ground. They climb only in the sense that their stems will proceed on a vertical path if secured (by you) to a support as they grow. "Climbing" roses are the most familiar example. Left to themselves, they'll simply mound, sprawl and, yes, scramble on the ground. They need appropriate attachment and a helping hand on a regular basis. Indicated with a **"S"** after the common name.

SMALL *(generally 8 to 12 feet)*

Aconitum bulbuliferum 'Monk Gone Wild'	CLIMBING MONKSHOOD	Tw
Aconitum volubile	WOLF'S-BANE	Tw
Aristolochia sempervirens	EVERGREEN DUTCHMAN'S PIPE	Tw
Asteranthera ovata	ESTRELLITA, LITTLE STAR	S
Berberidopsis beckleri	CLIMBING CORAL PLANT	S
Billardiera longiflora	TASMANIAN BLUEBERRY VINE	Tw
Campsis x *tagliabuana* 'Takarazuka Fresa'	SUMMER JAZZ FIRE TRUMPET VINE	S
Chrysojasminum (Jasminum) odoratissimum	SWEETEST JASMINE	Tw/S
Clematis alpina 'Pamela Jackman'	BLUE ALPINE CLEMATIS	Te
Clematis x *cartmanii* 'Avalanche'	AVALANCHE EVERGREEN CLEMATIS	Te/S
Clematis x *cartmanii* 'Joe'	JOE EVERGREEN CLEMATIS	Te
Clematis chiisanensis 'Lemon Bells'	YELLOW BELL CLEMATIS	Te
Clematis 'Delightful Scent'	SUGAR SWEET CLEMATIS	Te
Clematis 'Etoile Violette'	VITICELLA CLEMATIS	Te
Clematis 'Josephine'	JOSEPHINE CLEMATIS	Te
Clematis 'General Sikorski'	GENERAL SIKORSKI CLEMATIS	Te
Clematis otophora	YELLOW BELL CLEMATIS	Te
Clematis 'Mrs. George Jackman'	MRS. GEORGE JACKMAN CLEMATIS	Te
Clematis 'Niobe'	NIOBE CLEMATIS	Te
Clematis occidentalis	WESTERN BLUE VIRGINS' BOWER ❖	S
Clematis 'Pink Flamingo'	PINK ALPINE CLEMATIS	Te
Clematis 'Princess Diana'	PRINCESS DIANA CLEMATIS	Te
Clematis 'Rooguchi'	ROOGUCHI CLEMATIS	S
Clematis serratifolia	SAW-LEAF CLEMATIS	Te
Clematis 'Silver Moon'	SILVER MOON CLEMATIS	Te
Clematis tangutica	GOLDEN-BELL CLEMATIS	Te
Clematis 'Westerplatte'	WESTERPLATTE CLEMATIS	Te
Codonopsis convolvulacea ssp. *grey-wilsonii*	CLIMBING BELLFLOWER	Tw
Codonopsis lanceolata	BONNET BELLFLOWER	Tw
Codonopsis pilosula	POOR-MAN'S GINSENG	Tw
Codonopsis vinciflora	BLUE BONNET BELLFLOWER	Tw/S
Dactylicapnos (Dicentra) scandens	CLIMBING YELLOW BLEEDING HEART	Te
Ercilla spicata (E. volubilis)	CHILEAN CLIMBER	C
Jasminum beesianum	RED JASMINE	Tw
Lapageria rosea	CHILEAN BELLFLOWER	Tw
Mitraria coccinea	CHILEAN MITRE FLOWER	S
Rosa 'Jeanne Lajoie'	CLIMBING MINIATURE ROSE	S
Rosa 'New Dawn'	NEW DAWN ROSE	S
Trachelospermum asiaticum 'Theta'	BIRD-FOOT STAR JASMINE	S
Tropaeolum leptophyllum	CLIMBING NASTURTIUM	S
Tropaeolum speciosum	RED NASTURTIUM	Tw
Tropaeolum tricolor	THREE-COLORED NASTURTIUM	Tw
Tropaeolum tuberosum var. *lineomaculatum* 'Ken Aslet'	MASHUA	Tw

MEDIUM *(generally 12 to 24 feet)*

Akebia quinata	CHOCOLATE VINE Tw
Chrysojasminum (Jasminum) humile f. *wallichianum*	NEPAL JASMINE Tw/S
Clematis 'Betty Corning'	BETTY CORNING CLEMATIS Te
Clematis cirrhosa	WINTER CLEMATIS Te
Clematis 'Polish Spirit'	POLISH SPIRIT CLEMATIS Te
Clematis tibetana	TIBETAN CLEMATIS Te
Decumaria sinensis	CHINESE WOOD VAMP C
Holboellia brachyandra 'Heavenly Ascent'	HOLBOELLIA VINE Tw
Hydrangea seemannii	SEEMANN'S HYDRANGEA C/S
Jasminum x *stephanense*	STEPHAN'S JASMINE Tw/S
Lonicera acuminata (L. henryi)	HENRY'S HONEYSUCKLE Tw
Lonicera ciliosa	ORANGE HONEYSUCKLE ❖ S
Lonicera x *tellmanniana*	RED-GOLD HONEYSUCKLE Tw
Passiflora x *belotii (P.* x *alato-caerulea)*	BLUE PASSION FLOWER Te/Tw
Pileostegia viburnoides	CLIMBING HYDRANGEA C
Schisandra rubriflora	CHINESE MAGNOLIA VINE Tw
Stauntonia purpurea	SAUSAGE VINE Tw

LARGE *(generally 24 feet and upwards of 100 feet)*

Actinidia kolomikta (male form)	KOLOMIKTA VINE S
Actinidia tetramera var. *maloides*	ROSY CRABAPPLE KIWI S
Campsis x *tagliabuana*	HYBRID TRUMPET CREEPER S
Clematis armandii	EVERGREEN CLEMATIS Te
Clematis montana	ANEMONE CLEMATIS Te
Clematis paniculata	SWEET AUTUMN CLEMATIS Te
Hedera algeriensis 'Glorie de Marengo'	VARIEGATED ALGERIAN IVY C
Hedera colchica 'Dentata Variegata'	VARIEGATED PERSIAN IVY C
Holboellia coriacea	SAUSAGE VINE Tw
Holboellia angustifolia ssp. *trifoliata* (= "Heronswood form"?)	SAUSAGE VINE Tw
Hydrangea anomala	CLIMBING HYDRANGEA Tw/C
Hydrangea petiolaris	CLIMBING HYDRANGEA Tw/C
Hydrangea (Schizophragma) hydrangeoides	JAPANESE HYDRANGEA VINE C
Hydrangea integrifolia	EVERGREEN CLIMBING HYDRANGEA C
Parthenocissus henryana	SILVER-VEIN CREEPER C
Parthenocissus quinquefolia	VIRGINIA CREEPER C
Parthenocissus tricuspidata 'Veitchii'	BOSTON IVY C
Vitis californica	PACIFIC GRAPE ❖ Te
Vitis coignetiae	CRIMSON GLORY VINE Te
Vitis 'Roger's Red'	ROGER'S RED GRAPE Te
Vitis vinifera 'Incana'	DUSTY MILLER GRAPE VINE Te
Vitis vinifera 'Purpurea'	PURPLE-LEAF GRAPE VINE Te

GROUNDCOVERS

Any plant which covers the ground, usually densely and flatly, can be described as a "ground cover." But some plants do a much better, more effective, and more efficient job of doing so. Some are woody-stemmed (low, spreading shrubs and subshrubs), some are rhizomatous-rooting herbaceous perennials (the more familiar types), and some grow slowly but tightly, in a "caespitose" (clumping) fashion with the advantage of covering the ground so densely that few, if any, weeds can find a footing. Make sure you select a groundcover suited to the size of your plot.

* = will tolerate various degrees of traffic; potential lawn substitute, some are mowable

FOR SMALL SPACES

Alchemilla alpina	ALPINE LADY'S-MANTLE
Asarum splendens	SPLENDID WILD GINGER
Bergenia dwarf hybrids (planted closely)	DWARF BERGENIA
Cardamine trifolia	THREE-LEAF CARDAMINE
Carex siderosticha var. *ciliatomarginata* 'Treasure Island'	CREEPING SEDGE
Clinopodium (Micromeria, Satureja) douglasii	YERBA BUENA ❖
Gaultheria ovatifolia	WESTERN TEABERRY ❖
Gazania linearis	TREASURE FLOWER
Glandora (Lithodora) prostrata 'Grace Ward', 'Heavenly Blue'	LITHODORA
Helianthemum nummularium	SUN ROSE
Hosta, smaller cultivars (such as the "Mouse" series; planted densely)	HOSTA
Leptinella gruveri*	MINIATURE BRASS BUTTONS
Leptinella squalida*	NEW ZEALAND BRASS BUTTONS
Mukdenia rossii 'Karasuba'	MUKDENIA
Omphalodes verna	CREEPING FORGET-ME-NOT
Ophiopogon formosanum	TAIWAN MONDO GRASS
Ophiopogon japonicus 'Gyoku-ryu'	DWARF MONDO GRASS
Phedimus (Sedum) kamtschaticus	KAMSCHATKA SEDUM, ORANGE STONECROP
Phedimus (Sedum) spurius	CAUCASIAN STONECROP
Phlox adsurgens	WOODLAND PHLOX ❖
Phlox caespitosa	TUFTED PHLOX ❖
Phlox nana	SANTA FE PHLOX
Pratia (Lobelia) pedunculata 'County Park'	SUPER STAR CREEPER
Saxifraga x geum 'Dentata'	TOOTHED SAXIFRAGE
Sedum divergens	SPREADING STONECROP ❖
Sedum oreganum	OREGON STONECROP ❖
Sedum spathulifolium	BROAD-LEAVED STONECROP ❖
Sedum tetractinum	CHINESE STONECROP
Teucrium aroanium	GRAY CREEPING GERMANDER
Thymus praecox ssp *praecox (T. polytrichus* ssp. *britannicus)* especially the cultivars 'Elfin', 'Minus'	MOTHER-OF-THYME

FOR MEDIUM SPACES

Alchemilla alpina	ALPINE LADY'S-MANTLE
Arctostaphylos uva-ursi 'Wood's Compact'	WOOD'S COMPACT BEARBERRY
Asarum caudatum	WILD GINGER ❖
Asarum europaeum	EUROPEAN WILD GINGER
Campanula poscharskyana	SERBIAN BELLFLOWER
Ceratostigma plumbaginoides	DWARF PLUMBAGO
Corethrogyne (Lessingia) filaginifolia 'Silver Carpet'	TRAILING SAND ASTER
Cotoneaster adpressus 'Little Gem'	COMPACT COTONEASTER
Epilobium (Zauschneria) canum ssp. *garrettii* 'Orange Carpet'	CALIFORNIA FUCHSIA
Epimedium trailing hybrids	HYBRID EPIMEDIUM
Falkia repens	OORTJIES, LITTLE EARS
Festuca rubra var. *juncea* 'Patrick's Point'*	BLUE CREEPING FESCUE ❖
*Fragaria chiloensis**	BEACH STRAWBERRY❖
Gaultheria procumbens 'Winter Splash'	VARIEGATED WINTERGREEN
Hakonechloa macra and cultivars	JAPANESE FOREST GRASS
Hebe pinguifolia 'Pagei'	PAGE'S HEBE
Hebe 'Wingletye'	WINGLETYE HEBE
*Leptinella gruveri**	MINIATURE BRASS BUTTONS
*Leptinella squalida**	NEW ZEALAND BRASS BUTTONS
Muehlenbeckia axillaris 'Nana'*	CREEPING WIRE VINE
Myrteola nummularia	CRANBERRY-MYRTLE
Ophiopogon clarkei	HIMALAYAN MONDO GRASS
Ophiopogon planiscapus 'Nigrescens'	BLACK MONDO GRASS
Oxalis oregana evergreen types*	EVERGREEN REDWOOD SORREL ❖
Pachysandra axillaris 'Windcliff Fragrant'	WINDCLIFF FRAGRANT PACHYSANDRA
Petrosedum (Sedum) rupestre	BLUE SEDUM
Phedimus (Sedum) kamtschaticus	KAMSCHATKA SEDUM, ORANGE STONECROP
Phedimus (Sedum) spurius	CAUCASIAN STONECROP
Phlox diffusa	SPREADING PHLOX ❖
Phlox divaricata	WOODLAND PHLOX
Pimelea prostrata	NEW ZEALAND DAPHNE
Pratia (Lobelia) pedunculata 'County Park'	SUPER STAR CREEPER
Ruscus x *microglossus*	GROUNDCOVER BUTCHERS BROOM
Saxifraga stolonifera	STRAWBERRY BEGONIA
Sedum divergens	SPREADING STONECROP ❖
Sedum tetractinum	CHINESE STONECROP
Teucrium cossonii "Majoricum"	FRUITY GERMANDER
Thymus cherierioides	SILVER NEEDLE THYME
Thymus x *citriodorus*	LEMON THYME
Thymus herba-barona	CARAWAY-SCENTED THYME
Thymus polytrichus ssp. *brittanicus* (*T. praecox* ssp. *arcticus*) 'Creeping Pink', 'Hall's', 'Reiter'	CREEPING THYME
Thymus serpyllum	WOOLLY THYME

FOR LARGE SPACES

Arctostaphylos 'Pacific Mist'	PACIFIC MIST MANZANITA
Arctostaphylos uva-ursi	KINNIKINNICK, BEARBERRY ❖
Baccharis tricuneata (B. magellanica) low form	CHRISTMAS BUSH
*Carex inops (C. pensylvanica)**	CREEPING SEDGE ❖
*Carex pansa**	DUNE SEDGE, MEADOW SEDGE ❖
*Carex praegracilis**	FIELD SEDGE ❖
*Carex tumulicola**	FOOTHILL SEDGE ❖
Ceanothus 'Centennial'	CENTENNIAL CALIFORNIA LILAC
Ceanothus gloriosus 'Anchor Bay'	ANCHOR BAY CALIFORNIA LILAC
Cotoneaster adpressus 'Little Gem'	COMPACT COTONEASTER
Cotoneaster dammeri	BEARBERRY COTONEASTER
Cotoneaster hodjingensis (C. glaucophyllus)	GRAY-LEAF COTONEASTER
Cotoneaster procumbens 'Queen of Carpets'	GROUND-HUGGING COTONEASTER
Cotoneaster salicifolius 'Repens'	SPREADING WILLOW-LEAF COTONEASTER
Epimedium trailing hybrids	HYBRID EPIMEDIUM
Festuca rubra var. *juncea* 'Patrick's Point'*	BLUE CREEPING FESCUE ❖
*Fragaria chiloensis**	BEACH STRAWBERRY❖
Grevillea australis "Prostrate"	TASMANIAN ALPINE GREVILLEA
Hakonechloa macra and cultivars	JAPANESE FOREST GRASS
Hebe decumbens	CREEPING HEBE
Juniperus communis selections	COMMON JUNIPER ❖
Leptospermum humifusum 'Horizontalis' ("Prostrate Form")	
	PROSTRATE TASMANIAN MANUKA
Leptospermum rupestre "Low Form"	CREEPING TEA TREE
Lonicera crassifolia	CREEPING HONEYSUCKLE
Lonicera pileata	BOX-LEAF HONEYSUCKLE
Mahonia repens	CREEPING OREGON-GRAPE ❖
Muehlenbeckia axillaris	CREEPING WIRE VINE
Oxalis oregana evergreen types*	EVERGREEN REDWOOD SORREL ❖
Pachysandra axillaris 'Windcliff Fragrant'	WINDCLIFF FRAGRANT PACHYSANDRA
Pachysandra procumbens	ALLEGHENY SPURGE
Pachysandra terminalis	JAPANESE SPURGE
Podocarpus lawrencei 'Purple King'	PURPLE KING MOUNTAIN PLUM-PINE
*Rubus calycinoides (R. hayata-koidzumii)**	CREEPING TAIWAN BRAMBLE
Symphoricarpos x *chenaultii* 'Hancock'	CHENAULT CORALBERRY
Thymus polytrichus ssp. *brittanicus (T. praecox* ssp. *arcticus)*	
'Creeping Pink', 'Reiter'	CREEPING THYME
Vancouveria hexandra	WHITE INSIDE-OUT FLOWER ❖
*Waldsteinia ternata**	BARREN STRAWBERRY

For dense groundcovers that suppress weeds, see the section "PROBLEM AREAS, PLANT PROBLEMS."

PERENNIALS & BULBS

Although commonly considered separate types of plants (usually based on arbitrarily assigned growth habits), both perennials and bulbs fill the same spaces and needs in the garden. Hence why I combined them here. More important to the selection decision, aside from sun or shade or something in-between, is their height.

TALL *(3 to 6 feet tall)*

Acanthus spinosus	BEAR'S BREECH
Actaea racemosa	BLACK BUGBANE, BLACK COHOSH
Actaea simplex Atropurpurea Group	BLACK BANEBERRY, BLACK BUGBANE
Agave many hardy species	CENTURY PLANT
Alcea rugosa	UKRAINIAN HOLLYHOCK
Amicia zygomeris	YOKE-LEAVED AMICIA
Aralia cordata including 'Sun King'	JAPANESE SPIKENARD
Aruncus dioicus var. *acuminatus*	SYLVAN GOAT'S-BEARD ❖
Baptisia australis and hybrids	FALSE INDIGO
Boltonia asteroides	WHITE DOLL'S DAISY, FALSE CHAMOMILE, FALSE ASTER
Campanula lactiflora	MILKY BELLFLOWER
Campanula latiloba	GREAT BELLFLOWER
Canna x *generalis*	CANNA, CANNA-LILY
Canna glauca 'Panache'	PANACHE CANNA
Cardiocrinum species	GIANT HIMALAYAN LILIES
Caryopteris divaricata	BUTTERFLY BLUEBEARD
Cephalaria gigantea	GIANT YELLOW SCABIOUS
Darmera peltata	UMBRELLA PLANT
Dierama adelphicum	FAIRY WAND, ANGEL'S FISHING ROD
Dierama dracomontanum	DRAKENBERG WANDFLOWER
Dierama grandiflorum	ANGEL'S FISHING ROD
Digitalis ferruginea	RUSTY FOXGLOVE
Disporum longistylum	CHINESE FAIRY BELLS
Echinops bannaticus	GLOBE THISTLE
Echinops tienschanicum	GIANT GLOBE THISTLE
Eremurus himalaicus	HIMALAYAN FOXTAIL LILY
Eremurus hybrids	FOXTAIL LILY
Eremurus stenophyllus	DESERT CANDLE
Eutrochium (Eupatorium) dubium 'Little Joe'	LITTLE JOE PYE WEED
Eutrochium (Eupatorium) maculatum Atropurpureum Group	
	BLACK-LEAF JOE PYE WEED ❖
Filipendula rubra	QUEEN OF THE PRAIRIE
Gunnera tinctoria	GIANT RHUBARB, CHILEAN RHUBARB
Hedychium species and hybrids	FLOWERING GINGER
Helianthus angustifolius 'First Light'	FIRST LIGHT SWAMP SUNFLOWER
Helianthus angustifolius 'Gold Lace'	GOLD LACE SWAMP SUNFLOWER
Helianthus angustifolius 'Matanzas Creek'	MATANZAS CREEK SUNFLOWER
Helianthus 'Lemon Queen'	LEMON QUEEN PERENNIAL SUNFLOWER
Helianthus maximiliani 'Dakota Sunshine'	DAKOTA SUNSHINE SUNFLOWER

Helianthus maximiliani 'Santa Fe'	SANTA FE SUNFLOWER
Helianthus x *multiflorus* 'Capenoch Star'	CAPENOCH STAR SUNFLOWER
Helianthus x *multiflorus* 'Meteor'	METEOR SUNFLOWER
Helianthus x *multiflorus* 'Sunshine Daydream'	SUNSHINE DAYDREAM SUNFLOWER
Hemerocallis citrina 'Yao Ming'	CITRON DAYLILY, LONG YELLOW DAYLILY
Hibiscus 'Pink Teacups'	PINK TEACUPS HARDY MALLOW
Hibiscus 'Rubra'	RUBRA HYBRID MALLOW
Hosta, especially 'Blue Mammoth', 'Blue Wu', 'Empress Wu', 'Eola Sapphire', 'Jurassic Park', 'Komodo Dragon', 'Mikado', 'Sum and Substance, 'Sum of All', 'T Rex'	HOSTA
Iris x *pseudata* hybrids	PSEUDATA IRIS
Iris Spuria hybrids	SPURIA IRIS
Kirengeshoma palmata Koreana Group *(K. koreana)*	KOREAN WAXBELLS
Kniphofia 'Lola'	LOLA TORCH LILY
Kniphofia northiae	GIANT POKER
Leymus cinereus	GREAT BASIN WILDRYE ❖
Lilium columbianum	TIGER LILY ❖
Lilium davidii	CREEPING LILY
Lilium formosanum "Giant Form"	GIANT TAIWAN LILY
Lilium martagon hybrids (most)	TURK'S CAP LILY
Lilium x *sulphurgale* 'Vico Gold'	GIANT YELLOW LILY
Lilium washingtonianum	WASHINGTON LILY, CASCADE LILY ❖
Lobelia tupa	DEVIL'S TOBACCO
Lupinus polyphyllus	BROADLEAF LUPINE ❖
Melica subulata	ALASKA ONIONGRASS ❖
Miscanthus sinensis	CHINESE SILVER-GRASS
Polygonatum huanum (P. kingianum)	
SIBERIAN SOLOMON'S SEAL, ORANGE-FLOWERING SOLOMON' SEAL	
Polystichum munitum	SWORD FERN ❖
Rheum palmatum	CHINESE RHUBARB
Rodgersia aesculifolia	FINGER-LEAF RODGERSIA
Rodgersia pinnata	FEATHER LEAF RODGERSIA
Rudbeckia 'Herbstsonne' ('Autumn Sun')	CONEFLOWER
Rudbeckia laciniata 'Hortensia'	GOLDEN GLOW RUDBECKIA
Rudbeckia subtomentosa 'Henry Eilers'	SWEET CONEFLOWER
Salvia barrelieri	NORTH AFRICAN SAGE
Salvia nutans	NODDING SAGE
Sidalcea campestris	MEADOW CHECKERMALLOW ❖
Sidalcea cusickii	CUSICK'S SIDALCEA, CUSICK'S CHECKERMALLOW ❖
Sidalcea hendersonii	HENDERSON'S CHECKER MALLOW
Solidago rugosa 'Fireworks'	GOLDENROD
Stipa gigantea	GIANT FEATHER GRASS
Thalictrum delavayi 'Hewitt's Double'	DOUBLE-FLOWERED MEADOW RUE
Veronicastrum sibericum	JAPANESE CULVER'S ROOT
Woodwardia fimbriata	GIANT CHAIN FERN ❖
Xerophyllum tenax	BEAR GRASS, INDIAN BASKET GRASS ❖
Yucca many hardy species	YUCCA
Zantedeschia aethiopica 'White Giant'	GIANT CALLA-LILY

MEDIUM *(1 to 3 feet tall)*

Achillea 'Moonshine'	MOONSHINE YARROW
Aconitum x cammarum 'Bicolor'	MONKSHOOD
Aconitum carmichaelii	AZURE MONKSHOOD
Aconitum lycoctonum	NORTHERN WOLFS-BANE
Aconitum napellus	COMMON MONKSHOOD
Actaea (Cimicifuga) simplex	BUGBANE
Adelinia (Cynoglossum) grande	GRAND HOUND'S TONGUE ❖
Adiantum pedatum	MAIDENHAIR FERN ❖
Ageratina altissima 'Chocolate'	PURPLE-LEAF BUGBANE
Allium 'Serendipity'	SERENDIPITY ALLIUM
Allium wallichii	HIMALAYAN ONION
Amsonia ciliata	FRINGED BLUE STAR
Amsonia hubrichtii	THREADLEAF BLUE STAR
Amsonia illustris	OZARK BLUE STAR
Amsonia tabernaemontana	EASTERN BLUE STAR
Anemonopsis macrophylla	FALSE ANEMONE
Aquilegia formosa	WESTERN RED COLUMBINE ❖
Arisaema consanguineum	HIMALAYAN COBRA LILY
Arisaema ringens	COBRA LILY
Arisaema sikokianum	JAPANESE COBRA LILY
Arisaema triphyllum	JACK-IN-THE-PULPIT
Artemisia versicolor 'Sea Foam'	CURLICUE SAGE
Aruncus aethusifolius	KOREAN GOATSBEARD, DWARF GOAT'S-BEARD
Aruncus dioicus var. *vulgaris* 'Zweiweltenkind' ("Child of Two Worlds")	GOAT'S-BEARD
Aruncus 'Misty Lace'	MISTY LACE GOAT'S-BEARD
Aspidistra elatior	CAST-IRON PLANT
Aster ageratoides 'Ezo Murasaki'	ASIAN ASTER
Aster x frikartii	FRIKART'S ASTER
Aster tongolensis	EAST INDIES ASTER
Astrantia major	GREAT MASTERWORT
Athyrium filix-femina	LADY FERN ❖
Betonica (Stachys) macrantha 'Robusta'	BIG BETONY
Betonica (Stachys) officinalis	WOOD BETONY
Blechnum (Struthiopteris) spicant	DEER FERN ❖
Brunnera macrophylla	SIBERIAN BUGLOSS
Calanthe sieboldii	JAPANESE GROUND ORCHID
Camassia cusickii	CAMAS ❖
Camassia howellii	HOWELL'S CAMAS ❖
Camassia leichtlinii	LARGE CAMAS, GREAT CAMAS ❖
Camassia quamash	CAMAS ❖
Campanula 'Sarastro'	SARASTRO BELLFLOWER
Carex densa	DENSE SEDGE ❖
Carex elata 'Aurea'	BOWLE'S GOLDEN SEDGE
Carex microptera	SMALL WINGED SEDGE ❖
Carex obnupta	SLOUGH SEDGE ❖
Ceratostigma willmottianum	CHINESE PLUMBAGO
Chaerophyllum hirsutum 'Roseum'	PINK HAIRY CHERVIL

Chelonopsis yagiharana (C. moschata)	JAPANESE TURTLEHEAD
Chrysanthemum x *rubellum*	HARDY CHRYSANTHEMUM
Chrysanthemum zawadskii	MANCHURIAN CHRYSANTHEMUM
Deinanthe caerulea x *bifida*	HERBACEOUS HYDRANGEA
Deschampsia caespitosa	TUFTED HAIRGRASS ❖
Dierama dracomontanum	DRAKENBERG WANDFLOWER
Digitalis grandiflora	LARGE YELLOW FOXGLOVE
Disporopsis bakeri (D. pernyi 'Bill Baker')	EVERGREEN SOLOMON'S SEAL
Disporopsis pernyi	EVERGREEN SOLOMON'S SEAL
Disporum uniflorum	FAIRY BELLS
Epipactis gigantea 'Serpentine Knight'	STREAM ORCHID
Epipactis 'Sabine'	HYBRID STREAM ORCHID
Eryngium agavifolium	AGAVE-LEAF SEA HOLLY
Eryngium alpinum	ALPINE SEA HOLLY
Eryngium amethystinum	BLUE SEA HOLLY
Eryngium bourgatii	MEDITERRANEAN SEA HOLLY
Farfugium japonicum	LEOPARD PLANT
Festuca idahoensis	IDAHO FESCUE ❖
Filipendula purpurea 'Elegans'	JAPANESE MEADOWSWEET
Fritillaria affinis (F. lanceolata)	CHOCOLATE LILY ❖
Fritillaria camschatcensis	INDIAN RICE ❖
Glaucidium palmatum	JAPANESE WOOD POPPY
Helenium autumnale and hybrids	MOUNTAIN SNEEZEWEED ❖
Helianthus angustifolius 'Low Down'	LOW DOWN SWAMP SUNFLOWER
Helianthus x *multiflorus* 'Happy Days'	DWARF PERENNIAL SUNFLOWER
Helianthus salicifolius 'Table Mountain'	WILLOW-LEAF SUNFLOWER
Heliopsis helianthoides	FALSE SUNFLOWER
Helleborus argutifolius	CORSICAN HELLEBORE
Helleborus hybrids such as Winter Plum', 'Great White', 'Searchlight', 'Fresco', 'Great White Double', 'Pink Frost Double', 'Winter Plum Double'	TALL HELLEBORES
Hesperantha (Schizostylis) coccinea	CRIMSON FLAG
Hosta hybrids (almost all fit this size category)	HOSTA
Hosta sieboldiana var. *elegans*	GIANT HOSTA
Hylotelephium (Sedum) Autumn hybrids ('Autumn Charm', 'Autumn Delight', 'Autumn Fire', 'Autumn Joy')	HYBRID AUTUMN SEDUM
Hylotelephium (Sedum) spectabile	SHOWY STONECROP, AUTUMN SEDUM, BORDER SEDUM
Hylotelephium (Sedum) telephium	BORDER SEDUM
Incarvillea delavayi	GARDEN GLOXINIA
Iris bracteata	SISKIYOU IRIS ❖
Iris cristata	DWARF CRESTED IRIS
Iris douglasiana	DOUGLAS IRIS ❖
Iris innominata	GOLDEN IRIS ❖
Iris missouriensis	ROCKY MOUNTAIN IRIS ❖
Iris 'Nada'	BUTTERFLY IRIS
Iris PCH hybrids	PACIFIC COAST IRIS HYBRIDS
Iris sanguinea	BLOOD IRIS
Iris siberica	SIBERIAN IRIS
Iris pallida	DALMATIAN IRIS

Iris tenax	OREGON IRIS, TOUGH-LEAF IRIS ❖
Isodon umbrosus	ISODON
Leontodon (Microseris) rigens	HAWKBITS
Leucanthemum x superbum, especially 'Becky'	SHASTA DAISY
Liatris ligulistylis	MEADOW BLAZING STAR
Lilium rosthornii	ROSTHORN'S LILY
Linaria (*purpurea* Hybrid) 'Natalie'	NATALIE TOADFLAX
Meconopsis 'Lingholm' (*M.* x sheldonii; "Fertile Blue Group")	HIMALAYAN POPPY
Mertensia ciliata	FRINGED LUNGWORT ❖
Mirabilis jalapa (often grown as an annual)	FOUR-O'CLOCKS
Monarda mildew-free hybrids:	BEE BALM

    'Blue Stocking', 'Blue Wreath', 'Colrain Red', 'Dark Ponticum',
    'Gardenview Scarlet', 'Grand Marshall', 'Marshall's Delight', 'Purple Rooster',
    'Raspberry Wine', 'Violet Queen'

Ophiopogon planiscapus 'Nigrescens'	BLACK MONDO GRASS
Paeonia emodi	HIMALAYAN PEONY
Pedicularis groenlandica	ELEPHANT-HEAD LOUSEWORT ❖
Penstemon azureus	AZURE PENSTEMON ❖
Penstemon grandiflorus	LARGE BEARDTONGUE
Penstemon richardsonii	RICHARDSON'S BEARDTONGUE ❖
Penstemon serrulatus	CASCADE PENSTEMON, COAST PENSTEMON ❖
Phlomis cashmeriana	KASHMIR-SAGE
Phlomis viscosa	STICKY JERUSALEM-SAGE
Phlomoides (Phlomis) tuberosa	SAGE-LEAF MULLEIN
Polygonatum odoratum var. *pluriflorum* 'Variegatum'	VARIEGATED SOLOMON'S SEAL
Polypodium glycyrrhiza	LICORICE FERN ❖
Polystichum neolobatum	ASIAN SABER FERN
Primula sieboldii	SIEBOLD'S PRIMROSE
Psephellus (Centaurea) simplicicaulis	LILAC CORNFLOWER
Pulmonaria longifolia ssp. *cevennensis*	LONGLEAF LUNGWORT
Rodgersia podophylla	MAYAPPLE RODGERSIA
Rudbeckia fulgida var. *sullivantii* 'Goldsturm'	BLACK-EYED SUSAN
Salvia heldreichiana	HELDREICH'S SAGE
Salvia nemorosa	PURPLE WOOD SAGE
Salvia spathacea	HUMMINGBIRD SAGE
Salvia x sylvestris	BLUE MEADOW SAGE, BLUE WOOD SAGE
Salvia transylvanica	TRANSYLVANIAN SAGE
Salvia verticillata	LILAC SAGE
Saruma henryi	UPRIGHT WILD GINGER
Sidalcea hendersonii	HENDERSON'S CHECKER MALLOW ❖
Sidalcea oregana	OREGON CHECKER MALLOW ❖
Sphaeralcea munroana	ORANGE GLOBE MALLOW ❖
Symphyotrichum ericoides 'Blue Star'	BLUE STAR ASTER
Thermopsis chinensis 'Sophia'	CHINESE BUSH PEA
Thermopsis montana	MOUNTAIN GOLD-BANNER ❖
Uvularia grandiflora	LARGE-FLOWERED BELLWORT
Verbascum hybrids	MULLEIN
Watsonia angusta	SCARLET BUGLE FLOWER

SHORT *(1 inch to 12 inches tall)*

* = low and slow growers suitable for "edging" (where the flower bed meets the lawn or other, distinct garden area)

Allium acuminatum	HOOKER'S ONION ❖
Allium amplectens	SLIM-LEAF ONION ❖
Allium cernuum	NODDING ONION ❖
Allium (?lusitanicum hybrid*)* 'Summer Beauty'*	SUMMER BEAUTY MOUNTAIN GARLIC
Allium sacculiferum*	NORTHERN PLAINS CHIVE
Anaphalis margaritacea	COMMON PEARLY EVERLASTING ❖
Androsace (Douglasia) laevigata*	SMOOTH DOUGLASIA ❖
Anemone occidentalis	WESTERN PASQUE FLOWER ❖
Anemonoides (Anemone) nemorosa	WOOD ANEMONE
Arisaema candidissimum	PINK COBRA LILY
Arisarum proboscideum	MOUSE PLANT
Asarum caudatum	WESTERN WILD GINGER
Asarum europaeum	EUROPEAN WILD GINGER
Asarum hartwegii	HARTWEG'S WILD GINGER
Asarum marmoratum	MARBLED WILD GINGER ❖
Asarum fauriei var. *takaoi*	JAPANESE WILD GINGER
Asarum splendens	SPLENDID WILD GINGER
Asplenium trichomanes	SPLEENWORT ❖
Beesia deltophylla	FALSE BUGBANE
Bergenia ciliata	FUZZY-LEAVED BERGENIA
Bergenia cordifolia	HEART-LEAVED BERGENIA
Bergenia hybrids	HYBRID BERGENIA
Bloomeria (Triteleia) crocea	GOLDEN STARS ❖
Brodiaea coronaria	HARVEST BRODIAEA ❖
Brodiaea elegans ssp. *hooveri*	HARVEST LILY ❖
Calochortus elegans var. *elegans*	ELEGANT CAT'S EAR ❖
Calylophus hartwegii	HARTWEG'S SUNDROPS
Campanula rotundifolia*	BLUEBELL BELLFLOWER ❖
Campanula portenschlagiana	DALMATIAN BELLFLOWER
Campanula poscharskyana	SERBIAN BELLFLOWER
Cardamine trifolia	THREE-LEAF CARDAMINE
Carex brevicaulis	SHORT-STEMMED SEDGE ❖
Carex flacca 'Blue Zinger'	BLUE SEDGE
Carex scaposa*	CHINESE PINK FAIRY SEDGE
Carex siderosticha variegated cultivars	VARIEGATED BROADLEAF SEDGE
Carex oshimensis cultivars*	VARIEGATED JAPANESE SEDGE
Ceratostigma plumbaginoides	DWARF PLUMBAGO
Clematis columbiana	ROCK CLEMATIS ❖
Clematis hirsutissima var. *hirsutissima*	HAIRY CLEMATIS ❖
Codonopsis ovata	BONNET BELLFLOWER
Corydalis scouleri*	SCOULER'S CORYDALIS ❖
Darmera peltata 'Nana'	DWARF UMBRELLA PLANT
Dianella revoluta 'Baby Bliss'	BABY BLISS FLAX LILY
Dicentra formosa*	PACIFIC OR WESTERN BLEEDING-HEART ❖

Dichelostemma capitatum ssp. *capitatum*	BLUEDICKS ❖
Dichelostemma congestum	OOKOW, FIELD CLUSTER LILY, HARVEST LILY ❖
Dichelostemma ida-maia	FIRECRACKER FLOWER ❖
Dichelostemma x venustum	SNAKE-LILY ❖
*Dodecatheon cusickii**	CUSICK'S SHOOTING-STAR ❖
*Dodecatheon hendersonii**	SHOOTING STAR, MOSQUITO BILL ❖
Dryopteris arguta	COASTAL WOOD FERN ❖
Dryopteris expansa (D. austriaca)	SPREADING WOOD FERN ❖
Epimedium species and hybrids	BISHOP'S HAT, EPIMEDIUM
Eriogonum latifolium	COAST BUCKWHEAT ❖
*Eriogonum ovalifolium**	OVAL-LEAF BUCKWHEAT ❖
*Eriogonum umbellatum**	SULPHUR BUCKWHEAT ❖
Eriophyllum lanatum	OREGON SUNSHINE, WOOLLY SUNFLOWER ❖
Erodium chrysanthum	HERONSBILL, STORKSBILL
Erythronium elegans	COAST RANGE FAWN-LILY ❖
Erythronium grandiflorum	YELLOW AVALANCHE-LILY, GLACIER-LILY ❖
Erythronium revolutum	MAHOGANY FAWN-LILY, COAST FAWN-LILY ❖
Filipendula 'Kahome'	DWARF JAPANESE MEADOWSWEET
Geranium x cantabrigiense	HARDY GERANIUM
Geranium cinereum	HARDY GERANIUM
Geranium macrorrhizum	HARDY GERANIUM
Geranium renardii	HARDY GERANIUM
Geranium x riversleaianum	HARDY GERANIUM
Geranium wlassovianum	HARDY GERANIUM
Geum hybrids*	GEUM, AVENS
Gymnocarpium disjunctum	PACIFIC OAK FERN ❖
Gymnocarpium dryopteris	WESTERN OAK FERN ❖
*Hacquetia epipactis**	BROAD-LEAVED SANICLE, HACQUETIA
Hakonechloa macra cultivars	JAPANESE FOREST GRASS
Helianthemum nummularium and hybrids	SUN ROSE
Helleborus foetidus	STINKING HELLEBORE
Helleborus hybrids	HYBRID HELLEBORE
Hosta hybrids (hundreds of small and miniature cultivars)*	HOSTA
Hosta tokudama	SILVER HEART HOSTA
Hylotelephium (Sedum) cauticola 'Lidakense'	LIDAKENSE CLIFF STONECROP
Hylotelephium (Sedum) sieboldii	OCTOBER DAPHNE SEDUM
Hylotelephium (Sedum) 'Vera Jameson'*	PURPLE AUTUMN SEDUM
*Iris chrysophylla**	YELLOW-LEAF IRIS ❖
Iris koreana 'Firefly Shuffle'	KOREAN WOODLAND IRIS
Iris PCH hybrids*	PACIFIC COAST IRIS HYBRIDS
Iris purdyi	PURDY'S IRIS ❖
Iris tenax	OREGON IRIS, TOUGH-LEAF IRIS ❖
Iris tenuis	CLACKAMAS IRIS ❖
*Lewisia cotyledon**	SISKIYOU LEWISIA ❖
*Lewisiopsis tweedyi**	TWEEDY'S LEWISIA ❖
Luzula multiflora	WOODRUSH❖
Monarda 'Petite Delight'	DWARF BEE BALM
Mukdenia rossii 'Karasuba'	MUKDENIA
Myriopteris (Cheilanthes) gracillima	LACE LIP FERN ❖

*Olsynium (Sisyrinchium) douglasii***	DOUGLAS' BLUE-EYED-GRASS ❖
Omphalodes verna	CREEPING FORGET-ME-NOT
*Oncostema (Scilla) peruviana***	PORTUGUESE SQUILL
Ophiopogon japonicus 'Nanus'	DWARF MONDO GRASS
Opuntia fragilis	BRITTLE PRICKLY PEAR ❖
Oxalis nidulans 'Pom-Pom'	POM-POM SORREL
Penstemon barrettiae	BARRETT'S BEARDTONGUE ❖
Penstemon cardwellii	CARDWELL'S PENSTEMON ❖
Penstemon davidsonii	DAVIDSON'S BEARDTONGUE ❖
Penstemon newberryi var. *berryi*	BERRY'S MOUNTAIN PRIDE ❖
Penstemon speciosus	SHOWY PENSTEMON ❖
Phedimus (Sedum) kamtschaticus	KAMSCHATKA SEDUM, ORANGE STONECROP
Phedimus (Sedum) spurius	TWO-ROW STONECROP
Phegopteris connectilis (Thelypteris phegopteris)	NORTHERN BEECH FERN ❖
Phlox 'Minnie Pearl'	MINNIE PEARL PHLOX
*Polemonium carneum***	SALMON POLEMONIUM ❖
Polypodium scouleri	LEATHER-LEAF FERN ❖
Polystichum imbricans	CLIFF SWORD FERN ❖
Polystichum lemmonii	LEMMON'S SWORD FERN ❖
Polystichum scopulinum	MOUNTAIN HOLLY FERN ❖
Pulmonaria 'Benediction'	LUNGWORT
*Rhodiola pachyclados***	AFGHAN SEDUM
*Rhodanthemum (Chrysanthemum) hosmariense***	MOROCCAN DAISY
Saxifraga fortunei	FORTUNE SAXIFRAGE
Saxifraga x urbium 'Primuloides'	MINIATURE LONDON PRIDE
Sedum spathulifolium	BROAD-LEAF STONECROP ❖
*Sempervivum arachnoideum***	HENS AND CHICKS, HOUSELEEK
Sisyrinchium bellum	WESTERN BLUE-EYED GRASS ❖
Sisyrinchium californicum	GOLDEN-EYED GRASS ❖
Solidago 'Little Lemon'	LITTLE LEMON GOLDENROD
Stachys coccinea	SCARLET BETONY
Thalictrum (Anemonella) thalictroides	RUE-ANEMONE
*Titanotrichum oldhamii***	OLDHAM'S GOLD WOODLAND FOXGLOVE
Trillium albidum	GIANT WHITE WAKE-ROBIN
Trillium chloropetalum	GIANT TRILLIUM
Trillium grandiflorum	GREAT WHITE TRILLIUM
Trillium kurabayashii	GIANT PURPLE TRILLIUM ❖
Trillium ovatum	WESTERN WHITE TRILLIUM, WAKE ROBIN ❖
Triteleia (Brodiaea) hyacinthina	WHITE TRIPLET-LILY ❖
Triteleia grandiflora	LARGE-FLOWERED TRIPLET-LILY, WILD HYACINTH ❖
Triteleia ixioides	PRETTYFACE ❖
Veronica liwanensis	TURKISH SPEEDWELL
Veronica (Parahebe) perfoliata	DIGGER'S SPEEDWELL
*Viola adunca***	EARLY BLUE VIOLET, WESTERN DOG VIOLET ❖
Viola alba ssp. *dehnhardtii***	PARMA VIOLET
Viola 'Dancing Geisha', 'Silver Samurai'*	HYBRID VIOLET
Waldsteinia ternata	BARREN STRAWBERRY
Woodsia scopulina	CLIFF FERN, MOUNTAIN CLIFF FERN ❖

GRASSES AND GRASS-LIKE PLANTS

Their texture — sometimes fine, sometimes bold — gives these plants a special use in the landscape. Some of them possess a strong vertical presence which can add interest to an otherwise flat landscape, one which might be a little too moundy or too "soft." Many complement a garden pond or stream (real or composed only of rocks). Some find a fitting place with a "meadow" theme. The bamboos, at the end, help create an Asian themed landscape or a tropical feel.

TALL *(over 5 feet tall in bloom)*

Austrostipa ramosissima	AUSTRALIAN PLUME GRASS
Calamagrostis x acutiflora 'Karl Foerster'	FEATHER REED GRASS
Cannomois grandis	BELL REED
Chondropetalum elephantinum	LARGE CAPE RUSH
Dierama pendulum	FAIRY WAND, HAIR BELL
Erianthus ravennae	RAVENNA GRASS
Leymus (Elymus) mollis	AMERICAN DUNE-GRASS ❖
Miscanthus 'Andante'	ANDANTE MAIDEN GRASS
Miscanthus gracillimus	JAPANESE SILVER GRASS
Miscanthus sinensis	CHINESE SILVER-GRASS
Miscanthus transmorrisonensis	EVERGREEN EULALIA
Nolina nelsonii	NELSON'S BLUE BEAR GRASS
Restio (Ischyrolepis) subverticillata	DUNE RESTIO
Rhodocoma capensis	CAPE RESTIO
Rhodocoma gigantea	DEKRIET, GIANT RESTIO
Stipa gigantea	GIANT FEATHER GRASS
Thamnochortus rigidus	CAPE REED

MEDIUM *(2 to 5 feet tall)*

Aciphylla glaucescens	BLUE SPEARGRASS
Anemanthele lessoniana	GOSSAMER GRASS, NEW ZEALAND WIND GRASS
Arrhenatherum elatius var. *bulbosa*	TALL OAT GRASS
Calamagrostis brachytricha	KOREAN FEATHER REED GRASS
Calamagrostis nutkaensis	PACIFIC REEDGRASS ❖
Chionochloa rubra	RED TUSSOCK GRASS
Chondropetalum tectorum	SMALL CAPE RUSH
Deschampsia caespitosa	TUFTED HAIRGRASS
Dierama adelphicum	FAIRY WAND, ANGEL'S FISHING ROD
Dierama dracomontanum	DRAKENBERG WANDFLOWER
Dierama grandiflorum	ANGEL'S FISHING ROD
Dierama pulcherrimum	FAIRY WAND, ANGEL'S FISHING ROD
Dierama reynoldsii	ANGEL'S FISHING ROD
Helictotrichon sempervirens	BLUE OAT GRASS
Iris typhifolia	CATTAIL IRIS
Juncus patens 'Elk Blue', 'Occidental Blue'	SPREADING RUSH
Libertia peregrinans	ORANGE SWORD

Luzula sylvatica 'Aurea'	GOLDEN WOODRUSH
Luzula sylvatica 'Marginata'	VARIEGATED WOODRUSH
Melica subulata	ALASKA ONIONGRASS
Miscanthus sinensis 'Little Kitten'	DWARF CHINESE SILVER GRASS
Molinia caerulea	VARIEGATED MOOR GRASS
Muhlenbergia rigens	DEER GRASS
Muhlenbergia reverchonii 'Undaunted'	RUBY MUHLY
Stipa barbata	SILVER FEATHER GRASS
Stipa gigantea 'Little Giant'	LITTLE GIANT FEATHER GRASS
Vahlodea (Deschampsia) atropurpurea	MOUNTAIN HAIRGRASS ❖

SHORT *(under 2 feet)*

Acorus calamus 'Variegatus'	GHOST SWEET FLAG
Acorus gramineus 'Golden Lion'	GOLDEN SWEETFLAG
Acorus gramineus 'Ogon'	GOLDEN VARIEGATED SWEETFLAG
Calamagrostis foliosa	MENDOCINO REED GRASS
Carex comans 'Olive Oil'	KHAKI SEDGE
Carex conica 'Snowline'	HIME KAN SUGE
Carex elata 'Aurea'	BOWLE'S GOLDEN SEDGE
Carex flacca 'Blue Zinger'	BLUE SEDGE
Carex hachijoensis 'Evergold'	EVERGOLD SEDGE
Carex morrowii 'Ice Dance'	ICE DANCE SEDGE
Carex oshimensis many cultivars	JAPANESE SEDGE
Carex phyllocephala 'Sparkler'	SPARKLER PALM SEDGE
Carex scaposa	PINK FAIRY SEDGE
Carex trifida 'Rekohu Sunrise'	MUTTONBIRD SEDGE
Chondropetalum tectorum "dwarf form"	DWARF CAPE RUSH
Corynephorus canescens 'Spiky Blue'	BLUE HAIR GRASS
Elymus (Agropyron) magellanicum	CHILEAN BLUE WHEAT GRASS
Festuca roemeri	ROEMER'S FESCUE
Hakonechloa macra and cultivars	JAPANESE FOREST GRASS
Iris missouriensis	WESTERN BLUE-FLAG ❖
Iris tenax	OREGON IRIS, TOUGH-LEAF IRIS ❖
Isolepis (Scirpus) cernua	FIBER-OPTIC GRASS
Juncus effusus 'Big Twister', 'Spiralis'	COMMON RUSH
Liriope platyphylla 'Peter's Pick'	PETER'S PICK HARDY MONKEY GRASS
Luzula nivea	SNOWY WOODRUSH
Ophiopogon formosanum	TAIWAN MONDO GRASS
Ophiopogon japonicus and cultivars	MONDO GRASS
Ophiopogon planiscapus and cultivars	MONDO GRASS
Ophiopogon umbraticola 'Sparkler'	CHINESE MONDO GRASS
Reineckea carnea	RIBBON LILY OR RIBBON GRASS
Sesleria autumnalis	AUTUMN MOOR GRASS
Sisyrinchium bellum	WESTERN BLUE-EYED GRASS
Sisyrinchium californicum	GOLDEN-EYED GRASS ❖

CLUMPING BAMBOOS *Hardy in the Western PNW*

Bambusa multiplex 'Riviereorum'	CHINESE GODDESS BAMBOO
Borinda angustissima	NARROW LEAF CLUMPING BAMBOO
Borinda contracta	BLUE MOUNTAIN BAMBOO
Borinda (Fargesia) fungosa	CHOCOLATE BAMBOO
Borinda (Fargesia) lushiensis	RED-STEM BAMBOO
Borinda macclureana	TIBETAN MOUNTAIN BAMBOO
Borinda (Fargesia) papyrifera	WHITE WAX BORINDA
Borinda (Fargesia) yunnanensis	YUNNAN FOUNTAIN BAMBOO
Chusquea culeou	CHILEAN BAMBOO
Chusquea culeou "Hillier's Form"	COMPACT CHILEAN BAMBOO
Fargesia dracocephala (F. apicirubens)	DRAGON'S HEAD BAMBOO
Fargesia dracocephala 'White Dragon'	STRIPED DRAGON'S HEAD BAMBOO
Fargesia rufa (F. dracocephala 'Rufa'*)*	RED DRAGON'S HEAD BAMBOO
Fargesia denudata	DENUDATA BAMBOO
Fargesia murielae	UMBRELLA BAMBOO
Fargesia nitida	BLUE FOUNTAIN
Fargesia robusta	ROBUST BAMBOO
Fargesia robusta 'Wolong'	LARGE-LEAVED ROBUST BAMBOO
Fargesia scabrida	ORANGE-STEM BAMBOO
X Hibanobambusa tranquillans 'Shiroshima'	SHIROSHIMA BAMBOO
Himalayacalamus planatus (H. asper)	MALINGE NAGALO BAMBOO
Thamnocalamus crassinodus	TIBETAN BAMBOO
Thamnocalamus crassinodus 'Mendocino'	KNOBBY TIBETAN BAMBOO
Thamnocalamus tesselatus	BERGBAMBOES, MOUNTAIN BAMBOO
Yushania (Borinda) boliana	HIMALAYAN BLUE MOUNTAIN BAMBOO
Yushania confusa	GUADUA BAMBOO

FALL-PLANTED, SPRING-BLOOMING BULBS

When gardeners hear the word "bulb," this is the category they most think of. This does duplicate the bulbs included in the list previously but it does so in a planting season way. This list also includes many more bulbs — pretty much all of the spring-blooming bulbs which can be planted in the fall in the Pacific Northwest.

Allium 'Ambassador'	ORNAMENTAL ONION
Allium amplectens 'Graceful Beauty'	ORNAMENTAL ONION ❖
Allium atropurpureum	ORNAMENTAL ONION
Allium beesianum	BLUE ALLIUM
Allium (Nectaroscordum) bulgaricum siculum	SICILIAN HONEY LILY
Allium caeruleum	BLUE ORNAMENTAL ONION
Allium cernuum	NODDING ONION ❖
Allium cristophii	STAR OF PERSIA, PERSIAN ONION
Allium 'Firmament'	ORNAMENTAL ONION
Allium 'Gladiator'	ORNAMENTAL ONION
Allium 'Globemaster'	ORNAMENTAL ONION
Allium jesdianum	ORNAMENTAL ONION
Allium karataviense (including white 'Ivory Queen')	TURKESTAN ONION
Allium macleanii (A. elatum)	ORNAMENTAL ONION
Allium 'Mars'	ORNAMENTAL ONION
Allium 'Miami'	ORNAMENTAL ONION
Allium 'Mt. Everest'	ORNAMENTAL ONION
Allium neopolitanum cowanii	GUERNSEY STAR-OF-BETHLEHEM
Allium nigrum (A. multibulbosum)	BLACK GARLIC
Allium oreophilum	PINK LILY LEEK
Allium 'Ostara'	ORNAMENTAL ONION
Allium 'Purple Sensation'	ORNAMENTAL ONION
Allium rosenbachianum	SHOWY ONION
Allium roseum	ROSY GARLIC
Allium schubertii	TUMBLEWEED ONION
Allium (Nectaroscordum) tripedale	PINK HONEY LILY
Anemone x *fulgens*	FLAME ANEMONE
Anemonoides (Anemone) blanda	GRECIAN WINDFLOWER
Arisaema dracontium	DRAGONROOT
Arisaema candidissimum	PINK COBRA LILY
Arisaema consanguineum	HIMALAYAN COBRA LILY
Arisaema kishidae	JAPANESE COBRA-LILY
Arisaema ringens	COBRA LILY
Arisaema sikokianum	JAPANESE COBRA LILY
Arisaema taiwanensis	TAIWAN CORBA LILY
Arisarum proboscideum	MOUSE PLANT
Arum concinnatum	CRETE ARUM
Asphodeline lutea	KING'S SPEAR
Asphodelus aestivus	SUMMER ASPHODEL
Bellevalia (Muscari) pycnantha	GIANT GRAPE HYACINTH
Brimeura amethystina	AMETHYST HYACINTH
Brodiaea californica	CALIFORNIA BRODIAEA

Brodiaea coronaria	CROWN BRODIAEA ❖
Brodiaea elegans	HARVEST BRODIAEA ❖
Camassia cusickii	CUSICK'S QUAMASH ❖
Camassia leichtlinii	WILD HYACINTH ❖
Camassia leichtlinii 'Alba'	WHITE WILD HYACINTH ❖
Camassia leichtlinii 'Semi-plena'	DOUBLE-FLOWERED WILD HYACINTH
Camassia quamash	CAMAS, QUAMASH ❖
Colchicum bulbocodium (C. vernum)	SPRING MEADOW SAFFRON
Convallaria majalis	LILY-OF-THE-VALLEY
Convallaria majalis 'Albostriata'	STRIPED LILY-OF-THE-VALLEY
Corydalis elata	BLUE CORYDALIS
Corydalis hybrids	FUMEWORT
Corydalis quantmeyeriana 'Chocolate Stars'	CHOCOLATE STARS FUMEWORT
Corydalis shimienensis 'Berry Exciting'	GOLDEN-LEAF FUMEWORT
Corydalis solida	FUMEWORT
Crocus chrysanthus	GOLDEN CROCUS
Crocus tommasinianus	TOMMASINI'S CROCUS
Crocus vernus and hybrids	SPRING CROCUS
Cyclamen coum	HARDY CYCLAMEN, EASTERN SOWBREAD
Cyclamen hederifolium	IVY-LEAF CYCLAMEN
Cyclamen pseudibericum	FALSE IBERIAN SOWBREAD
Cyclamen repandum	SPRING SOWBREAD
Cypella herbertii	HERBERT'S GOBLET FLOWER
Dichelostemma (Brodiaea) congestum	OOKOW ❖
Dichelostemma ida-maia	FIRECRACKER FLOWER
Dichelostemma 'Pink Diamond'	PINK DIAMOND FIRECRACKER FLOWER
Dracunculus vulgaris	VOODOO LILY
Eranthis hyemalis (including "Cilicica Group")	WINTER ACONITE
Erythronium 'Pagoda'	PAGODA FAWN-LILY
Erythronium grandiflorum var. grandiflorum	AVALANCHE-LILY, GLACIER-LILY ❖
Erythronium oregonum	OREGON FAWN-LILY ❖
Erythronium revolutum	COAST FAWN-LILY, PINK FAWN-LILY ❖
Fritillaria affinis (F. lanceolata)	CHOCOLATE LILY ❖
Fritillaria assyriaca	TURKISH FRITILLARY
Fritillaria bucharica 'Giant'	RUSSIAN FRITILLARY
Fritillaria camschatcensis	BLACK SARANA ❖
Fritillaria eduardii	EDUARD'S FRITILLARIA
Fritillaria michailovskyi	MICHAEL'S FLOWER
Fritillaria pontica	PONTIC FRITILLARY
Fritillaria raddeana	PERSIAN FRITILLARY
Galanthus elwesii	GIANT SNOWDROPS
Galanthus nivalis	SNOWDROPS
Galanthus plicatus	PLEATED SNOWDROPS
Geranium malviflorum	MALLOW-FLOWERED CRANESBILL
Gladiolus 'Rosy Cheeks'	ROSY CHEEKS GLADIOLUS
Gladiolus dalenii 'Bolivian Peach'	BOLIVIAN PEACH GLADIOLUS
Gladiolus dalenii var. *primulinus*	CAROLINA PRIMROSE
Gladiolus italicus	ITALIAN GLADIOLUS
Hyacinthella glabrescens	TURKISH HYACINTH

Hyacinthoides hispanica (NOT *H.* x massartiana)	SPANISH BLUEBELL
Ipheion uniflorum	SPRING STARFLOWER
Iris bucharica	BUKHARA IRIS
Iris danfordiae	DWARF IRIS, DANFORD IRIS
Iris histrioides	MINI IRIS
Iris x hollandica	DUTCH IRIS
Iris latifolia	ENGLISH IRIS
Iris persica	PERSIAN IRIS
Iris reticulata and hybrids	RETICULATED IRIS
Iris (Hermodactylus) tuberosa	SNAKE'S-HEAD IRIS
Iris xiphium	SPANISH IRIS
Leucojum aestivum	SUMMER SNOWFLAKE
Leucojum vernum	SPRING SNOWFLAKE
Muscari latifolium	GRAPE HYACINTH
Muscari macrocarpum	YELLOW GRAPE HYACINTH
Muscari neglectum	STARCH GRAPE HYACINTH
Narcissus 'February Gold'	MINIATURE DAFFODIL
Narcissus 'Jack Snipe'	MINIATURE DAFFODIL
Narcissus 'King Alfred'	KING ALFRED DAFFODIL
Narcissus 'Mount Hood'	WHITE TRUMPET DAFFODIL
Narcissus 'Mrs. Langtry'	HEIRLOOM DAFFODIL
Narcissus 'Replete'	DOUBLE DAFFODIL
Narcissus 'Rosy Clouds'	DOUBLE PINK DAFFODIL
Narcissus 'Saint Keverne'	GOLDEN TRUMPET DAFFODIL
Narcissus 'Tahiti'	TAHITI DAFFODIL
Narcissus 'Tête-à-tête'	MINIATURE DAFFODIL
Narcissus bulbocodium	HOOP-PETTICOAT
Narcissus cyclamineus and hybrids (including some of the above)	
	CYCLAMEN-FLOWERED DAFFODIL
Narcissus x *italicus* 'Thalia'	ITALIAN ANGEL'S TEARS
Narcissus jonquilla	JONQUILS
Narcissus papyraceus	PAPERWHITE
Narcissus poeticus var. *recurvus*	PHEASANT'S EYE DAFFODIL
Narcissus tazetta	MULTI-FLOWERED NARCISSUS
Oncostema (Scilla) peruviana	PORTUGUESE SQUILL
Ornithogalum magnum	EASTERN STAR
Ornithogalum narbonense	SOUTHERN STAR-OF-BETHLEHEM
Ornithogalum ponticum	STAR-OF-BETHLEHEM
Oxalis adenophylla	SILVER SHAMROCK, PINK BUTTERCUPS
Oxalis heterophylla	VARIED-LEAF SORREL
Oxalis nidulans 'Pom Pom'	POM-POM SORRELL
Oxalis triangularis	FALSE SHAMROCK
Oxalis versicolor	CANDY CANE SHAMROCK
Oxalis violacea	VIOLET WOOD SORREL
Pseudomuscari (Muscari, Bellavalia) azureum	AZURE GRAPE HYACINTH
Pseudomuscari (Muscari, Bellavalia) forniculatum	TURKISH GRAPE HYACINTH
Puschkinia scilloides	STRIPED SQUILL
Scilla bifolia	ALPINE SQUILL
Scilla (Chionodoxa) forbesii	FORBES' GLORY-OF-THE-SNOW

Scilla litardierei (S. pratensis)	AMETHYST MEADOW SQUILL, DALMATIAN SCILLA
Scilla (Chionodoxa) luciliae	GLORY OF THE SNOW
Scilla mischtschenkoana ("Tubergeniana")	EARLY SQUILL, WHITE SQUILL
Scilla (Chionodoxa) sardensis	SARDINIAN GLORY OF THE SNOW
Scilla siberica	WOOD SQUILL
Trillium chloropetalum	GIANT WAKEROBIN ❖
Trillium cuneatum	WOOD-LILY
Trillium erectum	WAKE ROBIN
Trillium grandiflorum 'Flore Pleno'	DOUBLE-FLOWERED TRILLIUM
Trillium kurabayashii	GIANT PURPLE WAKEROBIN ❖
Trillium luteum	YELLOW TRILLIUM
Triteleia (Brodiaea) hyacinthina	WHITE TRIPLET-LILY ❖
Triteleia laxa 'Queen Fabiola'	ITHURIEL'S SPEAR ❖
Tulipa clusiana	LADY TULIP
Tulipa clusiana var. *chrysantha*	GOLDEN LADY TULIP
Tulipa clusiana 'Cynthia'	ROSE AND GOLD TULIP
Tulipa clusiana 'Lady Jane'	CANDY-STRIPE TULIP
Tulipa clusiana var. *stellata*	STAR TULIP
Tulipa dasystemon	DASYSTEMON TULIP
Tulipa linifolia (including *T. batalinii*)	BOKHARA TULIP, FLAX-LEAF TULIP
Tulipa orphanidea (including *T. whittallii*)	ANATOLIAN TULIP, COTTAGE TULIP
Tulipa sprengeri	SPRENGER'S TULIP
Tulipa sylvestris	WOODLAND TULIP
Tulipa urumiensis (T. tarda)	LATE TULIP, TARDY TULIP
Watsonia angusta	SCARLET BUGLE FLOWER
Zantedeschia aethiopica	CALLA-LILY

Note that many of these spring-blooming bulbs naturalize better with a dry-soil rest period during the summer months.

"Daffodils, that come before the swallow dares, and take the winds of March with beauty."
~~ William Shakespeare

FALL-PLANTED BULBS
FOR SUMMER AND FALL BLOOM

All of these can be planted as early as July or as soon as bulbs are available.

Acis autumnalis	AUTUMN SNOWFLAKE
Allium wallichii	HIMALAYAN ONION
X Amarine tubergenii	VAN TUBERGEN'S AMARINE LILY
X Amarygia parkeri	HYBRID AMARYLLIS
Amaryllis belladonna	NAKED LADY
Barnardia (Scilla) japonica	JAPANESE SQUILL
Colchicum x agrippinum	AUTUMN CROCUS, MEADOW SAFFRON
Colchicum autumnale and cultivars	AUTUMN CROCUS
Colchicum bornmuelleri	AUTUMN CROCUS
Colchicum byzantinum	BYZANTINE MEADOW SAFFRON
Colchicum hybrids (such as 'Giant', 'Lilac Wonder', 'Violet Queen', 'Waterlily')	
	AUTUMN CROCUS
Colchicum speciosum	AUTUMN CROCUS
Colchicum variegatum	SPOTTED AUTUMN CROCUS
Crocus goulimyi	PELOPONNESE CROCUS
Crocus imperati	ITALIAN CROCUS
Crocus kotschyanus	KOTSCHY'S CROCUS
Crocus laevigatus	LATE CROCUS
Crocus longiflorus	ITALIAN CROCUS
Crocus medius	LATE-AUTUMN CROCUS
Crocus niveus	FALL CROCUS
Crocus ochroleucus	YELLOW CROCUS
Crocus pulchellus	TURKISH CROCUS
Crocus serotinus	LATE CROCUS
Crocus speciosus	BIEBERSTEIN'S CROCUS
Cyclamen graecum	GREEK CYCLAMEN
Eremurus himalaicus	HIMALAYAN FOXTAIL LILY
Eremurus hybrids	FOXTAIL LILY
Eremurus stenophyllus	DESERT CANDLE
Eucomis autumnalis	AUTUMN PINEAPPLE LILY
Eucomis bicolor	VARIEGATED PINEAPPLE LILY
Eucomis comosa	WINE PINEAPPLE LILY
Eucomis 'Nani'	DWARF PINEAPPLE LILY
Eucomis pole-evansii	TALL PINEAPPLE LILY
Gladiolus (tubergenii) 'Charm'	SWORD LILY
Gladiolus communis var. *byzantinus*	BYZANTINE GLADIOLUS
Gladiolus flanaganii	SUICIDE LILY
Gladiolus oppositiflorus ssp. *salmoneus*	SALMON GLADIOLUS
Gladiolus (papilio hybrid*)* 'Ruby'	RUBY GLADIOLUS
Gladiolus saundersii	SAUNDER'S GLADIOLUS
Hyacinthoides (Scilla) lingulata	AUTUMN BLUEBELL
Impatiens arguta	BLUE DREAM IMPATIENS
Impatiens flanaganae	FLANAGAN'S IMPATIENS

Impatiens puberula	SOFT PINK BALSAM
Impatiens tinctoria	PAINTED IMPATIENS
Lilium Asiatic hybrids	ASIATIC LILY
Lilium columbianum	TIGER LILY
Lilium formosanum (including var. *pricei*)	FORMOSA LILY
Lilium henryi	HENRY'S LILY
Lilium jankae	BALKAN LILY
Lilium lancifolium	TURK'S-CAP LILY
Lilium mackliniae	SHIRUI LILY
Lilium martagon and hybrids	MARTAGON LILY
Lilium nepalense	NEPAL LILY
Lilium Oriental hybrids	ORIENTAL LILY
Lilium pardalinum	SHASTA LILY
Lilium regale	REGAL LILY
Lilium sargentiae	SARGENT'S LILY
Lilium speciosum	RUBRUM LILY
Lilium szovitsianum	SZOVITS' LILY
Lilium taliense	FRAGRANT TURK'S-CAP LILY
Lilium x testaceum	NANKEEN LILY
Lilium wallichianum	LONG-FLOWERED LILY
Lycoris aurea	YELLOW SPIDER LILY
Lycoris radiata	RED SPIDER LILY
Lycoris sprengeri	SURPRISE LILY, MAGIC LILY
Lycoris x squamigera	RESURRECTION LILY, MAGIC LILY
Moraea spathulata	YELLOW BUTTERFLY LILY
Nerine bowdenii and hybrids	SPIDER LILY
Nerine sarniensis and hybrids	GUERNSEY LILY
Nomocharis aperta	NOMOCHARIS LILY
Nomocharis x notabilis	HYBRID NOMOCHARIS LILY
Nomocharis pardanthina	NOMOCHARIS LILY
Nomocharis saluenensis	NOMOCHARIS LILY
Notholirion bulbiferum	NEPAL LILY
Notholirion campanulatum	ANCIENT LILY
Notholirion macrophyllum	BHUTAN LILY
Notholirion thomsonianum	ROSY HIMALAYAN LILY
Ornithogalum (Galtonia) candicans	SUMMER HYACINTH
Ornithogalum (Galtonia) princeps	BERG LILY
Ornithogalum (Galtonia) viridiflora	GREEN SUMMER HYACINTH
Oxalis fabaefolia	RABBIT'S EARS
Oxalis purpurea	PURPLE WOOD SORREL
Oxalis triangularis	LOVE PLANT, PURPLE SHAMROCK
Pancratium illyricum	SEA LILY
Pancratium maritimum	SEA LILY
Phalocallis (Cypella) coelestis	GOBLET FLOWER
Pinellia cordata	MINIATURE GREEN DRAGON
Prospero (Scilla) autumnale	AUTUMN SQUILL
Scilla bifolia	TWO-LEAF SQUILL
Sternbergia lutea	AUTUMN DAFFODIL

SPRING-PLANTED BULBS
FOR SUMMER-INTO-FALL BLOOM

Achimenes x grandiflora	MAGIC FLOWER
Agave amica (Polianthes tuberosa)	TUBEROSE
Begonia boliviensis	BOLIVIAN BEGONIA
Begonia Non-stop hybrids	NON-STOP BEGONIAS
Begonia x tuberhybrida	TUBEROUS BEGONIA
Canna x generalis	CANNA-LILY*
Dahlia hybrids	DAHLIA*
Gladiolus murielae (G. callianthus, Acidanthera)	ABYSSINIAN SWORD-LILY
Gladiolus hybrids	GLADIOLUS*
Tigridia pavonia	MEXICAN SHELL FLOWER
Zantedeschia albomaculata	SPOTTED CALLA
Zantedeschia elliottiana	GOLDEN CALLA
Zantedeschia hybrids	HYBRID CALLA-LILY
Zantedeschia pentlandii	PURPLE-THROATED CALLA
Zantedeschia rehmannii	RED/PINK CALLA

* In the mildest areas with sandy soils, many of the cultivars within these species will winter over with just a light mulch. Otherwise, these are dug out of the ground as soon as the first good frost damages the foliage and then they are stored inside.

For the most dependable and longest-lasting flower show, it's a good idea to start these in pots before planting to the ground. A good time to do this is in February-March and usually into 1-gallon containers. If they are big bulbs or they become too large in the 1-gallon container before it's time to put out, transplant them to larger containers to grow on more. Once put into pots and initially soaked, they are grown outdoors in the sunniest spot possible and watered again only when new growth appears. Whenever temperatures are expected to drop below 40°F, whether night or day, they can and should be brought indoors; they are returned to the outdoors when temperatures are expected to be above that temp.

HARDY SUCCULENT PLANTS

It is important that these be planted in very well-drained soil. Although they tolerate any amount of cold the PNW can throw at them, a wet soil will do them in. Most of these are best in full sun, some are shade tolerant and a few require at least some shade.

CACTACEAE

Cylindropuntia echinocarpa	GOLDEN CHOLLA
Cylindropuntia echinocarpa 'Silver Fox'	SILVER CHOLLA
Cylindropuntia imbricata	TREE CHOLLA
Cylindropuntia imbricata var. *arborescens* forms and cultivars	TREE CHOLLA
Cylindropuntia imbricata var. *viridiflora*	GREEN-FLOWERED TREE CHOLLA
Cylindropuntia whipplei	WHIPPLE CHOLLA
Cylindropuntia whipplei 'Snow Leopard'	SNOW LEOPARD CHOLLA
Echinocactus texensis	HORSE CRIPPLER CACTUS
Echinocereus canus x *E. russanthus*	HYBRID HEDGEHOG CACTUS
Echinocereus coccineus	SCARLET HEDGEHOG CACTUS
Echinocereus enneacanthus	STRAWBERRY HEDGEHOG
Echinocereus fendleri	FENDLER'S HEDGEHOG
Echinocereus knippelianus	PEYOTE VERDE
Echinocereus reichenbachii	LACE HEDGEHOG CACTUS
Echinocereus reichenbachii ssp. *baileyi*	BAILEY'S HEDGEHOG CACTUS
Echinocereus reichenbachii var. *caespitosus*	CLUMPING HEDGEHOG CACTUS
Echinocereus triglochidiatus	KING CUP CACTUS
Echinocereus triglochidiatus var. *mohavensis*	MOJAVE HEDGEHOG CACTUS
Echinocereus triglochidiatus var. *mojavensis* f. *inermis*	GEOMAJI CACTUS
Echinocereus triglochidiatus 'White Sands'	WHITE SANDS HEDGEHOG CACTUS
Echinocereus viridiflorus	NYLON HEDGEHOG CACTUS
Echinocereus viridiflorus var. *davisii*	DAVIS' HEDGEHOG CACTUS
Echinocereus viereckii ssp. *morricalii*	CLUSTERING HEDGEHOG CACTUS
Echinocereus viridiflorus	NYLON HEDGEHOG CACTUS
Echinocereus weedenii x *E. russanthus*	HYBRID HEDGEHOG CACTUS
Echinomastus intertextus	WHITE FISHHOOK CACTUS
Echinopsis oxygona	EASTER-LILY CACTUS
Epithelantha micromeris	BUTTON CACTUS
Escobaria (Coryphantha, and all the others*) hesteri*	HESTER'S FOXTAIL CACTUS
Escobaria organensis	ORGAN MOUNTAIN FOXTAIL CACTUS
Escobaria minima	NELLIE CORY CACTUS
Escobaria missouriensis	MISSOURI FOXTAIL CACTUS
Escobaria orcuttii	ORCUTT PINCUSHION CACTUS
Escobaria sneedii	CARPET FOXTAIL CACTUS
Escobaria sneedii var. *leei*	LEE'S PINCUSHION CACTUS
Escobaria sneedii var. *sneedii*	SNEED'S PINCUSHION CACTUS
Escobaria vivipara	COMMON BEEHIVE CACTUS ❖
Escobaria vivipara var. *arizonica*	ARIZONA HEDGEHOG
Grusonia (Corynopuntia) clavata "Giant Form"	GIANT CLUB CHOLLA
Gymnocalycium bruchii	CHIN CACTUS

Hamatocactus bicolor	TWISTED-RIB CACTUS
Maihueniopsis darwinii	DARWIN'S CACTUS
Maihueniopsis (Maihuenia) poepigii	MAIHUÉN
Mammillaria wrightii	WRIGHT'S NIPPLE CACTUS
Mammillaria heyderi	HEYDER PINCUSHION CACTUS
Opuntia arenaria	DUNE PRICKLYPEAR
Opuntia aurea including 'Coombe's Winter Glow'	GOLDEN PRICKLYPEAR
Opuntia basilaris	BEAVERTAIL PRICKLYPEAR
Opuntia basilaris var. *brachyclada*	SHORT-JOINT BEAVERTAIL
Opuntia cacanapa 'Ellisiana'	ELLISIANA SPINELESS PRICKLY PEAR
Opuntia x *columbiana*	COLUMBIA PRICKLYPEAR ❖
Opuntia cymochila	GRASSLAND PRICKLYPEAR
Opuntia davisii including 'Copper King'	DAVIS' GOLDEN CHOLLA
Opuntia debreczyi including 'Alberta Sunset', 'Apache'	WESTERN PRICKLYPEAR
Opuntia erinacea	MOJAVE PRICKLY PEAR
Opuntia fragilis, including 'Black Cat', 'Nevada Cushion'	BRITTLE PRICKLYPEAR ❖
Opuntia fragilis var. *denudata*	POTATO CACTUS
Opuntia gilvescens	PANCAKE CACTUS
Opuntia heacockiae	HEACOCK'S PRICKLYPEAR
Opuntia humifusa including 'Barr's Dwarf'	PRICKLYPEAR
Opuntia humifusa 'Inermis'	SPINELESS PRICKLYPEAR
Opuntia Hybrids (many)	HYBRID PRICKLYPEAR
Opuntia kleiniae	CANDLE CHOLLA
Opuntia leptocaulis	DESERT CHRISTMAS CACTUS, PENCIL CACTUS
Opuntia macrocentra	PURPLE PRICKLYPEAR
Opuntia macrorhiza	TWIST SPINE PRICKLYPEAR
Opuntia phaeacantha including 'Mesa Sky', 'Persimmon', 'Plum'	TULIP PRICKLYPEAR
Opuntia polyacantha including 'Crystal Tide', 'Nebraska Orange', 'Peter Pan' 'Taylor's Red'	PRICKLYPEAR ❖
Opuntia polyacantha var. *hystricina* 'Bernalillo'	BERNALILLO PRICKLYPEAR
Opuntia polyacantha var. *nicholii*	NAVAJO BRIDGE PRICKLYPEAR
Opuntia polyacantha var. *polyacantha* 'Wavy Gravy'	WAVY GRAVY PRICKLYPEAR
Opuntia polyacantha var. *rhodantha,* especially 'Chinle', 'Grand Mesa Peach', 'Hanksville Rose', 'Snowball'	COLORADO PRICKLYPEAR
Opuntia pottsii var. *montana*	POTT'S PRICKLYPEAR
Opuntia x *rutila*	HYBRID PRICKLYPEAR
Opuntia sanguinicola	TEXAS PRICKLYPEAR
Opuntia x *tortispina*	TWISTED SINE PRICKLYPEAR
Pediocactus nigrispinus	HEDGEHOG CACTUS, SNOWBALL CACTUS
Pediocactus simpsonii	MOUNTAIN BALL CACTUS
Sclerocactus parviflorus	SMALL-FLOWER FISHHOOK CACTUS
Sclerocactus spinosior	DESERT VALLEY FISHHOOK CACTUS

OTHER SUCCULENTS

Agave asperrima	SCABROUS CENTURY PLANT
Agave bracteosa	CANDELABRUM AGAVE
Agave 'Desert Love'	DESERT LOVE HYBRID CENTURY PLANT
Agave ferdinandi-regis	KING FERDINAND AGAVE
Agave harvardiana	HAVARD'S CENTURY PLANT
Agave multifilifera 'Basaseachic Falls'	B. F. MANY-HAIRED CENTURY PLANT
Agave nickelsiae	KING FERDINAND CENTURY PLANT
Agave ovatifolia	WHALE'S TONGUE CENTURY PLANT
Agave x *ovatispina* 'Blue Rapture'	BLUE RAPTURE HYBRID CENTURY PLANT
Agave parryi ssp. *neomexicana*	NEW MEXICO AGAVE
Agave x pseudoferox 'Bellville'	BELLVILLE CENTURY PLANT
Agave victoriae-reginae	QUEEN VICTORIA CENTURY PLANT
Aloe polyphylla	SPIRAL ALOE
Aloiampelos (Aloe) striatula	HARDY ALOE
X Aloinanthus (*Aloinopsis spathulata* X *Nanathus* sp.) hybrids	HYBRID LIVING STONE
Aloinopsis x 'Psychedelic" (no, this is not hallucinogenic)	PSYCHEDELIC LIVING STONE
Aloinopsis spathulata	HARDY LIVING STONE
Aristaloe (Aloe) aristata	LACE ALOE
Bergeranthus jamesii	CLUMPING ICE PLANT
Beschorneria septentrionalis	FALSE RED AGAVE
Bukiniczia cabulica	VARIEGATED STATICE
Crassula sarcocaulis	BONSAI CRASSULA
Crassula setulosa	HAIRY CUSHION CRASSULA
Dasylirion wheeleri	SPOON YUCCA, DESERT SPOON
Delosperma 'Alan's Apricot'	APRICOT ICE PLANT
Delosperma basauticum 'Sunfire'	YELLOW ICE PLANT
Delosperma cooperi including 'Mesa Verde', 'Table Mountain'	
	COOPER'S HARDY PURPLE ICE PLANT
Delosperma dyeri including 'Red Mountain'	DYER'S ICE PLANT
Delosperma deleeuwiae	HARDY PURPLE ICE PLANT
Delosperma 'Fire Spinner'	FIRE SPINNER ICE PLANT
Delosperma floribunda 'Starburst'	STARBURST ICE PLANT
Delosperma lavisiae	DRAKENSBERG ICE PLANT
Delosperma nubigenum	HARDY YELLOW ICE PLANT
Delosperma sutherlandii	SUTHERLAND'S ICE PLANT
Dudleya cymosa	LIVE-FOREVER
Dudleya farinosa	CHALKY LIVE-FOREVER
Dyckia choristaminea	HARDY MINI BROMELIAD
Euphorbia griffithii 'Fireglow'	FIREGLOW SPURGE
Euphorbia schillingii	SCHILLING'S SPURGE
Hesperaloe parviflora	RED-FLOWERED YUCCA
Hylotelephium (Sedum) Autumn hybrids ('Autumn Charm', 'Autumn Delight', 'Autumn Fire', 'Autumn Joy')	HYBRID AUTUMN SEDUM
Hylotelephium (Sedum) cauticola 'Lidakense'	LIDAKENSE CLIFF STONECROP
Hylotelephium (Sedum) ewersii	PINK MONGOLIAN STONECROP
Hylotelephium (Sedum) hybrids (many including 'Vera Jameson')	HYBRID SEDUMS
Hylotelephium (Sedum) populifolium	POPLAR-LEAVED STONECROP

Hylotelephium (Sedum) spectabile	
	SHOWY STONECROP, AUTUMN SEDUM, BORDER SEDUM
Hylotelephium (Sedum) telephium	BORDER SEDUM
Hylotelephium (Sedum) telephioides	ALLEGHANY STONECROP
Hylotelephium (Sedum) ussuriense	TURKISH SEDUM
Hylotelephium (Sedum) verticillatum	CHINESE STONECROP
Jovibarba 'Belansky Tetra'	BELANSKY TETRA JOVIBARBA
Jovibarba heuffelii	BEARD OF JUPITER
Jovibarba hirta	BEARD OF JUPITER
Lewisia columbiana var. *columbiana*	COLUMBIAN LEWISIA
Lewisia cotyledon and hybrids	SISKIYOU LEWISIA
Lewisiopsis tweedyi	TWEEDY'S LEWISIA
Nolina nelsonii	NELSON'S BLUE BEAR GRASS
Orostachys malacophyllus	CHINESE DUNCE CAPS
Orostachys minuta	IWARENGE DUNCE-CAPS
Orostachys spinosa	SPINY PENNYWORT
Orostachys thyrsiflora	DUNCE-CAPS
Petrosedum (Sedum) polytrichoides	SPANISH STONECROP
Petrosedum (Sedum) rupestre	BLUE SEDUM
Petrosedum (Sedum) sediforme	PALE SEDUM
Phedimus (Sedum) ellacombianus	YELLOW STONECROP
Phedimus (Sedum) kamtschaticus	KAMSCHATKA SEDUM, ORANGE STONECROP
Phedimus (Sedum) middendorfianus	CHINESE MOUNTAIN STONECROP
Phedimus (Sedum) obtusifolius	MOUNDING STONECROP
Phedimus (Sedum) spurius	CAUCASIAN STONECROP
Phedimus (Sedum) stoloniferus	RUNNING FALSE STONECROP
Prometheum (Rosularia) muratdaghense	TURKISH STONECROP
Prometheum (Rosularia) rechingeri	RECHINGER'S HENS-AND-CHICKS
Rhodiola integrifolia	KING'S CROWN ❖
Rhodiola pachyclados	AFGHAN SEDUM
Rhodiola rosea	ROSEROOT, GOLDEN ROOT
Rosularia chrysantha	TURKISH HENS-AND-CHICKS
Rosularia platyphylla	TURKISH STONECROP
Rosularia rosulata	ROSETTE-LEAF SEDUM
Rosularia sedoides	ROSULARIA
Rosularia sempervivoides	SEMPERVIVELLA
Saxifraga 'Canis Dalmatica'	DALMATIAN DOG SAXIFRAGE
Saxifraga cochlearis	SILVER SAXIFRAGE
Saxifraga 'Cockscomb'	COCKSCOMB SAXIFRAGE
Saxifraga cotyledon	PYRAMIDAL SAXIFRAGE
Saxifraga x *geum* 'Dentata'	TOOTHED SAXIFRAGE
Saxifraga paniculata	LIFELONG SAXIFRAGE
Saxifraga 'Peachtree'	DWARF CUSHION SAXIFRAGE
Saxifraga x *urbium*	LONDON PRIDE
Saxifraga 'Whitehill'	WHITEHILL SAXIFRAGE
Saxifraga x *zimmeter*	HYBRID SAXIFRAGE
Sedum album	WHITE STONECROP
Sedum anglicum	ENGLISH STONECROP
Sedum dasyphyllum	CORSICAN STONECROP

Sedum divergens	SPREADING STONECROP ❖
Sedum 'Elizabeth'	ELIZABETH STONECROP
Sedum floriferum	STONECROP
Sedum forsterianum	ROCK STONECROP
Sedum 'Fulda Glow'	FULDA GLOW STONECROP
Sedum glaucophyllum	CLIFF STONECROP
Sedum lanceolatum	LANCE-LEAVED STONECROP ❖
Sedum oreganum	OREGON STONECROP ❖
Sedum oregonense	CREAMY FLOWERED STONECROP ❖
Sedum pachyclados	AFGHAN SEDUM
Sedum palmeri	PALMER'S SEDUM
Sedum reflexum (S. rupestre) including 'Angelina'	BLUE STONECROP
Sedum sexangulare	TASTELESS SEDUM
Sedum spathulifolium	BROAD-LEAVED STONECROP ❖
Sedum stenopetalum	WORM-LEAF STONECROP
Sedum tetractinum	CHINESE STONECROP
Sempervivum arachnoideum and cultivars	COBWEB HOUSE-LEEK, HENS-AND-CHICKS
Sempervivum grandiflorum	HENS-AND-CHICKS
Sempervivum heuffelii	HENS-AND-CHICKS
Sempervivum hybrids	HENS-AND-CHICKS
Sempervivum marmoreum	HENS-AND-CHICKS
Sempervivum tectorum	HENS-AND-CHICKS
Sempervivum villosum	HENS-AND-CHICKS
Umbilicus (Chiastophyllum) oppositifolium	LAMB'S TAIL, GOLD DROP
Yucca angustissima	NARROW-LEAF YUCCA
Yucca baccata	BANANA YUCCA
Yucca baileyi	NAVAJO YUCCA
Yucca desmettiana	SOFT-LEAVED YUCCA
Yucca elata var. *verdiensis*	ARIZONA YUCCA
Yucca faxoniana	FAXON YUCCA
Yucca filamentosa	ADAM'S NEEDLE
Yucca glauca (Y. angustifolia)	SOAPWEED YUCCA
Yucca harrimaniae	HARRIMAN'S YUCCA
Yucca harrimaniae var. *neomexicana*	NEW MEXICO BAYONET
Yucca linearifolia	LINEAR-LEAF YUCCA
Yucca x pollyjeaniae *(Y. harrimaniae* x *Y. glauca)*	COLORADO BAYONET
Yucca x schottii	SCHOTT'S YUCCA
Yucca thompsoniana	THOMPSON'S YUCCA

HARDY TERRESTRIAL ORCHIDS

Almost all require special soil or growing conditions. All need to be protected from snails and slugs. Some would probably be at their best in well-maintained containers.

Bletilla hybrids	CHINESE GROUND ORCHID
Bletilla ochracea	CHINESE BUTTERFLY ORCHID
Bletilla striata	CHINESE GROUND ORCHID
Bletilla x *yokohama* 'Sweet Lips'	SWEET LIPS GROUND ORCHID
Calanthe aristulifera	SMALL SPIKE CALANTHE
Calanthe x bicolor	HYBRID CALANTHE
Calanthe discolor	EBINE
Calanthe hybrids (Hizen, Kojima, Takane, Kozu Spice series)	HYBRID CALANTHE
Calanthe kawakamiense	TAIWAN CALANTHE ORCHID
Calanthe nipponica	GOLDEN SPIRITUAL CALANTHE ORCHID
Calanthe okinawensis	RYUKYU EBINE
Calanthe reflexa	BACK-BENT CALANTHE
Calanthe striata (C. seiboldii)	YELLOW EBINE
Calanthe tricarinata	HAIRY MONKEY ORCHID
Calopogon tuberosus	TUBEROUS GRASS-PINK
Calypso bulbosa	FAIRY SLIPPER ❖
Cremastra appendiculate	HANDLE ORCHID
Cremastra variabilis	VARIABLE HANDLE ORCHID
Cymbidium goeringii	HARDY CYMBIDIUM
Cymbidium tracyanum	TRACY'S CYMBIDIUM
Cypripedium acaule	PINK LADY'S SLIPPERS
Cypripedium x barbii	HYBRID LADY'S SLIPPERS
Cypripedium calceolus	EUROPEAN YELLOW LADY'S SLIPPERS
Cypripedium californicum	CALIFORNIA LADY'S SLIPPERS
Cypripedium x columbianum	HYBRID LADY'S SLIPPERS ❖
Cypripedium fargesii	FARGES' PINK LADY'S SLIPPERS
Cypripedium fasciolatum	STRIPED LADY'S SLIPPER
Cypripedium flavum	CHINESE LADY'S SLIPPERS
Cypripedium formosana	FORMOSAN LADY'S SLIPPERS
Cypripedium franchetii	FRANCHET'S LADY SLIPPER
Cypripedium guttatum	SPOTTED LADY'S SLIPPERS
Cypripedium henryi	HENRY'S LADY'S SLIPPERS
Cypripedium hybrids	HYBRID CYPRIPEDIUMS
Cypripedium japonicum	JAPANESE LADY'S SLIPPERS
Cypripedium macranthos	SHOWY LADY'S SLIPPERS
Cypripedium montanum	NORTHWEST MOUNTAIN LADY SLIPPER ORCHID ❖
Cypripedium parviflorum var pubescens	LARGE YELLOW LADY'S SLIPPER
Cypripedium passerinum	SPARROW'S-EGG LADY'S-SLIPPER
Cypripedium plectrochilum	DWARF LADY'S SLIPPERS
Cypripedium pubescens	YELLOW LADY'S SLIPPERS, MOCCASIN FLOWER
Cypripedium reginae	QUEEN'S LADY SLIPPERS
Cypripedium smithii	SMITH'S LADY'S SLIPPERS
Cypripedium tibeticum	TIBETAN LADY'S SLIPPERS

Cypripedium x ventricosum	INFLATED LADY'S SLIPPERS
Dactylorhiza elata	ROBUST MARSH ORCHID
Dactylorhiza (*D. foliosa* X *D. purpurella*) 'Foliorella'	MARSH ORCHID
Dactylorhiza fuchsii	COMMON SPOTTED MARSH ORCHID
Dactylorhiza hybrids	HYBRID MARSH ORCHID
Dactylorhiza maculata	HEATH SPOTTED ORCHID
Dactylorhiza majalis	BROAD-LEAVED MARSH ORCHID
Dactylorhiza pardalina	LEOPARD MARSH ORCHID
Dactylorhiza praetermissa	SOUTHERN MARSH ORCHID
Dactylorhiza purpurella	NORTHERN MARSH ORCHID
Dactylorhiza sambuciina	ELDER-FLOWERED ORCHID
Dactylorhiza sphagnicola	SPHAGNUM ORCHID
Epipactis gigantea, especially 'Serpentine Knight'	STREAM ORCHID ❖
Epipactis helleborine	BROAD-LEAVED HELLEBORINE
Epipactis palustris	MARSH HELLEBORINE
Epipactis royleana	HIMALAYAN HELLEBORINE
Epipactis 'Sabine'	SABINE HELLEBORINE
Epipactis thunbergii	JAPANESE STREAM ORCHID
Goodyera oblongifolia	RATTLESNAKE-PLANTAIN
Gymnadenia conopsea	FRAGRANT ORCHID
Liparis kumokiri	JAPANESE TWAYBLADE ORCHID
Oreorchis patens	COMMON OREORCHIS
Pleione albiflora	WHITE-FLOWERED PLEIONE
Pleione bulbocodioides (*P. formosana*)	PEACOCK ORCHID
Pleione x confusa 'Golden Gate'	GOLDEN GATE PEACOCK ORCHID
Pleione hookerianum	HOOKER'S PLEIONE
Pleione hybrids (many)	HYBRID PLEIONES
Pleione saxicola	AUTUMN PEACOCK ORCHID
Pleione yunnanensis	YUNNAN PEACOCK ORCHID
Ponerorchis graminifolia	SATSUMA PLOVER ORCHID
Pogonia ophioglossoides	ROSE POGONIA
Spiranthes cernua 'Chadds Ford'	CHADDS FORD NODDING LADIES' TRESSES
Spiranthes odorata	FRAGRANT LADY'S TRESSES
Spiranthes romanzoffiana	HOODED LADIES' TRESSES ❖

"The orchid is Mother Nature's masterpiece." ~~ Robyn Nola

SPRING ("COOL SEASON") ANNUALS, BIENNIALS

Many suitable for fall bloom, as well, but most are not at their best for summer. Biennials are marked "(b)" and are best sown in late summer and/or planted out in fall.

TALL *(over 3 feet)*

Alcea rosea (b)	HOLLYHOCK
Campanula pyramidalis (b)	CHIMNEY BELLFLOWER
Lathyrus odoratus	SWEET PEA
Lavatera trimestris	ROSE MALLOW
Verbascum bombyciferum (b)	GIANT SILVER MULLEIN

MEDIUM *(1 to 3 feet)*

Antirrhinum majus (often acts like a perennial)	SNAPDRAGON
Arctotis venusta (stoaechadifolia)	BLUE-EYED AFRICAN DAISY
Dianthus barbatus (b)	SWEET WILLIAM
Erythranthe (Mimulus) naiandina 'Mega'	SPUNKY MONKEY FLOWER
Lathyrus odoratus	SWEET PEA
Matthiola incana	STOCK
Molucella laevis	BELLS-OF-IRELAND
Pericallis (Senecio) x *hybridus* 'Giovanna's Select'	TALL CINERARIA
Salvia argentea (b)	SILVER SAGE
Scabiosa atropurpurea	PINCUSHION FLOWER
Trachymene coerulea	BLUE LACE FLOWER

SHORT *(under 1 foot)*

Anchusa capensis	CAPE FORGET-ME-NOT
Antirrhinum majus	SNAPDRAGON
Arctotis fastuosa	CAPE DAISY
Bellis perennis	ENGLISH DAISY
Brachyscome iberidifolia	SWAN RIVER DAISY
Brassica oleracea var. Acephala	FLOWERING CABBAGE, KALE
Calendula officinalis	POT MARIGOLD
Campanula medium (b)	CANTERBURY BELLS, CUP-AND-SAUCER
Clarkia amoena	GODETIA ❖
Coleostephus myconis (Chrysanthemum multicaule)	YELLOW CLUMP DAISY
Dianthus barbatus (b)	SWEET WILLIAM
Dianthus chinensis and hybrids	PINKS
Erythranthe (Mimulus) x *hybridus*	MONKEY FLOWER
Limonium sinuatum	ANNUAL STATICE
Lobelia erinus	LOBELIA
Matthiola incana	STOCK
Mauranthemum (Leucanthemum, Chrysanthemum) paludosum	WHITE CLUMP DAISY

Myosotis sylvatica (b)	WOOD FORGET-ME-NOT
Nemesia strumosa	NEMESIA
Nemesia versicolor	NEMESIA
Pericallis (Senecio) x hybridus	CINERARIA
Primula malacoides	FAIRY PRIMROSE
Primula obconica	GERMAN PRIMROSE
Schizanthus pinnatus, S. x wisetonensis	BUTTERFLY FLOWER
Viola cornuta	VIOLA
Viola tricolor	JOHNNY-JUMP-UP
Viola x wittrockiana (b)	PANSY
Xanthisma texanum	TEXAS SLEEPY DAISY

HARDIEST FALL-INTO-WINTER ANNUALS

For late summer sowing or early fall planting. Many will survive through the following spring and even possibly well beyond it, depending on weather. (b) indicates biennials, which when planted in fall will bloom the following spring-summer.

Antirrhinum majus	SNAPDRAGON
Bellis perennis	ENGLISH DAISY
Brassica oleracea	FLOWERING CABBAGE, FLOWERING KALE
Calendula officinalis	CALENDULA
Centaurea cineraria	VELVET CINERARIA, DUSTY MILLER
Dianthus chinensis and hybrids (b)	PINKS
Erysimum cheiri (b)	ENGLISH WALLFLOWER
Lathyrus odoratus	SWEET PEA
Lobularia maritima	SWEET ALYSSUM
Matthiola incana	STOCK
Jacobaea maritima	DUSTY MILLER
Myosotis sylvatica (b)	WOOD FORGET-ME-NOT
Papaver crocea/nudicaule (b)	ICELAND POPPY
Primula hybrids	ENGLISH PRIMROSE
Viola cornuta hybrids	VIOLA
Viola x wittrockiana (b)	PANSY

SUMMER AND INTO FALL ("WARM SEASON") ANNUALS, BIENNIALS, AND TENDER PERENNIALS

Flowers and foliage to plant out after hard frosts and when soil begins to warm.

ANNUALS

Tall (over 3 feet)

Alcea rosea (annual types)	HOLLYHOCK
Amaranthus caudatus	LOVE-LIES-BLEEDING
Centaurea americana	BASKET-FLOWER
Cleome hasslerana	SPIDER FLOWER
Cosmos bipinnatus (some strains)	COSMOS
Helianthus annuus	SUNFLOWER
Helianthus debilis ssp. *cucumerifolius* (including 'Italian White')	BEACH SUNFLOWER
Nicotiana sylvestris	FLOWERING TOBACCO
Persicaria orientale	KISS-ME-OVER-THE-GARDEN GATE
Ricinus communis	CASTOR BEAN
Tithonia rotundifolia	MEXICAN SUNFLOWER
Zinnia (best in driest, hottest spots only)	ZINNIA

Medium (1 to 3 feet)

Callistephus chinensis	CHINA ASTER
Celosia argentea var. *cristata*	COCKSCOMB
Celosia argentea var. *plumosa*	FEATHERED COCKSCOMB
Celosia argentea var. *spicata*	WHEAT CELOSIA, SILVER FEATHER
Cleome hasslerana	SPIDER FLOWER
Coreopsis tinctoria	CALLIOPSIS ❖
Cosmos bipinnatus	COSMOS
Cosmos sulphureus	YELLOW COSMOS
Cynoglossum amabile	CHINESE FORGET-ME-NOT
Helianthus annuus	SUNFLOWER
Datura inoxia	MOONFLOWER
Impatiens balsamina	BALSAM
Lavatera trimestris	ROSE MALLOW
Mirabilis jalapa (usually a perennial in gardens)	FOUR-O'CLOCKS
Molucella laevis	BELLS-OF-IRELAND
Nicotiana alata	FLOWERING TOBACCO
Nicotiana x *sanderae*	FLOWERING TOBACCO
Salpiglossus sinuata	PAINTED TONGUE
Salvia splendens	SCARLET SAGE
Scabiosa atropurpurea	PINCUSHION FLOWER
Tagetes erecta	AFRICAN MARIGOLD
Tropaeolum majus	NASTURTIUM
Zinnia (best in driest, hottest spots only)	ZINNIA

Begonia semperflorens	BEGONIA
Browallia speciosa	AMETHYST FLOWER
Calibrachoa x hybrida	MILLION BELLS
Callistephus chinensis	CHINA ASTER
Celosia argentea var. *cristata*	COCKSCOMB
Celosia argentea var. *plumosa*	FEATHERED COCKSCOMB
Convolvulus tricolor	BUSH MORNING GLORY
Cynoglossum amabile	CHINESE FORGET-ME-NOT
Dahlia hybrids	DAHLIA
Dianthus chinensis hybrids	ANNUAL PINKS
Dorotheanthus bellidiformis	LIVINGSTONE DAISY
Eustoma russellianum (E. grandiflorum; Lisianthus)	SWEET LISSIE, PRAIRIE GENTIAN
Impatiens balsamina	BALSAM
Lobelia erinus	TRAILING LOBELIA
Nolana humifusa	NOLANA
Nolana paradoxa	CHILEAN BELLFLOWER
X *Petchoa (Petunia* x *Calibrachoa* hybrid)	PETCHOA
Petunia axillaris, P. integrifolia	"WILD" PETUNIAS
Petunia × atkinsiana	HYBRID PETUNIA
Phlox drummondii	ANNUAL PHLOX
Portulaca grandiflora	MOSS ROSE
Salvia splendens	SCARLET SAGE
Sanvitalia procumbens	CREEPING ZINNIA
Tagetes erecta	AFRICAN MARIGOLD
Tagetes filifolia	IRISH LACE
Tagetes patula	FRENCH MARIGOLD
Tagetes tenuifolia	SIGNET MARIGOLD
Thymophylla tenuiloba	GOLDEN FLEECE
Torenia fournieri	BLUEWINGS, WISHBONE FLOWER
X *Torelus (Torenia x Mimulus hybrids)*	HYBRID MONKEYS
Tropaeolum majus	NASTURTIUM
Zinnia angustifolia	NARROW-LEAF ZINNIA
Zinnia elegans and hybrids	ZINNIA
Zinnia haageana	MEXICAN ZINNIA

TENDER & SHORT-LIVED PERENNIALS

These are the plants which are often followed by "treat as annuals" in references. Although they will grow through frost-free winters, our winters can't be described as such, hence this category.

Alcea ficifolia hybrids	ANTWERP HOLLYHOCK
Alcea rugosa	RUSSIAN HOLLYHOCK
Angelonia angustifolia	SUMMER SNAPDRAGON
Asclepias curassavica	SUNSET FLOWER
Catanache caerulea	CUPID'S-DART
Cerinthe major 'Purpurascens'	HONEYWORT

Delphinium grandiflorum	CHINESE DELPHINIUM
Digitalis x *valinii (X Digiplexis)*	DIGIPLEXIS
Glandularia (Verbena) x *hybrida*	GARDEN VERBENA
Heliotropium arborescens	CHERRY PIE
Monarda 'Bergamo Bouquet'	BUTTERFLY MONARDA
Monarda citriodora	LEMON BEE-BALM
Nicotiana langsdorfii	LANGSDORF'S TOBACCO
Osteospermum x *Dimorphotheca* hybrids	AFRICAN DAISY
Salvia coccinea	TEXAS SAGE
Salvia farinacea	MEALY-CUP SAGE
Salvia guaranitica	BLUE HUMMINGBIRD SAGE

BIENNIALS

Although usually considered spring-into-summer "annuals," these plants are best planted in early autumn (from seed sown in late summer) for growing their foliage and roots through winter and then blooming in late spring into summer and often through summer into fall.

Alcea rosea	HOLLYHOCK
Campanula medium	CANTERBURY BELLS, CUP-AND-SAUCER
Campanula pyramidalis	CHIMNEY BELLFLOWER
Dianthus barbatus	SWEET WILLIAM
Erysimum cheiri	ENGLISH WALLFLOWER
Eryngium giganteum	MISS WILMOTT'S GHOST
Ipomopsis aggregata	SKYROCKET, SCARLET GILIA ❖
Verbascum bombyciferum	GIANT SILVER MULLEIN

TENDER HERBACEOUS VINES

Cobaea scandens	CUP-AND-SAUCER VINE
Eccremocarpus scaber	CHILEAN GLORY VINE
Lablab purpureus	HYACINTH BEAN
Ipomoea x *imperialis*	HYBRID MORNING GLORY
Ipomoea lobata	FIRECRACKER VINE
Ipomoea x *multifida*	CARDINAL CLIMBER
Ipomoea nil	JAPANESE MORNING GLORY
Ipomoea quamoclit	CYPRESS VINE
Ipomoea tricolor	MORNING GLORY
Lophospermum (Asarina) erubescens	CREEPING GLOXINIA
Lophospermum (Asarina) scandens	CLIMBING SNAPDRAGON
Maurandella (Asarina) antirrhiniflora	VIOLET TWINING SNAPDRAGON
Phaseolus coccineus	SCARLET RUNNER BEAN
Scyphanthus elegans (S. grandiflorus)	LITTLE NUN, MONJITA
Thunbergia alata	BLACK-EYED SUSAN VINE

SUMMER FOLIAGE

Some of these can be planted out and left until hard frosts render them "ugly-beyond-belief." Most can be grown in pots or potted up after summer and wintered over by moving indoors when temperatures are expected below 32°F.

Alternanthera dentata	RUBY LEAF
Alternanthera ficoidea	JOSEPH'S COAT
Amaranthus cruentus x *powellii*	HOPI RED DYE
Amaranthus tricolor	AMARANTH, CHINESE SPINACH
Begonia (many)	BEGONIA
Canna warscewiczii	MEXICAN CANNA
Canna 'Minerva', 'Pretoria', 'Red King Humbert', 'Stuttgart', 'Tropicana', Tropicanna Series, 'Wyoming'	CANNAS
Centaurea cineraria	VELVET CINERARIA, DUSTY MILLER
Coleus (*Plectranthus*) *argentatus*	SILVER SPURFLOWER
Coleus (*Solenostemon*) *scuttellarioides*	COLEUS
Coleus (incorrectly *Perilla*) "Magilla"	MAGILLA PERILLA
Cynara cardunculus (may act as a biennial)	CARDOON
Dahlia Hybrida dark-leafed forms	DAHLIA
Ensete ventricosum 'Maurelii'	RED ABYSSINIAN BANANA
Euphorbia marginata	SNOW-ON-THE-MOUNTAIN
Helichrysum petiolare	LICORICE PLANT
Hibiscus acetosella	RED SHIELD
Hypoestes phyllostachya	POLKA-DOT PLANT
Ipomoea batatas	ORNAMENTAL SWEET POTATO
Iresine herbstii	BLOODLEAF
Jacobaea maritima	DUSTY MILLER
Manihot esculenta 'Variegata'	VARIEGATED TAPIOCA
Musa acuminata 'Zebrina'	STRIPED BANANA
Pennisetum glaucum	ORNAMENTAL PEARL MILLET
Pennisetum macrostachyum 'Burgundy Giant'	BURGUNDY GIANT FOUNTAIN GRASS
Perilla frutescens var. *purpurascens*	BEEFSTEAK PLANT, RED SHISO
Ricinus communis	CASTOR BEAN
Salvia argentea	SILVER SAGE
Salvia discolor	ANDEAN SILVER-LEAF SAGE
Senecio candicans 'Angel Wings'	DUSTY MILLER
Senecio niveoaureus	SILVER FEATHERS
Senecio vira-vira	DUSTY MILLER
Strobilanthes dyerianus	PERSIAN SHIELD
Strobilanthes gossypinus	SILVER PERSIAN SHIELD
Tradescantia (*Setcreasea*) *pallida* 'Purpurea'	PURPLE HEART

SITE

SPECIFIC

Most often, the choice of a plant is dictated by the environmental conditions as delineated herein. Creativity follows. To be fair, most plants are adaptable to a wide range of conditions.

Look for the symbol ❖ which indicates a native plant.

SUN

This list contains plants suited to sun from just about sun-up to sun-down. Although many garden references describe "full sun" as anything more than six hours, our cooler weather and more frequent cloudiness generally dictates that plants requiring full sun are best in garden spots with more than eight hours of sun in a day. This is only a sampling; the majority of the plants in this entire book are adaptable to full sun. All of these on this list are at their best in all-day sun. Which means they will tolerate even what many in the PNW consider "baking, hot afternoon sun."

BULBS

Acis autumnalis	AUTUMN SNOWFLAKE
Allium (Nectaroscordum) bulgaricum siculum	SICILIAN HONEY LILY
Allium atropurpureum	ORNAMENTAL ONION
Allium beesianum	BLUE ALLIUM
Allium cernuum	NODDING ONION ❖
Allium cristophii	STAR OF PERSIA, PERSIAN ONION
Allium 'Globemaster'	ORNAMENTAL ONION
Allium karataviense	TURKESTAN ONION
Allium neopolitanum cowanii	GUERNSEY STAR-OF-BETHLEHEM
Allium rosenbachianum	SHOWY ONION
Allium roseum	ROSY GARLIC
Allium schubertii	TUMBLEWEED ONION
Allium (Nectaroscordum) tripedale	PINK HONEY LILY
X Amarygia parkeri	HYBRID AMARYLLIS
Amaryllis belladonna	NAKED LADY
Anemone x fulgens	FLAME ANEMONE
Brodiaea californica	CALIFORNIA BRODIAEA
Brodiaea coronaria	CROWN BRODIAEA ❖
Brodiaea elegans	HARVEST BRODIAEA
Colchicum x agrippinum	AUTUMN CROCUS, MEADOW SAFFRON
Colchicum autumnale	AUTUMN CROCUS
Colchicum byzantinum	BYZANTINE MEADOW SAFFRON
Colchicum hybrids (such as 'Giant', 'Lilac Wonder', 'Violet Queen', 'Waterlily')	
	AUTUMN CROCUS
Colchicum speciosum	AUTUMN CROCUS
Colchicum variegatum	SPOTTED AUTUMN CROCUS
Crocus goulimyi	PELOPONNESE CROCUS
Crocus imperati	ITALIAN CROCUS
Crocus laevigatus	LATE CROCUS
Crocus longiflorus	ITALIAN CROCUS
Crocus niveus	FALL CROCUS
Crocus ochroleucus	YELLOW CROCUS
Crocus pulchellus	TURKISH CROCUS
Crocus serotinus	LATE CROCUS
Crocus chrysanthus	GOLDEN CROCUS
Crocus tommasinianus	TOMMASINI'S CROCUS
Dichelostemma (Brodiaea) congestum	OOKOW

Dracocephalum argunense (or D. austriacum)	DRAGON'S HEAD
Eremurus himalaicus	HIMALAYAN FOXTAIL LILY
Eremurus hybrids	FOXTAIL LILY
Eremurus stenophyllus	DESERT CANDLE
Fritillaria affinis (F. lanceolata)	CHOCOLATE LILY ❖
Fritillaria assyriaca	TURKISH FRITILLARY
Fritillaria bucharica 'Giant'	RUSSIAN FRITILLARY
Fritillaria eduardii	EDUARD'S FRITILLARIA
Fritillaria pontica	PONTIC FRITILLARY
Fritillaria michailovskyi	MICHAEL'S FLOWER
Gladiolus (tubergenii) 'Charm'	SWORD LILY
Gladiolus 'Rosy Cheeks'	ROSY CHEEKS GLADIOLUS
Gladiolus communis var. *byzantinus*	BYZANTINE GLADIOLUS
Gladiolus dalenii var. *primulinus*	CAROLINA PRIMROSE
Gladiolus italicus	ITALIAN GLADIOLUS
Gladiolus oppositiflorus ssp. *salmoneus*	SALMON GLADIOLUS
Gladiolus saundersii	SAUNDER'S GLADIOLUS
Iris xiphium	SPANISH IRIS
Lilium Asiatic hybrids	ASIATIC LILY
Lilium columbianum	TIGER LILY
Lilium Oriental hybrids	ORIENTAL LILY
Lilium sargentiae	SARGENT'S LILY
Lilium x testaceum	NANKEEN LILY
Lycoris aurea	YELLOW SPIDER LILY
Lycoris radiata	RED SPIDER LILY
Lycoris sprengeri	SURPRISE LILY, MAGIC LILY
Lycoris x squamigera	RESURRECTION LILY, MAGIC LILY
Muscari latifolium	GRAPE HYACINTH
Narcissus 'February Gold'	MINIATURE DAFFODIL
Narcissus 'Jack Snipe'	MINIATURE DAFFODIL
Narcissus 'King Alfred'	KING ALFRED DAFFODIL
Narcissus 'Mount Hood'	WHITE TRUMPET DAFFODIL
Narcissus 'Mrs. Langtry'	HEIRLOOM DAFFODIL
Narcissus 'Replete'	DOUBLE DAFFODIL
Narcissus 'Rosy Clouds'	DOUBLE PINK DAFFODIL
Narcissus 'Saint Keverne'	GOLDEN TRUMPET DAFFODIL
Narcissus 'Tahiti'	TAHITI DAFFODIL
Narcissus (cyclamineus) 'Tête-à-tête'	MINIATURE DAFFODIL
Narcissus x *italicus* 'Thalia'	ITALIAN ANGEL'S TEARS
Narcissus jonquilla	JONQUILS
Narcissus poeticus var. *recurvus*	PHEASANT'S EYE DAFFODIL
Nerine bowdenii and hybrids	SPIDER LILY
Nerine sarniensis and hybrids	GUERNSEY LILY
Oncostema (Scilla) peruviana	PORTUGUESE SQUILL
Ornithogalum narbonense	SOUTHERN STAR-OF-BETHLEHEM
Ornithogalum ponticum	STAR-OF-BETHLEHEM
Prospero (Scilla) autumnale	AUTUMN SQUILL
Pseudomuscari (Muscari, Bellavalia) azureum	AZURE GRAPE HYACINTH
Pseudomuscari (Muscari, Bellavalia) forniculatum	TURKISH GRAPE HYACINTH

Scilla bifolia	TWO-LEAF SQUILL
Sternbergia lutea	AUTUMN DAFFODIL
Triteleia 'Queen Fabiola'	ITHURIEL'S SPEAR
Triteleia (Brodiaea) hyacinthina	WHITE TRIPLET-LILY ❖
Tulipa clusiana and forms	LADY TULIP
Tulipa dasystemon	DASYSTEMON TULIP
Tulipa linifolia (including *T. batalinii*)	BOKHARA TULIP, FLAX-LEAF TULIP
Tulipa orphanidea (including *T. whittallii*)	ANATOLIAN TULIP, COTTAGE TULIP
Tulipa sprengeri	SPRENGER'S TULIP
Tulipa urumiensis (*T. tarda*)	LATE TULIP, TARDY TULIP

PERENNIALS

Acanthus syriacus	SYRIAN ACANTHUS
Achillea clavennae	SILVER YARROW
Achillea filipendulina	YARROW
Achillea 'Moonshine'	MOONSHINE YARROW
Aloiampelos (Aloe) striatula	HARDY ALOE
Amsonia ciliata	FRINGED BLUE STAR
Amsonia hubrichtii	THREADLEAF BLUE STAR
Amsonia illustris	OZARK BLUE STAR
Amsonia tabernaemontana	EASTERN BLUE STAR
Artemisia versicolor 'Sea Foam'	CURLICUE SAGE
Artemisia lactiflora Guizhou Group	WHITE MUGWORT
Aster x frikartii	FRIKART'S ASTER
Baptisia australis	BLUE FALSE INDIGO
Baptisia hybrids	FALSE INDIGO
Calylophus hartwegii	HARTWEG'S SUNDROPS
Campanula 'Birch Hybrid'	BIRCH'S BELLFLOWER
Campanula lactiflora	MILKY BELLFLOWER
Campanula rotundifolia	HAREBELL
Cephalaria gigantea	GIANT YELLOW SCABIOUS
Coreopsis verticillata	THREAD-LEAF COREOPSIS
Digitalis ferruginea	RUSTY FOXGLOVE
Digitalis grandiflora	LARGE YELLOW FOXGLOVE
Dracocephalum grandiflorum	DRAGON'S HEAD
Echinops ritro	GLOBE THISTLE
Epilobium (Zauschneria) septentrionalis	CALIFORNIA FUCHSIA
Erodium chrysanthum	HERONSBILL, STORKSBILL
Eryngium agavifolium	AGAVE-LEAF SEA HOLLY
Eryngium alpinum	ALPINE SEA HOLLY
Eryngium amethystinum	BLUE SEA HOLLY
Geranium x cantabrigiense cultivars	HARDY GERANIUM
Geranium cinereum 'Laurence Flatman'	ASHY CRANESBILL
Geranium macrorrhizum, especially 'Album', 'Bevan's Variety', 'Czakor', 'Ingwersen's Variety'	BIG-ROOTED CRANESBILL
Geranium x procurrens, especially 'Ann Folkard', 'Anne Thomson'	HARDY GERANIUM
Geranium renardii	CAUCASIAN CRANESBILL

Geranium x *riversleaianum*	CRANESBILL
Geranium wlassovianum	HARDY GERANIUM
Geum hybrids	GEUM, AVENS
Gillenia trifoliata	BOWMAN'S ROOT
Gypsophila cerastioides	ALPINE BABY'S BREATH
Helenium autumnale and hybrids	SNEEZEWEED ❖
Helianthemum nummularium	SUN ROSE
Helictotrichon sempervirens	BLUE OAT GRASS
Heliopsis helianthoides	FALSE SUNFLOWER
Hemerocallis hybrids	DAYLILIES

Hosta sun-tolerant types such as: 'August Moon', 'Guacamole', 'Halcyon'
  'Krossa Regal', 'Minuteman', 'Patriot', 'Sun Power'   HOSTA

Hylotelephium (Sedum) cauticola 'Lidakense'	LIDAKENSE CLIFF STONECROP
Hylotelephium (Sedum) ewersii	PINK MONGOLIAN STONECROP
Hylotelephium (Sedum) spectabile	

SHOWY STONECROP, AUTUMN SEDUM, BORDER SEDUM

Hylotelephium (Sedum) 'Vera Jameson'	PURPLE AUTUMN SEDUM
Iris pallida	DALMATIAN IRIS
Iris tenax	OREGON IRIS, TOUGH-LEAF IRIS ❖
Jovibarba heuffelii	HENS-AND-CHICKS
Jovibarba hirta	HENS-AND-CHICKS
Kniphofia hybrids	TORCH LILY
Lathyrus vernus	SPRING VETCHLING
Leptinella squalida 'Platt's Black'	BRASS BUTTONS
Leucanthemum x *superbum* 'Becky'	SHASTA DAISY
Liatris ligulistylis	MEADOW BLAZING STAR
Linaria (purpurea Hybrid) 'Natalie'	NATALIE TOADFLAX
Lobelia tupa	TABACO DEL DIABLO, DEVIL'S TOBACCO
Nepeta racemosa 'Walker's Low'	CATMINT
Opuntia fragilis	BRITTLE PRICKLY PEAR ❖
Opuntia humifusa 'Inermis'	SPINELESS PRICKLY PEAR
Opuntia phaeacantha	TULIP PRICKLY PEAR
Opuntia polyacantha	PLAINS PRICKLY PEAR
Paeonia peregrina	BALKAN PEONY
Paeonia daurica ssp. *mlokosewitschii*	"MOLLY'S WITCH" PEONY
Paeonia lactiflora hybrids	COMMON PEONY
Paeonia officinalis ssp. *huthii (P. villosa, P. mollis)*	HAIRY COMMON PEONY
Paeonia veitchii	CHINESE WOODLAND PEONY
Papaver Oriental hybrids	ORIENTAL POPPY
Penstemon attenuatus	TAPER-LEAVED PENSTEMON ❖
Penstemon azureus	AZURE PENSTEMON ❖
Penstemon barrettiae	BARRETT'S BEARDTONGUE ❖
Penstemon cardwellii	CARDWELL'S PENSTEMON ❖
Penstemon davidsonii	DAVIDSON'S BEARDTONGUE ❖
Penstemon grandiflorus	LARGE BEARDTONGUE
Penstemon kunthii	MEXICAN BEARDTONGUE
Penstemon richardsonii	RICHARDSON'S BEARDTONGUE ❖
Penstemon rupicola	ROCK PENSTEMON ❖
Penstemon serrulatus	CASCADE PENSTEMON, COAST PENSTEMON ❖

Penstemon speciosus	SHOWY PENSTEMON ❖
Penstemon subserratus	FINE-TOOTHED PENSTEMON ❖
Penstemon venustus	LOVELY PENSTEMON, BEAUTIFUL PENSTEMON ❖
Penstemon wilcoxii	WILCOX'S PENSTEMON ❖
Phedimus (Sedum) kamtschaticus	KAMSCHATKA SEDUM, ORANGE STONECROP
Phedimus (Sedum) spurius	TWO-ROW STONECROP
Phedimus (Sedum) stoloniferus	RUNNING FALSE STONECROP
Phlomis russeliana	STICKY JERUSALEM-SAGE
Psephellus simplicicaulis	LILAC CORNFLOWER
Rhodiola pachyclados	AFGHAN SEDUM
Rhodanthemum (Chrysanthemum) hosmariense	MOROCCAN DAISY
Rudbeckia fulgida var. *sullivantii* 'Goldsturm'	BLACK-EYED SUSAN
Salvia nemorosa	PURPLE WOOD SAGE
Salvia x sylvestris	VIOLET WOOD SAGE
Salvia verticillata	LILAC SAGE
Salvia yangii (Perovskia atriplicifolia)	RUSSIAN SAGE
Sedum 'Bertram Anderson'	STONECROP
Sedum cyaneum	BLUE STONECROP
Sedum kimnachii	MEXICAN SEDUM
Sedum selskianum	AMUR SEDUM
Sempervivum species and hybrids	HENS AND CHICKS, HOUSELEEK
Solidago 'Golden Baby'	GOLDEN BABY GOLDENROD
Solidago 'Little Lemon'	LITTLE LEMON GOLDENROD
Solidago (X Solidaster) x luteus	SOLIDASTER
Solidago rugosa 'Fireworks'	GOLDENROD
Thermopsis chinensis 'Sophia'	CHINESE BUSH PEA
Thermopsis montana	MOUNTAIN GOLD-BANNER ❖

VINES

Campsis x tagliabuana	HYBRID TRUMPET CREEPER
Clematis species and hybrids	CLEMATIS
Jasminum x stephanense	STEPHAN'S JASMINE
Lonicera acuminata (L. henryi)	HENRY'S HONEYSUCKLE
Lonicera x tellmanniana	RED-GOLD HONEYSUCKLE
Passiflora x belotii (*P.* x alato-caerulea)	BLUE PASSION FLOWER
Rosa "climbing" hybrids	CLIMBING ROSES
Solanum crispum 'Glasnevin'	CHILEAN POTATO VINE
Tropaeolum hardy perennial species	HARDY NASTURTIUM

SHRUBS

Arbutus unedo cultivars	COMPACT STRAWBERRY TREE
Arctostaphylos densiflora 'Howard McMinn'	MANZANITA
Berberis x gladwynensis 'William Penn'	WILLIAM PENN BARBERRY
Berberis x ottawensis 'Royal Cloak'	PURPLE-LEAF JAPANESE BARBERRY

Berberis darwinii	DARWIN'S BARBERRY
Berberis thunbergii f. *atropurpurea*	PURPLE-LEAF JAPANESE BARBERRY
Berberis verruculosa	WARTY BARBERRY
Brachyglottis 'Otari Cloud'	OTARI CLOUD DAISY BUSH
Calluna vulgaris	HEATHER
Caryopteris x *clandonensis*	BLUEBEARD
Caryopteris incana	BLUEBEARD
Ceanothus 'Skylark' ('Victoria')	VICTORIA CALIFORNIA LILAC
Cistus hybrids	WHITE ROCKROSE
Cotinus coggygria purple forms	PURPLE SMOKEBUSH
Daphne x *burkwoodii* 'Carol Mackie'	VARIEGATED HYBRID DAPHNE
Daphne x *medfordensis* 'Lawrence Crocker'	LAWRENCE CROCKER DWARF DAPHNE
Daphne x *transatlantica*	HYBRID DAPHNE
Daphne tangutica	DAPHNE
Elaeagnus x *submacrophylla* (*E.* x *ebbingei*)	HYBRID ELAEAGNUS
Elaeagnus pungens	ELAEAGNUS
Erica carnea	WINTER HEATH
Erica cinerea	BELL HEATHER
Erica x *darleyensis*	DARLEY DALE HEATH
Elsholtzia stauntonii	CHINESE MINT SHRUB
Forsythia x *intermedia*	FORSYTHIA
Fothergilla gardenii	DWARF WITCH ALDER
Fothergilla 'Mount Airy'	WITCH ALDER
Grevillea victoriae	ROYAL GREVILLEA
Hebe cupressoides	HEBE
Hebe 'Emerald Gem'	EMERALD GEM HEBE
Hebe 'Hinerua'	HINERUA HEBE
Hebe odora	BOXWOOD HEBE
Hebe topiaria	TOPIARISTS' HEBE
Hibiscus syriacus	ROSE-OF-SHARON
Hydrangea arborescens	SMOOTH HYDRANGEA
Hydrangea paniculata	PANICLE HYDRANGEA
Linnaea (Abelia) 'Edward Goucher'	GLOSSY ABELIA
Linnaea (Abelia) x *grandiflora*	GLOSSY ABELIA
Lonicera pileata	BOX-LEAF HONEYSUCKLE
Mahonia x *media*	HYBRID MAHONIA
Notholithocarpus densiflorus var. *echinoides*	SHRUB TANOAK ❖
Osmanthus x *burkwoodii*	BURKWOOD'S SWEET OLIVE
Osmanthus delavayi	SWEET OLIVE
Philadelphus 'Belle Etoile'	MOCK ORANGE
Physocarpus opulifolius	NINEBARK
Pieris 'Brouwer's Beauty'	LILY-OF-THE-VALLEY SHRUB
Pieris japonica	LILY-OF-THE-VALLEY SHRUB, ANDROMEDA
Prostanthera cuneata	ALPINE MINT BUSH
Pyracantha 'Mohave'	FIRETHORN
Ribes sanguineum	FLOWERING CURRANT ❖
Rosa glauca	RED-STEM ROSE
Rosa rugosa	JAPANESE BEACH ROSE
Salvia rosmarinus (Rosmarinus officinalis)	ROSEMARY

Sambucus nigra 'Black Lace'	PURPLE CUT-LEAF ELDERBERRY
Sambucus nigra 'Black Beauty'	PURPLE-LEAF BLACK ELDER
Sophora davidii	DAVID'S MOUNTAIN LAUREL
Spiraea betulifolia	BIRCH-LEAF SPIREA ❖
Spiraea japonica	JAPANESE SPIRAEA
Spiraea thunbergii	THUNBERG'S SPIREA, BRIDALWREATH SPIREA
Syringa pubescens ssp. *patula* 'Miss Kim'	DWARF KOREAN LILAC
Teucrium aroanium	GRAY CREEPING GERMANDER
Teucrium cossonii "Majoricum"	FRUITY GERMANDER
Vaccinium ovatum	EVERGREEN HUCKLEBERRY ❖
Viburnum x bodnantense 'Dawn'	PINK DAWN VIBURNUM
Viburnum carlesii	KOREAN SPICE VIBURNUM
Viburnum davidii	DAVID'S VIBURNUM
Weigela florida	WEIGELA
Yucca filamentosa	ADAM'S NEEDLE
Yucca flaccida	ADAM'S NEEDLE
Yucca linearifolia	NARROW-LEAFED BEAKED YUCCA
Yucca recurvifolia	CURVE-LEAF YUCCA

"I'm like a plant; I reach for the sun." ~~ Carole King

SHADE

Shade is generally difficult to describe. In this context, it is less than 6 hours of sun in a day. Where there is less than 3 hours of any direct sunlight per day ("deep shade"), consider those plants marked with an ✓. Many of the plants listed here are *variegated* selections of shade-loving species; a welcome quality in areas of darkness.

SMALL TREES
For understory

Acer circinatum	VINE MAPLE ❖
Acer crataegifolium	HAWTHORN MAPLE
Acer griseum	PAPER-BARK MAPLE
Acer japonicum f. *aconitifolium*	FERN-LEAF FULL MOON MAPLE
Acer palmatum	JAPANESE MAPLE
Acer pseudosieboldianum	KOREAN MAPLE
Acer triflorum	THREE-FLOWER MAPLE, ROUGH-BARK MAPLE ✓
Amelanchier x grandiflora	SERVICEBERRY
Carpinus betulus	EUROPEAN HORNBEAM ✓
Carpinus caroliniana	AMERICAN HORNBEAM ✓
Carpinus japonica	JAPANESE HORNBEAM ✓
Cephalotaxus harringtonia	COW-TAIL PINE, PLUM YEW ✓
Cercis canadensis 'Little Woody'	LITTLE WOODY REDBUD
Clerodendrum trichotomum	HARLEQUIN GLORYBOWER
Clethra barbinervis	JAPANESE CLETHRA
Cornus alternifolia	PAGODA DOGWOOD
Cornus controversa 'Variegata'	WEDDING CAKE TREE
Cornus x elwinortonii cultivars	HYBRID DOGWOODS
Cornus kousa	KOREAN DOGWOOD
Cornus mas 'Variegata'	VARIEGATED CORNELIAN CHERRY
Eucryphia glutinosa	NIRRHE
Hoheria sexstylosa	LACEBARK, RIBBON-WOOD
Ostrya virginiana	HOP-HORNBEAM
Oxydendrum arboreum	SOURWOOD
Parrotia subaequalis	CHINESE IRONWOOD
Ptelea trifoliata	COMMON HOPTREE
Pterostyrax hispidus	EPAULETTE TREE
Raukaua laetevirens	TRAUMEN
Staphylea holocarpa (including 'Rosea')	CHINESE BLADDERNUT
Stewartia serrata	JAPANESE STEWARTIA
Stewartia monadelpha	ORANGE-BARK STEWARTIA
Styrax wuyuanensis	CHINESE SNOWBELL
Thuja plicata 'Zebrina	VARIEGATED WESTERN RED-CEDAR ❖✓
Tsuga heterophylla 'Thorsen's Weeping'	WEEPING WESTERN HEMLOCK ❖✓
Tsuga diversifolia	NORTHERN JAPANESE HEMLOCK

SHRUBS
Including some very small trees

Acer shirasawanum f. *aureum*	FULL MOON MAPLE
Acer circinatum	VINE MAPLE ❖✓
Acer crataegifolium 'Veitchii'	VARIEGATED HAWTHORN MAPLE
Aucuba omeiensis	JAPANESE LAUREL✓
Aucuba japonica especially variegated forms	JAPANESE LAUREL✓
Buxus sempervirens 'Aureovariegata'	VARIEGATED BOXWOOD✓
Camellia hiemalis	SNOW CAMELLIA
Camellia japonica	CAMELLIA, JAPANESE CAMELLIA
Camellia reticulata	FOREST CAMELLIA
Camellia sasanqua	SASANQUA CAMELLIA
Camellia x *vernalis* (includes 'Yuletide')	HYBRID CAMELLIA
Camellia x *williamsii*	HYBRID CAMELLIA
Cephalotaxus harringtonia	COW-TAIL PINE, PLUM YEW
Chamaecyparis obtusa Dwarf forms	DWARF HINOKI CYPRESS
Clethra barbinervis 'Takeda Nishiki'	FIRST SNOW JAPANESE CLETHRA
Cornus alba 'Elegantissima'	VARIEGATED RED-TWIG DOGWOOD
Corylopsis glabrescens 'Longwood Chimes'	WINTER HAZEL
Corylopsis sinensis var. *sinensis*	CORYLOPSIS
Daphne bholua	HARDY DAPHNE
Daphne x *burkwoodii* 'Carol Mackie'	CAROL MACKIE DAPHNE
Daphne x *medfordensis* 'Lawrence Crocker'	LAWRENCE CROCKER DAPHNE
Daphne odora 'Aureomarginata'	VARIEGATED DAPHNE
Daphne tangutica	TANGUTICA DAPHNE
Daphne x *transatlantica* cultivars	DAPHNE
Decaisnea fargesii	BLUE BEAN SHRUB
Dichroa (*Hydrangea*) *febrifuga*	BLUE EVERGREEN HYDRANGEA
Disanthus cercidifolius	REDBUD HAZEL
Edgeworthia chrysantha	PAPERBUSH✓
Elaeagnus x *submacrophylla* (*E.* x *ebbingei*) 'Gilt Edge'	
	GILT EDGE HYBRID ELAEAGNUS✓
Eleutherococcus sieboldianus 'Variegatus'	VARIEGATED FIVE-LEAF ARALIA✓
Enkianthus campanulatus cultivars	ENKIANTHUS
Enkianthus perulatus	WHITE ENKIANTHUS
Eurya japonica 'Sea Brocade'	SEA BROCADE EURYA
Fatsia japonica 'Annelise', 'Murakumo nishiki' ('Camouflage'), 'Spider's Web',	
'Variegata'	VARIEGATED JAPANESE FATSIA✓
Fuchsia fulgens	BRILLIANT FUCHSIA
Fuchsia 'Riccartonii'	HARDY FUCHSIA
Fuchsia magellanica, especially white-flowered and variegated forms	
	MAGELLAN FUCHSIA
Fuchsia regia ssp. *reitzii*	RED BRAZILIAN PRINCESS
Hamamelis x *intermedia*	HYBRID WITCH-HAZEL✓
Hydrangea aspera (including *H. a.* Villosa)	ROUGH-LEAF HYDRANGEA
Hydrangea macrophylla cultivars	HYDRANGEA
Hydrangea quercifolia	OAKLEAF HYDRANGEA
Hydrangea serrata	MOUNTAIN HYDRANGEA

Ilex crenata	JAPANESE HOLLY
Itea virginica 'Little Henry'	LITTLE HENRY SWEETSPIRE
Kerria japonica 'Picta'	JAPANESE KERRIA✓
Leucothoe fontanesiana	LEUCOTHOE
Magnolia stellata 'Royal Star'	ROYAL STAR MAGNOLIA
Mahonia x media cultivars	HYBRID MAHONIA
Microbiota decussata	SIBERIAN CYPRESS
Morella (Myrica) californica	CALIFORNIA WAX MYRTLE ❖
Myrteola nummularia	CRANBERRY-MYRTLE
Osmanthus x burkwoodii	HYBRID SWEET OLIVE✓
Osmanthus delavayi	SWEET OLIVE✓
Osmanthus heterophyllus, especially variegated forms	VARIEGATED FALSE HOLLY✓
Pieris 'Forest Flame'	LILY-OF-THE-VALLEY BUSH
Pieris formosa var. *forrestii*	CHINESE PIERIS
Pieris japonica cultivars	JAPANESE PIERIS, ANDROMEDA
Rhododendron species and hybrids	RHODODENDRON, AZALEA
Ribes laurifolium	EVERGREEN CURRANT
Ruscus colchicus	BUTCHER'S BROOM✓
Sarcococca confusa	SWEETBOX✓
Sarcococca hookeriana var. *hookeriana*	SWEETBOX✓
Sarcococca hookeriana var. *humilis*	DWARF SWEETBOX✓
Sarcococca orientalis	ASIAN SWEETBOX✓
Sarcococca ruscifolia	SWEETBOX✓
Skimmia japonica	SKIMMIA
Taxus brevifolia 'Nana'	DWARF PACIFIC YEW ❖✓
Thuja plicata 'Pygmaea', 'Whipcord'	DWARF RED-CEDAR ❖✓
Tsuga canadensis especially dwarf, prostrate forms	DWARF CANADIAN HEMLOCK
Vaccinium ovatum, especially 'Cascade Sunburst'	EVERGREEN HUCKLEBERRY ❖✓
Viburnum x burkwoodii cultivars	BURKWOOD VIBURNUM
Viburnum furcatum	SCARLET-LEAVED VIBURNUM
Viburnum plicatum f. *tomentosum*	DOUBLE-FILE VIBURNUM

VINES

Actinidia tetramera var. *maloides*	ROSY CRABAPPLE KIWI
Berberidopsis corallina	CORAL PLANT
X *Fatshedera lizei*	FATSHEDERA, BOTANICAL WONDER
X *Fatshedera lizei* 'Annemieke'	GOLDEN VARIEGATED FATSHEDERA
Hedera algeriensis 'Glorie de Marengo'	VARIEGATED ALGERIAN IVY✓
Hedera colchica 'Dentata Variegata'	VARIEGATED PERSIAN IVY✓
Hydrangea anomala	CLIMBING HYDRANGEA
Hydrangea (Schizophragma) hydrangeoides 'Moonlight'	JAPANESE HYDRANGEA VINE✓
Hydrangea integrifolia	EVERGREEN CLIMBING HYDRANGEA
Hydrangea petiolaris (*H. anomala petiolaris*)	CLIMBING HYDRANGEA
Hydrangea seemannii	MEXICAN CLIMBING HYDRANGEA
Lonicera ciliosa	WESTERN ORANGE HONEYSUCKLE ❖
Lonicera x tellmanniana	RED-GOLD HONEYSUCKLE

Parthenocissus henryana	SILVER-VEIN CREEPER
Parthenocissus quinquefolia	VIRGINIA CREEPER
Stauntonia purpurea	SAUSAGE VINE✓
Vitis coignetiae	JAPANESE GRAPE

GROUND COVERS
* will tolerate various degrees of traffic; some are mowable.

Asarum sieboldii	KOREAN WILD GINGER
Asarum caudatum	WESTERN WILD GINGER ❖✓
Asarum europaeum	EUROPEAN WILD GINGER✓
Asarum ichangensis 'Silver Lining'	SILVER LINING GINGER✓
Asarum splendens	SPLENDID WILD GINGER✓
Asarum fauriei var. *takaoi* 'Pitter Patter'	JAPANESE WILD GINGER✓
Astilbe chinensis var. *pumila*	DWARF CHINESE ASTILBE
Berberis buxifolia 'Nana'	DWARF BOX-LEAF BARBERRY
Cardamine trifolia	THREE-LEAF CARDAMINE
Carex inops (C. pensylvanica)*	CREEPING SEDGE ❖
Carex pansa*	MEADOW SEDGE ❖
Carex siderosticha var. *ciliatomarginata* 'Treasure Island'	
	CREEPING BROAD-LEAF SEDGE
Carex tumulicola*	FOOTHILL SEDGE ❖
Carex oshimensis cultivars	VARIEGATED JAPANESE SEDGE
Clinopodium (Micromeria, Satureja) douglasii	YERBA BUENA ❖
Cotoneaster adpressus 'Little Gem'	COMPACT COTONEASTER
Cotoneaster procumbens 'Queen of Carpets'	GROUND-HUGGING COTONEASTER
Epimedium brachyrrhizum	BISHOP'S HAT
Epimedium epsteinii	BISHOP'S HAT
Epimedium grandiflorum	BISHOP'S HAT
Epimedium pauciflorum	BISHOP'S HAT
Epimedium x perralchicum	BISHOP'S HAT
Epimedium perralderianum	BISHOP'S HAT
Epimedium pinnatum	BISHOP'S HAT
Epimedium x rubrum	BISHOP'S HAT
Epimedium x versicolor	BISHOP'S HAT
Epimedium x warleyense	BISHOP'S HAT
Euonymus fortunei 'Wolong Ghost'	SILVER-VEINED WINTER CREEPER
Fuchsia procumbens	CREEPING FUCHSIA
Galium odoratum	SWEET WOODRUFF
Hakonechloa macra and cultivars	JAPANESE FOREST GRASS
Hosta, especially dwarf and miniature cultivars, planted densely	HOSTA
Leptinella gruveri*	MINIATURE BRASS BUTTONS
Leptinella squalida*	NEW ZEALAND BRASS BUTTONS
Liriope muscari cultivars especially variegated types	LILYTURF✓
Lonicera crassifolia	CREEPING HONEYSUCKLE
Luzuriaga radicans	QUILINEJA
Mahonia repens	CREEPING OREGON-GRAPE ❖
Muehlenbeckia axillaris 'Nana'*	CREEPING WIRE VINE

Myrteola nummularia	CRANBERRY-MYRTLE
Omphalodes verna	CREEPING FORGET-ME-NOT
Ophiopogon clarkei	HIMALAYAN MONDO GRASS
Ophiopogon japonicus 'Gyoku-ryu'	DWARF MONDO GRASS
Ophiopogon planiscapus 'Juru'	VARIEGATED DWARF MONDO GRASS✓
Ophiopogon planiscapus 'Little Tabby'	STRIPED DWARF MONDO GRASS✓
Ophiopogon planiscapus 'Nigrescens'	BLACK MONDO GRASS✓
Oxalis oregana (evergreen form)	EVERGREEN REDWOOD SORREL ❖✓
Pachysandra procumbens	ALLEGHENY SPURGE
Phlox divaricata	WOODLAND PHLOX
Ribes davidii var. *davidii*	DAVID'S CURRANT
Rubus calycinoides (R. hayata-koidzumii, R. pentalobus)	CREEPING RASPBERRY
Rubus nepalensis	CREEPING BRAMBLE
Rubus x *tricolor* 'Betty Ashburner'	HYBRID CREEPING BRAMBLE
Saxifraga stolonifera 'Tricolor'	STRAWBERRY BEGONIA
Trachelospermum asiaticum especially variegated forms	ASIAN STAR JASMINE
Tsuga canadensis 'Cole's Prostrate'	PROSTRATE CANADIAN HEMLOCK ❖
Tsuga heterophylla 'Thorsen's Weeping'	THORSEN'S WEEPING HEMLOCK ❖
Vancouveria hexandra	INSIDE-OUT FLOWER ❖✓
Vinca minor variegated forms	TRAILING PERIWINKLE
Viola 'Dancing Geisha', 'Silver Samurai'	HYBRID VIOLET✓
*Waldsteinia ternata**	BARREN STRAWBERRY

CLUMPING BAMBOOS

Borinda angustissima	NARROW LEAF CLUMPING BAMBOO
Borinda (Fargesia) fungosa	CHOCOLATE BAMBOO
Borinda (Fargesia) lushiensis	RED-STEM BAMBOO
Borinda (Fargesia) papyrifera	WHITE WAX BORINDA
Borinda (Fargesia) yunnanensis	YUNNAN FOUNTAIN BAMBOO
Fargesia denudata	DENUDATA BAMBOO
Fargesia dracocephala (F. apicirubens)	DRAGON'S HEAD BAMBOO
Fargesia murielae	UMBRELLA BAMBOO
Fargesia nitida	BLUE FOUNTAIN
Fargesia robusta	ROBUST BAMBOO
Fargesia scabrida	ORANGE-STEM BAMBOO

PERENNIALS INCLUDING FERNS, GRASSES

Acanthus caroli-alexandri	BEAR'S BREECH
Acanthus 'Holland Days'	HOLLAND DAYS BEAR'S BREECH
Acanthus mollis	BEAR'S BREECH
Acanthus mollis 'Rue Ledan'	RUE LEDAN BEAR'S BREECH
Acanthus mollis 'Tasmanian Angel'	TASMANIAN ANGEL BEAR'S BREECH
Acanthus 'Morning's Candle'	BEAR'S BREECH
Acanthus spinosus	BEAR'S BREECH
Acanthus 'Summer Beauty'	SUMMER BEAUTY BEAR'S BREECH

Acanthus 'Whitewater'	WHITEWATER BEAR'S BREECH
Actaea matsumurae 'White Pearl'	WHITE PEARL JAPANESE BUGBANE
Actaea pachypoda	WHITE BANEBERRY, DOLL'S EYE
Actaea rubra	RED BANEBERRY
Adiantum aleuticum	WESTERN MAIDENHAIR FERN ❖✓
Adiantum venustum	HIMALAYAN MAIDENHAIR FERN
Anemonoides (Anemone) x lipsiensis	HYBRID WOOD ANEMONE
Anemonoides (Anemone) nemorosa	WOOD ANEMONE
Anemonoides (Anemone) pseudoaltaica	ASTER-FLOWERED ANEMONE
Anemonopsis macrophylla	FALSE ANEMONE
Asarum caudatum	WESTERN WILD GINGER ❖
Asarum europaeum	EUROPEAN WILD GINGER
Asarum ichangensis 'Silver Lining'	SILVER LINING GINGER
Asarum splendens	SPLENDID WILD GINGER
Asarum fauriei var. *takaoi* 'Pitter Patter'	JAPANESE WILD GINGER
Aspidistra elatior especially variegated cultivars	CAST IRON PLANT✓
Aspidistra ibanensis 'Flowing Fountains'	F. F. CAST IRON PLANT✓
Aspidistra sichuanensis 'Spek-Tacular'	CHINESE CAST IRON PLANT✓
Aspidistra zongbayi	YUNNAN SUNBEAM✓
Asplenium scolopendrium	HART'S-TONGUE FERN✓
Asplenium trichomanes	MAIDENHAIR SPLEENWORT✓
Astelia nervosa	ASTELIA
Astilboides tabularis	SHIELD-LEAF
Athyrium niponicum var. *pictum* cultivars	JAPANESE PAINTED FERN
Athyrium otophorum	EARED LADY FERN
Austroblechnum (Blechnum) penna-marina	ANTARCTIC HARD-FERN✓
Beesia calthifolia	GINGER-LEAF FALSE BUGBANE✓
Beesia deltophylla	BEESIA✓
Begonia grandis 'Heron's Pirouette'	HERON'S PIROUETTE BEGONIA✓
Begonia grandis ssp. *evansiana*	HARDY BEGONIA✓
Bergenia species and hybrids	BERGENIA
Berneuxia thibetica	RED PLANT
Blechnum (Struthiopteris) spicant	DEER FERN ❖✓
Brunnera macrophylla variegated cultivars	SIBERIAN BUGLOSS✓
Calanthe arisanensis	JAPANESE GROUND ORCHID
Calanthe "Kajima" series	CALANTHE ORCHID✓
Calanthe sieboldii	CALANTHE ORCHID✓
Campanula latifolia	BELLFLOWER
Campanula takesimana	BELLFLOWER
Cardamine glandulifera	TOOTH-LEAF LADY'S SMOCK
Cardamine quinquefolia	LADY'S SMOCK, CUCKOO FLOWER
Cardamine trifolia	THREE-LEAF CARDAMINE✓
Cardiocrinum species	GIANT HIMALAYAN LILY
Carex caryophyllea 'Beatlemania'	TUFTED SEDGE
Carex hachijoensis 'Evergold'	EVERGOLD SEDGE
Carex flaccosperma	BLUE WOOD SEDGE
Carex oshimensis 'Everillo', 'Eversheen' and many others	JAPANESE SEDGE
Carex siderosticha 'Banana Boat', 'Snow Cap'	COLORED SEDGE
Clematis repens	TWINKLE BELL CLEMATIS✓

Coniogramme intermedia	BAMBOO FERN✓
Coniogramme japonica	JAPANESE BAMBOO FERN✓
Cyrtomium caryotideum	HOLLY FERN✓
Cyrtomium falcatum	JAPANESE HOLLY FERN✓
Cyrtomium fortunei	FORTUNE'S HOLLY FERN✓
Cyrtomium macrophyllum	LARGE-LEAF HOLLY FERN✓
Deinanthe bifida	FALSE HYDRANGEA
Dicentra formosa 'Bacchanal'	BLEEDING HEART, DICENTRA ❖
Dicentra 'Langtrees'	BLEEDING HEART
Dicentra 'Luxuriant'	FRINGED BLEEDING HEART
Diphylleia cymosa	UMBRELLA LEAF
Disporopsis arisanensis	EVERGREEN SOLOMON SEAL✓
Disporopsis bakeri (*D. pernyi* 'Bill Baker')	EVERGREEN SOLOMON'S SEAL✓
Disporopsis 'Lily Pads'	LILY PADS SOLOMON'S SEAL✓
Disporopsis pernyi	EVERGREEN SOLOMON'S SEAL✓
Disporum cantoniense 'Night Heron'	CANTON FAIRY BELLS
Disporum megalanthum	LARGE-FLOWERED FAIRY BELLS
Disporum sessile	JAPANESE FAIRY BELLS
Disporum uniflorum	FAIRY BELLS
Dryopteris crassirhizoma	THICK-STEMMED WOOD FERN✓
Dryopteris cycadina	SHAGGY SHIELD FERN✓
Dryopteris erythrosora	AUTUMN FERN✓
Dryopteris lepidopoda	SUNSET FERN✓
Dryopteris sieboldii	SIEBOLD'S WOOD FERN✓
Dryopteris wallichiana	WALLICH'S WOOD FERN✓
Dysosma (*Podophyllum*) *delavayi,* many cultivars	MARBLED MAYAPPLE✓
Dysosma (*Podophyllum*) *pleianthum*	CHINESE MAYAPPLE✓
Dysosma (*Podophyllum*) *versipellis* 'Spotty Dotty'	SPOTTY DOTTY MAYAPPLE
Epimedium species and hybrids	BISHOP'S HAT
Farfugium japonicum cultivars	LEOPARD PLANT
Gentiana asclepiadea	WILLOW-LEAF GENTIAN
Glaucidium palmatum	JAPANESE WOOD POPPY
Gymnocarpium disjunctum	COMMON OAK FERN ❖✓
Hakonechloa macra cultivars	VARIEGATED JAPANESE FOREST GRASS
Helleborus hybrids	HELLEBORES
Helleborus argutifolius	CORSICAN HELLEBORE
Helleborus foetidus	STINKING HELLEBORE✓
Helleborus liguricus	ITALIAN HELLEBORE✓
Heloniopsis orientalis	ORIENTAL SWAMP PINK
Hepatica nobilis	HEPATICA
Hosta hybrids (a multitude)	PLANTAIN LILY, HOSTA
Hosta sieboldiana	PLANTAIN LILY✓
Ichtyoselmis (*Dicentra*) *macrantha*	CHINESE BLEEDING HEART
Impatiens 'Heronswood'	PINK HARDY IMPATIENS
Impatiens namchabarwensis	BLUE DIAMOND IMPATIENS
Impatiens omeiana 'Ice Storm'	SILVER HARDY IMPATIENS
Impatiens stenantha	HARDY IMPATIENS
Iris cristata	CRESTED IRIS
Iris foetidissima	GLADWIN IRIS✓

Iris henryi	CHINESE WOODLAND IRIS
Iris japonica	FRINGED IRIS✓
Iris 'Nada'	BUTTERFLY IRIS
Jeffersonia dubia	ASIAN TWINLEAF
Kirengeshoma palmata Koreana Group (*K. koreana*)	KOREAN WAXBELLS
Lamprocapnos (Dicentra) spectabilis	OLD-FASHIONED BLEEDING HEART
Lepisorus bicolor	SCHEZUAN RIBBON FERN✓
Leucosceptrum stellipilum	JAPANESE SHRUB MINT
Ligularia 'Britt-Marie Crawford'	LEOPARD PLANT✓
Ligularia 'King Kong'	LEOPARD PLANT✓
Ligularia 'The Rocket'	LEOPARD PLANT✓
Liriope muscari, especially variegated cultivars	BIG BLUE LILYTURF✓
Maianthemum (Smilacina) henryi	FRAGRANT FALSE SOLOMON'S SEAL
Maianthemum oleraceum	ASIAN FALSE SOLOMON'S SEAL
Meconopsis 'Lingholm' (*M.* x *sheldonii*; "Fertile Blue Group")	HIMALAYAN POPPY
Omphalodes cappadocica	CAPPADOCIAN NAVELWORT
Ophiopogon planiscapus 'Juru'	VARIEGATED DWARF MONDO GRASS✓
Ophiopogon planiscapus 'Little Tabby'	STRIPED DWARF MONDO GRASS✓
Ophiopogon planiscapus 'Nigrescens'	BLACK MONDO GRASS✓
Ourisia 'Loch Ewe'	HYBRID OURISIA
Ourisia coccinea	SCARLET OURISIA
Ourisia macrophylla	NEW ZEALAND MOUNTAIN FOXGLOVE
Pachyphragma macrophyllum	CAUCASIAN PENNYCRESS
Paeonia mairei	WOODLAND PEONY
Paeonia veitchii	CHINESE WOODLAND PEONY
Paris incompleta	PARIS
Paris japonica	JAPANESE PARIS
Paris polyphylla	MULTI-LEAF PARIS
Petasites japonicus var. *giganteus*	GIANT JAPANESE BUTTERBUR
Podophyllum 'Kaleidoscope'	KALEIDOSCOPE MAYAPPLE
Polygonatum biflorum (*P. commutatum*) 'Bigfoot'	GIANT SOLOMON'S SEAL✓
Polygonatum humile 'Shiro Shima'	GIANT SOLOMON'S SEAL✓
Polygonatum odoratum 'Byakko'	PAINTED SOLOMON'S SEAL✓
Polygonatum odoratum 'Prince Charming'	PRINCE CHARMING SOLOMON'S SEAL✓
Polygonatum odoratum var. *pluriflorum* 'Variegatum'	VARIEGATED SOLOMON'S SEAL✓
Polystichum makinoi	MAKINOI'S HOLLY FERN✓
Polystichum munitum	SWORD FERN✓
Polystichum neolobatum	ASIAN SABER FERN✓
Polystichum polyblepharum	JAPANESE TASSEL FERN✓
Polystichum setiferum Divisilobum Group	SOFT SHIELD FERN✓
Polystichum setiferum Plumosomultilobum Group	PLUMOSE SOFT SHIELD FERN✓
Polystichum tsus-simense	KOREAN ROCK FERN✓
Primula florindae	TIBETAN PRIMROSE
Primula sieboldii	SIEBOLD'S PRIMROSE
Primula vulgaris	PRIMROSE
Pteridophyllum racemosum	WOODLAND POPPY
Pulmonaria 'Benediction'	LUNGWORT
Pulmonaria longifolia ssp. *cevennensis*	LONGLEAF LUNGWORT✓
Pulmonaria rubra 'Rachel Vernie'	RED-FLOWERED LUNGWORT

Rodgersia aesculifolia	FINGER-LEAF RODGERSIA
Rodgersia pinnata 'Chocolate Wings'	CHOCOLATE WINGS RODGERSIA
Rodgersia podophylla	RODGERSIA
Salvia glabrescens	JAPANESE WOODLAND SAGE
Sanguinaria canadensis	BLOODROOT
Saruma henryi	WILD GINGER✓
Saxifraga fortunei	SAXIFRAGE
Saxifraga stolonifera variegated cultivars	STRAWBERRY BEGONIA✓
Saxifraga x urbium 'Primuloides'	MINIATURE LONDON PRIDE✓
Shortia galacifolia	OCONEE BELLS
Sinopodophyllum (Podophyllum) hexandrum var. *chinense*	HIMALAYAN MAYAPPLE
Smilacina racemosa	FALSE SOLOMON'S SEAL✓
Soldanella 'Spring Symphony'	HYBRID SNOWBELL
Soldanella carpatica	CARPATHIAN SNOWBELL
Speirantha convallarioides	FALSE LILY-OF-THE-VALLEY✓
Syneilesis aconitifolia	TATTERED UMBRELLA PLANT
Syneilesis subglabrata (S. intermedia)	UMBRELLA PLANT✓
Tellima grandiflora	FRAGRANT FRINGECUP ❖
Thalictrum ichangense	ICHANG MEADOW-RUE
Thalictrum (Anemonella) thalictroides	RUE ANEMONE
Titanotrichum oldhamii	FOXGLOVE GESNERIAD✓
Tricyrtis formosana 'Gilt Edge'	VARIEGATED TOAD LILY✓
Uvularia grandiflora	LARGE-FLOWERED MERRY-BELLS
Vancouveria hexandra	INSIDE-OUT FLOWER
Woodwardia unigemmata	JEWELED CHAIN FERN✓
Ypsilandra thibetica	FRAGRANT YPSILANDRA✓
Zingiber mioga	WOODLAND GINGER✓

BULBS

Arisaema dracontium	DRAGONROOT✓
Arisaema candidissimum	PINK COBRA LILY
Arisaema consanguineum	HIMALAYAN COBRA LILY
Arisaema kishidae	JAPANESE COBRA-LILY
Arisaema ringens	COBRA LILY✓
Arisaema sikokianum	JAPANESE COBRA LILY
Arisaema triphyllum	JACK-IN-THE-PULPIT✓
Arisarum proboscideum	MOUSE PLANT✓
Convallaria majalis, especially 'Albostriata'	LILY-OF-THE-VALLEY
Corydalis solida	FUMEWORT
Crocosmia aurea (not hybrids)	FALLING STARS
Cyclamen coum	HARDY CYCLAMEN, EASTERN SOWBREAD
Cyclamen hederifolium	IVY-LEAF CYCLAMEN
Dracunculus vulgaris	VOODOO LILY
Eranthis hyemalis	WINTER ACONITE
Erythronium grandiflorum var. *grandiflorum*	AVALANCHE-LILY, GLACIER-LILY ❖
Erythronium oregonum	OREGON FAWN-LILY ❖
Erythronium 'Pagoda'	PAGODA FAWN-LILY

Erythronium revolutum	COAST FAWN-LILY, PINK FAWN-LILY ❖
Galanthus nivalis	SNOWDROPS
Hyacinthoides hispanica (NOT *H.* x massartiana)	SPANISH BLUEBELL
Impatiens arguta	BLUE DREAM IMPATIENS
Impatiens flanaganae	FLANAGAN'S IMPATIENS
Impatiens puberula	SOFT PINK BALSAM
Impatiens tinctoria	PAINTED IMPATIENS
Lilium columbianum	TIGER LILY ❖
Lilium henryi	HENRY'S LILY
Lilium lancifolium	TIGER LILY
Lilium martagon and hybrids	MARTAGON LILY
Lilium mackliniae	SHIRUI LILY
Lilium regale	REGAL LILY
Lilium sargentiae	SARGENT'S LILY
Lilium szovitsianum	SZOVITS' LILY
Lilium speciosum	RUBRUM LILY
Lilium wallichianum	LONG-FLOWERED LILY
Nomocharis aperta	NOMOCHARIS LILY
Nomocharis saluenensis	NOMOCHARIS LILY
Scilla siberica	SIBERIAN SQUILL
Trillium chloropetalum	GIANT WAKEROBIN ❖
Trillium cuneatum	WOOD-LILY
Trillium grandiflorum 'Flore Pleno'	DOUBLE-FLOWERED TRILLIUM
Trillium kurabayashii	GIANT PURPLE WAKEROBIN ❖
Trillium luteum	YELLOW TRILLIUM

ANNUALS

Begonia semperflorens	BEGONIA
Browallia speciosa	AMETHYST FLOWER
Campanula medium	CANTERBURY BELLS, CUP-AND-SAUCER
Campanula pyramidalis	CHIMNEY BELLFLOWER
Clarkia amoena	GODETIA
Clarkia unguiculata (C. elegans)	CLARKIA
Coleus (Solenostemon) scuttellarioides	COLEUS
Erythranthe (Mimulus) x hybridus	MONKEY FLOWER
Impatiens balsamina	BALSAM
Impatiens walleriana	IMPATIENS
Malcomia maritima	VIRGINIA STOCK
Matthiola longipetala bicornis	EVENING-SCENTED STOCK
Myosotis sylvatica	WOOD FORGET-ME-NOT
Nicotiana sylvestris	FLOWERING TOBACCO
Nicotiana x sanderae	FLOWERING TOBACCO
Pericallis (Senecio) x hybridus	CINERARIA
Primula malacoides	FAIRY PRIMROSE
Primula obconica	GERMAN PRIMROSE
X Torelus (*Torenia x Mimulus hybrids*)	HYBRID MONKEYS
Tropaeolum majus	NASTURTIUM

SEASONAL BULBS (Summer into Fall)

Achimenes hybrids	MAGIC FLOWER
Begonia hybrids	BEGONIA
Eucomis species and hybrids	PINEAPPLE-LILY
Zantedeschia hybrids	CALLA-LILIES

CLAY/HEAVY SOIL

Although most plants are adaptable to pretty much any kind of soil, this list represents those which thrive in the heaviest versions abundant in our Western PNW lowlands. Keep in mind that clay isn't a bad thing; clay actually holds nutrients better than sandy soils and plants of any kind in these heavy soils require no supplemental feeding. It may be hard digging — a disadvantage to the gardener's back — but it's a better support for these landscape candidates. And once the landscape is planted, no more digging or tilling is involved.

TREES

Acer campestre	HEDGE MAPLE
Acer griseum	PAPER-BARK MAPLE
Acer negundo 'Sensation'	SEEDLESS BOXELDER
Acer palmatum	JAPANESE MAPLE
Arbutus unedo	STRAWBERRY TREE
Asimina triloba	PAW-PAW
Betula nigra	RIVER BIRCH
Cercidiphyllum japonicum	KATSURA
Cercis species	REDBUD
Cornus kousa	KOREAN DOGWOOD
Cotinus obovatus	SMOKE TREE
Cryptomeria japonica	JAPANESE PLUME CEDAR
Ginkgo biloba	GINKGO
Ilex x altaclarensis	HIGHCLERE HOLLY
Magnolia species and hybrids	MAGNOLIA
Malus sargentii	SARGENT CRABAPPLE
Metasequoia glyptostroboides	DAWN REDWOOD
Parrotia persica	PERSIAN IRONWOOD
Syringa reticulata	TREE LILAC
Syringa reticulata ssp. *pekinensis*	PEKIN LILAC, CHINESE TREE LILAC

SHRUBS

Aucuba japonica	JAPANESE LAUREL
Berberis x stenophylla	HEDGE BARBERRY
Berberis wilsoniae	WILSON'S BARBERRY
Buddleja species and hybrids (not *B. davidii*)	BUTTERFLY BUSH
Calluna vulgaris	SCOTCH HEATHER
Camellia japonica	CAMELLIA
Carpenteria californica cultivars	BUSH ANEMONE
Cercis occidentalis	CALIFORNIA REDBUD
Chaenomeles species and hybrids	FLOWERING QUINCE
Cistus x dansereaui 'Jenkyn Place'	JENKYN PLACE ROCKROSE
Clethra alnifolia	SUMMERSWEET
Cornus sericea (C. stolonifera)	RED OSIER DOGWOOD ❖
Corylopsis pauciflora	BUTTERCUP WINTER HAZEL

Cryptomeria japonica dwarf cultivars	JAPANESE PLUME CEDAR
Dasiphora (Potentilla) fruticosa ssp. *floribunda*	CINQUEFOIL ❖
Deutzia species and hybrids	DEUTZIA
Enkianthus campanulatus	ED-VEIN ENKIANTHUS
Erica carnea	WINTER HEATH
Forsythia x *intermedia*	BORDER FORSYTHIA
Fothergilla gardenii	DWARF FOTHERGILLA
Hibiscus syriacus	ROSE-OF-SHARON
Hydrangea species	HYDRANGEA
Itea virginica	SWEETSPIRE
Kerria japonica	JAPANESE KERRIA
Lindera benzoin	SPICE BUSH
Lonicera fragrantissima	WINTER HONEYSUCKLE
Notholithocarpus densiflorus var. *echinoides*	SHRUB TANOAK ❖
Philadelphus coronaria	MOCK ORANGE
Phlomis italica	BALEARIC ISLAND-SAGE
Pieris species and hybrids	LILY-OF-THE-VALLEY SHRUB
Physocarpus opulifolius	NINEBARK
Pyracantha species and hybrids	FIRETHORN
Rhus aromatica	FRAGRANT SUMAC
Ribes odoratum	CLOVE CURRANT
Rosa hybrids and almost all species	ROSE
Sambucus canadensis	COMMON ELDERBERRY
Sambucus nigra ssp. *nigra*	BLACK ELDERBERRY ❖
Sarcococca species	SWEET BOX
Spiraea nipponica 'Snowmound'	SPIREA
Syringa vulgaris	LILAC
Weigela florida and hybrids	WEIGELA

PERENNIALS & BULBS

Achillea filipendulina	FERNLEAF YARROW
Achillea tomentosa	WOOLLY YARROW
Aconitum species and hybrids	MONKSHOOD
Amsonia species	BLUE-STAR
Anemonastrum (Anemone) canadense	MEADOW ANEMONE ❖
Aquilegia species	COLUMBINE ❖
Arisaema species	COBRA LILY, JACK-IN-THE-PULPIT
Aruncus dioicus	GOATSBEARD ❖
Asarum caudatum	WILD GINGER ❖
Asclepias incarnata	SWAMP MILKWEED
Aster x frikartii	FRIKART'S ASTER
Astilbe species and hybrids	ASTILBE
Astrantia major	MASTERWORT
Baptisia australis and hybrids	FALSE INDIGO
Bergenia species and hybrids	BERGENIA
Blechnum (Struthiopteris) spicant	DEER FERN ❖
Boltonia asteroides var. *latisquama* 'Snowbank'	FALSE ASTER

Brunnera macrophylla	SIBERIAN BUGLOSS
Camassia leichtlinii	CAMASS ❖
Campanula lactiflora	MILKY BELLFLOWER
Cardiocrinum giganteum	GIANT LILY
Ceratostigma plumbaginoides	BLUE PLUMBAGO
Eryngium yuccifolium	RATTLESNAKE MASTER
Eutrochium (Eupatorium) species and hybrids	JOE-PYE WEED
Geum hybrids	AVENS
Glaucidium palmatum	JAPANESE WOOD POPPY
Helenium species and hybrids	SNEEZEWEED ❖
Helianthus species and hybrids	SUNFLOWER
Heliopsis helianthoides	SMOOTH OXEYE
Helleborus species and hybrids	HELLEBORE
Hemerocallis	DAYLILY
Heuchera hybrids	CORAL BELLS
Hibiscus species and hybrids	ROSE-MALLOW
Hosta species and hybrids	HOSTA
Hylotelephium (Sedum) spectabile	SHOWY STONECROP, AUTUMN SEDUM
Iris siberica and hybrids	SIBERIAN IRIS
Leucanthemum x superbum	SHASTA DAISY
Leucojum species	SNOWFLAKE
Liatris spicata	BLAZING STAR, GAYFEATHER
Ligularia species and hybrids	LEOPARD PLANT
Liriope muscari	LILY TURF
Lysimachia species	LOOSESTRIFE
Miscanthus sinensis	SILVER GRASS
Monarda species and hybrids	BEE BALM, BERGAMOT
Narcissus species and hybrids	NARCISSUS, DAFFODIL
Pachysandra terminalis	JAPANESE PACHYSANDRA
Phlox divaricata	WOODLAND PHLOX
Primula species and hybrids	PRIMROSES
Rudbeckia fulgida	BLACK-EYED SUSAN
Rudbeckia subtomentosa	SWEET CONEFLOWER
Salvia species (most)	SALVIA, SAGE
Salvia yangii (Perovskia atriplicifolia)	RUSSIAN SAGE
Scutellaria incana	DOWNY SKULLCAP
Solidago species and hybrids	GOLDENROD ❖
Symphyotrichum (Aster) ericoides	HEATH ASTER
Thermopsis chinensis 'Sophia'	CHINESE BUSH PEA
Watsonia angusta	SCARLET BUGLE FLOWER
Yucca species and hybrids	YUCCA

SANDY SOIL

Sandy soils definitely lean toward the dry, warm, and (alliteration intended) lean side. For the permanent landscape, these plants will be quite happy here.

TREES

Acer campestre	HEDGE MAPLE
Acer negundo	BOXELDER ❖
Acer tataricum	TATARIAN MAPLE
Amelanchier species and hybrids	SERVICEBERRY ❖
Araucaria araucana	MONKEY PUZZLE
Castanea sativa	CHESTNUT
Cedrus deodara	DEODAR CEDAR
Celtis occidentalis	HACKBERRY
Cercidiphyllum japonicum	KATSURA
Cercis siliquastrum	LOVE TREE
Cotinus coggygria	SMOKE TREE
Crataegus species and hybrids	HAWTHORN
Cupressus arizonica	ARIZONA CYPRESS
Ginkgo biloba	GINKGO
Gymnocladus dioicus	KENTUCKY COFFEETREE
Juniperus communis	COMMON JUNIPER ❖
Juniperus scopulorum	ROCKY MOUNTAIN JUNIPER
Koelreuteria paniculata	GOLDEN RAIN TREE
Pinus contorta var. *contorta*	SHORE PINE ❖
Quercus garryana	GARRY OAK ❖
Tilia tomentosa	SILVER LINDEN
Trachycarpus fortunei	CHINESE WINDMILL PALM
Ulmus glabra 'Camperdownii'	CAMPERDOWN ELM
Ulmus parvifolia	LACEBARK ELM, CHINESE ELM
Ulmus pumila	SIBERIAN ELM
Zelkova serrata	KEAKI

SHRUBS

Arctostaphylos uva-ursi	KINNIKINNICK ❖
Artemisia species and hybrids	WORMWOOD ❖
Brachyglottis 'Sunshine'	DAISY BUSH
Calluna vulgaris	SCOTS HEATHER
Caryopteris x clandonensis	BLUE BEARD
Choisya ternata	MEXICAN ORANGE
Cistus hybrids	ROCK ROSE
Corylus cornuta var. *californica*	WESTERN HAZELNUT ❖
Cotinus coggygria	SMOKE TREE
Daphne bholua	PAPER DAPHNE
Edgeworthia chrysantha	PAPER BUSH

Escallonia species and hybrids	ESCALLONIA
Fabiana imbricata 'Violacea'	CHILEAN HEATHER
Grevillea species and cultivars	GREVILLEA
Hebe species and hybrids	HEBE
Hibiscus syriacus	ROSE-OF-SHARON
Indigofera pendula	WEEPING INDIGO
Juniperus communis	COMMON JUNIPER ❖
Linnaea (Abelia) 'Edward Goucher'	ABELIA
Mahonia x media	MAHONIA
Olearia x haastii	STARRY DAISY BUSH
Olearia x mollis 'Zennorensis'	SAW-LEAF DAISY BUSH
Osmanthus x burkwoodii	BURKWOOD'S OSMANTHUS
Osmanthus delavayi	DELAVAY TEA-OLIVE
Penstemon fruticosus	SHRUBBY PENSTEMON ❖
Philadelphus species and hybrids	MOCK ORANGE ❖
Phlomis fruticosa	JERUSALEM-SAGE
Phlomis russeliana	JERUSALEM-SAGE
Physocarpus opulifolius	NINEBARK
Rosa pimpinellifolia	BURNETT ROSE
Rosa rugosa	JAPANESE BEACH ROSE
Salvia rosmarinus (Rosmarinus officinalis)	ROSEMARY
Spiraea nipponica	SPIREA
Stachyurus praecox	STACHYURUS
Yucca species and hybrids	YUCCA

VINES

Campsis x tagliabuana	HYBRID TRUMPET CREEPER
Parthenocissus quinquefolia	VIRGINIA CREEPER

PERENNIALS & BULBS

Acanthus species and hybrids	BEAR'S BREECH
Achillea species and hybrids	YARROW ❖
Agastache aurantiaca	HUMMINGBIRD HYSSOP
Allium acuminatum	TAPER-TIP ONION ❖
Allium cernuum	NODDING ONION ❖
Allium cristophii	STARS OF PERSIA
Allium rosenbachianum	PURPLE ONION
Allium schubertii	SHUBERT'S ONION
Aloiampelos (Aloe) striatula	HARDY ALOE
Anemonoides (Anemone) nemorosa	WOOD ANEMONE
Artemisia species and hybrids	WORMWOOD ❖
Baptisia species and hybrids	FALSE INDIGO
Calylophus hartwegii	HARTWEG'S SUNDROPS
Campanula persicifolia	PEACH-LEAF BELLFLOWER
Cephalaria gigantea	GIANT SCABIOUS

Coreopsis verticillata	THREAD-LEAF COREOPSIS
Corethrogyne (Lessingia) filaginifolia 'Silver Carpet'	TRAILING SAND ASTER
Dahlia x hybrida	DAHLIA
Delosperma species and hybrids	HARDY ICE PLANTS
Dianthus species and hybrids	PINKS, CARNATION
Dicentra formosa	WESTERN BLEEDING HEART ❖
Dichelostemma (Brodiaea) congesta	HARVEST LILY ❖
Dierama pulcherrimum	ANGEL'S FISHING ROD
Digitalis thapsi	SPANISH FOXGLOVE
Echinops ritro	GLOBE THISTLE
Eremurus species and hybrids	FOXTAIL-LILY
Eriophyllum lanatum	OREGON SUNSHINE, WOOLLY SUNFLOWER ❖
Eryngium species and hybrids	SEA HOLLY
Fragaria chiloensis	BEACH STRAWBERRY ❖
Glandularia (Verbena) bipinnatifida	DAKOTA MOCK VERVAIN
Helianthemum nummularium	ROCK ROSE
Helichrysum arenarium	SANDY EVERLASTING
Helictotrichon sempervirens	BLUE-OAT GRASS
Kniphofia hybrids	RED-HOT-POKER, TORCH LILY
Lamprocapnos (Dicentra) spectabilis	OLD-FASHIONED BLEEDING HEART
Lavandula species and hybrids	LAVENDER
Lavatera x clementii	TREE MALLOW
Liatris ligulistylis	MEADOW BLAZING STAR
Liatris spicata	GAYFEATHER
Linaria (purpurea Hybrid) 'Natalie'	NATALIE TOADFLAX
Nepeta species and hybrids	CAT MINT
Nerine bowdenii and hybrids	GUERNSEY LILY
Origanum libanoticum	CASCADING HOPFLOWER OREGANO
Salvia yangii (Perovskia atriplicifolia) and hybrids	RUSSIAN SAGE
Polemonium pulcherrimum	SHOWY JACOB'S LADDER ❖
Rhodanthemum (Chrysanthemum) hosmariense	MOROCCAN DAISY
Salvia species and hybrids	SAGE
Sedum (including *Hylotelephium, Petrosedum, Phedimus, Pseudosedum, Rhodiola*) species	
	STONECROP, SEDUM ❖
Sisyrinchium californicum	YELLOW-EYED GRASS ❖
Solidago species and hybrids	GOLDENROD ❖
Symphyotrichum oblongifolium	AROMATIC ASTER
Tigridia pavonia	MEXICAN SHELL FLOWER
Triteleia (Brodiaea) hyacinthina	WHITE TRIPLET-LILY ❖
Yucca species and hybrids	YUCCA

SHALLOW SOIL

For areas with natural or artificial (e.g., "construction compaction") hardpan.

TREES

Albizzia julibrissin	SILK TREE
Cedrus atlantica	ATLAS CEDAR
Crinodendron hookerianum	CHILEAN LANTERN TREE
Ficus carica	FIG
Pinus species (most)	PINES
Trachycarpus fortunei	CHINEE WINDMILL PALM
Ulmus pumila	SIBERIAN ELM

SHRUBS

Arctostaphylos species	MANZANITA ❖
Artemisia species	WORMWOOD, SAGE BRUSH ❖
Ceanothus thyrsiflorus	BLUE BLOSSOM
Ceratostigma willmottianum	CHINESE PLUMBAGO
Chamaerops humilis	MEDITERRANEAN FAN PALM
Cotoneaster species	COTONEASTER
Indigofera species	INDIGO
Juniperus species	JUNIPERS ❖
Lavandula angustifolia	ENGLISH LAVENDER
Mahonia species	GRAPE-HOLLY, BARBERRY, MAHONIA
Phlomis fruticosa	JERUSALEM-SAGE
Physocarpus opulifolius	NINEBARK
Pyracantha species	FIRETHORN
Rhus species	SUMACS

VINES

Lonicera x tellmanniana	RED-GOLD HONEYSUCKLE
Muehlenbeckia species	WIRE VINE

PERENNIALS

Antennaria microphylla	ROSY PUSSYTOES ❖
Anacyclus pyrethrum var. *depressus*	MT. ATLAS DAISY
Abronia species	SAND VERBENA ❖
Asclepias tuberosa	BUTTERFLY WEED
Baptisia australis	BLUE FALSE INDIGO
Callirhoe involucrata	PURPLE POPPY MALLOW
Coreopsis grandiflora	LARGE-FLOWERED TICKSEED

Coreopsis verticillata	THREAD-LEAF COREOPSIS
Dierama pendulum	ANGEL'S FISHING ROD, FAIRY WAND
Dudleya cymosa	LIVE-FOREVER
Echinacea purpurea	PURPLE CONEFLOWER
Epilobium (Zauschneria) canum including ssp. *garrettii*	CALIFORNIA FUCHSIA
Epilobium (Zauschneria) septentrionalis 'Select Mattole'	CALIFORNIA FUCHSIA
Epimedium x versicolor 'Sulphureum'	BISHOP'S HAT
Glandularia (Verbena) bipinnatifida	DAKOTA MOCK VERVAIN
Glandularia (Verbena) canadensis	ROSE MOCK VERVAIN
Heliopsis helianthoides var. scabra	OX EYE
Helleborus hybrids	HELLEBORE
Iris germanica	BEARDED IRIS
Iris unguicularis	WINTER IRIS
Kniphofia uvaria and hybrids	RED-HOT-POKER, TORCH-LILY
Linaria (purpurea Hybrid) 'Natalie'	NATALIE TOADFLAX
Lysimachia nummularia	CREEPING JENNY
Nepeta racemosa (N. mussinii)	EASTERN CAT-MINT
Oenothera fremontii	TRAILING EVENING-PRIMROSE
Oenothera fruticosa	SUNDROPS
Oenothera macrocarpa (O. missouriensis)	EVENING-PRIMROSE
Ophiopogon japonica	MONDO GRASS
Opuntia fragilis	PRICKLY PEAR
Origanum dictamnus	CRETE DITTANY
Phedimus species	ASIAN STONECROPS
Rudbeckia fulgida	BLACK-EYED SUSAN
Sedum species	STONECROP ❖
Sempervivum species	HOUSE-LEEK
Stachys byzantina (S. lanata)	LAMB'S EARS
Stokesia laevis	STOKE'S ASTER
Symphyotrichum (Aster) chilense	PACIFIC ASTER
Symphyotrichum (Aster) ericoides	HEATH ASTER
Thymus serpyllum	CREEPING THYME
Tropaeolum (perennial species)	PERENNIAL NASTURTIUM
Verbena rigida	SLENDER VERBENA, TUBEROUS VERBENA
Veronica liwanensis	SPEEDWELL
Veronica (Parahebe) perfoliata	DIGGER'S SPEEDWELL
Yucca species	YUCCA

POOR SOIL

Overtly sandy soil, overused farmland, or "soils" as a result of construction scour and compaction. These soils have lost their nutrients or are incapable, as is, of holding supplemental nutrients. These are the plants for reclaiming these grounds. Additionally, don't forget to use "cover crops" where appropriate and regularly apply organic mulches using homemade compost.

TREES

Abies concolor	WHITE FIR ❖
Acer buergerianum	TRIDENT MAPLE
Acer campestre	FIELD MAPLE
Acer tataricum ssp. *ginnala*	AMUR MAPLE
Acer negundo	BOX ELDER
Alnus cordata	ITALIAN ALDER
Alnus rubra	RED ALDER ❖
Araucaria araucana	MONKEY PUZZLE
Castanea sativa	ITALIAN CHESTNUT
Cedrus deodara	DEODAR CEDAR
Celtis australis	EUROPEAN HACKBERRY
Cephalotaxus harringtonia	JAPANESE PLUM YEW
Cercidiphyllum japonicum	KATSURA
Cercis siliquastrum	LOVE TREE
X *Chitalpa tashkentensis*	CHITALPA
Corylus colurna	TURKISH FILBERT
Cotinus coggygria	SMOKE TREE
Fraxinus latifolia	OREGON ASH ❖
Fraxinus ornus	FLOWERING ASH
Ginkgo biloba	GINKGO
Hamamelis x *intermedia*	HYBRID WITCH-HAZEL
Hesperocyparis (Cupressus) bakeri	BAKER CYPRESS
Juniperus scopulorum	ROCKY MOUNTAIN JUNIPER
Koelreuteria paniculata	GOLDEN RAIN TREE
Picea omorika	SERBIAN SPRUCE
Picea orientalis	ORIENTAL SPRUCE
Picea pungens	BLUE SPRUCE
Pinus species	PINE ❖
Platanus x *acerifolia*	LONDON PLANETREE
Pseudotsuga menziesii	DOUGLAS-FIR ❖
Quercus garryana	GARRY OAK
Sequoiadendron giganteum	GIANT REDWOOD
Syringa reticulata	JAPANESE TREE LILAC
Trachycarpus fortunei	WINDMILL PALM
Ulmus pumila	SIBERIAN ELM
Zelkova serrata	KEAKI

SHRUBS

Amelanchier alnifolia	WESTERN SERVICEBERRY, JUNEBERRY, SASKATOON ❖
Arbutus unedo	STRAWBERRY TREE
Arctostaphylos species	MANZANITA ❖
Artemisia species	SAGEBRUSH ❖
Berberis	BARBERRIES
Brachyglottis (Senecio) greyi and hybrids	YELLOW DAISY BUSH
Buddleja species and hybrids (not *B. davidii*)	BUTTERFLY BUSH
Calluna vulgaris	HEATHER
Caryopteris x clandonensis	BLUEBEARD
Ceratostigma willmottianum	PLUMBAGO
Chamaerops humilis	MEDITERRANEAN FAN PALM
Chaenomeles speciosa	FLOWERING QUINCE
Choisya ternata	MEXICAN MOCK ORANGE
Cistus hybrids	ROCKROSE
Cornus sericea	RED-TWIG DOGWOOD
Corokia cotoneaster	COROKIA
Cotinus coggygria	SMOKE TREE
Cotoneaster (most)	COTONEASTER
Dasiphora fruticosa ssp. *floribunda*	SHRUBBY CINQUEFOIL
Elaeagnus species and hybrids	SILVERBERRY
Escallonia species and hybrids	ESCALLONIA
Euonymus fortunei	WINTERCREEPER
Fabiana imbricata 'Violacea'	CHILEAN HEATHER
Fargesia nitida	BLUE FOUNTAIN BAMBOO
Forsythia species and hybrids	FORSYTHIA
Fuchsia (hardy kinds)	HARDY FUCHSIA
Garrya elliptica	SILK-TASSEL
Gaultheria shallon	SALAL ❖
X *Halimiocistus sahucii*	HYBRID ROCKROSE
X *Halimiocistus wintonensis*	HYBRID ROCKROSE
Halimium lasianthum	WOOLLY ROCKROSE
Halimium ocymoides	GOLDEN ROCKROSE
Hebe species and hybrids	HEBE
Hibiscus syriacus	ROSE-OF-SHARON
Holodiscus discolor	OCEAN SPRAY
Hydrangea paniculata	PANICLE HYDRANGEA
Juniperus species	JUNIPERS
Kerria japonica	JAPANESE KERRIA
Lavandula species and hybrids	LAVENDERS
Lavatera species and hybrids	ROSE MALLOW
Leptodermis oblonga	HIMALAYAN LILAC
Linnaea (Abelia) species and hybrids	ABELIA
Linnaea (Kolkwitzia) amabilis	BEAUTYBUSH
Mahonia species and hybrids	UPRIGHT BARBERRIES
Microbiota decussata	SIBERIAN CARPET CYPRESS
Morella (Myrica) californica	PACIFIC WAX MYRTLE ❖
Olearia species and hybrids	DAISY-BUSH

Osmanthus x burkwoodii	BURKWOOD'S OSMANTHUS
Penstemon fruticosus	SHRUBBY PENSTEMON
Philadelphus species	MOCK ORANGE
Phlomis fruticosa	JERUSALEM-SAGE
Physocarpus opulifolius	NINEBARK
Rhus species	SUMACS
Ribes species	CURRANTS
Rosa pimpinellifolia	BURNETT ROSE
Rosa rugosa	RUGOSA ROSE
Ruscus species	BUTCHER'S BROOM
Salvia rosmarinus (Rosmarinus officinalis)	ROSEMARY
Sambucus species	ELDERBERRY
Sarcococca species	SWEETBOX
Skimmia japonica	JAPANESE SKIMMIA
Spiraea japonica	SUMMER SPIREA
Spiraea x vanhouttei	BRIDAL WREATH
Symphoricarpos species and hybrids	SNOWBERRY
Viburnum species	VIBURNUM
Vitex agnus-castus	CHASTE TREE
Zauschneria (Epilobium) species and hybrids	HUMMINGBIRD TRUMPETS

VINES

Fallopia aubertii	SILVER LACE VINE
X Fatshedera lizei	FATSHEDERA
Hedera algeriensis 'Glorie de Marengo'	VARIEGATED IVY
Hedera colchica 'Dentata Variegata'	PERSIAN IVY
Jasminum x stephanense	STEPHAN'S JASMINE
Lonicera x tellmanniana	RED-GOLD HONEYSUCKLE
Muehlenbeckia species	WIRE VINE
Rosa wichuraiana	MEMORIAL ROSE
Tropaeolum species	PERENNIAL NASTURTIUMS
Wisteria species	WISTERIA

PERENNIALS

Abronia latifolia	SAND VERBENA ❖
Acanthus species	BEAR'S BREECH
Achillea species	YARROW
Aethionema cordifolia	LEBANON STONE CRESS
Aethionema grandiflorum	PERSIAN STONE CRESS
Agastache species	GINT HYSSOP, HUMMINGBIRD MINT
Alstroemeria hybrids	INCA LILY
Amaryllis belladonna	NAKED LADY
Anemanthele lessoniana	NEW ZEALAND GOSSAMER GRASS
Antennaria species	PUSSYTOES ❖
Armeria species	THRIFT ❖

Artemisia species	WORMWOOD ❖
Baptisia species and hybrids	FALSE INDIGO
Calamagrostis species and hybrids	FEATHER REED GRASS
Calylophus hartwegii	HARTWEG'S SUNDROPS
Campanula carpatica	CARPATHIAN BELLFLOWER
Campanula portenschlagiana	DALMATIAN BELLFLOWER
Campanula poscharskyana	SERBIAN BELLFLOWER
Carex (some)	SEDGE ❖
Centranthus ruber	RED VALERIAN, JUPITER'S BEARD
Cerastium tomentosum	SNOW-IN-SUMMER
Ceratostigma plumbaginoides	DWARF PLUMBAGO
Chamaenerion (Epilobium) angustifolia	FIREWEED ❖
Chionochloa rubra	RED TUSSOCK GRASS
Coreopsis verticillata	THREAD-LEAF COREOPSIS
Delosperma species	ICE PLANT
Dianthus species and hybrids	PINKS, CARNATION
Dracocephalum argunense (or D. austriacum)	FUJI BLUE DRAGON'S HEAD
Echinops species	GLOBE THISTLE
Epimedium species and hybrids	BISHOP'S CAP, BARRENWORT
Eriogonum umbellatum	SULFUR BUCKWHEAT ❖
Eriophyllum lanatum	OREGON SUNSHINE, WOOLLY SUNFLOWER ❖
Eryngium species	SEA HOLLY
Euphorbia species	SPURGE
Gaillardia aristata	BLANKET FLOWER ❖
Geranium macrorrhizum	BIG-ROOT GERANIUM
Geranium renardii	RENARD GERANIUM
Glaucium species	HORNED POPPY
Gypsophila repens	CREEPING BABY'S BREATH
Helictotrichon sempervirens	BLUE OAT GRASS
Heliopsis helianthoides	FALSE SUNFLOWER
Hesperantha (Schizostylis) coccineus	RIVER LILY, CRIMSON FLAG
Hemerocallis species and hybrids	DAYLILY
Helianthemum nummularium	SUN ROSE
Helianthus most species	SUNFLOWER
Iberis species	CANDYTUFT
Hosta species and hybrids	PLANTAIN-LILY
Iris germanica	BEARDED IRIS
Iris unguicularis	WINTER IRIS
Kniphofia uvaria and hybrids	RED-HOT POKER, TORCH LILY
Lewisia cotyledon	BITTER ROOT ❖
Leymus mollis	AMERICAN DUNE GRASS ❖
Liatris ligulistylis	MEADOW BLAZING STAR
Liatris spicata	GAYFEATHER
Lilium species and hybrids	LILIES
Liriope muscari	BIG BLUE LILYTURF
Mirabilis jalapa	FOUR-O'CLOCKS
Monardella species	MOUNTAIN BALM, COYOTE MINT
Nepeta species and hybrids	CATMINTS
Oenothera species and hybrids	EVENING PRIMROSE

Opuntia fragilis	PRICKLY PEAR ❖
Papaver orientale and hybrids	ORIENTAL POPPY
Penstemon davidsonii	DAVIDSON'S BEARDTONGUE ❖
Penstemon rupicola	ROCK PENSTEMON ❖
Psephellus (Centaurea) simplicicaulis	LILAC CORNFLOWER
Rhodanthemum (Chrysanthemum) hosmariense	MOROCCAN DAISY
Romneya coulteri	MATILLIJA POPPY
Rudbeckia species	CONEFLOWER
Salvia species and hybrids	SAGE
Salvia yangii (Perovskia atriplicifolia)	RUSSIAN SAGE
Sedum species	STONECROP ❖
Sempervivum species and hybrids	HOUSE-LEEK
Solidago species	GOLDENROD ❖
Stachys byzantina (S. lanata)	LAMB'S EARS
Thermopsis chinensis 'Sophia'	CHINESE BUSH PEA
Thymus species and hybrids	THYME
Tradescantia virginiana (including *T.* x *andersoniana*)	SPIDERWORT
Tropaeolum (perennial species)	PERENNIAL NASTURTIUM
Woodwardia fimbriata	GIANT CHAIN FERN
Yucca species	YUCCA

ANNUALS

Amaranthus caudatus	LOVE-LIES-BLEEDING
Centaurea moschata	SWEET-SULTAN
Clarkia amoena	GODETIA ❖
Cleome spinosa	SPIDER FLOWER
Coreopsis tinctoria	CALLIOPSIS ❖
Eschscholzia californica	CALIFORNIA POPPY ❖
Gaillardia pulchella	BLANKET FLOWER
Impatiens balsamina	GARDEN BALSAM
Lobularia maritima	SWEET ALYSSUM
Petunia × atkinsiana	HYBRID PETUNIA
Portulaca grandiflora	ROSE MOSS
Tropaeolum majus	NASTURTIUM

»» More ...

NITROGEN FIXERS FOR NITROGEN-POOR SOILS

Due to the fact that most "poor" soils have been stripped of any living component that would ordinarily be in native soils, it's necessary to inoculate these plants at planting time. For many, there are inoculants for sale. Most, however, will need a special treatment which involves bringing in just a bit of native soil from nearby.

Albizia julibrissin	PERSIAN SILK TREE
Alnus species	ALDERS ❖
Argyrocytisus battandieri	MOROCCAN PINEAPPLE BROOM
Ceanothus species	CEANOTHUS ❖
Cercis canadensis	EASTERN REDBUD
Cercis occidentalis	CALIFORNIA REDBUD ❖
Cercis siliquastrum	LOVE TREE
Cercocarpus species	MOUNTAIN MAHOGANY ❖
Chamaebatia foliolosa	MOUNTAIN MISERY
Elaeagnus x *submacrophylla (E.* x ebbingei)	HYBRID ELAEAGNUS
Glycyrrhiza glabra	LICORICE, EUROPEAN
Glycyrrhiza lepidota	AMERICAN LICORICE
Gymnocladus dioica	KENTUCKY COFFEE TREE
Hippophae rhamnoides	SEA BUCKTHORN, SEABERRY
Elaeagnus multiflora	CHERRY SILVERBERRY
Indigofera gerardiana	HIMALAYAN INDIGO
Indigofera kirilowii	CHINESE INDIGO
Indigofera pendula	WEEPING INDIGO
Lathyrus japonicus	BEACH PEA ❖
Lupinus albifrons	SILVER-LEAF LUPINE ❖
Lupinus arboreus	TREE LUPINE ❖
Lupinus latifolius (L. arcticus)	ARCTIC LUPINE ❖
Lupinus polyphyllus	BROADLEAF LUPINE ❖
Lupinus rivularis	STREAMBANK LUPINE ❖
Maackia amurensis	AMUR MAACKIA
Morella (Myrica) californica	PACIFIC WAX MYRTLE ❖
Pinus contorta ssp. *contorta*	SHORE PINE ❖
Populus species	POPLARS ❖
Robinia species	BLACK LOCUST
Salix species	WILLOWS ❖
Shepherdia canadensis	BUFFALOBERRY ❖
Styphnolobium (Sophora) japonica	JAPANESE PAGODA TREE
Thermopsis chinensis 'Sophia'	CHINESE BUSH PEA

DRY SITES

Most of our area is flush with rain (pun intended). But we do have our drier microclimates and even gardens in the wettest zones have their dry spots. It might be an area with a rocky, gravelly under-layer. Or a steep slope. Or a bed surrounded by concrete, asphalt, rocks, or other material which otherwise warm and wick the soil. It's tempting here to open the door to "climate change," but I won't. Or did I?

TREES

Abies concolor	WHITE FIR
Abies nebrodensis	SICILIAN FIR
Acer ginnala	FLAME MAPLE
Acer glabrum var. *douglasii*	DOUGLAS MAPLE ❖
Acer griseum	PAPER-BARK MAPLE
Acer negundo 'Sensation'	SEEDLESS BOXELDER
Butia odorata (B. capitata)	JELLY PALM, PINDO PALM
Calocedrus decurrens	INCENSE-CEDAR ❖
Carpinus caroliniana	AMERICAN HORNBEAM
Cedrus atlantica	ATLAS CEDAR
Cephalotaxus harringtonia	JAPANESE PLUM YEW
Cercis siliquastrum	LOVE TREE
Chamaecyparis pisifera	SAWARA FALSE CYPRESS
Chrysolepis chrysophylla	GOLDEN CHINQUAPIN ❖
Cornus kousa	KOUSA DOGWOOD
Cotinus obovatus	AMERICAN SMOKE TREE
Ficus johannis ssp. *afghanistanica*	AFGHAN FIG
Ginkgo biloba	GINKGO
Halesia tetraptera	SILVERBELLS
Juniperus species (most)	JUNIPERS
Koelreuteria paniculata	GOLDEN RAIN TREE
Magnolia x loebneri	LOEBNER HYBRID MAGNOLIA
Malus species	CRABAPPLE
Picea breweriana	BREWER'S WEEPING SPRUCE ❖
Picea species (most)	SPRUCE
Pinus aristata	BRISTLE-CONE PINE
Pinus contorta var. *contorta*	SHORE PINE ❖
Pinus species (most)	PINE
Quercus chrysolepis	CANYON LIVE OAK ❖
Quercus garryana	GARRY OAK, OREGON WHITE OAK ❖
Quercus kelloggii	CALIFORNIA BLACK OAK ❖
Styphnolobium (Sophora) japonica	JAPANESE PAGODA TREE
Syringa reticulata	JAPANESE TREE LILAC
Taxus species (most)	YEW
Ulmus parvifolia	LACEBARK ELM
Zelkova serrata	KEAKI

SHRUBS

Amorpha nana	FRAGRANT DWARF FALSE INDIGO
Arctostaphylos columbiana	BRISTLY OR HAIRY MANZANITA ❖
Arctostaphylos densiflora 'Howard McMinn'	MANZANITA
Arctostaphylos x media (natural hybrid)	HYBRID MANZANITA ❖
Arctostaphylos pajaroensis 'Paradise'	PARADISE MANZANITA
Brachyglottis 'Otari Cloud'	OTARI CLOUD DAISY BUSH
Calluna vulgaris	HEATHER
Carpenteria californica cultivars	BUSH ANEMONE
Ceanothus thyrsiflorus	BLUEBLOSSOM, CALIFORNIA LILAC ❖
Cistus hybrids	ROCK ROSE
Clethra alnifolia	SWEET PEPPERBUSH
Comptonia peregrina	SWEETFERN
Cornus mas	CORNELIAN CHERRY DOGWOOD
Dasiphora (Potentilla) fruticosa	BUSH CINQUEFOIL ❖
Fatsia japonica	JAPANESE FATSIA
Garrya elliptica	SILK-TASSEL ❖
Grevillea miqueliana var. *moroka*	ROUND-LEAF GREVILLEA
Helichrysum splendidum	CAPE GOLD
Hibiscus syriacus	ROSE-OF-SHARON
Ilex crenata	JAPANESE HOLLY
Ilex x meserveae	MESERVE HOLLY
Juniperus communis selections	COMMON JUNIPER ❖
Juniperus maritima	SEASIDE JUNIPER ❖
Juniperus scopulorum	ROCKY MOUNTAIN JUNIPER
Notholithocarpus densiflorus var. *echinoides*	SHRUB TANOAK ❖
Mahonia piperiana	PIPER'S OREGON-GRAPE
Monardella villosa ssp. *franciscana*	COYOTE MINT ❖
Osmanthus delavayi	DELAVAY TEA-OLIVE
Penstemon fruticosus	SHRUBBY PENSTEMON, BUSH PENSTEMON ❖
Philadelphus lewisii	WESTERN MOCK ORANGE ❖
Philadelphus madrensis	DESERT MOUNTAIN MOCK ORANGE
Phlomis italica	BALEARIC ISLAND-SAGE
Physocarpus opulifolius	NINEBARK
Rhus aromatica	FRAGRANT SUMAC
Rhus trilobata	SKUNKBUSH SUMAC ❖
Rhus typhina	STAGHORN SUMAC
Ribes sanguineum	RED CURRANT ❖
Rosa rugosa	JAPANESE BEACH ROSE
Sophora davidii	DAVID'S MOUNTAIN LAUREL
Spiraea species	SPIREA
Syringa laciniata	CUT-LEAF LILAC
Yucca linearifolia	NARROW-LEAFED BEAKED YUCCA

»» More…

VINES

Clematis occidentalis	WESTERN BLUE VIRGINS' BOWER ❖
Vitis californica	PACIFIC GRAPE ❖

GROUNDCOVERS

Arctostaphylos 'Pacific Mist'	PACIFIC MIST MANZANITA
Arctostaphylos uva-ursi	KINNIKINNICK, BEARBERRY ❖
Baccharis tricuneata (B. magellanica) low form	CHRISTMAS BUSH
Carex pansa	DUNE SEDGE, MEADOW SEDGE ❖
Carex praegracilis	FIELD SEDGE ❖
Carex tumulicola	FOOTHILL SEDGE ❖
Ceanothus prostratus	PROSTRATE CEANOTHUS
Cerastium tomentosum	SNOW-IN-SUMMER
Epilobium (Zauschneria) canum ssp. *garrettii* 'Orange Carpet'	CALIFORNIA FUCHSIA
Juniperus communis selections	COMMON JUNIPER ❖
Mahonia repens	CREEPING OREGON-GRAPE ❖
Petrosedum (Sedum) rupestre	BLUE SEDUM
Phedimus (Sedum) kamtschaticus	KAMSCHATKA SEDUM, ORANGE STONECROP
Phedimus (Sedum) spurius	CAUCASIAN STONECROP
Rhus aromatica 'Gro-Low'	GRO-LOW FRAGRANT SUMAC
Sedum divergens	SPREADING STONECROP ❖
Sedum lanceolatum	LANCE-LEAVED STONECROP ❖
Sedum oreganum	OREGON STONECROP ❖
Sedum oregonense	CREAMY FLOWERED STONECROP ❖
Sedum sexangulare	TASTELESS SEDUM
Sedum spathulifolium	BROAD-LEAVED STONECROP ❖
Sedum stenopetalum	WORM-LEAF STONECROP
Sedum tetractinum	CHINESE STONECROP
Teucrium aroanium	GRAY CREEPING GERMANDER
Teucrium cossonii "Majoricum"	FRUITY GERMANDER

PERENNIALS & BULBS

Achillea clavennae	SILVER YARROW
Achillea 'Moonshine'	YELLOW YARROW
Agastache aurantiaca	GOLDEN HUMMINGBIRD MINT
Agave many species	AGAVE
Allium acuminatum	HOOKER'S ONION ❖
Allium cernuum	NODDING ONION ❖
Allium cristophii	STARS OF PERSIA
Aloiampelos (Aloe) striatula	HARDY ALOE
Anaphalis margaritacea	COMMON PEARLY EVERLASTING ❖
Anchusa azurea 'Dropmore'	ITALIAN BUGLOSS
Armeria maritima	SEA THRIFT
Artemisia 'Powis Castle'	POWIS CASTLE WORMWOOD

Asclepias fascicularis	NARROW-LEAVED MILKWEED ❖
Asphodeline lutea	YELLOW ASPHODEL
Balsamorhiza incana	HOARY BALSAMROOT ❖
Baptisia australis	FALSE INDIGO
Baptisia hybrids	FALSE INDIGO
Bloomeria (Triteleia) crocea	GOLDEN STARS ❖
Brodiaea coronaria	HARVEST BRODIAEA ❖
Brodiaea elegans ssp. *hooveri*	HARVEST LILY ❖
Calylophus hartwegii	HARTWEG'S SUNDROPS
Caryopteris divaricata	BUTTERFLY BLUEBEARD
Centranthus ruber	JUPITER'S BEARD, RED VALERIAN
Clematis fremontii	FREMONT'S LEATHER FLOWER
Clematis hirsutissima var. *hirsutissima*	DOUGLAS CLEMATIS, HAIRY CLEMATIS ❖
Coreopsis verticillata	THREAD-LEAF COREOPSIS
Dianthus gratianopolitanus	CHEDDAR PINK
Dichelostemma capitatum ssp. *capitatum*	BLUEDICKS ❖
Dichelostemma congestum	OOKOW, FIELD CLUSTER LILY, HARVEST LILY ❖
Dichelostemma ida-maia	FIRECRACKER FLOWER ❖
Dichelostemma x *venustum*	SNAKE-LILY ❖
Dierama pulcherrimum	ANGEL'S FISHING ROD
Dracocephalum argunense (or D. austriacum)	DRAGON'S HEAD
Echinops bannaticus	GLOBE THISTLE
Echinops ritro	GLOBE THISTLE
Epilobium (Zauschneria) canum ssp. *latifolium*	HUMMINGBIRD TRUMPET ❖
Eremurus himalaicus	HIMALAYAN FOXTAIL LILY
Eremurus hybrids	FOXTAIL LILY
Eremurus stenophyllus	DESERT CANDLE
Eriogonum elatum	RUSH BUCKWHEAT ❖
Eriogonum latifolium	COAST BUCKWHEAT ❖
Eriogonum ovalifolium	OVAL-LEAF BUCKWHEAT ❖
Eriogonum umbellatum	SULPHUR BUCKWHEAT ❖
Eriophyllum lanatum	OREGON SUNSHINE, WOOLLY SUNFLOWER ❖
Eryngium alpinum	ALPINE SEA HOLLY
Eryngium amethystinum	BLUE SEA HOLLY
Eryngium bourgatii	MEDITERRANEAN SEA HOLLY
Festuca idahoensis	IDAHO FESCUE ❖
Fritillaria x *gentneri*	GENTNER'S FRITILLARY ❖
Fritillaria recurva	SCARLET FRITILLARY ❖
Gazania linearis	TREASURE FLOWER
Helianthella uniflora var. *douglasii*	LITTLE SUNFLOWER ❖
Helianthus cusickii	CUSICK'S SUNFLOWER ❖
Helichrysum arenarium	SANDY EVERLASTING
Helictotrichon sempervirens	BLUE OAT GRASS
Hyacinthoides (Scilla) lingulata	AUTUMN BLUEBELL
Hylotelephium (Sedum) spectabile	
	SHOWY STONECROP, AUTUMN SEDUM, BORDER SEDUM
Hylotelephium (Sedum) 'Vera Jameson'	PURPLE AUTUMN SEDUM
Kniphofia hybrids	TORCH LILY, RED-HOT POKER
Leptosiphon nuttallii	NUTTALL'S LINANTHUS ❖

121

Lewisia cotyledon	SISKIYOU LEWISIA ❖
Leymus cinereus	GREAT BASIN WILDRYE ❖
Liatris ligulistylis	MEADOW BLAZING STAR
Linaria (purpurea Hybrid) 'Natalie'	NATALIE TOADFLAX
Lomatium columbianum	COLUMBIA DESERT PARSLEY ❖
Olsynium (Sisyrinchium) douglasii	DOUGLAS' BLUE-EYED-GRASS ❖
Origanum libanoticum	CASCADING HOPFLOWER OREGANO
Penstemon azureus	AZURE PENSTEMON ❖
Penstemon grandiflorus	LARGE BEARDTONGUE
Penstemon kunthii	MEXICAN BEARDTONGUE
Penstemon newberryi var. *berryi*	BERRY'S MOUNTAIN PRIDE ❖
Penstemon rupicola	ROCK PENSTEMON ❖
Phlox nana	SANTA FE PHLOX
Rhodanthemum (Chrysanthemum) hosmariense	MOROCCAN DAISY
Rudbeckia subtomentosa	SWEET CONEFLOWER
Salvia x *sylvestris*	WOOD SAGE
Salvia transylvanica	TRANSYLVANIAN SAGE
Salvia yangii (Perovskia atriplicifolia)	RUSSIAN SAGE
Saxifraga occidentalis	WESTERN SAXIFRAGE ❖
Scutellaria incana	DOWNY SKULLCAP
Sisyrinchium bellum	WESTERN BLUE-EYED GRASS ❖
Sisyrinchium californicum	GOLDEN-EYED GRASS ❖
Sisyrinchium idahoense	BLUE-EYED GRASS ❖
Sphaeralcea munroana	ORANGE GLOBE MALLOW ❖
Teucrium hircanicum	IRANIAN GERMANDER
Thermopsis chinensis 'Sophia'	CHINESE BUSH PEA
Thermopsis montana	MOUNTAIN GOLD-BANNER ❖
Triteleia bridgesii	BRIDGES' TRITELEIA ❖
Triteleia grandiflora	LARGE-FLOWERED TRIPLET-LILY, WILD HYACINTH ❖
Triteleia (Brodiaea) hyacinthina	WHITE TRIPLET-LILY ❖
Triteleia ixioides	PRETTYFACE ❖
Veratrum californicum var. *californicum*	CALIFORNIA FALSE-HELLEBORE ❖
Vernonia lettermannii	THREADLEAF IRONWEED
Wyethia angustifolia	NARROWLEAF WYETHIA ❖
Yucca selected species	YUCCA

See many more candidates in "HARDY SUCCULENT PLANTS"

WET AREAS

The PNW definitely has its share of wet areas. In the shade, in the low spots, in the drainage zone, over a hardpan. There's engineered drainage solutions and then there's this "Right Plant, Right Place" approach. These are also suitable for planting along creeks and streams.

TREES

Acer circinatum	VINE MAPLE ❖
Acer negundo 'Sensation'	SEEDLESS BOXELDER
Acer rubrum	RED MAPLE
Alnus glutinosa	EUROPEAN BLACK ALDER
Amelanchier alnifolia	WESTERN SERVICEBERRY, JUNEBERRY, SASKATOON ❖
Betula nigra	RIVER BIRCH
Carpinus caroliniana	AMERICAN HORNBEAM
Chamaecyparis thyoides	ATLANTIC WHITE CEDAR
Fitzroya cupressoides	PATAGONIAN CYPRESS
Frangula (Rhamnus) purshiana	CASCARA ❖
Fraxinus latifolia	OREGON ASH ❖
Lagarostrobos (Dacrydium) franklinii	HUON PINE
Metasequoia glyptostroboides	DAWN REDWOOD
Nyssa sylvatica	SOUR GUM
Sambucus racemosa	RED ELDERBERRY ❖
Taxodium ascendens (T. distichum var. *imbricatum)*	POND CYPRESS
Taxodium distichum	BALD CYPRESS
Taxodium mucronatum	MONTEZUMA CYPRESS
Taxus brevifolia	PACIFIC YEW ❖
Thuja occidentalis	AMERICAN ARBORVITAE
Thuja orientalis	ORIENTAL ARBORVITAE
Thuja plicata	WESTERN ARBORVITAE, RED-CEDAR ❖
Thujopsis dolabrata	HIBA CEDAR
Zelkova serrata	KEAKI

SHRUBS

Amelanchier alnifolia	WESTERN SERVICEBERRY, JUNEBERRY, SASKATOON ❖
Aronia arbutifolia	RED CHOKEBERRY
Aronia melanocarpa	BLACK CHOKEBERRY
Calycanthus floridus	SWEETSHRUB
Cephalanthus occidentalis	BUTTON BUSH
Clethra alnifolia	SUMMERSWEET
Cornus alba 'Sibirica'	SIBERIAN DOGWOOD
Cornus amomum	SILKY DOGWOOD
Cornus racemosa	GRAY DOGWOOD
Cornus sericea	RED-OSIER DOGWOOD ❖
Frangula (Rhamnus) purshiana	CASCARA ❖
Itea virginica	VIRGINIA SWEETSPIRE
Leucothoe fontanesiana	DROOPING LEUCOTHOE

Lindera benzoin	SPICE BUSH
Oplopanax horridus	DEVIL'S CLUB ❖
Physocarpus capitatus	PACIFIC NINEBARK ❖
Ribes divaricatum var. *divaricatum*	WAX CURRANT ❖
Ribes lacustre	SWAMP GOOSEBERRY ❖
Rosa nutkana	NOOTKA ROSE ❖
Rosa pisocarpa	PEA-FRUIT ROSE ❖
Rosa wichuraiana	MEMORIAL ROSE
Rosa woodsii	WOOD'S ROSE ❖
Salix sitchensis	SITKA WILLOW ❖
Sambucus racemosa	RED ELDERBERRY ❖
Spiraea douglasii	DOUGLAS SPIREA ❖
Spiraea splendens	SUBALPINE OR MOUNTAIN SPIREA ❖
Symphoricarpos albus	COMMON SNOWBERRY ❖
Thujopsis dolabrata 'Nana'	DWARF HIBA CEDAR
Tsuga canadensis 'Jervis'	DWARF CANADIAN HEMLOCK
Vaccinium corymbosum	HIGHBUSH BLUEBERRY
Vaccinium ovatum	EVERGREEN HUCKLEBERRY ❖

PERENNIALS

Aconitum napellus	COMMON MONKSHOOD
Acorus gramineus 'Ogon'	GOLDEN VARIEGATED SWEETFLAG
Actaea racemosa	BLACK COHOSH
Adiantum aleuticum	MAIDENHAIR FERN ❖
Alchemilla mollis	LADY'S MANTLE
Allium cernuum	NODDING ONION ❖
Aruncus aethusifolius	KOREAN GOATSBEARD, DWARF GOAT'S-BEARD
Aruncus dioicus	GOAT'S-BEARD ❖
Asarum caudatum	WILD GINGER ❖
Astilbe x arendsii	ASTILBE
Astilbe chinensis var. *pumila*	DWARF CHINESE ASTILBE
Athyrium filix-femina	LADY FERN ❖
Blechnum (Struthiopteris) spicant	DEER FERN ❖
Brunnera macrophylla	SIBERIAN BUGLOSS
Camassia leichtlinii	GIANT CAMAS ❖
Camassia quamash	COMMON CAMAS ❖
Carex tumulicola	FOOTHILL SEDGE ❖
Carex elata 'Aurea'	BOWLE'S GOLDEN SEDGE
Carex mertensiana (C. columbiana)	MERTEN'S SEDGE ❖
Ceratostigma plumbaginoides	PLUMBAGO
Coptis asplenifolia	FERN-LEAF GOLDTHREAD
Corydalis scouleri	SCOULER'S CORYDALIS ❖
Dactylorhiza species and hybrids	MARSH ORCHID
Darmera (Peltiphyllum) peltata	UMBRELLA PLANT ❖
Delphinium trolliifolium	COLUMBIAN LARKSPUR ❖
Deschampsia caespitosa	TUFTED HAIRGRASS ❖
Dicentra formosa	PACIFIC OR WESTERN BLEEDING-HEART ❖
Diphylleia cymosa	UMBRELLA LEAF

Dryopteris arguta	COASTAL WOOD FERN ❖
Dryopteris expansa	SPREADING WOOD FERN ❖
Erythranthe (Mimulus) cardinalis	RED MONKEYFLOWER
Erythranthe (Mimulus) guttatus	YELLOW MONKEYFLOWER ❖
Erythranthe (Mimulus) lewisii	PINK MONKEYFLOWER ❖
Eutrochium (Eupatorium) dubium 'Little Joe'	LITTLE JOE PYE WEED
Eutrochium maculatum	JOE-PYE-WEED ❖
Eutrochium (Eupatorium) purpureum	JOE PYE WEED
Gunnera manicata	GIANT RHUBARB
Gymnocarpium dryopteris	OAK FERN ❖
Helianthus angustifolius	SWAMP SUNFLOWER
Hemerocallis species and cultivars	DAYLILY
Iris ensata	JAPANESE WATER IRIS
Iris "Pseudata" hybrids	PSEUDATA IRIS
Iris x robusta 'Gerald Darby'	GERALD DARBY IRIS
Juncus effusus	SOFT RUSH ❖
Juncus inflexus	BLUE RUSH
Juncus patens	SPREADING RUSH ❖
Lamprocapnos (Dicentra) spectabilis	BLEEDING HEART
Ligularia dentata 'Desdemona'	LEOPARD PLANT
Ligularia przewalskii	LEOPARD PLANT
Oxalis oregana	REDWOOD SORREL ❖
Pedicularis groenlandica	ELEPHANT-HEAD LOUSEWORT ❖
Penstemon serrulatus	CASCADE PENSTEMON, COAST PENSTEMON ❖
Persicaria amplexicaulis	BISTORT, MOUNTAIN FLEECE
Persicaria polymorpha	GIANT FLEECEFLOWER
Persicaria virginiana 'Painter's Palette'	PAINTED KNOTWEED
Phlox divaricata	BLUE PHLOX
Primula "Candelabra" species and hybrids	CANDELABRA PRIMROSE
Pulmonaria species and hybrids	LUNGWORT
Rheum palmatum	CHINESE RHUBARB
Rodgersia species	RODGERSIAS
Sidalcea hendersonii	HENDERSON'S CHECKER MALLOW ❖
Symphyotrichum (Aster) chilense	PACIFIC ASTER, WETLAND ASTER ❖
Tellima grandiflora	FRAGRANT FRINGECUP ❖
Tiarella cordifolia	FOAM FLOWER ❖
Trillium ovatum	WESTERN WHITE TRILLIUM, WAKE ROBIN ❖
Zantedeschia aethiopica	CALLA-LILY

See also "PONDS."

COASTAL GARDENS

These plants will put up with the windier conditions, the salty air and possibly saltier soil, and the lighter soil (many will grow in pure beach sand).

* = good for stabilizing sandy soil

TREES

Abies balsamea	BALSAM FIR
Abies grandis	GRAND FIR ❖
Arbutus menziesii	MADRONE ❖
Arbutus unedo	STRAWBERRY TREE
Betula pendula	EUROPEAN BIRCH
Carpinus betulus	HORNBEAM
Chamaecyparis pisifera	SAWARA FALSE CYPRESS
Castanea sativa	CHESTNUT
Crataegus laevigata	HAWTHORN
Ginkgo biloba	GINKGO
Ilex x altaclerensis	HIGHCLERE HOLLY
Juniperus maritima	SEASIDE JUNIPER ❖
Juniperus scopulorum cultivars	ROCKY MOUNTAIN JUNIPER
Laurus nobilis	GRECIAN BAY LAUREL
Picea sitchensis	SITKA SPRUCE ❖
Pinus contorta var. *contorta**	SHORE PINE ❖
Pinus nigra	AUSTRIAN PINE
Pseudotsuga menziesii*	DOUGLAS-FIR ❖
Thuja occidentalis	NORTHERN WHITE CEDAR
Thuja plicata*	WESTERN RED-CEDAR ❖
Tilia cordata	LITTLELEAF LINDEN
Trachycarpus fortunei	CHINESE WINDMILL PALM

SHRUBS

Amelanchier alnifolia	WESTERN SERVICEBERRY, JUNEBERRY, SASKATOON ❖
Arbutus unedo 'Compacta'	STRAWBERRY TREE
Arctostaphylos 'Austin Griffins'	MANZANITA
Arctostaphylos columbiana	HAIRY MANZANITA ❖
Arctostaphylos uva-ursi	KINNICK-KINNICK ❖
Aronia arbutifolia	RED CHOKEBERRY
Azara microphylla	SMALL-LEAF AZARA
Berberis species and hybrids	BARBERRY
Brachyglottis species and hybrids	YELLOW DAISY BUSH
Calluna vulgaris	SCOTCH HEATHER
Ceratostigma willmottianum	SHRUBBY BLUE PLUMBAGO
Chaenomeles species	FLOWERING QUINCE

Choisya species and hybrids	MEXICAN MOCK ORANGE
Clethra alnifolia	SUMMERSWEET
Comptonia peregrina	SWEETFERN
Cordyline australis	CABBAGE PALM
Cornus sericea	RED-OSIER DOGWOOD
Corokia cotoneaster	COROKIA
Corylus cornuta var. *californica*	HAZELNUT ❖
Cotinus coggygria	SMOKE TREE
Cotoneaster species	COTONEASTER
Dasiphora (Potentilla) fruticosa	CINQUEFOIL
Dichroa (Hydrangea) febrifuga	BLUE EVERGREEN HYDRANGEA
Elaeagnus x *submacrophylla* (*E.* x *ebbingei*)	HYBRID ELAEAGNUS
Erica carnea	WINTER HEATH
Escallonia species and hybrids	ESCALLONIA
Euonymus japonicus	EVERGREEN EUONYMUS
Forsythia hybrids	FORSYTHIA
Fuchsia magellanica	HARDY FUCHSIA
Fuchsia 'Mrs. Popple'	MRS. POPPLE FUCHSIA
Gaultheria shallon*	SALAL ❖
Griselinia littoralis	PAPAUMA
Hebe species and hybrids	HEBE
Hibiscus syriacus	ROSE OF SHARON
Holodiscus discolor*	OCEANSPRAY ❖
Jovellana violacea	VIOLET TEACUP FLOWERS
Juniperus many species	JUNIPERS
Linnaea (Abelia) x grandiflora	ABELIA
Lonicera hispidula	CHAPARRAL HONEYSUCKLE, HAIRY HONEYSUCKLE ❖
Lonicera involucrata	BLACK TWINBERRY ❖
Lonicera ligustrina var. *yunnanensis* (*L. nitida*)	BOX-LEAF HONEYSUCKLE
Lonicera pileata	BOX-LEAF HONEYSUCKLE
Lupinus arboreus	TREE LUPINE ❖
Morella (Myrica) californica	PACIFIC WAX MYRTLE ❖
Melicytus crassifolius*	THICK-LEAVED MAHOE
Olearia species and hybrids	DAISY BUSH
Pachystegia insignis	MARLBOROUGH ROCK DAISY
Pieris floribunda	MOUNTAIN ANDROMEDA
Pinus mugo	MUGO PINE
Pittosporum tenuifolium	KOHUHU
Prostanthera cuneata	ALPINE MINT BUSH
Pseudowintera colorata	MOUNTAIN HOROPITO
Pyracantha species and hybrids	FIRETHORN
Rhododendron macrophyllum	PACIFIC RHODODENDRON ❖
Rhus aromatica*	FRAGRANT SUMAC
Rhus glabra*	SMOOTH SUMAC
Rhus typhina*	STAGHORN SUMAC
Ribes odoratum	CLOVE CURRAN
Ribes sanguineum	RED-FLOWERING CURRANT
Rosa gymnocarpa	BALD-HIP ROSE ❖
Rosa rubiginosa	SWEET BRIAR

Rosa rugosa and hybrids	JAPANESE BEACH ROSE
Rosa spinosissima	SCOT'S ROSE
Salvia rosmarinus (Rosmarinus officinalis)	ROSEMARY
Salix hookeriana*	BEACH WILLOW ❖
Salix scouleriana*	SCOULER'S WILLOW ❖
Sambucus nigra	BLACK ELDERBERRY
Sambucus racemosa	RED ELDERBERRY
Sambucus canadensis	COMMON ELDER
Solanum crispum 'Glasnevin'	CHILEAN POTATO BUSH
Spiraea douglasii	WESTERN SPIREA ❖
Spiraea species and cultivars	SPIREA
Symphoricarpos albus*	SNOWBERRY ❖
Syringa x laciniata	CUT-LEAF LILAC
Syringa meyeri 'Palibin'	KOREAN LILAC
Syringa vulgaris	COMMON LILAC
Thamnocalamus tesselatus	BERGBAMBOES, MOUNTAIN BAMBOO
Viburnum x *bodnantense* cultivars	HYBRID VIBURNUM
Viburnum davidii	DAVID VIBURNUM

GROUNDCOVERS

Arctostaphylos uva-ursi	BEARBERRY ❖
Ceanothus gloriosus 'Anchor Bay'	ANCHOR BAY CALIFORNIA LILAC
Ceanothus gloriosus 'Heart's Desire'	HEART'S DESIRE CALIFORNIA LILAC
Ceanothus thyrsiflorus 'Yankee Point'	YANKEE POINT CALIFORNIA LILAC
Corethrogyne (Lessingia) filaginifolia 'Silver Carpet'	TRAILING SAND ASTER
Festuca rubra var. *juncea* 'Patrick's Point'	BLUE FESCUE ❖
Fragaria chiloensis	BEACH STRAWBERRY ❖
Gazania linearis	TREASURE FLOWER
Helianthemum nummularium cultivars	ROCKROSE
Juniperus horizontalis	CREEPING JUNIPER
Rhus aromatica 'Gro-Low'	FRAGRANT SUMAC
Teucrium chamaedrys 'Prostratum' (*T.* x lucidrys)	LOW WALL GERMANDER

VINES

Billardiera longiflora	PURPLE APPLE-BERRY
Hydrangea anomala	CLIMBING HYDRANGEA
Hydrangea petiolaris	CLIMBING HYDRANGEA
Hydrangea seemannii	SEEMANN'S CLIMBING HYDRANGEA
Muehlenbeckia complexa	WIRE VINE
Parthenocissus quinquefolia	VIRGINIA CREEPER
Tropaeolum tuberosum var. *lineamaculatum* 'Ken Aslet'	MASHUA

PERENNIALS & BULBS

Abronia latifolia	SAND VERBENA ❖
Achillea species and hybrids	YARROW
Actaea (Cimicifuga) racemosa	SNAKEROOT, BLACK COHOSH
Agapanthus hardy hybrids	LILY-OF-THE-NILE
Alchemilla mollis	LADY'S MANTLE
Allium species and hybrids	ORNAMENTAL ONIONS, GARLIC
Amsonia species	BLUE STAR
Aquilegia hybrids	COLUMBINE
Arabis species	ROCK CRESS
Armeria maritima	SEA THRIFT
Artemisia species	WORMWOOD
Asclepias tuberosa	BUTTERFLY WEED
Aurinia saxatilis	BASKET-OF-GOLD
Baptisia australis and hybrids	FALSE BLUE INDIGO
Bergenia species and hybrids	BERGENIA
Calamagrostis nutkaensis	PACIFIC REEDGRASS ❖
Calystegia (Convolvulus) soldanella	BEACH MORNING GLORY ❖
Carex macrocephala	BIG-HEAD SEDGE ❖
Centranthus ruber	JUPITER'S BEARD, RED VALERIAN
Ceratostigma plumbaginoides	BLUE PLUMBAGO
Clematis non-climbing herbaceous species	CLEMATIS
Coreopsis species	TICKSEED
Corynephorus canescens 'Spiky Blue'	BLUE HAIR GRASS
Crocus species and hybrids	CROCUS
Delosperma species and hybrids	ICE PLANTS
Dianthus species and hybrids	PINKS
Dierama pulcherrimum	ANGEL'S FISHING ROD
Echinops species	GLOBE THISTLE
Erigeron glaucus cultivars	SEASIDE DAISY
Eryngium species and hybrids	ERYNGO, SEA HOLLY
Erythronium revolutum	PINK FAWN-LILY ❖
Gaillardia x *grandiflora*	BLANKET FLOWER
Geranium species and hybrids	HARDY GERANIUMS
Gladiolus communis ssp. *byzantinus*	BYZANTINE GLADIOLUS
Glandora (Lithodora) prostrata 'Grace Ward', 'Heavenly Blue'	LITHODORA
Glehnia littoralis var. *leiocarpa*	AMERICAN SILVER-TOP ❖
Grindelia integrifolia var. *macrophylla*	GUM PLANT ❖
Helictotrichon sempervirens	BLUE OAT GRASS
Hemerocallis species and hybrids	DAYLILY
Hesperantha (Schizostylis) coccinea	CRIMSON FLAG, SCARLET RIVER LILY
Hibiscus moscheutos	ROSE MALLOW
Hosta species and hybrids	HOSTA
Kniphofia species and hybrids	RED-HOT POKER, TORCH LILY
Lamprocapnos (Dicentra) spectabilis	JAPANESE BLEEDING HEART
Lathyrus japonicus	BEACH PEA ❖
*Lathyrus littoralis**	BEACH PEAVINE, SILKY BEACH VETCHLING ❖
Lavandula stoechas	SPANISH LAVENDER

Lavatera maritima	SEA MALLOW
Leucanthemum x superbum	SHASTA DAISY
Leymus (Elymus) mollis*	AMERICAN DUNE-GRASS ❖
Limonium bellidifolium	CASPIA, MATTED SEA LAVENDER
Lupinus littoralis	BEACH LUPINE ❖
Mertensia maritima var. *maritima*	OYSTER PLANT ❖
Nepeta x faassenii	CATMINT
Nerine bowdenii	GUERNSEY LILY
Nipponanthemum nipponicum	MONTAUK DAISY
Ophiopogon planiscapus 'Nigrescens'	BLACK MONDO GRASS
Opuntia fragilis	BRITTLE PRICKLY PEAR ❖
Paeonia lactiflora hybrids	PEONY
Papaver orientale hybrids	ORIENTAL POPPY
Phlox subulata	CREEPING PHLOX
Rhodanthemum (Chrysanthemum) hosmariense	MOROCCAN DAISY
Phormium species and hybrids	NEW ZEALAND FLAX
Polystichum munitum*	WESTERN SWORD FERN ❖
Pulsatilla vulgaris	PASQUE FLOWER
Rudbeckia fulgida var. *sullivantii* 'Goldsturm'	GOLDSTURM BLACK-EYED SUSAN
Salvia yangii (Perovskia atriplicifolia)	RUSSIAN SAGE
Saxifraga x urbium 'Primuloides'	MINIATURE LONDON PRIDE
Scilla (Chionodoxa) luciliae	GLORY OF THE SNOW
Sedum (including *Hylotelephium, Petrosedum, Phedimus, Rhodiola*) species	SEDUM
Sempervivum species	HENS-AND-CHICKS
Solidago species	GOLDENROD
Stachys byzantina (S. lanata)	LAMB'S EARS
Tulipa species (not hybrids)	"WILD" TULIPS
Veronica (Parahebe) perfoliata	DIGGER'S SPEEDWELL
Yucca species	YUCCA

BETWEEN PAVERS, FLAGSTONE, STEPPING STONES

The spaces between pavers, flagstones or stepping stones are often marginally suitable for growing plants. Space-wise, it's simply too small for growing plants with wide bases. With the heat of the stone, the gritty soil between it, and the difficulty in providing any supplemental water, it's prone to severe dryness at times. Finally, there's the matter of traffic, especially serious in patio areas and pathways. The following are the candidates that will tolerate this troika of stress.

Acaena 'Blue Haze'	BLUE HAZE NEW ZEALAND BURR
Acaena inermis 'Purpurea'	PURPLE NEW ZEALAND BURR
Acaena microphylla	NEW ZEALAND BURR
Achillea ageratifolia	GREEK YARROW
Achillea x *lewisii* 'King Edward'	TRAILING YARROW
Achillea serbica	SERBIAN YARROW
Alchemilla alpina	ALPINE LADY'S-MANTLE
Antennaria dioica 'Rubra'	PINK PUSSY-TOES
Arenaria balearica	CORSICAN SANDWORT
Bolax gummifera (Azorella trifurcata) 'Nana'	CUSHION BOLAX
Chamaemelum nobile	ROMAN CHAMOMILE
Dianthus deltoides	MAIDEN PINK
Erodium reichardii (E. chamaedryoides)	ALPINE GERANIUM
Falkia repens	OORTJIES, LITTLE EARS
Gypsophila cerastioides	TRAILING BABY'S BREATH
Herniaria glabra	GREEN CARPET, RUPTUREWORT
Isotoma fluviatilis (can be thuggish)	BLUE STAR CREEPER
Leptinella gruveri	MINIATURE BRASS BUTTONS
Leptinella (Cotula) squalida	NEW ZEALAND BRASS BUTTONS
Mazus reptans	CREEPING MAZUS
Mentha pulegium	PENNYROYAL
Mentha requienii	CORSICAN MINT
Ophiopogon japonicus 'Compactus', 'Gyoku-ryu', 'Nanus'	DWARF MONDO GRASS
Phyla nodiflora	FOGFRUIT
Potentilla neumanniana 'Nana'	ALPINE CINQUEFOIL
Pratia (Lobelia) pedunculata 'County Park'	SUPER STAR CREEPER
Sagina subulata	IRISH MOSS
Sagina subulata 'Aurea'	SCOTCH MOSS
Scleranthus biflorus	NEW ZEALAND ASTROTURF
Scleranthus uniflorus	NEW ZEALAND MOSS
Sedum acre	GOLD MOSS SEDUM
Stachys corsica	CORSICAN TRAILING LAMB'S EAR
Stachys densiflora	CREEPING BETONY
Thymus cherierioides	SILVER NEEDLE THYME
Thymus x *citriodorus* including 'Leprechaun'	LEMON THYME
Thymus herba-barona	CARAWAY-SCENTED THYME
Thymus praecox ssp. *arcticus* 'Albus', 'Mint'	WHITE MOSS THYME
Thymus praecox ssp. *arcticus* 'Languinosus'	WOOLLY THYME

Thymus praecox ssp *praecox (T. polytrichus* ssp. *britannicus)*	MOTHER-OF-THYME
especially the cultivars 'Elfin', 'Minus', 'Pseudolanuginosus'	
Thymus serpyllum 'Annie Hall', 'Pink Chintz'	CREEPING THYME
Trifolium repens 'Purpurascens Quadrifolium'	BLACK-LEAVED CLOVER
Veronica alpina	ALPINE SPEEDWELL
Veronica liwanensis	TURKISH SPEEDWELL
Veronica nummularia	MONEYWORT SPEEDWELL
Veronica pectinata	WOOLLY SPEEDWELL
Veronica repens	CREEPING SPEEDWELL
Veronica whitleyi	WHITLEY'S SPEEDWELL

FOR VERTICAL ACCENT AT THE EDGES

In the more natural designs, it doesn't hurt to plant a few, more upright plants just at the sides of the pathway, out of traffic yet close enough to provide seasonal surprises.

Acis (Leucojum) autumnalis	AUTUMN SNOWFLAKE
Aquilegia bertolonii	BERTOLONI COLUMBINE
Armeria maritima	THRIFT, SEA PINK ❖
Brimeura amethystina	AMETHYST HYACINTH
Brodiaea coronaria	CROWN BRODIAEA ❖
Brodiaea elegans	HARVEST BRODIAEA ❖
Campanula carpatica	CARPATHIAN HAREBELL
Campanula cochlearifolia	FAIRY THIMBLES
Crocus species and hybrids	CROCUS
Dianthus plumarius	COTTAGE PINK
Dichelostemma (Brodiaea) congestum	OOKAW, CLUSTER LILY ❖
Fritillaria michailovskyi	MICHAEL'S FLOWER
Hyacinthoides (Scilla) lingulata	AUTUMN BLUEBELL
Lewisia longipetala hybrids	LONG-PETALLED LEWISIA
Narcissus cyclamineus and hybrids	CYCLAMINEUS NARCISSUS
Oxalis adenophylla	SILVER SHAMROCK
Papaver alpinum	ALPINE POPPY, DWARF POPPY
Penstemon hirsutus 'Pygmaeus'	DWARF HAIRY PENSTEMON
Pseudomuscari (Muscari, Bellavalia) azureum	AZURE GRAPE HYACINTH
Rhodohypoxis baurii	RED STAR
Sempervivum species and hybrids	HOUSELEEK, HEN AND CHICKS
Sternbergia lutea	AUTUMN DAFFODIL
Triteleia (Brodiaea) hyacinthina	WHITE TRIPLET-LILY ❖
Triteleia laxa	ITHURIEL'S SPEAR ❖
Tulipa orphanidea (including *T. whittallii*)	ANATOLIAN TULIP, COTTAGE TULIP
Tulipa urumiensis (T. tarda)	LATE TULIP, TARDY TULIP
Viola corsica	CORSICAN VIOLET

OVER A SEPTIC SYSTEM

Shallow rooted, of course. Emphasis on native plants.

* = for sites that are dry/sandy and sunny

GROUNDCOVERS

Antennaria microphylla*	ROSY PUSSYTOES ❖
Antennaria neglecta*	FIELD PUSSYTOES ❖
Armeria maritima*	SEA PINK ❖
Asarum caudatum	WILD GINGER ❖
Asarum marmoratum	MARBLED WILD GINGER ❖
Carex inops (*C. pensylvanica*)	LONG-STOLONED SEDGE ❖
Carex pansa*	DUNE SEDGE, MEADOW SEDGE ❖
Carex praegracilis	FIELD SEDGE ❖
Carex tumulicola*	FOOTHILL SEDGE ❖
Cerastium tomentosum	SNOW-IN-SUMMER
Clinopodium (*Micromeria, Satureja*) *douglasii*	YERBA BUENA ❖
Eriogonum ternatum*	TERNATE BUCKWHEAT ❖
Festuca rubra (can make a lawn)	CREEPING RED FESCUE ❖
Festuca rubra var. *juncea* 'Patrick's Point'	BLUE CREEPING FESCUE ❖
Fragaria chiloensis*	BEACH STRAWBERRY ❖
Fragaria vesca	WOODLAND STRAWBERRY ❖
Fragaria virginiana var. *platypetala*	WILD STRAWBERRY ❖
Gaultheria procumbens	WINTERGREEN
Gazania linearis	TREASURE FLOWER
Linnaea borealis	TWINFLOWER ❖
Pachysandra terminalis	PACHYSANDRA
Phlox adsurgens	WOODLAND PHLOX ❖
Phlox austromontana	MOUNTAIN PHLOX ❖
Phlox caespitosa	CLUSTERED PHLOX ❖
Phlox diffusa	SPREADING PHLOX ❖
Phlox hoodii	HOOD'S PHLOX ❖
Sagina subulata	IRISH MOSS OR SCOTCH MOSS
Sedum divergens*	SPREADING STONECROP ❖
Sedum lanceolatum*	LANCE-LEAVED STONECROP ❖
Sedum oreganum*	OREGON STONECROP ❖
Sedum oregonense*	CREAMY FLOWERED STONECROP ❖
Sedum spathulifolium*	BROAD-LEAVED STONECROP ❖
Sempervivum tectorum	HENS AND CHICKS
Thymus species	THYME
Tolmiea menziesii	PIGGYBACK PLANT ❖
Whipplea modesta	WHIPPLE VINE, MODESTY ❖

PERENNIALS & BULBS

*Allium acuminatum**	HOOKER'S ONION ❖
*Allium amplectens**	SLIM-LEAF ONION ❖
*Allium cernuum**	NODDING ONION ❖
*Allium crenulatum**	SCALLOPED ONION ❖
*Allium douglasii**	DOUGLAS' ONION ❖
*Allium falcifolium**	SICKLE-LEAF ONION ❖
Allium geyeri var. *geyeri**	GEYER'S ONION ❖
*Allium lemmonii**	LEMMON'S ONION ❖
*Allium siskiyouense**	SISKIYOU ONION ❖
Allium tolmiei var. *tolmiei**	TOLMIE'S ONION ❖
*Anaphalis margaritacea**	COMMON PEARLY EVERLASTING ❖
Aquilegia formosa	WESTERN RED COLUMBINE ❖
Armeria maritima	SEA THRIFT
Asarum marmoratum	MARBLED WILD GINGER ❖
Astilbe x arendsii	ASTILBE
Aurinia saxatilis	BASKET OF GOLD
Blechnum (Struthiopteris) spicant	DEER FERN ❖
*Bloomeria (Triteleia) crocea**	GOLDEN STARS ❖
*Brodiaea coronaria**	HARVEST BRODIAEA ❖
Brodiaea elegans ssp. *hooveri**	HARVEST LILY ❖
Calochortus coxii	COX'S MARIPOSA LILY ❖
Calochortus elegans var. *elegans*	ELEGANT CAT'S EAR ❖
Calochortus eurycarpus	BIGPOD MARIPOSA LILY ❖
Calochortus howellii	HOWELL'S MARIPOSA LILY ❖
Calochortus macrocarpus var. *macrocarpus**	SAGEBRUSH MARIPOSA LILY ❖
Calochortus tolmiei	TOLMIE'S CAT'S EAR ❖
Calochortus umpquaensis ssp. *umpquaensis*	UMPQUA MARIPOSA LILY ❖
Calochortus uniflorus	LARGE-FLOWERED STAR-TULIP ❖
Campanula rotundifolia	BLUEBELL BELLFLOWER ❖
Campanula species	CAMPANULA, BELLFLOWER
Carex brevicaulis	SHORT-STEMMED SEDGE ❖
Carex densa	DENSE SEDGE ❖
Carex microptera	SMALL WINGED SEDGE ❖
Carex obnupta	SLOUGH SEDGE ❖
Clematis columbiana	ROCK CLEMATIS ❖
Clematis hirsutissima var. *hirsutissima*	DOUGLAS CLEMATIS, HAIRY CLEMATIS ❖
Clintonia uniflora	BLUE BEAD ❖
Convallaria majalis	LILY OF THE VALLEY
Corydalis scouleri	SCOULER'S CORYDALIS ❖
Deschampsia caespitosa	TUFTED HAIRGRASS ❖
Dianthus species	PINKS
Dicentra formosa	PACIFIC OR WESTERN BLEEDING-HEART ❖
Dichelostemma capitatum ssp. *capitatum**	BLUEDICKS ❖
Dichelostemma congestum	OOKOW, FIELD CLUSTER LILY, HARVEST LILY ❖
Dichelostemma ida-maia	FIRECRACKER FLOWER ❖
Dichelostemma x venustum	SNAKE-LILY ❖
Dodecatheon austrofrigidum	FRIGID SHOOTING STAR ❖

Dodecatheon cusickii	CUSICK'S SHOOTING-STAR ❖
Dodecatheon hendersonii	SHOOTING STAR, MOSQUITO BILL ❖
Erythronium citrinum	LEMON FAWN-LILY, CREAM FAWN-LILY ❖
Erythronium elegans	COAST RANGE FAWN-LILY ❖
Erythronium grandiflorum	YELLOW AVALANCHE LILY, GLACIER LILY ❖
Erythronium hendersonii	HENDERSON'S FAWN-LILY ❖
Erythronium howellii	HOWELL'S FAWN-LILY ❖
Erythronium klamathense	KLAMATH FAWN-LILY ❖
Erythronium montanum	AVALANCHE-LILY ❖
Erythronium oreganum	OREGON FAWN-LILY ❖
Erythronium revolutum	MAHOGANY FAWN-LILY, COAST FAWN-LILY ❖
Festuca idahoensis*	IDAHO FESCUE ❖
Fritillaria affinis (F. lanceolata)	CHOCOLATE LILY ❖
Fritillaria atropurpurea	SPOTTED FRITILLARY ❖
Fritillaria camschatcensis	INDIAN RICE ❖
Fritillaria glauca	SISKIYOU FRITILLARY ❖
Fritillaria pudica*	YELLOW BELLS ❖
Fritillaria recurva	SCARLET FRITILLARY ❖
Fritillaria x gentneri	GENTNER'S FRITILLARY ❖
Heuchera micrantha	SMALL- FLOWERED ALUMROOT, CORALBELLS ❖
Heuchera sanguinea	CORAL BELL
Hyacinthoides (Scilla) lingulata	AUTUMN BLUEBELL
Iberis sempervirens	CANDYTUFT
Iris bracteata	SISKIYOU IRIS ❖
Iris chrysophylla	YELLOW-LEAF IRIS ❖
Iris douglasiana	DOUGLAS IRIS ❖
Iris innominata	GOLDEN IRIS ❖
Iris missouriensis	ROCKY MOUNTAIN IRIS ❖
Iris purdyi	PURDY'S IRIS ❖
Iris tenax	OREGON IRIS, TOUGH-LEAF IRIS ❖
Iris tenuis	CLACKAMAS IRIS ❖
Lavandula angustifolia	ENGLISH LAVENDER
Leptosiphon nuttallii	NUTTALL'S LINANTHUS ❖
Lewisia columbiana var. *columbiana**	COLUMBIAN LEWISIA ❖
Lewisia cotyledon*	SISKIYOU LEWISIA ❖
Lupinus albicaulis	SICKLE-KEELED LUPINE ❖
Lupinus grayi	SIERRA LUPINE ❖
Melica subulata	ALASKA ONIONGRASS ❖
Olsynium (Sisyrinchium) douglasii*	DOUGLAS' BLUE-EYED-GRASS ❖
Oxalis oregana	REDWOOD SORREL ❖
Oxalis suksdorfii	WESTERN YELLOW OXALIS ❖
Penstemon attenuatus	TAPER-LEAVED PENSTEMON, SULPHUR PENSTEMON ❖
Penstemon azureus*	AZURE PENSTEMON ❖
Penstemon barrettiae	BARRETT'S BEARDTONGUE ❖
Penstemon cardwellii	CARDWELL'S PENSTEMON ❖
Penstemon davidsonii	DAVIDSON'S BEARDTONGUE ❖
Penstemon davidsonii var. *praeteritus*	TIMBERLINE PENSTEMON ❖
Penstemon ellipticus	ROCKY LEDGE BEARDTONGUE ❖
Penstemon euglaucus	GLAUCUS PENSTEMON ❖

Penstemon newberryi var. *berryi*	BERRY'S MOUNTAIN PRIDE ❖
Penstemon ovatus	BROAD-LEAVED PENSTEMON ❖
Penstemon payettensis	PAYETTE BEARDTONGUE ❖
Penstemon richardsonii	RICHARDSON'S BEARDTONGUE ❖
Penstemon rupicola	ROCK PENSTEMON ❖
Penstemon serrulatus	CASCADE PENSTEMON, COAST PENSTEMON ❖
Penstemon speciosus	SHOWY PENSTEMON ❖
Penstemon subserratus	FINE-TOOTHED PENSTEMON ❖
Penstemon venustus	LOVELY PENSTEMON, BEAUTIFUL PENSTEMON ❖
Penstemon wilcoxii	WILCOX'S PENSTEMON ❖
Polemonium carneum	SALMON POLEMONIUM ❖
Polypodium scouleri	LEATHER-LEAF FERN ❖
Polystichum imbricans	CLIFF SWORD FERN ❖
Polystichum lemmonii	LEMMON'S SWORD FERN ❖
Polystichum munitum	SWORD FERN ❖
Polystichum scopulinum	MOUNTAIN HOLLY FERN ❖
Pulsatilla vulgaris	PASQUE FLOWER
Rhodanthemum (Chrysanthemum) hosmariense	MOROCCAN DAISY
Saxifraga occidentalis	WESTERN SAXIFRAGE ❖
Silene hookeri	HOOKER'S INDIAN-PINK ❖
*Sisyrinchium bellum**	WESTERN BLUE-EYED GRASS ❖
*Sisyrinchium californicum**	GOLDEN-EYED GRASS ❖
Sisyrinchium hitchcockii	HITCHCOCK'S BLUE-EYED-GRASS ❖
*Sisyrinchium idahoense**	BLUE-EYED GRASS ❖
Stenanthium occidentale	WESTERN FEATHERBELLS ❖
Synthyris (Veronica) missurica ssp. *stellata*	COLUMBIA KITTEN-TAILS ❖
Synthyris (Veronica) reniformis	SPRING QUEEN, KITTEN TAILS ❖
Tellima grandiflora	FRINGECUP ❖
Trillium albidum ssp. *albidum (T. chloropetalum)*	GIANT TRILLIUM ❖
Trillium kurabayashii	GIANT PURPLE TRILLIUM ❖
Trillium ovatum	WESTERN WHITE TRILLIUM, WAKE ROBIN ❖
Trillium parviflorum	SMALL-FLOWERED TRILLIUM ❖
*Triteleia (Brodiaea) hyacinthina**	WHITE TRIPLET-LILY ❖
*Triteleia bridgesii**	BRIDGES' TRITELEIA ❖
*Triteleia grandiflora**	LARGE-FLOWERED TRIPLET-LILY, WILD HYACINTH ❖
*Triteleia hendersonii**	HENDERSON'S TRITELEIA ❖
*Triteleia ixioides**	PRETTYFACE ❖
Viola adunca	EARLY BLUE VIOLET, WESTERN DOG VIOLET ❖
Viola glabella	STREAM VIOLET, YELLOW WOOD VIOLET ❖
*Viola trinervata**	SAGEBRUSH VIOLET ❖

ANNUALS

Ageratum houstonianum	FLOSS FLOWER
Begonia semperflorens	WAX BEGONIA
Clarkia amoena	FAREWELL-TO-SPRING ❖
Clarkia pulchella	PINK FAIRIES ❖
Coleus (Plectranthus) scutellarioides	COLEUS

Collomia grandiflora	GRAND COLLOMIA, MOUNTAIN COLLOMIA ❖
Coreopsis tinctoria var. *atkinsoniana**	COLUMBIA COREOPSIS ❖
Dianthus barbatus	SWEET WILLIAM
*Eschscholzia californica**	CALIFORNIA POPPY ❖
Gilia capitata	GLOBE GILIA, BLUEFIELD GILIA ❖
*Ipomopsis aggregata**	SKYROCKET, SCARLET GILIA ❖
Lobelia erinus	LOBELIA
Lobularia maritima	SWEET ALYSSUM
Madia elegans	ELEGANT TARWEED ❖
Nemophila menziesii	BABY BLUE-EYES ❖
Pelargonium x hortorum	GERANIUM
Petunia × atkinsiana	HYBRID PETUNIA
Salvia farinacea	MEALY SAGE
Salvia coccinea	SCARLET SAGE
Tagetes species	MARIGOLDS
Valeriana (Plectritis) congesta	SEA BLUSH ❖
Zinnia elegans	ZINNIA

A CALENDAR OF BLOOM

We can garden 365 days of the year here and we can have plants blooming that whole time. We are not stuck with a short but wonderfully refreshing Spring bloom, a peak of bloom in Summer, and then a waning show in Fall with no flower color in Winter, as is so common in gardens here.

Besides the four familiar seasons, one must consider the overlap in seasons, because, simply put, plants can't read your calendar.

There is also **"A CALENDAR OF FLOWER SEED SOWING"** at the end of this chapter.

In addition to color from flowers, there's much more that can add interest to the garden and should be used as prominently as flowers, particularly when it comes to the winter season. Look in the ORNAMENTAL CONSIDERATIONS section for:

"COLORFUL FOLIAGE" *(8 to 12 months of the year)*
"FALL FOLIAGE"
"STRIKING EVERGREEN FOLIAGE" *(Good looking all year long)*
"DRAMATIC/BOLD FOLIAGE" *(Mostly spring through fall; a few are evergreen)*
"FINE-TEXTURED FOLIAGE"
"BERRIES/FRUITS, FALL INTO WINTER"
"BEAUTIFUL BARK"
"MULTI-SEASON ACCENT PLANTS"

Look for the symbol ❖ which indicates a native plant.

WINTER FLOWERS

This is the expected down time in the PNW garden. Yet there is a good many flowering plants which can help brighten up the landscape. Combine these with hundreds more evergreen plants, especially those with colorful or unusual foliage, along with fruiting trees, shrubs, and vines, and don't forget the extra-special deciduous plants with beautiful bark or overall eye-grabbing structure.

Abeliophyllum distichum	WHITE FORSYTHIA
Arbutus x reyorum 'Marina'	MARINA STRAWBERRY TREE
Bergenia crassifolia and some hybrids	BERGENIA
Calluna vulgaris 'Autumn Glow', 'Barja', 'Saint Nick'	
	COMMON HEATHER, SCOTS HEATHER
Camellia 'Buttermint'	BUTTERMINT CAMELLIA
Camellia 'Buttons 'n Bows'	BUTTONS 'N BOWS CAMELLIA
Camellia x 'Elina Cascade'	HYBRID CAMELLIA
Camellia 'Fairy Blush'	FAIRY BLUSH CAMELLIA
Camellia japonica	JAPANESE CAMELLIA
Camellia x lutchuensis 'Cinnamon Cindy'	CINNAMON CANDY CAMELLIA
Camellia x lutchuensis 'High Fragrance'	HIGH FRAGRANCE CAMELLIA
Camellia 'Minato-no-Akebono'	FRAGRANT WINTER CAMELLIA
Camellia 'Pink Icicle'	PINK ICICLE CAMELLIA
Camellia reticulata	FOREST CAMELLIA
Camellia 'Taylor's Perfection'	TAYLOR'S PERFECTION CAMELLIA
Camellia transarisanensis	CAMELLIA
Camellia 'Valley Knudsen'	VALLEY KNUDSEN CAMELLIA
Camellia x vernalis 'Egao', 'Shibori-Egao' (variegated version) SMILING FACE CAMELLIA	
Camellia x vernalis 'Yuletide'	YULETIDE CAMELLIA
Camellia x williamsii	HYBRID CAMELLIA
Camellia 'Winter's Snowman'	WINTER'S SNOWMAN CAMELLIA
Camellia 'Yume'	YUME CAMELLIA
Chimonanthus praecox	WINTERSWEET
Clematis armandii	ARMAND CLEMATIS, EVERGREEN CLEMATIS
Clematis cirrhosa	FERN-LEAVED CLEMATIS
Clematis clarkeana (Clematis anshunensis)	CHINESE WINTER CLEMATIS
Clematis tangutica	GOLDEN CLEMATIS
Clematis urophylla	WINTER BEAUTY CLEMATIS
Cornus mas	CORNELIAN CHERRY
Crocus tommasinianus	WOODLAND CROCUS
Daphne bholua	NEPALESE PAPER PLANT
Daphne odora cultivars	WINTER DAPHNE
Edgeworthia chrysantha	PAPER BUSH
Eranthis hyemalis	WINTER ACONITE

Erica carnea   WINTER HEATH
   from earliest within this season to latest within this season, by group:
   -- *Erica carnea* 'Queen Mary'
   -- *Erica carnea* 'Robert Jan', 'Golden Starlet', 'King George', 'Lesley Sparkes'
   -- *Erica carnea* 'Pirbright Rose'
   -- *Erica carnea* 'Cecelia M. Beale', 'Jean', 'Pink Mist', 'Wanda', 'Rubina'
   -- *Erica carnea* 'Accent', 'Adrienne Duncan', 'Altadena', 'Nathalie', 'Sarolyn',
     'Sherwood Creeping', 'Waquoit Mac'
   -- *Erica carnea* 'Alan Coates', 'Pink Cloud', 'Red Rover', 'Rosalinde Schorn'
Erica x *darleyensis* (long bloomer) 'Furzey'   DARLEY DALE HEATH
Erica x *darleyensis*   DARLEY DALE HEATH
   from earliest within this season to latest within this season, by group:
   -- *Erica* x *darleyensis* 'Archie Graham', 'Mrs. Parris' Red', 'N. R. Webster',
     'Perfect Polly', 'White Perfection'
   -- *Erica* x *darleyensis* 'Alice', 'Beacon Hill', 'Coral Bells', 'Lena', 'Lucie'
Erica erigena 'W.T. Rackliff'   IRISH HEATH
Erica glandulosa   GLANDULAR HEATH
Erica mackayana 'Andevalensis'   MACKAY'S HEATH
Erica speciosa   SHOWY HEATH
Forsythia suspensa ssp. *sieboldii*   WEEPING FORSYTHIA
Forsythia viridissima var. *koreana* 'Kumson'   KUMSON FORSYTHIA
Galanthus nivalis   SNOWDROP
Garrya elliptica   WAVYLEAF SILKTASSEL ❖
Garrya x *issaquahensis*   HYBRID SILKTASSEL
Gelsemium sempervirens   CAROLINA JESSAMINE
Grevillea australis   SOUTHERN GREVILLEA
Grevillea 'Poorinda Leanne' ('Poorinda Queen')   LEANNE GREVILLEA
Grevillea 'The Precious'   THE PRECIOUS GREVILLEA
Grevillea victoriae   ROYAL GREVILLEA
Hacquetia epipactis   BROAD-LEAVED SANICLE, HACQUETIA
Hamamelis x *intermedia* cultivars   HYBRID WITCH-HAZEL
Helleborus argutifolius, *H. foetidus*, *H.* hybrids   HELLEBORES
X *Heucherella* cultivars   FOAMY BELLS
Iris lazica (*Iris unguicularis* ssp. *lazica*)   LAZISTAN IRIS, BLACK SEA IRIS
Iris unguicularis   WINTER IRIS
Jasminum nudiflorum   WINTER JASMINE
Lonicera sempervirens 'Major Wheeler'   MAJOR WHEELER HONEYSUCKLE
Magnolia (*Michelia*) *cavaleriei* var. *platypetala*   BROAD-PETAL MICHELIA
Mahonia aquifolium   OREGON-GRAPE ❖
Mahonia japonica   JAPANESE MAHONIA
Mahonia x *lindsayae* 'Cantab'   CANTAB WINTER BARBERRY
Mahonia x *media* cultivars   WINTER BARBERRY
Oxalis nidulans 'Pom Pom'   POM-POM SORRELL
Prunus mume   JAPANESE APRICOT
Prunus x *subhirtella* 'Autumnalis', 'Autumnalis Rosea'   WINTER-FLOWERING CHERRY
Rhododendron dauricum   DAHURIAN/DAURIAN RHODODENDRON
Rhododendron barbatum   BEARDED RHODODENDRON

Rhododendron hybrids ('Abigale', 'Babylon', 'Bodega Crystal Pink', 'Bo-Peep', 'Bric-a-Brac', 'Christmas Cheer', 'Conemaugh', 'Etta Boroughs', 'Goosander', 'Harry Carter', 'Helen Scott Richey', 'Lee's Scarlet', 'Nobleanum Album', 'Nobleanum Coccineum', 'Nobleanum Venustum', 'Olive', 'Peter Faulk', 'Pink Prelude', 'Pink Snowflakes', 'Pioneer', 'PJM Elite', 'Praecox', 'Promise of Spring', 'Red Majesty', 'Quaver', 'Rosa Mundi', 'Seta', 'Sausalito', 'Tessa', 'Tessa Bianca', 'Vemus', 'Wisp')	HYBRID RHODODENDRONS
Rhododendron irroratum	IRRORATUM RHODODENDRON
Rhododendron lanigerum	RHODODENDRON
Rhododendron moupinense	EARLY-FLOWERING RHODODENDRON
Rhododendron (Azalea) mucronulatum	KOREAN AZALEA
Rhododendron strigilosum	RHODODENDRON
Rhododendron praevernum	RHODODENDRON
Ribes laurifolium	EVERGREEN CURRANT
Ribes malvaceum	CHAPARRAL CURRANT
Sarcococca confusa	CHRISTMAS BOX, CONFUSED SWEET BOX
Sarcococca hookeriana	HIMALAYAN SWEET BOX
Sarcococca hookeriana var. *humilis*	DWARF SWEET BOX
Sarcococca ruscifolia	FRAGRANT SWEET BOX
Sarcococca saligna	NARROW-LEAF SWEETBOX
Stachyurus praecox	STACHYURUS
Viburnum x bodnantense 'Charles Lamont', 'Dawn'	HYBRID VIBURNUM
Viburnum farreri	FRAGRANT VIBURNUM
Viburnum grandiflorum f. *foetens* (*V. foetens*)	HIMALAYAN CRANBERRY BUSH
Viburnum x pragense	PRAGUE VIBURNUM

DON'T FORGET:

"STRIKING EVERGREEN FOLIAGE"
"BERRIES/FRUITS FALL INTO WINTER"
"BEAUTIFUL BARK"
"MULTI-SEASON ACCENT PLANTS"

EARLY SPRING FLOWERS

This is the tease of Spring or, to use a cliché, the harbingers of Spring.

Aurinia saxatilis	BASKET-OF-GOLD
Bergenia cordifolia	HEARTLEAF BERGENIA
Calluna vulgaris	SCOTCH HEATHER
Cardamine quinquefolia	FIVE-LEAVED CUCKOO FLOWER
Chrysosplenium macrophyllum	GIANT GOLDEN SAXIFRAGE
Clematis x cartmanii 'Joe'	JOE CLEMATIS
Corylopsis pauciflora	BUTTERCUP WITCHHAZEL
Cyclamen coum	HARDY CYCLAMEN, EASTERN SOWBREAD
Cyclamen pseudibericum	FALSE IBERIAN CYCLAMEN
Daphne mezereum	FEBRUARY DAPHNE
Darmera peltata (including 'Nana')	UMBRELLA PLANT
Edgeworthia papyrifera	ORIENTAL PAPERBUSH
Eranthis hyemalis	WINTER ACONITE
Erica arborea var. *alpina*	ALPINE TREE HEATH
Erica arborea 'Golden Joy'	TREE HEATH
Erica baccans	BERRY-FLOWER HEATH
Erica canaliculata	CHANNELED HEATH, CHRISTMAS HEATH
Erica carnea	WINTER HEATH

    from earliest within this season to latest within this season, by group:
- *Erica carnea* 'Mrs. Sam Doncaster', 'R.B. Cooke', 'Snow Queen'
- *Erica carnea* 'Ann Sparkes, 'Atrorubra, 'Aurea', 'Bell's Extra Special', 'Etta Rose', 'Ken's Golden Star', 'Pink Spangles', 'Polly Bigguns', 'Porter's Red', 'Rosy Gem', 'Ruby Glow', 'Springwood White', 'Vivellii'
- *Erica carnea* 'Beoley Pink', 'Heathwood', 'Ice Princess', 'Martin', 'Moonlight', 'Saskia', 'Scatterley', 'Schneesturm', 'Tanja', 'Treasure Trove', 'Vivellii Aurea', 'Westwood Yellow'
- *Erica carnea* 'Bright Jewel', 'March Seedling', 'Tatjana', 'Winter Snow', 'Winter Sport', 'Wintersonne'
- *Erica carnea* 'Rosantha', 'Thomas Kingscote'

Erica x darleyensis	DARLEY DALE HEATH

    from earliest within this season to latest within this season, by group:
- *Erica* x darleyensis 'Ada S. Collings', 'Goldrush', 'Irish Treasure', 'Katia', 'Pink Harmony', 'Silberschmelze', 'White Glow'
- *Erica* x darleyensis 'Cross' Puzzle', 'Dunreggan', 'Epe', 'Erecta', 'Eva Gold', 'J. W. Porter', 'Jack H. Brummage', 'Jenny Porter', 'Lyra', 'Margaret Porter'
- *Erica* x darleyensis 'Mary Helen'
- *Erica* x darleyensis 'Citzler's Rosa'
- *Erica* x darleyensis 'Spring Surprise', 'White Spring Surprise'

Erica erigena 'Brightness', 'Coccinea', 'Ewan Jones', 'Golden Lady', 'Hibernica', 'Irish Salmon', 'Ivory', 'Maxima', 'Nana', 'Thing Nee'	IRISH HEATH
Erica lusitanica 'George Hunt', 'Sheffield Park'	PORTUGUESE HEATH
Erica x oldenburgensis 'Ammerland', 'Oldenburg'	OLDENBERG HEATH
Erica 'Winter Fire'	WINTER FIRE HEATH
Galanthus elwesii	GIANT SNOWDROP

Galanthus ikariae	SNOWDROP
Galanthus plicatus	CRIMEAN SNOWDROP
Garrya elliptica	WAVYLEAF SILKTASSEL ❖
Gladiolus oppositiflorus ssp. *salmoneus*	HARDY SALMON GLADIOLUS
Grevillea australis	SOUTHERN GREVILLEA
Grevillea 'Canberra Gem'	SPIDER FLOWER
Hacquetia epipactis	BROAD-LEAVED SANICLE, HACQUETIA
Helleborus x *ballardiae*	HYBRID HELLEBORE
Helleborus lividus	MAJORCAN HELLEBORE
Iris lazica (Iris unguicularis ssp. *lazica)*	LAZISTAN IRIS, BLACK SEA IRIS
Lonicera x *purpusii* 'Winter Beauty'	WINTER BEAUTY HONEYSUCKLE
Oemleria cerasiformis	OSOBERRY, INDIAN PLUM ❖
Primula many species	PRIMROSES
Prunus x subhirtella 'Autumnalis' 'Autumnalis Rosea'	WINTER-FLOWERING CHERRY
Pulmonaria longifolia ssp. *cevennensis*	LUNGWORT
Rhododendron hybrids ('Cilpinense', 'Dora Amateis', 'Elya', HYBRID RHODODENDRONS 'Ginney Gee', 'Lucy Lou', 'Mary Fleming', 'P.J.M.', Rosamundi, 'Shamrock', 'Small Gem', 'Small Wonder', 'Snow Lady', 'Grace Seabrook', 'Unknown Warrior')	
Rhododendron calophytum	BEAUTIFUL-FACE RHODODENDRON
Rhododendron ciliatum	FRINGE-LEAFED RHODODENDRON
Rhododendron hodgsonii	HODGON'S RHODODENDRON
Rhododendron leucaspis	RHODODENDRON
Rhododendron macabeanum	MACABE RHODODENDRON
Rhododendron oreodoxa	RHODODENDRON
Rhododendron principis	RHODODENDRON
Rhododendron racemosum	RACEMOSE RHODODENDRON
Rhododendron recurvoides	NARROW-LEAF RHODODENDRON
Rhododendron rubiginosum	RUBIGINOSE RHODODENDRON
Rhododendron russatum	PURPLISH-BLUE RHODODENDRON
Rhododendron (Azalea) schlippenbachii	ROYAL AZALEA
Rhododendron sutchuenense	SZECHWAN RHODODENDRON
Stachyurus praecox	EARLY SPIKE-TAIL
Trillium ovatum	PACIFIC TRILLIUM
Viburnum x *bodnantense* 'Charles Lamont'	HYBRID VIBURNUM
Viburnum grandiflorum f. *foetens* (*V. foetens*)	HIMALAYAN CRANBERRY BUSH

SPRING FLOWERS

Most gardeners look forward to spring more than they do to any other season so it's a good thing there's this wealth of plant material to create the explosion of bloom required of a good spring garden.

Adelinia (Cynoglossum) grande	PACIFIC HOUND'S TONGUE ❖
Akebia quinata	CHOCOLATE VINE
Allium karataviense including 'Ivory Queen'	TURKESTAN ONION
Allium neapolitanum cowanii	DAFFODIL GARLIC
Amelanchier x grandiflora	SERVICEBERRY
Amsonia hubrichtii	BLUESTAR
Androsace (Douglasia) laevigata	CLIFF DWARF-PRIMROSE ❖
Anemone x fulgens	SCARLET WINDFLOWER
Anemonoides (Anemone) blanda	GRECIAN WINDFLOWER
Anemonoides (Anemone) x *lipsiensis*	HYBRID WOOD ANEMONE
Anemonoides (Anemone) nemorosa	WOOD ANEMONE
Anemonoides (Anemone) pseudoaltaica	ASTER-FLOWERED ANEMONE
Arabis species	ROCK CRESS
Arctostaphylos columbiana	HAIRY MANZANITA ❖
Arisaema ringens	COBRA-LILY
Arisarum proboscideum	MOUSE PLANT
Armeria maritima	SEA PINK ❖
Arum concinnatum	LORDS-AND-LADIES
Aruncus aethusifolius	KOREAN GOATSBEARD, DWARF GOAT'S-BEARD
Asphodelus lutea	KING'S- SPEAR
Beesia deltophylla	BEESIA
Berberis x *gladwynensis* 'William Penn'	WILLIAM PENN BARBERRY
Berberis jamesiana 'Exuberant'	EXUBERANT BARBERRY
Berberis julianae	WINTERGREEN BARBERRY
Berberis x *stenophylla*	HYBRID BARBERRY
Bergenia ciliata	HAIRY-LEAF BERGENIA
Bergenia hybrids	BERGENIA
Bletilla striata	CHINESE GROUND ORCHID
Brunnera macrophylla	SIBERIAN BUGLOSS
Calanthe sieboldii	SIEBOLD'S JAPANESE ORCHID
Camassia howellii	HOWELL'S CAMAS ❖
Campanula portenschlagiana	DALMATIAN BELLFLOWER
Ceanothus cuneatus var. *rigidus* 'Snowball'	SNOWBALL LILAC
Cercis canadensis	REDBUD
Cercis siliquastrum	LOVE TREE
Chaenomeles hybrids	JAPANESE FLOWERING QUINCE
Chionanthus retusus	CHINESE FRINGE TREE
Clematis armandii	EVERGREEN CLEMATIS
Clematis 'Constance'	CONSTANCE CLEMATIS
Cornus alternifolia	PAGODA DOGWOOD
Cornus mas	CORNELIAN CHERRY
Cornus x *elwinortonii* (including 'Hyperion', 'Rosy Teacups', 'Venus')	DOGWOOD
Corydalis solida	FUMEWORT

Corylopsis glabrescens	FRAGRANT WINTER HAZEL
Corylopsis sinensis	CHINESE FRAGRANT WINTER HAZEL
Corylopsis spicata	SPIKE WINTER HAZEL
Corylus avellana 'Contorta'	HARRY LAUDER'S WALKING STICK
Crataegus × lavallei	LAVALLE HAWTHORN
Crocus chrysanthus	GOLDEN CROCUS
Crocus x luteus	CROCUS
Cyclamen repandum	SPRING SOWBREAD
Daboecia azorica 'Arthur P. Dome'	AZORES HEATH
Daphne x burkwoodii	BURKWOOD'S DAPHNE
Daphne genkwa	LILAC DAPHNE
Daphne retusa	DWARF DAPHNE
Davidia involucrata	DOVE TREE
Dicentra formosa	WESTERN BLEEDING HEART ❖
Disporopsis pernyi	EVERGREEN SOLOMON'S SEAL
Disporum uniflorum	FAIRY BELLS
Dracunculus vulgaris	DRAGON-LILY
Edgeworthia chrysantha	ORIENTAL PAPERBUSH
Embothrium coccineum	CHILEAN FIRE-TREE
Enkianthus perulatus	WHITE ENKIANTHUS
Epimedium brachyrrhizum, brevicornu, x cantabrigiense,	BARRENWORT
dolichostemon, epsteinii, grandiflorum, myrianthum, x perralchicum,	
perralderianum, pinnatum, pubescens, x rubrum, *sempervirens,* x versicolor,	
x warleyense, x youngianum	
Erica arborea 'Estrella Gold', 'Spring Smile'	TREE HEATH
Erica australis and cultivars 'Holehird', 'Mr. Robert', 'Riverslea'	SPANISH HEATH
Erica azorica (*Erica scoparia* ssp. *azorica*)	AZOREAN HEATH
Erica erigena 'Alba, 'Brian Proudley', 'Superba'	IRISH HEATH
Erica scoparia 'Minima'	BESOM HEATH, GREEN HEATHER
Erica spiculifolia f. *albiflora*	WHITE-FLOWERED BALKAN HEATH
Erica umbellata	DWARF SPANISH HEATH
Erodium chrysanthum	HERONSBILL, STORKSBILL
Erysimum species	WALLFLOWER
Erythronium grandiflorum var. *grandiflorum*	YELLOW AVALANCHE-LILY ❖
Erythronium oregonum	WHITE FAWN-LILY ❖
Erythronium 'Pagoda'	PAGODA FAWN-LILY
Erythronium revolutum	COAST FAWN-LILY ❖
Forsythia x intermedia cultivars	FORSYTHIA
Fothergilla gardenii	DWARF WITCHALDER
Fothergilla 'Mount Airy'	MOUNT AIRY WITCHALDER
Fritillaria affinis, assyriaca, bucharica (especially 'Giant'), *eduardii,*	FRITILLARY
x gentneri, *pontica, pudica, raddeana, recurva*	
Glandora (*Lithodora*) *diffusa*	PURPLE GROMWELL
Helleborus x ericsmithii	HYBRID HELLEBORE
Iberis sempervirens	EVERGREEN CANDYTUFT
Iris cristata	DWARF CRESTED IRIS
Iris douglasiana	DOUGLAS' IRIS ❖
Iris ensata	JAPANESE WATER IRIS
Iris henryi	CHINESE WOODLAND IRIS

Iris PCH hybrids	PACIFIC COAST HYBRID IRISES
Iris reticulata and hybrids	NETTED IRIS
Iris xiphium	SPANISH IRIS
Iris tenax	OREGON IRIS, TOUGH-LEAVED IRIS ❖
Kerria japonica	JAPANESE KERRIA
Lapageria rosea	CHILEAN BELLFLOWER
Leucojum aestivum	SUMMER SNOWFLAKE
Leucojum vernum	SPRING SNOWFLAKE
Lindera obtusiloba	JAPANESE SPICEBUSH
Linnaea (Abelia) species and hybrids	ABELIA
Liriope muscari	BLUE LILYTURF
Magnolia 'Galaxy'	GALAXY MAGNOLIA
Magnolia 'Inspiration'	INSPIRATION MAGNOLIA
Magnolia x kewensis 'Wada's Memory'	WADA'S MEMORY MAGNOLIA
Magnolia kobus	KOBUSHI
Magnolia laevifolia (Michelia yunnanensis)	YUNNAN MAGNOLIA
Magnolia x loebneri 'Leonard Messel', 'Merrill'	LOBNER MAGNOLIA
Magnolia x soulangeana 'Rustica Rubra'	SAUCER MAGNOLIA
Magnolia stellata 'Centennial Blush', 'Chrysanthemumiflora', 'Jane Platt', 'Rosea'	STAR MAGNOLIA
Mahonia nervosa	CASCADE OREGON-GRAPE ❖
Malus fusca	PACIFIC CRABAPPLE ❖
Malus 'Golden Raindrops', 'Royal Raindrops'	RAINDROPS CRABAPPLE
Melliodendron xylocarpum	CHINESE PARASOL
Mukdenia rossii 'Karasuba'	RED-LEAVED MUKDENIA
Muscari armeniacum	GRAPE HYACINTH
Muscari latifolium	BROAD-LEAVED GRAPE HYACINTH
Narcissus (large flowers, best naturalizers:) 'King Alfred', 'Mrs. Langtry', 'Replete', 'Rosy Clouds', 'Tahiti', 'Mount Hood', 'Saint Keverne'	DAFFODILS
Narcissus (small flowers, best naturalizers:) 'February Gold', 'Jack Snipe', 'Tête-à-tête'	CYCLAMINEUS DAFFODILS
Narcissus x italicus 'Thalia'	ORCHID NARCISSUS
Narcissus jonquilla	JONQUIL
Narcissus poeticus var. *recurvus*	PHEASANT'S EYE
Olsynium (Sisyrinchium) douglasii	DOUGLAS' GRASSWIDOW ❖
Omphalodes cappadocica	CAPPADOCIAN NAVELWORT
Omphalodes verna	BLUE-EYED MARY
Osmanthus x burkwoodii	BURKWOOD'S OSMANTHUS
Osmanthus delavayi	DELAVAY'S OSMANTHUS
Osmanthus suavis	SWEET OLIVE
Paeonia cambessedesii	MAJORCAN PEONY
Paeonia daurica ssp. *mlokosewitschii*	MOLLY-THE-WITCH PEONY
Paeonia peregrina	BALKAN PEONY
Paeonia rockii	ROCK'S TREE PEONY
Parrotia persica	PERSIAN IRONWOOD
Phlox most trailing species	CREEPING PHLOX
Pieris formosa	CHINESE PIERIS
Pieris japonica	LILY-OF-THE-VALLEY SHRUB, ANDROMEDA
Primula kisoana	JAPANESE PRIMROSE

Prunus 'Gyoiko', 'Pink Perfection', 'Tai-Haku'	FLOWERING CHERRY
Prunus mume	JAPANESE APRICOT
Pseudocydonia sinensis	CHINESE QUINCE
Pseudomuscari (Muscari, Bellavalia) azureum	AZURE GRAPE HYACINTH
Pseudomuscari (Muscari, Bellavalia) forniculatum	FALSE GRAPE HYACINTH
Pulmonaria 'Benediction'	LUNGWORT
Rhododendron glaucophyllum	ROSY RHODODENDRON
Rhododendron (Azalea) Mollis/Ghent/Exbury hybrids	
Rhododendron most species and hybrids	RHODODENDRON

    (including and especially 'Baden', 'Capistrano', 'Dreamland', 'Edith Bosley',
    'Elsie Watson', 'Fred Peste', 'Girard's Crimson', 'Girard's Fuchsia', 'Glacier',
    'Hachmann's Charmant', 'Hardy Gardenia', 'Herbert', 'Hino-crimson', 'Hinode-giri',
    'Horizon Monarch', 'Janet Blair', 'Kalinka', 'Ken Janeck', 'Lemon Dream',
    'Manda Sue', 'Mardi Gras', 'Markeeta's Prize', 'Mrs. Furnivall', 'Nancy Evans',
    'Naselle', 'Noble Mountain', 'Odee Wright', 'Queen Alice', 'Skookum', 'Snowbird',
    'Taurus', 'The Hon. Jean Marie de Montague')

Ribes aureum	GOLDEN CURRANT ❖
Saruma henryi	UPRIGHT WILD GINGER
Scilla bifolia	ALPINE SQUILL
Scilla siberica	SIBERIAN SQUILL
Sedum ternatum	WHORLED STONECROP
Spiraea thunbergii	THUNBERG'S MEADOWSWEET
Stachys coccinea	SCARLET BETONY
Staphylea holocarpa (including 'Innocence', 'Rosea')	CHINESE BLADDERNUT
Syringa microphylla	LITTLELEAF LILAC
Syringa vulgaris	LILAC
Thalictrum (Anemonella) thalictroides	RUE-ANEMONE
Thermopsis chinensis 'Sophia'	CHINESE BUSH PEA
Trillium kurabayashii	GIANT PURPLE WAKEROBIN ❖
Tulipa orphanidea (including *T. whittallii*)	ANATOLIAN TULIP, COTTAGE TULIP
Tulipa sylvestris	WOODLAND TULIP
Tulipa urumiensis (*T. tarda*)	LATE TULIP, TARDY TULIP
Uvularia grandiflora	LARGE-FLOWERED BELLWORT
Veronica liwanensis	TURKISH SPEEDWELL
Viburnum carlesii	KOREAN SPICE VIBURNUM

DON'T FORGET:

"COLORFUL FOLIAGE"
"DRAMATIC/BOLD FOLIAGE"
"FINE-TEXTURED FOLIAGE"
"MULTI-SEASON ACCENT PLANTS"

LATE SPRING INTO EARLY SUMMER FLOWERS

Plants don't pay attention to the calendar. Some bloom later in the season we call spring and make their way easily into the season we call Summer in an uninterrupted procession.

Abutilon x hybridum 'Cascade Dawn'	CHINESE LANTERN, FLOWERING MAPLE
Allium acuminatum	TAPER-TIP ONION ❖
Allium amplectens	NARROWLEAF ONION ❖
Allium cristophii	STAR-OF-PERSIA
Allium roseum	ROSY GARLIC
Amelanchier alnifolia	WESTERN SERVICEBERRY, JUNEBERRY, SASKATOON ❖
Amsonia tabernaemontana	BLUESTAR
Anemone narcissiflora	NARCISSUS ANEMONE
Aquilegia hybrids	COLUMBINE
Arctostaphylos columbiana	HAIRY MANZANITA ❖
Astilbe species and hybrids	ASTILBE
Baptisia hybrids	FALSE INDIGO
Bloomeria (Triteleia) crocea	GOLDEN STARS ❖
Brodiaea californica	CALIFORNIA BRODIAEA
Brodiaea coronaria	HARVEST BRODIAEA ❖
Brodiaea elegans	ELEGANT CLUSTER-LILY ❖
Callianthe (Abutilon) megapotamica	BRAZILIAN BELLFLOWER
Calluna vulgaris 'Alex Warwick'	COMMON HEATHER, SCOTS HEATHER
Calycanthus occidentalis	WESTERN SPICEBUSH
Camassia leichtlinii (including 'Alba', 'Semi-plena')	GREAT CAMAS ❖
Camassia quamash	CAMAS, QUAMASH ❖
Campanula poscharskyana	SERBIAN BELLFLOWER
Clematis columbiana	ROCK CLEMATIS ❖
Clematis hirsutissima var. *hirsutissima*	HAIRY CLEMATIS ❖
Clematis montana	HIMALAYAN CLEMATIS
Daboecia x scotica 'Ben', 'Katherine's Choice', 'Silverwells'	
	WILLIAM BUCHANAN HEATH
Daphne x medfordensis 'Lawrence Crocker'	LAWRENCE CROCKER DAPHNE
Daphne x rollsdorfii 'Wilhelm Schacht'	WILHELM SCHACHT DAPHNE
Dasiphora (Potentilla) fruticosa	POTENTILLA, CINQUEFOIL
Dicentra formosa plus hybrids and cultivars	PACIFIC BLEEDING HEART ❖
Dichelostemma (Brodiaea) congestum	FIELD CLUSTER-LILY ❖
Dichroa (Hydrangea) versicolor	EVERGREEN HYDRANGEA
Digitalis species (not *D. purpurea*)	FOXGLOVE
Dodecatheon cusickii	DARK-THROAT SHOOTING STAR ❖
Epimedium davidii	DAVID'S BARRENWORT
Epipactis gigantea	STREAM ORCHID ❖
Eremurus himalaicus	HIMALAYAN FOXTAIL LILY
Eremurus hybrids	FOXTAIL LILY
Eremurus stenophyllus	DESERT CANDLE
Erica caffra	WATER HEATH, SWEET-SCENTED HEATH
Erica x stuartii 'Irish Lemon'	STUART'S HEATH
Erica spiculifolia 'Balkan Rose', "red form"	BALKAN HEATH
Eriophyllum lanatum	OREGON SUNSHINE, WOOLLY SUNFLOWER ❖

Fuchsia regia	BRINCO DE PRINCESA
Geranium cinereum 'Laurence Flatman'	LAWRENCE FLATMAN GERANIUM
Gladiolus communis var. *byzantinus*	BYZANTINE CORNFLAG
Gladiolus italicus	ITALIAN GLADIOLUS
Glandora (Lithodora) diffusa	PURPLE GROMWELL
Hebe 'Sky Blue'	SKY BLUE HEBE
Helianthemum nummularium and hybrids	SUN ROSE
Heloniopsis orientalis	ORIENTAL SWAMP-PINK
Hyacinthoides hispanica (NOT *H.* x *massartiana*)	SPANISH BLUEBELL
Hypericum cerastioides	TRAILING ST. JOHNS-WORT
Ipheion uniflorum	SPRING STARFLOWER
Lewisia cotyledon and hybrids	SISKIYOU LEWISIA
Lonicera ferdinandii (L. versicaria)	KOREAN HONEYSUCKLE
Mahonia repens	TRAILING OREGON-GRAPE ❖
Melittis melissophyllum	BASTARD BALM
Oncostema (Scilla) peruviana	PORTUGUESE SQUILL
Ourisia macrophylla	MOUNTAIN FOXGLOVE
Paeonia emodi	HIMALAYAN PEONY
Paeonia Intersectional hybrids	INTERSECTIONAL TREE PEONY
Paeonia lactiflora hybrids	PEONY
Paeonia obovata	GRASS PEONY
Parrotiopsis jacquemontiana	HIMALAYAN HAZEL
Philadelphus lewisii (including 'Goose Creek')	LEWIS' MOCK ORANGE ❖
Phyllodoce aleutica	MOUNTAIN-HEATH
Polygonatum odoratum var. *pluriflorum*	SCENTED SOLOMON'S SEAL
Primula denticulata	DRUMSTICK PRIMULA
Primula sieboldii	SIEBOLD'S PRIMROSE
Puschkinia scilloides	STRIPED SQUILL
Rhododendron hybrids ('Anah Kruschke', 'Azurro',	RHODODENDRON HYBRIDS
'Blue Boy', 'Blue Danube', 'Double Winner', 'Fantastica', 'Goldflimmer' 'Trail Blazer',	
'Very Berry', 'Vulcan's Flame', 'Vulcan')	
Rhododendron macrophyllum	PACIFIC RHODODENDRON
Rhododendron (Azalea) occidentale and "Occidental hybrids"	WESTERN AZALEA
("Koster" hybrids, "Albicans" hybrids)	
Ribes sanguineum	RED-FLOWERING CURRANT ❖
Scabiosa caucasica	PINCUSHION FLOWER
Styrax japonicus (including 'Pink Chimes', 'Snowcone')	JAPANESE SNOWBELL
Thalictrum species and hybrids	MEADOW-RUE
Trillium chloropetalum	GIANT WAKEROBIN ❖
Trillium grandiflorum	LARGE-FLOWERED TRILLIUM
Tulipa clusiana and forms	LADY TULIP
Tulipa clusiana var. *chrysantha*	GOLDEN LADY TULIP
Uvularia grandiflora	LARGE-FLOWERED BELLWORT
Veronica species and hybrids	SPEEDWELL
Viburnum plicatum f. *tomentosum* 'Mariesii'	DOUBLEFILE VIBURNUM
Viburnum trilobum (V. opulus var. *americanum)*	AMERICAN CRANBERRY BUSH ❖
Viola cornuta	VIOLA, HORNED VIOLET
Wyethia angustifolia	NARROW-LEAF MULE'S EARS ❖
Xerophyllum tenax	BEAR GRASS, INDIAN BASKET GRASS ❖

SUMMER FLOWERS

This is the time when we become more casually interactive with our gardens. That is, we begin to relax and actually enjoy our gardens. For most PNW gardeners, this is the "peak" of the bloom season (hence why this list is the longest).

Acanthus caroli-alexandri, A. hungaricus, A. mollis, A. spinosus	BEAR'S-BREECH
Acanthus 'Holland Days'	HOLLAND DAYS BEAR'S-BREECH
Achillea 'Moonshine'	MOONSHINE YARROW
Aconitum lycoctonum	WOLFSBANE
Aconitum napellus	MONKSHOOD
Adina rubella	CHINESE BUTTONBUSH
Agastache species and hybrids	GIANT HYSSOP, HUMMINGBIRD MINT
Allium atropurpureum	MAROON ALLIUM
Allium 'Gladiator'	GLADIATOR ONION
Allium schubertii	TUMBLEWEED ONION
Allium 'Silver Spring'	SILVER SPRING ONION
Allium (?lusitanicum hybrid*)* 'Summer Beauty'	SUMMER BEAUTY MOUNTAIN GARLIC
Aquilegia formosa	WESTERN COLUMBINE
Arisaema candidissimum	PINK-FLOWERED WHITE STRIPE JACK-IN-THE-PULPIT
Aruncus dioicus	GOAT'S-BEARD ❖
Asarina procumbens	CREEPING SNAPDRAGON
Aster tongolensis	EAST INDIES ASTER
Baptisia australis	BLUE FALSE INDIGO
Betonica (Stachys) macrantha 'Robusta'	BIG BETONY
Betonica (Stachys) officinalis	WOOD BETONY
Callicarpa bodinieri	BODINIER'S BEAUTYBERRY
Callicarpa dichotoma	BEAUTYBERRY
Calluna vulgaris	COMMON HEATHER, SCOTS HEATHER

from earliest within this season to latest within this season, by group:
-- *Calluna vulgaris* 'Aberdeen', 'Alba Jae', 'Alba Rigida', 'Anneke', 'Arina', 'Barbara Fleur',
'Bernadette', 'Boreray', 'Braeriach', 'Corbett's White', 'Fraser's Old Gold',
'Green Cardinal', 'Insriach Bronze', 'Oiseval', 'Orange Max', 'Rock Spray', 'Soay'
-- *Calluna vulgaris* 'Alba Minor', 'Alportii Praecox', 'Arran Gold', 'Branchy Anne',
'Bray Head', 'Carmina', 'Fire King', 'Hoyerhagen', 'Janice Chapman', 'Loch Turret',
'Martha Hermann', 'Pat's Gold', 'Radnor', 'Ross Hutton', 'Silver Knight', 'Silver Queen',
'Sir John Charrington', 'Spider', 'Tenuis', 'Tino', 'Waquoit Red', 'White Mite'

Calochortus elegans var. *elegans*	ELEGANT MARIPOSA-LILY
Campanula latiloba	GREAT BELLFLOWER
Campanula 'Sarastro'	SARASTRO BELLFLOWER
Campsis x *tagliabuana* 'Indian Summer', 'Madame Galen'	TRUMPET VINE
Cautleya spicata	CHINESE BUTTERFLY GINGER
Ceanothus x *delileanus* 'Topaze'	HARDY HYBRID CEANOTHUS
Cephalaria gigantea	GIANT YELLOW SCABIOUS
Ceratostigma willmottianum	CHINESE PLUMBAGO
X *Chitalpa tashkentensis*	CHITALPA
Clematis 'Betty Corning'	BETTY CORNING CLEMATIS
Clematis large-flowered hybrids	CLEMATIS
Clematis viticella and hybrids	ITALIAN CLEMATIS

Clethra barbinervis	JAPANESE CLETHRA
Codonopsis ovata	KASHMIR BELLFLOWER
Codonopsis pilosula	POOR-MAN'S GINSENG
Coreopsis species and hybrids	TICKSEED
Corydalis scouleri	SCOULER'S FUMEWORT ❖
Crocosmia x *crocosmiiflora* cultivars and other hybrids	MONTBRETIA
Cypella herbertii	HERBERT'S GOBLET FLOWER
Daboecia cantabrica 'Alberta White', 'Amelie', 'Vanessa'	IRISH HEATH
Daphne x napolitana	ITALIAN DAPHNE
Deinanthe caerulea x *bifida*	HYBRID FALSE HYDRANGEA
Dichelostemma ida-maia (including 'Pink Diamond')	FIRECRACKER FLOWER
Dichroa (Hydrangea) febrifuga	BLUE EVERGREEN HYDRANGEA
Dierama dracomontanum	DRAKENBERG WANDFLOWER
Digitalis ferruginea	RUSTY FOXGLOVE
Digitalis grandiflora	YELLOW FOXGLOVE
Disporum longistylum (D. cantoniense) 'Night Heron'	SOLOMON'S SEAL
Enkianthus campanulatus	RED-VEIN ENKIANTHUS
Erica ciliaris 'White Wings'	DORSET HEATH
Erica cinerea	GRAY HEATH, BELL HEATH

from earliest within this season to latest within this season, by group:
-- *Erica cinerea* 'Coccinea', 'Golden Drop', 'Green Drop', 'Gurnsey Plum',
  'Harry Fulcher', 'Pygmaea', 'Violacea'
-- *Erica cinerea* 'Atrosanguinea', 'C.D. Eason', 'Golden Sport', 'Knap Hill Pink',
  'Lorna Ann Hutton', 'P.S. Patrick', 'Rosea', 'Stephen Davis', 'Velvet Night', 'West End'
-- *Erica cinerea* 'Bucklebury Red', 'Colligan Bridge', 'Fiddler's Gold', 'Grandiflora',
  'Heidebrand', 'Providence', 'Rock Pool', 'Schizopetala'
-- *Erica cinerea* 'Baylay's Variety', 'Celebration', 'Kerry Cherry', 'Mrs. Ford', 'Neptune',
  'Vivienne Patricia', 'Windlebook'
-- *Erica cinerea* 'Constrast', 'Iberian Beauty'

Erica curvifolia	WATER HEATH
Erica mackayana 'Donegal', 'Galicia', 'Shining Light'	MACKAY'S HEATH
Erica manipuliflora 'Don Richards'	AUTUMN HEATH
Erica x stuartii 'Irish Orange'	STUART'S HEATH

Erica tetralix 'Daphne Underwood', 'George Fraser', 'Gratis', 'Helma', 'Mollis',
  'Pink Glow', 'Riko', 'Rosea', 'Rubra', 'Swedish Yellow'

BOG HEATHER, CROSS-LEAF HEATHER

Erica vagans 'Carnea', 'Miss Waterer', 'Mrs. Donaldson', 'Pyrenees Pink'

CORNISH HEATH, WANDERING HEATH

Erica x williamsii 'Phantom', 'Gold Button'	WILLIAMS' HEATH
Eriogonum umbellatum	SULPHUR BUCKWHEAT ❖
Eryngium alpinum, E. amethystinum, E. bourgatii	ERYNGO
Erythranthe (Mimulus) lewisii	PINK MONKEY FLOWER
Eucryphia glutinosa 'Flore Pleno'	DOUBLE-FLOWERED BRUSH BUSH
Filipendula 'Kahome'	DWARF MEADOWSWEET
Filipendula kamtschatica	GIANT MEADOWSWEET
Fritillaria camschatcensis	CHOCOLATE LILY
Fuchsia bracelinae	BRACIE'S FUCHSIA
Fuchsia 'Genii'	HARDY FUCHSIA
Fuchsia hatschbachii	HATSCHBACH'S FUCHSIA

Fuchsia 'Hawkshead'	HAWKSHEAD FUCHSIA
Gaultheria (X *Gaulnettya*) *wisleyensis*	GAULNETTYA
Geranium x cantabrigiense	HYBRID GERANIUM
Geranium endressii 'Wargrave Pink'	WARGRAVE PINK GERANIUM
Geranium 'Johnson's Blue'	JOHNSON'S BLUE GERANIUM
Geranium renardii	RENARD GERANIUM
Geranium x riversleaianum	HYBRID GERANIUM
Geranium wlassovianum	LATE GERANIUM
Geum hybrids	GEUM
Gladiolus dalenii var. *primulinus*	CAROLINA PRIMROSE
Gladiolus saundersii	LESOTHO LILY
Glaucidium palmatum	JAPANESE WOOD POPPY
Gunnera tinctoria	CHILEAN GIANT RHUBARB
Hebe 'Blue Mist', 'Patty's Purple', 'Paula', 'Sapphire', 'Walter Buccleugh', 'Youngii'	HYBRID HEBES
Hebe odora	BOXWOOD HEBE
Hebe topiaria	TOPIARIST'S HEBE
Hemerocallis species and hybrids	DAYLILIES
Heuchera micrantha	CREVICE ALUMROOT
Hoheria lyallii	MOUNTAIN LACEBARK
Holodiscus discolor	OCEANSPRAY ❖
Hosta fortunei	PLANTAIN LILY
Hydrangea (*Schizophragma*) *hydrangeoides*	JAPANESE HYDRANGEA VINE
Hydrangea anomala	CLIMBING HYDRANGEA
Hydrangea arborescens	SMOOTH HYDRANGEA, WILD HYDRANGEA
Hydrangea chinensis (including var. *lobbii*)	CHINESE HYDRANGEA
Hydrangea integrifolia	EVERGREEN CLIMBING HYDRANGEA
Hydrangea macrophylla and its many cultivars	
	BIGLEAF HYDRANGEA, FRENCH HYDRANGEA
Hydrangea petiolaris (*H. anomala petiolaris*)	CLIMBING HYDRANGEA
Hydrangea quercifolia	OAKLEAF HYDRANGEA
Hydrangea seemannii	EVERGREEN CLIMBING HYDRANGEA
Hylotelephium (*Sedum*) 'Vera Jameson'	VERA JAMESON SEDUM
Impatiens arguta, I. namchabarwensis, I. stenantha	HARDY IMPATIENS
Incarvillea delavayi	HARDY GLOXINIA
Iris ensata "Kaempferi"	JAPANESE IRIS
Iris latifolia	ENGLISH IRIS
Iris Spuria hybrids	SPURIA IRIS
Itea 'Henry's Garnet', 'Little Henry'	DWARF SWEETSPIRE
Itea virginica	VIRGINIA SWEETSPIRE
Jasminum x stephanense	STEPHAN JASMINE
Kalmia latifolia	MOUNTAIN LAUREL
Kirengeshoma palmata Koreana Group *(K. koreana)*	KOREAN WAXBELLS
Lamprocapnos (*Dicentra*) *spectabilis*	OLD-FASHIONED BLEEDING HEART
Leontodon (*Microseris*) *rigens*	HAWKBITS
Leucothoe fontanesiana 'Zeblid'	DROOPING LAUREL
Liatris ligulistylis	MEADOW BLAZING STAR
Ligularia 'Britt-Marie Crawford'	BRITT-MARIE CRAWFORD LEOPARD PLANT
Ligularia stenocephala 'The Rocket'	THE ROCKET

Lilium henryi	HENRY'S LILY
Lilium martagon and hybrids	TURK'S CAP LILY
Lilium Oriental hybrids	ORIENTAL LILIES
Lilium regale	REGAL LILY
Lilium sargentiae	SARGENT'S LILY
Lilium taliense	YUNNAN TURK'S CAP LILY
Lilium x testaceum	NANKEEN LILY
Lilium washingtonianum	MT. HOOD LILY, SHASTA LILY ❖
Linnaea borealis	TWINFLOWER ❖
Lonicera acuminata (L. henryi)	HENRY'S HONEYSUCKLE
Lonicera ciliosa	WESTERN TRUMPET HONEYSUCKLE ❖
Lonicera crassifolia	CREEPING HONEYSUCKLE
Lycoris sprengeri	ELECTRIC BLUE SPIDER LILY
Magnolia sieboldii	OYAMA MAGNOLIA
Moraea spathulata	YELLOW BUTTERFLY LILY
Nepeta species and hybrids	CATMINT
Nomocharis pardanthina	NOMOCHARIS
Notholirion bulbiferum, N. campanulatum, N. macrophyllum, N. thomsonianum	
	HIMALAYAN LILIES
Olearia x *oleifolia* 'Waikariensis'	DAISY-ON-A-STICK
Ornithogalum (Galtonia) candicans	SUMMER HYACINTH
Ornithogalum narbonense	NARBONNE STAR-OF-BETHLEHEM
Oxalis purpurea	PURPLE WOOD-SORREL
Oxalis triangularis	PURPLE FALSE SHAMROCK
Oxydendrum arboreum	SOURWOOD
Papaver (Meconopsis) cambrica	WELSH POPPY
Papaver Oriental hybrids	ORIENTAL POPPY
Penstemon davidsonii	DAVIDSON'S PENSTEMON ❖
Penstemon serrulatus	CASCADE PENSTEMON, COAST PENSTEMON ❖
Petrosedum (Sedum) rupestre	BLUE SEDUM
Phalocallis (Cypella) coelestis	GOBLET FLOWER
Phedimus (Sedum) kamtschaticus	KAMSCHATKA STONECROP
Phedimus (Sedum) spurius	CAUCASIAN STONECROP
Philadelphus lewisii	PACIFIC MOCK ORANGE ❖
Phlox diffusa	SPREADING PHLOX ❖
Phygelius capensis and hybrids	CAPE FUCHSIA
Pileostegia viburnoides	CLIMBING HYDRANGEA
Primula beesiana, P. bulleyana, P. poissonii, P. pulverulenta	CANDELABRA PRIMROSE
Prostanthera cuneata	ALPINE MINT BUSH
Psephellus (Centaurea) simplicicaulis	LILAC CORNFLOWER
Rhodiola pachyclados	AFGHAN SEDUM
Rhododendron albiflorum	WHITE-FLOWERED RHODODENDRON
Rhododendron (Azalea) arborescens	SWEET AZALEA, TREE AZALEA
Rhododendron auriculatum	RHODODENDRON
Rhododendron (Azalea) bakeri	CUMBERLAND AZALEA
Rhododendron degronianum ssp. *yakushimanum* hybrids (the "Yaks")	
	YAK RHODODENDRON
Rhododendron decorum ssp. *diaprepes*	GREAT WHITE RHODODENDRON
Rhododendron discolor	RHODODENDRON

Rhododendron facetum	RHODODENDRON
Rhododendron fauriei (*R. brachycarpum*)	FAURIEI RHODODENDRON
Rhododendron ferrugineum	RUSTY-LEAF ALPENROSE
Rhododendron hemsleyanum	HEMSLEY'S RHODODENDRON
Rhododendron hirsutum	HAIRY RHODODENDRON
Rhododendron hybrids ('Aladdin', 'Azonea', 'Europa', 'Good News', 'Independence Day', 'Midsummer', 'Pearce's American Beauty', 'Polar Bear', 'Romany Chal')	HYBRID RHODODENDRONS
Rhododendron maximum	ROSEBAY RHODODENDRON
Rhododendron serotinum	RHODODENDRON
Rhododendron (Azalea) viscosum	SWEET AZALEA
Rhododendron (Azalea) viscosum ssp. *serrulatum*	HAMMOCKSWEET AZALEA
Rhododendron wardii	WARD'S RHODODENDRON
Rodgersia aesculifolia, R. pinnata, R. podophylla	RODGERSIA
Rosa gallica	GALLIC ROSE
Rosa hybrids	ROSE
Rosa mulliganii	MULLIGAN ROSE, RAMBLING ROSE
Roscoea alpina, R. "Family Jewels" hybrids, *R. humeana, R. praecox, R. purpurea* "Gigantea", *R. purpurea* f. *rubra* ('Red Gurkha')	MOUNTAIN ROSCOE-LILY
Salvia hians, S. nemorosa, S. verticillata	PERENNIAL SAGE
Saxifraga stolonifera	STRAWBERRY SAXIFRAGE
Sedum divergens, S. sexangulare, S. stenopetalum, S. tetractinum	SEDUM
Sidalcea oregana	OREGON CHECKERBLOOM ❖
Spiraea splendens (*S. densiflora*)	ROSE MEADOWSWEET
Stewartia monadelpha (including 'Black Dog')	TALL STEWARTIA
Stewartia pseudocamellia	JAPANESE STEWARTIA
Stewartia 'Scarlet Sentinel'	SCARLET SENTINEL STEWARTIA
Thalictrum delavayi 'Hewitt's Double'	CHINESE MEADOWRUE
Titanotrichum oldhamii	CHINESE FOXGLOVE
Triteleia laxa 'Queen Fabiola'	ITHURIEL'S SPEAR
Tropaeolum polyphyllum	WREATH NASTURTIUM
Tropaeolum tricolor	PERENNIAL NASTURTIUM VINE
Veronica (Parahebe) perfoliata	DIGGER'S SPEEDWELL
Viburnum trilobum (*V. opulus* var. *americanum*)	AMERICAN CRANBERRY BUSH ❖
Vitex agnus-castus	CHASTE TREE
Weigela florida	WEIGELA
Yucca filamentosa, flaccida, gloriosa, rostrata	YUCCAS

LATE SUMMER INTO FALL FLOWERS

Many of the Summer bloomers (a few noted in this list, too) will continue a bit into Fall. This is a more comprehensive list. The gardener must make sure that the flowering show doesn't simply dwindle away at this time.

Acanthus 'Morning Candle'	MORNING CANDLE ACANTHUS
Achillea ptarmica 'Peter Cottontail'	DOUBLE-FLOWERED SNEEZEWORT
Acis (Leucojum) autumnalis	AUTUMN SNOWFLAKE
Agastache species and hybrids	GIANT HYSSOP, HUMMINGBIRD MINT
Allium wallichii	WALLICH'S ONION
X *Amarine tubergenii*	VAN TUBERGEN'S AMARINE LILY
X *Amarygia parkeri*	HYBRID NAKED LADIES
Amaryllis belladonna	NAKED LADY
Anemonopsis macrophylla	FALSE ANEMONE
Aster x frikartii	ITALIAN ASTER
Astrantia major	GREAT MASTERWORT
Begonia chitoensis	HARDY TAIWAN BEGONIA
Begonia grandis ssp. *evansiana*	HARDY BEGONIA
Berberidopsis corallina	CORAL PLANT
Boltonia asteroides	STAR ASTER
Calluna vulgaris	COMMON HEATHER, SCOTS HEATHER

(most cultivars fit here; eliminate those listed within other seasons)
Some examples, from earliest within this season to latest within this season, by group:
-- *Calluna vulgaris* 'Alissa Diane', 'Allegretto', 'Allegro', 'Amanda Wain', 'Barnett Anley'
-- *Calluna vulgaris* 'Red Pimpernel', 'Underwoodii'
-- *Calluna vulgaris* 'Alba Aurea', 'Alba Elata', 'Alba Plena', 'Amy', 'C.W. Nix',
  'Carole Chapman', 'Catherine Anne', 'Corbett's Red', 'Cuprea', 'Dainty Bess',
  'Dark Star', 'Darkness', 'Darleyensis', 'David Platt', 'E. Hoare', 'Ellie Barbour',
  'Else Frye', 'Elsie Purnell', 'Flore Pleno', 'Fortyniner Gold', 'Fred J. Chapple',
  'Galaxy', 'Golden Angie', 'Golden Feather', 'Goldsworth Crimson',
  'Hammondii Rubifolia', 'Heidesinfonie', 'Hiemalis', 'Isobel Hughes',
  'Long White', 'Lyndon Proudley', 'Molecule', 'Mousehole', 'My Dream',
  'Oxshott Common', 'Penhale', 'Peter Sparkes', 'Pyramidalis', 'Ralph Purnell', 'Red Rug',
  'Robert Chapman', 'Roma', 'Rotfuchs', 'Ruby Slinger', 'Sister Anne', 'Skipper',
  'Spitfire', 'Spring Torch', 'Sunrise', 'Sunset', 'Wickwar Flame'
-- *Calluna vulgaris* 'Agnes', 'Anette', 'Anouk', 'Charmglo', 'Ginkle's Glorie',
  'Highland Rose', 'Jeanette', 'Jette', 'Leonie', 'Lianne', 'Melanie', 'Merlyn', 'Michelle',
  'Miranda', 'Pink Alicia', 'Renate', 'Sabine', 'Salena', 'Sandy', 'Schurig' s Sensation',
  'Selly', 'Svenja', 'Theresa', 'Veluwe', 'Veronique', 'Wynanda'

Campanula takesimana	KOREAN BELLFLOWER
Campanula lactiflora	MILKY BELLFLOWER
Caryopteris divaricata	BUTTERFLY BLUEBEARD
Caryopteris incana	BLUEBEARD
Ceratostigma plumbaginoides	CHINESE PLUMBAGO
Chrysanthemum x rubellum	HARDY CHRYSANTHEMUM
Chrysanthemum zawadskii	MANCHURIAN CHRYSANTHEMUM
Chelonopsis yagiharana (C. moschata)	JAPANESE TURTLEHEAD

Clematis x durandii	DURAND'S CLEMATIS
Clematis 'Etoile Violette'	VIOLET STAR CLEMATIS
Clematis repens	TWINKLE BELL CLEMATIS
Clematis tangutica, C. texensis, and their hybrids	CLEMATIS
Clerodendrum trichotomum	HARLEQUIN GLORYBOWER
Clethra alnifolia	SUMMERSWEET
Clethra barbinervis	JAPANESE CLETHRA
Colchicum hybrids (such as 'Giant', 'Lilac Wonder', 'Violet Queen', 'Waterlily')	
	AUTUMN CROCUS
Colchicum speciosum	GIANT MEADOW SAFFRON
Crinodendron patagua	LILY-OF-THE-VALLEY TREE

Daboecia cantabrica 'Alba', 'Arielle', 'Atropurpurea', 'Blueless',   IRISH HEATH
  'Cinderella', 'Creeping White', 'David Moss', 'Hookstone Purple', 'Polifolia',
  'Praegerae', 'Rubra', 'Silversmith', 'Waley's Red', 'White Blum'

Daboecia x *scotica* 'Bearsden', 'Ellen Norris',   WILLIAM BUCHANAN HEATH
  'Seattle Purple', 'Tabramhill', 'William Buchanan'

Erica chamissonis	GRAHAMSTOWN HEATH

Erica ciliaris 'Aurea', 'Corfe Castle' 'David McClintock', 'Globosa',   DORSET HEATH
  'Mawiana', 'Mrs. C. H. Gill', 'Stoborough', 'Wych'

Erica cinerea   GRAY HEATH, BELL HEATH
  from earliest within this season to latest within this season, by group:
  -- *Erica cinerea* 'Alba', 'Alba Minor', 'Ashdown Forest', 'Atropurpurea', 'Atrorubens',
    'C.G. Best', 'Caldy Island', 'Carnea', 'Frances', 'G. Osmond', 'Glencairn', 'Katinka',
    'Lime Soda', 'Pentreath', 'Purple Beauty', 'Rosabella', 'Rose Queen', 'Rozanne Waterer',
    'Ruby', 'Ruby Chalice', 'Sherry', 'Splendens'
  -- *Erica cinerea* 'Appleblossom', 'Cindy', 'Hardwick's Rose', 'Plummer's Seedling
  -- *Erica cinerea* 'Cevennes', 'Champs Hill', 'Dunkelroter Kobald', 'Eden Valley',
    'Golden Hue', 'Goldilocks'
  -- *Erica cinerea* 'Constance', 'Foxhollow Mahogany', 'Hookstone Lavender', 'Lilacina',
    'Miss Waters', 'Pink Ice'

Erica x *garforthensis* 'Tracy Wilson'	GARFORTH HEATH
Erica x *gaudificans* (*E. spiculifola* x *bergiana*?) 'Edewecht Blush'	EDEWECHT HEATH

Erica x *griffithsii* 'Ashlea Gold', 'Heaven Scent', 'Jacqueline', 'Valerie Griffiths'
                                       GRIFFITH'S HEATH

Erica x *krameri* 'Otto', 'Rudi'	KRAMER'S HEATH
Erica mackayana 'Dr. Ronald Gray', 'Plena'	MACKAY'S HEATH
Erica terminalis 'Thelma Woolner'	CORSICAN HEATH, UPRIGHT HEATH

Erica tetralix 'Alba', 'Con Underwood', 'Dänemark', 'Foxhome', 'Hookstone Pink',
  'L.E. Underwood', 'Melbury White', 'Pink Star', 'Ruth's Gold', 'Tina'
                 BOG HEATHER, CROSS-LEAF HEATHER

Erica vagans   CORNISH HEATH, WANDERING HEATH
  from earliest within this season to latest within this season, by group:
  -- *Erica vagans* 'Mrs. D.F. Maxwell'
  -- *Erica vagans* 'Ida M. Britten'
  -- *Erica vagans* 'Alba', 'Diana Hornibrook', 'Fiddlestone', 'French White',
    'George Underwood', 'Golden Triumph', 'Highway One', 'Holden Pink', 'J.C. Fletcher',
    'Keira', 'Kevernensis Alba', 'Leucantha', 'Lyonesse', 'Nana', 'Yellow John'
  -- *Erica vagans* 'Birch Glow', 'Cornish Cream', 'St Keverne'

Erica verticillata	WHORL HEATH, SOUTH AFRICAN HEATH

157

Erica x watsonii 'Cherry Turpin', 'Claire Elise', 'Dawn', 'Mary', 'Pearly Pink'
WATSON'S HEATH

Erica x williamsii 'Cow-y-Jack', 'David Coombe', 'Gwavas',   WILLIAMS' HEATH
  'Ken Wilson', 'Lizard Downs', 'P.D. Williams'

Eriogonum latifolium	SEASIDE BUCKWHEAT
Eryngium agavifolium	AGAVE-LEAF SEA HOLLY
Elsholtzia stauntonii	CHINESE MINT SHRUB
Eucomis autumnalis	PINEAPPLE LILY
Eucryphia glutinosa	NIRRHE, BRUSH BUSH
Eutrochium (Eupatorium) dubium 'Little Joe'	DWARF JOE PYE WEED
Eutrochium (Eupatorium) maculatum	PURPLE JOE PYE WEED ❖
Fuchsia fulgens	BRILLIANT FUCHSIA
Fuchsia hatschbachii	HATSCHBACH'S FUCHSIA
Fuchsia 'Lord Byron', 'Mrs. Popple', 'Riccartonii'	HARDY FUCHSIAS
Gentiana asclepiadea	WILLOW GENTIAN
Gladiolus (tubergenii) 'Charm'	CHARM GLADIOLUS
Helenium autumnale and hybrids	SNEEZEWEED
Helianthus 'Lemon Queen'	LEMON QUEEN PERENNIAL SUNFLOWER
Heliopsis helianthoides	FALSE SUNFLOWER
Heptacodium miconioides	SEVEN SONS FLOWER
Hesperantha (Schizostylis) coccinea	CRIMSON FLAG
Hibiscus moscheutos hybrids	ROSE MALLOW
Hibiscus syriacus	ROSE OF SHARON
Hydrangea paniculata	PANICLED HYDRANGEA
Hydrangea serrata	TEA OF HEAVEN, MOUNTAIN HYDRANGEA
Hylotelephium (Sedum) cauticola 'Lidakense'	LIDAKENSE CLIFF STONECROP
Hylotelephium (Sedum) ewersii	PINK MONGOLIAN STONECROP
Hylotelephium (Sedum) sieboldii	OCTOBER DAPHNE

Hylotelephium (Sedum) spectabile
SHOWY STONECROP, AUTUMN SEDUM, BORDER SEDUM

Impatiens flanaganae, I. puberula, I. tinctoria	HARDY IMPATIENS
Isodon (Plectranthus, Rabdosia) longitubus	TRUMPET SPURFLOWER.
Itea ilicifolia	HOLLY-LEAF SWEETSPIRE
Lagerstroemia 'Arapaho', 'Natchez'	CREPE MYRTLE
Lavatera cachmeriana	KASHMIR TREE MALLOW
Leucanthemum x superbum 'Becky'	SHASTA DAISY
Ligularia fischeri	GOMCHWI
Lilium rosthornii	ROSTHORN'S LILY
Lilium wallichianum	HIMALAYAN LILY
Linnaea (Abelia) x grandiflora	ABELIA
Lobelia tupa	TUPA, TABACO DEL DIABLO
Nerine bowdenii and hybrids	JERSEY LILY
Nipponanthemum (Chrysanthemum) nipponicum	NIPPON DAISY
Oxalis versicolor	CANDY CANE SORREL
Pancratium maritimum	SEA LILY
Passiflora x belotii *(P.* x alato-caerulea*)*	PASSION FLOWER
Penstemon serrulatus	CASCADE PENSTEMON
Persicaria amplexicaulis	BISTORT, MOUNTAIN FLEECE
Platycodon grandiflorus (with deadheading)	BALLOON FLOWER

Poliothyrsis sinensis	CHINESE PEARLBLOOM
Prospero (Scilla) autumnale	AUTUMN SQUILL
Roscoea auriculata	EARED ROSCOEA
Rostrinucula dependens	WEEPING ROSTRINICULA
Rudbeckia laciniata	CUT-LEAF CONEFLOWER
Rudbeckia nitida 'Autumn Sun'	AUTUMN SUN BLACK-EYED SUSAN
Rudbeckia fulgida var. *sullivantii* 'Goldsturm'	GOLDSTURM BLACK-EYED SUSAN
Salvia azurea var. *grandiflora*	PITCHER SAGE
Salvia x *sylvestris*	WOOD SAGE
Salvia yangii (Perovskia) including other species and hybrids	RUSSIAN SAGE
Sanguisorba hakusanensis	KOREAN MOUNTAIN BURNET, LILAC SQUIRREL
Solanum crispum 'Glasnevin'	CHILEAN POTATO BUSH/VINE
Solidago rugosa 'Fireworks'	ROUGH GOLDENROD
Symphyotrichum 'Little Carlow'	LITTLE CARLOW ASTER
Syringa microphylla	LITTLE-LEAF LILAC
Tanacetum ptarmiciflorum	SILVER LACE BUSH
Teucrium hircanicum	IRANIAN GERMANDER
Tricyrtis flava	DWARF GOLDEN TOAD-LILY
Tricyrtis formosana	TAIWAN TOAD-LILY
Tricyrtis hirta	JAPANESE TOAD-LILY
Tricyrtus hybrids (many)	HYBRID TOAD-LILIES
Tricyrtis lasiocarpa	AMETHYST TOAD LILY
Tricyrtis latifolia	EAST ASIAN TOAD-LILY
Tricyrtis macranthopsis	KII PENINSULA TOAD-LILY
Tricyrtis ohsumiensis	DWARF YELLOW TOAD-LILY
Tropaeolum speciosum, T. tuberosum 'Ken Aslet'	PERENNIAL NASTURTIUM VINE
Vernonia gigantea	GIANT IRONWEED
Veronicastrum sibericum	JAPANESE CULVER'S ROOT
Yucca x *schottii*	SCHOTT'S YUCCA
Yucca recurvifolia	CURVE-LEAF YUCCA
Zantedeschia aethiopica	CALLA-LILY

TENDER BULBS

All the preceding plants are perennial, in that they don't need to be dug up and stored for the winter time. But don't forget about the seasonal plants such as these tender summer bulbs; most will take their flowering into fall.

Agave amica (Polianthes tuberosa) (f)	TUBEROSE
Begonia tuberous hybrids	BEGONIA
Canna hybrids	CANNA-LILY
Dahlia hybrids	DAHLIA
Eucomis species and hybrids	PINEAPPLE-LILY
Gladiolus hybrids	GLADIOLUS
Gladiolus murielae (Acidanthera)	PEACOCK IRIS
Tigridia pavonia	MEXICAN SHELL FLOWER
Zantedeschia hybrids	CALLA-LILIES

FALL FLOWERS

This is the perfect time for a punch of bloom to remind us that we live in the PNW where gardening is a 365-days-a-year event.

Aconitum carmichaelii	CHINESE MONKSHOOD
Ageratina altissima 'Chocolate'	CHOCOLATE SNAKEROOT
Arbutus unedo cultivars	STRAWBERRY TREE
Aster ageratoides 'Ezo Murasaki'	ASIAN ASTER
Begonia grandis	HARDY BEGONIA
Calluna vulgaris	COMMON HEATHER, SCOTS HEATHER

from earliest within this season to latest within this season, by group:
-- *Calluna vulgaris* 'Alice Knight', 'Alison Yates', 'Annabel', 'Annemarie', 'Applecross',
'Beoley Crimson', 'Beoley Silver', 'Blueness', 'Golden Carpet', 'Grijsje', 'Guinea Gold',
'Hollandia', 'Indian Summer', 'John F. Letts', 'Late Crimson Gold', 'Lime Glade',
'Sally Anne Proudley', 'Serlei Aurea', 'Waquoit Edna', 'Westphalia', 'White Star'
-- *Calluna vulgaris* 'Christin', 'Hibernica', 'Jimmy Dyce', 'Mrs. Pat', 'Perestrojka',
'Roodkapje', 'Roter Oktober', 'Serlei Grandiflora', 'Spook', 'Susanne'
-- *Calluna vulgaris* 'Athene', 'Bonita', 'Bronze Beauty', 'E. F. Brown', 'Helena', 'Hilda',
'Rosita', 'Sylvana', 'Tessa'

Camellia sasanqua most cultivars	SASANQUA CAMELLIA
Caryopteris hybrids	BLUEBEARD
Chrysanthemum x *morifolium*	MUMS
Clematis paniculatum	SWEET AUTUMN CLEMATIS
Colchicum x *agrippinum*	HYBRID AUTUMN CROCUS
Colchicum autumnale	AUTUMN CROCUS
Colchicum byzantinum	BYZANTINE MEADOW SAFFRON
Colchicum variegatum	SÜRINCAN
Crocus goulimyi	FALL CROCUS
Crocus laevigatus	MEADOW SAFFRON
Crocus longiflorus	LONG-FLOWERED SAFFRON
Crocus pulchellus	AUTUMN CROCUS
Cyclamen graecum	GREEK CYCLAMEN
Cyclamen hederifolium	PERSIAN VIOLET
Erica ciliaris 'Ram'	DORSET HEATH
Erica mammosa	NINE-PIN HEATH
Erica manipuliflora 'Korçula'	AUTUMN HEATH
Erica vagans 'Valerie Proudley'	CORNISH HEATH, WANDERING HEATH
Farfugium japonicum	LEOPARD PLANT
Galanthus nivalis ssp. *reginae-olgae*	QUEEN OLGA'S SNOWDROP
Hamamelis virginiana	AMERICAN WITCH-HAZEL
Heptacodium miconioides	SEVEN SON FLOWER
Hesperantha (Schizostylis) coccinea	CRIMSON FLAG
Hibiscus moscheutos and hybrids	ROSE MALLOW
Hylotelephium (Sedum) "Autumn Hybrids"	AUTUMN SEDUM
Iberis sempervirens 'Autumn Beauty'	AUTUMN BEAUTY CANDYTUFT
Impatiens omeiana	HARDY IMPATIENS
Isodon (Plectranthus, Rabdosia) longitubus	TRUMPET SPURFLOWER
Isodon umbrosus	ISODON

Lagerstroemia indica 'Dynamite', 'Red Rocket'	CREPE MYRTLE
Leucosceptrum stellipilum	JAPANESE SHRUB MINT
Leucanthemella serotinum	GIANT SHASTA DAISY
Lilium rosthornii	ROSTHORN'S LILY
Linnaea (Abelia) x grandiflora	ABELIA
Lycoris aurea	GOLDEN SPIDER-LILY
Lycoris radiata	RED SPIDER-LILY
Nerine sarniensis and hybrids	GUERNSEY-LILY
Oxalis fabaefolia	RABBIT'S EARS
Persicaria amplexicaulis	BISTORT, MOUNTAIN FLEECE
Rhododendron fastigiatum	DWARF RHODODENDRON
Rhododendron impeditum	DWARF PURPLE RHODODENDRON
Rhododendron (Azalea) prunifolium	PLUM-LEAF AZALEA
Rhododendron hybrids ('Bob's Blue', 'Bluebird', 'Camubia', 'Elizabeth', 'Ernie Dee', 'Yellowhammer')	HYBRID RHODODENDRONS
Salvia glabrescens	JAPANESE WOODLAND SAGE
Salvia yangii (Perovskia atriplicifolia)	RUSSIAN SAGE
Solidago rugosa 'Fireworks'	FIREWORKS GOLDENROD
Sternbergia lutea	AUTUMN DAFFODIL
Symphyotrichum (Aster) lateriflorus 'Prince', 'Lady in Black'	CALICO ASTER
Symphyotrichum (Aster) oblongifolium	AROMATIC ASTER
Tricyrtis ishiiana	WEEPING TOAD-LILY
Tricyrtis macrantha	WEEPING GOLDEN TRICYRTIS
Tricyrtis macropoda	PAGODA TOAD-LILY
Tricyrtis nana 'Karasuba'	CROW LEAF DWARF TOAD-LILY
Viburnum x bodnantense 'Dawn'	HYBRID VIBURNUM

HARDIEST SUMMER ANNUALS
The ones that will take it through the first several frosts of fall; to be planted in late spring.

Agrostis nebulosa	CLOUD GRASS
Calibrachoa x hybrida	`MILLION BELLS
Cenchrus x advena *(Pennisetum setaceus)* 'Rubrum'	PURPLE FOUNTAIN GRASS
Cenchrus (Pennisetum) elegans 'Burgundy Giant'	BURGUNDY GIANT FOUNTAIN GRASS
Cleome hassleriana	CLEOME
Coreopsis tinctoria	CALLIOPSIS ❖
Cosmos bipinnatus	COSMOS
Glandularia (Verbena) x hybrida	GARDEN VERBENA
Nicotiana x sanderae	JASMINE TOBACCO
Pelargonium x hortorum	ZONAL GERANIUMS
Pelargonium x domesticum	REGAL GERANIUMS
Petunia × atkinsiana	HYBRID PETUNIA
Rudbeckia hirta	BLACK-EYED SUSAN
Salvia farinacea	MEALY-CUP SAGE
Salvia viridis (S. horminum)	CLARY SAGE
Tagetes erecta	AFRICAN MARIGOLD
Tagetes patula	FRENCH MARIGOLD

FALL INTO WINTER FLOWERS

And of course we have the climate which allows some plants to connect the circle of seasons.

Aconitum carmichaelii (Arendsii Group) 'Arendsii'	AZURE MONKSHOOD
Arbutus x *reyorum* 'Marina'	MARINA STRAWBERRY TREE
Arbutus unedo 'Compacta'	COMPACT STRAWBERRY TREE
Calluna vulgaris 'Alexandra', 'Amanda',	COMMON HEATHER, SCOTS HEATHER
'Battle of Arnhem', 'Johnson's Variety', 'Juliane', 'October White'	
Camellia 'Fairy Blush'	FAIRY BLUSH CAMELLIA
Camellia hiemalis 'Chansonette'	CHANSONETTE CAMELLIA
Camellia reticulata	FOREST CAMELLIA
Camellia sasanqua	SASANQUA CAMELLIA
Camellia x *vernalis* 'Yuletide'	YULETIDE CAMELLIA
Camellia 'Yume'	YUME CAMELLIA
Clematis cirrhosa	WINTER CLEMATIS
Colchicum variegatum	SÜRINCAN
Crocus imperati	ITALIAN CROCUS
Crocus laevigatus	MEADOW SAFFRON
Crocus serotinus	LATE CROCUS
Cyclamen cilicium	CILICIAN CYCLAMEN
Cyclamen mirabile	TURKISH CYCLAMEN
Daboecia cantabrica 'Heather Yates'	IRISH HEATH
Erica x *arendsiana* 'Ronsdorf'	AREND'S HEATH
Erica carnea 'Early Red', 'Eileen Porter'	WINTER HEATH
Erica coccinea	TASSEL HEATH
Erica cruenta	CRIMSON HEATH
Erica curvifolia	WATER HEATH
Erica x *darleyensis* 'Alba'	WHITE DARLEY DALE HEATH
Erica formosa	WHITE HEATH
Erica gracilis	CAPE HEATH
Erica manipuliflora 'Ian Cooper'	AUTUMN HEATH
Galanthus nivalis ssp. *reginae-olgae*	QUEEN OLGA'S SNOWDROP
Grevillea victoriae	ROYAL GREVILLEA
Hamamelis virginiana	AMERICAN WITCH-HAZEL
Helleborus niger 'Jacob', 'Josef Lemper'	EARLY HELLEBORE
Mahonia eurybracteata 'Soft Caress'	SOFT CARESS MAHONIA
Mahonia x *media* cultivars	WINTER MAHONIA
Viburnum x *bodnantense* 'Dawn'	HYBRID VIBURNUM

HARDIEST FALL-INTO-WINTER ANNUALS
Many will survive into the following spring and even possibly through it.

Antirrhinum majus	SNAPDRAGON
Bellis perennis	ENGLISH DAISY
Brassica oleracea	FLOWERING CABBAGE, FLOWERING KALE
Calendula officinalis	CALENDULA

Centaurea cineraria	VELVET CINERARIA, DUSTY MILLER
Dianthus barbatus	SWEET WILLIAM
Dianthus chinensis and hybrids	PINKS
Erysimum cheiri	ENGLISH WALLFLOWER
Jacobaea maritima	DUSTY MILLER
Lobularia maritima	SWEET ALYSSUM
Matthiola incana	STOCK
Papaver crocea/nudicaule	ICELAND POPPY
Primula hybrids	ENGLISH PRIMROSE
Viola cornuta hybrids	VIOLA
Viola x wittrockiana	PANSY

FLOWERS FOR A LONG SEASON

These are the plants which will fill an entire season or, better, will distinctly overlap at least two seasons. They are for those who would luxuriate in the dependability of a strong flowering show. Certainly for the small garden where each chosen plant must pay well for its space. Note that many of the perennials among these may be shooting stars — they will so exhaust themselves pushing flowers that two or three years may be their life expectancy. Check these show-stoppers against the "TWEENERS" list. With MANY Of these, a major deadheading into the stems after a first good flush often leads to continued blooming or second bloom cycle later. Not included here are annual flowers, which, as a category, bloom longer than any others.

Abelia x grandiflora	GLOSSY ABELIA
Achillea 'Coronation Gold', 'Little Moonshine', 'Moonshine'	YELLOW YARROW
Achillea millefolium hybrids	YARROW
Aesculus x carnea 'Briotii'	RED HORSE CHESTNUT
Agastache hybrids	HYBRID HYSSOPS, HUMMINGBIRD MINT
Allium 'Millennium'	MILLENNIUM ORNAMENTAL ONION
Anemone x hybrida	JAPANESE ANEMONE
Antirrhinum glutinosum	GUMMY SNAPDRAGON
Arbutus unedo	STRAWBERRY TREE
Asclepias tuberosa	BUTTERFLY WEED
Aster x frikartii	FRIKART'S ASTER
Astilbe chinensis var. *pumila*	CHINESE ASTILBE???
Begonia grandis	HARDY BEGONIA
Betonica (Stachys) officinalis 'Hummelo', 'Pink Cotton Candy'	WOOD BETONY
Boltonia asteroides var. *latisquama* 'Snowbank	FALSE ASTER
Buddleia hybrids (not *B. davidii*)	BUTTERFLY BUSH
Callirhoe involucrata	POPPY MALLOW
Campanula carpatica	CARPATHIAN BELLFLOWER, TUSSOCK BELLFLOWER
Canna x generalis	CANNA-LILY
Caryopteris x clandonensis	BLUE BEARD
Centranthus ruber	JUPITER'S BEARD, RED VALERIAN
Ceratostigma plumbaginoides	DWARF PLUMBAGO
Clerodendrum trichotomum var. *fargesii*	GLORYBOWER
Coreopsis grandiflora	LARGE-FLOWERED TICKSEED
Coreopsis 'Mercury Rising'	MERCURY RISING COREOPSIS
Coreopsis verticillata 'Moonbeam'	MOONBEAM THREAD-LEAF COREOPSIS
Cornus hybrids	DOGWOODS
Cotinus coggygria	SMOKE TREE
Dahlia x hybrida	DAHLIA
Daphne bholua	NEPALESE PAPER PLANT
Daphne x medfordensis 'Lawrence Crocker'	LAWRENCE CROCKER DAPHNE
Daphne (D. odora X *D. bholua)* 'Perfume Princess'	PERFUME PRINCESS DAPHNE
Daphne x transatlantica including 'Eternal Fragrance', 'Jim's Pride'	HYBRID DAPHNE
Delosperma species and hybrids	HARDY ICE PLANT
Dianthus Allwoodii hybrids	PINKS
Dianthus 'Georgia Peach Pie', 'Key Lime'	PERENNIAL PINK
Dicentra formosa and hybrids	BLEEDING HEART ❖

Dasiphora (Potentilla) fruticosa	SHRUBBY CINQUEFOIL ❖
Echinacea purpurea	PURPLE CONEFLOWER
Epilobium (Zauschneria) canum ssp. *latifolium*	
	HUMMINGBIRD TRUMPET, CALIFORNIA FUCHSIA
Erica carnea 'December Red', 'Jennifer Anne', 'Praecox Rubra',	WINTER HEATH
'Prince of Wales', 'Queen of Spain', 'Rosy Morn', 'Winter Beauty', 'Winterfreude'	
Erica x *darleyensis* 'Winter Surprise', 'Winter Treasure'	DARLEY DALE HEATH
Erica erigena 'Irish Dusk'	IRISH HEATH
Eriophyllum lanatum	WOOLY SUNFLOWER ❖
Erysimum hybrids including 'Bowles' Mauve', 'Pastel Patchwork'	SHRUBBY WALLFLOWER
Eutrochium (Eupatorium) dubium 'Little Joe'	LITTLE JOE PYE WEED
Fuchsia 'Double Otto'	DOUBLE OTTO HARDY FUCHSIA
Fuchsia fulgens	BRILLIANT FUCHSIA
Fuchsia hatschbachii	HATSCHBACH'S FUCHSIA
Fuchsia magellanica	MAGELLAN FUCHSIA
Fuchsia procumbens	CREEPING FUCHSIA
Fuchsia 'Santa Claus'	SANTA CLAUS FUCHSIA
Gaillardia x *grandiflora*	BLANKET FLOWER
Geranium 'Rozanne'	ROZANNE HARDY GERANIUM
Glandularia (Verbena) canadensis	ROSE MOCK VERVAIN
Grevillea juniperina cultivars	JUNIPER-LEAF GREVILLEA
Helianthus salicifolius	WILLOW-LEAF SUNFLOWER
Heliopsis helianthoides	FALSE SUNFLOWER
Helleborus hybrids	HELLEBORES
Heptacodium miconioides	SEVEN-SON FLOWER
Hesperantha (Schizostylis) coccineus	RIVER LILY, CRIMSON FLAG
X *Heucherella* hybrids	FOAMY BELLS
Hibiscus syriacus	ROSE-OF-SHARON
Hydrangea arborescens	TREE HYDRANGEA, SMOOTH HYDRANGEA
Hydrangea macrophylla 'Endless Summer'	ENDLESS SUMMER HYDRANGEA
Hydrangea paniculata	PANICLED HYDRANGEA
Hydrangea serrata reblooming cultivars	MOUNTAIN HYDRANGEA
Hylotelephium (Sedum) 'Autumn Joy'	AUTUMN JOY SEDUM
Iberis sempervirens	EVERGREEN CANDYTUFT
Iris 'Immortality'	REPEAT-BLOOMING BEARDED IRIS
Knautia macedonica	KNAUTIA, MACEDONIAN SCABIOUS
Koelreuteria paniculata	GOLDEN RAIN TREE
Lagerstroemia hybrids 'Arapaho', 'Natchez'	HYBRID CRAPE MYRTLE
Lagerstroemia indica 'Dynamite', 'Red Rocket'	CRAPE MYRTLE
Lavandula species and hybrids	LAVENDER
Leucanthemum x *superbum*	SHASTA DAISY
Liatris aspera	BLAZING STAR
Libertia chilensis (Libertia formosa)	NEW ZEALAND SATIN FLOWER, CHILEAN-IRIS
Linum perenne	BLUE FLAX
Lobelia cardinalis hybrids	CARDINAL FLOWER
Matthiola incana	STOCK
Mazus reptans	CREEPING MAZUS
Miscanthus sinensis	JAPANESE SILVER-GRASS

Monarda mildew-free hybrids: BEE BALM
    'Blue Stocking', 'Blue Wreath', 'Colrain Red', 'Dark Ponticum',
    'Gardenview Scarlet', 'Grand Marshall', 'Marshall's Delight', 'Petite Delight',
    'Purple Rooster', 'Raspberry Wine', 'Violet Queen'

Nepeta hybrids	CATMINT
Oenothera (Gaura) lindheimeri and hybrids	GAURA, BEEBLOSSOM
Oenothera macrocarpa (O. missouriensis)	BIG-POD EVENING PRIMROSE
Persicaria amplexicaulis	MOUNTAIN FLEECE
Phedimus (Sedum) ellacombianus	YELLOW STONECROP
Phygelius capensis and hybrids	CAPE FUCHSIA
Platycodon grandiflorus	BALLOON FLOWER
Primula x polyantha and Acaulis groups	ENGLISH PRIMROSE
Prostanthera ovalifolia	PURPLE MINT BUSH
Rosa hybrids	ROSES
Rudbeckia hirta and hybrids	BLACK-EYED SUSAN, GLORIOSA DAISY
Salvia guaranitica	ANISE-SCENTED SAGE, HUMMINGBIRD SAGE
Salvia x jamensis *(Salvia microphylla* X *S. greggii),* including 'Hot Lips'	BUSH SAGE
Salvia nemorosa	PURPLE WOOD SAGE
Salvia rosmarinus (Rosmarinus officinalis)	ROSEMARY
Salvia x sylvestris	BLUE MEADOW SAGE, BLUE WOOD SAGE
Salvia yangii (Perovskia atriplicifolia) and hybrids	RUSSIAN SAGE
Saponaria x lempergii 'Max Frei'	SOAPWORT
Scabiosa columbariae	PINCUSHION FLOWER
Solidago 'Golden Baby'	GOLDEN BABY GOLDENROD
Solidago 'Little Lemon'	LITTLE LEMON GOLDENROD
Solidago (X Solidaster) x luteus	SOLIDASTER
Solidago rugosa 'Fireworks'	GOLDENROD
Stylophorum diphyllum	CELANDINE POPPY
Symphyotrichum (Aster) chilense	PACIFIC ASTER ❖
Tradescantia virginiana (including *T.* x andersoniana)	SPIDERWORT
Tricyrtis formosana	TOAD LILY
Verbascum hybrids	MULLEIN
Veronica spicata	SPIKED SPEEDWELL
Veronicastrum sibericum	JAPANESE CULVER'S ROOT

A CALENDAR OF FLOWER SEED SOWING

Annuals, biennials, and a few short-lived perennials and tender perennials treated as annuals

WINTER (GROUP 1) – SOWING INDOORS – 4 to 6 weeks and then transplanted in spring.
Especially important to provide a proper "hardening-off" period before planting outside.

Anchusa capensis	CAPE FORGET-ME-NOT
Antirrhinum majus	SNAPDRAGON
Arctotis fastuosa	CAPE DAISY
Arctotis venusta (A. stoaechadifolia)	BLUE-EYED AFRICAN DAISY
Bellis perennis	ENGLISH DAISY
Coleostephus myconis (Chrysanthemum multicaule)	YELLOW CLUMP DAISY
Dianthus chinensis hybrids	ANNUAL PINKS
Erythranthe (Mimulus) x *hybridus*	MONKEY FLOWER
Erythranthe (Mimulus) naiandina 'Mega'	SPUNKY MONKEY FLOWER
Impatiens balsamina	BALSAM
Lathyrus odoratus	SWEET PEA
Matthiola incana	STOCK
Mauranthemum (Leucanthemum, Chrysanthemum) paludosum	WHITE CLUMP DAISY
Molucella laevis	BELLS-OF-IRELAND
Nemesia strumosa	NEMESIA
Nemesia versicolor	NEMESIA
Primula malacoides	FAIRY PRIMROSE
Primula obconica	GERMAN PRIMROSE
Scabiosa atropurpurea	PINCUSHION FLOWER
Schizanthus pinnatus, S. x *wisetonensis*	BUTTERFLY FLOWER
Senecio vira-vira	DUSTY MILLER
X Torelus (*Torenia x Mimulus hybrids*)	HYBRID MONKEYS
Trachymene coerulea	BLUE LACE FLOWER

Tender & Short-Lived Perennials
The "treat as annuals" perennials.

Catanache caerulea	CUPID'S-DART
Centaurea cineraria	VELVET CINERARIA, DUSTY MILLER
Cynara cardunculus	CARDOON
Delphinium grandiflorum	CHINESE DELPHINIUM
Digitalis x *valinii* (X Digiplexis)	DIGIPLEXIS
Jacobaea maritima (Senecio cineraria)	DUSTY MILLER
Monarda 'Bergamo Bouquet'	BUTTERFLY MONARDA
Monarda citriodora	LEMON BEE-BALM
Senecio candicans 'Angel Wings'	DUSTY MILLER

LATE WINTER (GROUP 2) -- SOWING INDOORS – 6 to 8 weeks and then transplanted in very late spring or early summer. Includes some tender perennials.

Alcea rosea (annual types)	HOLLYHOCK
Amaranthus caudatus	LOVE-LIES-BLEEDING
Angelonia angustifolia	SUMMER SNAPDRAGON
Asclepias curassavica	SUNSET FLOWER
Begonia semperflorens	BEGONIA
Browallia speciosa	AMETHYST FLOWER
Celosia argentea var. *cristata*	COCKSCOMB
Celosia argentea var. *plumosa*	FEATHERED COCKSCOMB
Celosia argentea var. *spicata*	WHEAT CELOSIA, SILVER FEATHER
Coleus (Solenostemon) scuttellarioides	COLEUS
Dahlia hybrids	DAHLIA
Datura inoxia	MOONFLOWER
Euphorbia marginata	SNOW-ON-THE-MOUNTAIN
Eustoma russellianum (E. grandiflorum; Lisianthus)	
	SWEET LISSIE, PRAIRIE GENTIAN
Glandularia (Verbena) x hybrida	GARDEN VERBENA
Heliotropium arborescens	CHERRY PIE
Hibiscus acetosella	RED SHIELD
Impatiens walleriana	IMPATIENS
Limonium sinuatum	ANNUAL STATICE
Lobelia erinus	LOBELIA
Mirabilis jalapa (often a perennial in gardens)	FOUR-O'CLOCKS
Nicotiana alata	FLOWERING TOBACCO
Nicotiana langsdorfii	LANGSDORF'S TOBACCO
Nicotiana sylvestris	FLOWERING TOBACCO
Nicotiana x sanderae	FLOWERING TOBACCO
Nolana humifusa	NOLANA
Nolana paradoxa	CHILEAN BELLFLOWER
Osteospermum x *Dimorphotheca* hybrids	AFRICAN DAISY
Pericallis (Senecio) x hybridus	CINERARIA
Petunia axillaris, P. integrifolia	"WILD" PETUNIAS
Petunia × atkinsiana	HYBRID PETUNIA
Ricinus communis	CASTOR BEAN
Salpiglossus sinuata	PAINTED TONGUE
Salvia coccinea	TEXAS SAGE
Salvia farinacea	MEALY-CUP SAGE
Salvia guaranitica	BLUE HUMMINGBIRD SAGE
Salvia splendens	SCARLET SAGE
Sanvitalia procumbens	CREEPING ZINNIA
Tithonia rotundifolia	MEXICAN SUNFLOWER
Torenia fournieri	BLUEWINGS, WISHBONE FLOWER
Zinnia (best in driest, hottest spots only)	ZINNIA

SPRING – DIRECT SOWING

For cut flower production (those adaptable to such), sow in succession every 2 weeks up to summer

Agrostemma gracilis (usually sold as *A. githago*)	CORNCOCKLE
Amberboa (Centaurea) moschata	SWEET SULTAN
Ammi majus	(of florist') QUEEN ANNE'S LACE
Anchusa capensis	CAPE FORGET-ME-NOT
Brachyscome iberidifolia	SWAN RIVER DAISY
Calendula officinalis	POT MARIGOLD
Centaurea americana	BASKET-FLOWER
Centaurea cyanus	CORNFLOWER, BACHELORS' BUTTONS
Clarkia amoena	GODETIA ❖
Clarkia unguiculata (C. elegans)	CLARKIA
Coleostephus myconis (Chrysanthemum multicaule)	YELLOW CLUMP DAISY
Consolida ajacis (C. ambigua)	ROCKET LARKSPUR
Coreopsis tinctoria	CALLIOPSIS ❖
Dimorphotheca sinuata	AFRICAN DAISY
Eschscholzia californica	CALIFORNIA POPPY
Glebionis (Chrysanthemum) coronaria	GARLAND DAISY
Glebionis (Chrysanthemum) segetum	CORN MARIGOLD
Gypsophila elegans	ANNUAL BABY'S-BREATH
Iberis amara "Hyacinthiflora"	HYACINTH-FLOWERED CANDYTUFT
Iberis amara	ROCKET CANDYTUFT
Iberis umbellata	CANDYTUFT
Ismelia (Chrysanthemum) carinata	TRICOLOR DAISY
Lathyrus odoratus	SWEET PEA
Lavatera trimestris	ROSE MALLOW
Linaria maroccana	BABY SNAPDRAGON
Lobularia maritima	SWEET ALYSSUM
Malcomia maritima	VIRGINIA STOCK
Malope trifida	MALOPE
Matthiola longipetala bicornis	EVENING-SCENTED STOCK
Molucella laevis	BELLS-OF-IRELAND
Monarda citriodora	LEMON BEE-BALM
Nigella damascena	LOVE-IN-A-MIST
Nigella orientalis	NUTMEG FLOWER
Papaver rubrifragum var. *atlanticum*	MOROCCAN POPPY
Papaver somniferum	PEONY POPPY
Phacelia tanacetifolia	TANSY-LEAF PHACELIA
Reseda odorata	MIGNONETTE
Stylomecon heterophylla	WIND POPPY
Trifolium incarnatum	CRIMSON CLOVER
Tropaeolum majus	NASTURTIUM

SPRING – PLANTING SEEDLINGS of Group 1

LATE SPRING (GROUP 3) – SOWING INDOORS – 1 to 3 weeks (no more) and then
transplanted in very late spring to early summer

Amaranthus cruentus x *powellii*	HOPI RED DYE
Amaranthus tricolor	AMARANTH, CHINESE SPINACH
Brachyscome iberidifolia	SWAN RIVER DAISY
Callistephus chinensis	CHINA ASTER
Callistephus chinensis	CHINA ASTER
Cleome hasslerana	SPIDER FLOWER
Convolvulus tricolor	BUSH MORNING GLORY
Coreopsis tinctoria	CALLIOPSIS ❖
Cosmos bipinnatus	COSMOS
Cosmos sulphureus	YELLOW COSMOS
Cynoglossum amabile	CHINESE FORGET-ME-NOT
Cynoglossum amabile	CHINESE FORGET-ME-NOT
Dorotheanthus bellidiformis	LIVINGSTONE DAISY
Lobelia erinus	TRAILING LOBELIA
Phlox drummondii	ANNUAL PHLOX
Portulaca grandiflora	MOSS ROSE
Scabiosa atropurpurea	PINCUSHION FLOWER
Tagetes erecta	AFRICAN MARIGOLD
Tagetes filifolia	IRISH LACE
Tagetes patula	FRENCH MARIGOLD
Tagetes tenuifolia	SIGNET MARIGOLD
Thymophylla tenuiloba	GOLDEN FLEECE
Zinnia angustifolia	NARROW-LEAF ZINNIA
Zinnia elegans and hybrids	ZINNIA
Zinnia haageana	MEXICAN ZINNIA

Tender Herbaceous Vines

Cobaea scandens	CUP-AND-SAUCER VINE
Eccremocarpus scaber	CHILEAN GLORY VINE
Ipomoea x *imperialis*	HYBRID MORNING GLORY
Ipomoea lobata	FIRECRACKER VINE
Ipomoea x *multifida*	CARDINAL CLIMBER
Ipomoea nil	JAPANESE MORNING GLORY
Ipomoea quamoclit	CYPRESS VINE
Ipomoea tricolor	MORNING GLORY
Lophospermum (Asarina) erubescens	CREEPING GLOXINIA
Lophospermum (Asarina) scandens	CLIMBING SNAPDRAGON
Maurandella (Asarina) antirrhiniflora	VIOLET TWINING SNAPDRAGON
Scyphanthus elegans (S. grandiflorus)	LITTLE NUN, MONJITA
Thunbergia alata	BLACK-EYED SUSAN VINE

LATE SPRING (MAY) – DIRECT SOWING to the ground
Almost all are well-suited to "scatter sowing" (a la for "wildflowers").

Callistephus chinensis	CHINA ASTER
Centaurea americana	BASKET-FLOWER
Cleome hasslerana	SPIDER FLOWER
Convolvulus tricolor	BUSH MORNING GLORY
Coreopsis tinctoria	CALLIOPSIS
Cosmos bipinnatus	COSMOS
Cosmos sulphureus	YELLOW COSMOS
Cynoglossum amabile	CHINESE FORGET-ME-NOT
Dorotheanthus bellidiformis	LIVINGSTONE DAISY
Gaillardia pulchella	BLANKET FLOWER
Helianthus annuus	SUNFLOWER
Helianthus debilis ssp. cucumerifolius (including 'Italian White')	BEACH SUNFLOWER
Lupinus mutabilis (L. hartwegii)	MEXICAN LUPINE
Scabiosa atropurpurea	PINCUSHION FLOWER
Tagetes erecta	AFRICAN MARIGOLD
Tagetes filifolia	IRISH LACE
Tagetes patula	FRENCH MARIGOLD
Tagetes tenuifolia	SIGNET MARIGOLD
Thymophylla tenuiloba	GOLDEN FLEECE
Tropaeolum majus	NASTURTIUM
Xanthisma texanum	TEXAS SLEEPY DAISY
Xerochrysum (Helichrysum) bracteatum	STRAWFLOWER
Zinnia species and hybrids	ZINNIA

LATE MAY-EARLY JUNE – PLANTING SEEDLINGS of Groups 2 and 3

EARLY SUMMER – DIRECT SOWING to the ground

Amaranthus cruentus x *powellii*	HOPI RED DYE
Amaranthus tricolor	AMARANTH, CHINESE SPINACH
Cleome hasslerana	SPIDER FLOWER
Helianthus annuus	SUNFLOWER
Helianthus debilis ssp. cucumerifolius (e.g., 'Italian White')	BEACH SUNFLOWER
Zinnia angustifolia	NARROW-LEAF ZINNIA
Zinnia elegans and hybrids	ZINNIA
Zinnia haageana	MEXICAN ZINNIA

Tender Herbaceous Vines

Lablab purpureus	HYACINTH BEAN
Phaseolus coccineus	SCARLET RUNNER BEAN

LATE SUMMER – DIRECT SOWING to the ground for fall into winter bloom

Brachyscome iberidifolia	SWAN RIVER DAISY
Calendula officinalis	POT MARIGOLD
Centaurea cyanus	CORNFLOWER, BACHELORS' BUTTONS
Lobularia maritima	SWEET ALYSSUM

LATE SUMMER (4) – SOWING INDOORS – 4 to 6 weeks for transplanting in fall
(This is also the best time and method for seeding most true perennials)

Antirrhinum majus	SNAPDRAGON
Brassica oleracea var. Acephala	FLOWERING CABBAGE, FLOWERING KALE
Centaurea cineraria	VELVET CINERARIA, DUSTY MILLER
Jacobaea maritima	DUSTY MILLER
Matthiola incana	STOCK
Primula hybrids	ENGLISH PRIMROSE
Viola cornuta hybrids	VIOLA

Biennials

Alcea rosea	HOLLYHOCK
Bellis perennis	ENGLISH DAISY
Campanula medium	CANTERBURY BELLS, CUP-AND-SAUCER
Campanula pyramidalis	CHIMNEY BELLFLOWER
Dianthus barbatus	SWEET WILLIAM
Eryngium giganteum	MISS WILMOTT'S GHOST
Erysimum cheiri	ENGLISH WALLFLOWER
Ipomopsis aggregata	SKYROCKET, SCARLET GILIA
Myosotis sylvatica	WOOD FORGET-ME-NOT
Salvia argentea	SILVER SAGE
Verbascum bombyciferum	GIANT SILVER MULLEIN
Viola x wittrockiana	PANSY

Not-Quite-Perennials

Alcea ficifolia and hybrids	ANTWERP HOLLYHOCK
Alcea rugosa	RUSSIAN HOLLYHOCK
Antirrhinum majus	SNAPDRAGON
Bellis perennis	ENGLISH DAISY
Cynara cardunculus	CARDOON
Dianthus chinensis and hybrids	PINKS
Erysimum cheiri	ENGLISH WALLFLOWER
Myosotis alpestris	ALPINE FORGET-ME-NOT
Papaver crocea/nudicaule	ICELAND POPPY
Viola tricolor	JOHNNY-JUMP-UP

FALL – PLANTING SEEDLINGS of Group 4

172

FALL – DIRECT SOWING for late winter and spring bloom (and maybe longer; some will germinate in fall while others will wait until spring). Almost all are well-suited to "scatter sowing" (a la for "wildflowers"). For an authentic "wildflower meadow," focus on the PNW natives.

Agrostemma gracilis (usually sold as *A. githago*)	CORNCOCKLE
Amberboa (Centaurea) moschata	SWEET SULTAN
Ammi majus	(of florist') QUEEN ANNE'S LACE
Anchusa capensis	CAPE FORGET-ME-NOT
Calendula officinalis	POT MARIGOLD
Centaurea cyanus	CORNFLOWER, BACHELORS' BUTTONS
Clarkia amoena	GODETIA
Clarkia amoena ssp. *lindleyi*	FAREWELL-TO-SPRING ❖
Clarkia bottae	BOTTAE'S CLARKIA
Clarkia pulchella	PINK FAERIES ❖
Clarkia purpurea ssp. *quadrivulnera*	WINE CUPS CLARKIA, FOUR-SPOT ❖
Clarkia rubicunda	RUBY CHALICE CLARKIA
Clarkia unguiculata (C. elegans)	CLARKIA
Collinsia grandiflora	LARGE-FLOWERED BLUE-EYED MARY ❖
Collinsia heterophylla	CHINESE HOUSES
Collinsia parviflora	SMALL-FLOWERED BLUE-EYED MARY ❖
Collomia grandiflora	LARGE-FLOWERED COLLOMIA ❖
Consolida ajacis (C. ambigua)	ROCKET LARKSPUR
Coreopsis tinctoria	CALLIOPSIS ❖
Crocidium multicaule	GOLD-STAR, SPRING-GOLD ❖
Dianthus barbatus	SWEET WILLIAM
Eschscholzia californica	CALIFORNIA POPPY
Gilia capitata	QUEEN ANNE'S THIMBLES ❖
Gilia tricolor	BIRD'S EYE GILIA
Glebionis (Chrysanthemum) coronaria	GARLAND DAISY
Glebionis (Chrysanthemum) segetum	CORN MARIGOLD
Gypsophila elegans	ANNUAL BABY'S-BREATH
Iberis amara "Hyacinthiflora"	HYACINTH-FLOWERED CANDYTUFT
Iberis amara	ROCKET CANDYTUFT
Iberis umbellata	CANDYTUFT
Ipomopsis aggregata	SKYROCKET, SCARLET GILIA ❖
Ismelia (Chrysanthemum) carinata	TRICOLOR DAISY
Lathyrus odoratus	SWEET PEA
Lavatera trimestris	ROSE MALLOW
Layia platyglossa	COASTAL TIDY-TIPS ❖
Leptosiphon bicolor	BABY-STARS ❖
Limnanthes douglasii	DOUGLAS' MEADOWFOAM ❖
Linanthus androsaceus	FALSE BABY STARS
Linanthus grandiflorus	MOUNTAIN PHLOX ❖
Linaria maroccana	BABY SNAPDRAGON
Linaria reticulata	PURPLE-NET TOADFLAX, CROWN OF JEWELS
Linum grandiflorum	SCARLET FLAX
Lobularia maritima	SWEET ALYSSUM

Lunaria annua	HONESTY
Lupinus bicolor ssp. *bicolor*	FAIRY LUPINE, FIELD LUPINE ❖
Lupinus densiflorus	GOLDEN LUPINE
Lupinus nanus	SKY LUPINE ❖
Lupinus polycarpus	SMALL-FLOWERED LUPINE ❖
Lupinus succulentus	ARROYO LUPINE
Madia elegans	ELEGANT TARWEED ❖
Malcomia maritima	VIRGINIA STOCK
Malope trifida	MALOPE
Matthiola longipetala bicornis	EVENING-SCENTED STOCK
Microsteris gracilis	SLENDER PHLOX ❖
Monarda citriodora	LEMON BEE-BALM
Myosotis sylvatica	WOOD FORGET-ME-NOT
Nemophila maculata	FIVE-SPOT ❖
Nemophila menziesii	BABY BLUE-EYES ❖
Nigella damascena	LOVE-IN-A-MIST
Nigella orientalis	NUTMEG FLOWER
Nuttallanthus texanus	BLUE TOADFLAX ❖
Papaver commutatum	FLANDERS POPPY
Papaver dubium	LONG-HEAD POPPY
Papaver glaucum	TULIP POPPY
Papaver rhoeas	CORN POPPY, SHIRLEY POPPY
Papaver rubrifragum var. *atlanticum*	MOROCCAN POPPY
Papaver somniferum	PEONY POPPY
Phacelia campanularia	CALIFORNIA BLUEBELL
Phacelia linearis	THREAD-LEAF PHACELIA ❖
Phacelia tanacetifolia	TANSY-LEAF PHACELIA
Rhinanthus minor (a hemi-parasite on grasses)	LITTLE YELLOW RATTLE ❖
Silene coeli-rosa	ROSE-OF-HEAVEN
Stylomecon heterophylla	WIND POPPY
Trifolium incarnatum	CRIMSON CLOVER
Trifolium microcephalum	PINK CLOVER ❖
Trifolium willldenowii	SAND CLOVER ❖
Triodanis perfoliata	VENUS'-LOOKING-GLASS ❖
Vaccaria hispanica (*V. pyramidata*)	COW-COCKLE
Valeriana (*Plectritis*) *congesta* ssp. *congesta*	SEA-BLUSH ❖
Viola tricolor	JOHNNY-JUMP-UP

"Wildflowers don't care where they grow." ~~ Dolly Parton

PROBLEM AREAS, PLANT PROBLEMS

The Pacific Northwest, this "greatest place to garden," comes with a compendium of inherent problems and potential problems. It rains a lot and that sets up conditions for slugs and diseases. It is forested, even in most suburbs, and that sometimes casts heavy shade. Many of us are surrounded by nature at its most natural, which includes deer and rabbits and more. It's good to know that there are plenty of plants which can reduce or eliminate the potential for destruction.

Look for the symbol ❖ which indicates a native plant.

175

SLOPES AND EROSION MANAGEMENT

These plants have several means to help hold a slope — its soil and its water — in place. It could be a matter of providing a canopy which breaks the force of falling rain. Many of them have a fine but dense canopy capable of actually catching and holding rain or runoff water, preventing it from moving further and more dangerously down the slope. It might be an extensive, lateral root system which holds the soil particles in place near the surface. Or it could be a system of deep roots which keeps the layers of soil from sliding. Usually best to plant a variety of species on a slope to optimize all of these capabilities. Emphasis on native plants.

* = for dry slopes
◗ = suitable for wet slopes or streamside erosion management

TREES

Abies grandis*	GRAND FIR ❖
Abies lasiocarpa*	SUBALPINE FIR ❖
Abies procera*	NOBLE FIR ❖
Acer circinatum◗	VINE MAPLE ❖
Alnus rubra	RED ALDER ❖
Amelanchier x grandiflora	SERVICEBERRY
Arbutus menziesii*	MADRONE ❖
Cornus nuttallii*	PACIFIC DOGWOOD ❖
Crataegus douglasii	BLACK HAWTHORN ❖
Frangula (Rhamnus) purshiana◗	CASCARA ❖
Fraxinus latifolia	OREGON ASH ❖
Picea sitchensis*	SITKA SPRUCE ❖
Pinus contorta*	SHORE PINE, LODGEPOLE PINE ❖
Populus tremuloides*	QUAKING ASPEN ❖
Pseudotsuga menziesii*	DOUGLAS FIR ❖
Quercus garryana*	OREGON WHITE OAK ❖
Sambucus caerulea*	BLUE ELDERBERRY ❖
Thuja plicata*	WESTERN RED-CEDAR ❖
Tsuga mertensiana*	MOUNTAIN HEMLOCK ❖

SHRUBS

Acer circinatum◗	VINE MAPLE ❖
Amelanchier alnifolia*	WESTERN SERVICEBERRY, JUNEBERRY, SASKATOON ❖
Arctostaphylos canescens var. *sonomensis*	SONOMA MANZANITA
Arctostaphylos uva-ursi*	KINNIKINNICK ❖
Arctostaphylos x media*	HYBRID MANZANITA ❖
Baccharis pilularis*	COYOTE BRUSH ❖
Berberis darwinii*	DARWIN'S BARBERRY
Calluna vulgaris	SCOTCH HEATHER
Ceanothus integerrimus*	DEER BRUSH ❖
Cercocarpus ledifolius	CURL-LEAF MOUNTAIN-MAHOGANY ❖
Cistus spp. and cultivars	ROCKROSE

176

Cornus sericea (C. stolonifera) ♦   RED-TWIG DOGWOOD ❖
Corylus cornuta var. californica♦   HAZELNUT ❖
Cotoneaster horizontalis   ROCK-SPRAY
Elaeagnus x submacrophylla (E. x ebbingei)*   HYBRID ELAEAGNUS
Erica carnea   WINTER HEATH
Gaultheria shallon*   SALAL ❖
Grevillea miqueliana var. moroka   ROUND-LEAF GREVILLEA
Holodiscus discolor*   OCEANSPRAY ❖
Juniperus communis*   COMMON JUNIPER ❖
Lonicera hispidula*   CHAPARRAL HONEYSUCKLE, HAIRY HONEYSUCKLE ❖
Lonicera involucrata   BLACK TWINBERRY ❖
Mahonia (Berberis) aquifolium♦*   TALL OREGON-GRAPE ❖
Mahonia nervosa*   CASCADE OREGON-GRAPE ❖
Mahonia repens*   CREEPING OREGON-GRAPE ❖
Morella (Myrica) californica   CALIFORNIA WAX MYRTLE ❖
Philadelphus lewisii*   MOCK ORANGE ❖
Physocarpus capitatus♦   NINEBARK ❖
Podocarpus lawrencei 'Purple King'   PURPLE KING MOUNTAIN PLUM-PINE
Quercus vacciniifolia*   HUCKLEBERRY OAK ❖
Rhododendron macrophyllum   PACIFIC RHODODENDRON ❖
Rhus aromatica 'Gro-Low'   FRAGRANT SUMAC
Rhus glabra*   SMOOTH SUMAC ❖
Ribes aureum*   GOLDEN CURRANT ❖
Ribes sanguineum*   RED-FLOWERING CURRANT ❖
Rosa gymnocarpa*   BALD-HIP ROSE ❖
Rosa nutkana*   NOOTKA ROSE ❖
Rosa pisocarpa*   CLUSTERED ROSE ❖
Rosa rugosa   JAPANESE BEACH ROSE
Rubus calycinoides (Rubus hayata-koidzumii, Rubus pentalobus)
          TAIWAN CREEPING RUBUS
Sambucus caerulea*   ELDERBERRY ❖
Sambucus racemosa♦   RED ELDERBERRY ❖
Sorbus sitchensis   SITKA MOUNTAIN ASH ❖
Spiraea betulifolia var. lucida*   BIRCH-LEAF SPIREA ❖
Spiraea densiflora*   SUBALPINE SPIREA ❖
Symphoricarpos albus♦   SNOWBERRY ❖
Symphoricarpos mollis*   CREEPING SNOWBERRY ❖
Vaccinium ovatum*   EVERGREEN HUCKLEBERRY ❖
Vaccinium parvifolium*   RED HUCKLEBERRY ❖

HERBACEOUS

Achillea millefolium*   COMMON YARROW ❖
Anaphalis margaritacea*   PEARLY EVERLASTING ❖
Aruncus dioicus*   GOATSBEARD ❖
Asarum caudatum*   WILD GINGER ❖
Asclepias speciosa*   SHOWY MILKWEED ❖
Athyrium felix-femina♦   LADY FERN ❖

177

*Balsamorhiza deltoidea***	DELTOID BALSAMROOT ❖
*Baptisia australis***	BLUE FALSE INDIGO
Blechnum (Struthiopteris) spicant◆	DEER FERN ❖
Camassia leichtlinii	GREAT CAMAS ❖
Camassia quamash	COMMON CAMAS ❖
Carex obnupta◆	SLOUGH SEDGE ❖
*Carex pansa***	DUNE SEDGE, MEADOW SEDGE ❖
Carex praegracilis	FIELD SEDGE ❖
*Carex tumulicola***	FOOTHILL SEDGE ❖
Deschampsia caespitosa	TUFTED HAIRGRASS ❖
*Dicentra formosa***	PACIFIC BLEEDING HEART ❖
Dryopteris austriaca	WOOD FERN ❖
*Festuca idahoensis***	IDAHO FESCUE ❖
*Festuca roemeri***	ROEMER'S FESCUE ❖
Fragaria chiloensis	BEACH STRAWBERRY ❖
*Fragaria vesca***	WOODLAND STRAWBERRY ❖
*Heuchera chlorantha***	MEADOW ALUMROOT ❖
*Heuchera micrantha***	SMALL-FLOWERED ALUMROOT ❖
*Juncus effusus***	COMMON RUSH ❖
Juncus patens◆	SPREADING RUSH ❖
Leymus (Elymus) mollis	AMERICAN DUNE-GRASS ❖
*Lupinus rivularis***	STREAMBANK LUPINE ❖
*Luzula parviflora***	SMALL-FLOWERED WOOD RUSH ❖
Maianthemum dilatatum◆	FALSE LILY-OF-THE-VALLEY ❖
Polypodium glycyrrhiza◆	LICORICE FERN ❖
Polystichum munitum◆	SWORD FERN ❖
*Sisyrinchium bellum***	BLUE-EYED GRASS ❖
Sisyrinchium californicum	YELLOW-EYED GRASS ❖
*Solidago canadensis***	GOLDENROD ❖
*Symphyotrichum (Aster) subspicatum***	DOUGLAS ASTER ❖
Tolmiea menziesii◆	PIGGY-BACK PLANT ❖
*Vancouveria hexandra***	WHITE INSIDE-OUT FLOWER ❖

UNDER TREES
(the "Woodland Garden")

Trees not only cast shade (sometimes deep shade), they also compete for soil space, for water, and for nutrients. Against most plants, they win that competition. These are the plants which hold their own in that competition. In the toughest, rootiest zones, go with those marked with an asterisk (*).

SMALLER TREES

Acer circinatum	VINE MAPLE ❖
Amelanchier alnifolia	WESTERN SERVICEBERRY, JUNEBERRY, SASKATOON ❖
Frangula (Rhamnus) purshiana *	CASCARA, FALSE-BUCKTHORN ❖
Magnolia sieboldii	OYAMA MAGNOLIA
Parrotia subaequalis	CHINESE IRONWOOD
Ptelea trifoliata	HOP TREE
Taxus brevifolia	PACIFIC YEW ❖

SHRUBS

Arbutus unedo *	STRAWBERRY TREE
Aronia x *prunifolia*	PURPLE CHOKEBERRY
Aucuba japonica *	JAPANESE LAUREL
Berberis buxifolia 'Nana'*	DWARF BOX-LEAF BARBERRY
Berberis x *lologensis*	HYBRID EVERGREEN BARBERRY
Berberis x *stenophylla*	GOLDEN BARBERRY
Buxus sinica var. *insularis* 'Wintergreen'	KOREAN BOXWOOD
Cotoneaster simonsii *	SIMON'S COTONEASTER
Danae racemosa *	ALEXANDRIAN LAUREL
Elaeagnus x *submacrophylla* (*E.* x *ebbingei*) 'Limelight'	HYBRID ELAEAGNUS
Euonymus japonicus	EVERGREEN SPINDLE
Fatsia japonica *	JAPANESE ARALIA
Forsythia x *intermedia*	FORSYTHIA
Garrya elliptica	COAST SILK-TASSEL
Gaultheria shallon *	SALAL ❖
Kerria japonica 'Pleniflora'	JAPANESE KERRIA
Lonicera fragrantissima	WINTER HONEYSUCKLE
Lonicera ligustrina var. *yunnanensis (L. nitida)*	BOX-LEAF HONEYSUCKLE
Mahonia aquifolium *	OREGON-GRAPE ❖
Mahonia nervosa *	CASCADE OREGON-GRAPE ❖
Osmanthus x *burkwoodii*	BURKWOOD TEA-OLIVE
Osmanthus heterophyllus 'Goshiki', 'Variegatus'	HOLLY OSMANTHUS
Philadelphus 'Innocence'	MOCK ORANGE
Physocarpus capitatus *	NINEBARK
Pieris 'Forest Flame'	FOREST FLAME PIERIS
Pieris japonica	LILY-OF-THE-VALLEY SHRUB, ANDROMEDA
Rhododendron 'Gomer Waterer'	RHODODENDRON

179

Rhododendron 'Praecox'	RHODODENDRON
Ribes divaricatum	WILD GOOSEBERRY ❖
Rosa gymnocarpa	DWARF ROSE ❖
Ruscus aculeatus*	BUTCHER'S BROOM
Ruscus hypophyllum*	SPANISH BUTCHER'S BROOM
Sambucus nigra ssp. *nigra*	BLACK ELDERBERRY ❖
Skimmia japonica	SKIMMIA
Stephanandra incisa and cultivars	CUT-LEAF STEPHANANDRA
Symphoricarpos albus*	COMMON SNOWBERRY ❖
Symphoricarpos mollis	CREEPING SNOWBERRY ❖
Vaccinium ovatum*	EVERGREEN HUCKLEBERRY ❖
Viburnum davidii	DAVID VIBURNUM
Viburnum opulus	EUROPEAN CRANBERRY BUSH ❖
Viburnum trilobum (*V. opulus* var. *americanum*)	AMERICAN CRANBERRY BUSH ❖

VINES

Asteranthera ovata	ESTRELLITA, LITTLE STAR
Clematis occidentalis var. *grosseserrata*	WESTERN BLUE VIRGINS' BOWER ❖
Lonicera ciliosa	ORANGE HONEYSUCKLE ❖
Parthenocissus henryana	SILVER-VEIN CREEPER
Pileostegia viburnoides*	CLIMBING HYDRANGEA
Stauntonia hexaphylla	SAUSAGE VINE
Vitis californica	CALIFORNIA GRAPE
Vitis coignetiae	CRIMSON GLORY VINE
Vitis girdiana	SOUTHERN CALIFORNIA GRAPE

GROUNDCOVERS

Arctostaphylos uva-ursi	KINNIKINNICK, BEARBERRY ❖
Asarum caudatum*	WILD GINGER ❖
Asarum marmoratum	MARBLED WILD GINGER ❖
Bergenia hybrids*	BERGENIA
Carex glauca (C. flacca)*	BLUE SEDGE
Carex inops (C. pensylvanica)	LONG-STOLONED SEDGE ❖
Carex siderosticha var. *ciliatomarginata* 'Treasure Island'*	CREEPING SEDGE
Carex tumulicola	BERKELEY SEDGE ❖
Clinopodium (Micromeria, Satureja) douglasii	YERBA BUENA ❖
Coptis asplenifolia	FERN-LEAF GOLDTHREAD
Cotoneaster salicifolius 'Gnom'*	DWARF WILLOW-LEAF COTONEASTER
Epimedium trailing species and hybrids*	BARRENWORT
Erica carnea	WINTER HEATH
Euonymus fortunei*	WINTER CREEPER
Fragaria vesca	WOODLAND STRAWBERRY ❖
Gaultheria ovatifolia	WESTERN TEABERRY ❖
Gaultheria procumbens	WINTERGREEN
Linnaea borealis	TWINFLOWER ❖

*Mahonia repens**	CREEPING OREGON-GRAPE ❖
*Oxalis oregana**	REDWOOD SORREL ❖
*Pachysandra procumbens**	ALLEGHENY SPURGE
Pachysandra terminalis	JAPANESE PACHYSANDRA
Phlox adsurgens	WOODLAND PHLOX ❖
Phlox austromontana	MOUNTAIN PHLOX ❖
Rhododendron 'Wombat'	LOW RHODODENDRON
Rubus tricolor	CHINESE BRAMBLE
Ruscus x *microglossus**	GROUNDCOVER BUTCHERS BROOM
Sarcococca hookeriana var. *humilis**	CHRISTMAS BOX
Saxifraga stolonifera variegated cultivars*	STRAWBERRY BEGONIA
*Trachelospermum asiaticum**	ASIAN STAR JASMINE
*Vaccinium scoparium**	GROUSEBERRY ❖
*Vancouveria hexandra**	WHITE INSIDE-OUT FLOWER ❖
*Vancouveria chrysantha**	SISKIYOU INSIDE-OUT FLOWER ❖
*Vinca minor**	DWARF PERIWINKLE
*Whipplea modesta**	WHIPPLE VINE, MODESTY ❖

PERENNIALS & BULBS

*Acanthus mollis**	BEAR'S BREECH
*Acanthus spinosus**	BEAR'S BREECH
Aconitum columbianum	MONKSHOOD ❖
Actaea matsumurae 'White Pearl'	WHITE PEARL JAPANESE BUGBANE
Actaea pachypoda	WHITE BANEBERRY, DOLL'S EYE
Actaea rubra	RED BANEBERRY
Adelinia (Cynoglossum) grande	GRAND HOUND'S TONGUE ❖
Adiantum venustum	HIMALAYAN MAIDENHAIR FERN
*Alchemilla mollis**	LADY'S MANTLE
*Anemonoides (Anemone) nemorosa**	WOOD ANEMONE
Aquilegia formosa	WESTERN RED COLUMBINE ❖
*Arisarum proboscideum**	MOUSE PLANT
Aruncus dioicus	SYLVAN GOAT'S-BEARD ❖
*Asarum caudatum**	WESTERN WILD GINGER
*Asarum europaeum**	EUROPEAN WILD GINGER
Asarum ichangensis 'Silver Lining'*	SILVER LINING GINGER
*Asarum marmoratum**	MARBLED WILD GINGER ❖
*Asarum sieboldii**	KOREAN WILD GINGER
*Asarum splendens**	SPLENDID WILD GINGER
Asarum fauriei var. *takaoi* 'Pitter Patter'*	JAPANESE WILD GINGER
*Aspidistra elatior**	CAST IRON PLANT
Aspidistra ibanensis 'Flowing Fountains'*	CAST IRON PLANT
Aspidistra sichuanensis 'Spek-Tacular'*	CHINESE CAST IRON PLANT
*Aspidistra zongbayi**	YUNNAN SUNBEAM
*Asplenium scolopendrium**	HART'S TONGUE FERN
Astilbe chinensis var. *pumila*	DWARF CHINESE ASTILBE
Athyrium niponicum var. *pictum*	JAPANESE PAINTED FERN
Austroblechnum (Blechnum) penna-marina	ANTARCTIC HARD-FERN

Begonia grandis	HARDY BEGONIA
Bergenia ciliata*	FUZZY-LEAF BERGENIA
Bergenia cordifolia*	HEART-LEAF BERGENIA, PIG-SQUEAK
Bergenia hybrids and other species*	BERGENIA
Blechnum (Struthiopteris) spicant*	DEER FERN ❖
Brunnera macrophylla cultivars*	SIBERIAN BUGLOSS
Carex albicans*	WHITE-TINGED SEDGE
Carex flaccosperma*	BLUE WOOD SEDGE
Carex inops (C. pensylvanica)	CREEPING SEDGE
Carex muskingumensis	PALM SEDGE
Clematis occidentalis var. *dissecta*	CUT-LEAF BLUE VIRGINS' BOWER ❖
Colchicum autumnale	MEADOW SAFFRON, AUTUMN CROCUS
Coniogramme intermedia	BAMBOO FERN
Coniogramme japonica	JAPANESE BAMBOO FERN
Cornus x unalaschkensis	BUNCHBERRY ❖
Cyclamen species*	HARDY CYCLAMEN, SOWBREAD
Cyrtomium caryotideum	HOLLY FERN
Cyrtomium falcatum	JAPANESE HOLLY FERN
Cyrtomium fortunei	FORTUNE'S HOLLY FERN
Cyrtomium macrophyllum	LARGE-LEAF HOLLY FERN
Deschampsia caespitosa*	TUFTED HAIR GRASS ❖
Dicentra formosa	PACIFIC OR WESTERN BLEEDING-HEART ❖
Diphylleia cymosa	UMBRELLA LEAF
Disporopsis arisanensis*	EVERGREEN SOLOMON SEAL
Disporopsis bakeri (D. pernyi 'Bill Baker')*	EVERGREEN SOLOMON'S SEAL
Disporopsis 'Lily Pads'	LILY PADS SOLOMON'S SEAL
Disporopsis pernyi*	EVERGREEN SOLOMON'S SEAL
Disporum cantoniense 'Night Heron'	CANTON FAIRY BELLS
Disporum megalanthum	LARGE-FLOWERED FAIRY BELLS
Disporum sessile	JAPANESE FAIRY BELLS
Disporum uniflorum	FAIRY BELLS
Dryopteris arguta	COASTAL WOOD FERN ❖
Dryopteris crassirhizoma	THICK-STEMMED WOOD FERN
Dryopteris cycadina	SHAGGY SHIELD FERN
Dryopteris erythrosora	AUTUMN FERN
Dryopteris expansa (D. austriaca)	COMMON WOOD FERN ❖
Dryopteris filix-mas	MALE FERN ❖
Dryopteris lepidopoda	SUNSET FERN
Dryopteris sieboldii	SIEBOLD'S WOOD FERN
Dryopteris wallichiana	WALLICH'S WOOD FERN
Dysosma (Podophyllum) versipellis 'Spotty Dotty'	SPOTTY DOTTY MAYAPPLE
Epimedium brachyrrhizum*	BISHOP'S HAT
Epimedium brevicornu*	BISHOP'S HAT
Epimedium dolichostemon*	BISHOP'S HAT
Epimedium epsteinii*	BISHOP'S HAT
Epimedium grandiflorum*	BISHOP'S HAT
Epimedium lishihchenii*	BISHOP'S HAT
Epimedium myrianthum 'Mottled Madness'*	BISHOP'S HAT
Epimedium pauciflorum*	BISHOP'S HAT

Epimedium x perralchicum*	BISHOP'S HAT
*Epimedium perralderianum**	BISHOP'S HAT
*Epimedium pinnatum**	BISHOP'S HAT
*Epimedium platypetalum**	BISHOP'S HAT
*Epimedium pubescens**	BISHOP'S HAT
Epimedium x rubrum*	RED BARRENWORT
Epimedium x warleyense*	BISHOP'S HAT
Epimedium x youngianum*	BISHOP'S HAT
Epimedium x versicolor 'Sulphureum'*	BISHOP'S HAT
Erythronium elegans	COAST RANGE FAWN-LILY ❖
Erythronium oreganum	OREGON FAWN-LILY ❖
Erythronium revolutum	MAHOGANY FAWN-LILY, COAST FAWN-LILY ❖
Gymnocarpium disjunctum	PACIFIC OAK FERN ❖
Gymnocarpium dryopteris	WESTERN OAK FERN ❖
Hacquetia epipactis	BROAD-LEAVED SANICLE, HACQUETIA
Hakonechloa macra cultivars*	JAPANESE FOREST GRASS
*Helleborus argutifolius**	CORSICAN HELLEBORE
*Helleborus foetidus**	STINKING HELLEBORE
Helleborus hybrids*	HELLEBORES
Helleborus liguricus	ITALIAN HELLEBORE
*Heuchera micrantha**	SMALL- FLOWERED ALUMROOT, CORALBELLS ❖
Hosta species and hybrids*	HOSTA
Hyacinthoides hispanica (NOT *H.* x massartiana)	SPANISH BLUEBELL
Ichtyoselmis (Dicentra) macrantha	CHINESE BLEEDING HEART
*Iris foetidissima**	GLADWIN IRIS
Iris 'Nada'	BUTTERFLY IRIS
Lamprocapnos (Dicentra) spectabilis	OLD-FASHIONED BLEEDING HEART
Lepisorus bicolor	SCHEZUAN RIBBON FERN
*Lilium columbianum**	TIGER LILY ❖
Lilium parvum	SIERRA TIGER LILY ❖
Linnaea borealis	TWINFLOWER ❖
Liriope muscari	LILYTURF
*Luzula multiflora**	WOOD-RUSH ❖
*Luzula sylvatica**	WOOD RUSH
*Maianthemum (Smilacina) racemosa**	FALSE SOLOMON'S SEAL ❖
Melica uniflora f. *albida*	WOOD MELIC
Mertensia ciliata	FRINGED LUNGWORT ❖
Milium effusum 'Aureum'	GOLDEN WOOD MILLET
Muehlenbeckia axillaris 'Nana'	CREEPING WIRE VINE
Muhlenbergia rigens	DEER GRASS
Myriopteris (Cheilanthes) gracillima	LACE LIP FERN ❖
Ophiopogon japonicus	MONDO GRASS
Ophiopogon planiscapus 'Juru'	VARIEGATED DWARF MONDO GRASS
Ophiopogon planiscapus 'Little Tabby'	STRIPED DWARF MONDO GRASS
Ophiopogon planiscapus 'Nigrescens'	BLACK MONDO GRASS
Paris polyphylla	MULTI-LEAF PARIS
Phlox divaricata	WOODLAND PHLOX
Polemonium carneum	SALMON POLEMONIUM ❖
Polygonatum biflorum (P. commutatum) 'Bigfoot'*	GIANT SOLOMON'S SEAL

183

Polygonatum huanum (P. kingianum)	
	SIBERIAN SOLOMON'S SEAL, ORANGE-FLOWERING SOLOMON' SEAL
Polygonatum humile 'Shiro Shima'*	GIANT SOLOMON'S SEAL
Polygonatum odoratum 'Byakko'*	PAINTED SOLOMON'S SEAL
Polygonatum odoratum 'Prince Charming'*	P. C. SOLOMON'S SEAL
Polygonatum odoratum var. *pluriflorum* 'Variegatum'*	VARIEGATED SOLOMON'S SEAL
Polypodium glycyrrhiza	LICORICE FERN ❖
Polypodium vulgare	COMMON POLYPODY
Polystichum acrostichoides	CHRISTMAS FERN
Polystichum lemmonii	LEMMON'S HOLLY FERN, LEMMON'S SWORD FERN ❖
Polystichum munitum*	SWORD FERN ❖
Polystichum neolobatum	ASIAN SABER FERN
Polystichum setiferum	SOFT SHIELD FERN
Pulmonaria longifolia ssp. *cevennensis**	LONGLEAF LUNGWORT
Saxifraga x urbium 'Primuloides'	MINIATURE LONDON PRIDE
Speirantha convallarioides*	FALSE LILY-OF-THE-VALLEY
Tellima grandiflora*	FRINGECUP
Tiarella species and hybrids	FOAMFLOWER
Trachystemon orientalis	EARLY-FLOWERING BORAGE
Trautvetteria caroliniensis	FALSE BUGBANE ❖
Trillium albidum ssp. *albidum (T. chloropetalum)*	GIANT TRILLIUM ❖
Trillium kurabayashii	GIANT PURPLE TRILLIUM ❖
Trillium ovatum*	WESTERN WHITE TRILLIUM, WAKE ROBIN ❖
Uvularia grandiflora*	LARGE-FLOWERED BELLWORT
Viola glabella	STREAM VIOLET, YELLOW WOOD VIOLET ❖
Waldsteinia ternata	BARREN STRAWBERRY
Woodwardia fimbriata	GIANT CHAIN FERN ❖
Woodwardia unigemmata	JEWELED CHAIN FERN

PLANTING UNDER TREES, *the process*

1. Protect the tree.
2. Start small.
3. Dig small holes.
4. Use a few cultivars/species.
5. Plant a lot.
6. Plant in masses throughout the zone (not just in a circle).
7. Emphasize foliage.
8. Plant in fall.
9. Water by hand until small plants are established.
10. Use groundcovers to be your "mulch."
11. Consider trimming up lower branches of the trees.

"There is a serene and settled majesty to woodland scenery that enters into the soul and delights and elevates it, and fills it with noble inclinations." ~~ Washington Irving

DEEP SHADE

Less than 3 hours of any direct sunlight per day.

TREES

Acer circinatum	VINE MAPLE ❖
Acer triflorum	THREE-FLOWER MAPLE, ROUGH-BARK MAPLE
Carpinus betulus	HORNBEAM
Carpinus japonica	JAPANESE HORNBEAM
Cephalotaxus harringtonia	COW-TAIL PINE, PLUM YEW
Thuja plicata smaller cultivars	WESTERN RED-CEDAR ❖
Tsuga heterophylla 'Thorsen's Weeping'	WEEPING WESTERN HEMLOCK ❖

SHRUBS

Aucuba omeiensis	JAPANESE LAUREL
Aucuba japonica 'Mr. Goldstrike'	VARIEGATED JAPANESE AUCUBA
Aucuba japonica 'Rozannie'	ROZANNIE JAPANESE AUCUBA
Aucuba japonica 'Serratifolia'	SAW-TOOTHED JAPANESE AUCUBA
Buxus sempervirens 'Aureovariegata'	VARIEGATED BOXWOOD
Edgeworthia chrysantha	PAPERBUSH
Elaeagnus x *submacrophylla* (*E.* x *ebbingei*) 'Gilt Edge'	
	VARIEGATED HYBRID ELAEAGNUS
Elaeagnus pungens 'Maculata'	GOLDEN ELAEAGNUS
Eleutherococcus sieboldianus 'Variegatus'	VARIEGATED FIVE-LEAF ARALIA
Fatsia japonica many variegated cultivars	VARIEGATED JAPANESE FATSIA
Hamamelis x *intermedia*	HYBRID WITCH-HAZEL
Hydrangea serrata 'O-amacha Nishiki'	GOLD DUST MOUNTAIN HYDRANGEA
Kerria japonica 'Picta'	JAPANESE KERRIA
Leucothoe fontanesiana	LEUCOTHOE
Mahonia nervosa	CASCADE OREGON-GRAPE ❖
Mahonia repens	CREEPING OREGON-GRAPE ❖
Microbiota decussata	SIBERIAN CYPRESS
Osmanthus x *burkwoodii*	HYBRID SWEET OLIVE
Osmanthus delavayi	SWEET OLIVE
Osmanthus heterophyllus cultivars	FALSE HOLLY
Ruscus colchicus	BUTCHER'S BROOM
Sarcococca confusa	SWEETBOX
Sarcococca hookeriana	SWEETBOX
Sarcococca orientalis	ASIAN SWEETBOX
Sarcococca ruscifolia	SWEETBOX
Taxus brevifolia 'Nana'	DWARF PACIFIC YEW ❖
Vaccinium ovatum	EVERGREEN HUCKLEBERRY ❖

VINES

Hedera algeriensis 'Glorie de Marengo'	VARIEGATED ALGERIAN IVY
Hedera colchica 'Dentata Variegata'	VARIEGATED PERSIAN IVY
Hydrangea (Schizophragma) hydrangeoides 'Moonlight'	JAPANESE HYDRANGEA VINE
Stauntonia purpurea	SAUSAGE VINE

PERENNIALS
Including ferns and some bulbs

Adiantum aleuticum	WESTERN MAIDENHAIR FERN ❖
Arisaema dracontium	DRAGONROOT
Arisaema ringens	COBRA LILY
Arisaema triphyllum	JACK-IN-THE-PULPIT
Arisarum proboscideum	MOUSE PLANT
Asarum caudatum	WESTERN WILD GINGER ❖
Asarum europaeum	EUROPEAN WILD GINGER
Asarum ichangensis 'Silver Lining'	SILVER LINING GINGER
Asarum splendens	SPLENDID WILD GINGER
Asarum fauriei var. *takaoi* 'Pitter Patter'	JAPANESE WILD GINGER
Aspidistra elatior especially variegated cultivars	CAST IRON PLANT
Aspidistra ibanensis 'Flowing Fountains'	FLOWING FOUNTAINS CAST IRON PLANT
Aspidistra sichuanensis 'Spek-Tacular'	CHINESE CAST IRON PLANT
Aspidistra zongbayi	YUNNAN SUNBEAM
Asplenium scolopendrium	HART'S-TONGUE FERN
Asplenium trichomanes	MAIDENHAIR SPLEENWORT
Austroblechnum (Blechnum) penna-marina	ANTARCTIC HARD-FERN
Beesia calthifolia	GINGER-LEAF FALSE BUGBANE
Beesia deltophylla	BEESIA
Begonia grandis 'Heron's Pirouette'	HERON'S PIROUETTE BEGONIA
Begonia grandis ssp. *evansiana*	HARDY BEGONIA
Blechnum (Struthiopteris) spicant	DEER FERN ❖
Brunnera macrophylla variegated cultivars	SIBERIAN BUGLOSS
Calanthe "Kajima" series	CALANTHE ORCHID
Calanthe sieboldii	CALANTHE ORCHID
Cardamine trifolia	THREE-LEAF CARDAMINE
Clematis repens	TWINKLE BELL CLEMATIS
Coniogramme intermedia	BAMBOO FERN
Coniogramme japonica	JAPANESE BAMBOO FERN
Cyclamen coum	HARDY CYCLAMEN, EASTERN SOWBREAD
Cyclamen hederifolium	IVY-LEAF CYCLAMEN
Cyrtomium caryotideum	HOLLY FERN
Cyrtomium falcatum	JAPANESE HOLLY FERN
Cyrtomium fortunei	FORTUNE'S HOLLY FERN
Cyrtomium macrophyllum	LARGELEAF HOLLY FERN
Disporopsis arisanensis	EVERGREEN SOLOMON'S SEAL
Disporopsis bakeri (*D. pernyi* 'Bill Baker')	EVERGREEN SOLOMON'S SEAL
Disporopsis 'Lily Pads'	LILY PADS SOLOMON'S SEAL

186

Disporopsis pernyi	EVERGREEN SOLOMON'S SEAL
Dryopteris crassirhizoma	THICK-STEMMED WOOD FERN
Dryopteris cycadina	SHAGGY SHIELD FERN
Dryopteris erythrosora	AUTUMN FERN
Dryopteris lepidopoda	SUNSET FERN
Dryopteris sieboldii	SIEBOLD'S WOOD FERN
Dryopteris wallichiana	WALLICH'S WOOD FERN
Dysosma (Podophyllum) pleianthum	CHINESE MAYAPPLE
Dysosma (Podophyllum) versipellis 'Spotty Dotty'	SPOTTY DOTTY MAYAPPLE
Gymnocarpium disjunctum	COMMON OAK FERN ❖
Helleborus foetidus	STINKING HELLEBORE
Helleborus liguricus	ITALIAN HELLEBORE
Hosta sieboldiana 'Elegans'	PLANTAIN LILY
Hosta sieboldiana 'Great Expectations'	PLANTAIN LILY
Lepisorus bicolor	SCHEZUAN RIBBON FERN
Ligularia 'Britt-Marie Crawford'	LEOPARD PLANT
Ligularia 'King Kong'	LEOPARD PLANT
Ligularia 'The Rocket'	LEOPARD PLANT
Liriope muscari 'Okina'	SILVER LILYTURF
Liriope muscari 'Silver Midget'	DWARF LILYTURF
Luzuriaga radicans	QUILINEJA
Maianthemum (Smilacina) racemosa	FALSE SOLOMON'S SEAL ❖
Ophiopogon planiscapus cultivars	MONDO GRASS
Oxalis oregana (evergreen form)	EVERGREEN REDWOOD SORREL
Polygonatum commutatum 'Bigfoot'	GIANT SOLOMON'S SEAL
Polygonatum humile 'Shiro Shima'	GIANT SOLOMON'S SEAL
Polygonatum odoratum 'Byakko'	PAINTED SOLOMON'S SEAL
Polygonatum odoratum 'Prince Charming'	PRINCE CHARMING SOLOMON'S SEAL
Polygonatum odoratum var. *pluriflorum* 'Variegatum'	VARIEGATED SOLOMON'S SEAL
Polystichum makinoi	MAKINOI'S HOLLY FERN
Polystichum munitum	SWORD FERN ❖
Polystichum neolobatum	ASIAN SABER FERN
Polystichum polyblepharum	JAPANESE TASSEL FERN
Polystichum setiferum Plumosomultilobum Group	PLUMOSE SOFT SHIELD FERN
Polystichum setiferum Divisilobum Group	SOFT SHIELD FERN
Polystichum tsus-simense	KOREAN ROCK FERN
Pulmonaria longifolia ssp. *cevennensis*	LONGLEAF LUNGWORT
Saruma henryi	WILD GINGER
Saxifraga stolonifera variegated cultivars	STRAWBERRY BEGONIA
Saxifraga x *urbium* 'Primuloides'	MINIATURE LONDON PRIDE
Speirantha convallarioides	FALSE LILY-OF-THE-VALLEY
Syneilesis subglabrata (S. intermedia)	UMBRELLA PLANT
Tricyrtis formosana 'Gilt Edge'	VARIEGATED TOAD LILY
Vancouveria hexandra	INSIDE-OUT FLOWER ❖
Woodwardia unigemmata	JEWELED CHAIN FERN
Ypsilandra thibetica	FRAGRANT YPSILANDRA
Zingiber mioga	WOODLAND GINGER

See also "PLANTS FOR A SHADE GARDEN" for a complete list of shady-side plants.

HELL STRIP

A phrase originally applied to the strip of soil between the sidewalk and the street, notoriously hard to grow plants of any kind in due to several factors: minimal room, lack of convenient water, heat reflected from paved surfaces, and possible foot traffic. It now applies to any narrow (2 to 3 feet or less) planting bed with similar limiting factors.

Essentially, these are the lowest maintenance plants for ANY small area on the dry side. Almost all of these are also suited to under the eaves of a house or, more creatively, to a grand English garden concept called the "Gravel Garden" whereby the surface of the soil is mulched with a uniform pea gravel (or similar sized material).

Acaena microphylla	NEW ZEALAND BURR
Acaena 'Blue Haze'	BLUE HAZE NEW ZEALAND BURR
Acaena inermis 'Purpurea'	PURPLE NEW ZEALAND BURR
Achillea ageratifolia	GREEK YARROW
Achillea clavennae	SILVER YARROW
Achillea filipendulina	FERN-LEAF YARROW
Achillea x lewisii 'King Edward'	TRAILING YARROW
Achillea millefolium and especially hybrids	COMMON YARROW
Achillea 'Moonshine'	MOONSHINE YARROW
Achillea serbica	SERBIAN YARROW
Achillea x taygetea	HYBRID YARROW
Agastache aurantiaca	GOLDEN GIANT HYSSOP
Agastache barberi	ARIZONA HYSSOP
Agastache cana 'Rosita'	ROSITA HUMMINGBIRD-MINT
Agastache hybrids	HUMMINGBIRD-MINT
Allium acuminatum	HOOKER'S ONION ❖
Allium amplectens	SLIM-LEAF ONION ❖
Allium cernuum	NODDING ONION ❖
Allium cristophii	STARS OF PERSIA
Anaphalis margaritacea	COMMON PEARLY EVERLASTING ❖
Anemone drummondii	WINDFLOWER ❖
Anemone occidentalis	WESTERN PASQUE FLOWER ❖
Antennaria dioica 'Rubra'	PINK PUSSY-TOES
Antirrhinum sempervirens	SPANISH SNAPDRAGON
Aquilegia flavescens	YELLOW COLUMBINE ❖
Aquilegia formosa	WESTERN COLUMBINE ❖
Arenaria balearica	CORSICAN SANDWORT
Artemisia 'Powis Castle'	POWIS CASTLE WORMWOOD
Artemisia schmidtiana 'Silver Mound'	SILVER MOUND
Asclepias fascicularis	NARROW-LEAVED MILKWEED ❖
Asclepias tuberosa	BUTTERFLYWEED
Asphodeline lutea	YELLOW ASPHODEL
Baptisia hybrids	FALSE INDIGO
Berberis buxifolia 'Nana'	DWARF BOX-LEAF BARBERRY
Bloomeria (Triteleia) crocea	GOLDEN STARS ❖
Brodiaea coronaria	HARVEST BRODIAEA ❖

Brodiaea elegans ssp. *hooveri*	HARVEST LILY ❖
Callirhoe involucrata	PURPLE POPPY MALLOW
Calylophus hartwegii	HARTWEG'S SUNDROPS
*Campanula rotundifolia**	BLUEBELL BELLFLOWER ❖
Carex albula	BLONDE SEDGE
Carex buchananii	LEATHERLEAF SEDGE
Caryopteris x clandonensis Dwarf cultivars	DWARF BLUEBEARD
Centaurea hypoleuca	PINK CORNFLOWER
Centaurea ragusina	PERENNIAL DUSTY MILLER
Centranthus ruber	JUPITER'S BEARD, RED VALERIAN
Cerastium tomentosum	SNOW-IN-SUMMER
Cistus x bornetianus 'Jester'	JESTER ROCKROSE
Cistus x canescens 'Albus'	WHITE ROCKROSE
Cistus x crispatus 'Warley Rose'	WARLEY ROSE ROCKROSE
Cistus x dansereaui 'Jenkyn Place'	JENKYN PLACE ROCKROSE
Cistus x obtusifolius	COMPACT WHITE ROCKROSE
Cistus 'Snowfire'	SNOWFIRE ROCKROSE
Clematis hirsutissima var. *hirsutissima*	HAIRY CLEMATIS ❖
Comptonia peregrina	SWEETFERN
Coreopsis verticillata	THREAD-LEAF COREOPSIS
Corethrogyne (Lessingia) filaginifolia 'Silver Carpet'	TRAILING SAND ASTER
Dasiphora (Potentilla) fruticosa	SHRUBBY CINQUEFOIL ❖
Delosperma cooperi	COOPER'S HARDY PURPLE ICE PLANT
Delosperma nubigenum	CLOUD-LOVING ICE PLANT
Dianthus Allwoodii hybrids	PINKS
Dianthus deltoides	MAIDEN PINK
Dianthus gratianopolitanus	CHEDDAR PINK
Dianthus plumarius	COTTAGE PINK
Dichelostemma capitatum ssp. *capitatum*	BLUEDICKS ❖
Dichelostemma congestum	OOKOW, FIELD CLUSTER LILY, HARVEST LILY ❖
Dodecatheon austrofrigidum	FRIGID SHOOTING STAR ❖
Dodecatheon hendersonii	SHOOTING STAR, MOSQUITO BILL ❖
Dracocephalum argunense (or *D. austriacum*)	DRAGON'S HEAD
Dudleya farinosa	CHALKY LIVE-FOREVER
Echinops bannaticus	GLOBE THISTLE
Epilobium (Zauschneria) canum ssp. *latifolium*	HUMMINGBIRD TRUMPET ❖
Erica x darleyensis	DARLEY DALE HEATH
Eriogonum elatum	RUSH BUCKWHEAT ❖
Eriogonum latifolium	COAST BUCKWHEAT ❖
Eriogonum ovalifolium	OVAL-LEAF BUCKWHEAT ❖
Eriogonum ternatum	TERNATE BUCKWHEAT ❖
Eriogonum umbellatum	SULPHUR BUCKWHEAT ❖
Eriophyllum lanatum	OREGON SUNSHINE, WOOLLY SUNFLOWER ❖
Eryngium alpinum	ALPINE SEA HOLLY
Eryngium amethystinum	BLUE SEA HOLLY
Eryngium bourgatii	MEDITERRANEAN SEA HOLLY
Eryngium planum	FLAT SEA HOLLY
Festuca idahoensis	IDAHO FESCUE ❖
*Festuca roemeri**	ROEMER'S FESCUE ❖

Gaillardia x grandiflora	BLANKET FLOWER
Geranium maculatum	CRANESBILL GERANIUM
Geranium sanguineum	BLOODY CRANESBILL
Glandularia (Verbena) canadensis	ROSE MOCK VERVAIN
Grevillea juniperina cultivars	JUNIPER-LEAF GREVILLEA
Hebe pinguifolia 'Sutherlandii'	BLUE-LEAF HEBE
Helianthella uniflora var. *douglasii*	LITTLE SUNFLOWER ❖
Helianthemum nummularium (e)	SUN ROSE
Helictotrichon sempervirens	BLUE OAT GRASS
Hemerocallis species and hybrids	DAYLILIES
Herniaria glabra	GREEN CARPET, RUPTUREWORT
Heuchera micrantha	SMALL- FLOWERED ALUMROOT ❖
Hylotelephium (Sedum) Autumn hybrids ('Autumn Charm', 'Autumn Delight', 'Autumn Fire', 'Autumn Joy')	HYBRID AUTUMN SEDUM
Hylotelephium (Sedum) spectabile	SHOWY STONECROP, AUTUMN SEDUM, BORDER SEDUM
Hylotelephium (Sedum) 'Vera Jameson'	PURPLE AUTUMN SEDUM
Ilex crenata 'Dwarf Pagoda'	DWARF JAPANESE HOLLY
Iris confusa	BAMBOO IRIS
Iris purdyi	PURDY'S IRIS ❖
Iris germanica	BEARDED IRIS
Juniper communis 'Alpine Carpet'	ALPINE CARPET JUNIPER
Kniphofia species and hybrids	TORCH LILY, RED HOT POKER
Lavandula angustifolia	ENGLISH LAVENDER
Leucocrinum montanum	SAND-LILY ❖
Lewisia columbiana var. *columbiana*	COLUMBIAN LEWISIA ❖
Lewisia cotyledon	SISKIYOU LEWISIA ❖
Lewisiopsis tweedyi	TWEEDY'S LEWISIA ❖
Liatris ligulistylis	MEADOW BLAZING STAR
Liatris spicata	BLAZING STAR
Limonium latifolium	SEA LAVENDER
Linaria (purpurea Hybrid) 'Natalie'	NATALIE TOADFLAX
Lomatium columbianum	COLUMBIA DESERT PARSLEY ❖
Melaleuca (Callistemon) viridiflorus 'Xera's Hedgehog'	HEDGEHOG MOUNTAIN BOTTLEBRUSH
Mertensia longiflora	SAGEBRUSH BLUEBELLS ❖
Monarda punctata	SPOTTED BEE-BALM
Narcissus species and hybrids	NARCISSUS/DAFFODILS
Nepeta x faassenii 'Walkers Low'	WALKER'S LOW CATMINT
Oenothera fremontii	SHIMMER EVENING PRIMROSE
Olsynium (Sisyrinchium) douglasii	DOUGLAS' BLUE-EYED-GRASS ❖
Opuntia x columbiana	COLUMBIA PRICKLY PEAR ❖
Opuntia fragilis	BRITTLE PRICKLY PEAR ❖
Origanum x majoricum	HARDY MARJORAM
Penstemon azureus var. *azureus*	AZURE PENSTEMON ❖
Penstemon barrettiae	BARRETT'S BEARDTONGUE ❖
Penstemon cardwellii	CARDWELL'S PENSTEMON ❖
*Penstemon davidsonii**	DAVIDSON'S BEARDTONGUE ❖
Penstemon ellipticus	ROCKY LEDGE BEARDTONGUE ❖

Penstemon fruticosus	SHRUBBY PENSTEMON, BUSH PENSTEMON ❖
Penstemon newberryi var. *berryi*	BERRY'S MOUNTAIN PRIDE ❖
Penstemon pinifolius	PINE-LEAF PENSTEMON
Penstemon procerus var. *tolmiei**	TOLMIE'S PENSTEMON ❖
Penstemon richardsonii	RICHARDSON'S BEARDTONGUE ❖
Penstemon rupicola	ROCK PENSTEMON ❖
Petrosedum (Sedum) rupestre	BLUE SEDUM
Phedimus (Sedum) kamtschaticus	KAMSCHATKA SEDUM, ORANGE STONECROP
Phedimus (Sedum) spurius	CAUCASIAN STONECROP
Phlomis angustissima	DWARF GOLDEN TURKISH-SAGE
Phlomis fruticosa 'Nana'	DWARF JERUSALEM-SAGE
Phlomis italica	ITALIAN-SAGE
*Phlox diffusa**	SPREADING PHLOX ❖
Phlox subulata	ROCK PHLOX
Phyla nodiflora	FOGFRUIT
Pimelea prostrata	NEW ZEALAND DAPHNE
Potentilla nepalensis	NEPAL CINQUEFOIL
Potentilla neumanniana 'Nana'	DWARF SPOTTED CINQUEFOIL
Potentilla nivea	SNOW CINQUEFOIL
Prostanthera cuneata	ALPINE MINT BUSH
Psephellus (Centaurea) simplicicaulis	LILAC CORNFLOWER
Rhodanthemum (Chrysanthemum) hosmariense	MOROCCAN DAISY
Rudbeckia fulgida var. *sullivantii*	PERENNIAL BLACK-EYED SUSAN
Rudbeckia hirta	BLACK-EYED SUSAN
Salvia dorrii	PURPLE SAGE ❖
Salvia yangii (Perovskia atriplicifolia) and hybrids	RUSSIAN SAGE
Sedum acre	GOLD MOSS SEDUM
*Sedum divergens**	SPREADING STONECROP ❖
Sedum lanceolatum	LANCE-LEAVED STONECROP ❖
Sedum oreganum	OREGON STONECROP ❖
Sedum oregonense	CREAMY FLOWERED STONECROP ❖
Sedum sexangulare	TASTELESS SEDUM
Sedum spathulifolium	BROAD-LEAVED STONECROP ❖
Sedum stenopetalum	WORM-LEAF STONECROP
Sedum tetractinum	CHINESE STONECROP
Sempervivum many species and cultivars	HENS-AND-CHICKS
Sibbaldiopsis (Potentilla) tridentata	SHRUBBY FIVE FINGERS
Sisyrinchium bellum	WESTERN BLUE-EYED GRASS ❖
Sisyrinchium californicum	GOLDEN-EYED GRASS ❖
Sisyrinchium idahoense	BLUE-EYED GRASS ❖
Solidago elongata	WEST COAST GOLDENROD ❖
Solidago 'Little Lemon'	LITTLE LEMON GOLDENROD
Solidago multiradiata	NORTHERN GOLDENROD ❖
Sphaeralcea munroana	ORANGE GLOBE MALLOW ❖
Stachys byzantina (S. lanata) 'Silver Carpet'	TRAILING LAMB'S EARS
Stachys corsica	CORSICAN TRAILING LAMB'S EAR
Symphyotrichum (Aster) ericoides 'Snow Flurry'	TRAILING HEATH ASTER
Thermopsis chinensis 'Sophia'	CHINESE BUSH PEA
Thermopsis montana	MOUNTAIN GOLD-BANNER ❖

Thymus praecox ssp. *arcticus* 'Albus'	WHITE MOSS THYME
Thymus praecox ssp. *arcticus* 'Languinosus'	WOOLLY THYME
Thymus praecox ssp *praecox (T. polytrichus* ssp. *britannicus)*	MOTHER-OF-THYME
especially the cultivars 'Elfin', 'Minus', 'Pseudolanuginosus'	
Thymus serpyllum 'Pink Chintz'	CREEPING THYME
Thymus vulgaris 'Argenteus'	SILVER-EDGE THYME
Triteleia bridgesii	BRIDGES' TRITELEIA ❖
Triteleia grandiflora	LARGE-FLOWERED TRIPLET-LILY, WILD HYACINTH ❖
Triteleia hendersonii	HENDERSON'S TRITELEIA ❖
Triteleia (Brodiaea) hyacinthina	WHITE TRIPLET-LILY ❖
Triteleia ixioides	PRETTYFACE ❖
Tulipa clusiana including subspecies and forms	LADY TULIP
Tulipa dasystemon	DASYSTEMON TULIP
Tulipa linifolia (including *T. batalinii*)	BOKHARA TULIP, FLAX-LEAF TULIP
Tulipa orphanidea (including *T. whittallii*)	ANATOLIAN TULIP, COTTAGE TULIP
Tulipa sprengeri	SPRENGER'S TULIP
Tulipa sylvestris	WOODLAND TULIP
Tulipa urumiensis (T. tarda)	LATE TULIP, TARDY TULIP
Veronica liwanensis	TURKISH SPEEDWELL
Veronica pectinata	WOOLLY SPEEDWELL
Vitex agnus-castus 'Blue Puffball'	CHASTE "TREE"
Viola trinervata	SAGEBRUSH VIOLET ❖
Wyethia angustifolia	NARROWLEAF WYETHIA ❖

TREES FOR WINDY SITES

These are the trees that either resist or go-with-the-flow in areas of regular wind. Not a common situation in most of our area, mind you, but where it is, these trees can make a difference.

SMALL TO MEDIUM DECIDUOUS TREES

Acer campestre	HEDGE MAPLE
Amelanchier canadensis	SERVICEBERRY
Celtis australis	HACKBERRY
Cornus kousa and hybrids	DOGWOODS
Cotinus coggygria	SMOKETREE
Crataegus laevigata 'Paul's Scarlet'	SCARLET HAWTHORN
Crataegus douglasii	BLACK HAWTHORN ❖
Ilex x altaclarensis	HIGHCLERE HOLLY
Malus fusca	PACIFIC CRAB APPLE ❖
Prunus emarginata	BITTER CHERRY ❖
Salix hookeriana	COASTAL WILLOW ❖
Shepherdia argentea	SILVER BUFFALOBERRY ❖

TALL DECIDUOUS TREES

Liriodendron tulipifera	TULIP TREE
Populus hybrids	HYBRID POPLAR
Quercus garryana	GARRY OAK ❖
Salix alba var. *vitellina*	GOLDEN WILLOW
Taxodium mucronatum	MONTEZUMA CYPRESS

MEDIUM SIZE EVERGREEN TREES

Juniperus scopulorum	ROCKY MOUNTAIN JUNIPER
Juniperus virginiana	EASTERN RED-CEDAR
Picea pungens cultivars	COLORADO BLUE SPRUCE
Pinus contorta var. *contorta*	SHORE PINE ❖
Pinus nigra	AUSTRIAN PINE
Thamnocalamus tesselatus	BERGBAMBOES, MOUNTAIN BAMBOO
Thuja occidentalis	NORTHERN WHITE-CEDAR

»» More ...

TALL EVERGREEN TREES

Calocedrus decurrens	INCENSE-CEDAR ❖
Chamaecyparis lawsoniana	PORT ORFORD CEDAR ❖
Magnolia grandiflora	SOUTHERN MAGNOLIA
Picea abies	NORWAY SPRUCE
Picea pungens var. *glauca*	COLORADO BLUE SPRUCE
Pinus nigra	AUSTRIAN PINE
Pinus ponderosa	PONDEROSA PINE ❖
Pinus sylvestris	SCOTCH PINE
Pseudotsuga menziesii	DOUGLAS-FIR ❖

TIPS FOR TREES IN WINDY SITES

Plant young plants from small containers and be patient. Small plants adjust better to windy sites and become "one with the wind."

Plant trees in groves. Trees in tight colonies help support and protect each other against the full windy forces.

If you do stake newly-planted trees, stake them properly and only long enough for the root ball to put out roots and anchor itself. Do not leave stakes in beyond 18 months. An updated alternative to staking is to root-wash the tree before planting so that a root systems goes into the soil without a ball that would wobble around.

Prune older trees, by removing inner branches, to open them up. The less resistance against the wind, the less breakage.

DENSE GROUNDCOVERS FOR WEED SUPPRESSION

Where early spring weeds come up before the rest of the garden, it's best to consider the evergreen (e) types among this list. Select wisely; a few of these weed suppressors can become "weedy" themselves in the right location.

Alchemilla alpina	ALPINE LADY'S-MANTLE
Alchemilla mollis	LADY'S MANTLE
Arctostaphylos 'Emerald Carpet' (e)	EMERALD CARPET MANZANITA
Baccharis tricuneata (B. magellanica) low form	CHRISTMAS BUSH
Berberis buxifolia 'Nana' (e)	DWARF MAGELLAN BARBERRY
Bergenia ciliata (e)	FUZZY-LEAVED BERGENIA
Bergenia hybrids (e)	BERGENIA
Calluna vulgaris (e)	SCOTCH HEATHER
Carex flaccosperma (e)	BLUE WOOD SEDGE
Carex inops (C. pensylvanica) (e)	CREEPING SEDGE ❖
Carex pansa (e)	MEADOW SEDGE ❖
Carex siderosticha var. *ciliatomarginata* 'Treasure Island' (e)	
	CREEPING BROAD-LEAF SEDGE
Carex tumulicola (e)	FOOTHILL SEDGE ❖
Carex oshimensis cultivars (e)	VARIEGATED JAPANESE SEDGE
Ceanothus gloriosus cultivars (e)	POINT REYES CEANOTHUS
Ceratostigma plumbaginoides	DWARF PLUMBAGO
Chrysosplenium macrophyllum	GIANT GOLDEN SAXIFRAGE
Clinopodium (Micromeria, Satureja) douglasii (e)	YERBA BUENA ❖
Cotoneaster adpressus 'Little Gem'	COMPACT COTONEASTER
Cotoneaster dammeri (e)	BEARBERRY COTONEASTER
Cotoneaster hodjingensis (C. glaucophyllus) (e)	GRAY-LEAF COTONEASTER
Cotoneaster procumbens 'Queen of Carpets' (e)	Q. O. H. COTONEASTER
Cotoneaster salicifolius 'Repens' (e)	SPREADING WILLOW-LEAF COTONEASTER
Daboecia cantabrica (e)	IRISH HEATH
Delosperma lavisiae	DRAKENSBERG ICE PLANT
Epimedium leptorrhizum (e)	FAIRY WINGS, BISHOP'S HAT
Epimedium perralchicum (e)	FAIRY WINGS, BISHOP'S HAT
Epimedium perraldarianum (e)	FAIRY WINGS, BISHOP'S HAT
Epimedium pinnatum (e)	FAIRY WINGS, BISHOP'S HAT
Epimedium x *rubrum* 'Sweetheart' (e)	FAIRY WINGS, BISHOP'S HAT
Epimedium x *warleyense* (e)	FAIRY WINGS, BISHOP'S HAT
Festuca rubra var. *juncea* 'Patrick's Point' (e)	BLUE CREEPING FESCUE ❖
Gaultheria procumbens (e)	WINTERGREEN
Geranium macrorrhizum (e)	BIG-ROOT GERANIUM
Hebe decumbens (e)	CREEPING HEBE
Helianthemum nummularium (e)	SUN ROSE
Hosta sieboldiana	HOSTA
Juniperus procumbens 'Nana'	JAPANESE GARDEN JUNIPER
Lonicera crassifolia (e)	CREEPING HONEYSUCKLE
Mahonia repens (e)	CREEPING OREGON-GRAPE ❖
Microbiota decussata (e)	SIBERIAN CYPRESS

195

Mukdenia rossii 'Karasuba' (e)	MUKDENIA
Ophiopogon planiscapus 'Nigrescens' (e)	BLACK MONDO GRASS
Pachysandra procumbens	ALLEGHANY SPURGE
Pachysandra terminalis (e)	JAPANESE SPURGE
Persicaria affinis 'Superba' (e)	KNOTWEED
Phedimus (Sedum) kamtschaticus (e)	KAMSCHATKA SEDUM
Phedimus (Sedum) spurius (e)	DRAGON'S-BLOOD SEDUM
Phlox divaricata	WILD PHLOX
Phlox stolonifera (e)	CREEPING PHLOX
Phlox subulata (e)	CREEPING PHLOX
Rhus aromatica 'Gro-Low'	GRO-LOW SUMAC
Rubus calycinoides (R. hayata-koidzumii) (e)	CREEPING TAIWAN BLACKBERRY
Stachys byzantina (S. lanata) (e)	LAMB'S EARS
Thymus herba-barona (e)	CARAWAY-SCENTED THYME

WEED-SUPPRESSING SEASONAL COVER CROPS

Brassica rapa	TURNIPS
Brassica rapa var. *rapa*	MUSTARD
Brassica napus ssp. *napus*	RAPESEED
Fagopyrum esculentum	BUCKWHEAT
Helianthus annuus	SUNFLOWER
Hordeum vulgare	WINTER BARLEY
Raphanus sativus	RADISH (FORAGE)
Raphanus sativus var. *longipinnatus*	DAIKON RADISH
Secale cereale	WINTER CEREAL RYE
Sorghum × drummondii	SORGHUM-SUDANGRASS
Trifolium subterraneum	SUBTERRANEAN CLOVER

DEER RESISTANT

It is important to note that the species listed are deer *resistant*, not deer *proof*. Deer are likely to sample anything as they move through your yard, especially if it's near their routine pathways. Newly planted trees or shrubs are especially vulnerable and steps may need to be taken to protect them until they are more mature. The plants on this list are best used by planting them around the periphery of one's property as a discouraging (to the deer) buffer zone.

TREES

Abies species	TRUE FIRS ❖
Acer species	MAPLES
Aesculus indica	INDIAN HORSE CHESTNUT
Asimina triloba	PAWPAW
Betula nigra	RIVER BIRCH
Betula papyrifera	PAPER BIRCH ❖
Callitropsis (Chamaecyparis, Cupressus, Xanthocyparis) nootkatensis	
	ALASKA YELLOW-CEDAR ❖
Cedrus atlantica	ATLAS CEDAR
Cedrus deodara	DEODAR CEDAR
Cephalotaxus harringtonia	JAPANESE PLUM YEW
Cercidiphyllum japonicum	KATSURA TREE
Crataegus species and hybrids	HAWTHORN
Ficus johannis ssp. *afghanistanica*	AFGHAN FIG
Fraxinus latifolia	OREGON ASH ❖
Ginkgo biloba	GINKGO
Magnolia species and hybrids	MAGNOLIA
Microbiota decussata	RUSSIAN CYPRESS
Parrotia subaequalis	CHINESE IRONWOOD
Picea species	SPRUCES ❖
Pinus species	PINES
Pseudotsuga menziesii	DOUGLAS-FIR ❖
Quercus species	OAKS
Tsuga species	HEMLOCKS ❖
Umbellularia californica	OREGON MYRTLE, CALIFORNIA BAY ❖

SHRUBS

Arctostaphylos species	MANZANITAS ❖
Baeckea gunniana	HEATHMYRTLE
BAMBOOS (several genera and species)	BAMBOOS
Berberis species	BARBERRY
Buxus sempervirens	COMMON BOXWOOD
Calluna species	HEATHER
Calycanthus occidentalis	SPICEBUSH
Carpenteria californica cultivars	BUSH ANEMONE

Caryopteris x clandonensis	BLUE MIST SHRUB
Chaenomeles species and hybrids	JAPANESE QUINCE
Chrysojasminum species	YELLOW JASMINES
Corokia cotoneaster	COROKIA
Cotinus coggygria	SMOKETREE
Daphne species and hybrids	DAPHNE
Dasiphora (Potentilla) fruticosa	SHRUBBY CINQUEFOIL ❖
Erica species and hybrids	HEATH
Escallonia species and hybrids	ESCALLONIA
Elsholtzia stauntonii	CHINESE MINT SHRUB
Fatsia japonica	FATSIA
Frangula (Rhamnus) purshiana	CASCARA ❖
Garrya elliptica	COAST SILK-TASSEL ❖
Gaultheria shallon	SALAL ❖
Hydrangea species and hybrids	HYDRANGEA
Juniperus species	JUNIPER
Kerria japonica	KERRIA
Leptospermum species	TEA TREE
Leucothoe fontanesiana	DROOPING LEUCOTHOE
Mahonia aquifolium	OREGON-GRAPE ❖
Mahonia bealei	LEATHER-LEAF MAHONIA
Microbiota decussata	SIBERIAN CARPET CYPRESS
Morella (Myrica) californica	PACIFIC WAX MYRTLE ❖
Paxistima (Pachystima) myrsinites	OREGON BOXWOOD ❖
Phlomis italica	BALEARIC ISLAND-SAGE
Pieris floribunda	MOUNTAIN PIERIS
Pieris japonica	JAPANESE PIERIS, ANDROMEDA
Rhododendron species	RHODODENDRONS AND AZALEAS ❖
Rhus aromatica	FRAGRANT SUMAC
Rhus glabra	SMOOTH SUMAC ❖
Ribes species	CURRANTS AND GOOSEBERRIES ❖
Ruscus species	BUTCHER'S BROOMS
Salvia rosmarinus (Rosmarinus officinalis)	ROSEMARY
Sambucus racemosa	RED ELDERBERRY ❖
Sarcococca species	SWEET BOX
Skimmia japonica	JAPANESE SKIMMIA
Spiraea douglasii	DOUGLAS SPIREA ❖
Spiraea species and hybrids	SPIREA
Syringa species and hybrids	LILAC
Teucrium chamaedrys	WALL GERMANDER
Vaccinium ovatum	EVERGREEN HUCKLEBERRY ❖
Viburnum species	CRANBERRYBUSH ❖

GROUNDCOVERS

Arctostaphylos uva-ursi	KINNIKINNICK ❖
Asarum species	WILD GINGER
Bolax gummifera (Azorella trifurcata)	CUSHION BOLAX
Campanula poscharskyana	SERBIAN BELLFLOWER
Cardamine trifolia	THREE-LEAF CARDAMINE
Carex species and cultivars	SEDGES
Cerastium tomentosum	SNOW-IN-SUMMER
Ceratostigma plumbaginoides	DWARF PLUMBAGO
Fragaria chiloensis	BEACH STRAWBERRY ❖
Gaultheria ovatifolia	WESTERN TEABERRY ❖
Gaultheria procumbens	WINTERGREEN
Gazania linearis	TREASURE FLOWER
Juniperus species	JUNIPER
Pachysandra procumbens	ALLEGHENY SPURGE
Pachysandra terminalis	PACHYSANDRA
Thymus species	THYME

PERENNIALS & BULBS

Acanthus species	BEAR'S BREECH
Achillea filipendulina	YELLOW YARROW
Achillea millefolium	YARROW ❖
Acis autumnalis	AUTUMN SNOWDROPS
Aconitum species	MONKSHOOD
Acorus species	JAPANESE SWEET FLAG
Agastache species	GIANT HYSSOP, HUMMINGBIRD MINT
Agave many species	AGAVE
Allium species and hybrids	ORNAMENTAL ONIONS, GARLICS
X *Amarine tubergenii*	VAN TUBERGEN'S AMARINE LILY
X *Amarygia*	HYBRID NAKED LADIES
Amaryllis belladonna	NAKED LADIES
Amsonia species	AMSONIA
Anemone species	ANEMONE
Aquilegia formosa	WESTERN COLUMBINE ❖
Aquilegia hybrids	COLUMBINE
Arabis caucasica	ROCK-CRESS
Aralia spinosa	DEVIL'S WALKING STICK
Arisaema species	JACK-IN-THE-PULPIT
Armeria maritima	SEA THRIFT ❖
Artemisia ludoviciana	WESTERN MUGWORT
Aruncus species and hybrids	GOAT'S-BEARD
Asclepias species	MILKWEED
Asplenium scolopendrium	HART'S-TONGUE FERN
Aubrieta deltoidea	PURPLE ROCK-CRESS
Baptisia species and hybrids	FALSE INDIGO
Brunnera macrophylla	SIBERIAN BUGLOSS

Cactaceae species	CACTUS
Calamagrostis species	FEATHER REED GRASS
Campanula rotundifolia	HAREBELL ❖
Carex species	SEDGES ❖
Clematis fremontii	FREMONT'S LEATHER FLOWER
Colchicum species and hybrids	AUTUMN CROCUS
Convallaria majalis	LILY-OF-THE-VALLEY
Coreopsis verticillata	THREAD-LEAF COREOPSIS
Corydalis species	CORYDALIS
Cyrtomium falcatum	HOLLY FERN
Dennstaedtia punctilobula	HAY-SCENTED FERN
Dicentra eximia	FRINGED BLEEDING HEART
Dicentra formosa	WESTERN BLEEDING HEART ❖
Dierama dracomontanum	DRAKENBERG WANDFLOWER
Dierama reynoldsii	ANGEL'S FISHING ROD
Digitalis species and hybrids	FOXGLOVE
Drimia species	SQUILL
Dryopteris marginalis	WOOD FERN
Echinops ritro	GLOBE THISTLE
Eranthis species	WINTER ACONITE
Eremurus himalaicus	HIMALAYAN FOXTAIL LILY
Eremurus hybrids	FOXTAIL LILY
Eremurus stenophyllus	DESERT CANDLE
Erianthus ravennae	RAVENNA GRASS
Erigeron speciosus	WESTERN FLEABANE ❖
Erythranthe (Mimulus) guttatus	YELLOW MONKEY FLOWER ❖
Euphorbia species	EUPHORBIA
Fargesia species	CLUMP BAMBOO
FERNS (almost all)	FERNS
Festuca species	BLUE FESCUE
Fritillaria species	FRITILLARY
Galanthus nivalis	SNOWDROPS
Geranium species and hybrids	GERANIUM
GRASSES (almost all)	ORNAMENTAL GRASSES
Hakonechloa macra	HAKONECHLOA
Helictotrichon sempervirens	BLUE OAT GRASS
Helleborus species and hybrids	HELLEBORES
Hyacinthoides species	BLUEBELLS
Hyacinthus species	HYACINTH
Ipheion species	BLUE STAR FLOWER
Iris species	IRISES ❖
Isodon umbrosus	ISODON
Juncus species	HARD RUSH
Kniphofia hybrids	RED-HOT POKER, TORCH LILY
Lamprocapnos (Dicentra) spectabilis	BLEEDING HEART
Leucocoryne species	GLORY OF THE SUN
Leucojum species	SNOWDROPS
Leucosceptrum species	JAPANESE SHRUB MINT
Leymus arenarius	LYME GRASS

200

Liatris species	GAYFEATHER, BLAZING STAR
Ligularia species and hybrids	LEOPARD PLANT
Lupinus species	LUPINES ❖
Lycoris species and hybrids	SPIDER LILY
Mentha species	MINT
Miscanthus sinensis	JAPANESE SILVER-GRASS
Molinia caerulea	PURPLE MOOR GRASS
Muscari species	GRAPE HYACINTH
Narcissus species	NARCISSUS, JONQUILS, DAFFODILS
Nerine species and hybrids	GUERNSEY LILY
Origanum species	OREGANO
Ornithogalum species	STAR-OF-BETHLEHEM
Paeonia species and hybrids	PEONY
Papaver species	POPPY
Penstemon species	BEARDTONGUES ❖
Phlomis species	GREEK JERUSALEM SAGE
Phormium species and hybrids	NEW ZEALAND FLAX
Podophyllum species	MAY APPLE
Polystichum species	SWORD FERNS ❖
Primula sieboldii	SIEBOLD'S PRIMROSE
Prospero species	SQUILL
Pulmonaria saccharata	LUNGWORT
Ranunculus species	BUTTERCUP
Rhodanthemum (Chrysanthemum) hosmariense	MOROCCAN DAISY
Rodgersia species	RODGERS FLOWER
Rudbeckia fulgida var. *sullivantii*	BLACK-EYED SUSAN
Rudbeckia subtomentosa	SWEET CONEFLOWER
Salvia species and hybrids	SAGE
Salvia yangii (Perovskia atriplicifolia)	RUSSIAN SAGE
Scilla species	SQUILL
Sisyrinchium species	YELLOW-EYED AND BLUE-EYED GRASSES ❖
Stachys byzantina (S. lanata)	LAMB'S EAR
Sternbergia species	AUTUMN DAFFODIL
Symphyotrichum (Aster) subspicatum (S. douglasii)	DOUGLAS ASTER ❖
Thalictrum species	MEADOW RUE
Thermopsis chinensis 'Sophia'	CHINESE BUSH PEA
Trollius x cultorum	GLOBEFLOWER
Watsonia angusta	SCARLET BUGLE FLOWER
Yucca species	YUCCA

201

RABBIT RESISTANT

Although there's really not much that is totally rabbit-proof, these perennials and shrubs hold up better than most. Note that young, tender plants and newly transplanted plants are especially susceptible, and mature, larger plants are better able to withstand nibbling bunnies.

Achillea species and hybrids	YARROWS
Agastache species and hybrids	GIANT HYSSOP, HUMMINGBIRD MINT
Agave species and hybrids	AGAVE, CENTURY PLANT
Allium species and hybrids	ORNAMENTAL ONIONS
Amsonia species	BLUESTARS
Anemone species and hybrids	ANEMONES
Aquilegia species and hybrids	COLUMBINES
Arisaema species and hybrids	JACK-IN-THE-PULPITS, COBRA LILIES
Armeria species	SEA PINK, THRIFT
Artemisia species	SAGE, MUGWORT, WORMWOOD
Arum species	ARUM
Asarum species	WILD GINGER
Asclepias species	BUTTERFLY WEED, MILKWEED
Asphodeline species	KING'S SPEAR, YELLOW ASPHODEL
Asphodelus species	ASPHODEL
Astilbe species and hybrids	ASTILBE
Baptisia species and hybrids	FALSE INDIGO
Begonia species and hybrids	BEGONIA
Betonica, Stachys species	HEDGE NETTLE, BETONY, LAMB'S-EARS
Brachyglottis species and hybrids	DAISY BUSH
Buddleja species and hybrids (not *B. davidii*)	BUTTERFLY BUSH
Canna species and hybrids	CANNA-LILY
Carex species	SEDGES
Caryopteris species and hybrids	BLUEBEARDS
Centaurea cineraria	VELVET CINERARIA, DUSTY MILLER
Centaurea gymnocarpa	DUSTY MILLER
Cerastium tomentosum	SNOW-IN-SUMMER
Colchicum species and hybrids	AUTUMN CROCUS
Coreopsis species and hybrids	COREOPSIS
Crocosmia species and hybrids	CROCOSMIA
Dahlia species and hybrids	DAHLIAS
Delosperma species and hybrids	HARDY ICE PLANT
Delphinium species and hybrids	DELPHINIUM
Dicentra species and hybrids	BLEEDING HEART
Epilobium (Zauschneria) species and cultivars	CALIFORNIA FUCHSIA
Eremurus species and hybrids	FOXTAIL LILIES
Ericameria species	RABBITBRUSH
Eriogonum ovalifolium var. *nivale*	CUSHION BUCKWHEAT ❖
Erodium species and hybrids	STORK'S-BILLS
Eryngium species and hybrids	SEA HOLLY, ERYNGO
Euphorbia species and hybrids	EUPHORBIAS
Festuca species	FESCUES
Gaillardia species and hybrids	INDIAN PAINTBRUSH, BLANKET FLOWER

Geranium species and hybrids	HARDY GERANIUM
Geum species and hybrids	AVENS
Glandularia (Verbena) species	MOCK VERVAIN, VERBENA
Helichrysum italicum	CURRY PLANT
Hemerocallis species and hybrids	DAYLILIES
Hyacinthoides hispanica (NOT *H.* x *massartiana*)	SPANISH BLUEBELL
Hypericum species and hybrids	ST. JOHN'S-WORT
Iberis species	CANDYTUFT
Ilex species and hybrids	HOLLIES
Iris species and hybrids	IRIS
Jacobaea maritima	DUSTY MILLER
Juniperus species and cultivars	JUNIPERS
Kniphofia species and hybrids	RED HOT POKER, TORCH LILIES
Lamprocapnos (Dicentra) spectabilis	OLD-FASHIONED BLEEDING HEART
Lavandula species and hybrids	LAVENDERS
Leptospermum lanigerum	WOOLLY TEA TREE
Leucosceptrum species	JAPANESE SHRUB MINT
Lupinus species and hybrids	LUPINES
Mahonia species and hybrids	MAHONIA, BARBERRY, OREGON-GRAPE
Mandevilla laxa	CHILEAN JASMINE
Mentha species and hybrids	MINTS
Miscanthus species	SILVER GRASS
Monarda species and hybrids	BEE BALMS, BERGAMOT
Muhlenbergia species	MUHLY GRASSES
Myosotis species	FORGET-ME-NOTS
Narcissus species and hybrids	NARCISSUS, DAFFODILS, JONQUILS
Nepeta species and hybrids	CATMINT, CATNIP
Origanum species and hybrids	ORNAMENTAL OREGANOES
Pachysandra species	PACHYSANDRA
Papaver species	POPPIES
Penstemon species and hybrids	BEARDTONGUE
Phlomis species	JERUSALEM-SAGE
Phlox species and hybrids	PHLOX
Platycodon	BALLOON FLOWER
Pulmonaria species and hybrids	LUNGWORT
Rhazya species	ASIAN BLUESTARS
Rhodanthemum (Chrysanthemum) hosmariense	MOROCCAN DAISY
Rhododendron species and hybrids	RHODODENDRONS, AZALEAS
Ribes species and hybrids	CURRANTS, GOOSEBERRIES
Rudbeckia species and hybrids	BLACK-EYED SUSAN, CONEFLOWERS
Salvia rosmarinus (Rosmarinus officinalis)	ROSEMARY
Salvia species and hybrids	SAGES
Salvia yangii (Perovskia) including other species and hybrids	RUSSIAN SAGE
Santolina chamaecyparissus	LAVENDER COTTON
Scabiosa species	PINCUSHION FLOWERS
Sedum (including *Hylotelephium, Petrosedum, Phedimus, Rhodiola*) species and hybrids	SEDUMS, STONECROPS
Senecio candicans 'Angel Wings'	DUSTY MILLER
Senecio vira-vira	DUSTY MILLER

Tanacetum haradjanii (T. densum amanii)	SILVER LACE TANSY
Tanacetum ptarmiciflorum	SILVER LACE PLANT
Teucrium aroanium	GRAY CREEPING GERMANDER
Thermopsis chinensis 'Sophia'	CHINESE BUSH PEA
Thymus praecox 'Pseudolanuginosus'	WOOLLY THYME
Thymus species and hybrids	THYMES
Trachelospermum species	STAR JASMINE, ASIATIC JASMINE
Verbascum bombyciferum 'Arctic Summer'	GIANT SILVER MULLEIN
Verbascum densiflorum	DENSE-FLOWERED MULLEIN
Verbascum epixanthinum	YELLOW MULLEIN
Verbascum eriophorum	COTTON MULLEIN
Verbascum x splendidum	SPLENDID MULLEIN
Verbena species	VERBENA
Veronica (including *Parahebe*) species and hybrids	SPEEDWELL
Veronica pectinata	WOOLLY SPEEDWELL
Vinca species	PERIWINKLES
Zantedeschia species and hybrids	CALLA-LILIES

RODENT RESISTANT BULBS

These are rarely touched by scavenging rodents and are good deterrents to keep the rodents off other, tasty bulbs (e.g., tulips, crocus) when they are planted among and around them.

Acis (Leucojum) species	AUTUMN SNOWDROPS
Allium species and hybrids	ORNAMENTAL ONIONS
Amaryllis belladonna	NAKED LADY
X Amarine tubergenii	VAN TUBERGEN'S AMARINE LILY
X Amarygia	HYBRID NAKED LADY
Asphodeline species	KING'S SPEAR, YELLOW ASPHODEL
Asphodelus species	ASPHODEL
Beauverdia species	BEAUVERDIA
Chlidanthus fragrans	PERFUMED FAIRY LILY
Colchicum species and hybrids	AUTUMN CROCUS
Disporum species	FAIRY BELLS
Drimia species	SQUILL
Eranthis species and hybrids	WINTER ACONITES
Eremurus species and hybrids	FOXTAIL LILIES
Fritillaria species	FRITILLARIAS
Galanthus species and hybrids	SNOWFLAKES
Hyacinthoides species	BLUEBELLS
Hyacinthus species and hybrids	HYACINTH
Ipheion species	SPRING STARFLOWER
Ismene species and hybrids (not all are hardy here)	PERUVIAN DAFFODIL
Leucocoryne species	GLORY-OF-THE-SUN
Leucojum species and hybrids	SNOWFLAKES
Lycoris species and hybrids	SPIDER LILIES
Muscari species	GRAPE HYACINTH
Narcissus species and hybrids	NARCISSUS, DAFFODILS, JONQUILS
Nerine species and hybrids	SPIDER LILIES
Nothoscordum species	FALSE GARLIC
Ornithogalum species	STAR-OF-BETHLEHEM
Prospero species	AUTUMN HYACINTH
Scilla (including *Chionodoxa*) species and hybrids	BLUEBELLS
Sternbergia species and hybrids	AUTUMN DAFFODIL

SLUG AND SNAIL RESISTANT

Primarily herbaceous perennials although a few representative shrubs have been thrown in (almost all woody plants are slug/snail-resistant).

Achillea species and hybrids	YARROWS
Aconitum species and hybrids	MONKSHOOD
Actaea (Cimicifuga) species and hybrids	COHOSH
Alcea species	HOLLYHOCKS
Alchemilla species	LADY'S MANTLE
Allium species and hybrids	ORNAMENTAL ONION
Alyssum species and hybrids	MADWORT
Amaranthus species and hybrids	AMARANTH
Anaphalis species	PEARLY EVERLASTING
Anchusa species	ALKANET
Anemone species and hybrids	ANEMONE, WINDFLOWER
Anemone (Hepatica) nobilis	HEPATICA
Antennaria species	EVERLASTING, PUSSYTOES
Antirrhinum (depending on species)	SNAPDRAGONS
Aquilegia species and hybrids	COLUMBINE
Arabis species	ROCKCRESS
Armeria species and hybrids	SEA PINK, THRIFT
Artemisia species	WORMWOOD
Aruncus species and hybrids	GOATS-BEARDS
Aster species and hybrids	ASTER
Astilbe species and hybrids	ASTILBE
Astrantia major	MASTERWORT
Aubrieta species	FALSE ROCKCRESS
BAMBOOS	BAMBOO
Begonia species and hybrids	BEGONIA
Bellis perennis	ENGLISH DAISY
Bergenia species and hybrids	BERGENIA
Betonica, Stachys species and hybrids	HEDGE NETTLES, LAMB'S EARS
Brachyglottis species and hybrids	DAISY BUSH
Brunnera macrophylla	GREAT FORGET-ME-NOT
Calendula officinalis	CALENDULA
Callistephus chinensis	CHINA ASTER
Campanula (vulnerability depending on the species)	BELLFLOWERS
Carex species	SEDGES
Caryopteris species and hybrids	BLUEBEARD
Centaurea species	BLUETS, CORNFLOWERS, BASKET FLOWERS
Centranthus ruber	JUPITER'S BEARD, RED VALERIAN
Convallaria majallis	LILY OF THE VALLEY
Coreopsis verticillata	THREAD-LEAF COREOPSIS
Corydalis species and hybrids	FUMEWORT
Cosmos bipinnatus	COSMOS
Cotinus species and hybrids	SMOKE TREE
Cyclamen species	SOWBREAD, HARDY CYCLAMEN
Cymbalaria species	IVY-LEAVED TOADFLAX

Dasiphora (Potentilla) fruticosa	SHRUBBY CINQUEFOIL ❖
Delphinium species and hybrids	DELPHINIUM
Dianthus species and hybrids	CARNATION, PINKS, SWEET WILLIAM
Digitalis species and hybrids	FOXGLOVES
Dryas octopetala	MOUNTAIN AVENS
Echinacea (sometimes infested)	CONEFLOWERS
Echinops species	GLOBE THISTLES
Epimedium species and hybrids	BARRENWORT, BISHOP'S HAT
Erigeron species and hybrids	FLEABANES, DAISIES
Erysimum species and hybrids	WALLFLOWER
Eschscholzia californica	CALIFORNIA POPPY
Euphorbia species and hybrids	SPURGE
FERNS (many)	FERNS ❖
Festuca species	BLUE FESCUE
Filipendula species and hybrids	MEADOWSWEET
Forsythia species and hybrids	FORSYTHIA
Fritillaria species	FRITILLARY
Fuchsia species and hybrids	FUCHSIA
Fumaria species	ANNUAL FUMITORY, FUMEWORT
Gaillardia species and hybrids	BLANKET FLOWER
Galanthus species	SNOWDROP
Galium odoratum	SWEET WOODRUFF
Gaultheria shallon	SALAL
Gazania species and hybrids	GAZANIA
Geranium species and hybrids	HARDY GERANIUM, CRANESBILLS
Geum species and hybrids	AVENS
Gladiolus species and hybrids	GLADIOLA
Glandularia (Verbena) species and hybrids	MOCK VERVAIN, VERBENA
Glebionis segetum	CORN MARIGOLD
GRASSES	ORNAMENTAL GRASSES
Gypsophila paniculata	BABY'S BREATH
Hedychium species and hybrids	FLOWERING GINGERS
Helenium species and hybrids	SNEEZEWEED
Helianthemum nummularium	ROCKROSE
Helichrysum italicum	CURRY PLANT
Helipterum species	SILVER BELLS, AUSTRALIAN STRAWFLOWER
Helleborus species and hybrids	HELLEBORE
Hemerocallis (strongly varietal and location dependent)	DAYLILIES
Hesperis matronalis	DAME'S ROCKET, SWEET ROCKET
Heuchera species and hybrids	CORAL BELLS
X *Heucherella* hybrids	CORAL-BELLS x FOAMFLOWER
Hyacinthoides hispanica (NOT *H.* x massartiana)	SPANISH BLUEBELL
Hydrangea macrophylla	HYDRANGEA
Hydrangea paniculata	PANICLED HYDRANGEA
Hypericum species	ST. JOHN'S WORT
Iberis species	CANDYTUFT
Impatiens species	JEWELWEED, BALSAM
Inula helenium	ELECAMPANE
Iris ensata	JAPANESE IRIS

Iris sibirica	SIBERIAN IRIS
Iris (other species strongly dependent on variety and location)	IRIS
Jasminum species and hybrids	JASMINE
Juniperus species	JUNIPERS
Knautia macedonica	KNAUTIA, MACEDONIAN SCABIOUS
Lamprocapnos (Dicentra) spectabilis	OLD-FASHIONED BLEEDING HEART
Lathyrus species	PEAS, SWEET PEAS
Lavandula species and hybrids	LAVENDERS
Leucanthemum (depending on location)	SHASTA DAISY
Liatris (vulnerability dependents on the species)	BLAZING STAR, GAY FEATHER
Limonium species	SEA LAVENDER, STATICE
Linaria species and hybrids	TOADFLAX
Linnaea borealis	CREEPING TWINFLOWER
Lobelia species and hybrids	LOBELIA
Lobularia maritima	SWEET ALYSSUM
Lonicera species and hybrids	HONEYSUCKLES
Lychnis species and hybrids	CATCHFLIES
Lysimachia species and hybrids	LOOSESTRIFE
Malva (depending on the species and location)	MALLOWS
Meconopsis species and hybrids	HIMALAYAN POPPY
Monarda species and hybrids	BEE BALM
Muscari (including *Pseudomuscari, Leopoldia, Bellevalia*)	GRAPE HYACINTH
Musella lasiocarpa	GOLDEN LOTUS BANANA
Myosotis species	FORGET-ME-NOT
Narcissus species and hybrids	DAFFODILS, JONQUIL
Nemesia species and hybrids	NEMESIA
Nepeta species and hybrids	CATNIP, CATMINT
Nicotiana species and hybrids	FLOWERING TOBACCO
Nigella damascena	LOVE-IN-A-MIST
Oenothera species	EVENING PRIMROSE
Omphalodes species	BLUE-EYED-MARY
Oxalis species	OXALIS
Paeonia species and hybrids	PEONY
Papaver species and hybrids	POPPIES
Pelargonium species and hybrids	GERANIUM
Penstemon species and hybrids	BEARDTONGUE
Pericallis x hybrida	CINERARIA
Persicaria species	KNOTWEEDS, SMARTWEEDS
Phlox species and hybrids	PHLOX
Platycodon grandiflorus	BALLOON FLOWER
Polemonium species and hybrids	JACOB'S LADDER
Polemonium species and hybrids	JACOB'S LADDER ❖
Polygonatum species and hybrids	SOLOMON'S SEAL
Portulaca grandiflora	SUN ROSE
Potentilla species and hybrids	CINQUEFOILS
Primula species and hybrids	PRIMROSES
Pulmonaria species and hybrids	LUNGWORT
Pulsatilla species and hybrids	PASQUE FLOWER
Rhodiola species	MOUNTAIN STONECROP ❖

Rhododendron species and hybrids	RHODODENDRONS, AZALEAS
Rosa (depending on the species, cultivar)	ROSES
Rudbeckia species and hybrids	BLACK-EYED SUSAN
Salvia yangii (Perovskia) including other species and hybrids	RUSSIAN SAGE
Santolina species and hybrids	LAVENDER COTTON
Saxifraga species and hybrids	SAXIFRAGE, ROCKFOILS
Sedum (including *Hylotelephium, Petrosedum, Phedimus, Pseudosedum*)	SEDUMS, STONECROPS ❖
Sempervivum species and hybrids	HOUSELEEKS, HEN AND CHICKS
Senecio species and hybrids	DUSTY MILLERS, RAGWORTS, GROUNDSELS
Silene species and hybrids	CAMPION, CATCHFLY
Solidago species and hybrids	GOLDENROD
Spiraea species and hybrids	SPIREA
SUCCULENTS (almost all species of succulent plants)	SUCCULENTS
Symphyotrichum species and hybrids	ASTERS
Symphytum species and hybrids	COMFREY
Tanacetum parthenium	FEVERFEW
Teucrium species and hybrids	GERMANDERS
Thymus species and hybrids	THYMES
Tiarella species and hybrids	FOAMFLOWER
Trollius species and hybrids	GLOBEFLOWERS
Tropaeolum species	NASTURTIUMS
Tulipa species	TULIPS
Verbascum species and hybrids	MULLEINS
Verbena species	VERBENA
Veronica species and hybrids	SPEEDWELL
Viola (some species are vulnerable)	VIOLETS
Xeranthemum annuum	IMMORTELLE, EVERLASTING
Yucca species and hybrids	YUCCAS

PHYTOPHTHORA RESISTANT/TOLERANT

This root rot disease is prevalent in the Pacific Northwest particularly in soils with poor drainage. The leaves of infected plants appear drought stressed, sometimes turning dull green, yellow, red, or purple as they wilt. The list of susceptible species is long while, unfortunately, the list, as shown below, is short.

Aesculus x carnea 'Briotii'	RED HORSE CHESTNUT
Aesculus species and hybrids	BUCKEYE, HORSE CHESTNUT
Albizia julibrissin	SILK TREE
Alnus species	ALDER
Amaryllis belladonna	NAKED LADY
Amsonia species	BLUESTAR
Anemone species	ANEMONE
Aster species	ASTER
Baccharis species	COYOTE BRUSH
Betula nigra	RIVER BIRCH
Calycanthus species	SWEETSHRUB, SPICEBUSH
Canna species and hybrids	CANNA LILY
Carex species	ORNAMENTAL SEDGES
Chimonanthus praecox	WINTERSWEET
Cotoneaster species	COTONEASTER
Dahlia species	DAHLIA
Echinacea purpurea	PURPLE CONEFLOWER
Euonymus species	EUONYMUS
FERNS several species	FERNS
Fraxinus species	ASH
Gaillardia species	BLANKET FLOWER
Geranium species	HARDY GERANIUM, CRANESBILL
Ginkgo biloba	GINKGO
Gleditsia triacanthos var. *inermis*	HONEY LOCUST
GRASSES several species	ORNAMENTAL GRASSES
Iberis sempervirens	EVERGREEN CANDYTUFT
Ilex species and hybrids	HOLLIES
Linnaea (Abelia) species and hybrids	ABELIA
Liriodendron species and hybrids	TULIP TREE
Lychnis species	LYCHNIS, CAMPION
Lycoris radiata	SPIDER LILY
Magnolia species	MAGNOLIAS
Metasequoia glyptostroboides	DAWN REDWOOD
Monarda species	BEE BALM
Narcissus species	NARCISSUS, DAFFODIL
Nyssa sylvatica	BLACK GUM
Pachysandra species	PACHYSANDRA
Phlox subulata	CREEPING PHLOX, MOSS PHLOX
Podocarpus species	PODOCARPUS
Populus species	COTTONWOODS, POPLARS, ASPEN
Ribes species	CURRANTS, GOOSEBERRY
Rosa species and hybrids	ROSE

Salix species	WILLOWS
Symphyotrichum species	ASTER
Taxodium species	BALD CYPRESS
Tilia species	LINDEN
Trillium species	TRILLIUM
Ulmus species and hybrids	ELM
Zelkova serrata	KEAKI

VERTICILLIUM RESISTANT SMALL TREES

This is a very common soil-borne disease which gets into the stem tissues of plants, thereby plugging them and leading to chlorosis, wilting, and defoliation. One or more branches, usually on one side of the tree, wilt suddenly. Sometimes the leaves turn yellow before they wilt, or leaf margins turn brown and appear scorched. The susceptible list of plants is long, ranging from seasonal vegetables all the way to the biggest tree species. In trees, one good sign of the disease is a ring of discolored tissue in the branch. Here's a list of the better small-scale trees which can be considered where this disease is a problem.

Aesculus x carnea 'Briotii'	RED HORSE CHESTNUT
Abies smaller species and cultivars	FIR
Arbutus unedo	STRAWBERRY TREE
Arctostaphylos 'Austin Griffins'	AUSTIN GRIFFINS MANZANITA
Arctostaphylos manzanita 'St. Helena'	ST. HELENA MANZANITA
Azara microphylla	SMALL-LEAVED AZARA
Betula nigra 'Little King'	LITTLE KING RIVER BIRCH
Carpinus japonica	KUMA-SHIDE
Carpinus laxiflora	AKA-SHIDE
Cedrus smaller cultivars	CEDARS
Cercidiphyllum japonicum 'Claim Jumper'	GOLDEN KATSURA
Cercidiphyllum japonicum 'Heronswood Globe'	DWARF KATSURA
Clethra barbinervis (including its smaller 'Takeda Nishiki')	JAPANESE CLETHRA
Cornus 'Eddie's White Wonder'	EDDIE'S WHITE WONDER DOGWOOD
Cornus x elwinortonii hybrids	HYBRID DOGWOOD
Cornus kousa 'Satomi'	RED FLOWERING KOUSA DOGWOOD
Cornus kousa var. *chinensis* 'Milky Way'	MILKY WAY DOGWOOD
Crataegus x lavalleei	LAVALLÉE'S HAWTHORN
Crataegus viridis 'Winter King'	WINTER KING HAWTHORN
Cupressus smaller species	CYPRESSES
Embothrium coccineum	CHILEAN FIRE TREE
Emmenopterys henryi	EMMENOPTERYS
Eucryphia glutinosa	NIRRHE
Fagus sylvatica 'Purple Fountain'	PURPLE DWARF WEEPING BEECH
Fagus sylvatica 'Purpurea Tricolor'	TRICOLOR BEECH
Fagus sylvatica 'Zlatia'	GOLDEN BEECH
Ginkgo biloba 'Jade Butterfly'	DWARF GINKGO
Gleditsia triacanthos f. *inermis* 'Imperial'	IMPERIAL HONEY LOCUST
Halesia tetraptera 'Wedding Bells'	SILVER-BELLS
Hesperocyparis (*Cupressus*) species (smaller species)	CYPRESSES
Hydrangea paniculata 'Grandiflora'	PANICLE HYDRANGEA, PEE-GEE
Hydrangea paniculata 'Snow Mountain'	SNOW MOUNTAIN HYDRANGEA
Juniperus tree-like species	JUNIPERS
Larix smaller cultivars	LARCH
Luma apiculata	CHILEAN GUAVA
Maackia amurensis	AMUR MAACKIA
Melliodendron xylocarpum	CHINESE PARASOL
Parrotia persica	PERSIAN IRONWOOD

212

Picea smaller species and cultivars	SPRUCES
Pinus smaller species and cultivars	PINES
Pseudocydonia sinensis	CHINESE QUINCE
Quercus hypoleucoides	SILVERLEAF OAK
Quercus myrsinifolia	CHINESE EVERGREEN OAK
Rehderodendron macrocarpum	CHINESE REHDERODENDRON
Sciadopitys verticillata	JAPANESE UMBRELLA PINE
Staphylea holocarpa (including 'Rosea')	CHINESE BLADDERNUT
Stewartia monadelpha 'Black Dog'	BLACK-STEM STEWARTIA
Stewartia rostrata	BEAKED STEWARTIA
Stewartia 'Scarlet Sentinel'	SCARLET SENTINEL STEWARTIA
Styrax obassia (trained into standard)	FRAGRANT SNOWBELL
Taxus species	YEW
Tetradium (Evodia) daniellii	KOREAN EVODIA
Trochodendron aralioides	WHEEL TREE

Several conifer species have been included in this list. These are just a sampling of the many genera of conifers, all of which are verticillium resistant.

ASSERTIVE PLANTS

Good news, bad news. Considered overtly intrusive by many, these plants will grow "where nothing else will grow." If you plant these species, you must watch them carefully; they can become weedy — either by seeding or spreading vegetatively — in some garden sites. This list includes only those plants still sold in garden centers or through mail-order or, most likely, shared by friendly neighbors who "have plenty." Note that I have included a few of these in other, "recommended" lists; add this talent to these to help make your decision.

Aegopodium podagraria	BISHOP'S-WEED, GOUT-WEED
Ajuga reptans	CARPET BUGLE
Alchemilla mollis	LADY'S MANTLE
Anthriscus sylvestris	COW PARSLEY
Aquilegia vulgaris	EUROPEAN COLUMBINE
Artemisia ludoviciana and cultivars	WESTERN MUGWORT
BAMBOO, running types (several genera)	RUNNING BAMBOOS
Bellis perennis	ENGLISH DAISY
Borago officinalis	BORAGE
Calendula officinalis	CALENDULA
Campanula rapunculoides	CREEPING BELLFLOWER
Centaurea montana	PERENNIAL BACHELOR'S BUTTONS
Clematis terniflora	SWEET AUTUMN CLEMATIS
Convallaria majalis	LILY-OF-THE-VALLEY
Crocosmia most hybrids	CROCOSMIA
Digitalis purpurea	FOXGLOVE
Eriocapitella (Anemone) x *hybrida*	JAPANESE ANEMONE
Eschscholzia californica	CALIFORNIA POPPY
Euonymus alatus (maybe not 'Compacta')	BURNING BUSH
Euphorbia amygdaloides var. *robbiae*	EUPHORBIA
Euphorbia characias	EUPHORBIA
Galium odoratum	SWEET WOODRUFF
Houttuynia cordata	CHAMELEON PLANT
Hyacinthoides x *massartiana* (our common "bluebells")	SPANGLISH BLUEBELLS
Hypericum calycinum	CREEPING ST. JOHNS-WORT
Isotoma fluviatilis	BLUE STAR CREEPER
Leucanthemum x *superbum*, older cultivars	SHASTA DAISY
Leycesteria formosa	HIMALAYAN HONEYSUCKLE
Ligustrum (some species)	PRIVET
Linaria purpurea	PURPLE TOADFLAX
Lonicera japonica	JAPANESE HONEYSUCKLE
Lonicera tatarica	BUSH HONEYSUCKLE
Lysimachia ciliata	FRINGED LOOSESTRIFE
Lysimachia nummularia	CREEPING JENNY
Lysimachia punctata	LARGE YELLOW LOOSESTRIFE
Malva sylvestris 'Zebrina' (and other forms)	ZEBRA MALLOW
Melissa officinalis	LEMON BALM
Mentha species (most)	MINTS
Muscari armeniacum	GRAPE HYACINTH

214

Oenothera fruticosa	SUNDROPS
Origanum vulgare including subspecies, cultivars, and some hybrids	OREGANO
Ornithogalum umbellatum	STAR-OF-BETHLEHEM
Papaver (Meconopsis) cambricum	WELSH POPPY
Paulownia tomentosa	EMPRESS TREE
Physalis alkekengi	CHINESE LANTERN
Pseudofumaria (Corydalis) lutea	YELLOW CORYDALIS, ROCK FUMEWORT
Pyrus calleryana	CALLERY ("BRADFORD") PEAR
Romneya coulteri	MATILLIJA POPPY
Sedum (some species)	STONECROP
Silene (Lychnis) coronaria	ROSE CAMPION
Sorbaria sorbifolia	FALSE SPIREA
Symphytum officinale	COMFREY
Tanacetum parthenium	FEVERFEW
Vinca minor	TRAILING PERIWINKLE
Viola odorata, V. riviniana	VIOLETS
Wisteria sinensis (and maybe *Wisteria* species)	CHINESE WISTERIA

Then there are these few which are designated, legally, as "Invasive" or "Noxious" but are included here because an occasional garden center or mail-order source (especially out-of-state) still sells them or, more commonly, they are still shared by friendly gardeners.

Arum italicum	ITALIAN ARUM
Artemisia absinthium	ABSINTH
Berberis vulgaris	COMMON BARBERRY
Buddleja davidii (but see alternatives in the "SHRUBS" section)	BUTTERFLY BUSH
Cortaderia selloana	PAMPAS GRASS
Crataegus monogyna	ENGLISH HAWTHORN
Daucus carota ssp. *carota*	QUEEN ANNE'S LACE
Elaeagnus angustifolia	RUSSIAN OLIVE
Euphorbia myrsinites	MYRTLE SPURGE
Foeniculum vulgare	FENNEL
Gypsophila paniculata	BABY'S-BREATH
Hedera helix, Hedera hibernica	ENGLISH IVY
Hypericum perforatum	COMMON ST. JOHNSWORT
Iris pseudacorus	YELLOW FLAG IRIS
Lamium (Lamiastrum) galeobdolon	YELLOW ARCHANGEL
Prunus laurocerasus	ENGLISH LAUREL
Tanacetum vulgare	TANSY

215

PET-TOXIC PLANTS

Primarily based on the ASPCA database. All are toxic to dogs, cats, and horses, except as noted. Of course these are all "toxic" to various degrees but indicating such would need a complex system of coding. Suffice it to say, it's all dependent on how much you treasure your fur-babies and how much good research you want to do ("good research" = reading university and professional veterinarian websites).

Acer circinatum	VINE MAPLE
Acer rubrum (only horses)	RED MAPLE
Achillea millefolium	YARROWS
Aconitum species	MONKSHOOD
Actaea (including *Cimicifuga*) species	BUGBANE
Adonis species	PHEASANT'S EYE, SUMMER ADONIS
Aegopodium podagraria	BISHOP'S WEED
Aesculus species and hybrids	BUCKEYE, HORSE CHESTNUT
Ageratina species (only horses)	SNAKEROOT
Allium ampeloprasum	LEEK, ELEPHANT GARLIC
Allium cepa	ONION
Allium sativum	GARLIC
Allium schoenoprasm	CHIVES
Aloe vera	ALOE
Aloysia triphylla	LEMON VERBENA
Amaryllis belladonna (+ x Amarygia, x Amarine)	NAKED LADIES, AMARYLLIS
Ammi majus	FLORISTS' QUEEN ANNE'S LACE
Anemone species and hybrids	ANEMONE
Anemonopsis macrophylla	FALSE ANEMONE
Aquilegia species and hybrids	COLUMBINES
Aralia spinosa	DEVIL'S WALKING STICK
Arisaema species and hybrids	JACK-IN-THE-PULPIT, COBRA LILY
Arum species	LORD-AND-LADIES, ARUM
Asclepias species	MILKWEED, BUTTERFLYWEED
Beesia species	BEESIA
Begonia species and hybrids	BEGONIAS
Borago officinalis	BORAGE
Buxus species	BOXWOOD
Cannabis sativa	WEED
Carum carvi	CARAWAY
Catharanthus (Vinca) roseus	MADAGASCAR PERIWINKLE
Celastrus scandens	AMERICAN BITTERSWEET
Chamaemelum (Anthemis) nobilis	CHAMOMILE
Chamaenerion (Epilobium) angustifolium	FIREWEED
Chenopodium ambrosioides	EPAZOTE
Chrysanthemum species and hybrids	MUMS, ETC.
Clematis species and hybrids	CLEMATIS
Colchicum species and hybrids	AUTUMN CROCUS
Colocasia esculenta	TARO, ELEPHANT EARS
Consolida species	LARKSPUR
Convallaria majalis	LILY-OF-THE-VALLEY

Cordyline australis	CABBAGE TREE
CYCADS	CYCADS
Cyclamen species	CYCLAMEN
Cymbopogon citratus	LEMON GRASS
Cynoglossum species and hybrids (only horses)	HOUNDS-TONGUE, FORGET-ME-NOT
Dahlia hybrids	DAHLIA
Delphinium species and hybrids	DELPHINIUM
Dianthus caryophyllus	CARNATION
Digitalis species and hybrids	FOXGLOVE
Echium species (only horses)	BUGLOSS
Erigeron species and hybrids	SHOWY DAISY
Eucalyptus species	EUCALYPTUS
Euonymus species	BURNING BUSH, SPINDLE
Euphorbia species and hybrids	EUPHORBIA
Fagopyrum esculentum	BUCKWHEAT
Gardenia jasminoides	GARDENIA
Gladiolus species and hybrids	GLADIOLA
Hedera species	IVIES
Heliotropium arborescens (only horses)	HELIOTROPE
Helleborus species and hybrids	HELLEBORES
Hemerocallis species and hybrids (only cats)	DAYLILIES
Hippeastrum species and hybrids	AMARYLLIS
Hosta species and hybrids	HOSTA
Humulus lupulus (only dogs)	HOPS
Hyacinthus orientalis	HYACINTH
Hydrangea arborescens	HYDRANGEA
Hypericum species (only horses)	ST. JOHN'S-WORT
Ilex species and hybrids	HOLLY
Ipomoea species	MORNING GLORIES
Iris species and hybrids	IRIS
Juglans species	WALNUTS, HICKORIES
Kalanchoe species	KALANCHOE
Kalmia species	BOG LAUREL
Lantana camara and hybrids	LANTANA
Lathyrus latifolius	EVERLASTING PEA
Laurus nobilis	BAY LAUREL
Lavandula species and hybrids	LAVENDER
Leucothoe species and hybrids	DOGHOBBLE
Levisticum officinale	LOVAGE
Ligustrum species	PRIVET
Lilium species and hybrids (only cats)	LILIES
Lobelia species and hybrids	LOBELIA
Malus species and hybrids	APPLES, CRABAPPLES
Melia azedarach	CHINA BERRY
Mentha species	GARDEN MINTS
Nandina domestica	HEAVENLY BAMBOO
Narcissus species and hybrids	DAFFODILS, NARCISSUS, JONQUILS
Nicotiana species and hybrids	FLOWERING TOBACCO
Nigella damascena	LOVE-IN-A-MIST

Origanum majorana (only cats, dogs)	MARJORAM
Oxalis species	OXALIS, SHAMROCK PLANT
Paeonia species and hybrids	PEONIES
Pelargonium species and hybrids	GERANIUM
Petroselinum crispum	PARSLEY
Pieris species and hybrids	ANDROMEDA, LILY-OF-THE-VALLEY BUSH
Podocarpus species	YEW PINE
Podophyllum species	MAYAPPLE, UMBRELLA LEAF
Portulaca oleracea	MOSS ROSE
Prunus fruiting and ornamental species	APRICOT, CHERRIES, PEACHES, PLUMS, ETC., as well as ORNAMENTAL CHERRIES AND PLUMS
Pulsatilla species	PASQUE FLOWER
Quercus species (only horses)	OAKS
Ranunculus species	BUTTERCUPS
Raphanus species (only horses)	RADISH
Rheum species	ORNAMENTAL AND EDIBLE RHUBARBS
Rhododendron species and hybrids	RHODODENDRON, AZALEAS
Ricinus communis	CASTOR BEAN
Robinia species and hybrids	LOCUST
Rumex species	DOCK
Senecio species	RAGWORT
Solanum lycopersicum (Lycopersicum esculentum)	TOMATO
Solanum tuberosum	POTATO
Taxus species	YEW
Thalictrum species	MEADOW-RUE
Tradescantia species	SPIDERWORT
Trifolium hybridum (only horses)	ALSIKE CLOVER
Tulipa species and hybrids	TULIPS
Trollius species and hybrids	GLOBEFLOWER
Wisteria species	WISTERIA
Yucca species	YUCCA
Zantedeschia species and hybrids	CALLA-LILIES

FAST-GROWING TREES AND SHRUBS FOR QUICK COVER

Fast-growing plants can come with issues. Some are short-lived and some may be overly-vigorous. Although some are choice plants, many may have to be cut out after a few years. Always best to combine these rapid-growing species with slower-growing but choicer species.

Acer x freemanii 'Autumn Blaze'	AUTUMN BLAZE MAPLE
Acer grandidentata	BIGTOOTH MAPLE
Acer rubrum 'October Glory'	OCTOBER GLORY MAPLE
Betula nigra 'Heritage'	RIVER BIRCH
Betula papyrifera	PAPER BIRCH ❖
Cryptomeria japonica 'Radicans', 'Sekkan-sugi'	JAPANESE PLUME CEDAR
X *Cupressocyparis leylandii*	LEYLAND CYPRESS
Ginkgo biloba	GINKGO
Liriodendron tulipifera	TULIP TREE
Metasequoia glyptostroboides	DAWN REDWOOD
Populus hybrids	HYBRID POPLAR
Populus tremuloides	QUAKING ASPEN
Quercus acutissima	SAWTOOTH OAK
Thuja 'Green Giant'	GREEN GIANT ARBORVITAE
Amelanchier x grandiflora	SERVICEBERRY
Chaenomeles speciosa	FLOWERING QUINCE
Cornus sericea (*C. stolonifera*)	RED-TWIG DOGWOOD ❖
Cotinus 'Grace'	GRACE SMOKE TREE
Forsythia x intermedia	FORSYTHIA
Halimium species and hybrids	GOLDEN ROCKROSE
Hibiscus syriacus	ROSE-OF-SHARON
Hydrangea paniculata 'Grandiflora'	PEE-GEE HYDRANGEA
Kerria japonica	JAPANESE ROSE
Ligustrum x ibolium	NORTHERN PRIVET
Linnaea (Kolkwitzia) amabilis	BEAUTYBUSH
Philadelphus hybrids	MOCK ORANGE
Physocarpus opulifolius	NINEBARK
Ribes sanguineum	FLOWERING CURRANT ❖
Salix integra 'Hakuro Nishiki'	DAPPLED WILLOW
Sambucus nigra	ELDERBERRY
Spiraea cantoniensis	BRIDAL WREATH
Viburnum opulus	HIGHBUSH CRANBERRY
Vitex agnus-castus	CHASTE TREE

ATTRACTING BENEFICIAL INSECTS

Just about any plant which has tiny individual flowers in a cluster or spike or some such, is a pollinator and beneficial insect attractant. This includes pretty much any kind of daisy. A few of the most popular.

Achillea species and hybrids	YARROW lw, lb, hf, w
Anethum graveolens	DILL lw, lb, hf, w
Calendula officinalis	POT MARIGOLD lw, lb, hf
Carum carvi	CARAWAY lw, hf, w
Chamaemelum nobile	ROMAN CHAMOMILE lw, hf, w
Coriandrum sativum	CORIANDER lw, lb, hf, w
Cosmos bipinnatus	COSMOS lw, hf, w
Erigeron species and hybrids	FLEABANE lw, hf, w
Fagopyrum esculentum	BUCKWHEAT lb, hf, t
Foeniculum vulgare	FENNEL lw, lb, hf, w
Helianthus species and hybrids	SUNFLOWER lw, hf, w
Iberis species	CANDYTUFT lb, hf
Lavandula species and hybrids	LAVENDER hf
Lobularia maritima	SWEET ALYSSUM hf, w
Matricaria recutita	GERMAN CHAMOMILE lw, hf, w
Mentha species and hybrids (in containers)	MINTS hf
Penstemon species and hybrids	BEARDTONGUE lb, hf
Petroselinum crispum	PARSLEY hf, w, t
Sedum species	STONECROP hf, w
Tagetes tenuifolia	IRISH LACE MARIGOLD bb, lb, hf, w
Tanacetum parthenium	FEVERFEW hf
Thymus species and hybrids	THYMES hf, lb, lw, w, t
Trifolium species	CLOVERS hf, w, bb

Beneficial Insect Codes (and what they eat)

bb = big eyed bugs (mites, caterpillars, leafhoppers, thrips, whiteflies, various insect eggs)

db = damsel bugs (aphids, moth eggs, small caterpillars — corn earworm, European corn borer, cabbageworm — leafhoppers, small sawfly larvae, mites, asparagus beetle eggs and nymphs)

hf = hover flies (aphids, thrips)

lb = ladybugs (aphids, scale insects, adelgids, mites, and insect eggs)

lw = lacewings (aphids, caterpillars, insect eggs, spiders, mites)

mpb = minute pirate bugs (aphids, mites, thrips, psyllids, whiteflies, small caterpillars, insect eggs)

t = tachinid flies (caterpillars, beetle grubs, grasshoppers, sawfly larvae, fly maggots, earwigs)

w = parasitoid mini-wasps (aphids, beetle larvae, caterpillars, leaf-miners, mealybugs, sawfly larvae, scale, squash vine borers, stink bugs, whiteflies)

SPECIAL GARDENS, SPECIAL PLANTS

There are certainly gardens within gardens and there are plants which have special, welcomed talents.

Look for the symbol ❖ which indicates a native plant.

ATTRACTING BIRDS, BEES, BUTTERFLIES, AND HUMMINGBIRDS

Almost every flowering plant will attract birds, bees, butterflies, and/or hummingbirds. Simply put, if you plant flowers throughout your garden — as almost every gardener already does — you will attract these flying friends. It's better to dot the entire landscape with such plants rather than isolate them in a small "Butterfly (or whatever the creature) Garden." This lists shortcuts the process along with pointing out those favorites that are PNW native plants, which, for the bigger picture, are the most effective in maintaining the populations of our native birds, bees, etc.

What they attract:

Bi = songbirds; Be = bees and other pollinators; Bu = butterflies (* = larval food);
Hb = Hummingbirds; and ❖ = PNW native

ANNUALS, BIENNIALS

Carthamus tinctorius	SAFFLOWER Bi, Be, Bu
Cosmos bipinnatus	COSMOS Bi, Be, Bu
Cynara cardunculus	CARDOON Bi, Be, Bu, Hb
Phacelia tanacetifolia	LACY PHACELIA Be, Bu

BULBS

Allium acuminatum	TAPER-TIP ONION Be, ❖
Allium cernuum	NODDING ONION Be, Bu, Hb, ❖
Allium (Nectaroscordum) bulgaricum siculum	SICILIAN HONEY LILY Be
Amaryllis belladonna	NAKED LADIES Be, Hb
Anemonoides (Anemone) blanda	GRECIAN WINDFLOWER Be, Bu
Camassia cusickii	CUSICK'S QUAMASH Be, Bu, ❖
Camassia quamash	CAMAS, QUAMASH Be, Bu, ❖
Dichelostemma congestum	OOKOW Be, Bu, ❖
Dichelostemma ida-maia	FIRECRACKER FLOWER Be, Bu
Eucomis comosa	PINEAPPLE LILY B, Bu
Lilium columbianum	TIGER LILY Be, Bu, Hb, ❖
Lilium martagon	TURK'S CAP LILY Be, Bu, Hb
Lilium regale	REGAL LILY Be, Bu, Hb
Triteleia laxa	BLUE FOOL'S ONION Be, Bu, Hb

PERENNIALS

Achillea species and hybrids	YARROW	Be, Bu
Aconitum species and hybrids	MONKSHOOD	Be, Bu
Actaea species	BUGBANE	Be, Bu
Agastache species and hybrids	GIANT HYSSOP, HUMMINGBIRD MINT	Be, Bu, Hb
Ageratina altissima 'Chocolate'	PURPLE-LEAF BUGBANE	Be, Bu
Allium senescens	GERMAN GARLIC	Be, Bu, Hb
Amsonia species	BLUE STAR	Be, Bu
Anemonoides (Anemone) nemorosa	WOOD ANEMONE	Be, Bu
Aralia cordata	SPIKENARD	Bi, Be
Artemisia lactiflora	WHITE MUGWORT	Be, Bu
Aruncus dioicus	GOAT'S-BEARD	Be, Bu, ❖
Aster x frikartii	FRIKART'S ASTER	Be, Bu
Astrantia major	GREAT MASTERWORT	Be, Bu
Balsamorhiza deltoidea	PUGET BALSAMROOT	Bi, Be, Bu, ❖
Ceratostigma species	PLUMBAGO	Be, Bu, Hb
Coreopsis verticillata	THREAD-LEAF COREOPSIS	Be, Bu
Crocosmia hybrids	MONTBRETIA, CROCOSMIA	Be, Hb
Darmera peltata	UMBRELLA PLANT	Be, Bu
Dicentra formosa	WESTERN BLEEDING HEART	Be, Bu*, ❖
Digitalis species (not *D. purpurea*)	FOXGLOVE	Be, Bu
Dracocephalum grandiflorum	DRAGON'S HEAD	Be, Hb
Echinacea purpurea and hybrids	PURPLE CONEFLOWER	Bi, Be, Bu
Eriogonum species	BUCKWHEAT	Be, Bu, ❖
Eriophyllum lanatum	OREGON SUNSHINE, WOOLLY SUNFLOWER	Be, Bu, ❖
Eryngium species and hybrids	ERYNGO, SEA HOLLY	Be, Bu
Eurybia (Aster) divaricatus	WHITE WOOD ASTER	Be, Bu
Eutrochium (Eupatorium) species	JOE PYE WEED	Be, Bu, ❖
Fragaria chiloensis	BEACH STRAWBERRY	Bi, Be, Bu*, ❖
Geranium species and hybrids	HARDY GERANIUM	Be, Bu
Geum hybrids	GEUM, AVENS	Be, Bu
Helenium autumnale and hybrids	SNEEZEWEED	Bi, Be, Bu, ❖
Helianthemum nummularium	SUN ROSE	Be, Bu
Heuchera hybrids	CORAL BELLS	Be, Bu
Hosta species and hybrids	HOSTA	Be, Bu
Iris species and hybrids	IRIS	Be, Bu
Leucanthemum x superbum	SHASTA DAISY	Be, Bu
Leucosceptrum species	JAPANESE SHRUB MINT	Be, Bu, Hb
Lobelia tupa	DEVIL'S TOBACCO	Be, Bu, Hb
Lupinus polyphyllus	MEADOW LUPINE	Be, Bu*, ❖
Melittis melissophyllum	BASTARD BALM	Bu, Hb
Penstemon species and hybrids	PENSTEMON	Bi, Be, Hb, ❖
Persicaria amplexicaulis cultivars	BISTORT, MOUNTAIN FLEECE	Be, Bu
Phacelia hastata	SILVER-LEAF PHACELIA	Be, Bu, ❖
Primula pulverulenta	CANDELABRA PRIMROSE	Be, Bu, Hb
Rodgersia species	RODGERSIA	Be, Bu

223

Rudbeckia fulgida ssp. *sullivantii* 'Goldsturm'	BLACK-EYED SUSAN Be, Bu
Salvia species and hybrids	SAGE Be, Bu
Sedum species and hybrids	STONECROP Be, Bu, ❖
Smilacina racemosa	FALSE SOLOMON'S SEAL Be, Bu, ❖
Solidago species and hybrids	GOLDENROD Be, Bu
Symphyotrichum (Aster) species and hybrids	ASTER Be, Bu*
Trillium species	TRILLIUM Be, Hb, ❖
Vernonia species	IRONWEED Be, Bu, Hb
Viola langsdorfii	ALASKA VIOLET Be, Bu*, ❖

VINES

Campsis x tagliabuana	HYBRID TRUMPET CREEPER Be, Bu, Hb
Clematis armandii cultivars and hybrids	EVERGREEN CLEMATIS Be, Bu, Hb
Clematis hybrids	HYBRID CLEMATIS Be, Bu
Lonicera hispidula CHAPARRAL HONEYSUCKLE, HAIRY HONEYSUCKLE Bi, Hb, ❖
Lonicera ciliosa	ORANGE HONEYSUCKLE Bi, Be, Hb, ❖
Parthenocissus henryana	SILVER-VEIN CREEPER Bi
Parthenocissus quinquefolia	VIRGINIA CREEPER Bi
Parthenocissus tricuspidata	BOSTON IVY Bi

SHRUBS

Arbutus unedo	STRAWBERRY TREE Bi, Be, Hb
Arctostaphylos columbiana	HAIRY MANZANITA Bi, Bu, Hb, ❖
Berberis x gladwynensis 'William Penn'	WILLIAM PENN BARBERRY Bi, Be
Berberis darwinii	DARWIN'S BARBERRY Bi, Be, Bu
Callicarpa bodinieri	BEAUTYBERRY Bi, Be
Caryopteris species and hybrids	BLUEBEARD Be, Bu
Ceanothus hardy species	CALIFORNIA LILAC Be, Bu, Hb
Cistus species and hybrids	ROCKROSE Be, Bu
Cornus alba	TARTARIAN DOGWOOD Be, Bu
Cornus sericea	RED-TWIG DOGWOOD Be, Bu, ❖
Corylopsis species	WINTERHAZEL Be, Hb
Corylus cornuta var. *californica*	BEAKED HAZELNUT Bi, ❖
Cotoneaster species and hybrids	COTONEASTER Bi, Be
Daphne species and hybrids	DAPHNE Be, Bu
Enkianthus species	ENKIANTHUS Be, Bu
Erica species and hybrids	HEATH Be
Fothergilla species and hybrids	WITCH ALDER Be, Bu
Fuchsia species	HARDY FUCHSIA Be, Hb
Grevillea species and hybrids	GREVILLEA Be, Bu, Hb
Heptacodium miconioides	SEVEN-SON FLOWER Be, Bu, Hb
Hibiscus syriacus	ROSE-OF-SHARON Be, Bu
Holodiscus discolor	OCEAN SPRAY Bi, Be, Bu, ❖

Hydrangea macrophylla	HYDRANGEA Be, Bu
Linnaea (Abelia) x grandiflora	GLOSSY ABELIA Be, Bu
Lonicera involucrata	BLACK TWINBERRY Bi, Hb, ❖
Mahonia aquifolium	OREGON-GRAPE Be, Bu, ❖
Mahonia x media cultivars	HYBRID MAHONIA Bi, Hb
Monardella villosa ssp. *franciscana*	COYOTE MINT Be, Bu, ❖
Oemleria cerasiformis	INDIAN PLUM Bi, Be, ❖
Philadelphus lewisii	LEWIS' MOCK ORANG Bi, Be, ❖
Physocarpus capitatus	PACIFIC NINEBARK Bi, Be, Bu, ❖
Prostanthera cuneata	ALPINE MINT BUSH Be, Bu
Rhododendron macrophyllum	PACIFIC RHODODENDRON Be, Bu*, ❖
Rhododendron hybrids	HYBRID RHODODENDRON Be, Hb
Ribes acerifolium	MAPLE-LEAF CURRANT Bi, Be, Bu*, ❖
Ribes laxiflorum	TRAILING BLACK CURRANT Bi, Be, Bu*, ❖
Ribes sanguineum	RED-FLOWERED CURRANT Bi, Be, Bu*, Hb, ❖
Rosa hybrids	ROSE Be, Bu
Rosa mulliganii	MULLIGAN ROSE Be, Bu
Rubus parviflorus	THIMBLEBERRY Bi, Be, Hb, ❖
Rubus calycinoides (R. hayata-koidzumii)	CREEPING TAIWAN BRAMBLE Bi, Be
Salvia rosmarinus (Rosmarinus officinalis)	ROSEMARY Be
Salix scouleriana	SCOULER'S WILLOW Bi, Be, Bu*, ❖
Sambucus species	ELDERBERRY Bi, Be, Bu*, ❖
Spiraea betulifolia	BIRCH-LEAF SPIREA Be, Bu
Spiraea japonica cultivars	JAPANESE SPIRAEA Be, Bu
Spiraea splendens	ROSY SPIRAEA Be, Bu, ❖
Spiraea thunbergii	BRIDALWREATH SPIREA Be, Bu
Symphoricarpos albus	SNOWBERRY Bi, Be, Bu, ❖
Vaccinium membranaceum	MOUNTAIN HUCKLEBERRY Bi, Be, Bu*, ❖
Vaccinium ovalifolium	OVAL-LEAF BLUEBERRY Bi, Be, Bu*, ❖
Vaccinium ovatum	EVERGREEN HUCKLEBERRY Bi, Be, Bu*, Hb, ❖
Vaccinium parvifolium	RED HUCKLEBERRY Bi, Be, Bu*, ❖
Vaccinium hybrids	BLUEBERRY Bi, Be
Weigela florida cultivars	WEIGELA Be, Bu
Yucca species	YUCCA Be, Hb

TREES

Abies grandis	GRAND FIR Bi, ❖
Acer circinatum	VINE MAPLE Bi, Bu, ❖
Acer macrophyllum	BIG-LEAF MAPLE Bi, Bu, ❖
Amelanchier alnifolia	SERVICEBERRY, JUNEBERRY, SASKATOON Bi, Be, Bu, ❖
Amelanchier x grandiflora	HYBRID SERVICEBERRY Bi, Be, Bu
Arbutus menziesii	MADRONE Bi, Be, Hb, ❖
Arbutus x reyorum 'Marina'	MARINA MADRONE Bi, Be, Hb

Azara microphylla	BOX-LEAF AZARA, CHINCHIN Be
X Chitalpa tashkentensis	CHITALPA Be, Hb
Cornus alternifolia	PAGODA DOGWOOD Be, Bu
Cornus hybrids	HYBRID DOGWOODS Be, Bu
Cornus kousa	KOREAN DOGWOOD Be, Bu
Cornus mas	CORNELIAN CHERRY Bi, Be, Bu
Crataegus douglasii	PACIFIC HAWTHORN Bi, Be, ❖
Crataegus x *lavallei*	LAVALLE HAWTHORN Bi, Be
Magnolia kobus	KOBUSHI Bi, Be
Malus fusca	WASHINGTON CRABAPPLE Bi, Be, ❖
Malus hybrids	FLOWERING CRABAPPLE Bi, Be
Malus toringo ssp. *sargentii*	SARGENT'S CRABAPPLE Bi, Be
Pinus contorta var. *contorta*	SHORE PINE Bi, ❖
Prunus emarginata	BITTER CHERRY Bi, Be, Bu*, ❖
Quercus garryana	GARRY OAK Bi, Bu*, Hb, ❖
Sorbus alnifolia	KOREAN MOUNTAIN ASH Be, Bu
Styrax japonicus	JAPANESE SNOWBELL Be, Hb

"It's fun to think about plants not just as decorations but as functioning parts of our yard's ecosystem that attract wildlife to the garden. We have hummingbirds, tons of bees, and many monarch butterflies*. The kids love it!" ~~ Katherine Center

"What's a butterfly garden without butterflies?" ~~ Roy Rogers

[* = monarch butterflies do not use most of the western Pacific Northwest for their migrations.]

ROCK GARDEN PLANTS
Traditional but includes a few PNW native plants

A rock garden is a landscape which features and emphasizes rocks, including stones and boulders. Such rocks are the core of the design but gaps are left for plants. The plants are usually small though tiny trees and shrubs can be used especially to create shade for a shade-loving smaller plant or even for an entire woodland rock garden.

Because of the rockiness of such a landscape and the consequent warmth and fast drainage, the plants suitable for rock gardens are usually species that flourish in well-drained, low irrigation soils. Although most rock garden plants prefer dryish, sunny conditions, there are several within this listing which do best with average to even substantial water and some shade. Do check individual species for best conditions.

Achillea ageratifolia	GREEK YARROW
Achillea clavennae	SILVER YARROW
Acis (Leucojum) autumnalis	AUTUMN SNOWFLAKE
Aethionema armenum	PERSIAN CANDYTUFT
Aethionema grandiflorum	PERSIAN ROCKCRESS
Alchemilla alpina	ALPINE LADY'S MANTLE
Allium cernuum	NODDING ONION ❖
Allium oreophilum	PINK LILY LEEK
Allium sikkimense	HIMALAYAN ALLIUM
Allium thunbergii 'Ozawa'	JAPANESE ONION
Alyssum montanum	MOUNTAIN ALYSSUM
Anacyclus pyrethrum var. *depressus*	MOUNT ATLAS DAISY
Androsace lanuginosa	WOOLLY ROCK JASMINE
Androsace sarmentosa	COMMON ROCK JASMINE
Androsace (Vitaliana) primuliflora	PRIMROSE-FLOWERED VITALIANA
Anemone patens	PASQUEFLOWER, PRAIRIE-CROCUS ❖
Anemonoides (Anemone) apennina	APENNINE ANEMONE
Anemonoides (Anemone) blanda	GRECIAN WINDFLOWER
Antennaria dioica	PUSSYTOES
Antennaria microphylla	LITTLELEAF PUSSYTOES ❖
Antirrhinum glutinosum	GUMMY SNAPDRAGON
Antirrhinum sempervirens	SPANISH SNAPDRAGON
Aquilegia bertolonii	BERTOLONI COLUMBINE
Aquilegia flabellata	FAN COLUMBINE
Aquilegia oxysepala var. *kansuensis*	GANSU COLUMBINE
Arabis caucasica	SNOWCAP ROCKCRESS
Arabis procurrens	SPREADING ROCKCRESS
Arabis x sturii	DWARF ROCKCRESS
Arenaria montana	MOUNTAIN SANDWORT
Armeria juniperifolia	JUNIPER-LEAVED THRIFT
Armeria maritima	THRIFT, SEA PINK ❖
Artemisia pedemontana	DWARF WORMWOOD
Asplenium trichomanes	MAIDENHAIR SPLEENWORT ❖
Aster alpinus	ALPINE ASTER

227

Aubrieta deltoidea	PURPLE ROCKCRESS
Aurinia (Alyssum) saxatilis	BASKET-OF-GOLD
Barnardia (Scilla) japonica	JAPANESE SQUILL
Bellevalia (Muscari) pycnantha	GIANT GRAPE HYACINTH
Bergeranthus jamesii	CLUMPING ICE PLANT
Brimeura amethystina	AMETHYST HYACINTH
Brodiaea californica	CALIFORNIA BRODIAEA
Brodiaea coronaria	CROWN BRODIAEA ❖
Brodiaea elegans	HARVEST BRODIAEA ❖
Bukiniczia cabulica	VARIEGATED STATICE
Callirhoe involucrata	PURPLE POPPY-MALLOW
Calylophus hartwegii	HARTWEG'S SUNDROPS
Campanula carpatica	CARPATHIAN HAREBELL
Campanula cochlearifolia	FAIRY THIMBLES
Campanula garganica	ADRIATIC BELLFLOWER
Campanula portenschlagiana	DALMATIAN BELLFLOWER
Campanula poscharskyana	SERBIAN BELLFLOWER
Campanula rotundifolia	BLUEBELL ❖
Cerastium tomentosum	SNOW-IN-SUMMER
Chaenorhinum origanifolium	DWARF SNAPDRAGON
Clematis integrifolia "Dwarf Form"	DWARF GROUND CLEMATIS
Colchicum x *agrippinum*	AUTUMN CROCUS, MEADOW SAFFRON
Colchicum autumnale	AUTUMN CROCUS
Colchicum byzantinum	BYZANTINE MEADOW SAFFRON
Colchicum cilicicum	AUTUMN CROCUS
Colchicum hybrids	AUTUMN CROCUS
Colchicum speciosum	AUTUMN CROCUS
Colchicum variegatum	SPOTTED AUTUMN CROCUS
Coreopsis auriculata 'Nana'	DWARF COREOPSIS
Corydalis solida	FUMEWORT
Crocus goulimyi	PELOPONNESE CROCUS
Crocus imperati	ITALIAN CROCUS
Crocus laevigatus	LATE CROCUS
Crocus longiflorus	ITALIAN CROCUS
Crocus niveus	FALL CROCUS
Crocus ochroleucus	YELLOW CROCUS
Crocus pulchellus	TURKISH CROCUS
Crocus serotinus	LATE CROCUS
Crocus speciosus	BIEBERSTEIN'S CROCUS
Cyclamen cilicum	CILICIAN CYCLAMEN
Cyclamen graecum	GREEK CYCLAMEN
Cyclamen hederifolium	IVY-LEAFED CYCLAMEN
Daphne cneorum f. *verlotii* X *D. arbuscula*	ALPINE DAPHNE
Delosperma basauticum 'Sunfire'	YELLOW ICE PLANT
Delosperma cooperi	COOPER'S HARDY PURPLE ICE PLANT
Delosperma dyeri	ICE PLANT
Delosperma floribundum	PURPLE ICE PLANT
Delosperma nubigenum	YELLOW ICE PLANT
Dianthus alpinus	ALPINE PINK

Dianthus 'Blue Hills'	BLUE HILLS CHEDDAR PINK
Dianthus deltoides	MAIDEN PINK
Dianthus gratianopolitanus	CHEDDAR PINK
Dianthus petraeus ssp. *noeanus*	FRAGRANT SNOWFLAKE GARDEN PINK
Dianthus plumarius	COTTAGE PINK
Dichelostemma (Brodiaea) congestum	OOKAW, CLUSTER LILY ❖
Dierama trichorhizum	DIMINUTIVE FAIRY WAND
Dodecatheon meadia	SHOOTING STAR
Draba aizoides	YELLOW WHITLOW-GRASS
Dracocephalum argunense (or D. austriacum)	DRAGON'S HEAD
Dryas octopetala	MOUNTAIN AVENS
Edraianthus pumilio	SILVERY DWARF HAREBELL
Edraianthus serbicus	ROCK BELLS, GRASSY BELLS
Epilobium canum (Zauschneria californica) including ssp. *garrettii*	
	HUMMINGBIRD TRUMPET, CALIFORNIA FUCHSIA
Epimedium x *youngianum* 'Niveum'	YOUNG'S BARRENWORT
Eranthis hyemalis	WINTER ACONITE
Eremurus himalaicus	HIMALAYAN FOXTAIL LILY
Eremurus hybrids	FOXTAIL LILY
Eremurus stenophyllus	DESERT CANDLE
Erigeron compositus	CUT-LEAF DAISY ❖
Erigeron tweedyi	TWEEDY'S FLEABANE
Erinus alpinus	FAIRY FOXGLOVE
Eriogonum caespitosum	MAT BUCKWHEAT
Eriogonum ovalifolium	CUSHION BUCKWHEAT ❖
Eriogonum umbellatum	SULFUR BUCKWHEAT ❖
Eryngium planum 'Blue Hobbit'	DWARF SEA HOLLY
Erysimum kotschyanum	ALPINE WALLFLOWER
Erysimum pulchellum	BEAUTIFUL WALLFLOWER
Eucomis 'Nani'	DWARF PINEAPPLE LILY
Fritillaria michailovskyi	MICHAEL'S FLOWER
Geum triflorum "Dwarf Form"	DWARF PRAIRIE SMOKE ❖
Gentiana scabra	JAPANESE GENTIAN
Gentiana septemfida var. *lagodechiana*	LAGODEKHI CRESTED GENTIAN
Geranium x cantabrigiense	CAMBRIDGE CRANESBILL
Geranium cinereum	GRAY-LEAF CRANESBILL
Geranium dalmaticum	COMPACT ROSE CRANESBILL
Geranium magniflorum	CAPE CRANESBILL
Geranium sanguineum var. *lancastriense*	BLOODY CRANESBILL
Glandora (Lithodora) prostrata 'Grace Ward', 'Heavenly Blue'	LITHODORA
Glandularia (Verbena) bipinnatifida	DAKOTA MOCK VERVAIN
Globularia cordifolia	HEART-LEAVED GLOBE DAISY
Gypsophila repens	CREEPING BABY'S BREATH
Hebe buchananii 'Fenwickii'	SIR GEORGE FENWICK'S HEBE
Helianthemum nummularium	SUNROSE
Heuchera cylindrica	CORALBELLS
Heuchera rubescens	ALPINE CORALBELLS
Hosta venusta	HANDSOME PLANTAIN LILY
Hutchinsia alpina	CHAMOIS ROCK CRESS

Hyacinthoides (Scilla) lingulata	AUTUMN BLUEBELL
Hylotelephium (Sedum) pluricaule	ISLE OF SAKHALIN STONECROP
Hylotelephium (Sedum) sieboldii	OCTOBER DAPHNE
Iberis saxatilis	PERENNIAL CANDYTUFT
Iberis sempervirens	CANDYTUFT
Ipheion uniflorum	SPRING STARFLOWER
Iris cristata	DWARF CRESTED IRIS
Iris x pumila	DWARF IRIS
Iris reticulata	NETTED IRIS
Leucojum vernum	SPRING SNOWFLAKE
Lewisia columbiana var. *rupicola*	COLUMBIAN LEWISIA ❖
Lewisia cotyledon	SISKIYOU LEWISIA ❖
Lewisia longipetala hybrids	LONG-PETALLED LEWISIA
Lewisiopsis tweedyi	TWEEDY'S LEWISIA ❖
Lilium pumilum	CORAL LILY
Linum flavum 'Compactum'	DWARF GOLDEN FLAX
Linum perenne 'Saphir'	BLUE FLAX
Monardella macrantha	RED MONARDELLA
Myosotis pulvinaris	NEW ZEALAND FORGET-ME-NOT
Narcissus asturiensis	PIGMY DAFFODIL
Narcissus cyclamineus and hybrids	CYCLAMINEUS NARCISSUS
Narcissus Miniature hybrids/selections	MINIATURE DAFFODILS

'Baby Moon', 'Bell Song', 'Canaliculatus', 'February Gold', 'Hawera', 'Jack Snipe', 'Jetfire', 'Minnow', 'Rapture', 'Rip Van Winkle', 'Sundisc', 'Tete-a-Tete', 'Topolino'

Nepeta x 'Little Trudy'	DWARF CATMINT
Nerine filifolia	DWARF NERINE
Nerine sarniensis and hybrids	GUERNSEY LILY
Oenothera fremontii	SHIMMER EVENING PRIMROSE
Oenothera speciosa	WHITE EVENING PRIMROSE
Origanum libanoticum	CASCADING HOPFLOWER OREGANO
Oxalis adenophylla	SILVER SHAMROCK
Oxalis fabaefolia	RABBIT'S EARS
Oxalis lasiandra	PALM TREE OXALIS
Ozothamnus coralloides	CORAL SHRUB
Pachystegia insignis	MARLBOROUGH ROCK DAISY
Papaver alpinum	ALPINE POPPY, DWARF POPPY
Penstemon aridus	STIFF-LEAF PENSTEMON
Penstemon caespitosus	CREEPING PENSTEMON
Penstemon cardwellii	CARDWELL'S PENSTEMON ❖
Penstemon davidsonii and varieties	DAVIDSON'S PENSTEMON ❖
Penstemon fruticosus dwarf form	DWARF SHRUBBY PENSTEMON ❖
Penstemon hirsutus 'Pygmaeus'	DWARF HAIRY PENSTEMON
Penstemon pinifolius	PINE-LEAF PENSTEMON
Penstemon uintahensis	UINTA MOUNTAINS BEARDTONGUE
Penstemon virens	BLUE MIST PENSTEMON, FRONT RANGE PENSTEMON
Petrophytum caespitosum	MAT ROCK-SPIREA
Petrorhagia saxifraga	TUNIC FLOWER
Petrosedum (Sedum) rupestre	ROCKY STONECROP
Phedimus (Sedum) kamtschaticus	KAMSCHATKA SEDUM, ORANGE STONECROP

Phedimus (Sedum) middendorffianus	CHINESE MOUNTAIN STONECROP
Phedimus (Sedum) obtusifolius	MOUNDING STONECROP
Phedimus (Sedum) spurius	TWO-ROW STONECROP
Phemeranthus sediformis (Talinum okanoganense)	OKANOGAN FAME-FLOWER
Phlox divaricata	WILD BLUE PHLOX
Phlox nana	SANTA FE PHLOX
Phlox stolonifera	CREEPING PHLOX
Phlox subulata	MOSS PINK, CREEPING PHLOX
Phyteuma scheuchzeri	HORNED RAMPION
Polemonium reptans	CREEPING JACOB'S LADDER
Polygaloides (Polygala) chamaebuxus	SHRUBBY MILKWORT
Polystichum tsus-simense	DWARF HOLLY FERN
Potentilla nepalensis 'Miss Wilmott'	MISS WILMOTT CINQUEFOIL
Potentilla neumanniana	ALPINE CINQUEFOIL
Potentilla nitida	PINK CINQUEFOIL
Prospero (Scilla) autumnale	AUTUMN SQUILL
Pseudomuscari (Muscari, Bellavalia) azureum	AZURE GRAPE HYACINTH
Pseudomuscari (Muscari, Bellavalia) forniculatum	TURKISH GRAPE HYACINTH
Pterocephalus depressus	CARPETING PINCUSHION FLOWER
Pterocephalus perennis	MT. PARNASSUS PINCUSHION FLOWER
Pulsatilla vulgaris	EUROPEAN PASQUE FLOWER
Raoulia eximia	VEGETABLE SHEEP
Raoulia hookeri var. *albosericea* (*R. albosericea, R. australis* var. *albosericea*)	
	ALPINE VEGETABLE SHEEP
Rhodiola rosea	ROSEROOT, GOLDEN ROOT
Rhodanthemum (Chrysanthemum) hosmariense	MOROCCAN DAISY
Rhodohypoxis baurii	RED STAR
Sanguinaria canadensis	BLOODROOT
Saponaria ocymoides	ROCK SOAPWORT
Saponaria pumilio	DWARF PINK, DWARF SOAPWORT
Saxifraga 'Canis Dalmatica'	DALMATIAN DOG SAXIFRAGE
Saxifraga cochlearis	SILVER SAXIFRAGE
Saxifraga 'Cockscomb'	COCKSCOMB SAXIFRAGE
Saxifraga cotyledon	PYRAMIDAL SAXIFRAGE
Saxifraga moschata 'Peter Pan'	DWARF MOSSY SAXIFRAGE
Saxifraga oppositifolia	PURPLE ROBE SAXIFRAGE
Saxifraga 'Peachtree'	DWARF CUSHION SAXIFRAGE
Saxifraga x urbium	LONDON PRIDE
Saxifraga 'Whitehill'	WHITEHILL SAXIFRAGE
Saxifraga x zimmeter	HYBRID SAXIFRAGE
Scabiosa lucida	GLOSSY PINCUSHION FLOWER
Scilla bifolia	TWO-LEAF SQUILL
Scilla (Chionodoxa) luciliae	GLORY OF THE SNOW
Scilla mischtschenkoana 'Tubergeniana'	MISCZENKO SQUILL
Sedum grisebachii	GRISEBACH'S SEDUM
Sedum palmeri	PALMER'S SEDUM
Sempervivum species and hybrids	HOUSELEEK, HEN AND CHICKS
Sibbaldiopsis (Potentilla) tridentata	SHRUBBY FIVE-FINGERS
Silene acaulis	MOSS CAMPION ❖

Silene alpestris especially 'Flore Pleno' (double-flowered)   ALPINE CATCHFLY
Sisyrinchium montanum   BLUE-EYED GRASS ❖
Sternbergia lutea   AUTUMN DAFFODIL
Teucrium aroanium   GRAY CREEPING GERMANDER
Teucrium chamaedrys 'Prostratum' (*T.* x lucidrys)   LOW WALL GERMANDER
Teucrium cossonii "Majoricum"   FRUITY GERMANDER
Thalictrum kiusianum   DWARF MEADOW RUE
Thymus praecox ssp *praecox* (*T. polytrichus* ssp. *britannicus*)   MOTHER-OF-THYME
  Especially 'Elfin', 'Minus', 'Pseudolanuginosus'
Triteleia (Brodiaea) hyacinthina   WHITE TRIPLET-LILY ❖
Triteleia laxa   ITHURIEL'S SPEAR ❖
Tulipa cretica   CRETAN TULIP
Tulipa dasystemon   DASYSTEMON TULIP
Tulipa humilis   LOW-GROWING TULIP
Tulipa humilis 'Alba Coerulea Oculata'   BLUE-EYED TULIP
Tulipa linifolia (including *T. batalinii*)   BOKHARA TULIP, FLAX-LEAF TULIP
Tulipa orphanidea (including *T. whittallii*)   ANATOLIAN TULIP, COTTAGE TULIP
Tulipa sylvestris   WOODLAND TULIP
Tulipa urumiensis (T. tarda)   LATE TULIP, TARDY TULIP
Umbilicus (Chiastophyllum) oppositifolium   LAMB'S TAIL, GOLD DROP
Vernonia lettermannii   THREADLEAF IRONWEED
Veronica (Parahebe) catarractae   PARAHEBE
Veronica liwanensis   TURKISH SPEEDWELL
Veronica pectinata   WOOLLY SPEEDWELL
Veronica prostrata   PROSTRATE SPEEDWELL
Veronica thessalica   THESSALONIAN SPEEDWELL

DWARF CONIFERS FOR LARGER ROCK GARDENS

Abies balsamea 'Nana', 'Piccolo'	DWARF BALSAM FIR
Abies koreana 'Gait'	DWARF KOREAN FIR
Cedrus deodara dwarf cultivars	DWARF DEODAR CEDAR
Cephalotaxus harringtonia 'Duke Gardens'	DWARF PLUM YEW
Chamaecyparis obtusa many dwarf cultivars	DWARF HINOKI CYPRESS
Chamaecyparis pisifera many dwarf cultivars	DWARF SAWARA CYPRESS
Chamaecyparis thyoides many dwarf cultivars	DWARF ATLANTIC CEDAR
Cryptomeria japonica dwarf cultivars	DWARF PLUME CEDAR
Ginkgo biloba 'Mariken'	DWARF GINKGO
Juniperus communis selections	COMMON JUNIPER
Juniperus procumbens 'Nana'	JAPANESE GARDEN JUNIPER
Juniperus squamata cultivars	FLAKY JUNIPER
Larix kaempferi 'Haverbeck'	DWARF JAPANESE LARCH
Metasequoia glyptostroboides 'North Light'	DWARF VARIEGATED DAWN REDWOOD
Picea abies dwarf cultivars	DWARF NORWAY SPRUCE
Picea glauca dwarf cultivars	DWARF WHITE SPRUCE
Picea mariana 'Nana'	DWARF BLACK SPRUCE
Picea omorika 'Nana'	DWARF SERBIAN SPRUCE
Picea orientalis 'Bergman's Gem'	BERGMAN'S GEM ORIENTAL SPRUCE
Picea pungens dwarf cultivars	DWARF COLORADO SPRUCE
Pinus aristata 'Bashful #75'	BASHFUL BRISTLECONE PINE
Pinus cembra 'Blue Mound'	BLUE MOUND SWISS STONE PINE
Pinus contorta 'Spaan's Dwarf'	SPAAN'S DWARF SHORE PINE
Pinus heldreichii 'Compact Gem'	COMPACT BOSNIAN PINE
Pinus heldreichii var. *leucodermis* 'Schmidtii'	DWARF BOSNIAN PINE
Pinus monticola 'Nana'	DWARF WESTERN WHITE PINE
Pinus mugo dwarf cultivars (especially selections of ssp. *uncinata*)	MUGO PINE
Pinus pumila 'Dwarf Blue'	DWARF BLUE JAPANESE STONE PINE
Pinus strobus 'Pincushion'	DWARF EASTERN WHITE PINE
Pinus sylvestris dwarf cultivars	DWARF SCOTS PINE
Podocarpus alpinus 'Blue Gem'	ALPINE PLUM YEW
Podocarpus nivalis 'Otari'	OTARI PODOCARPUS
Sciadopitys verticillata 'Picola'	DWARF JAPANESE UMBRELLA PINE
Thuja occidentalis 'Sunkist', 'Teddy', 'Technito'	DWARF WHITE CEDARS
Thuja orientalis dwarfest cultivars	DWARF ORIENTAL ARBORVITAE
Thujopsis dolabrata 'Nana'	DWARF HIBA ARBORVITAE
Tsuga canadensis dwarf cultivars	DWARF HEMLOCK
Tsuga diversifolia 'Loowit'	DWARF NORTHERN JAPANESE HEMLOCK

WALL PLANTS

TO TUMBLE FROM THE TOP OF A WALL

Expanses of wall, given a plantable area above them, deserve and often demand a green waterfall of foliage to break up the monotony, soften the hard lines, and otherwise add interest to the scene.

Arctostaphylos 'Emerald Carpet'	EMERALD CARPET MANZANITA
Arctostaphylos uva-ursi	KINNIKINNICK, BEARBERRY ❖
Campanula portenschlagiana (muralis)	DALMATIAN BELLFLOWER
Campanula poscharskyana	SERBIAN BELLFLOWER
Ceanothus gloriosus 'Anchor Bay'	ANCHOR BAY CALIFORNIA LILAC
Cedrus deodara 'Prostrate Beauty'	TRAILING DEODAR CEDAR
Clematis columbiana	ROCK CLEMATIS ❖
Clematis hirsutissima var. *hirsutissima*	HAIRY CLEMATIS ❖
Convolvulus sabatius	BLUE ROCK MORNING GLORY
Corethrogyne (Lessingia) filaginifolia 'Silver Carpet'	TRAILING SAND ASTER
Delosperma species and cultivars	HARDY ICEPLANT
Epilobium (Zauschneria) canum ssp. *garrettii* 'Orange Carpet'	CALIFORNIA FUCHSIA
Grevillea australis "Prostrate"	TASMANIAN ALPINE GREVILLEA
Hebe 'Wingletye'	WINGLETYE HEBE
Hebe decumbens	CREEPING HEBE
Helianthemum nummularium	SUNROSE
Juniperus horizontalis 'Icee Blue'	ICEE BLUE JUNIPER
Lonicera crassifolia	CREEPING HONEYSUCKLE
Microcachrys tetragona	CREEPING STRAWBERRY PINE
Myrteola nummularia	CRANBERRY-MYRTLE
Origanum libanoticum	CASCADING HOPFLOWER OREGANO
Phlox diffusa	SPREADING PHLOX ❖
Phlox subulata	CREEPING PHLOX
Picea pungens 'Procumbens'	TRAILING BLUE SPRUCE
Saxifraga stolonifera	STRAWBERRY SAXIFRAGE
Sedum (many)	STONECROP
Stachys byzantina (S. lanata) 'Silver Carpet'	TRAILING LAMB'S EARS
Teucrium chamaedrys 'Prostratum' (*T.* x *lucidrys*)	LOW WALL GERMANDER
Teucrium cossonii "Majoricum"	FRUITY GERMANDER
Thymus cherierioides	SILVER NEEDLE THYME
Thymus 'Doone Valley'	LEMON THYME
Thymus herba-barona	CARAWAY-SCENTED THYME
Thymus praecox ssp. *arcticus* 'Albus'	WHITE MOSS THYME
Thymus praecox ssp. *arcticus* 'Languinosus'	WOOLLY THYME
Thymus praecox ssp *praecox* (*T. polytrichus* ssp. *britannicus*)	MOTHER-OF-THYME
Thymus serpyllum	CREEPING THYME
Tropaeolum polyphyllum	WREATH NASTURTIUM
Whipplea modesta	WHIPPLE VINE, MODESTY ❖

BETWEEN THE ROCKS OF THE WALL: PERENNIALS AND SUBSHRUBS

Rock and block walls without mortar and with soil filling the small gaps are prime opportunities to stuff a few special plants.

Aethionema grandiflorum	PERSIAN STONECRESS
Anacyclus pyrethrum var. *depressus*	MOUNT ATLAS DAISY
Androsace lanuginosa	WOOLLY ROCK JASMINE
Antirrhinum braun-blanquetii	SPANISH SNAPDRAGON
Antirrhinum molle	DWARF SNAPDRAGON
Antirrhinum sempervirens	SPANISH SNAPDRAGON
Aquilegia flabellata	JAPANESE FAN COLUMBINE
Asarina procumbens	TRAILING SNAPDRAGON
Aubrieta deltoidea	PURPLE ROCKCRESS
Aubrieta libanotica	LEBANESE ROCKCRESS
Aubrieta thessala	GREEK ROCKCRESS
Campanula poscharskyana	SERBIAN BELLFLOWER
Chamaemelum nobile	ROMAN CHAMOMILE
Corydalis species and hybrids	FUMEWORT
Dianthus gratianopolitanus	CHEDDAR PINKS
Epilobium canum (Zauschneria californica)	CALIFORNIA FUCHSIA
Erodium reichardii (E. chamaedryoides)	ALPINE GERANIUM
Erodium x variabile	DWARF HERONSBILL
Helianthemum nummularium	SUNROSE
Erysimum cheiri hybrids	WALLFLOWER
Glandora (Lithodora) diffusa	PURPLE GROMWELL
Jovibarba species	ROLLING HEN-AND-CHICKS
Lewisia cotyledon and hybrids	LEWISIA
Lewisiopsis tweedyi	TWEEDY'S LEWISIA
Nepeta x faassenii 'Jr. Walker'	DWARF CATMINT
Nepeta racemosa	DWARF CATNIP
Phlox stolonifera	CREEPING PHLOX
Phlox subulata	CREEPING PHLOX
Potentilla neumanniana 'Nana'	DWARF ALPINE CINQUEFOIL
Primula auricula	AURICULA PRIMROSE
Rhodanthemum (Chrysanthemum) hosmariense	MOROCCAN DAISY
Salvia officinalis	CULINARY SAGE
Saponaria x lempergii 'Max Frei'	HYBRID SOAPWORT
Saponaria pumilio	DWARF PINK, DWARF SOAPWORT
Saxifraga sarmentosa	STRAWBERRY SAXIFRAGE
Sedum (including *Petrosedum, Phedimus, Rhodiola)*	STONECROP
Sempervivum many species and hybrids	HENS N' CHICKS
Thymus vulgaris	THYME

ESPALIERS

Wall plants pruned in one plane: trained on trellis, wiring/cabling, or merely flat against a wall. Traditionally in some formal pattern but simply splayed against the wall or fencing is acceptable.

Acer circinatum	VINE MAPLE
Acer palmatum	JAPANESE MAPLE
Azara microphylla	AZARA
Camellia hiemalis 'Shishi-Gashira', 'Showa-No-Sakae', 'Showa Supreme'	
	HIEMALIS CAMELLIA
Camellia reticulata	FOREST CAMELLIA
Camellia sasanqua 'Appleblossom, 'Mine-No-Yuki', 'Tanya'	SUN CAMELLIA
Cercidiphyllum japonicum	KATSURA
Chaenomeles japonica 'Low-n-White', 'Minerva', 'Orange Delight'	JAPANESE QUINCE
Cornus kousa	KOREAN DOGWOOD
Garrya elliptica	TASSEL BUSH
Ginkgo biloba dwarf and semi-dwarf cultivars	GINKGO
Hamamelis x intermedia	HYBRID WITCH-HAZEL
Ilex x altaclarensis 'Wilsoni'	WILSON HOLLY
Ilex crenata	JAPANESE HOLLY
Loropetalum chinense	FRINGE FLOWER
Magnolia grandiflora 'Little Gem'	SOUTHERN MAGNOLIA
Magnolia stellata	STAR MAGNOLIA
Malus hybrids	FLOWERING CRABAPPLES
Osmanthus fragrans	FRAGRANT TEA-OLIVE
Pinus aristata	BRISTLECONE PINE
Podocarpus macrophyllus 'Maki'	DWARF YELLOWWOOD
Prunus triloba 'Multiplex'	FLOWERING ALMOND
Pyracantha crenatoserrata 'Graberi'	GRABER'S FIRETHORN
Ribes sanguineum	RED-FLOWERING CURRANT
Stewartia koreana	KOREAN STEWARTIA
Tilia cordata, especially dwarf cultivars	LITTLELEAF LINDEN
Viburnum x burkwoodii	BURKWOOD VIBURNUM
Viburnum tinus	LAURUSTINUS
Viburnum plicatum f. *tomentosum* 'Mariesii'	DOUBLEFILE VIBURNUM

Espalier-able Fruit Trees

Apple (on dwarf or semi-dwarf stock)
Apricot
Asian Apple (Apple-Pear)
Bay Laurel (*Laurus nobilis*)
Cherry

Fig
Mulberry, white
Pear (on dwarf or semi-dwarf stock)
Quince

A STUMPERY

Decaying stumps provide a fertile nursery for a great many woodland plants, including those listed here. These can be planted around a neo-rotting tree base and a few of these can even be plopped into the stump itself.

FERNS

Stumperies are sometimes known as "Ferneries"

Adiantum aleuticum (A. pedatum)	WESTERN MAIDENHAIR FERN ❖
Asplenium scolopendrium	HART'S TONGUE FERN
Asplenium trichomanes	MAIDENHAIR SPLEENWORT
Blechnum (Struthiopteris) spicant	DEER FERN ❖
Dryopteris affinis	SCALY MALE FERN
Dryopteris erythrosora	BUCKLER FERN
Gymnocarpium dryopteris	OAK FERN ❖
Dryopteris filix-mas	MALE FERN ❖
Dryopteris expansa	SPREADING WOOD FERN OR SHIELD FERN
Gymnocarpium disjunctum	PACIFIC OAK FERN ❖
Matteuccia struthiopteris	OSTRICH FERN
Phegopteris connectilis	NARROW BEECH FERN
Polypodium scouleri	LEATHERY POLYPODY ❖
Polystichum andersonii	ANDERSON'S HOLLY FERN ❖
Polystichum braunii	BRAUN'S HOLLY FERN
Polypodium glycyrrhiza	LICORICE FERN ❖
Polystichum munitum	WESTERN SWORD FERN ❖
Polystichum polyblepharum	JAPANESE TASSEL FERN
Woodwardia fimbriata	GIANT CHAIN FERN ❖

OTHER PLANTS

Anemonoides (Anemone) nemorosa	WOOD ANEMONE
Asteranthera ovata	ESTRELLITA, LITTLE STAR
Calypso bulbosa	FAIRY SLIPPER ORCHID ❖
Campanula species	BELLFLOWERS
Chimaphila menziesii	MENZIE'S PIPSISSEWA ❖
Chimaphila umbellata	PRINCE'S PINE ❖
Convallaria majalis	LILY-OF-THE-VALLEY
Cornus x *unalaschkensis* (including *C. canadensis*)	BUNCHBERRY ❖
Cypripedium montanum	MOUNTAIN LADYSLIPPER ❖
Dicentra formosa	BLEEDING HEART ❖
Epimedium species and hybrids	BARRENWORTS
Eriocapitella (Anemone) x *hybrida*	JAPANESE ANEMONE
Erythronium species	FAWN LILY, AVALANCHE LILY, DOG-TOOTH VIOLET ❖
Galanthus species	SNOWDROPS
Helleborus species and hybrids	HELLEBORES
Hosta species and hybrids	HOSTA

237

Hyacinthoides hispanica (NOT *H.* x massartiana)	SPANISH BLUE BELLS
Leucojum species	SNOWFLAKES
Liriope muscari	LILYTURF
Luzuriaga radicans	QUILINEJA
Moneses uniflora	WAX FLOWER ❖
Narcissus species and hybrids	DWARF NARCISSI
Polygonatum species and hybrids	SOLOMON'S SEAL
Primula species	PRIMROSE
Primula veris	COWSLIP
Rhododendron macrophyllum	PACIFIC RHODODENDRON ❖
Rodgersia aesculifolia	FINGER-LEAF RODGERSIA
Tellima grandiflora	FRINGE CUPS ❖
Thalictrum aquilegifolium	MEADOW-RUE
Trillium species	TRILLIUM ❖
Uvularia grandiflora	LARGE-FLOWERED BELLWORT
Vaccinium alaskaense	ALASKAN BLUEBERRY ❖
Vaccinium parvifolium	RED HUCKLEBERRY ❖
Vancouveria hexandra	BARRENWORT ❖

And don't forget the mosses and lichens.

For companion plants, see "PLANTING UNDER TREES (The Woodland Garden)"

CONTAINER PLANTS

    I have organized the bulk of this major list into three categories: "Spillers, Fillers, and Thrillers." These are the three types of plant habits which are used when building a mixed container. Yet all of them can be used as specimens unto themselves within a single container, provided their basic form is accommodated and matched to the container.

SPILLERS *(falling over the edge; also imminently suitable for hanging baskets)*

Seasonal container

Acalypha hispida	RED HOT CAT'S TAIL
Antirrhinum majus nanum pendula	TRAILING SNAPDRAGONS
Begonia boliviensis	SCARLET BEGONIA
Begonia x tuber-hybrida, hanging types	TUBEROUS BEGONIA
Calibrachoa x hybrida	MILLION BELLS
Chaenostoma (Sutera) cordatum	BACOPA
Coleus (Solenostemon) scutellarioides 'Trailing Rose' (*C. rehneltianus*)	TRAILING COLEUS
Dichondra argentea	SILVER FALLS
Eccremocarpus scaber	CHILEAN GLORY VINE
Fuchsia hybrids, hanging basket types	FUCHSIA
Glandularia (Verbena) x hybrida, trailing strains	TRAILING VERBENA
Helichrysum argyrophyllum	GOLDEN GUINEA EVERLASTING
Helichrysum petiolare	LICORICE PLANT
Ipomoea batatas	ORNAMENTAL SWEET POTATO
Lathyrus odoratus Dwarf types	SWEET PEA
Lobelia erinus, trailing types	LOBELIA
Lophospermum (Asarina) erubescens	CREEPING GLOXINIA
Lotus berthelotii, L. maculata, and hybrids	LOTUS VINE, PARROT'S-BEAK
Mandevilla (Dipladenia) splendens hybrids	SHINING MANDEVILLA
Pelargonium peltatum	IVY GERANIUM
X *Petchoa* (*Petunia* x *Calibrachoa* hybrid)	PETCHOA
Petunia × *atkinsiana*	HYBRID PETUNIAS
Nierembergia hippomanica	BLUE MOUNTAIN NIEREMBERGIA
Sanvitalia procumbens	CREEPING ZINNIA
Scaevola aemula and hybrids, trailing types	FAN FLOWER
Tradescantia (Setcreasea) purpurea	PURPLE HEART
Tropaeolum majus	NASTURTIUM

Perennial container

Antirrhinum glutinosum	GUMMY SNAPDRAGON
Aurinia saxatilis	BASKET-OF-GOLD
Campanula carpatica	CARPATHIAN HAREBELL
Campanula isophylla	ITALIAN BELLFLOWER
Campanula portenschlagiana	DALMATIAN BELLFLOWER
Clematis x *cartmanii* 'Pixie'	PIXIE CLEMATIS
Clematis repens	TWINKLE BELL CLEMATIS

Convolvulus sabatius	BLUE ROCK MORNING GLORY
Glechoma hederacea 'Variegata'	GROUND IVY
Hedera helix dwarf and variegated cultivars	ENGLISH IVY
Hydrocotyle sibthorpioides 'Crystal Snowflake'	MARSH PENNYWORT
Hylotelephium (Sedum) sieboldii	OCTOBER DAPHNE
Lysimachia alfredii 'Night Light'	NIGHT LIGHT MONEYWORT
Lysimachia nummularia including *aurea*	CREEPING JENNY
Origanum hybrids	ORNAMENTAL OREGANOES
Persicaria microcephala 'Red Dragon', 'Silver Dragon'	PAINTED KNOTWEED
Saxifraga sarmentosa	STRAWBERRY SAXIFRAGE
Thymus species	CREEPING THYME
Vinca minor, especially variegated forms	TRAILING PERIWINKLE

FILLERS *(filling around the edge)*

Seasonal Container

Angelonia	SUMMER SNAPDRAGON
Arctotis/Dimorphotheca/Osteospermum	AFRICAN DAISIES
Begonia semperflorens	WAX BEGONIA
Bellis perennis	ENGLISH DAISY
Brachyscome multifida hybrids	CUT-LEAF DAISY
Brassica oleracea	ORNAMENTAL CABBAGE/KALE
Coleus (Solenostemon) scutellarioides	COLEUS
Cuphea species	CUPHEA
Dahlia x hybrida (*bedding types*)	DAHLIA
Diascia species and hybrids	TWINSPUR
Gazania, especially Talent Series	SILVER GAZANIA
Gerbera hybrids	GERBERA DAISY
Heliotropium arborescens dwarf cultivars	HELIOTROPE
Iresine herbstii	BLOOD-LEAF
Lavandula stoechas	SPANISH LAVENDER
Lobelia erinus	LOBELIA
Nemesia species and hybrids	NEMESIA
Pelargonium many hybrids	GERANIUMS
Pentas lanceolata (dwarf cultivars)	EGYPTIAN STAR FLOWER
Primula hybrids	ENGLISH PRIMROSE
X Torelus (*Torenia x Mimulus hybrids*)	HYBRID MONKEYS
Viola cornuta hybrids	VIOLA
Viola x wittrockiana	PANSY

Perennial Container

Achillea hybrids (many)	YARROWS
Allium sacculiferum	NORTHERN PLAINS CHIVE
Anthemis punctata ssp. *cupaniana*	SICILIAN CHAMOMILE
Bergenia species and hybrids	BERGENIA
Carex (many)	SEDGES

240

Dianthus many types	PINKS
Helleborus hybrids	HYBRID HELLEBORE
Heuchera hybrids	CORALBELLS
Liriope muscari	LILY TURF
Ophiopogon japonicus	MONDO GRASS
Ophiopogon planiscapus 'Nigrescens'	BLACK MONDO GRASS
Phedimus (Sedum) spurius	CAUCASIAN STONECROP
Scabiosa columbariae	PINCUSHION FLOWER
Sempervivum species and hybrids	HENS-AND-CHICKS
Sisyrinchium 'Janet Kiner'	DWARF BLUE-EYED GRASS
Viola alba ssp. *dehnhardtii*	PARMA VIOLET
Viola 'Dancing Geisha', 'Silver Samurai'	HYBRID VIOLET
Zantedeschia aethiopica	CALLA-LILY

Bulbs

Allium neopolitanum 'Cowanii'	FLOWERING ONION
Cyclamen coum	HARDY CYCLAMEN, EASTERN SOWBREAD
Cyclamen hederifolium (shade)	HARDY CYCLAMEN
Dichelostemma pulchellum	BLUE DICKS, WILD HYACINTH
Fritillaria biflora	CHOCOLATE LILY, MISSION BELLS
Galanthus nivalis	SNOWDROP
Ipheion uniflorum	SPRING STAR FLOWER
Iris reticulata	RETICULATED IRIS
Leucojum vernum	SPRING SNOWFLAKE
Muscari armeniacum	GRAPE HYACINTH
Narcissus (tiny ones especially)	NARCISSUS, DAFFODIL
Oxalis nidulans 'Pom Pom'	POM-POM SORRELL
Triteleia grandiflora var. *grandiflora*	BLUE-LILY ❖
Triteleia (Brodiaea) hyacinthina	WHITE TRIPLET-LILY ❖
Triteleia laxa including 'Queen Fabiola'	PRETTY FACE, TRIPLET LILY
Tulipa clusiana and forms	LADY TULIP
Tulipa orphanidea (including *T. whittallii*)	ANATOLIAN TULIP, COTTAGE TULIP
Tulipa saxatilis (T. bakeri)	CANDIA TULIP, ROCK TULIP
Tulipa sylvestris	WOODLAND TULIP
Zantedeschia hybrids	CALLA-LILY

THRILLERS *(the central, upright accent)*

Seasonal Container

Antirrhinum majus	SNAPDRAGON
Campanula pyramidalis	CHIMNEY BELLFLOWER
Canna x *generalis*	CANNA
Helianthus annuus especially dwarf strains	SUNFLOWERS
Nicotiana sylvestris	FLOWERING TOBACCO
Pelargonium hybrids	GERANIUM
Rhodochiton atrosanguineus	PURPLE BELL VINE
Thunbergia alata	BLACK-EYED SUSAN VINE

Perennial Container

Achillea 'Moonshine'	MOONSHINE YARROW
Agapanthus (many; select hardy)	LILY-OF-THE-NILE
Alstroemeria hybrids	PERUVIAN LILY
Aspidistra elatior	CAST-IRON PLANT
Aster x frikartii	ITALIAN ASTER
Austrostipa ramosissima	AUSTRALIAN PLUME GRASS
BAMBOOS (many; select hardy species)	BAMBOO
Begonia grandis evansiana	HARDY BEGONIA
Betonica (Stachys) macrantha 'Robusta', 'Superba'	BIG BETONY
Chondropetalum tectorum	SMALL CAPE RUSH
Dierama species	FAIRY WAND, WAND FLOWER
Helictotrichon sempervirens	BLUE OAT GRASS
Hemerocallis (many)	DAYLILIES
Heuchera hybrids	CORAL BELLS
Hosta especially dwarf cultivars	HOSTA
Juncus effusus	BLUE/GRAY RUSH
Kniphofia (many)	RED-HOT POKER, TORCH LILY
Lavandula stoechas	SPANISH LAVENDER
Lilium (many)	LILIES
Penstemon hybrids (many)	BEARDTONGUE
Phygelius species and hybrids	CAPE FUCHSIA
Rehmannia elata	CHINESE SNAPDRAGON
Sisyrinchium striatum	SATIN FLOWER
Thamnochortus cinereus	SILVER REED
Trachelium caeruleum	THROATWORT, UMBRELLA FLOWER
Tricyrtis (many)	TOAD LILIES
Zantedeschia aethiopica	CALLA-LILY

SPECIMEN SHRUBS FOR BIG POTS/TUBS
Almost all are evergreen

Abies balsamea 'Nana', 'Piccolo'	DWARF BALSAM FIR
Acer circinatum 'Baby Buttons', 'Bort's Broom', 'Little Gem', 'Pacific Sprite'	
	DWARF VINE MAPLES
Arbutus unedo 'Elfin King', 'Oktoberfest'	DWARF STRAWBERRY TREE
Aucuba japonica 'Nana', 'Pacman', 'Petite Jade'	DWARF JAPANESE LAUREL
Azara microphylla	BOX-LEAF AZARA, CHINCHIN
Buxus sempervirens 'Vardar Valley'	DWARF BOXWOOD
Camellia x vernalis 'Yuletide'	CHRISTMAS CAMELLIA
Camellia x williamsii	HYBRID CAMELLIA
Cephalotaxus harringtonia 'Duke Gardens'	DWARF PLUM YEW
Chamaecyparis obtusa many dwarf cultivars	DWARF HINOKI CYPRESS
Chamaecyparis pisifera many dwarf cultivars	DWARF SAWARA CYPRESS
Chamaecyparis thyoides many dwarf cultivars	DWARF ATLANTIC CEDAR
Chondropetalum elephantinum	LARGE CAPE RUSH

242

Chondropetalum tectorum	SMALL CAPE RUSH
Chondropetalum tectorum "dwarf form"	DWARF CAPE RUSH
Cordyline australis	CABBAGE PALM
Corokia cotoneaster	COROKIA
Corylus avellana 'Contorta'	HARRY LAUDER'S WALKING STICK
Cryptomeria japonica dwarf cultivars	DWARF PLUME CEDAR
Daphne x transatlantica 'Eternal Fragrance'	DWARF DAPHNE
Erica x darleyensis	DARLEY DALE HEATH
X Fatshedera lizei	BOTANICAL WONDER
Fatsia japonica	JAPANESE FATSIA
Ginkgo biloba 'Mariken'	DWARF GINKGO
Hibiscus syriacus 'Little Kim'	DWARF ROSE OF SHARON
Hydrangea paniculata 'Bobo'	DWARF PANICLE HYDRANGEA
Hydrangea serrata 'Tiny Tuff Stuff'	DWARF MOUNTAIN HYDRANGEA
Ilex crenata 'Convexa'	CONVEX-LEAF JAPANESE HOLLY
Ilex crenata 'Northern Beauty'	JAPANESE HOLLY
Ilex crenata 'Mariesii'	CONGESTED JAPANESE HOLLY
Itea virginica 'Little Henry'	DWARF SWEETSPIRE
Leptecophylla juniperina ssp. *juniperina*	PINK MOUNTAIN BERRY
Kalmia latifolia 'Little Linda'	DWARF MOUNTAIN LAURE
Magnolia laevifolia (Michelia yunnanensis)	YUNNAN MAGNOLIA
Mahonia eurybracteata 'Soft Caress'	SOFT CARESS MAHONIA
Myrteola nummularia	CRANBERRY-MYRTLE
Osmanthus heterophyllus (several dwarf forms)	FALSE HOLLY
Osmanthus 'Kaori Hime'	FRAGRANT PRINCESS TEA-OLIVE
Physocarpus opulifolius especially dwarf purple-leaf forms	NINEBARK
Picea abies dwarf cultivars	DWARF NORWAY SPRUCE
Picea glauca dwarf cultivars	DWARF WHITE SPRUCE
Picea mariana 'Nana'	DWARF BLACK SPRUCE
Picea orientalis 'Bergman's Gem'	BERGMAN'S GEM ORIENTAL SPRUCE
Picea pungens dwarf cultivars	DWARF COLORADO SPRUCE
Pieris japonica 'Prelude'	JAPANESE PIERIS
Pinus cembra 'Blue Mound'	BLUE MOUND SWISS STONE PINE
Pinus heldreichii 'Compact Gem'	COMPACT BOSNIAN PINE
Pinus mugo dwarf cultivars	MUGO PINE
Pittosporum tenuifolium 'Marjorie Channon', 'Silver Sheen'	KOHUHU
Podocarpus nivalis 'Otari'	OTARI PODOCARPUS
Polygaloides (Polygala) chamaebuxus	SHRUBBY MILKWORT
Prunus caroliniana 'Compacta'	DWARF CAROLINA CHERRY
Rhododendron calostrotum ssp. *keleticum*	RHODODENDRON
Rhododendron campylogynum	RHODODENDRON
Rhododendron hanceanum 'Nanum'	RHODODENDRON

Rhododendron hybrids such as 'Carmen', 'Creeping Jenny', 'Curlew', 'Dopey', 'Egret',
  'Ernie Dee', 'Ginny Gee, 'Lori Eichelser', 'Moerheim', 'Ostbo's Red Elizabeth',
  'Patty Bee', 'Princess Anne', 'Ptarmigan', 'Ramapo', 'Shamrock', 'Wee Bee'

	HYBRID RHODODENDRON
Rhododendron kiusianum 'Komo Kulshan'	RHODODENDRON
Rhododendron lutescens	RHODODENDRON
Rhododendron nakaharae	RHODODENDRON

Rhododendron roxieanum var. *oreonastes*	RHODODENDRON
Rhododendron saluenense	RHODODENDRON
Rhododendron "Yak hybrids"	DWARF RHODODENDRON
Sophora prostrata 'Little Baby'	LITTLE BABY DWARF KOWHAI
Syringa 'Bloomerang', 'Scent and Sensibility', "Fairy Tale" series	DWARF LILAC
Thuja occidentalis 'Little Giant'	LITTLE GIANT ARBORVITAE
Thuja occidentalis 'Teddy'	TEDDY WHITE CEDAR
Thuja orientalis dwarf cultivars	DWARF ORIENTAL ARBORVITAE
Thujopsis dolabrata 'Nana'	DWARF HIBA ARBORVITAE
Tsuga canadensis dwarf cultivars	DWARF HEMLOCK
Tsuga diversifolia 'Loowit'	DWARF NORTHERN JAPANESE HEMLOCK
Vaccinium ovatum 'St. Andrews'	DWARF EVERGREEN HUCKLEBERRY
Yucca desmettiana	SOFT-LEAVED YUCCA

SMALL TREES FOR CONTAINERS

Acer palmatum (many dwarf cultivars)	JAPANESE MAPLE
Acer buergerianum 'Mino Yatsubusa'	DWARF TRIDENT MAPLE
Acer pictum 'Usugumo'	PAINTED MAPLE
Acer shirasawanum	HALF MOON MAPLE
Cercis canadensis 'Little Woody'	LITTLE WOODY REDBUD
Chamaecyparis obtusa 'Filicoides Compacta'	COMPACT FERN-SPRAY HINOKI CYPRESS
Cordyline australis	CABBAGE PALM
Crinodendron patagua	LILY-OF-THE-VALLEY TREE
Cryptomeria japonica 'Black Dragon'	JAPANESE CEDAR
Cryptomeria japonica 'Cristata'	CRESTED JAPANESE CEDAR
Ginkgo biloba 'Goldspire'	GOLDSPIRE GINKGO
Grevillea victoriae	ROYAL GREVILLEA
Juniperus chinensis 'Kaizuka'	HOLLYWOOD JUNIPER
Laurus nobilis	GRECIAN LAUREL
Luma apiculata (hardy form)	CHILEAN GUAVA
Magnolia grandiflora 'Little Gem'	LITTLE GEM MAGNOLIA
Magnolia laevifolia (*Michelia yunnanensis*)	YUNNAN MAGNOLIA
Malus toringo ssp. *sargentii* 'Tina'	DWARF CRABAPPLE
Metasequoia glyptostroboides 'North Light'	DWARF VARIEGATED DAWN REDWOOD
Pinus thunbergii 'Thundercloud'	JAPANESE BLACK PINE
Podocarpus totara 'Pendula'	WEEPING TOTARA
Sciadopitys verticillata 'Picola'	DWARF JAPANESE UMBRELLA PINE
Trachycarpus fortunei	WINDMILL PALM

»» More…

FRUIT TREES IN CONTAINERS

Temperate fruits

APPLE – dwarf (on Mark and M-27 rootstock); genetic dwarf 'Babe'
BLACKBERRY (not a tree)
BLUEBERRY (not a tree)
CHILEAN GUAVA (*Luma apiculata,* hardy form)
CHINESE QUINCE (*Pseudocydonia sinensis*)
CRANBERRY-MYRTLE *(Myrteola nummularia)* (not a tree)
FIG — 'Atreano', 'Chicago Hardy', 'Fignomenal', 'Little Miss Figgy', 'Lattarula',
    'Longue d'Aout', 'Olympian', 'Petite Negri', 'Neverella', 'Takoma Violet',
    'Vern's Brown Turkey', 'Verte', 'Violette de Bordeaux'
NECTARINE — genetic dwarves: 'Firecracker', 'Garden Beauty', 'Garden Delight',
    'Golden Flame', 'Nectar Babe', 'Necta Zee', 'Nectarina'
QUINCE (*Cydonia oblonga*)
PEACH — genetic dwarves: 'Bonanza II', 'Garden Gold', 'Garden Sun', 'Honey Babe',
    'Pix Zee'

Citrus fruits (on dwarf or semi-dwarf rootstock; to be brought in on cold winter nights)

CALAMONDIN
CITRON
ICHANG LEMON
KUMQUAT
LEMON — especially 'Meyer' (although not exactly a lemon)
LIME
LIMEQUAT
MANDARIN/TANGERINE
ORANGE
YUZU

Subtropical/Tropical Fruits (including some non-trees; to be brought in on cold winter nights)

BANANA – 'Extra Dwarf Cavendish'
CEYLON GOOSEBERRY, KITEMBILLA (*Dovyalis*)
GUAVA (*Psidium guajava* var. *nana*) "True Dwarf"
KEI APPLE (*Dovyalis caffra*)
MEXICAN GUAVA (*Psidium guajava*)
PAPAYA — 'TR Hovey'
PEPINO (*Solanum muricatum*)
PITANGA, PITAYA (*Hylocereus*)
STRAWBERRY GUAVA (and Lemon guava; *Psidium cattleianum*)

MISCELLANEOUS TENDER EDIBLES FOR CONTAINER GROWING
Suitable for growing outdoors until night temperatures are expected below 32°F (0°C)

Aloysia triphylla	LEMON VERBENA
Capparis spinosa inermis	CAPER
Colocasia esculenta	TARO, DASHEEN, CALLALOO
Cymbopogon citratus	LEMONGRASS
Lippia graveolens	MEXICAN OREGANO
Murraya koenigii	CURRY LEAF
Nopalea cochenillifera	NOPAL/NOPALES
Poliomintha longiflora	MEXICAN OREGANO
Salvia elegans	PINEAPPLE SAGE
Salvia rutilans	PINEAPPLE SAGE
Solanum annuum, S. frutescens	PEPPERS
Solanum muricatum	PEPINO
Solanum quitoense	NARANJILLA
Tagetes lucida	MEXICAN TARRAGON

BEST HERBS FOR CONTAINERS

BASIL	PARSLEY
BAY LEAF (tree)	ROSEMARY
CHIVES	SAGE
MARJORAM	SUMMER SAVORY
MINTS	THYME
OREGANO	WINTER SAVORY

CUTFLOWERS

Good for the home garden but all commercial quality (should you wish to go the business route). Harvest flowers in earliest morning with a bucket of hot water at the ready. Use a sharp scissors or knife and cut at a slight angle. Recut when creating the arrangement.

PERENNIALS

Plant in early spring or fall.

Achillea hybrids	YARROWS
Achillea ptarmica 'Peter Cottontail'	DOUBLE-FLOWERED SNEEZEWORT
Agapanthus hybrids	LILY-OF-THE-NILE
Allium 'Serendipity'	SERENDIPITY ALLIUM
Alstroemeria hybrids	PERUVIAN LILY, LILY OF THE INCAS
Astrantia major	GREAT MASTERWORT
Centaurea dealbata	PERSIAN CORNFLOWER
Centaurea hypoleuca	PINK CORNFLOWER
Cephalaria gigantea	GIANT SCABIOUS
Chrysanthemum Korean hybrids	HARDY MUM
Chrysanthemum x *morifolium* (selected hardy garden types)	MUM
Dendranthema zawadskii hybrids	ARCTIC DAISY
Dierama pulcherrimum and *D. pendulum*	FAIRY WAND
Echinops species	GLOBE THISTLE
Eryngium species and hybrids	SEA HOLLY, ERYNGO
Geum hybrids	AVENS
Helenium hybrids (especially 'Double Trouble')	HELEN'S FLOWER
Helianthus x *multiflorus* 'Happy Days'	DWARF PERENNIAL SUNFLOWER
Heliopsis helianthoides	FALSE SUNFLOWER
Helleborus hybrids	HELLEBORE
Leucanthemum x *superbum*	SHASTA DAISY

   Especially 'Aglaya', 'Banana Cream', 'Cream Puff', 'Old Court', 'Shaggy'

Liatris spicata	DENSE BLAZING STAR
Melittis melissophyllum	BASTARD BALM
Paeonia lactiflora hybrids	CHINESE PEONY, GARDEN PEONY
Rudbeckia 'Herbstsonne' ('Autumn Sun')	DOUBLE CONEFLOWER
Rudbeckia laciniata 'Hortensia'	GOLDEN GLOW RUDBECKIA
Rudbeckia subtomentosa 'Henry Eilers'	SWEET CONEFLOWER
Scabiosa caucasica	PINCUSHION FLOWER
Solidago (X *Solidaster*) *luteus*	GOLDEN SOLIDASTER
Solidago (Aster) ptarmicoides	PRAIRIE ASTER
Symphyotrichum (Aster) ericoides	HEATH ASTER
Thermopsis mollis	GOLD-BANNER
Trachelium caeruleum	THROATWORT, UMBRELLA FLOWER
Zantedeschia aethiopica (white species, not hybrids)	CALLA-LILY

"TWEENERS"

Good for 18 to 24 months; Plant plugs/seedlings in earliest spring.

Catanache caerulea "Amor" series	CUPID'S DART
Cerinthe major 'Purpurascens'	HONEYWORT
Coreopsis grandiflora	LARGE-FLOWERED TICKSEED
Dianthus barbatus	SWEET WILLIAM
Dianthus hybrids	CUTTING PINKS
Echinacea hybrids	CONEFLOWER
Monarda punctata	SPOTTED BEEBALM
Rudbeckia hirta hybrids	BLACK-EYED SUSAN
Rudbeckia triloba	BROWN-EYED SUSAN
Scabiosa columbaria	SMALL SCABIOUS
Silene (Lychnis) chalcedonica	MALTESE CROSS
Tanacetum parthenium 'Magic', 'Tetra White', 'Ultra Double White'	FEVERFEW

ANNUALS

For warm season sowing (late spring) for summer-fall bloom.

Callistephus chinensis	CHINA ASTER
Cerinthe majus	HONEYWORT
Cosmos bipinnatus "Cupcakes" strain, 'Double Click Cranberry'	COSMOS
Emilia coccinea	TASSEL FLOWER
Helianthus annuus	SUNFLOWER
Monarda 'Bergamo Bouquet'	BUTTERFLY MONARDA

For cool season sowing (earliest spring) for spring-into-summer bloom (some beyond).

Ammi majus	FLORISTS' QUEEN ANNE'S LACE
Antirrhinum majus	SNAPDRAGON
Best: "Liberty Classic" strain, "Madame Butterfly" strain, "Chantilly" series, "Aromas" series, "Rocket" series, 'Plumblossom Hybrid', 'Lipstick'	
Bupleurum rotundifolium	THOROW-WAX
Centaurea cyanus	CORNFLOWER, BACHELOR'S BUTTONS
Centaurea moschata	SWEET SULTAN
Clarkia amoena	GODETIA
Consolida ajacis (C. ambigua)	ROCKET LARKSPUR
Gypsophila elegans	ANNUAL BABY'S BREATH
Lathyrus odoratus	SWEET PEA
"Old Spice Mix", 'North Shore', 'Blue Celeste', 'Renaissance', 'April in Paris', 'Saltwater Taffy Swirls'	
Molucella laevis	BELLS-OF-IRELAND
Oralaya grandiflora	WHITE FINCH
Scabiosa atropurpurea	PINCUSHION FLOWER
'Ace of Spades', 'Snowmaiden', 'Beaujolais Bonnets', 'Fire King', 'Salmon Queen', 'Scarlet'	
Trachymene caerulea	BLUE LACE FLOWER

BULBS

Planted in Fall for Spring Bloom (these will naturalize).

Allium atropurpureum	ORNAMENTAL ONION
Allium (Nectaroscordum) bulgaricum siculum	SICILIAN HONEY LILY
Allium cernuum	NODDING ONION ❖
Allium cristophii	STAR OF PERSIA
Allium neopolitanum cowanii	GUERNSEY STAR-OF-BETHLEHEM
Allium macleanii (A. elatum)	ORNAMENTAL ONION
Allium 'Firmament'	ORNAMENTAL ONION
Allium roseum	ROSY GARLIC
Allium schubertii	TUMBLEWEED ONION
Allium (Nectaroscordum) tripedale	PINK HONEY LILY
Allium 'Hair'	HAIR ALLIUM
Allium 'Mars'	ORNAMENTAL ONION
Allium 'Mt. Everest'	ORNAMENTAL ONION
Allium 'Ostara'	ORNAMENTAL ONION
Allium 'Purple Sensation'	ORNAMENTAL ONION
Brodiaea californica	CALIFORNIA BRODIAEA
Brodiaea coronaria	CROWN BRODIAEA ❖
Brodiaea elegans	HARVEST BRODIAEA ❖
Dichelostemma congestum	CLUSTER LILY ❖
Eucomis hybrids	PINEAPPLE LILY
Fritillaria assyriaca	TURKISH FRITILLARY
Gladiolus communis var. *byzantinus*	BYZANTINE GLADIOLUS
Gladiolus dalenii 'Bolivian Peach'	BOLIVIAN PEACH GLADIOLUS
Gladiolus dalenii var. *primulinus*	CAROLINA PRIMROSE
Gladiolus italicus	ITALIAN GLADIOLUS
Gladiolus oppositiflorus ssp. *salmoneus*	SALMON GLADIOLUS
Gladiolus 'Rosy Cheeks'	ROSY CHEEKS GLADIOLUS
Gladiolus saundersii	SAUNDER'S GLADIOLUS
Gladiolus tubergenii	SWORD LILY
Narcissus jonquilla	JONQUILS
Narcissus pseudonarcissus (select naturalizing cultivars)	DAFFODILS
Narcissus x *italicus* 'Thalia'	ITALIAN ANGEL'S TEARS
Triteleia hyacinthina	WHITE TRIPLET-LILY ❖
Triteleia laxa 'Queen Fabiola'	ITHERIAL'S SPEAR ❖
Tulipa clusiana and cultivars	LADY TULIP
Tulipa sprengeri	SPRENGER'S TULIP
Tulipa sylvestris	WOODLAND TULIP

»» More ...

Planted Early Spring (in pots first if cold-wet outside)or in Late Spring for Summer Bloom.

Dahlia hybrids	DAHLIAS
Gladiolus murielae (Acidanthera)	ABYSSINIAN GLADIOLA
Gladiolus special hybrids	GLADIOLA
"Butterfly", "Cardinalis hybrids", *G.* x colvillei 'The Bride',	
Ornithogalum saundersiae	GIANT CHINCHERINCHEE
Watsonia borbonica and hybrids	BUGLE LILY

BEST LILIES (LILIUM) FOR CUTTING
Planted fall or earliest spring.

Asiatics

'Arbatax'
'Eyeliner'
'Kentucky'
'Lionheart'
'Pirandello'
'Royal Sunset'
'Suncrest'

Orientals

'Acapulco'
'Arabian Red'
'Pookie'
'Siberia'
'Sorbonne'

SPECIAL ROSES FOR CUTTING
"English Shrub" -- Old-fashioned-looking roses with scent. Need extra water; Planted bare-root in January-February-March.

'Abbaye de Cluny' (*apricot blend*)
'Charlotte' (*soft yellow*)
'Eglantyne' (*soft pink*)
'Frederic Mistral' (*light pink*)
'Golden Celebration' (*golden yellow*)
'Jean Giono' (*yellow-apricot blend*)
'Johann Strauss' (*pink-yellow*)
'Michelangelo' (*golden yellow*)

'Molineux' (*bright yellow*)
'Queen of Sweden' (*soft pink*)
'Rouge Royale' (*deep red*)
'Traviata' (*dark red*)
'Winchester Cathedral' (*white, palest blush*)
'Yves Piaget' (*deep mauve pink, fringed*)

PLANTS FOR CUT FOLIAGE

Annuals

Amaranthus cruentus	AMARANTH
Artemisia annua	SWEET ANNIE
Atriplex hortensis	ORNAMENTAL ORACH

Perennials

Artemisia ludoviciana 'Silver Queen', 'Valerie Finnis'	MUGWORT
Aspidistra elatior (many variegated cultivars)	CAST-IRON PLANT
Baptisia australis and hybrids	FALSE INDIGO
Comptonia peregrina	SWEETFERN
Coniogramme japonica	JAPANESE BAMBOO FERN
FERNS, primarily evergreen types	FERNS
Hosta species and hybrids	HOSTA
Lavandula species	LAVENDER
Paeonia lactiflora hybrids	PEONY
Polygonatum species	SOLOMON'S SEAL
Polystichum munitum	WESTERN SWORD FERN ❖
Stachys byzantina (S. lanata)	LAMB'S EARS
Xerophyllum tenax	BEAR GRASS, INDIAN BASKET GRASS ❖

Shrubs, Trees

Camellia species and hybrids	CAMELLIA
Chionanthus retusus	JAPANESE FRINGE TREE
Cornus mas 'Variegata'	VARIEGATED CORNELIAN CHERRY
Cotinus coggygria	SMOKE TREE
Danae racemosa	POET'S LAUREL
Euonymus japonicum	EUONYMUS
Gaultheria shallon	SALAL ❖
Hypericum x *inodorum* (for berries)	SANGRIA ST. JOHN'S WORT
Ilex, evergreen species except *I. aquifolium*	HOLLIES
Lavandula species and hybrids	LAVENDER
Leucothoe axillaris	COAST LEUCOTHOE
Leucothoe fontanesiana	DROOPING LEUCOTHOE
Lomatia myricoides	RIVER LOMATIA
Luma apiculata	CHILEAN GUAVA
Magnolia grandiflora	SOUTHERN MAGNOLIA
Myrtus communis	ROMAN MYRTLE
Osmanthus heterophyllus (many colorful cultivars)	HOLLY-LEAF OSMANTHUS
Paxistima (Pachystima) myrsinites	OREGON BOXWOOD ❖
Physocarpus opulifolius 'Diablo'	PURPLE NINEBARK
Pittosporum tenuifolium	KOHUHU
Ruscus hypoglossum	ITALIAN BUTCHER'S BROOM
Ruscus hypophyllum	SPANISH BUTCHER'S BROOM
Skimmia japonica	JAPANESE SKIMMIA
Symphoricarpos species and hybrids	SNOWBERRY
Umbellularia californica	PACIFIC BAY LAUREL
Vaccinium ovatum	EVERGREEN HUCKLEBERRY ❖
Viburnum davidii	DAVID'S VIBURNUM

WOODY BRANCHES FOR FORCING

Aesculus species and hybrids	HORSE CHESTNUT
Cercis species	REDBUDS
Chaenomeles species and hybrids	FLOWERING QUINCE
Cornus kousa and hybrids	DOGWOOD
Cornus mas	CORNELIAN CHERRY
Crataegus species and hybrids	HAWTHORN
Deutzia gracilis	SLENDER DEUTZIA
Deutzia scabra 'Flore-Pleno'	DOUBLE-FLOWERED FUZZY DEUTZIA
Forsythia species and hybrids	FORSYTHIA
Fothergilla species and hybrids	FOTHERGILLA
Hamamelis vernalis	OZARK WITCH-HAZEL
Kolkwitzia amabilis	BEAUTYBUSH
Lindera benzoin	SPICEBUSH
Magnolia species and hybrids, spring bloomers	MAGNOLIA
Malus species and hybrids	CRABAPPLES
Philadelphus species and hybrids	MOCK ORANGE
Prunus species and hybrids	ORNAMENTAL PLUMS, CHERRIES, APRICOTS
Rhododendron spring-bloomers, some	RHODODENDRON
Ribes odoratum	CLOVE CURRANT
Salix species, especially "pussy willows"	WILLOWS
Salix gracilistyla 'Mt. Asama'	MT. ASAMA PUSSY WILLOW
Spiraea cantoniensis	BRIDAL WREATH
Spiraea nipponica 'Snowmound'	SNOWMOUND SPIREA
Spiraea prunifolia 'Plena'	BRIDAL WREATH
Spiraea thunbergii	THUNBERG'S SPIREA, BRIDALWREATH SPIREA
Spiraea x *vanhouttei*	BRIDAL WREATH
Syringa species and hybrids	LILAC
Viburnum spring-blooming species	VIBURNUM

PLANTS FOR DRIED ARRANGEMENT MATERIAL

Achillea filipendulina	YARROW
Allium cristophii	STAR OF PERSIA
Allium schubertii	TUMBLEWEED ONION
Amaranthus caudatus	AMARANTH, LOVE-LIES-BLEEDING, TASSEL FLOWER
Amaranthus hypochondriacus	PRINCES' FEATHER
Ammobium elatum	WINGED EVERLASTING, DUTCH LACE
Anaphalis margaritacea	PEARLY EVERLASTING
Armeria maritima	SEA PINKS SEA THRIFT
Artemisia albula	ARTEMISIA, SILVER SAGE
Artemisia annua	SWEET ANNIE
Avena sativa	OATS
Briza maxima	QUAKING GRASS
Bromus madritensis	BROME GRASS
Capsicum species	CHILI PEPPERS

Celosia spicata	WHEAT CELOSIA
Coix lacryma-jobi	JOB'S TEARS
Consolida ajacis (C. ambigua)	ROCKET LARKSPUR
Echinops ritro	BLUE GLOBE THISTLE
Eleusine coracana	FINGER MILLET, DRAGON'S CLAW MILLET
Eryngium giganteum (biennial)	MISS WILMOTT'S GHOST
Fibigia clypeata	ROMAN SHIELDS, WISPY PILLOWS
Gomphrena globosa (needs heat)	GLOBE AMARANTH
Gypsophila paniculata	BABY'S BREATH
Helichrysum arenarium	SANDY EVERLASTING
Helipterum manglesii	RHODANTHE
Helipterum roseum	ACROCLINIUM, PAPER DAISY
Hordeum vulgare	BARLEY
Hydrangea macrophylla	HYDRANGEA
Hydrangea paniculata	SNOW BALL
Hydrangea quercifolia	OAK-LEAF HYDRANGEA
Iris foetidissima	GLADWIN IRIS
Lagurus ovatus	HARE'S TAIL BUNNY TAIL
Lavandula species	LAVENDER
Limonium bellidifolium	CASPIA, MATTED SEA LAVENDER
Limonium latifolium	ITALIAN SEA LAVENDER
Limonium sinuatum	ANNUAL STATICE
Limonium tataricum	GERMAN STATICE
Linum usitatissimum	FLAX
Lonas inodora	GOLDEN AGERATUM
Lunaria annua	HONESTY
Molucella laevis	BELLS-OF-IRELAND
Nigella damascena	LOVE-IN-A-MIST
Nigella orientalis	YELLOW FENNEL FLOWER
Papaver somniferum, especially "Hens-and-Chicks"	POPPY PODS
Pennisetum glaucum	ORNAMENTAL MILLET
Phalaris canariensis	CANARY GRASS
Physalis alkekengi var. *franchetii*	CHINESE LANTERN
Psylliostachys suworowii	RATTAIL STATICE, PINK POKER
Salvia farinacea	BLUE SALVIA
Scabiosa stellata	PAPER DRUMSTICKS
Secale cereale	RYE
Setaria italica	FOXTAIL MILLET
Setaria macrochaeta	MILLET
Sorghum bicolor	KASSABY SORGHUM
Sorghum vulgare var. *technicum*	BROOMCORN
Tanacetum camphoratum	DUNE TANSY
Triticum aestivum	EGYPTIAN WHEAT
Triticum aestivum ssp. *compactum*	CLUB WHEAT
Triticum durum	BLACK-BEARDED WHEAT
Triticum spelta	SPELT WHEAT
Uniola paniculata	SEA OATS
Xerochrysum (Helichrysum, Bracteantha) bracteatum	STRAWFLOWERS
Zea mays	ORNAMENTAL CORN

PONDS

Make sure your pond has no low edges and no pockets of still water to avoid mosquitoes. Small fish are also a good idea.

SUBMERSED PLANTS ("OXYGENATORS")

Ceratophyllum demersum	COON-TAIL❖
Elodea canadensis	AMERICAN WATERWEED❖
Elodea nuttallii	NUTTALL'S WATERWEED ❖
Fontinalis antipyretica	WATER MOSS❖
Ludwigia palustris	WATER PURSLANE
Najas flexilis	WATER NYMPH❖
Ranunculus aquatilis	WHITE WATER-BUTTERCUP❖

PLANTS WITH EMERGENT OR FLOATING LEAVES

Alisma traviale (*A. plantago aquatica*)	AMERICAN WATER-PLANTAIN❖
Aponogeton distachyus	WATER HAWTHORNE
Azolla filiculoides	WATER FERN❖
Brasenia schreberi	WATERSHIELD❖
Caltha palustris 'Plena'	DOUBLE MARSH MARIGOLD
Hydrocleys nymphoides	WATER POPPY
Lemna minor	DUCKWEED❖
Ludwigia peploides	PRIMROSE CREEPER
Ludwigia sedioides	MOSAIC PLANT
Menyanthes trifoliata	BOG BEAN❖
Nelumbo lutea	AMERICAN LOTUS
Nelumbo nucifera	SACRED LOTUS
Nuphar polysepala (*Nuphar lutea*)	YELLOW WATERLILY, SPATTERDOCK❖
Nymphaea odorata and other species and hybrids	HARDY WATER LILY
Nymphoides crenata	RUFFLED SNOWFLAKE
Nymphoides cristata	CRESTED WATER SNOWFLAKE
Nymphoides geminata	YELLOW SNOWFLAKE
Ranunculus aquatilis	WHITE WATER BUTTERCUP ❖
Sagittaria latifolia (*S. cuneata*)	DUCK POTATO❖

PLANTS FOR PERIPHERY

Pretty much anything from the bigger list of plants for "WET AREAS"

RAIN GARDEN

This is where excess water from natural runoff and roofs is directed, filtered, and captured. A bit of engineering math is involved to make sure the pond is big enough for whatever the wet clouds can produce.

Zone 1 = normal to frequent water saturation
Zone 2 = occasional standing water events
Zone 3 = least amount of water saturation but still moister than typical garden

ZONE 1

Acorus gramineus	SWEET FLAG
Athyrium filix-femina	LADY FERN ❖
Carex comans	NEW ZEALAND HAIR SEDGE
Carex mertensiana (C. columbiana)	MERTEN'S SEDGE ❖
Carex obnupta	SLOUGH SEDGE ❖
Cornus alba	TATARIAN DOGWOOD
Cornus sanguinea	BLOOD-TWIG DOGWOOD
Cornus sericea	RED OSIER DOGWOOD ❖
Hesperantha (Schizostylis) coccinea	CRIMSON FLAG
Geranium x cantabrigiense	HARDY GERANIUM
Iris douglasiana	DOUGLAS IRIS ❖
Iris tenax	OREGON IRIS, TOUGH-LEAF IRIS ❖
Juncus acuminatus	TAPER-TIPPED RUSH
Juncus ensifolius	DAGGER-LEAF RUSH ❖
Juncus patens	SPREADING RUSH
Lonicera involucrata	BLACK TWINBERRY ❖
Malus fusca	PACIFIC CRABAPPLE ❖
Ribes bracteosum	STINK CURRANT ❖
Rubus spectabilis	SALMONBERRY ❖
Salix purpurea 'Nana'	DWARF ARCTIC BLUE WILLOW
Sambucus nigra	BLACK ELDERBERRY
Scirpus microcarpus	SMALL-FRUITED BULRUSH
Sidalcea hendersonii	HENDERSON'S CHECKER-MALLOW ❖
Spiraea densiflora	ALPINE SPIREA ❖
Symphyotrichum (Aster) subspicatum	DOUGLAS ASTER ❖
Taxodium distichum 'Peve Minaret'	DWARF BALD CYPRESS

»» More...

ZONE 2

Acer circinatum	VINE MAPLE ❖
Acorus calamus	SWEET FLAG
Ajuga reptans	BUGLEWEED
Amelanchier alnifolia	WESTERN SERVICEBERRY, JUNEBERRY, SASKATOON ❖
Aquilegia formosa	WESTERN COLUMBINE
Asarum caudatum	WILD GINGER ❖
Betula nigra especially 'Heritage'	HERITAGE BIRCH
Blechnum (Struthiopteris) spicant	DEER FERN ❖
Calamagrostis brachytricha	KOREAN FEATHER REED GRASS
Camassia leichtlinii	LARGE OR GIANT CAMAS ❖
Camassia quamash	COMMON CAMAS ❖
Carex hachijoensis 'Evergold'	EVERGOLD SEDGE
Carex testacea	ORANGE NEW ZEALAND SEDGE
Cornus mas	CORNELIAN CHERRY
Cornus sericea	RED-TWIG DOGWOOD ❖
Corylus cornuta	BEAKED HAZELNUT ❖
Deschampsia caespitosa	TUFTED HAIR GRASS ❖
Frangula (Rhamnus) purshiana	CASCARA ❖
Fuchsia magellanica	HARDY FUCHSIA
Gaultheria shallon	SALAL ❖
Hemerocallis species and hybrids	DAYLILY
Hydrangea arborescens	SMOOTH HYDRANGEA
Iris sibirica	SIBERIAN IRIS
Iris unguicularis	WINTER IRIS
Lonicera pileata	BOX-LEAF HONEYSUCKLE
Mahonia aquifolium	OREGON-GRAPE ❖
Mahonia nervosa	CASCADE OREGON-GRAPE ❖
Mahonia repens	CREEPING OREGON-GRAPE ❖
Miscanthus sinensis	JAPANESE SILVER-GRASS
Molinia caerulea	MOOR GRASS
Persicaria affinis	HIMALAYAN FLEECE FLOWER
Physocarpus opulifolius	NINEBARK
Polystichum munitum	WESTERN SWORD FERN ❖
Rosa rugosa	JAPANESE BEACH ROSE
Rubus parviflorus	THIMBLEBERRY ❖
Sambucus caerulea	BLUE ELDERBERRY ❖
Symphoricarpos albus	SNOWBERRY ❖
Symphyotrichum (Aster) chilense	PACIFIC ASTER ❖
Tellima grandiflora	FRINGECUP ❖
Tiarella trifoliata	FOAMFLOWER ❖
Vaccinium ovatum	EVERGREEN HUCKLEBERRY ❖
Vancouveria hexandra	INSIDE-OUT FLOWER ❖

»» More…

Achillea millefolium and hybrids	YARROW ❖
Arbutus unedo	STRAWBERRY TREE
Astrantia major	MASTERWORT
Berberis thunbergii	BARBERRY
Fragaria chiloensis	BEACH STRAWBERRY ❖
Geum hybrids	GEUM
Hemerocallis	DAYLILIES
Hosta	HOSTA
Liatris spicata	GAYFEATHER
Mahonia aquifolium 'Compacta'	DWARF OREGON-GRAPE ❖
Malus 'Adirondack ', 'Beverly', 'Cardinal', 'Golden Raindrops', 'Lancelot', 'Lollipop', 'Molten Lava', 'Prairifire', 'Professor Sprenger', 'Ruby Tears', 'Tina'	CRABAPPLE
Parrotia persica	PERSIAN IRONWOOD
Penstemon species	BEARDTONGUE ❖
Ribes sanguineum	RED-FLOWERING CURRANT ❖
Spiraea japonica	SUMMER SPIREA
Stachys byzantina (S. lanata)	LAMB'S EARS
Viburnum trilobum (V. opulus var. *americanum)*	AMERICAN HIGHBUSH CRANBERRY ❖

Plus most of the plants on the list for "WET AREAS."

BARRIER

More than just a hedge – these plants bite back. For keeping animals, including the two-legged kind, away from a given area.

Agave asperrima	SCABROUS CENTURY PLANT
Agave harvardiana	HAVARD'S AGAVE
Agave x loferox 'Hacksaw'	HACKSAW HYBRID CENTURY PLANT
Agave ovatifolia	WHALE'S TONGUE CENTURY PLANT
Agave parryi ssp. *neomexicana*	NEW MEXICO HARDY CENTURY PLANT
Agave x pseudoferox 'Bellville'	BELLVILLE CENTURY PLANT
Berberis buxifolia	MAGELLAN BARBERRY
Berberis darwinii	DARWIN BARBERRY
Berberis x hybridogagnepainii 'Chenault'	CHENAULT BARBERRY
Berberis x stenophylla	HYBRID BARBERRY
Chamaerops humilis	MEDITERRANEAN FAN PALM
Chaenomeles (tall types)	FLOWERING QUINCE
Colletia hystrix	BARBED WIRE BRUSH
Elaeagnus x submacrophylla (*E.* x ebbingei)	HYBRID ELAEAGNUS
Gunnera tinctoria	CHILEAN GIANT RHUBARB
Ilex x altaclarensis 'Wilsoni'	WILSON'S HOLLY
Juniperus (the cultivars with immature [prickly] foliage)	JUNIPERS
Mahonia aquifolium	OREGON-GRAPE ❖
Mahonia x media	HYBRID MAHONIA
Melicytus crassifolius	THICK-LEAVED MAHOE
Olearia macrodonta	NEW ZEALAND HOLLY
Opuntia hardy species and hybrids	OPUNTIA, PRICKLY PEAR
Osmanthus armatus	TOOTHED SWEET OLIVE
Osmanthus heterophyllus	HOLLY-LEAF OSMANTHUS
Pyracantha x fortuneana 'Graberi'	FIRETHORN
Rhapidophyllum hystrix	NEEDLE PALM
Rhaphithamnus spinosus	PRICKLY MYRTLE
Ribes speciosum	FUCHSIA-FLOWERING GOOSEBERRY
Rosa canina	DOG ROSE
Rosa laevigata	CHEROKEE ROSE
Rosa nutkana	NOOTKA ROSE ❖
Rosa rugosa	JAPANESE BEACH ROSE
Rosa sericea ssp. *omeiensis* f. *pteracantha*	WINGED ROSE
Rubus parviflorus	THIMBLEBERRY ❖
Sophora davidii	DAVID'S MOUNTAIN LAUREL
Yucca aloifolia	SPANISH BAYONET
Yucca gloriosa	SPANISH DAGGER
Yucca linearifolia	NARROW-LEAFED BEAKED YUCCA
Zanthoxylum simulans	CHINESE-PEPPER, CHINESE PRICKLY-ASH

BULB COMPANIONS

Dying and dead bulb tops leave for a depressing landscape scene. Hence a good idea to cover the area with other plants which carry on simply to avoid a bare spot or, more so, to provide a continuation of color through the year. Many of these will also offer up flowers that bloom at the same time as the bulbs and may enhance the color scheme. Keep in mind that some bulbs are adamant about having a dry soil in the summertime; with these summer-dry bulb species, it's wise to either not plant over the top or to go with summer-drought-tolerant plants (several here).

ANNUALS

Antirrhinum majus	SNAPDRAGON
Callistephus chinensis	CHINA ASTER
Cleome hasslerana	SPIDER FLOWER
Convolvulus tricolor	BUSH MORNING GLORY
Cosmos bipinnatus	COSMOS
Impatiens balsamina	BALSAM
Lavatera trimestris	ROSE MALLOW
Nicotiana alata	FLOWERING TOBACCO
Nicotiana x sanderae	FLOWERING TOBACCO
Nolana humifusa	NOLANA
Nolana paradoxa	CHILEAN BELLFLOWER
Petunia × atkinsiana	HYBRID PETUNIA
Phlox drummondii	ANNUAL PHLOX
Salpiglossus sinuata	PAINTED TONGUE
Tagetes filifolia	IRISH LACE
Tagetes patula	FRENCH MARIGOLD
Tagetes tenuifolia	SIGNET MARIGOLD
Thymophylla tenuiloba	GOLDEN FLEECE
Zinnia (best in driest, hottest spots only)	ZINNIA

PERENNIALS

Achillea hybrids (many)	YARROWS
Aconitum lycoctonum	WOLFSBANE
Aconitum napellus	MONKSHOOD
Alstroemeria hybrids	PERUVIAN LILY
Artemisia 'Powis Castle'	SILKY WORMWOOD
Asarina procumbens	CREEPING SNAPDRAGON
Aster x frikartii	ITALIAN ASTER
Astrantia major	GREAT MASTERWORT
Betonica (Stachys) macrantha 'Robusta'	BIG BETONY
Betonica (Stachys) officinalis	WOOD BETONY
Calluna vulgaris	SCOTCH HEATHER
Calylophus hartwegii	HARTWEG'S SUNDROPS
Campanula takesimana	KOREAN BELLFLOWER

Campanula 'Sarastro'	SARASTRO BELLFLOWER
Campanula lactiflora	MILKY BELLFLOWER
Campanula latiloba	GREAT BELLFLOWER
Centranthus ruber	JUPITER'S BEARD, RED VALERIAN
Chrysanthemum X *rubellum*	HARDY CHRYSANTHEMUM
Coreopsis auriculata	TICKSEED
Digitalis ferruginea	RUSTY FOXGLOVE
Digitalis grandiflora	YELLOW FOXGLOVE
Epilobium (Zauschneria) (many)	CALIFORNIA FUCHSIA
Erica cinerea	BELL HEATHER/HEATH
Eriogonum latifolium	SEASIDE BUCKWHEAT
Eriogonum umbellatum	SULPHUR BUCKWHEAT
Galega x *hartlandii*	HYBRID GOAT'S-RUE
Geranium x *cantabrigiense*	CAMBRIDGE GERANIUM
Geranium cinereum 'Ballerina'	BALLERINA GERANIUM
Geranium endressii 'Wargrave Pink'	WARGRAVE PINK GERANIUM
Geranium x *oxonianum*	HYBRID GERANIUMS
Geranium 'Johnson's Blue'	JOHNSON'S BLUE GERANIUM
Geranium x *riversleaianum*	HYBRID GERANIUM
Geranium wlassovianum	LATE GERANIUM
Geum hybrids	GEUM
Heliopsis helianthoides	FALSE SUNFLOWER
Heuchera maxima and hybrids (many)	CORAL BELLS
Heuchera micrantha	CREVICE ALUMROOT ❖
Hylotelephium (Sedum) 'Vera Jameson'	VERA JAMESON SEDUM
Hylotelephium (Sedum) ewersii	PINK MONGOLIAN STONECROP
Hylotelephium (Sedum) sieboldii	OCTOBER DAPHNE
Hylotelephium (Sedum) spectabile	
SHOWY STONECROP, AUTUMN SEDUM, BORDER SEDUM	
Iberis sempervirens	EVERGREEN CANDYTUFT
Incarvillea delavayi	HARDY GLOXINIA
Lamprocapnos (Dicentra) spectabilis	OLD-FASHIONED BLEEDING HEART
Lewisia cotyledon and hybrids	SISKIYOU LEWISIA ❖
Nepeta 'Six Hills Giant'	GIANT CATMINT
Nepeta racemosa 'Walker's Low'	WALKER'S LOW CATMINT
Origanum dictamnus	CRETE DITTANY
Penstemon davidsonii	DAVIDSON'S PENSTEMON ❖
Phlomis lanata 'Pygmy'	DWARF PHLOMIS
Rhodanthemum (Chrysanthemum) hosmariense	MOROCCAN DAISY
Rhodiola pachyclados	AFGHAN SEDUM
Salvia hians, S. nemorosa, S. verticillata	PERENNIAL SAGE
Salvia x *sylvestris*	WOOD SAGE
Sanguisorba hakusanensis	KOREAN MOUNTAIN BURNET, LILAC SQUIRREL
Scabiosa columbariae 'Butterfly Blue', 'Pink Mist'	PINCUSHION FLOWER
Scabiosa ochroleuca	YELLOW PINCUSHION
Sidalcea oregana	OREGON CHECKERBLOOM ❖
Sisyrinchium striatum	SATIN FLOWER
Tanacetum ptarmiciflorum	SILVER LACE BUSH
Veronica (Parahebe) perfoliata	DIGGER'S SPEEDWELL

GROUNDCOVERS

Achillea ageratifolia	GREEK YARROW
Achillea x *lewisii* 'King Edward'	TRAILING YARROW
Achillea millefolium	YARROW ❖
Achillea serbica	SERBIAN YARROW
Aethionema grandiflorum	STONE CRESS
Cerastium tomentosum	SNOW-IN-SUMMER
Ceratostigma plumbaginoides	CHINESE PLUMBAGO
Dianthus deltoides	MAIDEN PINK
Epimedium trailing hybrids	HYBRID EPIMEDIUM
Erodium reichardii (E. chamaedryoides)	ALPINE GERANIUM
Fragaria chiloensis*	BEACH STRAWBERRY ❖
Gaultheria ovatifolia	WESTERN TEABERRY ❖
Gypsophila cerastioides	TRAILING BABY'S BREATH
Helianthemum nummularium	SUN ROSE
Origanum rotundifolium 'Hopleys'	ORNAMENTAL OREGANO
Phlox caespitosa	TUFTED PHLOX ❖
Phlox diffusa	SPREADING PHLOX ❖
Phlox divaricata	WOODLAND PHLOX
Sedum (including *Petrosedum, Phedimus*) hundreds of species and cultivars	STONECROP
Stachys corsica	CORSICAN TRAILING LAMB'S EAR
Stachys densiflora	CREEPING BETONY
Thymus x citriodorus	LEMON THYME
Thymus herba-barona	CARAWAY-SCENTED THYME
Thymus polytrichus ssp. *brittanicus (T. praecox* ssp. *arcticus)* 'Creeping Pink', 'Reiter'	CREEPING THYME
Veronica liwanensis	TURKISH SPEEDWELL
Veronica pectinata	WOOLLY SPEEDWELL
Veronica whitleyi	WHITLEY'S SPEEDWELL

261

FILLERS/"TWEENERS"

For TEMPORARILY filling in the empty spaces of a new landscape or bed. Fast-growing, short-lived perennials. Many often reseed but "volunteers" are easy to manage. See also "Fast-Growing Trees and Shrubs." Don't forget the judicious use of seasonal and even permanent cover crops.

Agastache foeniculum, A. occidentalis, A. rugosa and hybrids	GIANT HYSSOPS
Alcea ficifolia and hybrids	ANTWERP HOLLYHOCK
Anchusa azurea	ITALIAN BUGLOSS
Anthyllis vulneraria var. *coccinea*	RED LADY'S-FINGERS
Aquilegia species and hybrids	COLUMBINE
Bellis perennis	ENGLISH DAISY
Catanache caerulea	CUPID'S-DART
Cerinthe major 'Purpurascens'	HONEYWORT
Coreopsis grandiflora	LARGE-FLOWERED TICKSEED
Dianthus species (some species self-sow)	PINKS
Echium russicum	RUSSIAN BUGLOSS
Echinacea cultivars	CONEFLOWER
Erysimum linifolium (and other species)	"PERENNIAL" WALLFLOWER
Gaillardia x grandiflora	BLANKET FLOWER
Hesperis matronalis	DAME'S ROCKET
Heuchera cultivars	CORAL BELLS
Hibiscus radiatus	RUBY HIBISCUS, MONARCH ROSE-MALLOW
Monarda punctata	SPOTTED MONARDA
Knautia species	KNAUTIA
Leucanthemum x superbum	SHASTA DAISY
Linum perenne	BLUE FLAX
Lobelia cardinalis	CARDINAL FLOWER
Lobelia siphilitica	GREAT LOBELIA
Lupinus x regalis (*L.* x russellii)	RUSSELL LUPINE
Lychnis chalcedonica	MALTESE CROSS
Malva species	MALLOWS
Monarda citriodora	LEMON BEE-BALM
Papaver croceum/nudicaule	ICELAND POPPY
Penstemon gloxinioides hybrids	BEARD TONGUE
Rudbeckia hirta and hybrids	GLORIOSA DAISY, BLACK-EYED SUSAN
Rudbeckia triloba	BROWN-EYED SUSAN
Scabiosa columbariae	PINCUSHION FLOWER
Silene (Lychnis) coronaria	ROSE CAMPION
Sisyrinchium angustifolium	BLUE-EYED GRASS
Tanacetum coccineum	PAINTED DAISY
Tanacetum parthenium	FEVERFEW
Verbena bonariensis	PURPLE-TOP VERBENA

THE SMALL GARDEN

Selected plants for the landscape of a less-than-average scale. These are the biggest bangs for the buck, the smaller plants which do the necessary extra duty given the lesser space.

SMALL-ISH SHADE TREES

Acer buergerianum	TRIDENT MAPLE
Acer griseum	PAPERBARK MAPLE
Acer japonicum 'Vitifolium'	HALF-MOON MAPLE
Acer palmatum	JAPANESE MAPLE
'Beni Kawa', 'Crimson Queen', 'Fall's Fire', 'Katsura', 'Moonfire', 'Sherwood Flame', 'Shirazz', 'Shishigashira', 'Summergold'	
Acer shirasawanum 'Aureum'	GOLDEN FULL MOON MAPLE
Acer tataricum var. *ginnala*	AMUR MAPLE
Albizia julibrissin	SILK TREE
Betula nigra 'Heritage'	RIVER BIRCH
Cercis canadensis 'Forest Pansy'	FOREST PANSY REDBUD
Stewartia 'Scarlet Sentinel'	SCARLET SENTINEL STEWARTIA
Styrax japonicus	JAPANESE SNOWBELL

SMALL WEEPING TREES

Acer japonicum 'Abby's Weeping', 'Green Cascade'	WEEPING AMUR MAPLE
Acer palmatum 'Hana Matoi'	WEEPING JAPANESE MAPLE
Cercis canadensis 'Covey' ('Lavender Twist')	WEEPING REDBUD
Indigofera pendula	WEEPING INDIGO
Juniperus communis 'Horstmann'	HORSTMANN'S WEEPING JUNIPER
Juniperus scopulorum 'Tolleson's Blue Weeping'	TOLLESON'S WEEPING JUNIPER
Malus 'Louisa'	WEEPING CRABAPPLE
Picea omorika 'Pendula Bruns'	DWARF WEEPING SERBIAN SPRUCE
Podocarpus totara 'Pendula'	WEEPING TOTARA
Prunus mume 'W. B. Clarke'	WEEPING JAPANESE APRICOT
Prunus pendula 'Plena-rosea'	DOUBLE WEEPING CHERRY
Pyrus salicifolia 'Pendula'	WEEPING PEAR
Styrax japonicus 'Fragrant Fountain', 'Marley's Pink Parasol', 'Nightfall'	
	WEEPING JAPANESE SNOWBELL

SMALL SHRUBS *(under 3 feet)*
Including subshrubs ("woody perennials")

Aucuba japonica 'Pacman', 'Petite Jade'	DWARF JAPANESE LAUREL
Baeckea gunniana	HEATHMYRTLE
Berberis buxifolia 'Nana'	DWARF BOX-LEAF BARBERRY
Berberis x *stenophylla* 'Corallina Compacta'	MINIATURE HEDGE BARBERRY
Brachyglottis 'Otari Cloud'	OTARI CLOUD DAISY BUSH
Calluna vulgaris	HEATHER

263

Camellia sasanqua 'Jewel Box'　　　　　　　　　　　DWARF SUN CAMELLIA
Caryopteris x clandonensis dwarf cultivars　　　　　　　DWARF BLUEBEARD
Chaenomeles speciosa 'Contorta'　　　　CONTORTED FLOWERING QUINCE
Cistus x bornetianus 'Jester'　　　　　　　　　　　　JESTER ROCKROSE
Cistus x canescens 'Albus'　　　　　　　　　　　　　WHITE ROCKROSE
Cistus x crispatus 'Warley Rose'　　　　　　　WARLEY ROSE ROCKROSE
Cistus x dansereaui 'Jenkyn Place'　　　　　　JENKYN PLACE ROCKROSE
Cistus x heterocalyx 'Chelsea Bonnet'　　　CHELSEA BONNET ROCKROSE
Cistus x obtusifolius　　　　　　　　　　COMPACT WHITE ROCKROSE
Cistus 'Snowfire'　　　　　　　　　　　　　　SNOWFIRE ROCKROSE
Cornus sericea 'Kelseyi'　　　　KELSEY'S DWARF RED-OSIER DOGWOOD
Daphne x burkwoodii 'Carol Mackie'　　　　VARIEGATED HYBRID DAPHNE
Daphne x medfordensis 'Lawrence Crocker'　　　　　　DWARF DAPHNE
Daphne x transatlantica　　　　　　　　　　　　　HYBRID DAPHNE
Daphne tangutica　　　　　　　　　　　　　　　　　　DAPHNE
Dasiphora (Potentilla) fruticosa (selected cultivars)　SHRUBBY CINQUEFOIL ❖
Epilobium canum (Zauschneria californica) including ssp. *garrettii* CALIFORNIA FUCHSIA
Erica x darleyensis　　　　　　　　　　　　　　DARLEY DALE HEATH
Eriogonum caespitosum　　　　　　　　　　　　　MAT BUCKWHEAT
Eriogonum latifolium　　　　　　　　　　　　COAST BUCKWHEAT ❖
Eriogonum ovalifolium　　　　　　　　　　OVAL-LEAF BUCKWHEAT ❖
Eriogonum umbellatum　　　　　　　　　　SULPHUR BUCKWHEAT ❖
Forsythia x intermedia 'Fiesta'　　　　　　　VARIEGATED FORSYTHIA
Fuchsia 'Lord Byron'　　　　　　　　　　　　　　HARDY FUCHSIA
Grevillea juniperina cultivars　　　　　　　JUNIPER-LEAF GREVILLEA
Hebe 'Blue Mist'　　　　　　　　　　　　　　　BLUE MIST HEBE
Hebe buchananii 'Fenwickii'　　　　　　SIR GEORGE FENWICK'S HEBE
Hebe 'Emerald Gem'　　　　　　　　　　　　　　　　　HEBE
Hebe 'Hinerua'　　　　　　　　　　　　　　　　　　　HEBE
Hebe pinguifolia 'Sutherlandii'　　　　　　　　　　BLUE-LEAF HEBE
Hebe topiaria　　　　　　　　　　　　　　　　　　　HEBE
Helianthemum nummularium and hybrids　　　　　　　　SUN ROSE
Helichrysum splendidum　　　　　　　　　　　　　　CAPE GOLD
Hydrangea arborescens　　　　　　　　　　　SMOOTH HYDRANGEA
　　"Invincibelle" Series: 'Mini Mauvette', 'Ruby', 'Spirit II', 'Wee White'
Hydrangea macrophylla　　　　　　　　　　　DWARF HYDRANGEA
　　'Cherry Explosion', 'Cityline Paris', 'Cityline Rio', 'Endless Summer Crush',
　　'Everlasting Amethyst', 'Everlasting Revolution', 'Lanarth White',
　　'Let's Dance Blue Jangles', 'Let's Dance Rave', 'Let's Dance Rhythmic Blue',
　　'Mini Penny', 'Paraplu', 'Pia' (Pink Elf), 'Wedding Gown'
Hydrangea paniculata　　　　　　　　DWARF PANICLED HYDRANGEA
　　'Bobo', 'Bombshell', 'Fire Light Tidbit', 'Little Lime', 'Lavalamp Flare'
Hydrangea quercifolia　　　　　　　　DWARF OAK-LEAF HYDRANGEA
　　'Munchkin', 'Pee Wee', 'Sike's Dwarf'
Hydrangea serrata　　　　　　　　DWARF MOUNTAIN HYDRANGEA
　　'Little Geisha', 'Tuff Stuff'
Ilex crenata 'Dwarf Pagoda'　　　　　　　DWARF JAPANESE HOLLY
Ilex crenata 'Green Island'　　　　　　　　　JAPANESE HOLLY

Ilex x *meserveae* 'Little Rascal', 'Scallywag'	DWARF BLUE HOLLY
Ilex x 'Rock Garden'	ROCK GARDEN HOLLY
Kalmia latifolia 'Elf', 'Minuet'	DWARF MOUNTAIN LAUREL
Leptodermis oblonga	HIMALAYAN LILAC
Leptospermum namadgiensis	ALPINE TEA TREE
Leucothoe fontanesiana 'Zeblid'	DROOPING LAUREL
Lonicera pileata	BOX-LEAF HONEYSUCKLE
Myrteola nummularia	CRANBERRY-MYRTLE
Olearia x *oleifolia* 'Waikariensis'	HARDY DAISY-ON-A-STICK
Ozothamnus coralloides	CORAL SHRUB
Penstemon fruticosus	SHRUBBY PENSTEMON, BUSH PENSTEMON ❖
Pieris japonica 'Cavatine', 'Impish Elf', 'Little Heath'	
	DWARF LILY-OF-THE-VALLEY SHRUB
Polygaloides (Polygala) chamaebuxus	SHRUBBY MILKWORT
Prostanthera cuneata	ALPINE MINT BUSH
Rhodanthemum (Chrysanthemum) hosmariense	MOROCCAN DAISY
Rhododendron campylogynum	RHODODENDRON
Rhododendron hanceanum 'Nanum'	RHODODENDRON
Rhododendron hybrids including 'Carmen', 'Creeping Jenny', 'Curlew', 'Dopey',	
'Egret', 'Ernie Dee', 'Ginny Gee, 'Haaga', 'Lori Eichelser', 'Moerheim',	
'Ostbo's Red Elizabeth'. 'Patty Bee', 'Princess Anne', 'Ptarmigan', 'Ramapo',	
'Shamrock', 'Wee Bee'	DWARF RHODODENDRONS
Rhododendron kiusianum 'Komo Kulshan'	RHODODENDRON
Rhododendron lutescens	RHODODENDRON
Rhododendron roxieanum var. *oreonastes*	RHODODENDRON
Rhododendron saluenense	RHODODENDRON
Rhododendron "Yak hybrids"	DWARF RHODODENDRON
Sarcococca hookeriana var. *humilis*	SPREADING SWEET BOX
Sarcococca ruscifolia var. *chinensis*	WINTER SWEET BOX
Sibbaldiopsis (Potentilla) tridentata	SHRUBBY FIVE FINGERS
Spiraea betulifolia 'Tor'	BIRCH-LEAF SPIREA
Spiraea thunbergii	THUNBERG'S SPIREA, BRIDALWREATH SPIREA
Syringa 'Baby Kim'	BABY KIM DWARF LILAC
Syringa "Bloomerang Series"	BLOOMERANG DWARF LILACS
Teucrium chamaedrys	WALL GERMANDER
Vaccinium ovatum 'St. Andrews'	DWARF EVERGREEN HUCKLEBERRY
Viburnum carlesii 'Compactum', 'Spice Baby'	DWARF KOREAN SPICE VIBURNUM
Viburnum davidii	DAVID'S VIBURNUM
Viburnum farreri 'Nanum'	DWARF FRAGRANT VIBURNUM
Viburnum opulus 'Nanum'	DWARF EUROPEAN CRANBERRYBUSH
Viburnum plicatum f. *plicatum* 'Popcorn'	POPCORN VIBURNUM
Vitex agnus-castus 'Blue Puffball'	DWARF CHASTE TREE
Weigela 'Crimson Kisses'	CRIMSON KISSES WEIGELA

TALL BUT NARROW SHRUBS

Acer circinatum 'Pacific Sprite'	PACIFIC SPRITE VINE MAPLE
Berberis thunbergii 'Gold Pillar'	BERBERIS
Buxus sempervirens 'Dee Runk'	DEE RUNK BOXWOOD
Buxus sempervirens 'Graham Blandy'	GRAHAM BLANDY BOXWOOD
Camellia sasanqua "October Magic" series	UPRIGHT CAMELLIA
Cephalotaxus harringtonia 'Fastigiata'	COLUMNAR JAPANESE PLUM YEW
Chamaecyparis lawsoniana 'Chilworth Silver'	SILVER BLUE LAWSON'S CYPRESS
Chamaecyparis lawsoniana 'Grayswood Feather'	FEATHER LAWSON CYPRESS
Chamaecyparis obtusa 'Vokel's Upright'	UPRIGHT DWARF HINOKI CYPRESS
Cupressus sempervirens 'Tiny Tower'	TINY TOWER CYPRESS
Euonymus japonicus 'Aureo-marginatus', 'Chollipo', 'Greenspire'	EUONYMUS
Frangula alnus (Rhamnus frangula) 'Fine Line Improved'	FERNLEAF BUCKTHORN
Hibiscus syriacus 'Purple Pillar'	ROSE OF SHARON
Ilex x *aquipernyi* 'Meschick'	DRAGON LADY HOLLY
Ilex 'Carolina Sentinel'	CAROLINA SENTINEL HOLLY
Ilex crenata 'Mariesii'	JAPANESE HOLLY
Ilex crenata 'Patti O'	PATTI O HOLLY
Ilex crenata 'Sky Pencil'	SKY PENCIL HOLLY
Ilex x *meserveae* 'Castle Spire' *(female)*	BLUE HOLLY
Ilex x *meserveae* 'Castle Wall' *(male)*	BLUE HOLLY
Ilex 'National'	NATIONAL HOLLY
Juniperus chinensis 'Spartan'	SPARTAN JUNIPER
Juniperus communis 'Hibernica'	HIBERNICA JUNIPER
Juniperus communis 'Little Spire'	LITTLE SPIRE JUNIPER
Juniperus scopulorum 'Moonglow'	MOONGLOW JUNIPER
Podocarpus macrophyllus 'Maki'	DWARF YEW PINE
Sambucus nigra 'Black Tower'	BLACK TOWER ELDERBERRY
Taxus cuspidata 'Minute Westons'	DWARF NARROW JAPANESE YEW
Taxus x *media* 'Beanpole'	BEANPOLE YEW
Taxus x *media* 'Hicksii'	ANGLO-JAPANESE YEW
Taxus x *media* 'Stonehenge'	STONEHENGE ANGLO-JAPANESE YEW

DWARF CONIFERS

Abies balsamea 'Nana', 'Piccolo'	DWARF BALSAM FIR
Abies koreana 'Gait'	DWARF KOREAN FIR
Cephalotaxus harringtonia 'Duke Gardens'	DWARF PLUM YEW
Chamaecyparis obtusa many dwarf cultivars	DWARF HINOKI CYPRESS
Chamaecyparis pisifera many dwarf cultivars	DWARF SAWARA CYPRESS
Chamaecyparis thyoides many dwarf cultivars	DWARF ATLANTIC CEDAR
Cryptomeria japonica dwarf cultivars	DWARF PLUME CEDAR
Ginkgo biloba 'Mariken'	DWARF GINKGO
Juniperus communis selections	COMMON JUNIPER
Juniperus squamata cultivars	FLAKY JUNIPER
Larix kaempferi 'Haverbeck'	DWARF JAPANESE LARCH
Metasequoia glyptostroboides 'North Light'	DWARF VARIEGATED DAWN REDWOOD
Picea abies dwarf cultivars	DWARF NORWAY SPRUCE
Picea glauca dwarf cultivars	DWARF WHITE SPRUCE
Picea mariana 'Nana'	DWARF BLACK SPRUCE
Picea orientalis 'Bergman's Gem'	BERGMAN'S GEM ORIENTAL SPRUCE
Picea pungens dwarf cultivars	DWARF COLORADO SPRUCE
Pinus cembra 'Blue Mound'	BLUE MOUND SWISS STONE PINE
Pinus heldreichii 'Compact Gem'	COMPACT BOSNIAN PINE
Pinus mugo dwarf cultivars	MUGO PINE
Pinus strobus 'Pincushion'	DWARF EASTERN WHITE PINE
Podocarpus alpinus 'Blue Gem'	ALPINE PLUM YEW
Sciadopitys verticillata 'Picola'	DWARF JAPANESE UMBRELLA PINE
Thuja occidentalis 'Teddy'	TEDDY WHITE CEDAR
Thuja orientalis many dwarf cultivars	DWARF ORIENTAL ARBORVITAE
Thujopsis dolabrata 'Nana'	DWARF HIBA ARBORVITAE
Tsuga canadensis many dwarf cultivars	DWARF HEMLOCK
Tsuga diversifolia 'Loowit'	DWARF NORTHERN JAPANESE HEMLOCK

SMALL VINES

Aconitum bulbuliferum 'Monk Gone Wild'	CLIMBING MONKSHOOD
Aconitum hemsleyanum	SMALL CLIMBING MONKSHOOD
Billardiera longiflora	TASMANIAN BLUEBERRY VINE
Clematis alpina 'Pamela Jackman'	BLUE ALPINE CLEMATIS
Clematis x *cartmanii* 'Joe'	JOE EVERGREEN CLEMATIS
Clematis chiisanensis 'Lemon Bells'	LEMON BELLS CLEMATIS
Clematis 'Constance'	CONSTANCE ALPINE CLEMATIS
Clematis 'Josephine'	JOSEPHINE LARGE-FLOWERED CLEMATIS
Clematis 'General Sikorski'	GENERAL SIKORSKI CLEMATIS
Clematis 'Helsingborg'	HELSINGBORG ALPINE CLEMATIS
Clematis 'Pink Champagne'	PINK CHAMPAGNE LARGE-FLOWERED CLEMATIS
Clematis 'Madame Julia Correvon'	MADAME JULIA CORREVON CLEMATIS
Clematis 'Mrs. George Jackman'	MRS. GEORGE JACKMAN CLEMATIS
Clematis 'Niobe'	NIOBE LARGE-FLOWERED CLEMATIS

Clematis occidentalis	WESTERN BLUE VIRGINS' BOWER ❖
Clematis 'Pink Flamingo'	PINK FLAMINGO ALPINE CLEMATIS
Clematis 'The President'	THE PRESIDENT LARGE-FLOWERED CLEMATIS
Clematis 'Princess Diana'	PRINCESS DIANA CLEMATIS
Clematis 'Rooguchi'	ROOGUCHI CLEMATIS
Clematis serratifolia	SAW-LEAF CLEMATIS
Clematis 'Silver Moon'	SILVER MOON LARGE-FLOWERED CLEMATIS
Clematis tangutica	GOLDEN-BELL CLEMATIS
Clematis 'Warzawska Nike'	WARZAWSKA NIKE CLEMATIS
Clematis 'Westerplatte'	WESTERPLATTE LARGE-FLOWERED CLEMATIS
Codonopsis lanceolata	BONNET BELLFLOWER
Codonopsis pilosula	POOR-MAN'S GINSENG
Ercilla spicata (*E. volubilis*)	CHILEAN CLIMBER
Lapageria rosea	CHILEAN BELLFLOWER
Rosa 'Jeanne Lajoie'	CLIMBING MINIATURE ROSE
Rosa 'New Dawn'	NEW DAWN ROSE
Rosa 'Sally Holmes Climber'	CLIMBING SALLY HOLMES ROSE
Rosa 'Sombreuil'	SILVER PINK CLIMBING ROSE
Trachelospermum asiaticum 'Theta'	BIRD-FOOT STAR JASMINE
Tropaeolum leptophyllum	CLIMBING NASTURTIUM
Tropaeolum speciosum	RED NASTURTIUM
Tropaeolum tricolor	THREE-COLORED NASTURTIUM
Tropaeolum tuberosum var. *lineomaculatum* 'Ken Aslet'	MASHUA

SMALL-SCALE GROUNDCOVERS
* will tolerate various degrees of traffic; some are mowable (lawn substitute)

Acaena 'Blue Haze'	BLUE HAZE NEW ZEALAND BURR
Acaena microphylla	NEW ZEALAND BURR
Acaena inermis 'Purpurea'	PURPLE NEW ZEALAND BURR
Achillea ageratifolia	GREEK YARROW
Achillea clavennae	SILVER YARROW
Achillea x *lewisii* 'King Edward'*	TRAILING YARROW
Achillea x *taygetea*	HYBRID YARROW
Achillea tomentosa	WOOLLY YARROW
Achillea serbica	SERBIAN YARROW
Alchemilla alpina	ALPINE LADY'S-MANTLE
Antennaria dioica 'Rubra'	PINK PUSSY-TOES
Arenaria balearica	CORSICAN SANDWORT
Asarum caudatum	WILD GINGER ❖
Asarum europaeum	EUROPEAN WILD GINGER
Asarum marmoratum	MARBLED WILD GINGER ❖
Asarum splendens	SPLENDID WILD GINGER
Beesia deltophylla	FALSE BUGBANE
Bergenia 'Baby Doll', 'Beethoven', 'Ruby Elf', 'Dumbo'	DWARF BERGENIA
Calylophus hartwegii	HARTWEG'S SUNDROPS
Carex oshimensis cultivars	JAPANESE SEDGE
Carex siderosticha var. *ciliatomarginata* 'Treasure Island'	

	CREEPING BROAD-LEAF SEDGE
Chamaemelum nobile	ROMAN CHAMOMILE
Clinopodium (Micromeria, Satureja) douglasii	YERBA BUENA ❖
Delosperma species and hybrids	HARDY ICE PLANTS
Dianthus deltoides	MAIDEN PINK
Epimedium ecalcaratum	SPURLESS BARRENWORT
Erodium reichardii (E. chamaedryoides)	ALPINE GERANIUM
Festuca rubra var. *juncea* 'Patrick's Point'*	CREEPING BLUE FESCUE ❖
Gaultheria ovatifolia	WESTERN TEABERRY ❖
Gazania linearis	TREASURE FLOWER
Gypsophila cerastioides	TRAILING BABY'S BREATH
Helianthemum nummularium	SUN ROSE
Herniaria glabra	GREEN CARPET, RUPTUREWORT
Hosta, smaller cultivars (such as the "Mouse" series), planted densely	HOSTA
Isotoma fluviatilis (can be thuggish)	BLUE STAR CREEPER
*Leptinella gruveri**	MINIATURE BRASS BUTTONS
*Leptinella (Cotula) squalida**	NEW ZEALAND BRASS BUTTONS
Linnaea borealis	TWINFLOWER ❖
Lysimachia alfredii 'Night Light'	NIGHT LIGHT MONEYWORT
Mazus reptans	CREEPING MAZUS
Mukdenia rossii 'Karasuba'	MUKDENIA
Myrteola nummularia	CRANBERRY-MYRTLE
Omphalodes verna	CREEPING FORGET-ME-NOT
Ophiopogon japonicus 'Compactus', 'Gyoku-ryu', 'Nanus'	DWARF MONDO GRASS
Oxalis oregana Evergreen types*	EVERGREEN REDWOOD SORREL ❖
Petrosedum (Sedum) rupestre	BLUE SEDUM
Phedimus (Sedum) kamtschaticus	KAMSCHATKA SEDUM, ORANGE STONECROP
Phedimus (Sedum) spurius	CAUCASIAN STONECROP
Phlox adsurgens	WOODLAND PHLOX ❖
Phlox caespitosa	TUFTED PHLOX ❖
Phlox diffusa	SPREADING PHLOX ❖
Phlox divaricata	WOODLAND PHLOX
Pimelea prostrata	NEW ZEALAND DAPHNE
Potentilla neumanniana 'Nana'	ALPINE CINQUEFOIL
Pratia (Lobelia) pedunculata 'County Park'	SUPER STAR CREEPER
Sagina subulata	IRISH MOSS
Sagina subulata 'Aurea'	SCOTCH MOSS
Saxifraga x geum 'Dentata'	TOOTHED SAXIFRAGE
Saxifraga stolonifera	STRAWBERRY BEGONIA
Scleranthus biflorus	NEW ZEALAND ASTROTURF
Scleranthus uniflorus	NEW ZEALAND MOSS
Sedum divergens	SPREADING STONECROP ❖
Sedum lanceolatum	LANCE-LEAVED STONECROP ❖
Sedum oreganum	OREGON STONECROP ❖
Sedum oregonense	CREAMY FLOWERED STONECROP ❖
Sedum sexangulare	TASTELESS SEDUM
Sedum spathulifolium	BROAD-LEAVED STONECROP ❖
Sedum stenopetalum	WORM-LEAF STONECROP
Sedum tetractinum	CHINESE STONECROP

Stachys corsica	CORSICAN TRAILING LAMB'S EAR
Stachys densiflora	CREEPING BETONY
Symphyotrichum (Aster) ericoides 'Snow Flurry'	TRAILING HEATH ASTER
Thymus cherierioides	SILVER NEEDLE THYME
Thymus x *citriodorus*	LEMON THYME
Thymus 'Doone Valley'	DOONE VALLEY THYME
Thymus herba-barona	CARAWAY-SCENTED THYME
Thymus praecox ssp. *arcticus (T. polytrichus* ssp. *brittanicus)** especially the cultivars 'Creeping Pink', 'Reiter'	CREEPING THYME
Thymus praecox ssp. *arcticus* 'Albus'	WHITE MOSS THYME
Thymus praecox ssp. *arcticus* 'Languinosus'	WOOLLY THYME
Thymus praecox ssp *praecox* especially the cultivars 'Minus', 'Pseudolanuginosus'	MOTHER-OF-THYME
Thymus serpyllum 'Elfin', 'Pink Chintz'*	CREEPING THYME
Trifolium repens 'Purpurascens Quadrifolium'	BLACK-LEAVED CLOVER
Veronica alpina	ALPINE SPEEDWELL
Veronica liwanensis	TURKISH SPEEDWELL
Veronica nummularia	MONEYWORT SPEEDWELL
Veronica pectinata	WOOLLY SPEEDWELL
Veronica repens	CREEPING SPEEDWELL
Veronica umbrosa 'Georgia Blue'	GEORGIA BLUE SPEEDWELL
Veronica whitleyi	WHITLEY'S SPEEDWELL
Viola 'Dancing Geisha', 'Silver Samurai'	HYBRID VIOLET

PERENNIALS & BULBS *Under 12 inches tall*

Achillea 'Little Moonshine'	LITTLE MOONSHINE YARROW
Acis (Leucojum) autumnalis	AUTUMN SNOWFLAKE
Adiantum venustum	HIMALAYAN MAIDENHAIR
Aethionema grandiflorum	PERSIAN ROCKCRESS
Allium acuminatum	HOOKER'S ONION ❖
Allium amplectens	SLIM-LEAF ONION ❖
Allium cernuum	NODDING ONION ❖
Allium sacculiferum	NORTHERN PLAINS CHIVE
Allium thunbergii 'Ozawa'	JAPANESE ONION
Anacyclus pyrethrum var. *depressus*	MOUNT ATLAS DAISY
Androsace (Douglasia) laevigata	SMOOTH DOUGLASIA ❖
Anemonoides (Anemone) nemorosa	WOOD ANEMONE
Anemonoides (Anemone) sylvestris	SNOWDROP WINDFLOWER
Antirrhinum glutinosum	GUMMY SNAPDRAGON
Antirrhinum sempervirens	SPANISH SNAPDRAGON
Aquilegia flavescens	YELLOW COLUMBINE ❖
Arisaema candidissimum	PINK COBRA LILY
Arisarum proboscideum	MOUSE PLANT
Armeria juniperifolia	JUNIPER-LEAVED THRIFT
Armeria maritima	THRIFT, SEA PINK ❖
Artemisia pedemontana	DWARF WORMWOOD
Asarum hartwegii	HARTWEG'S WILD GINGER

Asarum marmoratum	MARBLED WILD GINGER ❖
Asarum fauriei var. *takaoi*	JAPANESE WILD GINGER
Asarum splendens	SPLENDID WILD GINGER
Asplenium trichomanes	SPLEENWORT ❖
Barnardia (Scilla) japonica	JAPANESE SQUILL
Bellevalia (Muscari) pycnantha	GIANT GRAPE HYACINTH
Bergenia hybrids	HYBRID BERGENIA
Bloomeria (Triteleia) crocea	GOLDEN STARS ❖
Brimeura amethystina	AMETHYST HYACINTH
Brodiaea coronaria	HARVEST BRODIAEA ❖
Brodiaea elegans ssp. *hooveri*	HARVEST LILY ❖
Callirhoe involucrata	PURPLE POPPY MALLOW
Calochortus elegans var. *elegans*	ELEGANT CAT'S EAR ❖
Campanula carpatica	CARPATHIAN HAREBELL
Campanula cochlearifolia	FAIRY THIMBLES
Campanula garganica	ADRIATIC BELLFLOWER
Carex buchananii	LEATHERLEAF SEDGE
Carex flacca 'Blue Zinger'	BLUE SEDGE
Carex siderosticha variegated cultivars	VARIEGATED BROADLEAF SEDGE
Carex oshimensis cultivars	VARIEGATED JAPANESE SEDGE
Clematis hirsutissima var. *hirsutissima*	HAIRY CLEMATIS ❖
Clematis integrifolia "Dwarf Form"	DWARF GROUND CLEMATIS
Codonopsis ovata	BONNET BELLFLOWER
Colchicum species and hybrids	AUTUMN CROCUS
Cyclamen cilicum	CILICIAN CYCLAMEN
Cyclamen coum	HARDY CYCLAMEN, EASTERN SOWBREAD
Cyclamen graecum	GREEK CYCLAMEN
Cyclamen hederifolium	IVY-LEAFED CYCLAMEN
Dianthus Allwoodii hybrids	PINKS
Dianthus 'Blue Hills'	BLUE HILLS CHEDDAR PINK
Dianthus deltoides	MAIDEN PINK
Dianthus gratianopolitanus	CHEDDAR PINK
Dianthus plumarius	COTTAGE PINK
Dicentra formosa	PACIFIC OR WESTERN BLEEDING-HEART ❖
Dichelostemma capitatum ssp. *capitatum*	BLUEDICKS ❖
Dichelostemma congestum	OOKOW, FIELD CLUSTER LILY, HARVEST LILY ❖
Dichelostemma ida-maia	FIRECRACKER FLOWER ❖
Dodecatheon cusickii	CUSICK'S SHOOTING-STAR ❖
Dodecatheon hendersonii	SHOOTING STAR, MOSQUITO BILL ❖
Dudleya farinosa	CHALKY LIVE-FOREVER
Edraianthus serbicus	ROCK BELLS, GRASSY BELLS
Erinus alpinus	FAIRY FOXGLOVE
Erodium chrysanthum	HERONSBILL, STORKSBILL
Eryngium planum 'Blue Hobbit'	DWARF SEA HOLLY
Eucomis 'Nani'	DWARF PINEAPPLE LILY
Filipendula 'Kahome'	DWARF JAPANESE MEADOWSWEET
Geranium cinereum	HARDY GERANIUM
Geranium renardii	HARDY GERANIUM
Geranium x riversleaianum	HARDY GERANIUM

Geranium wlassovianum	HARDY GERANIUM
Geum triflorum "Dwarf Form"	DWARF PRAIRIE SMOKE ❖
Geum hybrids	GEUM, AVENS
Globularia cordifolia	HEART-LEAVED GLOBE DAISY
Hemerocallis Dwarf hybrids	DAYLILIES
Hosta hybrids (hundreds of small and miniature cultivars)	HOSTA
Hosta tokudama	SILVER HEART HOSTA
Hyacinthoides (Scilla) lingulata	AUTUMN BLUEBELL
Hylotelephium (Sedum) species and hybrids	AUTUMN SEDUM
Iberis saxatilis	PERENNIAL CANDYTUFT
Ipheion uniflorum	SPRING STARFLOWER
Iris cristata	DWARF CRESTED IRIS
Iris PCH hybrids	PACIFIC COAST IRIS HYBRIDS
Iris reticulata	NETTED IRIS
Lewisia hybrids	HYBRID LEWISIA
Linaria (purpurea Hybrid) 'Natalie'	NATALIE TOADFLAX
Monarda 'Petite Delight'	DWARF BEE BALM
Mukdenia rossii 'Karasuba'	MUKDENIA
Myriopteris (Cheilanthes) gracillima	LACE LIP FERN ❖
Narcissus cantabricus	HOOP PETTICOAT DAFFODIL
Narcissus cyclamineus and hybrids	CYCLAMINEUS NARCISSUS

'Cha Cha', 'Cotinga', 'February Gold', 'Jack Snipe', ''Jenny', Jetfire',
'Peeping Tom', 'Tete-a-Tete', 'Velocity', 'Winter Waltz'

Narcissus Miniature hybrids/Selections	MINIATURE DAFFODILS

'Baby Moon', 'Bell Song', 'Canaliculatus', 'Hawera', 'Heart to Heart', 'Little Gem',
'Minnow', 'Rapture', 'Rip Van Winkle', 'Sundisc', 'Topolino'

Nepeta x 'Little Trudy'	DWARF CATMINT
Nerine filifolia	DWARF NERINE
Oncostema (Scilla) peruviana	PORTUGUESE SQUILL
Ophiopogon japonicus 'Nanus'	DWARF MONDO GRASS
Oxalis adenophylla	SILVER SHAMROCK
Oxalis fabaefolia	RABBIT'S EARS
Oxalis lasiandra	PALM TREE OXALIS
Pachystegia insignis	MARLBOROUGH ROCK DAISY
Penstemon caespitosus	CREEPING PENSTEMON
Penstemon newberryi var. *berryi*	BERRY'S MOUNTAIN PRIDE ❖
Penstemon rupicola	ROCK PENSTEMON ❖
Petrophytum caespitosum	MAT ROCK-SPIREA
Phegopteris connectilis (Thelypteris phegopteris)	NORTHERN BEECH FERN ❖
Phlomis angustissima	DWARF GOLDEN TURKISH-SAGE
Phlomis fruticosa 'Nana'	DWARF JERUSALEM-SAGE
Polemonium carneum	SALMON POLEMONIUM ❖
Polystichum tsus-simense	DWARF HOLLY FERN
Prospero (Scilla) autumnale	AUTUMN SQUILL
Pseudomuscari (Muscari, Bellavalia) azureum	AZURE GRAPE HYACINTH
Pseudomuscari (Muscari, Bellavalia) forniculatum	TURKISH GRAPE HYACINTH
Pterocephalus depressus	CARPETING PINCUSHION FLOWER
Pterocephalus perennis	MT. PARNASSUS PINCUSHION FLOWER
Pulmonaria 'Benediction'	LUNGWORT

Rhodiola pachyclados	AFGHAN SEDUM
Rhodohypoxis baurii	RED STAR
Rudbeckia fulgida var. *sullivantii* 'City Garden', 'Little Goldstar', 'Viette's Little Suzy'	DWARF BLACK-EYED SUSAN
Saponaria pumilio	DWARF PINK, DWARF SOAPWORT
Saxifraga 'Canis Dalmatica'	DALMATIAN DOG SAXIFRAGE
Saxifraga x urbium 'Primuloides'	MINIATURE LONDON PRIDE
Scilla (Chionodoxa) luciliae	GLORY OF THE SNOW
Sedum grisebachii	GRISEBACH'S SEDUM
Sedum hispanicum	SPANISH SEDUM
Sedum middendorffianum	CHINESE MOUNTAIN STONECROP
Sedum spathulifolium	BROAD-LEAF STONECROP ❖
Sempervivum species and hybrids	HENS AND CHICKS, HOUSELEEK
Silene alpestris especially 'Flore Pleno' (double-flowered)	ALPINE CATCHFLY
Sisyrinchium bellum	WESTERN BLUE-EYED GRASS ❖
Sisyrinchium californicum	GOLDEN-EYED GRASS ❖
Solidago 'Little Lemon'	LITTLE LEMON GOLDENROD
Stachys coccinea	SCARLET BETONY
Stachys spathulata (S. minima)	DWARF BETONY
Sternbergia lutea	AUTUMN DAFFODIL
Thalictrum kiusianum	DWARF MEADOW RUE
Thermopsis chinensis 'Sophia'	CHINESE YELLOW PEA BUSH
Titanotrichum oldhamii	OLDHAM'S GOLD WOODLAND FOXGLOVE
Triteleia (Brodiaea) hyacinthina	WHITE TRIPLET-LILY ❖
Triteleia grandiflora	LARGE-FLOWERED TRIPLET-LILY, WILD HYACINTH ❖
Triteleia ixioides	PRETTYFACE ❖
Tulipa dasystemon	DASYSTEMON TULIP
Tulipa linifolia (including *T. batalinii*)	BOKHARA TULIP, FLAX-LEAF TULIP
Tulipa orphanidea (including *T. whittallii*)	ANATOLIAN TULIP, COTTAGE TULIP
Tulipa sprengeri	SPRENGER'S TULIP
Tulipa sylvestris	WOODLAND TULIP
Tulipa urumiensis (T. tarda)	LATE TULIP, TARDY TULIP
Tulipa clusiana including subspecies and forms	LADY TULIP
Umbilicus (Chiastophyllum) oppositifolium	LAMB'S TAIL, GOLD DROP
Veronica (Parahebe) catarractae	PARAHEBE
Veronica (Parahebe) perfoliata	DIGGER'S SPEEDWELL
Viola alba ssp. *dehnhardtii*	PARMA VIOLET
Viola 'Dancing Geisha', 'Silver Samurai'	HYBRID VIOLET

ESPALIERS

Acer circinatum	VINE MAPLE
Acer palmatum	JAPANESE MAPLE
Azara microphylla	AZARA
Camellia hiemalis 'Shishi-Gashira', 'Showa-No-Sakae', 'Showa Supreme'	HIEMALIS CAMELLIA
Camellia sasanqua 'Appleblossom, 'Mine-No-Yuki', 'Tanya'	SUN CAMELLIA
Hamamelis x intermedia	HYBRID WITCH-HAZEL

Ilex crenata	JAPANESE MAPLE
Laurus nobilis	BAY LAUREL
Osmanthus fragrans	FRAGRANT TEA-OLIVE
Podocarpus macrophyllus 'Maki'	DWARF YELLOWWOOD
Prunus triloba 'Multiplex'	FLOWERING ALMOND
Ribes sanguineum	RED-FLOWERING CURRANT

Espaliered Fruit Trees

Apple (on dwarf or semi-dwarf stock)	Fig
Apricot	Mulberry, white
Asian Apple (Apple-Pear)	Pear (on dwarf or semi-dwarf stock)
Cherry	Quince

See also "CONTAINER PLANTS"

A MOON GARDEN

Silver foliage and/or white flowers to enhance, reflect, and magnify the light from the moon.
And/or night-blooming flowers, some with night-time fragrance (f),

Achillea white species and hybrids with emphasis on gray/silver foliage   YARROW
Agave amica (Polianthes tuberosa) (f)   TUBEROSE
Artemisia 'Powis Castle'   WORMWOOD
Artemisia schmidtiana   SILVER MOUND
Artemisia stellerana   BEACH WORMWOOD
Berlandiera lyrata (f)   CHOCOLATE FLOWER
Centaurea ragusina   PERENNIAL DUSTY MILLER
Chaenostoma (Sutera) cordatum   BACOPA
Cistus x *heterocalyx* 'Chelsea Bonnet'   CHELSEA BONNET ROCKROSE
Cleome hasslerana (white)   SPIDER FLOWER
Choisya ternata (f)   MEXICAN MOCK ORANGE
Clematis species and hybrids especially white forms   CLEMATIS
Cleome hassleriana   SPIDER FLOWER
Cosmos bipinnatus (white)   COSMOS
Dicentra eximia and hybrids (especially 'Alba', 'Snowdrift', 'Silversmith'
   BLEEDING HEART
Dicentra formosa (especially 'Langtrees' (bluish-green leaves, 'Pearl Drops'),
  'Margaret Fish' (bluish-gray-green), 'Quicksilver' (bluish-gray-green)
   WESTERN BLEEDING HEART ❖
Eriocapitella (Anemone) x *hybrida* (any white)   JAPANESE ANEMONE
Eriophyllum lanatum var. *lanatum*   WOOLLY SUNFLOWER
Euphorbia hypericifolia   DIAMOND FROST EUPHORBIA
Euphorbia marginata   SNOW-ON-THE-MOUNTAIN
Fothergilla gardenii 'Mount Airy'   DWARF FOTHERGILLA
Gaura lindheimeri   GAURA
Gladiolus tristis (f)   MARSH AFRIKANER
Helianthemum nummularium   ROCK ROSE, SUN ROSE
Helichrysum arenarium   SANDY EVERLASTING
Helichrysum splendidum   CAPE GOLD
Hesperis matronalis (f)   DAME'S ROCKET
X *Heucherella tiarelloides*, especially 'Cracked Ice', 'Quicksilver', 'Twilight'
   FOAMY FLOWER
Ipomoea alba (f)   MOON FLOWER
Jasminum x *stephanense* (f)   SPRING JASMINE
Lamprocapnos (Dicentra) spectabilis 'White Gold'   WHITE GOLD BLEEDING HEART
Leucanthemum x *superbum*   SHASTA DAISY
Lilium hybrids (f)   LILIES
Lobularia maritima (f)   SWEET ALYSSUM
Magnolia species and hybrids (f)   MAGNOLIA
Matthiola fruticulosa ssp. *perennis* 'Alba' (f)   PERENNIAL STOCK
Matthiola longipetala bicornis (f)   EVENING-SCENTED STOCK
Melianthus major   HONEY BUSH
Mentzelia lindleyi (f)   EVENING STAR

275

Mirabilis jalapa (f)	FOUR O'CLOCK
Narcissus species and hybrids	DAFFODILS, NARCISSUS, PAPERWHITES, JONQUIL
Nicotiana alata (f)	JESSAMINE TOBACCO
Nicotiana sylvestris (f)	WOODLAND TOBACCO
Oenothera fremontii	SHIMMER EVENING PRIMROSE
Oenothera glazioviana (f)	LARGE-FLOWERED EVENING PRIMROSE
Oenothera macrocarpa (f)	MISSOURI PRIMROSE
Origanum dictamnus	CRETE DITTANY
Osmanthus fragrans (f)	FRAGRANT TEA-OLIVE
X Petchoa (*Petunia* x *Calibrachoa* hybrid)	PETCHOA
Petunia × atkinsiana (preferably white, yellow, and pale violet forms)	HYBRID PETUNIA
Petunia axillaris	WHITE MOON PETUNIA
Philadelphus species and hybrids	MOCK ORANGE
Phlomis cashmeriana	KASHMIR-SAGE
Phlox subulata	CREEPING PHLOX
Rosa 'Sombreuil' (f)	SILVER PINK CLIMBING ROSE
Salvia argentea	SILVER SAGE
Senecio viravira	DUSTY MILLER
Stachys albotomentosa	HIDALGO
Stachys byzantina (S. lanata)	LAMBS' EARS
Tanacetum niveum	SNOWY TANSY
Tanacetum ptarmiciflorum	DUSTY MILLER
Teucrium polinum	SILVER GERMANDER
Tiarella cordifolia	FOAMFLOWER
Zaluzianskya capensis (f)	MIDNIGHT CANDY PHLOX

See also "BLUE/SILVER (TO NEAR WHITE) FOLIAGE" (within "COLORFUL FOLIAGE") and "WHITE" flowers within "THE FLOWER BORDER — BY COLOR."

A CHILDREN'S GARDEN

Easy, non-toxic plants to educate, entertain, and inspire.

PERENNIALS & BULBS

Achillea 'Moonshine'	MOONSHINE YARROW
Aquilegia formosa	WESTERN RED COLUMBINE ❖
Allium cernuum	NODDING ONION ❖
Aruncus dioicus	GOAT'S-BEARD ❖
Asarum caudatum	WESTERN WILD GINGER ❖
Bergenia hybrids	PIG-SQUEAK
Camassia quamash	CAMAS ❖
Dierama dracomontanum	DRAKENBERG WANDFLOWER
Fritillaria camschatcensis	INDIAN RICE ❖
Geranium macrorrhizum	HARDY GERANIUM
Helianthus 'Lemon Queen'	LEMON QUEEN PERENNIAL SUNFLOWER
Helianthus x *multiflorus* 'Happy Days'	DWARF PERENNIAL SUNFLOWER
Hosta especially the dwarf or the extra-large cultivars	HOSTAS
Hylotelephium (Sedum) spectabile and hybrids	
	SHOWY STONECROP, AUTUMN SEDUM, BORDER SEDUM
Hylotelephium (Sedum) sieboldii	OCTOBER DAPHNE
Leucanthemum x *superbum*, especially 'Becky'	SHASTA DAISY
Lilium washingtonianum	WASHINGTON LILY, CASCADE LILY ❖
Phedimus (Sedum) kamtschaticus	KAMSCHATKA SEDUM, ORANGE STONECROP
Phlomis viscosa	STICKY JERUSALEM-SAGE
Platycodon grandiflorus	BALLOON FLOWER
Rudbeckia fulgida var. *sullivantii* 'Goldsturm'	BLACK-EYED SUSAN
Salvia spathacea	HUMMINGBIRD SAGE
Salvia transylvanica	TRANSYLVANIAN SAGE
Sempervivum species and hybrids	HENS-AND-CHICKS, HOUSELEEK
Stachys byzantina (*S. lanata*)	LAMB'S EARS
Viola alba ssp. *dehnhardtii*	PARMA VIOLET

ANNUALS

Amaranthus caudatus	LOVE-LIES-BLEEDING
Antirrhinum majus	SNAPDRAGON
Alcea rosea	HOLLYHOCK
Brassica oleracea	FLOWERING CABBAGE, FLOWERING KALE
Calendula officinalis	CALENDULA
Clarkia amoena	GODETIA ❖
Cucurbita species	GOURDS
Dianthus barbatus	SWEET WILLIAM
Eschscholzia californica	CALIFORNIA POPPY
Helianthus annuus	SUNFLOWER

Ipomoea batatas	SWEET POTATO VINE
Lathyrus odoratus	SWEET PEA
Lobularia maritima	SWEET ALYSSUM
Lunaria annua	HONESTY
Molucella laevis	BELLS-OF-IRELAND
Myosotis sylvatica	WOOD FORGET-ME-NOT
Tagetes erecta, T. patula	MARIGOLDS
Tropaeolum majus	NASTURTIUM
Verbascum bombyciferum	GIANT SILVER MULLEIN
Viola cornuta hybrids	VIOLA
Viola tricolor	JOHNNY-JUMP-UP
Viola x wittrockiana	PANSY
Zinnia elegans	ZINNIA

EDIBLES

CARROTS
CORN
LETTUCE
PUMPKINS
RADISHES
SNAP PEAS
SUMMER SQUASH
TOMATOES

APPLES
BLUEBERRIES
STRAWBERRIES

"When I was a really young child, I felt like I could see fairies. I was convinced there were fairies in my grandmother's garden." ~~ Noel Fielding

ORNAMENTAL FEATURES

Design leads to another way of looking at "right plant, right place." The "place," whether the entire landscape or a part of it, may be best fit with a particular color or other decorative element.

Look for the symbol ❖ which indicates a native plant.

THE FLOWER BORDER — BY COLOR

Perennials, annuals, and bulbs; including native plants and "wildflowers." For those who understand and appreciate the concept of color schemes or at least the basics of how colors add value to a good landscape.

Color can be utilized in the garden to bring life and excitement to the landscape; to accent important areas that you want noticed (for example the front door); to blend the exterior environment with structural colors to tie the overall design; to complement the colors of other plants; to attract animals and insects, such as birds and butterflies; to create a mood; to balance bed and landscape designs; and to provide variety and interest through the seasons.

Colors can be used to visually change distance and size perspective.

Warm colors and light tints such as red, orange, yellow and white advance an object or area toward the observer. They make objects look closer, they draw one's attention. Be careful putting warm colors near areas where you don't want people to focus, such as service or functional areas. Instead, place them at the points that you want people to look, such as entrances and focal points.

Cool colors and deep shades such as blue, most violets, some greens and black recede and can be used to make the house — or other objects — appear farther from the street. These subdued colors make objects look farther away.

Colors can influence moods. Cool colors are restful; the softer blues, pinks, greens, and violets — especially pastels — produce a calming, tranquil effect. They also create a visually "cool" atmosphere.

Warm colors express action; they are best used in filtered light or against a green or dark background; they attract the eye, making things stand out and provide drama. For instance, a few red flowers or a red tree or shrub can become a focal point or accent in a garden where most of the colors are far more muted. Warm colors excite the intellect and they create a bright and happy atmosphere.

Then there's white and its associates on the spectrum. White tends to be the great unifier, providing a neutral, yet somewhat uplifting spirit. White ties all colors together or buffers them. Plants with "clashing" colors frequently can be planted in close proximity, creating an attractive arrangement, if separated by lots of white flowers (or green foliage). White provides the perfect background for any darker color (one of a different tint). Plants with gray, silvery, WOOLLY, and/or pale blue foliage have the same perception and use. And white flowers and silver foliage reflect light at dusk and night, almost appearing to glow at times.

Abbreviations within this list:

* = *indicates this plant comes in at least one other color form, sometimes several*
❖ = *indicates a PNW native plant*

WHITE

Perennials

Acanthus mollis	BEAR'S BREECH
Acanthus spinosus	BEAR'S BREECH
Acanthus x spinosissimus	SPINY BEAR'S BREECHES
Actaea matsumurae	JAPANESE BUGBANE
Actaea racemosa	BLACK BUGBANE, BLACK COHOSH
Actaea (Cimicifuga) simplex	BUGBANE
Agapanthus (many)	LILY-OF-THE-NILE*
Anemone occidentalis	WESTERN PASQUE FLOWER ❖
Anemonoides (Anemone) nemorosa	WOOD ANEMONE
Anemonopsis macrophylla	FALSE ANEMONE
Antirrhinum sempervirens	SPANISH SNAPDRAGON
Aruncus dioicus var. *vulgaris* 'Zweiweltenkind' ("Child of Two Worlds")	GOAT'S-BEARD
Aruncus 'Guinea Fowl'	FEATHERY GOAT'S-BEARD
Asarina procumbens	CREEPING SNAPDRAGON
Asclepias verticillata	WHORLED MILKWEED
Astrantia major	GREAT MASTERWORT*
Baptisia hybrids	FALSE INDIGO*
Bergenia hybrids	HYBRID BERGENIA*
Campanula lactiflora	MILKY BELLFLOWER*
Campanula latiloba	GREAT BELLFLOWER*
Cardiocrinum giganteum	GIANT HIMALAYAN LILY
Centranthus ruber	JUPITER'S BEARD, RED VALERIAN*
Chrysanthemum x morifolium	MUM*
Chrysanthemum zawadskii	MANCHURIAN CHRYSANTHEMUM*
Delphinium elatum hybrids	DELPHINIUM*
Dianthus caryophyllus	CARNATION*
Dianthus deltoides, D. gratianopolitanus, D. plumarius	PINKS*
Dicentra formosa and hybrids	PACIFIC OR WESTERN BLEEDING-HEART* ❖
Dierama pulcherrimum	FAIRY WAND, WAND FLOWER*
Disporopsis pernyi	EVERGREEN SOLOMON'S SEAL
Echinops bannaticus 'Albus', 'Star Frost'	WHITE GLOBE THISTLE
Epimedium grandiflorum	BISHOP'S HAT*
Eriocapitella (Anemone) x hybrida 'Honorine Jobert'	JAPANESE ANEMONE*
Eriogonum ovalifolium	OVAL-LEAF BUCKWHEAT❖*
Erodium chrysanthum	HERONSBILL, STORKSBILL
Erodium x variable	CRANESBILL*
Geranium renardii	HARDY GERANIUM*
Glandularia (Verbena) canadensis	ROSE MOCK VERVAIN, HARDY VERBENA*
Gypsophila cerastioides	KASHMIR BABY'S-BREATH*
Hedychium 'Vanilla Ice'	VANILLA ICE HARDY GINGER LILY
Hedychium spicatum	PERFUME GINGER
Helianthemum nummularium 'St. Mary's', 'The Bride'	SUNROSE
Helleborus hybrids (many)	LENTEN ROSE*
Helleborus lividus	MAJORCAN HELLEBORE*
Hemerocallis (many)	DAYLILIES*

Hesperantha (Schizostylis) coccinea 'Alba'	CRIMSON FLAG*
Heuchera hybrids (many)	CORAL BELLS*
Heuchera micrantha	ALUM ROOT
Hibiscus moscheutos and hybrids	ROSE MALLOW*
Iberis sempervirens	EVERGREEN CANDYTUFT
Iris douglasiana	DOUGLAS IRIS*
Iris chrysophylla	YELLOW-LEAF IRIS ❖
Iris cristata	DWARF CRESTED IRIS*
Iris PCH hybrids	PACIFIC COAST IRIS HYBRIDS*
Iris purdyi	PURDY'S IRIS ❖
Iris siberica hybrids	SIBERIAN IRIS*
Iris Spuria hybrids	SPURIA IRIS*
Iris tenax	OREGON IRIS, TOUGH-LEAF IRIS ❖*
Iris tenuis	CLACKAMAS IRIS ❖*
Iris unguicularis	WINTER IRIS*
Kniphofia 'Lightning Bug'	WHITE TORCH-LILY
Lamprocapnos (Dicentra) spectabilis	OLD-FASHIONED BLEEDING HEART*
Leucanthemella serotinum	GIANT DAISY
Leucanthemum x *superbum*, especially 'Becky'	SHASTA DAISY
Lewisia cotyledon and hybrids	SISKIYOU LEWISIA ❖*
Liatris species, white forms	BLAZING STAR, GAYFEATHER*
Lupinus x *regalis* (*L.* x *russellii*)	RUSSELL LUPINE*
Omphalodes verna 'Alba'	CREEPING FORGET-ME-NOT
Paeonia emodi	HIMALAYAN PEONY
Paeonia lactiflora hybrids	CHINESE/GARDEN PEONY*
Penstemon 'Holly's White'	WHITE BEARDTONGUE
Phlox paniculata, P. maculate	SUMMER PHLOX, TALL PHLOX
Primula denticulata	DRUMSTICK PRIMROSE*
Primula japonica	JAPANESE PRIMROSE*
Primula x juliana	JULIANA PRIMROSE*
Primula sieboldii	SIEBOLD'S PRIMROSE*
Rhodiola pachyclados	AFGHAN SEDUM
Rhodanthemum (Chrysanthemum) hosmariense	MOROCCAN DAISY
Romneya coulteri	MATILLIJA POPPY
Salvia x *sylvestris*	BLUE MEADOW SAGE, BLUE WOOD SAGE*
Saxifraga fortunei	FORTUNE SAXIFRAGE
Saxifraga x urbium 'Primuloides'	MINIATURE LONDON PRIDE
Symphyotrichum (Aster) ericoides 'Monte Cassino'	HEATH ASTER
Thalictrum (Anemonella) thalictroides	RUE-ANEMONE*
Trachelium caeruleum	THROATWORT, UMBRELLA FLOWER*
Tricyrtis hirta 'Alba', 'White Towers'	WHITE TOAD LILY
Veronica gentianoides 'Tissington White'	TISSINGTON WHITE SPEEDWELL
Veronica longifolia 'Vernique White'	WHITE VERONICA
Veronica spicata 'White Wands'	WHITE WANDS SPIKE SPEEDWELL
Veronicastrum sibericum	JAPANESE CULVER'S ROOT*
Viola alba ssp. *dehnhardtii*	PARMA VIOLET*
Xerophyllum tenax	BEAR GRASS, INDIAN BASKET GRASS ❖
Yucca species	YUCCA
Zantedeschia aethiopica	CALLA-LILY

Bulbs

Acis autumnalis	AUTUMN SNOWFLAKE
Agave amica (Polianthes tuberosa)	TUBEROSE
Allium amplectens	SLIM-LEAF ONION❖
Allium karataviense 'Ivory Queen'	WHITE TURKESTAN ONION
Allium 'Mt. Everest'	ORNAMENTAL ONION
Allium neopolitanum cowanii	GUERNSEY STAR-OF-BETHLEHEM
Allium nigrum (A. multibulbosum)	BLACK GARLIC
Allium stipitatum 'White Giant'	PERSIAN SHALLOT
Amaryllis belladonna (and x Amarygia)	NAKED LADY*
Anemone coronaria 'Mount Everest', 'The Bride'	POPPY-FLOWERED ANEMONE
Anemonoides (Anemone) blanda	GRECIAN WINDFLOWER
Anticlea (Zigadenus) elegans	MOUNTAIN STAR-LILY
Begonia x tuberhybrida	TUBEROUS BEGONIA*
Calochortus albus	WHITE GLOBE LILY, FAIRY LANTERN
Calochortus elegans var. *elegans*	ELEGANT CAT'S EAR ❖
Calochortus venustus albus	WHITE MARIPOSA LILY
Camassia cusickii 'Alba'	WHITE CUSICK'S QUAMASH
Camassia leichtlinii 'Alba'	WHITE WILD HYACINTH
Camassia leichtlinii 'Semi-plena'	DOUBLE-FLOWERED WILD HYACINTH
Colchicum 'Innocence'	AUTUMN CROCUS
Corydalis solida	FUMEWORT*
Crocus chrysanthus and hybrids	SNOW CROCUS*
Crocus niveus	FALL CROCUS*
Crocus ochroleucus	YELLOW CROCUS
Cyclamen hederifolium	HARDY CYCLAMEN*
Cyclamen pseudibericum	FALSE IBERIAN SOWBREAD*
Dahlia x hybrida	DAHLIA*
Erythronium oregonum	OREGON-FAWN LILY
Eucomis autumnalis	PINEAPPLE LILY*
Fritillaria meleagris alba	WHITE CHECKERED LILY
Fritillaria persica 'Ivory Bells'	WHITE PERSIAN FRITILLARIA
Galanthus nivalis	SNOWDROPS
Galanthus plicatus	PLEATED SNOWDROPS
Gladiolus murielae (G. callianthus, Acidanthera)	ABYSSINIAN SWORD LILY
Gladiolus hybrids	GLADIOLUS*
Hyacinthoides hispanica (NOT *H.* x massartiana)	SPANISH BLUEBELL*
Ipheion uniflorum	SPRING STAR FLOWER*
Iris x hollandica	DUTCH IRIS*
Iris reticulata and hybrids	RETICULATED IRIS*
Iris tingitana alba	WHITE AFRICAN IRIS
Leucojum aestivum	SUMMER SNOWFLAKE
Leucojum vernum	SPRING SNOWFLAKE
Lilium Asiatic hybrids	ASIATIC LILY*
Lilium candidum	MADONNA LILY
Lilium formosanum (including *var. pricei*)	FORMOSA LILY
Lilium martagon and hybrids	MARTAGON LILY*
Lilium Oriental hybrids	ORIENTAL LILY*

Lilium regale	REGAL LILY
Lilium sargentiae	SARGENT'S LILY
Lilium taliense	FRAGRANT TURK'S-CAP LILY
Lilium x testaceum	NANKEEN LILY
Lilium wallichianum	LONG-FLOWERED LILY
Lilium washingtonianum	WASHINGTON LILY, CASCADE LILY ❖
Narcissus cantabricus	SPANISH NARCISSUS
Narcissus x italicus 'Thalia'	ITALIAN ANGEL'S TEARS
Narcissus papyraceus 'Erlicheer'	PAPERWHITES
Narcissus poeticus var. *recurvus*	PHEASANT'S EYE DAFFODIL
Narcissus pseudonarcissus 'Bridal Crown' 'Mount Hood', 'Vigil'	WHITE DAFFODILS
Narcissus tazetta 'Cheerfulness', 'Silver Chimes'	WHITE NARCISSUS
Narcissus triandrus 'Hawera'	WHITE NARCISSUS
Nerine bowdenii and hybrids	SPIDER LILY*
Nerine sarniensis and hybrids	GUERNSEY LILY*
Notholirion bulbiferum	NEPAL LILY
Notholirion campanulatum	ANCIENT LILY
Notholirion macrophyllum	BHUTAN LILY
Ornithogalum arabicum	STAR OF BETHLEHEM
Ornithogalum (Galtonia) candicans	SUMMER HYACINTH
Ornithogalum magnum	EASTERN STAR
Ornithogalum narbonense	SOUTHERN STAR-OF-BETHLEHEM
Ornithogalum ponticum	STAR-OF-BETHLEHEM
Ornithogalum reverchonii	IBERIAN STAR
Oxalis adenophylla	SILVER SHAMROCK, PINK BUTTERCUPS
Oxalis purpurea	CAPE SORRELL*
Oxalis versicolor	CANDY CANE SHAMROCK*
Pancratium illyricum	SEA LILY
Pancratium maritimum	SEA LILY
Puschkinia scilloides	STRIPED SQUILL*
Ranunculus asiaticus "La Bella" strain	ITALIAN RANUNCULUS*
Scilla (Chionodoxa) luciliae	GLORY OF THE SNOW*
Tigridia pavonia	TIGER FLOWER, MEXICAN SHELL FLOWER*
Trillium albidum	GIANT WHITE WAKE-ROBIN
Trillium grandiflorum 'Flore Pleno'	DOUBLE-FLOWERED TRILLIUM
Trillium ovatum	WESTERN WHITE TRILLIUM, WAKE ROBIN ❖
Triteleia (Brodiaea) hyacinthina	WHITE TRIPLET-LILY ❖
Triteleia (Brodiaea) laxa 'Silver Queen'	WHITE ITHURIEL'S SPEAR ❖
Tulipa clusiana	LADY TULIP
Tulipa clusiana 'Lady Jane'	CANDY-STRIPE TULIP*
Zantedeschia albomaculata and some hybrids	SPOTTED CALLA

Annuals

Agastache foeniculum, A. rugosa, A. urticifolia	GIANT HYSSOPS*
Ageratum houstonianum	FLOSS FLOWER*
Agrostemma gracilis 'Ocean Pearl'	CORNCOCKLE
Alcea ficifolia	ANTWERP HOLLYHOCK*
Alcea rosea	HOLLYHOCK*

284

Amberboa (Centaurea) moschata	SWEET SULTAN*
Ammi majus (of florist')	QUEEN ANNE'S LACE
Antirrhinum majus	SNAPDRAGON*
Arctotis fastuosa	CAPE DAISY*
Arctotis venusta (A. stoaechadifolia)	BLUE-EYED AFRICAN DAISY
Argemone platyceros	PRICKLY POPPY
Argyranthemum frutescens	MARGUERITE DAISY*
Begonia semperflorens	BEGONIA*
Bellis perennis	ENGLISH DAISY*
Brachyscome iberidifolia	SWAN RIVER DAISY
Calibrachoa hybrids	MILLION BELLS*
Callistephus chinensis	CHINA ASTER*
Campanula medium	CANTERBURY BELLS, CUP-AND-SAUCER*
Campanula pyramidalis	CHIMNEY BELLFLOWER*
Catanache caerulea	CUPID'S DART*
Catharanthus roseus	MADAGASCAR PERIWINKLE*
Centaurea cyanus	CORNFLOWER, BACHELORS' BUTTONS*
Clarkia amoena	GODETIA* ❖
Clarkia unguiculata (elegans)	CLARKIA*
Cleome hasslerana	SPIDER FLOWER*
Convolvulus tricolor	BUSH MORNING GLORY*
Consolida ajacis (C. ambigua)	ROCKET LARKSPUR*
Cosmos bipinnatus	COSMOS*
Cynoglossum amabile	CHINESE FORGET-ME-NOT*
Datura inoxia	MOONFLOWER
Dianthus barbatus	SWEET WILLIAM*
Dianthus chinensis and hybrids	PINKS*
Dimorphotheca pluvialis	WHITE AFRICAN DAISY
Dorotheanthus bellidiformis	LIVINGSTONE DAISY*
Eryngium giganteum 'Miss Wilmott's Ghost'	MISS WILMOTT'S GHOST
Erythranthe (Mimulus) x *hybridus*	MONKEY FLOWER*
Eschscholzia californica	CALIFORNIA POPPY*
Eustoma russellianum (E. grandiflorum; Lisianthus)	SWEET LISSIE, PRAIRIE GENTIAN*
Gerbera hybrids	GERBERA DAISY*
Glandularia (Verbena) x *hybrida*	GARDEN VERBENA*
Glebionis (Chrysanthemum) segetum	CORN MARIGOLD*
Gomphrena globosa	GLOBE AMARANTH*
Gypsophila elegans	ANNUAL BABY'S-BREATH*
Iberis umbellata	CANDYTUFT*
Impatiens balsamina	BALSAM*
Impatiens walleriana	IMPATIENS*
Ipomoea quamoclit	CYPRESS VINE*
Ipomoea tricolor (and more)	MORNING GLORY*
Ismelia (Chrysanthemum) carinata	TRICOLOR DAISY*
Lathyrus odoratus	SWEET PEA*
Lavatera trimestris	ROSE MALLOW*
Linanthus androsaceus	FALSE BABY STARS*
Linanthus grandiflorus	MOUNTAIN PHLOX*
Limonium sinuatum	ANNUAL STATICE*

Linaria maroccana	BABY SNAPDRAGON*
Lobelia erinus	LOBELIA*
Lobularia maritima	SWEET ALYSSUM*
Lophospermum (Asarina) erubescens	CREEPING GLOXINIA*
Lophospermum (Asarina) scandens	CLIMBING SNAPDRAGON*
Lupinus mutabilis (hartwegii)	MEXICAN LUPINE*
Malope trifida	MALOPE*
Matthiola incana	STOCK*
Mauranthemum (Leucanthemum, Chrysanthemum) paludosum	CREEPING DAISY
Michauxia campanuloides	MICHAUX'S BELLFLOWER
Myosotis sylvatica	WOOD FORGET-ME-NOT*
Nemesia versicolor	NEMESIA*
Nemophila maculata	FIVE-SPOT
Nicotiana alata/sanderae	FLOWERING TOBACCO*
Nicotiana sylvestris	FLOWERING TOBACCO
Nierembergia caerulea 'Mont Blanc'	CUP FLOWER
Nierembergia repens (N. rivularis)	WHITE CUP
Nigella damascena	LOVE-IN-A-MIST*
Papaver croceum (nudicaule)	ICELAND POPPY*
Papaver rhoeas	CORN POPPY, SHIRLEY POPPY*
Papaver somniferum	PEONY POPPY*
Pericallis (Senecio) x *hybridus (Cineraria)*	CINERARIA*
Petunia × *atkinsiana*	PETUNIA*
Phlox drummondii	ANNUAL PHLOX*
Portulaca grandiflora	MOSS ROSE*
Primula malacoides	FAIRY PRIMROSE*
Primula obconica	GERMAN PRIMROSE*
Primula x *polyantha and Acaulis groups*	ENGLISH PRIMROSE*
Primula sinensis	CHINESE PRIMROSE*
Salvia coccinea 'Lactea', 'White Nymph'	TROPICAL SAGE
Salvia farinacea	MEALY-CUP SAGE*
Salvia splendens	SCARLET SAGE*
Scabiosa atropurpurea	PINCUSHION FLOWER*
Schizanthus pinnatus, S. x *wisetonensis*	BUTTERFLY FLOWER*
Silene coeli-rosa	ROSE-OF-HEAVEN*
Thunbergia alata	BLACK-EYED SUSAN VINE*
Torenia fournieri	WISHBONE FLOWER*
Trachymene coerulea	BLUE LACE FLOWER*
Vaccaria hispanica (V. pyramidata)	COW COCKLE*
Viola cornuta	VIOLA*
Viola x *wittrockiana*	PANSY*
Xerochrysum (Helichrysum) bracteatum	STRAWFLOWER*
Zinnia (best in hottest areas only)	ZINNIA

PINK

Perennials

Achillea 'Appleblossom', 'Heidi', 'Salmon Beauty'	HYBRID YARROWS
Aethionema grandiflorum	STONE CRESS
Alstroemeria hybrids	PERUVIAN LILY*
Armeria maritima	SEA PINK*
Astrantia major	GREAT MASTERWORT*
Begonia grandis evansiana	HARDY BEGONIA
Bergenia hybrids	HYBRID BERGENIA*
Betonica (Stachys) macrantha 'Robusta'	BIG BETONY
Betonica (Stachys) officinalis 'Pink Cotton Candy'	WOOD BETONY
Centranthus ruber	JUPITER'S BEARD, RED VALERIAN*
Chaerophyllum hirsutum 'Roseum'	PINK HAIRY CHERVIL
Chrysanthemum X rubellum	HARDY CHRYSANTHEMUM*
Darmera peltata	UMBRELLA PLANT
Dianthus caryophyllus	CARNATION*
Dianthus deltoides, D. gratianopolitanus, D. plumarius	PINKS*
Dicentra formosa	PACIFIC OR WESTERN BLEEDING-HEART* ❖
Dierama pulcherrimum	FAIRY WAND, WAND FLOWER*
Digitalis x mertonensis 'Summer King'	STRAWBERRY FOXGLOVE
Digitalis mariana	PINK FOXGLOVE
Digitalis thapsi	SPANISH FOXGLOVE
Dodecatheon hendersonii	SHOOTING STAR, MOSQUITO BILL ❖
Epimedium grandiflorum	BISHOP'S HAT*
Erigeron glaucus	SEASIDE DAISY, BEACH ASTER*
Eriocapitella (Anemone) x hybrida 'Party Dress', 'September Charm'	JAPANESE ANEMONE
Eriogonum latifolium	COAST BUCKWHEAT ❖
Erodium x variable	CRANESBILL*
Eutrochium (Eupatorium) dubium 'Little Joe'	LITTLE JOE PYE WEED
Eutrochium (Eupatorium) maculatum	JOE PYE WEED ❖
Filipendula purpurea 'Elegans'	JAPANESE MEADOWSWEET
Filipendula 'Kahome'	DWARF JAPANESE MEADOWSWEET
Geranium x antipodeum 'Stanhoe'	STANHOE GERANIUM
Geranium 'Bertie Crug'	BERTIE CRUG GERANIUM
Geranium x cantabrigiense	HARDY GERANIUMS*
Geranium cinereum	HARDY GERANIUM*
Geranium endressii 'Wargrave Pink'	W. P. GERANIUM
Geranium x oxonianum	HYBRID GERANIUMS*
Geranium x riversleaianum	HARDY GERANIUM*
Geum hybrids	GEUM, AVENS*
Glandularia (Verbena) 'Annie'	HEIRLOOM VERBENA
Glandularia (Verbena) canadensis	ROSE MOCK VERVAIN, HARDY VERBENA*
Gypsophila cerastioides	KASHMIR BABY'S-BREATH*
Helianthemum nummularium 'Annabel', 'Shot Silk', 'Wisley Pink'	SUN ROSE
Helleborus x ballardiae	HYBRID HELLEBORE
Helleborus x ericsmithii	HYBRID HELLEBORE

Helleborus x hybridus	LENTEN ROSE*
Helleborus lividus	MAJORCAN HELLEBORE*
Helleborus niger	CHRISTMAS ROSE*
Helleborus x sternii	HYBRID HELLEBORE*
Hemerocallis (many)	DAYLILIES*
Hesperantha (Schizostylis) coccinea 'Jennifer', 'Pink Princess'	CRIMSON FLAG*
Heuchera hybrids *(many)*	CORAL BELLS*
Hibiscus moscheutos and hybrids	ROSE MALLOW*
Hylotelephium (Sedum) sieboldii	OCTOBER DAPHNE SEDUM
Hylotelephium (Sedum) spectabile	
	SHOWY STONECROP, AUTUMN SEDUM, BORDER SEDUM
Hylotelephium (Sedum) telephium	BORDER SEDUM
Iris PCH hybrids	PACIFIC COAST IRIS HYBRIDS*
Iris tenax	OREGON IRIS, TOUGH-LEAF IRIS ❖*
Lewisia cotyledon and hybrids	SISKIYOU LEWISIA ❖*
Lupinus x regalis (*L.* x russellii)	RUSSELL LUPINE*
Origanum x 'Betty Rollins', 'Jim's Best'	ORNAMENTAL OREGANOS
Origanum rotundifolium 'Kent Beauty'	ORNAMENTAL OREGANO
Paeonia lactiflora hybrids	CHINESE/GARDEN PEONY*
Penstemon 'Dave Murray'	D. M. PENSTEMON
Penstemon 'Appleblossom', 'Frosty Pink', 'Hidcote Pink', 'Osprey', 'Pennington Gem', 'Thorn'	BEARDTONGUE
Penstemon richardsonii	RICHARDSON'S BEARDTONGUE ❖
Phedimus (Sedum) spurius	TWO-ROW STONECROP*
Phygelius 'Pink Elf', 'Pink Trumpet', 'Sunburst', 'Trewidden Pink'	CAPE FUCHSIA
Polemonium carneum	SALMON POLEMONIUM ❖
Primula japonica	JAPANESE PRIMROSE*
Primula sieboldii	SIEBOLD'S PRIMROSE*
Psephellus (Centaurea) simplicicaulis	LILAC CORNFLOWER
Rodgersia aesculifolia	FINGER-LEAF RODGERSIA
Rodgersia pinnata 'Elegans'	FEATHER LEAF RODGERSIA
Salvia x sylvestris	BLUE MEADOW SAGE, BLUE WOOD SAGE*
Scabiosa columbariae 'Pink Mist'	PINCUSHION FLOWER
Sidalcea campestris	MEADOW SIDALCEA ❖
Sidalcea oregana	OREGON CHECKER MALLOW ❖
Thalictrum (Anemonella) thalictroides	RUE-ANEMONE*
Tricyrtis formosana	TOAD LILY*
Veronicastrum sibericum	JAPANESE CULVER'S ROOT*
Zauschneria (Epilobium) 'Solidarity Pink'	PINK CALIFORNIA FUCHSIA

Bulbs

Allium (Nectaroscordum) bulgaricum siculum	SICILIAN HONEY LILY
Allium cernuum	NODDING ONION ❖
Allium karataviense	TURKESTAN ONION
Allium roseum	ROSY GARLIC
Allium 'Summer Beauty'	SUMMER BEAUTY ORNAMENTAL ONION
Allium (Nectaroscordum) tripedale	PINK HONEY LILY

X Amarine tubergenii	VAN TUBERGEN'S AMARINE LILY
Amaryllis belladonna (and x Amarygia)	NAKED LADY*
Anemone coronaria	POPPY-FLOWERED ANEMONE*
Anemonoides (Anemone) blanda 'Pink Star'	GRECIAN WINDFLOWER
Arisaema candidissimum	PINK COBRA LILY
Begonia x tuberhybrida	TUBEROUS BEGONIA*
Canna x generalis	CANNA*
Colchicum x agrippinum	AUTUMN CROCUS, MEADOW SAFFRON
Colchicum autumnale	AUTUMN CROCUS
Colchicum 'The Giant'	GIANT AUTUMN CROCUS
Colchicum 'Waterlily'	DOUBLE AUTUMN CROCUS
Corydalis solida	FUMEWORT*
Cyclamen graecum	GREEK CYCLAMEN
Cyclamen hederifolium	HARDY CYCLAMEN*
Cyclamen pseudibericum	FALSE IBERIAN SOWBREAD*
Dahlia x hybrida	DAHLIA*
Dichelostemma 'Pink Diamond'	PINK DIAMOND BRODIAEA
Erythronium revolutum	COAST FAWN-LILY, PINK FAWN-LILY
Gladiolus (tubergenii) 'Charm'	SWORD LILY
Gladiolus hybrids	GLADIOLUS*
Gladiolus oppositiflorus ssp. *salmoneus*	SALMON GLADIOLUS
Hyacinthoides hispanica (NOT *H.* x massartiana)	SPANISH BLUEBELL*
Impatiens flanaganae	FLANAGAN'S IMPATIENS
Lilium Asiatic hybrids	ASIATIC LILY*
Lilium mackliniae	SHIRUI LILY
Lilium martagon and hybrids	MARTAGON LILY*
Lilium Oriental hybrids	ORIENTAL LILY*
Lilium washingtonianum	WASHINGTON LILY, CASCADE LILY ❖
Lycoris sprengeri	SURPRISE LILY, MAGIC LILY
Lycoris x squamigera	RESURRECTION LILY, MAGIC LILY
Narcissus pseudonarcissus 'Accent', 'Mabel Taylor', 'Replete', 'Rosy Clouds' DAFFODILS	
Nerine bowdenii and hybrids	SPIDER LILY*
Nerine sarniensis and hybrids	GUERNSEY LILY*
Nomocharis aperta	NOMOCHARIS LILY
Nomocharis x notabilis	HYBRID NOMOCHARIS LILY
Nomocharis pardanthina	NOMOCHARIS LILY
Nomocharis saluenensis	NOMOCHARIS LILY
Notholirion thomsonianum	ROSY HIMALAYAN LILY
Oxalis confexula (C. depressa, C. inops)	WOOD SORREL
Oxalis purpurea	CAPE SORRELL*
Oxalis triangularis	LOVE PLANT, PURPLE SHAMROCK
Ranunculus asiaticus "La Bella" strain	ITALIAN RANUNCULUS*
Tigridia pavonia	TIGER FLOWER, MEXICAN SHELL FLOWER*
Tulipa clusiana	LADY TULIP
Zantedeschia 'Crystal Blush', 'Peach Chiffon', 'Pillow Talk', 'Pink Chiffon', 'Strawberry Parfait'	HYBRID CALLA-LILY
Zantedeschia rehmannii	RED/PINK CALLA

Annuals

Ageratum houstonianum	FLOSS FLOWER*
Alcea ficifolia	ANTWERP HOLLYHOCK*
Alcea rosea	HOLLYHOCK*
Amberboa (Centaurea) moschata	SWEET SULTAN*
Antirrhinum majus	SNAPDRAGON*
Aquilegia x hybrida	COLUMBINE*
Aquilegia vulgaris	ENGLISH COLUMBINE*
Argyranthemum frutescens	MARGUERITE DAISY*
Begonia semperflorens	BEGONIA*
Bellis perennis	ENGLISH DAISY*
Brachyscome iberidifolia	SWAN RIVER DAISY*
Calibrachoa hybrids	MILLION BELLS*
Callistephus chinensis	CHINA ASTER*
Campanula medium	CANTERBURY BELLS, CUP-AND-SAUCER*
Catharanthus roseus	MADAGASCAR PERIWINKLE*
Celosia argentea var. *cristata* (for warmest areas)	COCKSCOMB*
Centaurea cyanus	CORNFLOWER, BACHELORS' BUTTONS*
Clarkia amoena	GODETIA* ❖
Clarkia unguiculata (C. elegans)	CLARKIA*
Cleome hasslerana	SPIDER FLOWER*
Consolida ajacis (C. ambigua)	ROCKET LARKSPUR*
Convolvulus tricolor	BUSH MORNING GLORY*
Cosmos bipinnatus	COSMOS*
Cynoglossum amabile	CHINESE FORGET-ME-NOT*
Dahlia x hybrida	DAHLIA*
Dianthus barbatus	SWEET WILLIAM*
Dianthus chinensis and hybrids	PINKS*
Dorotheanthus bellidiformis	LIVINGSTONE DAISY*
Eustoma russellianum (E. grandiflorum; Lisianthus)	SWEET LISSIE, PRAIRIE GENTIAN*
Gerbera hybrids	GERBERA DAISY*
Glandularia (Verbena) x hybrida	GARDEN VERBENA*
Gomphrena globosa	GLOBE AMARANTH*
Gypsophila elegans	ANNUAL BABY'S-BREATH*
Iberis umbellata	CANDYTUFT*
Impatiens balsamina	BALSAM*
Impatiens walleriana	IMPATIENS*
Lablab purpureus	HYACINTH BEAN
Lathyrus odoratus	SWEET PEA*
Lavatera trimestris	ROSE MALLOW*
Linanthus androsaceus	FALSE BABY STARS*
Linanthus grandiflorus	MOUNTAIN PHLOX*
Limonium sinuatum	ANNUAL STATICE*
Linaria maroccana	BABY SNAPDRAGON*
Lobularia maritima	SWEET ALYSSUM*
Lophospermum (Asarina) erubescens	CREEPING GLOXINIA*
Lophospermum (Asarina) scandens	CLIMBING SNAPDRAGON*
Lupinus mutabilis (L. hartwegii)	MEXICAN LUPINE*

Malcomia maritima	VIRGINIA STOCK*
Malope trifida	MALOPE*
Matthiola incana	STOCK*
Matthiola longipetala bicornis	EVENING-SCENTED STOCK*
Myosotis sylvatica	WOOD FORGET-ME-NOT*
Nemesia versicolor	NEMESIA*
Nicotiana alata/sanderae	FLOWERING TOBACCO*
Nigella damascena	LOVE-IN-A-MIST*
Papaver rhoeas	CORN POPPY, SHIRLEY POPPY*
Papaver somniferum	PEONY POPPY*
Pericallis (Senecio) x hybridus (Cineraria)	CINERARIA*
Petunia × atkinsiana	PETUNIA*
Phlox drummondii	ANNUAL PHLOX*
Portulaca grandiflora	MOSS ROSE*
Primula malacoides	FAIRY PRIMROSE*
Primula obconica	GERMAN PRIMROSE*
Primula x polyantha and Acaulis groups	ENGLISH PRIMROSE*
Primula sinensis	CHINESE PRIMROSE*
Salvia coccinea 'Brenthurst', 'Coral Nymph'	TROPICAL SAGE
Salvia splendens	SCARLET SAGE*
Scabiosa atropurpurea	PINCUSHION FLOWER*
Schizanthus pinnatus, S. x wisetonensis	BUTTERFLY FLOWER*
Silene coeli-rosa	ROSE-OF-HEAVEN*
Torenia fournieri	WISHBONE FLOWER*
Trachymene coerulea	BLUE LACE FLOWER*
Vaccaria hispanica (V. pyramidata)	COW COCKLE*
Viola x wittrockiana	PANSY*
Xerochrysum (Helichrysum) bracteatum	STRAWFLOWER*
Zinnia elegans (best in hottest areas only)	ZINNIA*

ROSE

Perennials

Achillea hybrids	YARROWS
Alstroemeria hybrids	PERUVIAN LILY*
Androsace (Douglasia) laevigata	SMOOTH DOUGLASIA ❖
Armeria species	SEA PINK*
Astrantia major	GREAT MASTERWORT*
Bergenia cordifolia	BERGENIA*
Bergenia crassifolia	WINTER BERGENIA*
Bergenia hybrids	HYBRID BERGENIA*
Betonica (Stachys) officinalis 'Hummelo'	WOOD BETONY
Centranthus ruber	JUPITER'S BEARD, RED VALERIAN*
Chrysanthemum X rubellum	HARDY CHRYSANTHEMUM*
Dianthus caryophyllus	CARNATION*
Dianthus deltoides, D. gratianopolitanus, D. plumarius	PINKS*
Dicentra formosa	PACIFIC OR WESTERN BLEEDING-HEART* ❖

Dierama dracomontanum	DRAKENBERG WANDFLOWER
Dodecatheon hendersonii	SHOOTING STAR, MOSQUITO BILL ❖
Epimedium grandiflorum	BISHOP'S HAT*
Epimedium x rubrum	HYBRID EPIMEDIUM
Eriocapitella (Anemone) x hybrida 'Alice'	JAPANESE ANEMONE
Eriogonum ovalifolium	OVAL-LEAF BUCKWHEAT ❖*
Geranium cinereum	HARDY GERANIUM*
Geranium macrorrhizum	HARDY GERANIUM
Geranium x riversleaianum	HARDY GERANIUM*
Geum hybrids	GEUM, AVENS*
Glandularia (Verbena) canadensis	ROSE MOCK VERVAIN, HARDY VERBENA*
Glandularia (Verbena) tenera	MOSS VERBENA
Helianthemum nummularium 'Belgravia Rose'	ROCK ROSE, SUN ROSE
Helleborus x ballardiae	HYBRID HELLEBORE
Helleborus x ericsmithii	HYBRID HELLEBORE
Helleborus x hybridus	LENTEN ROSE*
Helleborus niger	CHRISTMAS ROSE*
Helleborus x sternii	HYBRID HELLEBORE*
Hemerocallis (many)	DAYLILIES*
Hesperaloe parviflora	RED YUCCA
Hesperantha (Schizostylis) coccinea	CRIMSON FLAG*
Heuchera hybrids *(many)*	CORAL BELLS*
Hibiscus moscheutos and hybrids	ROSE MALLOW*
Hibiscus 'Rubrum'	RUBRUM MALLOW
Hylotelephium (Sedum) Autumn hybrids ('Autumn Charm', 'Autumn Delight', 'Autumn Fire', 'Autumn Joy')	HYBRID AUTUMN SEDUM
Hylotelephium (Sedum) cauticola 'Lidakense'	LIDAKENSE CLIFF STONECROP
Hylotelephium (Sedum) 'Vera Jameson'	PURPLE AUTUMN SEDUM
Incarvillea delavayi	GARDEN GLOXINIA
Incarvillea zhongdianensis	YUNNAN TRUMPET FLOWER
Iris PCH hybrids	PACIFIC COAST IRIS HYBRIDS*
Lamprocapnos (Dicentra) spectabilis	OLD-FASHIONED BLEEDING HEART*
Lewisia cotyledon and hybrids	SISKIYOU LEWISIA❖*
Lilium Asiatic hybrids	ASIATIC LILY*
Lupinus x regalis (*L.* x russellii)	RUSSELL LUPINE*
Origanum 'Santa Cruz'	ORNAMENTAL OREGANO
Paeonia lactiflora hybrids	CHINESE/GARDEN PEONY*
Penstemon 'Garnet'	BEARDTONGUE
Penstemon mexicali 'Red Rocks'	RED PENSTEMON
Penstemon newberryi var. *berryi*	BERRY'S MOUNTAIN PRIDE ❖
Phedimus (Sedum) spurius	TWO-ROW STONECROP*
Primula japonica	JAPANESE PRIMROSE*
Ranunculus asiaticus "La Bella" strain	ITALIAN RANUNCULUS*
Sidalcea cusickii	CUSICK'S SIDALCEA, CUSICK'S CHECKERMALLOW ❖
Sidalcea hendersonii	HENDERSON'S CHECKER MALLOW ❖

Bulbs

Allium acuminatum	HOOKER'S ONION ❖
Amaryllis belladonna (and x Amarygia)	NAKED LADY*
Anemonoides (Anemone) blanda	GRECIAN WINDFLOWER*
Anemone coronaria 'Sylphide', 'The Admiral'	POPPY-FLOWERED ANEMONE
Begonia x tuberhybrida	TUBEROUS BEGONIA*
Canna x generalis	CANNA*
Corydalis solida	FUMEWORT*
Cyclamen hederifolium	HARDY CYCLAMEN*
Cyclamen pseudibericum	FALSE IBERIAN SOWBREAD*
Cyclamen repandum	SPRING SOWBREAD
Dahlia x hybrida	DAHLIA*
Dichelostemma ida-maia 'Pink Diamond'	PINK FIRECRACKER FLOWER
Gladiolus hybrids	GLADIOLUS*
Gladiolus italicus	ITALIAN GLADIOLUS
Gladiolus 'Rosy Cheeks'	ROSY CHEEKS GLADIOLUS
Hyacinthoides hispanica (NOT *H.* x massartiana)	SPANISH BLUEBELL*
Lilium Asiatic hybrids	ASIATIC LILY*
Lilium martagon and hybrids	MARTAGON LILY*
Lilium Oriental hybrids	ORIENTAL LILY*
Lilium speciosum	RUBRUM LILY
Nerine bowdenii and hybrids	SPIDER LILY*
Nerine sarniensis and hybrids	GUERNSEY LILY*
Oxalis purpurea	CAPE SORRELL*
Ranunculus asiaticus "La Bella" strain	ITALIAN RANUNCULUS*
Zantedeschia 'Cherry Chiffon', 'Garnet Glow', 'Gem Dark Eyes', 'Gem Rose', 'Hot Flashes', 'Lipstick', 'Parfait', 'Pink Diamond', 'Rubylite Rose', 'Sangria', 'Super Gem'	HYBRID CALLA-LILIES

Annuals

Agrostemma gracilis (A. githago)	CORNCOCKLE
Alcea ficifolia	ANTWERP HOLLYHOCK*
Alcea rosea	HOLLYHOCK*
Amberboa (Centaurea) moschata	SWEET SULTAN*
Antirrhinum majus	SNAPDRAGON*
Aquilegia vulgaris	ENGLISH COLUMBINE*
Begonia semperflorens	BEGONIA*
Bellis perennis	ENGLISH DAISY*
Brachyscome iberidifolia	SWAN RIVER DAISY*
Calibrachoa hybrids	MILLION BELLS*
Callistephus chinensis	CHINA ASTER*
Campanula medium	CANTERBURY BELLS, CUP-AND-SAUCER*
Celosia argentea var. *cristata* (for warmest areas)	COCKSCOMB*
Celosia argentea var. *cristata* 'Cramer's Amazon'	FLAMINGO FEATHER*
Centaurea cyanus	CORNFLOWER, BACHELORS' BUTTONS*
Clarkia amoena	GODETIA* ❖
Clarkia unguiculata (C. elegans)	CLARKIA*

Cleome hasslerana	SPIDER FLOWER*
Consolida ajacis (C. ambigua)	ROCKET LARKSPUR*
Convolvulus tricolor	BUSH MORNING GLORY*
Cosmos bipinnatus	COSMOS*
Dianthus barbatus	SWEET WILLIAM*
Dianthus chinensis and hybrids	PINKS*
Dorotheanthus bellidiformis	LIVINGSTONE DAISY*
Echinacea purpurea	PURPLE CONEFLOWER*
Erythranthe (Mimulus) x *hybridus*	MONKEY FLOWER*
Eustoma russellianum (E. grandiflorum; Lisianthus)	SWEET LISSIE, PRAIRIE GENTIAN*
Gerbera hybrids	GERBERA DAISY*
Glandularia (Verbena) x *hybrida*	GARDEN VERBENA*
Gomphrena globosa	GLOBE AMARANTH*
Gypsophila elegans	ANNUAL BABY'S-BREATH*
Iberis umbellata	CANDYTUFT*
Impatiens balsamina	BALSAM*
Impatiens walleriana	IMPATIENS*
Ipomoea quamoclit	CYPRESS VINE*
Lathyrus odoratus	SWEET PEA*
Lavatera trimestris	ROSE MALLOW*
Limonium sinuatum	ANNUAL STATICE*
Linaria maroccana	BABY SNAPDRAGON*
Lobelia erinus	LOBELIA*
Lobularia maritima	SWEET ALYSSUM*
Lophospermum (Asarina) scandens	CLIMBING SNAPDRAGON*
Lupinus mutabilis (L. hartwegii)	MEXICAN LUPINE*
Malope trifida	MALOPE*
Matthiola incana	STOCK*
Nicotiana alata/sanderae	FLOWERING TOBACCO*
Nigella damascena	LOVE-IN-A-MIST*
Petunia × *atkinsiana*	PETUNIA*
Phlox drummondii	ANNUAL PHLOX*
Portulaca grandiflora	MOSS ROSE*
Primula malacoides	FAIRY PRIMROSE*
Primula obconica	GERMAN PRIMROSE*
Primula x *polyantha* and Acaulis groups	ENGLISH PRIMROSE*
Primula sinensis	CHINESE PRIMROSE*
Salpiglossis sinuata	PAINTED TONGUE*
Salvia splendens	SCARLET SAGE*
Schizanthus pinnatus, S. x *wisetonensis*	BUTTERFLY FLOWER*
Silene coeli-rosa	ROSE-OF-HEAVEN*
Torenia fournieri	WISHBONE FLOWER*
Viola x *wittrockiana*	PANSY*
Xerochrysum (Helichrysum) bracteanthum	STRAWFLOWER*
Zinnia elegans (best in hottest areas only)	ZINNIA*

RED

Perennials

Achillea 'Beacon', 'Paprika'	HYBRID YARROWS
Astrantia major	GREAT MASTERWORT*
Bergenia cordifolia	BERGENIA*
Bergenia crassifolia	WINTER BERGENIA*
Bergenia hybrids	HYBRID BERGENIA*
Dianthus caryophyllus	CARNATION*
Dianthus 'Maraschino'	MARASCHINO PINK
Dicentra hybrids	BLEEDING HEART*
Geum hybrids	GEUM, AVENS*
Glandularia (Verbena) canadensis	ROSE MOCK VERVAIN, HARDY VERBENA*
Helianthemum nummularium 'Ben Ledi', 'Raspberry Ripple'	SUN ROSE
Helleborus x *hybridus*	LENTEN ROSE*
Heuchera hybrids *(many)*	CORAL BELLS*
Hibiscus coccineus	SCARLET ROSE MALLOW
Hibiscus moscheutos and hybrids	ROSE MALLOW*
Lamprocapnos (Dicentra) spectabilis 'Valentine'	OLD-FASHIONED BLEEDING HEART
Lobelia tupa	DEVIL'S TOBACCO
Paeonia lactiflora hybrids	CHINESE/GARDEN PEONY*
Penstemon 'Scarlet Queen'	BEARDTONGUE
Phygelius 'Devil's Tears'	CAPE FUCHSIA*
Primula auricula/hirsuta hybrids	BEARS' EARS*
Primula x *juliana*	JULIANA PRIMROSE*
Veronicastrum sibericum	JAPANESE CULVER'S ROOT*

Bulbs

Anemone coronaria 'His Excellency', 'Hollandia', 'The Governor'	
	POPPY-FLOWERED ANEMONE
Anemone x *fulgens*	FLAME ANEMONE
Begonia x *tuberhybrida*	TUBEROUS BEGONIA*
Canna x *generalis*	CANNA*
Corydalis solida	FUMEWORT*
Crocosmia 'Little Redhead'	MONTBRETIA
Dahlia x *hybrida*	DAHLIA*
Dichelostemma ida-maia	FIRECRACKER FLOWER
Gladiolus hybrids	GLADIOLUS*
Lilium Asiatic hybrids	ASIATIC LILY*
Lilium Oriental hybrids	ORIENTAL LILY*
Nerine bowdenii and hybrids	SPIDER LILY*
Nerine sarniensis and hybrids	GUERNSEY LILY*
Ranunculus asiaticus	RANUNCULUS*
Tulipa clusiana 'Lady Jane'	CANDY-STRIPE TULIP*
Tulipa sprengeri	SPRENGER'S TULIP

Annuals

Alcea rosea	HOLLYHOCK*
Antirrhinum majus	SNAPDRAGON*
Begonia semperflorens	BEGONIA*
Calibrachoa hybrids	MILLION BELLS*
Catharanthus roseus	MADAGASCAR PERIWINKLE*
Celosia argentea var. *cristata* (for warmest areas)	COCKSCOMB*
Clarkia amoena	GODETIA* ❖
Dahlia x hybrida	DAHLIA*
Dianthus barbatus	SWEET WILLIAM*
Dianthus chinensis and hybrids	PINKS*
Erythranthe (Mimulus) x *hybridus*	MONKEY FLOWER*
Gerbera hybrids	GERBERA DAISY*
Glandularia (Verbena) x *hybrida*	GARDEN VERBENA*
Gomphrena globosa	GLOBE AMARANTH*
Impatiens balsamina	BALSAM*
Impatiens walleriana	IMPATIENS*
Ipomoea x multifida	CARDINAL CLIMBER*
Ipomoea quamoclit	CYPRESS VINE*
Lathyrus odoratus	SWEET PEA*
Linum grandiflorum	SCARLET FLAX*
Matthiola incana	STOCK*
Nicotiana alata/*sanderae*	FLOWERING TOBACCO*
Petunia × atkinsiana	PETUNIA*
Phlox drummondii	ANNUAL PHLOX*
Salpiglossis sinuata	PAINTED TONGUE*
Salvia coccinea	TROPICAL SAGE*
Salvia splendens	SCARLET SAGE*
Scabiosa atropurpurea	PINCUSHION FLOWER*
Viola x wittrockiana	PANSY*
Zinnia (best in hottest areas only)	ZINNIA*

SCARLET

Perennials

Acanthus sennii	ETHIOPIAN BEAR'S BREECH
Alstroemeria	PERUVIAN LILY*
Chrysanthemum x morifolium	MUM*
Delosperma 'Red Mountain Flame'	SCARLET ICE PLANT
Geum hybrids	GEUM, AVENS*
Hemerocallis (many)	DAYLILIES*
Hesperantha (Schizostylis) coccinea 'Major'	CRIMSON FLAG*
Kniphofia hybrids (many)	RED-HOT POKER, TORCH LILY*
Lobelia laxiflora angustifolia	MEXICAN CARDINAL FLOWER
Lupinus x regalis (*L.* x russellii)	RUSSELL LUPINE*

Penstemon pinifolius	ROCKY MOUNTAIN PENSTEMON
Primula auricula/hirsuta hybrids	BEARS' EARS*
Stachys coccinea	SCARLET BETONY
Zauschneria (Epilobium) septentrionalis 'Select Mattole'	CALIFORNIA FUCHSIA

Bulbs

Anemone x fulgens	SCARLET WINDFLOWER
Begonia x tuberhybrida	TUBEROUS BEGONIA*
Canna x generalis	CANNA*
Crocosmia x crocosmiiflora 'Ember Glow', 'Krakatoa', 'Twilight Fairy Crimson',	
'Vulcan'	MONTBRETIA
Dahlia x hybrida	DAHLIA*
Dichelostemma ida-maia	FIRECRACKER FLOWER
Fritillaria affinis (F. lanceolata)	CHECKER-LILY
Gladiolus hybrids	GLADIOLUS*
Lilium Asiatic hybrids	ASIATIC LILY*
Lilium martagon and hybrids	MARTAGON LILY*
Lycoris radiata	RED SPIDER LILY
Ranunculus asiaticus	RANUNCULUS*
Tigridia pavonia	TIGER FLOWER, MEXICAN SHELL FLOWER*
Watsonia angusta	SCARLET BUGLE FLOWER
Watsonia latifolia	BROAD-LEAF BUGLE-LILY
Zantedeschia 'Blaze', 'Fire Glow', 'Flame'	HYBRID CALLA-LILY

Annuals

Antirrhinum majus	SNAPDRAGON*
Asclepias curassavica	SUNSET FLOWER
Begonia semperflorens	BEGONIA*
Calibrachoa hybrids	MILLION BELLS*
Celosia argentea var. *cristata* (for warmest areas)	COCKSCOMB*
Dahlia x hybrida	DAHLIA*
Eccremocarpus scaber	CHILEAN GLORY VINE*
Erysimum cheiri	WALLFLOWER*
Erythranthe (Mimulus) x hybridus	MONKEY FLOWER*
Eschscholzia californica	CALIFORNIA POPPY*
Gaillardia pulchella	BLANKET FLOWER*
Gerbera hybrids	GERBERA DAISY*
Gomphrena globosa	GLOBE AMARANTH*
Gomphrena haageana	RIO GRANDE GLOBE AMARANTH*
Impatiens walleriana	IMPATIENS*
Linaria maroccana	BABY SNAPDRAGON*
Linaria reticulata 'Flamenco'	SPANISH TOADFLAX
Nemesia strumosa	NEMESIA*
Papaver commutatum	FLANDERS POPPY
Papaver croceum (P. nudicaule)	ICELAND POPPY*

Phaseolus coccineus	SCARLET RUNNER BEAN
Portulaca grandiflora	MOSS ROSE*
Primula x polyantha and Acaulis groups	ENGLISH PRIMROSE*
Primula sinensis	CHINESE PRIMROSE*
Salpiglossis sinuata	PAINTED TONGUE*
Salvia coccinea 'Lady in Red'	TROPICAL SAGE
Salvia splendens	SCARLET SAGE*
Tropaeolum majus	NASTURTIUM*
Viola x wittrockiana	PANSY*
Xerochrysum (Helichrysum) bracteanthum	STRAWFLOWER*
Zinnia (best in driest, hottest areas only)	ZINNIA*

ORANGE
Including "brown-ish"

Perennials

Achillea 'Terra Cotta'	HYBRID YARROW
Alstroemeria	PERUVIAN LILY*
Aquilegia formosa	WESTERN RED COLUMBINE ❖
Baptisia hybrids	FALSE INDIGO*
Chrysanthemum x morifolium	MUM*
Chrysanthemum X rubellum	HARDY CHRYSANTHEMUM*
Delosperma 'Fire Spinner'	HARDY ICE PLANT
Delosperma micans	BICOLOR ICE PLANT
Dianthus caryophyllus	CARNATION*
Digitalis ferruginea	RUSTY FOXGLOVE
Digitalis 'Goldcrest'	GOLDCREST FOXGLOVE
Digitalis 'Honey Trumpets'	HONEY TRUMPETS FOXGLOVE
Digitalis laevigatus	GIRAFFE FOXGLOVE
Digitalis obscura	SUNSET FOXGLOVE
Digitalis parviflora 'Milk Chocolate'	CHOCOLATE FOXGLOVE
Digitalis 'Polkadot Pippa'	POLKADOT PIPPA FOXGLOVE
Epimedium x warleyense	HYBRID EPIMEDIUM
Epipactis gigantea	GIANT STREAM ORCHID
Epipactis 'Sabine'	HYBRID STREAM ORCHID
Erysimum 'Pastel Patchwork'	BUSH WALLFLOWER
Geum hybrids	GEUM, AVENS*
Glumicalyx goseloides	NODDING CHOCOLATE FLOWER
Hedychium hardy hybrids	GINGER-LILY
Helenium autumnale and hybrids	MOUNTAIN SNEEZEWEED* ❖
Helianthemum nummularium 'Apricot', 'Ben Nevis', 'Cheviot', 'Henfield Brilliant'	
	SUN ROSE*
Heliopsis helianthoides "Bleeding Hearts"	FALSE SUNFLOWER
Hemerocallis (many)	DAYLILIES*
Lewisia cotyledon and hybrids	SISKIYOU LEWISIA❖*
Lobelia laxiflora 'Candy Corn'	ORANGE LOBELIA
Kniphofia hybrids (many)	RED-HOT POKER, TORCH LILY*

Kniphofia thomsonii	ALPINE TORCH LILY
Papaver spicatum	TURKISH SPIKE POPPY
Penstemon 'Burnt Orange'	ORANGE BEARDTONGUE
Penstemon pinifolius 'Melon'	ROCKY MOUNTAIN PENSTEMON
Phygelius 'African Queen', 'Salmon Leap', 'Winchester Fanfare'	CAPE FUCHSIA
Primula bulleyana	CANDELABRA PRIMROSE
Primula chungensis	CHINESE CANDELABRA PRIMROSE
Primula veris	ENGLISH COWSLIP*
Sphaeralcea munroana	ORANGE GLOBE MALLOW ❖

Bulbs

Begonia x tuberhybrida	TUBEROUS BEGONIA*
Canna x generalis	CANNA*
Crocosmia x crocosmiiflora 'Bright Eyes', 'Debutante', 'Emily McKenzie', 'Severn Surprise', 'Star of the East',	MONTBRETIA
Dahlia x hybrida	DAHLIA*
Fritillaria eduardii	EDUARD'S FRITILLARIA
Gladiolus dalenii 'Boone', 'Halloweenie'	ORANGE GLADIOLUS
Gladiolus hybrids	GLADIOLUS*
Iris x hollandica	DUTCH IRIS*
Lilium Asiatic hybrids	ASIATIC LILY*
Lilium columbianum	TIGER LILY
Lilium henryi	HENRY'S LILY
Lilium jankae	BALKAN LILY
Lilium lancifolium	TURK'S-CAP LILY
Lilium martagon and hybrids	MARTAGON LILY*
Lilium pardalinum	SHASTA LILY
Lilium rosthornii	ROSTHORN'S LILY
Narcissus jonquilla 'Kinglet', 'Suzy'	ORANGE JONQUIL
Narcissus pseudonarcissus 'Bantam', 'Ceylon', 'Tahiti'	ORANGE DAFFODILS
Narcissus tazetta 'Geranium', 'Matador', 'Martha Washington', 'Sir Winston Churchill'	ORANGE NARCISSUS
Ranunculus asiaticus "La Bella" strain	ITALIAN RANUNCULUS*
Tigridia pavonia	TIGER FLOWER, MEXICAN SHELL FLOWER*
Tulipa clusiana chrysantha	GOLDEN LADY TULIP
Tulipa clusiana 'Cynthia'	ROSE AND GOLD TULIP
Tulipa linifolia (including *T. batalinii*)	BOKHARA TULIP, FLAX-LEAF TULIP
Tulipa orphanidea (including *T. whittallii*)	ANATOLIAN TULIP, COTTAGE TULIP
Zantedeschia 'Flame'	HYBRID CALLA-LILY

Annuals

Antirrhinum majus	SNAPDRAGON*
Arctotis fastuosa	CAPE DAISY*
Calendula officinalis	POT MARIGOLD*
Calibrachoa hybrids	MILLION BELLS*

299

Celosia argentea var. *cristata* (for warmest areas)	COCKSCOMB*
Cosmos sulphureus	ORANGE COSMOS*
Dahlia x hybrida	DAHLIA*
Digitalis lanata	GRECIAN FOXGLOVE
Dimorphotheca sinuata	AFRICAN DAISY*
Dorotheanthus bellidiformis	LIVINGSTONE DAISY*
Eccremocarpus scaber	CHILEAN GLORY VINE*
Erysimum x allionii	SIBERIAN WALLFLOWER
Erysimum cheiri	WALLFLOWER*
Erythranthe (Mimulus) x hybridus	MONKEY FLOWER*
Eschscholzia californica	CALIFORNIA POPPY*
Gaillardia pulchella	BLANKET FLOWER*
Gomphrena globosa	GLOBE AMARANTH*
Gomphrena haageana	RIO GRANDE GLOBE AMARANTH*
Ipomoea lobata	FIRECRACKER VINE
Nemesia strumosa	NEMESIA*
Papaver croceum (P. nudicaule)	ICELAND POPPY*
Papaver rubrifragum var. *atlanticum* 'Flore Pleno'	MOROCCAN POPPY
Portulaca grandiflora	MOSS ROSE*
Primula x polyantha and Acaulis groups	ENGLISH PRIMROSE*
Reseda odorata	MIGNONETTE
Salpiglossis sinuata	PAINTED TONGUE*
Stylomecon heterophylla	WIND POPPY
Tagetes erecta	AFRICAN MARIGOLD*
Tagetes patula	FRENCH MARIGOLD*
Tagetes tenuifolia	SIGNET MARIGOLD*
Thunbergia alata	BLACK-EYED SUSAN VINE*
Tithonia rotundifolia	MEXICAN SUNFLOWER*
Tropaeolum majus	NASTURTIUM*
Viola cornuta	VIOLA*
Viola x wittrockiana	PANSY*
Xerochrysum (Helichrysum) bracteanthum	STRAWFLOWER*
Zinnia elegans (best in driest, hottest areas only)	ZINNIA*

YELLOW/GOLD

Perennials

Achillea filipendulina	GOLDEN YARROW
Achillea 'Moonshine'	MOONSHINE YARROW
Achillea 'Anthea', 'Great Expectations', 'Schwellingberg'	HYBRID YARROWS
Achillea x taygetea	HYBRID YARROW
Aconitum lycoctonum	NORTHERN WOLFS-BANE
Alstroemeria hybrids	PERUVIAN LILY*
Anemonoides (Anemone) x lipsiensis	HYBRID WOOD ANEMONE
Baptisia hybrids	FALSE INDIGO*
Berlandiera lyrata	CHOCOLATE DAISY
Calanthe sieboldii	JAPANESE GROUND ORCHID

Calylophus hartwegii	HARTWEG'S SUNDROPS
Cephalaria gigantea	GIANT YELLOW SCABIOUS
Chrysanthemum x morifolium	MUM*
Coreopsis verticillata	THREAD-LEAF COREOPSIS
Dianthus caryophyllus	CARNATION*
Digitalis ambigua	TEMPLE BELLS FOXGLOVE
Digitalis davisiana	DAVIS' FOXGLOVE
Digitalis grandiflora	LARGE YELLOW FOXGLOVE
Disporum uniflorum	FAIRY BELLS
Epimedium davidii	BISHOP'S HAT
Epimedium ecalcaratum	SPURLESS BARRENWORT
Epimedium lishihchenii	BISHOP'S HAT
Epimedium x perralchicum	HYBRID EPIMEDIUM
Epimedium x versicolor 'Sulphureum'	HYBRID EPIMEDIUM
Eriogonum ovalifolium	OVAL-LEAF BUCKWHEAT ❖*
Eriogonum umbellatum	SULPHUR BUCKWHEAT ❖
Eriophyllum lanatum	OREGON SUNSHINE, WOOLLY SUNFLOWER ❖
Euphorbia 'Red Wing'	RED WING EUPHORBIA
Euphorbia rigida	GLAUCUS SPURGE
Geum hybrids	GEUM, AVENS*
Hedychium gardnerianum	KAHILI GINGER
Helenium autumnale and hybrids	MOUNTAIN SNEEZEWEED* ❖
Helianthemum nummularium 'Roxburgh Gold', 'Wisley Primrose'	SUN ROSE
Helianthus 'Lemon Queen'	LEMON QUEEN PERENNIAL SUNFLOWER
Heliopsis helianthoides	FALSE SUNFLOWER
Hemerocallis citrina	FRAGRANT DAYLILY
Hemerocallis dumortieri	FRAGRANT DAYLILY
Hemerocallis hybrids (many)	DAYLILIES*
Hemerocallis lilioasphodelus	LEMON LILY
Iris bracteata	SISKIYOU IRIS ❖
Iris innominata	GOLDEN IRIS ❖
Iris PCH hybrids	PACIFIC COAST IRIS HYBRIDS*
Iris Spuria hybrids	SPURIA IRIS*
Kniphofia hybrids (many)	RED-HOT POKER, TORCH LILY*
Leontodon (Microseris) rigens	HAWKBITS
Lewisia cotyledon and hybrids	SISKIYOU LEWISIA ❖*
Ligularia fischeri	GOMCHI
Lupinus x regalis (*L.* x russellii)	RUSSELL LUPINE*
Moraea alticola	YELLOW MORAEA
Oenothera fremontii	SHIMMER EVENING PRIMROSE
Opuntia fragilis	BRITTLE PRICKLY PEAR ❖
Phedimus (Sedum) kamtschaticus	KAMSCHATKA SEDUM, ORANGE STONECROP
Phlomis fruticosa	JERUSALEM SAGE
Phlomis russeliana	SYRIAN-SAGE
Phygelius 'Moonraker', 'Yellow Trumpet'	CAPE FUCHSIA
Primula auricula/hirsuta hybrids	BEARS' EARS*
Primula veris	ENGLISH COWSLIP*
Rudbeckia 'Herbstsonne' ('Autumn Sun')	CONEFLOWER
Rudbeckia fulgida var. *sullivantii* 'Goldsturm'	BLACK-EYED SUSAN

Saruma henryi	UPRIGHT WILD GINGER
Scabiosa ochroleuca	YELLOW PINCUSHION
Sedum spathulifolium	BROAD-LEAF STONECROP ❖
Sisyrinchium californicum	GOLDEN-EYED GRASS ❖
Sisyrinchium macrocarpum	CHILEAN GOLDEN-EYED GRASS
Sisyrinchium striatum	SATIN FLOWER
Solidago 'Little Lemon'	LITTLE LEMON GOLDENROD
Solidago (X Solidaster) x luteus	SOLIDASTER
Solidago rugosa 'Fireworks'	GOLDENROD
Thermopsis chinensis 'Sophia'	CHINESE YELLOW PEA BUSH
Thermopsis montana	MOUNTAIN GOLD-BANNER ❖
Titanotrichum oldhamii	OLDHAM'S GOLD WOODLAND FOXGLOVE
Tricyrtis latifolia	YELLOW TOAD-LILY
Tricyrtis macrantha	GOLDEN TOAD-LILY
Uvularia grandiflora	LARGE-FLOWERED BELLWORT
Viola glabella	STREAM VIOLET, YELLOW WOOD VIOLET ❖

Bulbs

Asphodeline lutea	KING'S SPEAR
Begonia x tuberhybrida	TUBEROUS BEGONIA*
Bloomeria (Triteleia) crocea	GOLDEN STARS
Canna x generalis	CANNA*
Chlidanthus fragrans	PERFUMED FAIRY LILY
Crocosmia x crocosmiiflora 'George Davidson', 'Jenny Bloom', 'Walberton Yellow'	MONTBRETIA
Crocus chrysanthus and hybrids	SNOW CROCUS*
Dahlia x hybrida	DAHLIA*
Eranthis hyemalis	WINTER ACONITE
Eremurus stenophyllus	YELLOW FOXTAIL LILY
Erythronium grandiflorum var. grandiflorum	AVALANCHE-LILY, GLACIER-LILY
Erythronium 'Pagoda'	PAGODA FAWN-LILY
Fritillaria raddeana	PERSIAN FRITILLARY*
Gladiolus dalenii var. primulinus	CAROLINA PRIMROSE
Gladiolus hybrids	GLADIOLUS*
Iris x hollandica	DUTCH IRIS*
Iris reticulata and hybrids	RETICULATED IRIS*
Iris xiphium	SPANISH IRIS*
Lilium Asiatic hybrids	ASIATIC LILY*
Lilium martagon and hybrids	MARTAGON LILY*
Lilium szovitsianum	SZOVITS' LILY
Lycoris aurea	YELLOW SPIDER LILY
Narcissus bulbocodium	HOOP PETTICOAT DAFFODIL
Narcissus cyclamineus 'February Gold', 'Jack Snipe', 'Jenny', 'Tête-à-tête'	DWARF DAFFODILS
Narcissus jonquilla	JONQUIL
Narcissus jonquilla hybrids 'Binkie', 'Sweetness', 'Trevithian'	YELLOW JONQUIL

Narcissus pseudonarcissus 'Arctic Gold', 'Carlton', 'Delibes', 'Festivity', 'Galway', 'King Alfred', 'Mrs. Langtry', 'Rustom Pasha', 'Saint Keverne', 'Wee Bee'	YELLOW DAFFODILS
Narcissus tazetta 'Yellow Cheerfulness'	YELLOW TAZETTA
Oxalis fabaefolia	RABBIT'S EARS
Ranunculus asiaticus "La Bella" strain	ITALIAN RANUNCULUS*
Sternbergia lutea	WINTER DAFFODIL
Tigridia pavonia	TIGER FLOWER, MEXICAN SHELL FLOWER*
Trillium luteum	YELLOW TRILLIUM
Triteleia ixioides	PRETTYFACE ❖
Tulipa clusiana var. *chrysantha*	GOLDEN TULIP
Tulipa dasystemon	DASYSTEMON TULIP
Tulipa linifolia (including *T. batalinii*)	BOKHARA TULIP, FLAX-LEAF TULIP
Tulipa sylvestris	WOODLAND TULIP
Tulipa urumiensis (T. tarda)	LATE TULIP, TARDY TULIP
Zantedeschia elliottiana	GOLDEN CALLA
Zantedeschia 'Gold Rush', 'Lemon Chiffon', 'Lemon Drop', 'Millennium Gold', 'Solar Flare', 'Sunshine'	HYBRID CALLA-LILY
Zantedeschia pentlandii	PURPLE-THROATED CALLA

Annuals

Alcea ficifolia	ANTWERP HOLLYHOCK*
Amberboa (Centaurea) moschata	SWEET SULTAN*
Antirrhinum majus	SNAPDRAGON*
Aquilegia x hybrida	COLUMBINE*
Argyranthemum frutescens	MARGUERITE DAISY*
Asclepias curassavica 'Apollo Yellow', 'Aurea', 'Silky Gold'	YELLOW SUNSET FLOWER
Calendula officinalis	POT MARIGOLD*
Calibrachoa hybrids	MILLION BELLS*
Celosia argentea var. *cristata* (for warmest areas)	COCKSCOMB*
Coleostephus myconis (Chrysanthemum multicaule)	YELLOW CLUMP DAISY
Coreopsis grandiflora	LARGE-FLOWERED TICKSEED
Coreopsis tinctoria	CALLIOPSIS*
Cosmos sulphureus	YELLOW COSMOS*
Dahlia x hybrida	DAHLIA*
Dimorphotheca sinuata	AFRICAN DAISY*
Eccremocarpus scaber	CHILEAN GLORY VINE*
Erysimum x allionii	SIBERIAN WALLFLOWER
Erysimum cheiri	WALLFLOWER*
Erythranthe (Mimulus) x hybridus	MONKEY FLOWER*
Eschscholzia californica	CALIFORNIA POPPY*
Gaillardia pulchella	BLANKET FLOWER*
Gerbera hybrids	GERBERA DAISY*
Glebionis (Chrysanthemum) segetum	CORN MARIGOLD*
Helianthus annuus	SUNFLOWER*
Ismelia (Chrysanthemum) carinatum	TRICOLOR DAISY*
Linanthus androsaceus	FALSE BABY STARS*

Limonium bonduellii	ANNUAL STATICE*
Linaria maroccana	BABY SNAPDRAGON*
Lupinus densiflorus	GOLDEN LUPINE
Matthiola incana	STOCK*
Meconopsis paniculata	PANICLED YELLOW POPPY
Nemesia strumosa	NEMESIA*
Nicotiana alata, N. x sanderae	FLOWERING TOBACCO*
Papaver croceum (P. nudicaule)	ICELAND POPPY*
Petunia × atkinsiana	PETUNIA*
Portulaca grandiflora	MOSS ROSE*
Primula x polyantha and Acaulis groups	ENGLISH PRIMROSE*
Rudbeckia hirta	BLACK-EYED SUSAN
Salpiglossis sinuata	PAINTED TONGUE*
Tagetes erecta	AFRICAN MARIGOLD*
Tagetes filifolia	IRISH LACE
Tagetes patula	FRENCH MARIGOLD*
Tagetes tenuifolia	SIGNET MARIGOLD*
Thunbergia alata	BLACK-EYED SUSAN VINE*
Thymophylla tenuiloba	GOLDEN FLEECE
Tropaeolum majus	NASTURTIUM*
Verbascum bombyciferum	GIANT SILVER MULLEIN
Viola cornuta	VIOLA*
Viola x wittrockiana	PANSY*
Xerochrysum (Helichrysum) bracteanthum	STRAWFLOWER*
Zinnia elegans (best in hottest areas only)	ZINNIA

GREEN

Perennials

Alstroemeria hybrids	PERUVIAN LILY*
Chrysanthemum x morifolium	MUM*
Dianthus caryophyllus	CARNATION*
Dianthus plumarius 'Charles Musgrave'	GREEN DIANTHUS
Digitalis viridis	GREEN FOXGLOVE
Eryngium agavifolium	AGAVE-LEAF SEA HOLLY
Euphorbia characias ssp. *wulfenii*	LARGE MEDITERRANEAN SPURGE
Euphorbia polychroma	SHINY EUPHORBIA
Helleborus argutifolius	CORSICAN HELLEBORE*
Helleborus foetidus	STINKING HELLEBORE
Helleborus lividus	MAJORCAN HELLEBORE*
Helleborus x sternii	HYBRID HELLEBORE*
Hemerocallis 'Green Puff'	GREEN DAYLILY
Heuchera cylindrica 'Greenfinch'	GREEN CORAL BELLS
Ismene 'Sulfur Queen'	SPIDER LILY
Lavandula viridis	LAVENDER
Primula auricula/hirsuta hybrids	BEARS' EARS*
Primula vulgaris 'Francesca'	GREEN PRIMROSE

Bulbs

Allium 'Hair'	HAIR ALLIUM
Anticlea (Zigadenus) elegans var. *glauca*	GREEN STARS
Arisaema dracontium	DRAGONROOT
Arisaema ringens	COBRA LILY
Arum concinnatum	CRETE ARUM
Eucomis bicolor 'Alba'	PINEAPPLE LILY
Fritillaria raddeana	PERSIAN FRITILLARY*
Gladiolus hybrids	GLADIOLUS*
Iris (Hermodactylus) tuberosa	SNAKE'S-HEAD IRIS
Narcissus jonquilla 'Vireo'	GREEN JONQUIL
Narcissus pseudonarcissus 'Green Island', 'St. Patty's Day'	GREEN DAFFODIL
Pinellia cordata	MINIATURE GREEN DRAGON

Annuals

Amaranthus caudatus 'Viridis'	GREEN THUMB AMARANTHUS
Molucella laevis	BELLS-OF-IRELAND
Nicotiana alata 'Lime Green'	FLOWERING TOBACCO
Nicotiana langsdorfii	JESSAMINE TOBACCO
Zinnia elegans 'Envy' (best in hottest areas only)	ZINNIA

BLUE

Perennials

Adelinia (Cynoglossum) grande	GRAND HOUND'S TONGUE ❖
Agapanthus (many)	LILY-OF-THE-NILE*
Allium sikkimense	TIBET ONION
Amsonia species	BLUE STAR
Amsonia tabernaemontana	EASTERN BLUE STAR
Anchusa azurea 'Dropmore'	ITALIAN BUGLOSS
Aquilegia x *hybrida* (short lived)	COLUMBINE*
Aster x frikartii	FRIKART'S ASTER
Baptisia australis	BLUE FALSE INDIGO
Baptisia hybrids	FALSE INDIGO*
Brunnera macrophylla	SIBERIAN BUGLOSS
Campanula carpatica	CARPATHIAN HAREBELL
Campanula lactiflora	BELLFLOWER*
Campanula olympica	GRECIAN BELLFLOWER
Campanula persicifolia	PEACH-LEAF BELLFLOWER*
Campanula portenschlagiana	DALMATIAN BELLFLOWER
Ceratostigma plumbaginoides	DWARF PLUMBAGO
Corydalis flexuosa 'Blue Panda'	FUMITORY
Delphinium elatum hybrids	DELPHINIUM*

Echinops ritro	GLOBE THISTLE
Echinops ritro ssp. *ruthenica*	SMALL GLOBE THISTLE
Eryngium alpinum	ALPINE SEA HOLLY
Eryngium amethystinum	BLUE SEA HOLLY
Eryngium bourgatii	MEDITERRANEAN SEA HOLLY
Eryngium maritimum	SEA HOLLY
Iris PCH hybrids	PACIFIC COAST IRIS HYBRIDS*
Iris siberica	SIBERIAN IRIS*
Iris unguicularis	WINTER IRIS*
Linum lewisii	BLUE FLAX ❖
Meconopsis gakyidiana	BHUTAN BLUE POPPY
Meconopsis 'Lingholm' (*M.* x *sheldonii*; "Fertile Blue Group")	HIMALAYAN POPPY
Mertensia ciliata	FRINGED LUNGWORT ❖
Omphalodes cappadocica	CAPPADOCIAN NAVELWORT
Omphalodes verna	CREEPING FORGET-ME-NOT
Penstemon azureus	AZURE PENSTEMON❖
Penstemon euglaucus	GLAUCUS PENSTEMON ❖
Pulmonaria 'Benediction'	LUNGWORT
Salvia uliginosa	BLUE SAGE
Sisyrinchium bellum	BLUE-EYED GRASS
Veronica liwanensis	TURKISH SPEEDWELL
Veronica peduncularis 'Georgia Blue'	SPEEDWELL

Bulbs

Allium beesianum	BLUE ALLIUM
Allium caeruleum	BLUE ALLIUM
Allium caesium	BLUE ALLIUM
Allium cyaneum	BLUE ALLIUM
Anemone coronaria 'Lord Lieutenant', 'Mr. Fokker'	POPPY-FLOWERED ANEMONE
Anemonoides (Anemone) blanda 'Blue Star'	GRECIAN WINDFLOWER
Brimeura amethystina	AMETHYST HYACINTH
Dichelostemma pulchellum	BLUE DICKS, WILD HYACINTH
Hyacinthoides hispanica (NOT *H.* x *massartiana*)	SPANISH BLUEBELL*
Hyacinthoides (Scilla) lingulata	AUTUMN BLUEBELL
Ipheion peregrinans 'Rolf Fiedler'	BLUE-STAR FLOWER
Iris reticulata and hybrids	RETICULATED IRIS*
Muscari armeniacum	GRAPE HYACINTH
Oncostema (Scilla) peruviana	PORTUGUESE SQUILL
Pseudomuscari (Muscari, Bellavalia) azureum	AZURE GRAPE HYACINTH
Puschkinia scilloides	STRIPED SQUILL*
Scilla bifolia	TWO-LEAF SQUILL
Scilla siberica	WOOD SQUILL
Triteleia laxa including 'Queen Fabiola'	
	PRETTY FACE, TRIPLET LILY, ITHURIEL'S SPEAR

Annuals

Ageratum houstonianum	FLOSS FLOWER*
Anchusa capensis	CAPE FORGET-ME-NOT*
Brachyscome iberidifolia	SWAN RIVER DAISY*
Browallia speciosa	AMETHYST FLOWER*
Calibrachoa hybrids	MILLION BELLS*
Callistephus chinensis	CHINA ASTER*
Campanula medium	CANTERBURY BELLS, CUP-AND-SAUCER*
Campanula pyramidalis	CHIMNEY BELLFLOWER*
Catharanthus roseus	MADAGASCAR PERIWINKLE*
Centaurea cyanus	CORNFLOWER, BACHELORS' BUTTONS*
Consolida ajacis (C. ambigua)	ROCKET LARKSPUR*
Convolvulus tricolor	BUSH MORNING GLORY*
Cynoglossum amabile	CHINESE FORGET-ME-NOT*
Delphinium grandiflorum	DWARF CHINESE DELPHINIUM*
Eustoma russellianum (E. grandiflorum; Lisianthus)	SWEET LISSIE, PRAIRIE GENTIAN*
Gilia capitata	QUEEN ANNE'S THIMBLES
Glandularia (Verbena) x *hybrida*	GARDEN VERBENA*
Ipomoea tricolor (and more species)	MORNING GLORY*
Lathyrus odoratus	SWEET PEA*
Limonium sinuatum	ANNUAL STATICE*
Lobelia erinus	LOBELIA*
Lupinus bicolor	FAIRY LUPINE
Lupinus mutabilis (L. hartwegii)	MEXICAN LUPINE*
Lupinus nanus	SKY LUPINE
Lupinus succulentus	ARROYO LUPINE
Myosotis sylvatica	WOOD FORGET-ME-NOT*
Nemesia versicolor	NEMESIA*
Nemophila menziesii	BABY BLUE-EYES
Nigella damascena	LOVE-IN-A-MIST*
Nolana humifusa	NOLANA*
Omphalodes linifolia	BLUE NAVELWORT
Pericallis (Senecio) x *hybridus*	CINERARIA*
Phacelia campanularia	CALIFORNIA BLUEBELL
Phacelia tanacetifolia	TANSY-LEAF PHACELIA
Salpiglossis sinuata	PAINTED TONGUE*
Salvia farinacea	MEALY-CUP SAGE*
Scabiosa atropurpurea	PINCUSHION FLOWER*
Trachymene coerulea	BLUE LACE FLOWER*
Viola cornuta	VIOLA*
Viola x *wittrockiana*	PANSY*

LILAC/LAVENDER

Perennials

Alstroemeria hybrids	PERUVIAN LILY*
Anemonoides (Anemone) nemorosa	WOOD ANEMONE*
Anemonopsis macrophylla	FALSE ANEMONE
Aquilegia x hybrida (short lived)	COLUMBINE*
Aquilegia vulgaris (short lived)	ENGLISH COLUMBINE*
Aster x frikartii	ITALIAN ASTER*
Aster tongolensis	EAST INDIES ASTER
Baptisia hybrids	FALSE INDIGO*
Betonica (Stachys) macrantha 'Robusta', 'Superba'	BIG BETONY
Campanula 'Birch's Hybrid'	BIRCH'S BELLFLOWER
Campanula lactiflora	MILKY BELLFLOWER*
Campanula latiloba	GREAT BELLFLOWER*
Campanula poscharskyana	SERBIAN BELLFLOWER
Campanula rotundifolia	BLUEBELL BELLFLOWER ❖
Catanache caerulea (a "tweener")	CUPID'S DART*
Chrysanthemum X rubellum	HARDY CHRYSANTHEMUM*
Clematis columbiana	ROCK CLEMATIS ❖
Codonopsis ovata	BONNET BELLFLOWER
Corydalis scouleri	SCOULER'S CORYDALIS ❖
Delphinium elatum hybrids	DELPHINIUM*
Echinops bannaticus	GLOBE THISTLE
Erigeron glaucus	SEASIDE DAISY, BEACH ASTER*
Eriocapitella (Anemone) x hybrida 'Queen Charlotte'	JAPANESE ANEMONE
Erysimum 'Bowle's Mauve'	BUSH WALLFLOWER
Erysimum 'Pastel Patchwork'	BUSH WALLFLOWER
Geranium x cantabrigiense	HARDY GERANIUMS*
Geranium himalayense	CARPET CRANESBILL
Geranium x oxonianum	HYBRID GERANIUMS*
Geranium renardii	HARDY GERANIUM*
Glandularia (Verbena) bipinnatifida	DAKOTA MOCK VERVAIN
Glandularia (Verbena) catherinae	LAVENDER VERBENA
Hemerocallis (many)	DAYLILIES*
Iris cristata	DWARF CRESTED IRIS*
Iris douglasiana	DOUGLAS IRIS
Iris innominata	GOLDEN IRIS ❖
Iris missouriensis	ROCKY MOUNTAIN IRIS ❖
Iris pallida	DALMATIAN IRIS
Iris PCH hybrids	PACIFIC COAST IRIS HYBRIDS*
Iris siberica	SIBERIAN IRIS*
Iris Spuria hybrids	SPURIA IRIS*
Iris tenax	OREGON IRIS, TOUGH-LEAF IRIS ❖*
Iris tenuis	CLACKAMAS IRIS ❖*
Iris unguicularis	WINTER IRIS*
Isodon (Rabdosia) longituba	TRUMPET SPUR-FLOWER*
Isodon umbrosus	ISODON

Lewisia cotyledon and hybrids	SISKIYOU LEWISIA ❖*
Lupinus latifolius	LUPINE
Lupinus polyphyllus	BROADLEAF LUPINE ❖
Nepeta racemosa 'Walker's Low'	CATMINT
Nepeta 'Six Hills Giant'	GIANT CATMINT
Origanum dictamnus	CRETE DITTANY
Origanum 'Rotkugel', 'Santa Cruz'	ORNAMENTAL OREGANOS
Penstemon 'Alice Hindley', 'Mother of Pearl'	BEARDTONGUE
Penstemon azureus	AZURE PENSTEMON ❖
Penstemon barrettiae	BARRETT'S BEARDTONGUE ❖
Penstemon cardwellii	CARDWELL'S PENSTEMON ❖
Penstemon davidsonii	DAVIDSON'S BEARDTONGUE ❖
Penstemon heterophyllus	FOOTHILL PENSTEMON
Penstemon speciosus	SHOWY PENSTEMON ❖
Penstemon spectabilis	ROYAL BEARDTONGUE
Phacelia bolanderi	WOODLAND PHACELIA ❖
Phlox bifida	SAND PHLOX
Phlox x henryae	MOSSY PHLOX
Primula denticulata	DRUMSTICK PRIMROSE*
Primula japonica	JAPANESE PRIMROSE*
Primula x juliana	JULIANA PRIMROSE*
Primula sieboldii	SIEBOLD'S PRIMROSE*
Rehmannia elata	CHINESE SNAPDRAGON
Salvia nutans	NODDING SAGE
Salvia yangii (Perovskia atriplicifolia) 'Blue Jean Baby'	RUSSIAN SAGE
Scabiosa anthemifolia	CHAMOMILE-LEAFED SCABIOSA
Scabiosa columbariae 'Butterfly Blue'	PINCUSHION FLOWER
Symphyotrichum (Aster) chilense	COAST ASTER ❖
Tricyrtis hirta	JAPANESE TOAD LILLY*
Tricyrtis 'Tojen'	TOAD LILY
Veronica (Parahebe) perfoliata	DIGGER'S SPEEDWELL
Viola alba ssp. *dehnhardtii*	PARMA VIOLET*

Bulbs

Anemonoides (Anemone) blanda 'Charmer'	GRECIAN WINDFLOWER
Anemone coronaria	POPPY-FLOWERED ANEMONE*
Brodiaea elegans	HARVEST BRODIAEA ❖
Calochortus uniflorus	MEADOW STAR TULIP
Camassia cusickii	CUSICK'S QUAMASH ❖
Camassia howellii	HOWELL'S CAMAS ❖
Camassia leichtlinii	WILD HYACINTH ❖
Camassia quamash	CAMAS, QUAMASH ❖
Colchicum byzantinum	BYZANTINE MEADOW SAFFRON
Colchicum 'Lilac Wonder'	LILAC AUTUMN CROCUS
Colchicum variegatum	SPOTTED AUTUMN CROCUS
Corydalis solida	FUMEWORT*
Crocus chrysanthus and hybrids	SNOW CROCUS*

Crocus goulimyi	PELOPONNESE CROCUS*
Crocus imperati	ITALIAN CROCUS
Crocus laevigatus	LATE CROCUS
Crocus longiflorus	ITALIAN CROCUS
Crocus niveus	FALL CROCUS*
Crocus pulchellus	TURKISH CROCUS
Crocus sativus	SAFFRON CROCUS
Crocus serotinus	LATE CROCUS
Crocus tommasinianus	TOMMASINI'S CROCUS
Dahlia x hybrida	DAHLIA*
Dichelostemma capitatum ssp. *capitatum*	BLUEDICKS ❖
Dichelostemma (Brodiaea) congesta	CLUSTER LILY ❖
Gladiolus hybrids	GLADIOLUS*
Hyacinthoides hispanica (NOT *H.* x massartiana)	SPANISH BLUEBELL*
Impatiens arguta	BLUE DREAM IMPATIENS
Impatiens puberula	SOFT PINK BALSAM
Ipheion uniflorum	SPRING STARFLOWER*
Iris x hollandica	DUTCH IRIS*
Iris reticulata and hybrids	RETICULATED IRIS*
Iris xiphium	SPANISH IRIS*
Oxalis purpurea	CAPE SORRELL*
Ranunculus asiaticus	RANUNCULUS*
Scilla (Chionodoxa) luciliae	GLORY OF THE SNOW*
Triteleia (Brodiaea) hyacinthina	WHITE TRIPLET-LILY*
Triteleia laxa	PRETTY FACE, TRIPLET LILY
Tulipa saxatilis (T. bakeri)	CANDIA TULIP, ROCK TULIP
Zantedeschia 'Amethyst', 'Gem Lavender', 'Plum Pretty', 'Regal'	HYBRID CALLA-LILY

Annuals

Agastache foeniculum, A. occidentalis, A. rugosa, A. urticifolia	GIANT HYSSOPS*
Ageratum houstonianum	FLOSS FLOWER*
Amberboa (Centaurea) moschata	SWEET SULTAN*
Brachyscome iberidifolia	SWAN RIVER DAISY*
Browallia speciosa	AMETHYST FLOWER*
Calibrachoa hybrids	MILLION BELLS*
Callistephus chinensis	CHINA ASTER*
Catharanthus roseus	MADAGASCAR PERIWINKLE*
Collinsia heterophylla	CHINESE HOUSES
Consolida ajacis (C. ambigua)	ROCKET LARKSPUR*
Eustoma russellianum (E. grandiflorum; Lisianthus)	SWEET LISSIE, PRAIRIE GENTIAN*
Gilia tricolor	BIRD'S EYE GILIA
Glandularia (Verbena) x hybrida	GARDEN VERBENA*
Heliotropium arborescens hybrid	HELIOTROPE*
Iberis umbellata	CANDYTUFT*
Impatiens walleriana	IMPATIENS*
Ipomoea tricolor (and more species)	MORNING GLORY*
Lathyrus odoratus	SWEET PEA*

Linanthus androsaceus	FALSE BABY STARS*
Limonium sinuatum	ANNUAL STATICE*
Linaria maroccana	BABY SNAPDRAGON*
Lobelia erinus	LOBELIA*
Lobularia maritima	SWEET ALYSSUM*
Lupinus mutabilis (L. hartwegii)	MEXICAN LUPINE*
Matthiola incana	STOCK*
Nemesia versicolor	NEMESIA*
Nigella damascena	LOVE-IN-A-MIST*
Papaver rhoeas	CORN POPPY, SHIRLEY POPPY*
Papaver setigerum	POPPY OF TROY
Papaver somniferum	PEONY POPPY*
Pericallis (Senecio) x hybridus	CINERARIA*
Petunia × atkinsiana	PETUNIA*
Primula malacoides	FAIRY PRIMROSE*
Primula sinensis	CHINESE PRIMROSE*
Scabiosa atropurpurea	PINCUSHION FLOWER*
Schizanthus pinnatus, S. x wisetonensis	BUTTERFLY FLOWER*
Silene coeli-rosa	ROSE-OF-HEAVEN*
Torenia fournieri	WISHBONE FLOWER*
Verbena bonariensis	PURPLE-TOP VERBENA
Viola cornuta	VIOLA*
Viola tricolor	JOHNNY-JUMP-UP*
Viola x wittrockiana	PANSY*

VIOLET/PURPLE

Perennials

Achillea 'Fiesta'	HYBRID YARROW
Aconitum x cammarum 'Bicolor'	MONKSHOOD
Aconitum carmichaelii	AZURE MONKSHOOD
Aconitum columbianum	MONKSHOOD ❖
Aconitum napellus	COMMON MONKSHOOD
Agapanthus (many)	LILY-OF-THE-NILE*
Baptisia hybrids	FALSE INDIGO*
Campanula primulifolia	VIOLET BELLFLOWER
Campanula portenschlagiana	DALMATIAN BELLFLOWER
Campanula 'Sarastro'	SARASTRO BELLFLOWER
Clematis hirsutissima var. *hirsutissima*	HAIRY CLEMATIS ❖
Clematis 'Stand by Me'	STAND BY ME BUSH CLEMATIS
Delosperma lavisiae	DRAKENSBERG ICE PLANT
Delphinium elatum hybrids	DELPHINIUM*
Delphinium trolliifolium	TROLLIUS-LEAF DELPHINIUM ❖
Dodecatheon cusickii	CUSICK'S SHOOTING-STAR ❖
Dracocephalum austriacum	PONTIC DRAGONS-HEAD
Geranium phaeum especially 'Raven'	DUCKY CRANESBILL
Geranium wlassovianum	HARDY GERANIUM

311

Glandularia (Verbena) canadensis	ROSE MOCK VERVAIN, HARDY VERBENA*
Iris cristata	DWARF CRESTED IRIS*
Iris douglasiana	DOUGLAS IRIS*
Iris lazica (Iris unguicularis ssp. *lazica)*	LAZISTAN IRIS, BLACK SEA IRIS
Iris missouriensis	ROCKY MOUNTAIN IRIS ❖
Iris PCH hybrids	PACIFIC COAST IRIS HYBRIDS*
Iris sanguinea	BLOOD IRIS
Iris siberica hybrids	SIBERIAN IRIS*
Iris Spuria hybrids	SPURIA IRIS*
Iris tenax	OREGON IRIS, TOUGH-LEAF IRIS ❖*
Iris tenuis	CLACKAMAS IRIS ❖*
Iris unguicularis	WINTER IRIS*
Isodon (Rabdosia) longituba	TRUMPET SPUR-FLOWER*
Lupinus polyphyllus	BROADLEAF LUPINE ❖
Lupinus x *regalis (L.* x *russellii)*	RUSSELL LUPINE*
Olsynium (Sisyrinchium) douglasii	DOUGLAS' BLUE-EYED-GRASS ❖
Origanum laevigatum 'Hopley's Purple'	ORNAMENTAL OREGANO
Origanum 'Xera Cascade'	XERA CASCADE OREGANO
Penstemon 'Burgundy Brew', 'Catherine de la Mare', 'Lavender Ruffles',	
'Midnight', 'Purple Passion', 'Raven', 'Sour Grapes'	BEARDTONGUE
Penstemon mexicali 'Pike's Peak Purple'	PENSTEMON
Penstemon serrulatus	CASCADE PENSTEMON, COAST PENSTEMON ❖
Primula beesiana	BEE'S CANDELABRA PRIMROSE
Primula capitata ssp. *mooreana*	PURPLE PRIMROSE
Primula denticulata	DRUMSTICK PRIMROSE*
Primula japonica	JAPANESE PRIMROSE*
Primula x *juliana*	JULIANA PRIMROSE*
Primula kisoana	KISOANA PRIMROSE
Pulmonaria 'Benediction'	LUNGWORT
Pulmonaria longifolia ssp. *cevennensis*	LONGLEAF LUNGWORT
Salvia barrelieri	BARRELIER'S SAGE
Salvia nemorosa	PURPLE WOOD SAGE
Salvia x *sylvestris*	BLUE MEADOW SAGE, BLUE WOOD SAGE*
Salvia transylvanica	TRANSYLVANIA SAGE
Salvia verticillata	LILAC SAGE
Sisyrinchium bellum	WESTERN BLUE-EYED GRASS❖
Thalictrum delavayi 'Hewitt's Double'	DOUBLE-FLOWERED MEADOW RUE
Trachelium caeruleum	THROATWORT, UMBRELLA FLOWER*
Tricyrtis formosana	FORMOSAN TOAD LILY
Tricyrtis 'Empress', 'Sinonome', 'Taipei Silk'	TOAD LILY
Verbena rigida	SLENDER VERVAIN, STIFF VERBENA
Veronica austriaca	SAW-LEAF SPEEDWELL
Veronicastrum sibericum	JAPANESE CULVER'S ROOT*
Viola adunca	EARLY BLUE VIOLET, WESTERN DOG VIOLET ❖
Viola alba ssp. *dehnhardtii*	PARMA VIOLET*

Bulbs

Allium amethystinum	AMETHYST ONION
Allium atropurpureum	ORNAMENTAL ONION
Allium cristophii	STAR OF PERSIA, PERSIAN ONION
Allium 'Firmament'	ORNAMENTAL ONION
Allium 'Gladiator'	ORNAMENTAL ONION
Allium 'Globemaster'	ORNAMENTAL ONION
Allium jesdianum	ORNAMENTAL ONION
Allium macleanii (A. elatum)	ORNAMENTAL ONION
Allium 'Mars'	ORNAMENTAL ONION
Allium 'Ostara'	ORNAMENTAL ONION
Allium 'Purple Sensation'	ORNAMENTAL ONION
Allium rosenbachianum	SHOWY ONION
Allium schubertii	TUMBLEWEED ONION
Allium sphaerocephalon	DRUMSTICKS
Arisarum proboscideum	MOUSE PLANT
Bellevalia (Muscari) pycnantha	GIANT GRAPE HYACINTH
Brodiaea californica	CALIFORNIA BRODIAEA
Brodiaea coronaria	CROWN BRODIAEA ❖
Brodiaea elegans ssp. *hooveri*	HARVEST LILY ❖
Colchicum 'Violet Queen'	VIOLET AUTUMN CROCUS
Corydalis solida	FUMEWORT*
Crocus chrysanthus and hybrids	SNOW CROCUS*
Crocus goulimyi	PELOPONNESE CROCUS*
Dahlia x *hybrida*	DAHLIA*
Dichelostemma congestum	OOKOW, FIELD CLUSTER LILY, HARVEST LILY ❖
Fritillaria persica	PERSIAN FRITILLARY
Gladiolus hybrids	GLADIOLUS*
Hyacinthella glabrescens	TURKISH HYACINTH
Hyacinthoides hispanica (NOT *H.* x *massartiana*)	SPANISH BLUEBELL*
Ipheion uniflorum	SPRING STARFLOWER*
Iris x hollandica	DUTCH IRIS*
Muscari latifolium	GRAPE HYACINTH
Oncostema (Scilla) peruviana	PORTUGUESE SQUILL
Oxalis purpurea	CAPE SORRELL*
Prospero (Scilla) autumnale	AUTUMN SQUILL
Pseudomuscari (Muscari, Bellavalia) forniculatum	TURKISH GRAPE HYACINTH
Triteleia grandiflora	LARGE-FLOWERED TRIPLET-LILY, WILD HYACINTH ❖
Triteleia (Brodiaea) hyacinthina	WHITE TRIPLET-LILY ❖*
Triteleia laxa 'Queen Fabiola'	ITHURIEL'S SPEAR
Tulipa saxatilis (T. bakeri)	CANDIA TULIP, ROCK TULIP

Annuals

Brachyscome iberidifolia	SWAN RIVER DAISY*
Calibrachoa hybrids	MILLION BELLS*
Callistephus chinensis	CHINA ASTER*
Catharanthus roseus	MADAGASCAR PERIWINKLE*

Cerinthe major purpurascens	BLUE HONEYWORT
Convolvulus tricolor	BUSH MORNING GLORY*
Dahlia x hybrida	DAHLIA*
Eustoma russellianum (E. grandiflorum; Lisianthus)	SWEET LISSIE, PRAIRIE GENTIAN*
Glandularia (Verbena) x hybrida	GARDEN VERBENA*
Heliotropium arborescens hybrid	HELIOTROPE*
Ipomoea tricolor (and more species)	MORNING GLORY*
Lathyrus odoratus	SWEET PEA*
Linaria maroccana	BABY SNAPDRAGON*
Lobelia erinus	LOBELIA*
Lobularia maritima	SWEET ALYSSUM*
Lophospermum (Asarina) scandens	CLIMBING SNAPDRAGON*
Lupinus mutabilis (L. hartwegii)	MEXICAN LUPINE*
Maurandella (Asarina) antirrhiniflora	VIOLET TWINING SNAPDRAGON
Nemophila maculata	FIVE-SPOT
Pericallis (Senecio) x hybridus	CINERARIA*
Petunia × atkinsiana	PETUNIA*
Primula x polyantha and Acaulis groups	ENGLISH PRIMROSE*
Primula sinensis	CHINESE PRIMROSE*
Salpiglossis sinuata	PAINTED TONGUE*
Salvia splendens	SCARLET SAGE*
Scabiosa atropurpurea	PINCUSHION FLOWER*
Schizanthus pinnatus, S. x wisetonensis	BUTTERFLY FLOWER*
Torenia fournieri	WISHBONE FLOWER*
Viola cornuta	VIOLA*
Viola tricolor	JOHNNY-JUMP-UP*
Viola x wittrockiana	PANSY*
Wulfenia x schwarzii	WULFENIA
Zinnia elegans (best in hottest areas only)	ZINNIA*

MAGENTA/BURGUNDY
Including "chocolate," mahogany, maroon, and near-black

Perennials

Chrysanthemum x morifolium	MUM*
Coreopsis 'Limerock Beauty'	HYBRID TICKSEED
Dianthus deltoides	MAIDEN PINK*
Dierama pulcherrimum and hybrids	FAIRY WAND, WAND FLOWER*
Dierama reynoldsii	ANGEL'S FISHING ROD
Epimedium epsteinii	BISHOP'S HAT
Geranium cinereum	HARDY GERANIUM*
Geranium sanguineum	BLOODY CRANESBILL
Helianthemum nummularium 'Dazzler', 'Mesa Wine', 'Raspberry Ripple'	SUNROSE
Helleborus x hybridus	LENTEN ROSE*
Helleborus x sternii	HYBRID HELLEBORE*
Hemerocallis (many)	DAYLILIES*

314

Iris Pacific Coast hybrids	PACIFIC COAST IRIS*
Iris siberica	SIBERIAN IRIS*
Knautia macedonica	KNAUTIA, MACEDONIAN SCABIOUS
Penstemon 'Bev Jensen', 'Blackbird', 'Enor', 'Raspberry Flair', 'Ruby' BEARDTONGUE	
Penstemon kunthii	MEXICAN BEARDTONGUE
Phygelius 'New Sensation'	CAPE FUCHSIA
Primula auricula/hirsuta hybrids	BEARS' EARS*
Primula pulverulenta	RED CANDELABRA PRIMROSE
Tricyrtis hirta 'Miyazaki'	JAPANESE TOAD LILY

Bulbs

Allium amethystinum 'Red Mohican'	RED MOHICAN ORNAMENTAL ONION
Arisaema kishidae	JAPANESE COBRA-LILY
Arisaema consanguineum	HIMALAYAN COBRA LILY
Arisaema sikokianum	JAPANESE COBRA LILY
Arisaema triphyllum	JACK-IN-THE-PULPIT
Arisarum proboscideum	MOUSE PLANT
Corydalis solida	FUMEWORT*
Cyclamen hederifolium	HARDY CYCLAMEN*
Dahlia x *hybrida*	DAHLIA*
Dracunculus vulgaris	VOODOO LILY
Fritillaria assyriaca	TURKISH FRITILLARY
Fritillaria bucharica 'Giant'	RUSSIAN FRITILLARY
Fritillaria camschatcensis	BLACK SARANA
Fritillaria affinis (F. lanceolata)	CHOCOLATE LILY
Fritillaria michailovskyi	MICHAEL'S FLOWER
Fritillaria pontica	PONTIC FRITILLARY
Gladiolus communis var. *byzantinus*	BYZANTINE GLADIOLUS
Gladiolus hybrids	GLADIOLUS*
Lilium Asiatic hybrids	ASIATIC LILY*
Lilium martagon and hybrids	MARTAGON LILY*
Lilium nepalense	NEPAL LILY
Tigridia pavonia	TIGER FLOWER, MEXICAN SHELL FLOWER*
Trillium chloropetalum	GIANT WAKE ROBIN
Trillium cuneatum	WOOD-LILY
Trillium kurabayashii	GIANT PURPLE WAKEROBIN

Annuals

Ageratum houstonianum	FLOSS FLOWER*
Agrostemma gracilis 'Purple Queen'	CORNCOCKLE
Alcea ficifolia	ANTWERP HOLLYHOCK*
Antirrhinum majus	SNAPDRAGON*
Aquilegia x *hybrida*	COLUMBINE*
Aquilegia vulgaris	ENGLISH COLUMBINE*
Calibrachoa hybrids	MILLION BELLS*

Callistephus chinensis	CHINA ASTER*
Catharanthus roseus	MADAGASCAR PERIWINKLE*
Centaurea cyanus	CORNFLOWER, BACHELORS' BUTTONS*
Cosmos bipinnatus	COSMOS*
Dahlia x hybrida	DAHLIA*
Dorotheanthus bellidiformis	LIVINGSTONE DAISY*
Glandularia (Verbena) x hybrida	GARDEN VERBENA*
Impatiens walleriana	IMPATIENS*
Lathyrus odoratus	SWEET PEA*
Linaria reticulata 'Velvet Red'	SPANISH TOADFLAX
Lobelia erinus	LOBELIA*
Matthiola incana	STOCK*
Petunia × atkinsiana	PETUNIA*
Phlox drummondii	ANNUAL PHLOX*
Primula x polyantha and Acaulis groups	ENGLISH PRIMROSE*
Primula sinensis	CHINESE PRIMROSE*
Salpiglossis sinuata	PAINTED TONGUE*
Salvia splendens	SCARLET SAGE*
Scabiosa atropurpurea	PINCUSHION FLOWER*
Torenia fournieri	WISHBONE FLOWER*
Viola x wittrockiana	PANSY*
Zinnia elegans (best in hottest areas only)	ZINNIA*

COLORFUL FOLIAGE

With the exception of common annuals, almost all flowering plants have a relatively short blooming season, usually less than four weeks. The rest of the year such plants are, as would be expected, just green. And not necessarily an exciting green. It's easy to add more "color" to the landscape with the following plants which offer their kind of color eight to twelve months of the year.

BLUE/SILVER (TO NEAR WHITE) FOLIAGE

Abies pinsapo 'Glauca'	BLUE SPANISH FIR
Abies procera 'Glauca'	BLUE NOBLE FIR
Abies procera 'Jeddeloh'	DWARF BLUE NOBLE FIR
Achillea clavennae	SILVER YARROW
Aciphylla glaucescens	BLUE SPEARGRASS
Aesculus hippocastanum 'Wisselink'	WISSELINK HORSE CHESTNUT
Agave ovatifolia 'Frosty Blue'	FROSTY BLUE AGAVE
Agave x *ovatispina* 'Blue Rapture'	BLUE RAPTURE HYBRID CENTURY PLANT
Agave parryi ssp. *neomexicana*	NEW MEXICO HARDY CENTURY PLANT
Agropyron magellanicum	CHILEAN BLUE WHEAT GRASS
Allium karataviense	TURKESTAN ONION
Antirrhinum glutinosum	GUMMY SNAPDRAGON
Arctostaphylos glandulosa ssp. *glandulosa* 'Demeter'	DEMETER OREGON MANZANITA ❖
Arctostaphylos silvicola 'Ghostly'	GHOSTLY BONNY DUNE MANZANITA
Artemisia abrotanum	SOUTHERNWOOD
Artemisia versicolor 'Sea Foam'	CURLICUE SAGE
Athyrium (Anisocampium) nipponicum silver-patterned cultivars	JAPANESE PAINTED FERN
Borinda contracta	BLUE MOUNTAIN BAMBOO
Brachyglottis 'Otari Cloud'	OTARI CLOUD DAISY BUSH
Brunnera macrophylla 'Jack Frost', 'Looking Glass'	SIBERIAN BUGLOSS
Bukiniczia cabulica	VARIEGATED STATICE
Caryopteris x *clandonensis* 'Sterling Silver'	STERLING SILVER BLUEBEARD
Centaurea dealbata	PERSIAN CORNFLOWER
Chamaecyparis lawsoniana 'Chilworth Silver'	SILVER BLUE LAWSON'S CYPRESS
Chamaecyparis lawsoniana 'Oregon Blue'	OREGON BLUE LAWSON CYPRESS
Chamaecyparis pisifera 'Iceberg'	ICEBERG SAWARA FALSE CYPRESS
Chamaerops humilis var. *cerifera*	BLUE MEDITERRANEAN FAN PALM
Chrysanthemum 'Snow Dome'	SNOW DOME MUM
Corynephorus canescens 'Spiky Blue'	BLUE HAIR GRASS
Cylindropuntia echinocarpa 'Silver Fox'	SILVER CHOLLA
Dianthus arenarius	SAND PINK
Dianthus 'Blue Hills'	BLUE HILLS CHEDDAR PINK
Dianthus caryophyllus and hybrids	CARNATIONS, PINKS
Dianthus plumarius	COTTAGE PINK
Dudleya farinosa	CHALKY LIVE-FOREVER
Echinops ritro	GLOBE THISTLE
Echinops ritro ssp. *ruthenicus*	SMALL GLOBE THISTLE
Edraianthus pumilio	SILVERY DWARF HAREBELL
Erodium chrysanthum	HERONSBILL, STORKSBILL

Eryngium giganteum 'Silver Ghost' (biennial)	SILVER GHOST
Geranium harveyi	SILVER GERANIUM
Hebe pinguifolia 'Sutherlandii'	BLUE-LEAF HEBE
Hebe topiaria	HEBE
Helichrysum arenarium	SANDY EVERLASTING
Helichrysum splendidum	CAPE GOLD
Helictotrichon sempervirens	BLUE OAT GRASS
Helleborus argutifolius	CORSICAN HELLEBORE
Helleborus x *ericsmithii* 'Silver Moon'	HYBRID HELLEBORE
Helleborus x *sternii*, e.g. 'Silver Dollar', "Broughton Beauty Strain"	HYBRID HELLEBORE
Hesperocyparis (Cupressus) arizonica cultivars	ARIZONA CYPRESS
Heuchera many cultivars	CORAL BELLS
Hosta 'Blue Angel', 'Blue Mouse Ears', 'Fragrant Blue', 'Halcyon'	BLUE HOSTA
Hosta sieboldiana var. *elegans*	HOSTA
Hylotelephium (Sedum) cauticola 'Lidakense'	LIDAKENSE CLIFF STONECROP
Hylotelephium (Sedum) sieboldii	OCTOBER DAPHNE SEDUM
Juncus patens 'Elk Blue', 'Occidental Blue'	SPREADING RUSH ❖
Leptospermum myrtifolium 'Silver Form'	SILVER CUNNINGHAM'S TEA TREE
Leptospermum sericeum	SILVER TEA TREE
Lupinus albifrons	SILVER-LEAF LUPINE ❖
Mahonia eurybracteata 'Cistus Silvers'	SILVER MAHONIA
Melianthus major 'Antonow's Blue'	BLUE HONEY BUSH
Oenothera macrocarpa ssp. *incana*	SILVER BLADE EVENING PRIMROSE
Olearia moschata	INCENSE PLANT
Papaver somniferum	PEONY POPPY
Pinus parviflora Glauca Group	BLUE-NEEDLED JAPANESE WHITE PINE
Podocarpus lawrencei 'Blue Gem'	BLUE MOUNTAIN PLUM-PINE
Phlebodium pseudoaureum (Polypodium areolatum)	BLUE RABBIT'S FOOT FERN
Rhododendron 'Snowbird'	SNOWBIRD AZALEA
Sedum spathulifolium 'Cape Blanco'	SPOON-LEAF STONECROP ❖
Sequoiadendron giganteum 'Glaucum'	BLUE-NEEDLED GIANT SEQUOIA
Tanacetum ptarmiciflorum	SILVER LACE PLANT
Thamnocalamus crassinodus 'Mendocino'	KNOBBY TIBETAN BAMBOO
Tsuga mertensiana 'Elizabeth'	DWARF MOUNTAIN HEMLOCK
Vaccinium 'Sunshine Blue'	BLUEBERRY
Veronica (Parahebe) perfoliata	DIGGER'S SPEEDWELL
Veronica spicata ssp. *incana* 'Pure Silver'	SILVER SPEEDWELL
Yucca cernua	NODDING SOAPWORT
Yucca rostrata 'Sapphire Skies'	SAPPHIRE SKIES BEAKED BLUE YUCCA
Yucca 'Silver Anniversary'	SILVER ANNIVERSARY SOAPWORT
Yushania (Borinda) boliana	HIMALAYAN BLUE MOUNTAIN BAMBOO

For "white" foliage, see "FUZZY, FURRY, WOOLLY, TOUCHY-FEELY FOLIAGE"

PURPLE, BRONZE, BLACKISH, COPPERY FOLIAGE

Acer palmatum 'Red Dragon', 'Tamuke yama', 'Wolff'   RED JAPANESE MAPLE
Actaea simplex 'Black Negligee', 'Brunette', 'Hillside Black Beauty'
                                                     PURPLE-LEAF SNAKEROOT
Ageratina altissima 'Chocolate'   SNAKEROOT
Berberis x *ottawensis* 'Royal Cloak'   PURPLE-LEAF JAPANESE BARBERRY
Berberis thunbergii f. *atropurpurea* many cultivars
                                       PURPLE-LEAF JAPANESE BARBERRY
Berberis thunbergii 'Rose Glow'   VARIEGATED JAPANESE BARBERRY
Betula x 'Royal Frost'   ROYAL FROST BIRCH
Calluna vulgaris 'Firefly', 'Spring Torch'   HEATHER
Carex tenuiculmis 'Cappuccino'   COFFEE SEDGE
Catalpa erubescens 'Purpurea'   PURPLE-LEAF CHINESE CATALPA
Cercis canadensis 'Forest Pansy'   FOREST PANSY REDBUD
Coleus (Plectranthus) argentatus   SILVER SPURFLOWER
Corylus avellana 'Red Dragon'   PURPLE LEAF CONTORTED FILBERT
Cotinus coggygria 'Royal Purple' (and others)   PURPLE SMOKEBUSH
Cotinus coggygria 'Winecraft Black'   BLACK SMOKE TREE
Cotinus 'Grace'   PURPLE SMOKEBUSH
Daphne x *houtteana* 'February Plum'   FEBRUARY PLUM DAPHNE
Disporum longistylum 'Night Heron'   CHINESE FAIRY BELLS
Dysosma (Podophyllum) 'Red Panda'   RED PANDA MAYAPPLE
Epimedium 'Black Sea'   HYBRID EPIMEDIUM
Epimedium grandiflorum 'Queen Esta'   BARRENWORT
Eucomis comosa 'Sparkling Burgundy'   PINEAPPLE LILY
Fagus sylvatica f. *atropurpurea*   COPPER BEECH
Fagus sylvatica 'Dawyck Purple', 'Rohan Obelisk' COLUMNAR PURPLE BEECH
Fagus sylvatica 'Riversii'   RIVERS' PURPLE BEECH
Fagus sylvatica 'Rohanii'   CUT-LEAF PURPLE BEECH
Geranium pratense 'Boom Chocolatta'   CHOCOLATTA GERANIUM
Heuchera 'Crimson Curls', 'Plum Pudding', 'Purple Petticoats', 'Sashay',
   'Velvet Night' among many others   PURPLE LEAF CORAL BELLS
Hibiscus 'Midnight Marvel'   BRONZE-LEAVED HIBISCUS
Hylotelephium (Sedum) 'Bertram Anderson', 'Cherry Tart', 'Dark Magic',
   'Purple Emperor'   STONECROP, SEDUM
Hylotelephium telephium ssp. *telephium* 'Red Cauli'   RED CAULI BORDER SEDUM
Hylotelephium (Sedum) 'Vera Jameson'   VERA JAMESON SEDUM
Leucothoe axillaris 'Curly Red'   RED DOG HOBBLE
Leycesteria crocothyrsos   YELLOW HIMALAYAN HONEYSUCKLE
Oxalis spiralis ssp. *vulcanicola* 'Plum Crazy'   PLUM CRAZY VOLCANIC SORREL
Osmanthus heterophyllus 'Purpureus'   PURPLE FALSE HOLLY
Physocarpus opulifolius 'Center Glow', 'Diabolo', 'Summer Wine'   PURPLE NINEBARK
Sambucus nigra 'Black Beauty'   PURPLE-LEAF BLACK ELDER
Sambucus nigra 'Black Prince', 'Black Lace'   PURPLE CUT-LEAF ELDERBERRY
Sempervivum arachnoideum ssp. *tomentosum* 'Stansfieldii'   HEN-AND-CHICKS
Yucca aloifolia 'Magenta Magic'   MAGENTA MAGIC YUCCA

GOLDEN/YELLOW FOLIAGE

Acanthus mollis 'Hollard's Gold'	GOLDEN BEAR'S BREECH
Acer shirasawanum 'Jordan'	GOLDEN FULL MOON MAPLE
Acorus gramineus 'Golden Lion'	GOLDEN SWEET FLAG
Aralia cordata 'Sun King'	SUN KING SPIKENARD
Baptisia 'IndiGold'	GOLDEN FALSE INDIGO
Berberis thunbergii 'Golden Carpet', 'Pow-Wow', 'Sunsation'	GOLDEN BARBERRY
Campanula garganica 'Dickson's Gold'	GOLD-LEAF ADRIATIC BELLFLOWER
Campanula portenschlagiana 'Aurea'	GOLDEN DALMATIAN BELLFLOWER
Carex elata 'Aurea'	BOWLE'S GOLDEN SEDGE
Chamaecyparis pisifera 'Filifera Aurea Nana'	DWARF GOLDEN THREADLEAF CYPRESS
Choisya ternata 'Goldfinger', 'Sundance'	MEXICAN ORANGE
Cornus sericea 'Hedgerows Gold'	GOLDEN RED-TWIG DOGWOOD
Corylopsis spicata 'Aurea'	GOLDEN-LEAF WINTERHAZEL
Corylopsis spicata 'Golden Spring'	GOLDEN WINTERHAZEL
Cotinus coggygria 'Golden Spirit'	GOLDEN SMOKETREE
Cryptomeria japonica 'Sekkan-sugi'	GOLDEN JAPANESE CEDAR
Fagus sylvatica 'Aurea Pendula'	GOLDEN WEEPING EUROPEAN BEECH
Lamprocapnos (Dicentra) spectabilis 'Gold Heart'	GOLD-LEAF BLEEDING HEART
Filipendula ulmaria 'Aurea'	GOLDEN MEADOWSWEET
Fuchsia genii 'Aurea'	GOLDEN HARDY FUCHSIA
Fuchsia magellanica 'Aurea'	GOLDEN FUCHSIA
Hakonechloa macra 'All Gold'	GOLDEN JAPANESE FOREST GRASS
Hakonechloa macra 'Aureola'	GOLD VARIEGATED JAPANESE FOREST GRASS
Hebe odora 'New Zealand Gold'	GOLDEN HEBE
Heuchera 'Citronelle', 'Lemon Love', 'Pretty Pistachio'	HEUCHERA
Hosta 'Age of Gold', 'Banana Puddin', 'Lemon Lime', 'Sum and Substance', 'Sun Power', 'Sun Mouse'	HOSTA
Humulus lupulus 'Aureus'	GOLDEN HOPS
Jasminum officinale 'Frojas'	FIONA SUNRISE JASMINE
Laurus nobilis 'Sicilian Sunshine'	GOLDEN BAY LAUREL
Leucosceptrum (Comanthosphace) japonicum 'Golden Angel'	GOLDEN ANGEL JAPANESE SHRUB MINT
Liriope muscari 'Peedee Ingot'	GOLDEN LIRIOPE
Lonicera ligustrina var. *yunnanensis* (*L. nitida*) 'Baggesen's Gold'	GOLDEN BOX-LEAF HONEYSUCKLE
Parthenocissus tricuspidata 'Fenway Park'	GOLDEN BOSTON IVY
Philadelphus coronarius 'Aureus'	GOLDEN MOCK ORANGE
Physocarpus opulifolius 'Dart's Gold', 'Nugget'	GOLDEN NINEBARK
Picea orientalis 'Aureospicata'	GOLDEN CAUCASIAN SPRUCE
Sambucus nigra 'Aurea'	GOLDEN BLACK ELDERBERRY
Sambucus racemosa 'Plumosa Aurea'	GOLDEN RED ELDERBERRY
Saxifraga stolonifera 'Harvest Moon'	GOLDEN STRAWBERRY BEGONIA
Sedum makinoi 'Ogon'	GOLDEN JAPANESE SEDUM
Spiraea japonica 'Gold Mound', Magic Carpet	JAPANESE SPIREA
Spiraea thunbergii 'Ogon'	GOLDEN BRIDALWREATH SPIREA
Trachystemon orientalis 'Sundew'	SUNDEW BLACK SEA COMFREY

VARIEGATED FOLIAGE

Acanthus mollis 'Tasmanian Angel'	VARIEGATED BEAR'S BREECH
Acer palmatum 'Shirazz'	PINK-VARIEGATED JAPANESE MAPLE
Acorus gramineus 'Ogon'	GOLDEN VARIEGATED SWEETFLAG
Actinidia tetramera var. *maloides*	ROSY CRABAPPLE KIWI
Amicia zygomeris 'John's Big Splash'	VARIEGATED YOKE-LEAVED AMICIA
Aspidistra elatior 'Lennon's Song', 'Sekko Kan', 'Snow Cap'	CAST IRON PLANT
Aspidistra ibanensis 'Flowing Fountains'	FLOWING FOUNTAINS CAST IRON PLANT
Aspidistra sichuanensis 'Spek-Tacular'	CHINESE CAST IRON PLANT
Aspidistra zongbayi	YUNNAN SUNBEAM
Astilbe chinensis 'Amber Moon'	AMBER MOON ASTILBE
Aucuba japonica many cultivars	JAPANESE LAUREL
Azara microphylla 'Variegata'	VARIEGATED BOX-LEAF AZARA
Bergenia 'Tubby Andrews''	TUBBY ANDREWS BERGENIA
Callianthe (Abutilon) megapotamica 'Variegata'	
	VARIEGATED BRAZILIAN BELLFLOWER
Camellia sinensis 'Variegata'	VARIEGATED TEA
Camellia sinensis var. *sinensis* 'Gold Splash'	GOLD SPLASH TEA
Cornus controversa 'Variegata'	WEDDING CAKE TREE
Cornus kousa 'Gold Star'	GOLD STAR DOGWOOD
Cornus kousa 'Sunsplash'	SUNSPLASH DOGWOOD
Cornus kousa 'Wolf Eyes'	WOLF EYES DOGWOOD
Cornus x *rutgersensis* 'Celestial Shadow'	CELESTIAL SHADOW DOGWOOD
Cornus x *rutgersensis* 'Stellar Pink'	STELLAR PINK DOGWOOD
Davidia involucrata 'Lady Sunshine'	VARIEGATED DOVE TREE
Disporum longistylum 'Moonlight'	MOONLIGHT SOLOMON SEAL
Elaeagnus x *submacrophylla* (*E.* x *ebbingei*) 'Gilt Edge'	
	VARIEGATED HYBRID ELAEAGNUS
Elaeagnus pungens 'Maculata'	GOLDEN ELAEAGNUS
Eucryphia lucida 'Spring Glow'	SPRING GLOW TASMANIAN LEATHERWOOD
Farfugium japonicum many cultivars	LEOPARD PLANT
Fargesia dracocephala 'White Dragon'	STRIPED DRAGON'S HEAD BAMBOO
X *Fatshedera lizei* 'Annemieke'	GOLDEN VARIEGATED FATSHEDERA
X *Fatshedera lizei* 'Variegata'	VARIEGATED FATSHEDERA
Fatsia japonica 'Annelise', 'Murakumo nishiki' ('Camouflage'), 'Spider's Web', 'Variegata'	VARIEGATED JAPANESE FATSIA
Filipendula palmata 'Variegata'	VARIEGATED SIBERIAN MEADOWSWEET
Forsythia x *intermedia* 'Fiesta'	VARIEGATED FORSYTHIA
Fuchsia fulgens 'Variegata'	VARIEGATED BRILLIANT FUCHSIA
Fuchsia procumbens 'Variegata'	VARIEGATED CREEPING FUCHSIA
Gaultheria procumbens 'Winter Splash'	VARIEGATED WINTERGREEN
Hakonechloa macra 'Albovariegata'	VARIEGATED JAPANESE FOREST GRASS
Hebe albicans 'Pink Elephant'	PINK ELEPHANT HEBE
Hedera algeriensis 'Glorie de Marengo'	VARIEGATED ALGERIAN IVY
Hedera colchica 'Dentata Variegata'	VARIEGATED PERSIAN IVY
Hedychium 'Vanilla Ice'	VANILLA ICE HARDY GINGER LILY

Hosta many cultivars	HOSTAS
Hydrangea serrata 'O-amacha Nishiki'	GOLD DUST MOUNTAIN HYDRANGEA
Hylotelephium (Sedum) 'Autumn Charm'	AUTUMN CHARM STONECROP
Hylotelephium erythrostictum (Sedum alboroseum) 'Mediovariegatum'	GOLD-SPOT SEDUM
Hylotelephium (Sedum) sieboldii f. *variegatum*	VARIEGATED OCTOBER DAPHNE
Hylotelephium (Sedum) sieboldii 'Mediovariegatum'	GOLD-SPOT OCTOBER DAPHNE
Hylotelephium (Sedum) spectabile 'Frosty Morn'	F. M. OCTOBER DAPHNE
Iris pallida 'Argentea Variegata'	VARIEGATED DALMATIAN IRIS
Iris pallida 'Variegata' ('Aureovariegata')	GOLDEN VARIEGATED DALMATIAN IRIS
Jasminum nudiflorum 'Argenteovariegatum'	VARIEGATED WINTER JASMINE
Jasminum officinale 'Argenteovariegatum'	VARIEGATED JASMINE
Linnaea (Abelia) x *grandiflora* 'Kaleidoscope'	GOLD-VARIEGATED ABELIA
Lonicera x *italica* 'Sherlite'	HARLEQUIN HONEYSUCKLE
Lonicera ligustrina var. *yunnanensis (L. nitida)* 'Lemon Beauty'	
	LEMON BEAUTY BOX-LEAF HONEYSUCKLE
Loropetalum chinense 'Irodori' ('Jazz Hands')	VARIEGATED FRINGE FLOWER
Metasequoia glyptostroboides 'North Light'	DWARF VARIEGATED DAWN REDWOOD
Miscanthus sinensis 'Gold Bar'	COMPACT VARIEGATED MAIDEN GRASS
Molinia caerulea ssp. *caerulea* 'Variegata'	VARIEGATED PURPLE MOOR GRASS
Osmanthus heterophyllus 'Variegatus'	VARIEGATED FALSE HOLLY
Parthenocissus quinquefolia 'Star Showers'	VARIEGATED VIRGINIA CREEPER
Phedimus (Sedum) kamtschaticus 'Variegatus'	VARIEGATED KAMSCHATKA SEDUM
Phedimus (Sedum) spurius 'Tricolor'	TRICOLOR SEDUM
Phedimus (Sedum) spurius 'Variegatus'	VARIEGATED TWO-ROW STONECROP
Phlox glaberrima 'Triple Play'	TRIPLE PLAY PHLOX
Pieris japonica 'Variegata'	VARIEGATED LILY-OF-THE-VALLEY SHRUB
Rhododendron 'Molten Gold'	VARIEGATED RHODODENDRON
Rhododendron 'Red and Gold'	VARIEGATED RHODODENDRON
Salix integra 'Hakuro-nishiki', 'Flamingo'	DAPPLED WILLOW
Saxifraga stolonifera 'Tricolor'	TRICOLOR STRAWBERRY BEGONIA
Scrophularia auriculata 'Variegata'	VARIEGATED WATER FIGWORT
Sedum 'Frosted Fire'	FROSTED FIRE SEDUM
Sedum makinoi 'Variegatum'	VARIEGATED JAPANESE SEDUM
Sedum selskianum 'Variegatum'	VARIEGATED AMUR STONECROP
Sedum takesimense 'Atlantis'	ATLANTIS SEDUM
Umbilicus (Chiastophyllum) oppositifolium 'Jim's Pride'	VARIEGATED LAMB'S TAIL
Vaccinium ovatum 'Cascade Sunburst'	VARIEGATED EVERGREEN HUCKLEBERRY
Veronica gentianoides 'Variegata'	VARIEGATED SPEEDWELL
Yucca aloifolia 'Mediopicta'	YELLOW-CENTERED SPANISH DAGGER
Yucca filamentosa 'Bright Edge', 'Color Guard', 'Variegata'	VARIEGATED YUCCA
Yucca flaccida 'Golden Sword'	VARIEGATED YUCCA
Yucca flaccida 'Wilder's Wonderful'	WILDER'S WONDERFUL FLACCID SOAPWORT
Yucca x *gloriosa* 'Variegata'	VARIEGATED MOUND-LILY SOAPWORT
Zingiber mioga 'Dancing Crane', 'White Feather'	JAPANESE GINGER

FALL FOLIAGE

These are the candidates for the "Autumn Color" many of us cherish for the nostalgia or romance as much as for the seasonal interest. Mostly shrubs, with some smallish trees and a few vines.

Acer 'Northern Glow'	NORTHERN GLOW MAPLE
Acer buergerianum	TRIDENT MAPLE
Acer circinatum 'Del's Dwarf', 'Little Gem', 'Pacific Sprite'	DWARF VINE MAPLE ❖
Acer circinatum especially 'Pacific Fire', 'Pacific Purple'	VINE MAPLE ❖
Acer glabrum var. *douglasii*	DOUGLAS MAPLE ❖
Acer griseum	PAPER-BARK MAPLE
Acer japonicum	AMUR MAPLE
Acer palmatum var. *dissectum* 'Viridis', 'Seiryu'	CUT-LEAF JAPANESE MAPLE
Acer palmatum 'Aka Kawa', 'Asagi Nichiki', 'Bonfire', 'Cornara Pygmy', 'Killarney', 'Koto Maru', 'Sharp's Pygmy', 'Winter Gold', 'Yellowbird')	
	DWARF JAPANESE MAPLE
Acer palmatum 'Bloodgood', 'Higasayama', 'Kihachijo', 'Osakazuki', 'Orido nishiki', 'Sango Kaku'	
	JAPANESE MAPLE
Acer pseudosieboldianum	KOREAN MAPLE
Acer shirasawanum 'Autumn Moon', 'Junihitoe', Moonrise', 'Sensu', 'Yasemin'	
	FULL-MOON MAPLE
Acer tataricum ssp. *ginnala* 'Flame'	AMUR MAPLE
Amelanchier alnifolia	WESTERN SERVICEBERRY, JUNEBERRY, SASKATOON ❖
Amelanchier alnifolia var. *pumila*	DWARF SERVICEBERRY ❖
Amelanchier x *grandiflora* 'Autumn Brilliance'	JUNEBERRY, SERVICEBERRY
Aronia melanocarpa 'Autumn Magic'	AUTUMN MAGIC BLACK CHOKEBERRY
Berberis koreana	KOREAN BARBERRY
Berberis jamesiana 'Exuberant'	JAMES' BARBERRY
Cercidiphyllum japonicum	KATSURA
Cladrastis kentukea	AMERICAN YELLOWWOOD
Clethra acuminata	CINNAMON CLETHRA
Clethra alnifolia	SUMMERSWEET
Cornus kousa and hybrids	KOREAN DOGWOOD
Cornus alba 'Kesselringii'	BLACK-TWIG DOGWOOD
Cornus sericea 'Bailey'	RED-OSIER DOGWOOD ❖
Cotinus 'Grace'	HYBRID SMOKETREE
Cotinus obovatus	AMERICAN SMOKETREE
Cotoneaster franchettii	GRAY COTONEASTER
Crataegus douglasii	DOUGLAS HAWTHORN ❖
Crataegus gaylussacia (*C. suksdorfii*)	KLAMATH HAWTHORN ❖
Diospyros kaki 'Ichi-Ki-Kei-Jiro', 'Izu'	DWARF PERSIMMON
Diospyros kaki many cultivars	JAPANESE PERSIMMON
Disanthus cercidifolius	REDBUD HAZEL
Enkianthus campanulatus	ENKIANTHUS
Enkianthus perulatus	WHITE ENKIANTHUS
Fothergilla 'Mount Airy'	WITCH ALDER
Fothergilla gardenii	DWARF WITCH ALDER
Franklinia alatamaha	FRANKLIN TREE

Fraxinus angustifolia 'Raywoodii'	RAYWOOD ASH
Ginkgo biloba 'Saratoga', 'Tremonia'	GINKGO
Ginkgo biloba 'Jade Butterflies', 'Spring Grove', 'Troll'	DWARF GINKGO
Hamamelis x *intermedia*	HYBRID WITCH-HAZEL
Hamamelis mollis	CHINESE WITCH-HAZEL
Hydrangea anomala	CLIMBING HYDRANGEA
Hydrangea petiolaris	CLIMBING HYDRANGEA
Hydrangea quercifolia	OAK-LEAF HYDRANGEA
Itea virginica	SWEETSPIRE
Lindera benzoin	SPICEBUSH
Lindera erythrocarpa	RED-BERRY SPICEBUSH
Lonicera involucrata	BLACK TWINBERRY ❖
Malus 'Adam'	CRABAPPLE
Nyssa sylvatica 'Wild Fire'	SOUR GUM
Oxydendrum arboreum	SOURWOOD
Parrotia persica	PERSIAN IRONWOOD
Parrotia subaequalis	CHINESE IRONWOOD
Parrotiopsis jacquemontiana	HATAB
Parthenocissus henryana	SILVER-VEIN CREEPER
Parthenocissus quinquefolia	VIRGINIA CREEPER
Parthenocissus tricuspidata	BOSTON IVY
Pistacia chinensis	CHINESE PISTACHE
Rhododendron menziesii (*Menziesia ferruginea*)	RUSTY MENZIESIA
Rhus aromatica 'Gro-Low'	FRAGRANT SUMAC
Rhus glabra	SMOOTH SUMAC
Rhus trilobata	SKUNKBUSH SUMAC
Rhus typhina 'Tiger Eyes'	DWARF SUMAC
Sambucus racemosa	RED ELDERBERRY ❖
Sorbus hupehensis 'Coral Cascade'	CHINESE ROWAN
Sorbus sargentiana	SARGENT'S MOUNTAIN ASH
Sorbus verrucosa var. *subulata*	VIETNAM MOUNTAIN ASH
Spiraea betulifolia	BIRCH-LEAF SPIREA ❖
Spiraea prunifolia	BRIDAL WREATH
Stachyurus praecox	STACHYURUS
Stewartia pseudocamellia	JAPANESE STEWARTIA
Styrax japonicus	JAPANESE SNOWBELL
Symphoricarpos albus	SNOWBERRY ❖
Tetracentron sinense	TETRACENTRON
Tilia cordata 'Summer Sprite'	LITTLELEAF LINDEN
Viburnum carlesii	KOREAN SPICE
Viburnum edule	HIGHBUSH CRANBERRY
Viburnum ellipticum	OVAL-LEAF VIBURNUM
Viburnum nudum	SMOOTH WINTEROD
Viburnum plicatum f. *tomentosum*	DOUBLE-FILE VIBURNUM
Viburnum trilobum (*V. opulus* var. *americanum*)	AMERICAN CRANBERRYBUSH ❖
Vitis coignetiae	CRIMSON GLORY VINE
Vitis vinifera 'Incana'	DUSTY MILLER GRAPE VINE

STRIKING EVERGREEN FOLIAGE

Among the many plants which hold onto the bulk of their foliage twelve months of the year all year long, there are these special lovelies which do so with style. If you're going to have a blob of green in the landscape, it might as well be something with added interest.

CONIFERS

Araucaria araucana	MONKEY PUZZLE TREE
Chamaecyparis obtusa 'Filicoides'	FERN-SPRAY HINOKI CYPRESS
Chamaecyparis obtusa 'Gracilis'	HINOKI CYPRESS
Chamaecyparis obtusa 'Spiralis'	SPIRAL HINOKI CYPRESS
Cryptomeria japonica 'Cristata'	CRESTED JAPANESE CEDAR
Fokienia (Chamaecyparis) hodginsii	FUJIAN CYPRESS
Pinus parviflora Glauca Group	BLUE-NEEDLED JAPANESE WHITE PINE
Pinus wallichiana	HIMALAYAN WHITE PINE
Sciadopitys verticillata	JAPANESE UMBRELLA PINE

BROADLEAVED EVERGREENS

Acer laevigatum 'Hóng Lóng'	RED DRAGON EVERGREEN CHINESE MAPLE
Aucuba japonica many cultivars	JAPANESE LAUREL
Azara microphylla	BOX-LEAF AZARA, CHINCHIN
Berberidopsis corallina	CORAL PLANT
Berberis darwinii	DARWIN'S BARBERRY
Berberis julianae	WINTERGREEN BARBERRY
Berberis verruculosa	WARTY BARBERRY
Butia odorata (B. capitata)	JELLY PALM, PINDO PALM
Danae racemosa	POET'S LAUREL
Desfontainia spinosa	CHILEAN HOLLY
Eucryphia moorei	PINKWOOD, PLUMWOOD, EASTERN LEATHERWOOD
X *Fatshedera lizei*	FATSHEDERA
Fatsia japonica	JAPANESE FATSIA
Fatsia polycarpa	FALSE CASTOR OIL PLANT
Hoheria angustifolia	NARROW-LEAVED LACEBARK
Mahonia eurybracteata 'Soft Caress'	SOFT CARESS MAHONIA
Mahonia gracilipes	CHINESE MAHONIA
Mahonia x media	HYBRID MAHONIA
Mahonia nervosa	CASCADE OREGON-GRAPE ❖
Metapanax (Dendropanax) delavayi	DELAVAY'S FALSE GINSENG
Osmanthus delavayi	SWEET OLIVE
Osmanthus heterophyllus cultivars, especially 'Goshiki'	FALSE HOLLY
Polylepis australis	TABAQUILLO, QUEÑOA
Quercus hypoleucoides	SILVERLEAF OAK
Quercus myrsinifolia	CHINESE EVERGREEN OAK
Rhododendron ambiguum	RHODODENDRON

Rhododendron brachycarpum	RHODODENDRON
Rhododendron bureavii	RHODODENDRON
Rhododendron calophytum	RHODODENDRON
Rhododendron caucasicum	RHODODENDRON
Rhododendron dauricum	RHODODENDRON
Rhododendron degronianum ssp. *yakushimanum*	RHODODENDRON
Rhododendron 'Everred'	RHODODENDRON
Rhododendron falconeri	RHODODENDRON
Rhododendron falconeri ssp. *eximeum*	RHODODENDRON
Rhododendron 'Fastigiatum'	RHODODENDRON
Rhododendron hemsleyanum	RHODODENDRON
Rhododendron 'Intrifast'	RHODODENDRON
Rhododendron 'Ken Janeck'	RHODODENDRON
Rhododendron macabeanum	RHODODENDRON
Rhododendron orbiculare ssp. *orbiculare*	RHODODENDRON
Rhododendron orerodoxa	RHODODENDRON
Rhododendron pachysanthum	RHODODENDRON
Rhododendron 'Ramapo'	RHODODENDRON
Rhododendron rex	RHODODENDRON
Rhododendron sinogrande	RHODODENDRON
Rhododendron sutchuenense	RHODODENDRON
Rhododendron 'Viking Silver'	RHODODENDRON
Rhododendron williamsianum	WILLIAMS RHODODENDRON
Rhododendron 'Wine and Roses'	RHODODENDRON
Rubus rolfei	CREEPING TAIWAN BRAMBLE
Sinopanax formosanus	CHINESE ARALIA
Trachycarpus fortunei including 'Wagnerianus'	CHINESE WINDMILL PALM
Trochodendron aralioides	WHEEL TREE
Viburnum davidii	DAVID'S VIBURNUM
Yucca species and hybrids	YUCCA

EVERGREEN FERNS

Adiantum hispidulum 'Mt. Haleakala'	MT. HALEAKALA ROSY MAIDENHAIR FERN
Adiantum venustum	HIMALAYAN MAIDENHAIR FERN
Arachniodes simplicior 'Variegata'	EAST INDIAN HOLLY FERN
Asplenium scolopendrium	HART'S-TONGUE FERN
Asplenium trichomanes	MAIDENHAIR SPLEENWORT
Athyrium 'Ghost'	GHOST FERN
Austroblechnum (*Blechnum*) *penna-marina*	ALPINE WATER FERN
Blechnum (*Struthiopteris*) *spicant*	DEER FERN ❖
Coniogramme intermedia cultivars	INTERMEDIATE BAMBOO FERN
Cyrtomium caryotideum	HOLLY FERN
Cyrtomium falcatum 'Rochfordianum'	ROCHFORD'S HOLLY FERN
Cyrtomium fortunei	FORTUNE'S HOLLY FERN
Cyrtomium macrophyllum	LARGE-LEAF HOLLY FERN
Dryopteris bissetiana	BEADED WOOD FERN
Dryopteris crassirhizoma	THICK-STEMMED WOOD FERN

Dryopteris cycadina	SHAGGY SHIELD FERN
Dryopteris erythrosora	AUTUMN FERN
Dryopteris intermedia	FANCY FERN
Dryopteris lepidopoda	SUNSET FERN
Dryopteris ludoviciana	SOUTHERN WOOD FERN
Dryopteris marginalis	MARGINAL SHIELD FERN
Dryopteris wallichiana	WALLICH'S WOOD FERN
Lepisorus pseudoussuriensis 'Taoshan'	TAOSHAN LEPISORUS FERN
Neolepisorus truncatus 'Lemon Lime'	LEMON LIME CHINESE TIGER-STRIPED FERN
Polystichum aculeatum	HARD SHIELD FERN
Polystichum makinoi	MAKINOI'S HOLLY FERN
Polystichum munitum	SWORD FERN ❖
Polystichum neolobatum	ASIAN SABER FERN
Polystichum polyblepharum	JAPANESE TASSEL FERN
Polystichum proliferum	MOTHER SHIELD FERN
Polystichum setiferum cultivars	SHIELD FERN
Polystichum tsus-simense	KOREAN ROCK FERN

EVERGREEN ORNAMENTAL GRASSES INCLUDING BAMBOOS
(and grass-like plants)

Acorus gramineus 'Ogon'	GOLDEN VARIEGATED SWEETFLAG
Calamagrostis x acutiflora 'Karl Foerster'	FEATHER REED GRASS
Carex many species and cultivars	SEDGES
Chionochloa rubra	RED TUSSOCK GRASS
Chusquea culeou	CHILEAN CLUMPING BAMBOO
Fargesia angustissima	UMBRELLA BAMBOO
Fargesia dracocephala (F. apicirubens)	DRAGON'S HEAD BAMBOO
Fargesia rufa (F. dracocephala 'Rufa')	RED DRAGON'S HEAD BAMBOO
Fargesia denudata	NAKED CLUMPING BAMBOO
Fargesia murielae	UMBRELLA BAMBOO
Fargesia nitida	BLUE FOUNTAIN BAMBOO
Fargesia robusta	ROBUST BAMBOO
Fargesia scabrida	ORANGE-STEM BAMBOO
Helictotrichon sempervirens	BLUE OAT GRASS
X *Hibanobambusa tranquillans* 'Shiroshima'	SHIROSHIMA BAMBOO
Himalayacalamus planatus (H. asper)	RED BAMBOO
Juncus effusus 'Big Twister', 'Spiralis'	COMMON RUSH
Juncus patens 'Elk Blue', 'Occidental Blue'	SPREADING RUSH
Ophiopogon planiscapus 'Nigrescens'	BLACK MONDO GRASS
Rhodocoma capensis	CAPE RESTIO
Sesleria autumnalis	AUTUMN MOOR GRASS
Shibataea kumasasa	ZIG-ZAG BAMBOO
Stipa gigantea	GIANT NEEDLE GRASS, GIANT FEATHER GRASS
Yushania confusa	GUADUA BAMBOO

EVERGREEN PERENNIALS

Agapanthus hardy evergreen types	LILY-OF-THE-NILE
Artemisia versicolor 'Sea Foam'	CURLICUE SAGE
Asarum almost all species and hybrids	WILD GINGER
Aspidistra species and cultivars	CAST IRON PLANT
Beesia deltophylla	BEESIA
Bergenia many species, hybrids, cultivars	BERGENIA
Callirhoe involucrata	WINE CUPS
Dianella revoluta	FLAX LILY
Dianthus species and hybrids	PINKS
Disporopsis pernyi	EVERGREEN SOLOMON'S SEAL
Disporopsis bakeri (*D. pernyi* 'Bill Baker)	BAKER'S SOLOMON'S SEAL
Disporum longistylum 'Night Heron'	CHINESE FAIRY BELLS
Epimedium davidii	BARRENWORT
Epimedium epsteinii	BARRENWORT
Epimedium ecalcaratum	SPURLESS BARRENWORT
Epimedium fargesii	BARRENWORT
Epimedium lishihchenii	BARRENWORT
Epimedium x perralchicum 'Fröhnleiten'	HYBRID EPIMEDIUM
Epimedium x warleyense 'Orangekönigin'	HYBRID EPIMEDIUM
Epimedium wushanense	EVERGREEN EPIMEDIUM
Eryngium species and hybrids	ERYNGO
Euphorbia x martinii 'Ascot Rainbow'	ASCOT RAINBOW SPURGE
Glandora (Lithodora) diffusa	PURPLE GROMWELL
Helleborus argutifolius especially 'Silver Lace'	CORSICAN HELLEBORE
Helleborus foetidus	STINKING HELLEBORE
Helleborus hybrids: 'Anna's Red', 'HGC Snow Fever,' 'Janet Starnes', 'Penny's Pink', 'Winter Moonbeam'	HYBRID HELLEBORE
Hesperaloe parviflora	RED YUCCA
X *Heucherella* hybrids	HEUCHERELLA
Iberis sempervirens	EVERGREEN CANDYTUFT
Iris japonica	JAPANESE EVERGREEN IRIS
Leptinella squalida 'Platt's Black'	BRASS BUTTONS
Luzuriaga radicans	QUILINEJA
Phedimus (Sedum) spurius many cultivars	TWO-ROW STONECROP
Phlox subulata	CREEPING PHLOX
Phormium colensoi	NEW ZEALAND MOUNTAIN FLAX
Potentilla neumanniana	ALPINE CINQUEFOIL
Pulmonaria species and hybrids	LUNGWORT
Sedum spathulifolium	SPOON-LEAF STONECROP ❖
Sempervivum arachnoideum	HENS AND CHICKS, HOUSELEEK
Synthyris (Veronica) cordata	HEART-LEAF SNOW QUEEN ❖
Synthyris (Veronica) reniformis	SPRING QUEEN ❖

SEE ALSO "HARDY SUCCULENT PLANTS"

DRAMATIC/BOLD FOLIAGE

Big leaves (wide or long) help make an overly-large garden look a bit smaller. They bring a far-away spot in the garden closer to the viewer. They lend an air of tropicalness to the landscape. Many also fit into the "specimen" concept (one important plant in one important spot).

SMALLISH TREES

Butia odorata (B. capitata)	JELLY PALM, PINDO PALM
Fokienia (Chamaecyparis) hodginsii	FUJIAN CYPRESS
Kalopanax septemlobus	CASTOR ARALIA
Rhapidophyllum hystrix	NEEDLE PALM
Sinopanax formosanus	ARALIAD
Trachycarpus fortunei (including *T. f. wagnerianus*)	CHINESE WINDMILL PALM

SHRUBS *(including hardy bamboos and cycads; of which many are marginally hardy in colder microclimates here)*

Aralia echinocaulis	ARALIAD
Aralia elata	JAPANESE ANGELICA TREE
Aralia spinosa	DEVIL'S WALKING-STICK
Aucuba japonica	JAPANESE LAUREL
Ceratozamia hildae	BAMBOO CYCAD
Ceratozamia latifolia	CYCAD
Chusquea culeou	CHILEAN BAMBOO
Cycas debaoensis	DEBAO FERN CYCAD
Cycas guizhouensis	GUIZHOU CYCAD
Cycas panzhihuaensis	DUKOU SAGO PALM
Cycas revoluta	SAGO PALM
Cycas taitungensis	TAITUNG CYCAD
Daphniphyllum macropodum	FALSE DAPHNE
Dasylirion wheeleri	SPOON YUCCA, DESERT SPOON
Desfontainia spinosa	ANDEAN HOLLY
Dioon edule 'Rio Verde'	CHESTNUT DIOON
Eleutherococcus sieboldianus	FIVE-FINGERED ARALIAD
Encephalartos friderici-guilielmi	WHITE-HAIRED CYCAD
Encephalartos lehmannii	KAROO CYCAD
Fargesia denudata	NAKED CLUMPING BAMBOO
Fargesia murielae	UMBRELLA BAMBOO
Fargesia nitida	OBEDIENT BLUE FOUNTAIN BAMBOO
Fargesia robusta	ROBUST BAMBOO
Fargesia scabrida	FOUNTAIN BAMBOO
Fatsia japonica cultivars	JAPANESE ARALIA
Fatsia polycarpa	GREEN FINGERS
Heptapleurum (Schefflera) alpinum, H. delavayi, H. fengii, H. gracilis, H. hoi, *H. impressum*	ARALIADS
Heptapleurum taiwanianum	YUAN SHAN HARDY SCHEFFLERA

X Hibanobambusa tranquillans 'Shiroshima'	SHIROSHIMA BAMBOO
Himalayacalamus planatus (H. asper)	MALINGE NAGALO
Hydrangea quercifolia	OAK-LEAF HYDRANGEA
Macrozamia communis	BURRAWANG
Metrapanax (Dendropanax) delavayi	ARALIAD
Phormium colensoi	COOK'S MOUNTAIN FLAX
Pseudopanax laetus	SHRUB PANAX
Rhododendron caucasicum	RHODODENDRON
Rhododendron dauricum	RHODODENDRON
Rhododendron oreodoxa	RHODODENDRON
Rhododendron sutchuenense	RHODODENDRON
Rhus typhina	STAGHORN SUMAC
Sambucus racemosa Cut-leaf forms	RED ELDERBERRY
Yucca elata var. *verdiensis*	ARIZONA YUCCA
Yucca rostrata	BEAKED BLUE YUCCA
Yucca thompsoniana	THOMPSON'S YUCCA

VINES

Ampelopsis glandulosa var. *brevipedunculata* 'Elegans'	PORCELAINBERRY
Boquila trifoliolata	VOQUICILLO, PILPIL, VOQUI
Clematis terniflora	SWEET AUTUMN CLEMATIS
X Fatshedera lizei	BOTANICAL WONDER
Hedera algeriensis 'Glorie de Marengo'	VARIEGATED ALGERIAN IVY
Ipomoea pandurata	WILD POTATO VINE
Pileostegia viburnoides	CLIMBING HYDRANGEA
Smilax laurifolia	LAUREL GREENBRIER

PERENNIALS

Acanthus caroli-alexandri	BEAR'S BREECH
Acanthus mollis	BEAR'S BREECH
Acanthus spinosus	BEAR'S BREECH
Aciphylla glaucescens	BLUE SPEARGRASS
Agapanthus hybrids	LILY-OF-THE-NILE
Agave many species	AGAVE
Aloe polyphylla	SPIRAL ALOE
Alpinia pumila	DWARF GINGER
Aralia cordata especially 'Sun King'	JAPANESE SPIKENARD
Aspidistra elatior	CAST IRON PLANT
Aspidistra sichuanensis	SICHUAN ASPIDISTRA
Astilboides tabularis	SHIELD LEAF
Begonia 'Eruption'	SPLIT-LEAF BEGONIA
Begonia grandis	HARDY BEGONIA
Begonia pedatifida	HARDY BEGONIA
Bergenia species and hybrids (most)	BERGENIA
Boehmeria platanifolia	SYCAMORE-LEAFED FALSE NETTLE

Brunnera macrophylla cultivars	SIBERIAN BUGLOSS
Calamagrostis x acutiflora 'Overdam'	VARIEGATED REED GRASS
Carex scaposa	PINK FAIRY SEDGE
Carex siderosticha	BROAD-LEAF SEDGE
Cautleya cathcartii, gracilis, spicata	HIMALAYAN GINGER
Cheilocostus lacerus	CREPE GINGER
Cynara cardunculus (may act as a biennial)	CARDOON
Darmera peltata	UMBRELLA PLANT
Diphylleia cymosa	AMERICAN UMBRELLALEAF
Dysosma (Podophyllum) delavayi, many cultivars	MARBLED MAYAPPLE
Epimedium wushanense	EVERGREEN EPIMEDIUM
Eryngium, especially *E. agavifolium, E. ebracteatum* var. *poterioides, E. planum lesseauxii,*	
E. venustum, E. yuccifolium	ERYNGO
Farfugium japonicum, especially 'Giganteum'	LEOPARD PLANT
Fascicularia bicolor, including *F. b.* ssp. *canaliculata (F. pitcairnifolia)*	BROMELIAD
Gunnera magellanica	CREEPING GUNNERA
Gunnera manicata	GIANT RHUBARB
Gunnera tinctoria	CHILEAN RHUBARB
Hibiscus 'Midnight Marvel'	MIDNIGHT MARVEL HIBISCUS
Hosta, especially 'Blue Mammoth', 'Blue Wu', 'Empress Wu',	GIANT HOSTA
'Eola Sapphire', 'Jurassic Park', 'Komodo Dragon', 'Mikado', 'Sum and Substance',	
'Sum of All', 'T Rex'	
Ischyrolepis subverticillata	BROOM RESTIO
Kniphofia northiae	GIANT POKER
Ligularia 'Britt-Marie Crawford'	LEOPARD PLANT
Ligularia 'King Kong'	LEOPARD PLANT
Ligularia przewalskii 'Dragon Wings'	DRAGON WINGS LIGULARIA
Melianthus major, including 'Antonow's Blue', 'Purple Haze'	HONEYBUSH
Musa basjoo	HARDY BANANA
Myosotidium hortensia	GIANT FORGET-ME-NOT
Petasites japonicus especially var. *giganteus*	SWEET COLTSFOOT
Podophyllum pleianthum	HIMALAYAN MAYAPPLE
Rheum palmatum	GIANT ORNAMENTAL RHUBARB
Rodgersia aesculifolia	FINGER-LEAF RODGERSIA
Rodgersia pinnata	PINNATE RODGER'S FLOWER
Rodgersia podophylla	BRONZE-LEAF RODGERSIA
Silphium terebinthinaceum	PRAIRIE DOCK
Sinopodophyllum (Podophyllum) hexandrum var. *chinense*	HIMALAYAN MAYAPPLE
Stachys byzantina (S. lanata) 'Countess Helen von Stein'	GIANT LAMB'S EAR
Syneilesis aconitifolia	SHREDDED UMBRELLA PLANT
Syneilesis palmata	PALM-LEAF MAYAPPLE
Zingiber mioga	MIOGA GINGER

FERNS

Arachniodes standishii	UPSIDE-DOWN FERN
Asplenium scolopendrium	HART'S-TONGUE FERN
Athyrium filix-femina (many cultivars)	LADY FERN
Athyrium niponicum (many cultivars)	JAPANESE PAINTED FERN

Coniogramme intermedia	BAMBOO FERN
Cyrtomium caryotideum	DWARF NET-VEIN HOLLYFERN
Cyrtomium falcatum	HOLLYFERN
Cyrtomium fortunei	ASIAN NET-VIEW HOLLYFERN
Dryopteris australis	DIXIE WOOD FERN
Dryopteris x celsa	LOG FERN
Dryopteris clintoniana	CLINTON'S WOOD FERN
Dryopteris goldiana	GIANT WOOD FERN
Myriopteris (Cheilanthes) lanosa	HAIRY LIP FERN
Polystichum acrostichoides	CHRISTMAS FERN
Polystichum braunii	BRAUN'S HOLLYFERN
Pyrrosia polydactyla	FIVE-FINGER TONGUE FERN
Woodwardia orientalis	ORIENTAL CHAIN FERN

BULBS

Arisaema amurense	AMUR JACK-IN-THE-PULPIT
Arisaema dracontium	GREEN DRAGON
Arisaema elephas	ELEPHANT COBRA LILY
Arisaema erubescens	BLUSHING COBRA LILY
Arisaema propinquum	WALLACH'S COBRA LILY
Arisaema serratum	JAPANESE JACK-IN-THE-PULPIT
Arisaema sikokianum	JAPANESE JACK-IN-THE-PULPIT
Arisaema triphyllum, especially 'Starburst'	JACK-IN-THE-PULPIT
Arisaema utile	SIKKIM COBRA LILY
Arum maculatum	CUCKOO-PINT
Dracunculus vulgaris	VOODOO LILY
Sauromatum venosum, especially 'Indian Giant'	VOODOO LILY

FINE-TEXTURED FOLIAGE

Ideally suited to the smaller garden, especially the "secret garden," where they can make spaces seem bigger. But they're also candidates for providing contrast in the larger landscape where huskier plants are also used. Some demand to be touched.

TREES

Acer circinatum 'Monroe'	LACE-LEAF VINE MAPLE ❖
Acer japonicum 'Aconitifolium'	CUT-LEAFED DOWNY MAPLE
Acer palmatum (many cultivars)	JAPANESE MAPLE
Acer pentaphyllum	CHINESE MAPLE, FIVE-LOBE MAPLE
Albizia julibrissin	SILK TREE
Alnus glutinosa 'Imperialis'	CUT-LEAF BLACK ALDER
Azara microphylla	SMALL-LEAFED AZARA
Cedrus deodara	DEODAR CEDAR
Cephalotaxus harringtonia	PLUM-YEW
Chamaecyparis lawsoniana 'Filiformis'	FEATHERY LAWSON CYPRESS ❖
Cryptomeria japonica	JAPANESE PLUME CEDAR
Eucalyptus pauciflora ssp. *niphophila*	ALPINE SNOW GUM
Fagus sylvatica f. *heterophylla* 'Aspleniifolia'	FERN-LEAF EUROPEAN BEECH
Fagus sylvatica 'Rohanii'	CUT-LEAF PURPLE BEECH
Fraxinus angustifolia ssp. *oxycarpa* 'Raywood'	CLARET ASH
Gymnocladus dioicus	KENTUCKY COFFEE TREE
Koelreuteria paniculata	GOLDEN RAIN TREE
Larix occidentalis	WESTERN LARCH ❖
Lyonothamnus floribundus ssp. *asplenifolius*	ISLAND IRONWOOD
Metasequoia glyptostroboides	DAWN REDWOOD
Microbiota decussata	SIBERIAN CYPRESS
Nothofagus antarctica	ANTARCTIC BEECH
Nothofagus dombeyi	COIGÜE
Picea breweriana	BREWER'S SPRUCE ❖
Pinus ayacahuite	MEXICAN WHITE PINE
Pinus bhutanica	BHUTAN WHITE PINE
Pinus wallichiana	HIMALAYAN WHITE PINE
Pseudolarix amabilis	GOLDEN LARCH
Pyrus salicifolia 'Pendula'	WEEPING WILLOW-LEAF PEAR
Salix x *sepulcralis* 'Chrysocoma'	GOLDEN WEEPING WILLOW
Sambucus nigra 'Black Beauty', 'Black Lace', 'Black Prince'	
	BLACK CUT-LEAF BLACK ELDERBERRY
Sambucus nigra 'Dart's Greenlace', f. *laciniata*	CUT-LEAF BLACK ELDERBERRY
Sciadopitys verticillata	JAPANESE UMBRELLA PINE
Sequoia sempervirens	COAST REDWOOD
Sorbus pseudohupehensis 'Pink Pagoda'	PINK PAGODA ROWAN
Styphnolobium (Sophora) japonicum	PAGODA TREE
Taxodium ascendens (*T. distichum* var. *imbricatum*) 'Greenfeather'	POND CYPRESS
Taxodium distichum	BALD CYPRESS
Taxodium mucronatum	MONTEZUMA CYPRESS

Tetradium (Euodia) daniellii	EUODIA
Torreya californica	CALIFORNIA NUTMEG
Tsuga heterophylla 'Thorsen's Weeping'	THORSEN'S WEEPING HEMLOCK
Ulmus parvifolia	CHINESE ELM
Vitex agnus-castus	CHASTE TREE
Xanthocyparis vietnamensis	VIETNAM CYPRESS

SHRUBS

Azara microphylla	SMALL-LEAF AZARA
Baeckea gunniana	HEATHMYRTLE
Betula pendula 'Trost's Dwarf'	TROST'S DWARF EUROPEAN WHITE BIRCH
Borinda angustissima	NARROW LEAF CLUMPING BAMBOO
Borinda macclureana	TIBETAN MOUNTAIN BAMBOO
Calluna vulgaris 'Firefly'	HEATHER
Chamaecyparis obtusa 'Sunlight Lace'	SUNLIGHT LACE DWARF HINOKI CYPRESS
Frangula alnus (Rhamnus frangula) 'Fine Line Improved'	FERNLEAF BUCKTHORN
Grevillea australis	SOUTHERN GREVILLEA
Grevillea 'Canberra Gem'	SPIDER FLOWER
Grevillea juniperina	JUNIPER-LEAVED GREVILLEA
Grevillea 'Neil Bell'	NEIL BELL GREVILLEA
Grevillea rivularis	CARRINGTON FALLS GREVILLEA
Lavandula multifida	FERNLEAF LAVENDER
Lavandula pinnata	LACE LAVENDER
Leptospermum minutifolium	SMALL LEAVED TEA TREE
Lonicera ligustrina var. *yunnanensis (L. nitida)* 'Twiggy'	
	TWIGGY BOX-LEAF HONEYSUCKLE
Mahonia eurybracteata 'Soft Caress'	SOFT CARESS BARBERRY
Morus alba 'Nuclear Blast'	DWARF TWISTED-LEAF MULBERRY
Nandina domestica 'Gulf Stream'	GULF STREAM HEAVENLY BAMBOO
Nandina domestica 'Moon Bay'	MOON BAY HEAVENLY BAMBOO
Pittosporum illiciodes 'Formosan Fingers'	FORMOSAN FINGERS PITTOSPORUM
Rhus typhina 'Dissecta'	CUT-LEAF STAGHORN SUMAC
Salix elaeagnos ssp. *angustifolia*	NARROW-LEAVED OLIVE WILLOW
Salvia rosmarinus (Rosmarinus officinalis)	ROSEMARY
Sambucus racemosa 'Laciniata', 'Moerheimii', 'Plumosa'	CUT-LEAF RED ELDERBERRY
Sambucus racemosa 'Tenuifolia'	THREAD-LEAF RED ELDERBERRY
Sambucus racemosa 'Golden Glow', 'Lemony Lace', Plumosa Aurea', 'Sutherland Gold'	GOLDEN CUT-LEAF RED ELDERBERRY
Sambucus racemosa 'Goldilocks'	DWARF GOLDEN CUT-LEAF RED ELDERBERRY
Spiraea cantoniensis 'Laceata'	DOUBLE BRIDALWREATH
Spiraea thunbergii	BABY'S-BREATH SPIREA
Stachyurus salicifolius 'Sparkler'	WILLOW-LEAF STACHYURUS
Vitex agnus-castus	CHASTE TREE

VINES

Akebia quinata	CHOCOLATE VINE
Gelsemium sempervirens	CAROLINA JASMINE
Jasminum x stephanense	STEPHAN JASMINE
Muehlenbeckia axillaris	ANGEL VINE, WIRE VINE
Rubus henryi var. *bambusarum*	BAMBOO-LEAVED RASPBERRY
Trachelospermum asiaticum 'Theta'	BIRD-FOOT STAR JASMINE

PERENNIALS *(including ferns, grasses, bamboos)*

Achillea 'Moonshine'	MOONSHINE YARROW
Achillea siberica	SIBERIAN YARROW
Adiantum x mairisii	MAIRIS' MAIDENHAIR FERN
Adiantum x tracyi	TRACY'S MAIDENHAIR FERN
Adiantum venustum	HIMALAYAN MAIDENHAIR FERN
Agropyron magellanicum	CHILEAN BLUE WHEAT GRASS
Amsonia 'Blue Ice'	BLUE ICE BLUE STAR
Amsonia ciliata 'Halfway to Arkansas'	HALFWAY TO ARKANSAS BLUE STAR
Amsonia hubrichtii	HUBRICHT'S BLUESTAR
Amsonia tabernaemontana var. *salicifolia*	WILLOW LEAF BLUE STAR
Anemanthele lessoniana	GOSSAMER GRASS, NEW ZEALAND WIND GRASS
Anemonopsis macrophylla	FALSE ANEMONE
Arachniodes standishii	UPSIDE-DOWN FERN
Artemisia absinthium	WORMWOOD
Artemisia arborescens 'Powis Castle'	POWIS CASTLE WORMWOOD
Artemisia frigida	PRAIRIE SAGEWORT ❖
Artemisia gmelinii	RUSSIAN WORMWOOD
Artemisia ludoviciana	WESTERN MUGWORT ❖
Artemisia ludoviciana 'Valerie Finnis'	VALERIE FINNIS ARTEMISIA
Artemisia mauiensis silver forms	MAUI WORMWOOD
Artemisia pedemontana	DWARF WORMWOOD
Artemisia schmidtiana 'Silver Mound'	SILVER MOUND WORMWOOD
Artemisia stelleriana 'Silver Brocade'	SILVER BROCADE ARTEMISIA
Artemisia versicolor 'Seafoam'	CURLICUE SAGE
Aruncus aethusifolius	DWARF GOAT'S-BEARD
Aruncus dioicus var. *pubescens* 'Kneiffii'	CUT-LEAF GOATS-BEARD
Aruncus hybrids 'Chantilly Lace', 'Fairy Hair', 'Misty Lace'	LACY GOAT'S-BEARD
Asplenium scolopendrium	HART'S-TONGUE FERN
Asplenium trichomanes	MAIDENHAIR SPLEENWORT
Astilbe x arendsii	ASTILBE
Astilbe chinensis var. *pumila*	DWARF CHINESE ASTILBE
Athyrium filix-femina (many cultivars)	LADY FERN
Athyrium niponicum (many cultivars)	JAPANESE PAINTED FERN
Athyrium otophorum	EARED LADY FERN
Austrostipa ramosissima	AUSTRALIAN PLUME GRASS
Borinda (Fargesia) fungosa	CHOCOLATE BAMBOO

Borinda (Fargesia) lushiensis	RED-STEM BAMBOO
Borinda (Fargesia) papyrifera	WHITE WAX BORINDA
Borinda (Fargesia) yunnanensis	YUNNAN FOUNTAIN BAMBOO
Calamagrostis acutiflora 'Overdam'	OVERDAM FEATHER GRASS
Calamagrostis brachytricha	KOREAN FEATHER REED GRASS
Calamagrostis foliosa	MENDOCINO REED GRASS
Calamagrostis nutkaensis	PACIFIC REEDGRASS ❖
Calamagrostis x *acutiflora* 'Karl Foerster'	FEATHER REED GRASS
Carex elata 'Aurea'	BOWLE'S GOLDEN SEDGE
Carex flacca 'Blue Zinger'	BLUE SEDGE
Carex hachijoensis 'Evergold'	EVERGOLD SEDGE
Carex morrowii 'Ice Dance'	ICE DANCE SEDGE
Carex oshimensis 'Everillo', 'Everest', 'Everlime', 'Everlite', 'Eversheen', 'Ice Cream'	VARIEGATED JAPANESE SEDGE
Carex tenuiculmis 'Cappuccino'	COFFEE SEDGE
Carex trifida 'Rekohu Sunrise'	MUTTONBIRD SEDGE
Caulophyllum thalictroides	COMMON BLUE COHOSH
Chaerophyllum hirsutum 'Roseum'	PINK HAIRY CHERVIL
Chionochloa rubra	RED TUSSOCK GRASS
Chusquea culeou	CHILEAN BAMBOO
Coniogramme intermedia cultivars	BAMBOO FERN
Coniogramme japonica	JAPANESE BAMBOO FERN
Coreopsis verticillata	THREAD-LEAF COREOPSIS
Corydalis flexuosa	BLUE FUMEWORT
Corydalis scouleri	SCOULER'S FUMEWORT ❖
Corydalis solida	FUMEWORT
Cyrtomium caryotideum	DWARF NET-VEIN HOLLYFERN
Deschampsia caespitosa	TUFTED HAIRGRASS
Dianthus species	COTTAGE PINKS
Dicentra formosa	WESTERN BLEEDING HEART
Dicentra hybrids	BLEEDING HEART
Dryopteris australis	DIXIE WOOD FERN
Dryopteris x celsa	LOG FERN
Dryopteris clintoniana	CLINTON'S WOOD FERN
Dryopteris goldiana	GIANT WOOD FERN
Dryopteris crassirhizoma	THICK-STEMMED WOOD FERN
Dryopteris cycadina	SHAGGY SHIELD FERN
Dryopteris erythrosora	AUTUMN FERN
Dryopteris lepidopoda	SUNSET FERN
Dryopteris sieboldii	SIEBOLD'S WOOD FERN
Dryopteris wallichiana	WALLICH'S WOOD FERN
Erianthus ravennae	RAVENNA GRASS
Fargesia denudata	DENUDATA BAMBOO
Fargesia dracocephala	DRAGON'S HEAD BAMBOO
Fargesia murielae	UMBRELLA BAMBOO
Fargesia nitida	BLUE FOUNTAIN
Fargesia robusta	ROBUST BAMBOO
Fargesia scabrida	ORANGE-STEM BAMBOO
Festuca glauca	BLUE FESCUE

Festuca roemeri	ROEMER'S FESCUE
Foeniculum vulgare (don't let it go to seed)	FENNEL
Gymnocarpium disjunctum	COMMON OAK FERN ❖
Hakonechloa macra and cultivars	JAPANESE FOREST GRASS
Helianthus angustifolius	SWAMP SUNFLOWER
Helictotrichon sempervirens	BLUE OAT GRASS
X *Hibanobambusa tranquillans* 'Shiroshima'	SHIROSHIMA BAMBOO
Himalayacalamus planatus (H. asper)	MALINGE NAGALO BAMBOO
Hosta 'Curly Fries'	CURLY FRIES HOSTA
Lamprocapnos (Dicentra) spectabilis	OLD-FASHIONED BLEEDING HEART
Lavandula multifida	FERNLEAF LAVENDER
Lepisorus bicolor	SCHEZUAN RIBBON FERN
Luzula nivea	SNOWY WOODRUSH
Luzula sylvatica 'Aurea'	GOLDEN WOODRUSH
Luzula sylvatica 'Marginata'	VARIEGATED WOODRUSH
Melica subulata	ALASKA ONIONGRASS ❖
Miscanthus sinensis	CHINESE SILVER-GRASS
Molinia caerulea 'Variegata'	VARIEGATED MOOR GRASS
Molinia caerulea ssp. *caerulea* 'Moorflamme'	PURPLE MOOR GRASS
Molinia caerulea ssp. *caerulea* 'Variegata'	VARIEGATED PURPLE MOOR GRASS
Muhlenbergia rigens	DEER GRASS
Myriopteris (Cheilanthes) lanosa	HAIRY LIP FERN
Ophiopogon japonicus 'Gyoku-ryu'	DWARF MONDO GRASS
Ophiopogon japonicus 'Pamela Harper'	STRIPED MONDO GRASS
Ophiopogon planiscapus	BIG MONDO GRASS
Ophiopogon planiscapus 'Juru'	VARIEGATED DWARF MONDO GRASS
Ophiopogon planiscapus 'Little Tabby'	STRIPED DWARF MONDO GRASS
Ophiopogon planiscapus 'Nigrescens'	BLACK MONDO GRASS
Ophiopogon umbraticola 'Sparkler'	CHINESE MONDO GRASS
Paeonia tenuifolia	FERN LEAF PEONY
Polemonium caeruleum	JACOBS LADDER
Polemonium carneum	ROYAL JACOB'S-LADDER ❖
Polystichum braunii	BRAUN'S HOLLY FERN ❖
Polystichum makinoi	MAKINOI'S HOLLY FERN
Polystichum munitum	SWORD FERN
Polystichum setiferum Plumosomultilobum Group	PLUMOSE SOFT SHIELD FERN
Polystichum tsus-simense	KOREAN ROCK FERN
Pulsatilla vulgaris	PASQUE FLOWER
Rhodocoma capensis	CAPE RESTIO
Salvia yangii (Perovskia atriplicifolia)	RUSSIAN SAGE
Selaginella apoda	MEADOW SPIKE-MOSS
Sesleria autumnalis	AUTUMN MOOR GRASS
Sisyrinchium bellum	WESTERN BLUE-EYED GRASS
Sisyrinchium californicum	GOLDEN-EYED GRASS
Sisyrinchium hitchcockii	HITCHCOCK'S BLUE-EYED-GRASS
Sisyrinchium idahoense	BLUE-EYED GRASS
Tanacetum ptarmiciflorum	SILVER LACE DUSTY MILLER
Thalictrum angustifolium	SHINING MEADOW-RUE
Thalictrum aquilegifolium	COLUMBINE MEADOW-RUE

Thalictrum dasycarpum	PURPLE MEADOW-RUE ❖
Thalictrum delavayi	CHINESE MEADOW-RUE
Thalictrum delavayi 'Hewitt's Double'	HEWITT'S DOUBLE MEADOW-RUE
Thalictrum dioicum	EARLY MEADOW-RUE
Thalictrum 'Elin'	ELIN MEADOW-RUE
Thalictrum fendleri	FENDLER'S MEADOW-RUE
Thalictrum flavum ssp. *glaucum*	YELLOW MEADOW-RUE
Thalictrum isopyroides	FOAMY MEADOW-RUE
Thalictrum kiusianum	DWARF MEADOW-RUE
Thalictrum minus 'Adiantifolium	FERN-LEAF MEADOW-RUE
Thalictrum occidentale	WESTERN MEADOWRUE ❖
Thalictrum rochebrunianum	LAVENDER MIST MEADOW RUE
Thalictrum (Anemonella) thalictroides	RUE-ANEMONE
Thamnocalamus crassinodus	TIBETAN BAMBOO
Thelypteris kunthii	ABUNDANT MAIDEN FERN
Vahlodea (Deschampsia) atropurpurea	MOUNTAIN HAIRGRASS
Vernonia lettermannii	THREADLEAF IRONWEED
Veronicastrum sibericum	JAPANESE CULVER'S ROOT
Woodwardia orientalis	ORIENTAL CHAIN FERN
Xerophyllum tenax	BEAR GRASS, INDIAN BASKET GRASS ❖

"The fabric of a garden is determined as much by its textures as by its tonal range and architectural flair." ~~ John Burnside

BERRIES/FRUITS, FALL INTO WINTER

Note that some of these plants produce fruit best when there are male and female plants in the same garden. Almost all of these are food for birds and other wildlife.

Actaea pachypoda	WHITE BANEBERRY
Acer tataricum 'Hot Wings'	HOT WINGS TATARIAN MAPLE
Arbutus unedo and cultivars	STRAWBERRY TREE
Arctostaphylos glauca	BIG BERRY MANZANITA
Arctostaphylos 'Monica'	MONICA MANZANITA
Arctostaphylos uva-ursi	KINNIKINNICK ❖
Aristotelia × fruserrata	WINEBERRY
Aronia arbutifolia	RED CHOKECHERRY
Aronia melanocarpa	BLACK CHOKECHERRY
Aronia × prunifolia	PURPLE CHOKEBERRY
Aucuba japonica (female cultivars; also need a male)	JAPANESE LAUREL
Azara petiolaris	HOLLY AZARA
Berberis darwinii	DARWIN'S BARBERRY
Berberis x gladwynensis 'William Penn'	WILLIAM PENN BARBERRY
Berberis jamesiana 'Exuberant'	JAMES' BARBERRY
Berberis koreana	KOREAN BARBERRY
Berberis wilsoniae	WILSON'S BARBERRY
Billardiera longiflora	CLIMBING BLUEBERRY
Callicarpa bodinieri	BEAUTYBERRY
Callicarpa dichotoma	BEAUTYBERRY
Callicarpa japonica 'Leucocarpa'	WHITE JAPANESE BEAUTYBERRY
Callicarpa kwangtungensis	CHINESE BEAUTYBERRY
Chionanthus retusus	CHINESE FRINGETREE
Clerodendrum trichotomum var. *fargesii*	GLORYBOWER
Cornus alba	TATARIAN DOGWOOD
Cornus amomum	SILKY DOGWOOD
Cornus alternifolia	PAGODA DOGWOOD
Cornus capitata	EVERGREEN DOGWOOD
Cornus kousa	KOREAN DOGWOOD
Cornus mas	CORNELIAN CHERRY
Cornus sericea	RED OSIER ❖
Cotinus coggygria 'The Velvet Fog'	DARK PINK SMOKEBUSH
Cotoneaster adpressus 'Little Gem'	COMPACT COTONEASTER
Cotoneaster dammeri	BEARBERRY COTONEASTER
Cotoneaster hodjingensis (*C. glaucophyllus*)	GRAY-LEAF COTONEASTER
Cotoneaster procumbens 'Queen of Carpets'	Q. o C. COTONEASTER
Cotoneaster salicifolius 'Repens'	SPREADING WILLOW-LEAF COTONEASTER
Cotoneaster x watereri 'Cornubia'	CORNUBIA COTONEASTER
Crataegus 'Autumn Glory'	AUTUMN GLORY HAWTHORN
Crataegus crus-galli 'Crusader'	CRUSADER CRABAPPLE
Crataegus douglasii	DOUGLAS HAWTHORN, BLACK HAWTHORN ❖
Crataegus x lavallei	LAVALLE HAWTHORN
Crataegus phaenopyrum	WASHINGTON HAWTHORNE

Crataegus pinnatifida	CHINESE HAWTHORNE
Crataegus tanacetifolia	TANSY-LEAF THORN
Crataegus viridis, especially 'Winter King'	GREEN HAWTHORN
Cudrania tricuspidata	CHE
Danae racemosa	POET'S LAUREL
Decaisnea fargesii	BLUE BEAN SHRUB
Diospyros kaki	JAPANESE PERSIMMON
Enkianthus cernuus f. *rubens*	DROOPING RED ENKIANTHUS
Elaeagnus x *submacrophylla* (*E.* x *ebbingei*)	HYBRID ELAEAGNUS
Elaeagnus multiflora	GOUMI BERRY
Euonymus phellomanus	CORK SPINDLE TREE
Euscaphis japonica	KOREAN SWEETHEART TREE
Frangula (Rhamnus) californica	COFFEEBERRY
Gaultheria mucronata 'Bell's Seedling'	PERNETTYA
Gaultheria ovatifolia	WESTERN TEABERRY ❖
Gaultheria procumbens	WINTERGREEN
Gaultheria (X *Gaulnettya*) 'Wisley Pearl'	GAULNETTYA
Hypericum x *inodorum*	SANGRIA ST. JOHN'S WORT
Ilex glabra	INKBERRY
Ilex x *meserveae* 'Blue Girl', 'Blue Princess'	BLUE HOLLY
Ilex opaca	AMERICAN HOLLY
Ilex verticillata 'Berry Poppins' + 'Mr. Poppins'	WINTERBERRY HOLLY
Koelreuteria paniculata	GOLDEN RAIN TREE
Leptecophylla juniperina ssp. *juniperina*	PINK MOUNTAIN BERRY
Lindera benzoin	SPICEBUSH
Lindera erythrocarpa	RED-BERRY SPICEBUSH
Lindera obtusiloba	JAPANESE SPICEBUSH
Lonicera pileata	BOX-LEAF HONEYSUCKLE
Luzuriaga radicans	QUILINEJA
Mahonia aquifolium	OREGON-GRAPE ❖
Mahonia x *media* cultivars	HYBRID MAHONIA
Malus species and hybrids (disease resistant cultivars)	CRABAPPLE
Melicytus crassifolius	THICK-LEAVED MAHOE
Myrceugenia parvifolia	PATAGÜILLA
Nyssa sylvatica	TUPELO
Oxycoccus oxycoccos	BOG CRANBERRY
Parthenocissus henryana	SILVER-VEIN CREEPER
Parthenocissus quinquefolia	VIRGINIA CREEPER
Parthenocissus tricuspidata	BOSTON IVY
Pseudocydonia sinensis	CHINESE QUINCE
Pyracantha coccinea hybrids	FIRETHORN
Rhamnus (Frangula) purshiana	CASCARA ❖
Rhaphithamnus spinosus	PRICKLY MYRTLE
Rhus aromatica	FRAGRANT SUMAC
Rhus glabra	SMOOTH SUMAC
Rhus trilobata	THREE LEAF SUMAC, SKUNKBUSH
Rhus typhina	STAGHORN SUMAC
Rosa davidii	FATHER DAVID'S ROSE
Rosa gallica	APOTHECARY ROSE

Rosa 'Geranium'	GERANIUM ROSE
Rosa glauca	RED-LEAF ROSE
Rosa moyesii	MOYES ROSE, MANCHURIAN ROSE
Rosa 'Robin Hood'	ROBIN HOOD ROSE
Rosa rugosa and hybrids	RUGOSA ROSE, JAPANESE BEACH ROSE
Rosa 'Sealing Wax' (Moyesii Hybrid)	SEALING WAX ROSE
Rosa woodsii var. *ultramontana*	WOOD'S ROSE
Skimmia japonica	SKIMMIA
X *Sorbaronia* 'Ivan's Beauty'	HYBRID MOUNTAIN ASH
Sorbus aria	WHITEBEAM
Sorbus scopulina	DWARF MOUNTAIN ASH
Sorbus verrucosa var. *subulata*	VIETNAM MOUNTAIN ASH
Symphoricarpos x *chenaultii* 'Hancock'	CHENAULT CORALBERRY
Symphoricarpos x *doorenbosii* 'Kordes Amethyst'	CORALBERRY
Symphoricarpos x *doorenbosii* 'Magic Berry'	INDIAN CURRANT
Symphoricarpos albus	SNOWBERRY ❖
Tetracentron sinense	TETRACENTRON
Vaccinium moupinense	HIMALAYAN BLUEBERRY
Viburnum betulifolium	BIRCH-LEAFED VIBURNUM
Viburnum 'Blue Muffin'	BLUE MUFFIN VIBURNUM
Viburnum dilatatum 'Cardinal Candy'	CARDINAL CANDY VIBURNUM
Viburnum edule	LOWBUSH CRANBERRY ❖
Viburnum ellipticum	OVAL-LEAF VIBURNUM
Viburnum nudum 'Brandywine'	BRANDYWINE VIBURNUM
Viburnum opulus and cultivars	EUROPEAN CRANBERRYBUSH
Viburnum opulus 'Xanthocarpum'	YELLOW-FRUITED VIBURNUM
Viburnum trilobum (V. opulus var. *americanum)* and cultivars	
	AMERICAN HIGH BUSH CRANBERRY ❖

BEAUTIFUL BARK

Bark can be intriguing, even eye-catching. It might be brightly colored, intricately or delicately patterned, huskily textured, or covered in striking shreds of exfoliation.

Acer capillipes	SNAKE-BARK MAPLE
Acer circinatum 'Pacific Fire'	PACIFIC FIRE VINE MAPLE ❖
Acer x *conspicuum* 'Phoenix'	ORANGE SNAKE-BARK MAPLE
Acer davidii	SNAKE-BARK MAPLE
Acer griseum	PAPER-BARK MAPLE
Acer palmatum 'Arakawa'	WARTY-BARK MAPLE
Acer palmatum 'Bihou'	YELLOW CORAL-BARK MAPLE
Acer palmatum 'Eddisbury', 'Sango Kaku'	CORAL-BARK MAPLE
Acer rufinerve 'Albolimbatum'	VARIEGATED RED-VEIN MAPLE
Acer tegmentosum 'Joe Witt'	MANCHURIAN STRIPED MAPLE
Acer triflorum	THREE-FLOWERED MAPLE
Arbutus 'Marina'	MARINA MADRONE
Arbutus menziesii	PACIFIC MADRONE ❖
Arctostaphylos columbiana	HAIRY MANZANITA ❖
Betula nigra 'Heritage', 'Little King'	RIVER BIRCH
Betula papyrifera 'Snowy'	PAPER BIRCH
Betula utilis var. *jacquemontii*	HIMALAYAN BIRCH
Carpenteria californica cultivars	BUSH ANEMONE ❖
Chusquea culeou	CHILEAN BAMBOO
Clethra acuminata	CINNAMON CLETHRA
Clethra fargesii	SWEET PEPPERBUSH
Cornus alba	TATARIAN DOGWOOD
Cornus kousa	KOREAN DOGWOOD
Cornus sericea 'Baileyi'	RED-OSIER DOGWOOD ❖
Fitzroya cupressoides	PATAGONIAN CYPRESS
Heptacodium miconioides	SEVEN-SON FLOWER
Hesperocyparis (*Cupressus*) *bakeri*	BAKER CYPRESS
Hesperocyparis (*Cupressus*) *forbesii*	TECATE CYPRESS
Maackia amurensis	AMUR MAACKIA
Parrotia persica	PERSIAN IRONWOOD
Parrotia subaequalis	CHINESE IRONWOOD
Polylepis australis	TABAQUILLO, QUEÑOA
Pseudocydonia sinensis	CHINESE QUINCE
Quercus suber	CORK OAK
Rhododendron ciliicalyx	RHODODENDRON
Stewartia koreana	KOREAN STEWARTIA
Stewartia monadelpha	ORANGE-BARK STEWARTIA
Stewartia pseudocamellia	JAPANESE STEWARTIA
Syringa reticulata ssp. *pekinensis*	PEKIN LILAC, CHINESE TREE LILAC
Ulmus parvifolia	LACEBARK ELM
Zelkova serrata	KEAKI

WEEPING TREES

There's an innate and elegant beauty in the cascading stems of these trees. They are in their element in Asian style gardens, near water features, and as complements to geometric hardscapes. You'll find many of these plants in the next category, "SPECIMENS AND ACCENTS," as well.

Acer japonicum 'Abby's Weeping', 'Green Cascade'	WEEPING AMUR MAPLE
Acer palmatum 'Hana Matoi'	WEEPING JAPANESE MAPLE
Alnus incana 'Pendula'	WEEPING ALDER
Betula nigra 'Summer Cascade'	WEEPING RIVER BIRCH
Betula pendula 'Youngii'	YOUNG'S WEEPING BIRCH
Carpinus betulus 'Pendula', 'Vienna Weeping'	WEEPING HORNBEAM
Cercidiphyllum japonicum 'Morioka Weeping', 'Pendulum	WEEPING KATSURA
Cercis canadensis 'Covey' ('Lavender Twist')	WEEPING REDBUD
Chamaecyparis lawsoniana 'Dik's Weeping'	DIK'S WEEPING PORT ORFORD CEDAR
Cornus kousa 'Weavers Weeping'	WEAVER'S WEEPING DOGWOOD
Callitropsis (Chamaecyparis, Cupressus, Xanthocyparis) nootkatensis 'Pendula'	
	WEEPING ALASKAN YELLOW-CEDAR
Diospyros kaki 'Pendula', 'Schibamichi Weeping'	JAPANESE WEEPING PERSIMMON
Fagus sylvatica 'Aurea Pendula', 'Purple Fountain'	WEEPING BEECH
Ginkgo biloba 'Pendula', 'Weeping Wonder'	WEEPING GINKGO
Hesperocyparis (Cupressus) macrocarpa 'Aurea Saligna'	WEEPING MONTEREY CYPRESS
Juniperus communis 'Horstmann'	HORSTMANN'S WEEPING JUNIPER
Juniperus formosana	FORMOSAN JUNIPER
Juniperus scopulorum 'Tolleson's Blue Weeping'	TOLLESON'S WEEPING JUNIPER
Lagarostrobos (Dacrydium) franklinii	HUON PINE
Larix decidua 'Puli'	WEEPING EUROPEAN LARCH
Larix kaempferi 'Pendula'	WEEPING LARCH
Morus alba 'Chaparral'	WEEPING MULBERRY
Pinus densiflora 'Pendula'	WEEPING JAPANESE RED PINE
Prunus mume 'W. B. Clarke'	WEEPING JAPANESE APRICOT
Prunus pendula 'Plena-rosea'	DOUBLE WEEPING CHERRY
Prunus serrulata 'Kiku-Shidare-Zakura'	CHEAL'S WEEPING CHERRY
Prunus serrulata 'Snow Fountains'	WHITE FOUNTAIN CHERRY
Prunus x *subhirtella* 'Pendula'	WEEPING HIGAN CHERRY
Prunus x *subhirtella* 'Pendula Double'	DOUBLE WEEPING CHERRY
Pyrus salicifolia 'Pendula'	WEEPING PEAR
Salix caprea 'Pendula'	WEEPING PUSSY WILLOW
Salix x *sepulcralis* 'Chrysocoma'	GOLDEN WEEPING WILLOW
Stewartia monadelpha 'Pendula'	WEEPING STEWARTIA
Styphnolobium (Sophora) japonica 'Pendula'	WEEPING JAPANESE PAGODA TREE
Styrax japonicus 'Fragrant Fountain', 'Marley's Pink Parasol', 'Nightfall'	
	WEEPING JAPANESE SNOWBELL
Taxodium distichum 'Falling Waters'	WEEPING BALD CYPRESS
Tilia tomentosa 'Petiolaris'	WEEPING SILVER LINDEN
Tsuga canadensis 'Pendula'	SARGENT'S WEEPING HEMLOCK
Tsuga heterophylla 'Thorsen's Weeping'	THORSEN'S WEEPING HEMLOCK
Ulmus glabra 'Camperdownii'	CAMPERDOWN ELM

SPECIMENS AND ACCENT PLANTS

Plants which can be used singularly (all by their lonesomes) to scream for attention, to redirect the eye, to create a "view" where there is no view. These are special plants requiring special places. Pruning shears used wisely and subtly often improve the already eye-catching character of the plant.

ARCHITEXTURAL PLANTS
Plants with strong, dramatic structure and overall form

Acanthus mollis	BEAR'S BREECH
Aloe polyphylla	SPIRAL ALOE
Araucaria araucana	MONKEY PUZZLE TREE
Athyrium niponicum	JAPANESE PAINTED FERN
Calamagrostis x acutiflora 'Karl Foerster'	FEATHER REED GRASS
Cedrus atlantica 'Pendula Glauca'	WEEPING BLUE ATLAS CEDAR
Chaenomeles speciosa 'Contorta'	CONTORTED FLOWERING QUINCE
Chamaerops humilis	MEDITERRANEAN FAN PALM
Chamaecyparis thyoides 'Glauca Pendula'	WEEPING WHITE CEDAR
Cordyline australis	CABBAGE PALM
Corokia cotoneaster	COROKIA
Corylus avellana 'Contorta'	HARRY LAUDER'S WALKING STICK
Danae racemosa	POET'S LAUREL
Disporum cantoniense 'Night Heron'	NIGHT HERON CHINESE FAIRY BELLS
Eryngium 'Big Blue'	BIG BLUE SEA HOLLY
X *Fatshedera lizei*	FATSHEDERA
Juncus effusus 'Big Twister', 'Spiralis'	COMMON RUSH
Juncus patens 'Elk Blue', 'Occidental Blue'	SPREADING RUSH
Juniperus chinensis 'Kaizuka'	HOLLYWOOD JUNIPER
Mahonia x media cultivars	MAHONIA
Morus alba 'Unryu'	CONTORTED WHITE MULBERRY
Phormium colensoi	NEW ZEALAND MOUNTAIN FLAX
Pinus bhutanica	BHUTAN WHITE PINE
Pinus densiflora 'Umbraculifera'	TANYOSHO PINE
Polylepis australis	TABAQUILLO, QUEÑOA
Rosa sericea ssp. *omeiensis* f. *pteracantha*	WINGED ROSE
Sciadopitys verticillata	JAPANESE UMBRELLA PINE
Sophora prostrata 'Little Baby'	LITTLE BABY DWARF KOWHAI
Trachycarpus fortunei, including 'Wagnerianus'	CHINESE WINDMILL PALM
Yucca species and hybrids	YUCCA

EXTRAVAGANT FLOWERING SPECIMEN TREES

Aesculus x carnea 'Briotii'	RED HORSE CHESTNUT
Catalpa ovata	CHINESE CATALPA
Cercis canadensis	REDBUD
Cornus 'Eddie's White Wonder'	EDDIE'S WHITE WONDER DOGWOOD
Cornus x elwinortonii 'Hyperion'	HYPERION DOGWOOD

Cornus x elwinortonii 'Rosy Teacups'	ROSY TEACUPS DOGWOOD'
Cornus x elwinortonii 'Venus'	VENUS DOGWOOD
Cornus kousa 'Satomi'	RED FLOWERING KOUSA DOGWOOD
Cornus kousa var. *chinensis* 'Milky Way'	MILKY WAY DOGWOOD
Davidia involucrata 'Sonoma'	DOVE TREE, HANDKERCHIEF TREE
Embothrium coccineum	CHILEAN FIRE TREE
Eucryphia glutinosa	NIRRHE
Garrya elliptica	SILKTASSEL
Magnolia denudata	YULAN
Magnolia 'Elizabeth' (*M. acuminata* x *M. denudata*)	YELLOW MAGNOLIA
Magnolia insignis	RED LOTUS TREE
Magnolia x kewensis 'Wada's Memory'	WADA'S MEMORY MAGNOLIA
Magnolia laevifolia (Michelia yunnanensis)	YUNNAN MAGNOLIA
Magnolia x loebneri 'Leonard Messel'	PINK LOBNER MAGNOLIA
Magnolia x loebneri 'Merrill'	MERRILL MAGNOLIA
Magnolia kobus	KOBUSHI
Magnolia sieboldii	OYAMA MAGNOLIA
Magnolia x soulangeana 'Rustica Rubra'	RUSTICA RUBRA SAUCER MAGNOLIA
Magnolia wilsonii	WILSON'S MAGNOLIA
Magnolia 'Vulcan'	VULCAN MAGNOLIA
Malus 'Golden Raindrops'	GOLDEN RAINDROPS CRABAPPLE
Malus 'Royal Raindrops'	ROYAL RAINDROPS CRABAPPLE
Melliodendron xylocarpum	CHINESE PARASOL
Oxydendrum arboreum	SOURWOOD
Prunus 'Gyoiko', 'Pink Perfection', 'Tai-Haku'	FLOWERING CHERRIES
Sorbus pseudohupehensis 'Pink Pagoda'	PINK PAGODA ROWAN
Styrax japonicus 'Pink Chimes'	PINK SNOWBELL
Styrax japonicus 'Snowcone'	JAPANESE SNOWBELL
Syringa reticulata	TREE LILAC

OTHER SPLASHY-BIG AND/OR EXOTIC FLOWER COLOR

Amaryllis belladonna, x Amarygia hybrids	NAKED LADY
Camellia (especially *C. reticulata*, *C.* x williamsii)	CAMELLIAS
Campsis x tagliabuana	HYBRID TRUMPET VINE
Cardiocrinum cathayanum	GIANT CATHAY LILY
Cardiocrinum cordatum	GIANT JAPANESE LILY
Cardiocrinum giganteum	GIANT HIMALAYAN LILY
Ceanothus species and hybrids	CALIFORNIA LILAC
Ceanothus x delileanus 'Gloire de Versailles'	HARDY HYBRID CEANOTHUS
Eremurus himalaicus	HIMALAYAN FOXTAIL LILY
Eremurus hybrids	FOXTAIL LILY
Eremurus stenophyllus	DESERT CANDLE
Eucomis species and hybrids	PINEAPPLE LILY
Fuchsia hardy species	FUCHSIA
Grevillea 'Audrey'	AUDREY GREVILLEA
Grevillea 'Canberra Gem'	SPIDER FLOWER

Grevillea 'Canterbury Gold'	CANTERBURY GOLD GREVILLEA
Grevillea x gaudichaudii	CREEPING GREVILLEA
Grevillea juniperina cultivars	JUNIPER-LEAF GREVILLEA
Grevillea 'Marshall Olbrich'	MARSHALL OLBRICH GREVILLEA
Grevillea miqueliana var. moroka	ROUND-LEAF GREVILLEA
Grevillea 'Neil Bell'	NEIL BELL GREVILLEA
Grevillea 'Poorinda Leanne' ('Poorinda Queen')	LEANNE GREVILLEA
Grevillea 'The Precious'	THE PRECIOUS GREVILLEA
Grevillea victoriae	ROYAL GREVILLEA
Hydrangea many species and cultivars	HYDRANGEA
Lavatera maritima	BEACH TREE MALLOW
Leonotis leonurus	LION'S-TAIL
Mandevilla laxa	CHILEAN JASMINE
Rosa single-flowered species and these hybrids	ROSES

'All A-Flutter'
'Altissimo'
'Betty Boop')
'Bill Reid'
'Campfire'
'Canary Bird'
'Dainty Bess'
'Deanna Krause'
'Excite'
'Flamingo Kolorscape'
'Fruit Punch'

'Golden Wings'
'Knock Out'
'Lemon Fizz Kolorscape'
'Mermaid'
'Mutabilis'
'Nancy Hayward'
'Oso Easy Cherry Pie'
'Pink Meidiland'
'Roy's Vision'
'Sally Holmes'
'Smiling Jean'

Zantedeschia aethiopica   CALLA-LILY

"A garden is a complex of aesthetic and plastic intentions; and the plant is, to a landscape artist, not only a plant — rare, unusual, ordinary, or doomed to disappearance — but it is also a color, a shape, a volume or an arabesque in itself." ~~ Roberto Burle Marx

MULTI-SEASON ACCENT PLANTS

Those which offer up some varied seasonal show during two or more seasons of the year. Could be a weeping tree with fall color or a spring bloomer showing off their berries from fall into winter.

Acer circinatum cultivars	VINE MAPLE❖
Acer x freemanii 'Autumn Blaze'	AUTUMN BLAZE MAPLE
Acer griseum	PAPER-BARK MAPLE
Acer japonicum 'Aconitifolium'	FERN-LEAF FULLMOON MAPLE
Acer japonicum 'Abby's Weeping', 'Green Cascade'	WEEPING AMUR MAPLE
Acer miyabei 'Morton'	MIYABE MAPLE
Acer palmatum 'Hana Matoi'	WEEPING JAPANESE MAPLE
Acer palmatum 'Sango-kaku'	CORAL-BARK JAPANESE MAPLE
Acer pseudosieboldianum	KOREAN MAPLE
Acer triflorum	THREE-FLOWERED MAPLE
Aesculus x neglecta 'Erythroblastos'	SUNRISE HORSE CHESTNUT, PAINTED BUCKEYE
Alnus incana 'Pendula'	WEEPING ALDER
Amelanchier x grandiflora	SERVICEBERRY
Araucaria araucana	MONKEY PUZZLE TREE
Aronia arbutifolia 'Brilliantissima'	BRILLIANT RED CHOKECHERRY
Bergenia cordifolia and hybrids	BERGENIA
Betula nigra 'Heritage'	HERITAGE BIRCH
Betula nigra 'Summer Cascade'	WEEPING RIVER BIRCH
Betula nigra 'Little King'	LITTLE KING RIVER BIRCH
Betula pendula 'Laciniata'	CUT-LEAF WEEPING BIRCH
Betula pendula 'Youngii'	YOUNG'S WEEPING BIRCH
Calamagrostis x acutiflora 'Karl Foerster'	FEATHER REED GRASS
Camellia x 'Elina Cascade'	HYBRID CAMELLIA
Carpinus betulus 'Pendula', 'Vienna Weeping'	WEEPING HORNBEAM
Cedrus atlantica 'Pendula'	WEEPING ATLAS CEDAR
Cercidiphyllum japonicum	KATSURA
Cercidiphyllum japonicum 'Morioka Weeping', 'Pendulum'	WEEPING KATSURA
Cercis canadensis 'Covey' ('Lavender Twist')	WEEPING REDBUD
Chamaecyparis lawsoniana 'Dik's Weeping'	WEEPING PORT ORFORD CEDAR
Clerodendrum trichotomum var. *fargesii*	HARLEQUIN GLORY-BOWER
Clethra alnifolia	SUMMERSWEET
Clethra barbinervis	JAPANESE CLETHRA
Cordyline australis, especially colored forms	CABBAGE PALM
Cornus alba 'Siberica'	RED-STEMMED OSIER
Cornus alternifolia 'Argentea'	VARIEGATED PAGODA DOGWOOD
Cornus mas 'Variegata'	VARIEGATED CORNELIAN CHERRY
Cornus sanguinea 'Arctic Sun', 'Midwinter Fire'	BLOODY DOGWOOD
Cornus sericea (C. stolonifera)	RED-OSIER DOGWOOD ❖
Cornus controversa 'Variegata'	WEDDING CAKE TREE
Cornus kousa 'Satomi'	RED FLOWERING KOUSA DOGWOOD
Cornus kousa var. *chinensis* 'Milky Way'	MILKY WAY DOGWOOD
Cornus kousa 'Weavers Weeping'	WEAVER'S WEEPING DOGWOOD

Corokia cotoneaster	COROKIA
Corylus avellana 'Burgundy Lace'	BURGUNDY CUT-LEAF FILBERT
Corylus avellana 'Contorta'	HARRY LAUDER'S WALKING STICK
Corylus avellana 'Red Dragon', 'Red Majestic'	RED CONTORTED FILBERT
Cotinus coggygria 'Golden Spirit'	GOLDEN SMOKETREE
Cotinus coggygria purple forms	PURPLE SMOKETREE
Cotoneaster 'Hessei'	HESSE'S COTONEASTER
Cotoneaster horizontalis	ROCKSPRAY COTONEASTER
Crataegus viridis 'Winter King'	WINTER KING HAWTHORN
Cryptomeria japonica 'Biroda'	DWARF JAPANESE CEDAR
Danae racemosa	POET'S LAUREL
Diospyros kaki	JAPANESE PERSIMMON
Enkianthus campanulatus	RED-VEIN ENKIANTHUS
Epimedium x perralchicum	HYBRID EPIMEDIUM
Epimedium wushu	SPINY-LEAF EPIMEDIUM
Eryngium proteiflorum	MEXICAN SEA HOLLY
Euphorbia x martinii 'Ascot Rainbow'	RAINBOW EUPHORBIA
Fagus sylvatica 'Aurea Pendula', 'Purple Fountain'	WEEPING BEECH
Fargesia dracocephala 'Garden Panda'	PANDA BAMBOO
X Fatshedera lizei, variegated forms	FATSHEDERA
Fothergilla 'Mt. Airy'	DWARF FOTHERGILLA
Ginkgo biloba 'Pendula', 'Weeping Wonder'	WEEPING GINKGO
Grevillea 'Audrey' (sold as 'Poorinda Constance')	AUDREY GREVILLEA
Halesia tetraptera	SILVER-BELLS
Hamamelis vernalis f. *carnea*	OZARK WITCH-HAZEL
Hamamelis x intermedia 'Diane'	DIANE WITCH-HAZEL
Heptacodium miconioides	SEVEN SONS FLOWER
Hydrangea quercifolia	OAKLEAF HYDRANGEA
Itea virginica 'Henry's Garnet'	VIRGINIA SWEETSPIRE
Juncus effusus 'Big Twister', 'Spiralis'	COMMON RUSH ❖
Juncus patens 'Elk Blue', 'Occidental Blue'	SPREADING RUSH ❖
Juniperus chinensis 'Kaizuka'	HOLLYWOOD JUNIPER
Larix decidua 'Puli'	WEEPING EUROPEAN LARCH
Larix kaempferi 'Pendula'	WEEPING LARCH
Leptospermum sericeum	SILVER TEA TREE
Maackia amurensis	AMUR MAACKIA
Mahonia eurybracteata 'Soft Caress'	SOFT CRESS BARBERRY
Malus 'Centurion'	CENTURION CRABAPPLE
Malus 'Golden Raindrops'	GOLDEN RAINDROPS CRABAPPLE
Malus 'Louisa'	WEEPING CRABAPPLE
Malus 'Royal Raindrops'	ROYAL RAINDROPS CRABAPPLE
Morus alba 'Chaparral'	WEEPING MULBERRY
Phlomis russeliana	TURKISH -SAGE
Phlomis tuberosa 'Amazone'	AMAZONE JERUSALEM-SAGE
Phormium colensoi	NEW ZEALAND MOUNTAIN FLAX
Physocarpus opulifolius 'Diablo'	PURPLE NINE-BARK
Picea breweriana	BREWER'S WEEPING SPRUCE ❖
Picea omorika 'Pendula Bruns'	WEEPING SERBIAN SPRUCE
Pinus densiflora 'Pendula'	WEEPING TANYOSHO PINE

Pinus densiflora 'Umbraculifera'	TANYOSHO PINE
Podocarpus lawrencei 'Purple King'	PURPLE KING MOUNTAIN PLUM-PINE
Prunus maackii	AMUR CHERRY
Prunus mume 'W. B. Clarke'	WEEPING JAPANESE APRICOT
Prunus pendula 'Plena-rosea'	DOUBLE WEEPING CHERRY
Prunus serrulata 'Kiku-Shidare-Zakura'	CHEAL'S WEEPING CHERRY
Prunus serrulata 'Snow Fountains'	WHITE WEEPING CHERRY
Prunus subhirtella 'Pendula Double'	DOUBLE WEEPING CHERRY
Prunus subhirtella 'Pendula'	WEEPING CHERRY
Pseudocydonia sinensis	CHINESE QUINCE
Pseudotsuga menziesii 'Graceful Grace'	WEEPING DOUGLAS-FIR ❖
Pyrus salicifolia 'Pendula'	WEEPING PEAR
Quercus hypoleucoides	SILVERLEAF OAK
Rehderodendron macrocarpum	CHINESE REHDERODENDRON
Rosa glauca (rubrifolia)	RED-LEAF ROSE
Rosa rugosa 'Frau Dagmar Hastrup'	JAPANESE BEACH ROSE
Sequoiadendron giganteum 'Pendulum'	WEEPING GIANT SEQUOIA
Sophora prostrata 'Little Baby'	LITTLE BABY DWARF KOWHAI
Sorbus pseudohupehensis 'Pink Pagoda'	PINK PAGODA ROWAN
Spiraea thunbergii 'Ogon'	OGON SPIREA
Stewartia monadelpha 'Pendula'	WEEPING STEWARTIA
Stewartia monadelpha	ORANGE-BARK STEWARTIA
Stewartia monadelpha 'Black Dog'	BLACK-STEM STEWARTIA
Stewartia pseudocamellia (especially var. *koreana*)	JAPANESE STEWARTIA
Stewartia 'Scarlet Sentinel'	SCARLET SENTINEL STEWARTIA
Styphnolobium japonica 'Pendula'	WEEPING JAPANESE PAGODA TREE
Styrax japonicus 'Marley's Pink Parasol'	WEEPING JAPANESE PINK SNOWBELL
Styrax japonicus 'Nightfall'	PURPLE WEEPING JAPANESE SNOWBELL
Styrax obassia	FRAGRANT SNOWBELL
Styrax wuyuanensis	CHINESE SNOWBELL
Syringa reticulata ssp. *pekinensis*	PEKIN LILAC, CHINESE TREE LILAC
Tetradium (Evodia) daniellii	KOREAN EVODI
Tilia tomentosa 'Petiolaris'	WEEPING SILVER LINDEN
Trachycarpus fortunei, including 'Wagnerianus'	CHINESE WINDMILL PALM
Tsuga canadensis 'Pendula	SARGENT'S WEEPING HEMLOCK ❖
Tsuga heterophylla 'Thorsen's Weeping'	THORSEN'S WEEPING HEMLOCK ❖
Ulmus glabra 'Camperdownii'	CAMPERDOWN ELM
Yucca species and hybrids (especially variegated forms)	YUCCA

FRAGRANT FLOWERS

"Flavors" range from subtle to "mile-away-nose-blaster" and from sweet to spicy. Some of these are strictly night blooming. Use such flowers along pathways, at key entrances, near the patio, outside and, especially with the night bloomers, under the bedroom window.

SMALL TREES

Amelanchier alnifolia	WESTERN SERVICEBERRY, JUNEBERRY, SASKATOON ❖
Argyrocytisus battandieri	MOROCCAN PINEAPPLE BROOM
Azara microphylla	SMALL-LEAVED AZARA
Chionanthus retusus	CHINESE FRINGE TREE
Clerodendrum trichotomum	HARLEQUIN GLORYBOWER
Crataegus douglasii	BLACK HAWTHORN ❖
Crataegus gaylussacia (C. douglasii ssp. *suksdorfii)*	KLAMATH HAWTHORN ❖
Maackia amurensis	AMUR MAACKIA
Magnolia 'Apollo', 'Athena', 'Heaven Scent'	MAGNOLIA
Magnolia compressa var. *langyuense*	DWARF ASIAN MAGNOLIA
Magnolia denudata	YULAN MAGNOLIA
Magnolia x *kewensis* 'Wada's Memory'	WADA'S MEMORY MAGNOLIA
Magnolia kobus	KOBUSHI
Magnolia laevifolia (Michelia yunnanensis)	YUNNAN MAGNOLIA
Magnolia x *loebneri* 'Ballerina', 'Leonard Messel', 'Spring Snow'	LOBNER MAGNOLIA
Magnolia sieboldii	OYAMA MAGNOLIA
Magnolia x *soulangeana* (several)	SAUCER MAGNOLIA
Magnolia stellata	STAR MAGNOLIA
Magnolia virginiana 'Henry Hicks', 'Moonglow', 'Tensaw'	SWEET BAY MAGNOLIA
Magnolia wilsonii	WILSON MAGNOLIA
Malus fusca	WESTERN CRABAPPLE ❖
Poliothyrsis sinensis	CHINESE PEARLBLOOM
Styrax japonicus	JAPANESE SNOWBELL
Styrax obassia	FRAGRANT SNOWBELL
Syringa reticulata	TREE LILAC
Syringa reticulata ssp. *pekinensis*	PEKIN LILAC, CHINESE TREE LILAC
Viburnum arbicolon 'Honey Tree'	HONEY TREE VIBURNUM

SHRUBS

Arctostaphylos columbiana	HAIRY MANZANITA ❖
Azara microphylla	SMALL-LEAF AZARA
Calycanthus x *raulstonii* 'Aphrodite'	APHRODITE SWEETSHRUB
Calycanthus occidentalis	SWEETSHRUB
Camellia 'Cinnamon Cindy', 'Fragrant Pink', 'Herme', 'High Fragrance', 'Minato-no-Akebono', 'Scentuous', 'Spring Mist', 'Spring Sonnet', 'Sweet Emily Kate'	FRAGRANT CAMELLIAS
Camellia sasanqua 'Setsugekka'	FRAGRANT AUTUMN CAMELLIA
Ceanothus cuneatus var. *cuneatus*	BUCK BRUSH ❖

350

Ceanothus velutinus	SNOWBRUSH ❖
Chimonanthus praecox	WINTERSWEET, JAPANESE ALLSPICE
Choisya ternata	MEXICAN ORANGE BLOSSOM
Chrysojasminum (Jasminum) floridum	SHOWY JASMINE
Chrysojasminum (Jasminum) parkeri	DWARF JASMINE
Clethra alnifolia	SUMMERSWEET
Corylopsis glabrescens	FRAGRANT WINTER HAZEL
Daphne bholua	NEPALESE PAPER PLANT
Daphne x *burkwoodii* 'Carol Mackie'	CAROL MACKIE DAPHNE
Daphne cneorum	GARLAND DAPHNE
Daphne x *medfordensis* 'Lawrence Crocker'	LAWRENCE CROCKER DAPHNE
Daphne odora 'Aureomarginata'	VARIEGATED WINTER DAPHNE
Daphne (odora X *bholua)* 'Perfume Princess'	PERFUME PRINCESS DAPHNE
Daphne x *rollsdorfii* 'Wilhelm Schacht'	WILHELM SCHACHT DAPHNE
Daphne tangutica	DWARF DAPHNE
Daphne x *transatlantica* 'Eternal Fragrance', 'Jim's Pride', 'Summer Ice'	HYBRID DAPHNE
Deutzia gracilis	SLENDER DEUTZIA
Deutzia scabra 'Flore-Pleno'	DOUBLE-FLOWERED FUZZY DEUTZIA
Edgeworthia chrysantha	PAPERBUSH
Eucryphia milliganii	DWARF LEATHERWOOD
Fothergilla gardenii	DWARF WITCHALDER
Fothergilla 'Mount Airy'	MOUNT AIRY DWARF WITCHALDER
Grevillea australis	SOUTHERN GREVILLEA
Hamamelis x *intermedia* especially 'Doerak', 'Limelight'	HYBRID WITCH-HAZEL
Hamamelis mollis especially 'Early Bouquet', 'Wisley Supreme'	CHINESE WITCH-HAZEL
Hamamelis vernalis especially 'Lombard's Weeping', 'New Year's Gold', 'Orange Surprise'	OZARK WITCH-HAZEL
Holodiscus discolor	OCEANSPRAY ❖
Leptodermis oblonga	HIMALAYAN LILAC
Lindera obtusiloba	JAPANESE SPICEBUSH
Linnaea (Abelia) x *grandiflora*	GLOSSY ABELIA
Lomatia polymorpha	MOUNTAIN GUITAR PLANT
Lonicera ferdinandii (L. versicaria)	KOREAN HONEYSUCKLE
Magnolia (Michelia) figo	BANANA SHRUB
Mahonia aquifolium	OREGON-GRAPE ❖
Mahonia x *media*	HYBRID MAHONIA
Mahonia nervosa	CASCADE OREGON-GRAPE ❖
Morella (Myrica) californica	PACIFIC WAX MYRTLE ❖
Olearia x *haastii*	FRAGRANT DAISY BUSH
Osmanthus x *burkwoodii*	BURKWOOD TEA-OLIVE
Osmanthus x *fortunei* 'San Jose'	SAN JOSE HOLLY-LEAF OSMANTHUS
Osmanthus fragrans	FRAGRANT TEA-OLIVE
Paeonia rockii and hybrids	ROCK'S TREE PEONY
Philadelphus 'Belle Etoile', 'Buckley's Quill', 'Glacier', 'Manteau d'Hermine', 'Virginal'	MOCK ORANGE
Philadelphus coronarius	MOCK ORANGE
Philadelphus lewisii	LEWIS' MOCK ORANGE ❖
Philadelphus madrensis	DESERT MOUNTAIN MOCK ORANGE
Philadelphus microphyllus	LITTLE-LEAF MOCK ORANGE

Rhododendron arborescens	TREE RHODODENDRON
Rhododendron canescens	MOUNTAIN AZALEA
Rhododendron (Azalea) 'Daviesii'	GHENT AZALEA
Rhododendron formosum	TAIWAN RHODODENDRON
Rhododendron japonicum	JAPANESE RHODODENDRON
Rhododendron (Azalea) luteum	YELLOW RHODODENDRON
Rhododendron (Azalea) molle	CHINESE AZALEA
Rhododendron (Azalea) occidentale	WESTERN AZALEA ❖
Rhododendron mucronulatum	KOREAN RHODODENDRON
Rhododendron (Azalea) prinophyllum	ROSE-SHELL AZALEA
Rhododendron hybrids: 'I Get Misty', 'Koromo Shikibu', 'Star Scent', 'Whitney White'	EVERGREEN AZALEA
Rhododendron hybrids: 'Admiral Semmes', 'Atlanta', 'Cannon's Double', 'Choice Cream', 'Choptank Rose', 'Colin Kendrick', 'Daviesii', 'Fragrant Star', 'Irene Koster', 'Jolie Madame', 'Klondyke', 'Late Date', 'Late Lady', 'Mt. St. Helens', 'My Mary', 'Narcissiflora', 'Rosy Cheeks', 'Snowbird', 'Stonewall Jackson', 'Washington State Centennial'	DECIDUOUS AZALEA
Ribes odoratum	CLOVE CURRANT
Rosa (many – see separate list: "DISEASE-FREE ROSES")	ROSES
Rosa nutkana	NOOTKA ROSE ❖
Sarcococca confusa	FRAGRANT SARCOCOCCA
Sarcococca hookeriana var. *humilis*	HIMALAYAN SWEET BOX
Sarcococca ruscifolia	FRAGRANT SWEETBOX
Syringa x chinensis	CHINESE LILAC
Syringa 'Josée'	JOSÉE LILAC
Syringa x laciniata	CUT-LEAF LILAC
Syringa meyeri 'Palibin'	MEYER LILAC, KOREAN LILAC
Syringa x persica	PERSIAN LILAC
Syringa pubescens ssp. *patula* 'Miss Kim'	MISS KIM LILAC
Syringa tomentella	FUZZY LILAC
Syringa vulgaris (especially older cultivars)	COMMON LILAC
Viburnum x bodnantense 'Dawn'	DAWN VIBURNUM
Viburnum x burkwoodii	BURKWOOD VIBURNUM
Viburnum x carlcephalum	HYBRID VIBURNUM
Viburnum carlesii	KOREAN SPICE VIBURNUM
Viburnum 'Chesapeake'	CHESAPEAKE VIBURNUM
Viburnum farreri	FRAGRANT VIBURNUM
Viburnum x juddii	JUDD VIBURNUM
Viburnum odoratissimum var. *awabuki*	AWABUKI SWEET VIBURNUM
Viburnum x pragense	PRAGUE VIBURNUM
Viburnum utile	SERVICE VIBURNUM

VINES

Chrysojasminum (Jasminum) humile	YELLOW JASMINE
Chrysojasminum (Jasminum) humile f. *wallichianum*	NEPAL JASMINE
Chrysojasminum (Jasminum) odoratissimum	SWEETEST JASMINE

Clematis armandii	EVERGREEN CLEMATIS
Clematis x cartmanii 'Avalanche'	AVALANCHE EVERGREEN CLEMATIS
Clematis 'Delightful Scent'	SUGAR SWEET CLEMATIS
Clematis montana	ANEMONE CLEMATIS
Clematis terniflora	SWEET AUTUMN VIRGIN'S BOWER
Clematis x triternata 'Rubromarginata'	HYBRID CLEMATIS
Holboellia brachyandra 'Heavenly Ascent'	HOLBOELLIA VINE
Holboellia coriacea	SAUSAGE VINE
Jasminum beesianum	RED JASMINE
Jasminum officinale	COMMON JASMINE
Jasminum officinale f. *affine*	POET'S JASMINE
Jasminum x stephanense	STEPHAN'S JASMINE
Lonicera acuminata (L. henryi)	HENRY'S HONEYSUCKLE
Lonicera x heckrottii	GOLDFLAME HONEYSUCKLE
Mandevilla laxa	CHILEAN JASMINE
Rosa climbers 'Candy Land', 'Constance Spry'	CLIMBING ROSE

PERENNIALS, BULBS

Actaea simplex	BUGBANE
Androsace lanuginosa	WOOLLY ROCK JASMINE
Androsace sarmentosa	COMMON ROCK JASMINE
Clematis integrifolia 'Hakurei'	SOLITARY CLEMATIS
Clematis recta	GROUND VIRGIN'S BOWER
Crinum x powellii	POWELL LILY
Dianthus caryophyllus and hybrids	CARNATION
Dianthus petraeus ssp. *noeanus*	FRAGRANT SNOWFLAKE GARDEN PINK
Dicentra formosa var. *formosa*	BLEEDING HEART ❖
Erysimum capitatum	WALLFLOWER ❖
Galium oreganum	SWEET WOODRUFF ❖
Glumicalyx goseloides	NODDING CHOCOLATE FLOWER
Hosta 'Fragrant Blue', 'Fragrant Bouquet', 'So Sweet'	FRAGRANT HOSTAS
Hyacinthoides hispanica (NOT *H.* x massartiana)	SPANISH BLUEBELL
Hyacinthus orientalis	HYACINTH
Iris confusa	BAMBOO IRIS
Iris germanica hybrids	BEARDED IRIS
Lilium auratum hybrids	JAPANESE GOLDEN-RAYED LILY
Lilium cernuum	NODDING LILY
Lilium lankongense	TURKS-CAP LILY
Lilium leucanthum var. *centifolium*	BLACK DRAGON LILY
Lilium parryi	LEMON LILY ❖
Lilium regale and hybrids	REGAL LILIES
Lilium speciosum and hybrids	JAPANESE LILY
Lilium washingtonianum	CASCADE LILY ❖
Linnaea borealis var. *longiflora*	TWINFLOWER ❖
Maianthemum (Smilacina) henryi	FRAGRANT FALSE SOLOMON'S SEAL
Matthiola fruticulosa ssp. *perennis*	PERENNIAL STOCK
Narcissus x italicus 'Thalia'	ITALIAN ANGEL'S TEARS

Narcissus jonquilla and hybrids	JONQUIL
Narcissus poeticus and hybrids	POET'S NARCISSUS
Narcissus tazetta cultivars	BUNCH-FLOWER DAFFODIL
Oenothera fruticosa	SUNDROPS
Pachysandra axillaris 'Windcliff Fragrant'	WINDCLIFF FRAGRANT PACHYSANDRA
Paeonia cambessedesii	MAJORCAN PEONY
Paeonia emodi	HIMALAYAN PEONY

Paeonia lactiflora hybrids 'August Dessert', 'Bouquet Perfect', 'Chestine Gowdy',
   'Cora Stubbs', 'Diana Parks', 'Duchesse de Nemours', 'Henry Bockstoce', 'Hermione',
   'Kansas', 'Madame Calot', 'Mme. Emile Lemoine', 'Mme. de Verneville',
   'Myrtle Gentry', 'Noemie Demay', 'Philomele', 'Pink Hawaiian Coral',
   'Romantic Lace', 'Sea Shell'   PEONY

Phlox 'Minnie Pearl'	MINNIE PEARL PHLOX
Phlox stolonifera	CREEPING PHLOX
Polemonium 'Heaven Scent'	FRAGRANT JACOB'S LADDER
Saponaria officinalis	SOAPWORT, BOUNCING BET
Sinningia tubiflora	HARDY WHITE GLOXINIA
Tellima grandiflora	FOAM FLOWER ❖
Viola alba ssp. *dehnhardtii*	PARMA VIOLET
Viola odorata	SWEET VIOLET

ANNUALS, BIENNIALS *(including tropicals treated as such)*

Dianthus barbatus	SWEET WILLIAM
Erysimum cheiri	ENGLISH WALLFLOWER
Heliotropium arborescens	HELIOTROPE
Lathyrus odoratus	SWEET PEA
Matthiola incana	STOCK
Matthiola longipetala bicornis	EVENING-SCENTED STOCK
Mirabilis jalapa	FOUR O'CLOCK
Nicotiana x sanderae	FLOWERING TOBACCO
Nicotiana sylvestris	GIANT FLOWERING TOBACCO
Zaluzianskya capensis	NIGHT PHLOX

"I know that if odor were visible, as color is, I'd see the summer garden in rainbow clouds."
~~ Robert Bridges

SCENTED FOLIAGE

Not including common leafy herbs. Rule of thumb: almost all of these would prefer to be in a lean dry soil in sunshine. The trees will help create that natural forest smell while the smaller plants are good near the patio or along a pathway where their leaves can be touched, crushed, and sniffed.

TREES

Abies balsamea	BALSAM FIR
Abies bracteata	INCIENSO
Abies concolor	WHITE FIR
Abies fraseri	FRASER FIR
Abies grandis	GRAND FIR ❖
Calocedrus decurrens	INCENSE CEDAR
Cedrus species	ATLAS AND DEODAR CEDARS
Cercidiphyllum japonicum	KATSURA
Chamaecyparis lawsoniana	LAWSON CYPRESS ❖
Clerodendrum trichotomum var. *fargesii* (the variety *fargesii* only)	HARLEQUIN BOWER
Hesperocyparis (Cupressus) bakeri	BAKER CYPRESS
Hesperocyparis (Cupressus) macnabiana	MACNAB'S CYPRESS
Hesperocyparis (Cupressus) macrocarpa	MONTEREY CYPRESS
Callitropsis (Chamaecyparis, Cupressus, Xanthocyparis) nootkatensis	
	ALASKA YELLOW-CEDAR ❖
Drimys winteri	WINTER'S BARK
Juniperus chinensis 'Kaizuka'	HOLLYWOOD JUNIPER
Larix decidua	EUROPEAN LARCH
Larix occidentalis	WESTERN LARCH ❖
Laurus 'Saratoga'	SARATOGA BAY LAUREL
Nothaphoebe cavaleriei	NOTHAPHOEBE
Peumus boldus	BOLDO
Picea abies	NORWAY SPRUCE
Picea pungens	COLORADO BLUE SPRUCE
Pinus monophylla	ONE-LEAF PIÑON
Pinus parviflora	JAPANESE WHITE PINE
Pinus ponderosa	PONDEROSA PINE ❖
Pinus sylvestris	SCOTS PINE
Pseudotsuga menziesii	DOUGLAS-FIR
Sequoia sempervirens	COAST REDWOOD
Thuja occidentalis	ARBORVITAE
Thuja plicata	WESTERN RED-CEDAR ❖
Tsuga heterophylla	WESTERN HEMLOCK ❖
Tsuga mertensiana	MOUNTAIN HEMLOCK ❖
Umbellularia californica	CALIFORNIA BAY ❖

»» More...

SHRUBS

Baeckea gunniana	HEATHMYRTLE
Calycanthus occidentalis	CALIFORNIA ALLSPICE
Caryopteris incana	BLUEBEARD
Caryopteris x clandonensis	BLUE MIST
Choisya ternata	MEXICAN ORANGE BLOSSOM
Cistus, especially *Cistus* x pagei	ROCKROSE
Clerodendrum trichotomum var. *fargesii* (the variety *fargesii* only)	HARLEQUIN BOWER
Colquhounia elegans	COLQUHOUNIA
Elsholtzia stauntonii	CHINESE MINT SHRUB
Gaultheria procumbens	WINTERGREEN
Juniperus communis	COMMON JUNIPER ❖
Lavandula x allardii	SWEET LAVENDER
Lavandula 'Goodwin Creek Grey'	LAVENDER
Lavandula x intermedia	LAVANDINS
Lindera benzoin	SPICEBUSH
Melianthus major	HONEYBUSH
Monardella odoratissima	MOUNTAIN MONARDELLA ❖
Olearia moschata	INCENSE PLANT
Philotheca myoporoides	LONG-LEAF WAX FLOWER
Phlomis fruticosa	JERUSALEM-SAGE
Prostanthera cuneata	ALPINE MINT BUSH
Rhododendron 'PJM Elite'	HYBRID RHODODENDRON
Rhus aromatica	FRAGRANT SUMAC
Rhus aromatica 'Gro-Low'	GRO-LOW FRAGRANT SUMAC
Rosa eglanteria (R. rubiginosa)	SWEET BRIAR
Salvia rosmarinus (Rosmarinus officinalis)	ROSEMARY
Sambucus nigra	BLACK ELDERBERRY
Teucrium chamaedrys	WALL GERMANDER
Teucrium fruticans	BUSH GERMANDER
Teucrium marum	CAT THYME
Vitex agnus-castus	CHASTE TREE

PERENNIALS

Achillea 'Moonshine'	YARROW
Agastache 'Blue Fortune'	BLUE FORTUNE HYBRID HYSSOP
Agastache cana	HUMMINGBIRD MINT
Agastache foeniculum (A. anisatum)	ANISE-HYSSOP
Agastache hybrids (many)	HYBRID HYSSOP
Agastache pallidiflora (A. austromontana)	ROSE-HYSSOP
Agastache rugosa	KOREAN MINT
Agastache rupestris	LICORICE-MINT
Agastache urticifolia	GIANT HYSSOP ❖
Anthriscus sylvestris	LADY'S LACE
Artemisia abrotanum	SOUTHERNWOOD
Artemisia absinthium	ABSINTH, WORMWOOD

Artemisia annua (annual)	SWEET ANNIE
Artemisia chamaemelifolia	CHAMOMILE WORMWOOD
Artemisia lactiflora	WHITE MUGWORT
Artemisia ludoviciana cultivars	WESTERN MUGWORT ❖
Artemisia vulgaris	COMMON MUGWORT
Asarum caudatum	WESTERN WILD GINGER
Ballota acetabulosa	GREEK HOREHOUND
Ballota pseudodictamnus	GRECIAN HOREHOUND
Calamintha grandiflora	LARGE-FLOWERED CALAMINT
Calamintha nepeta	LESSER CALAMINT
Chamaemelum nobile	ROMAN CHAMOMILE
Clinopodium (Micromeria) douglasii	YERBA BUENA ❖
Comptonia peregrina	SWEET-FERN
Dracocephalum rupestre	DRAGONHEAD
Foeniculum vulgare 'Purpureum' (don't let it go to seed)	BRONZE FENNEL
Galium odoratum	SWEET WOODRUFF
Geranium x cantabrigiense	HARDY GERANIUM, CRANESBILL
Geranium macrorrhizum	BIGROOT GERANIUM
Geranium x riversleaianum	HARDY GERANIUM
Helichrysum italicum	CURRY PLANT
Hierochloe odorata	SWEET GRASS ❖
Lavandula angustifolia	ENGLISH LAVENDER
Lavandula dentata	FRENCH LAVENDER
Lavandula pinnata	FERNLEAF LAVENDER
Marrubium incanum	SILVER HOREHOUND
Marrubium rotundifolium	SILVER EDGED HOREHOUND
Matricaria recutita (annual)	GERMAN CHAMOMILE
Melittis melissophyllum	BASTARD BALM
Mentha requienii	CORSICAN MINT
Micromeria fruticosa	LITTLE MINT, WHITE-LEAVED SAVORY
Monarda fistulosa 'Claire Grace'	WILD BEE BALM
Monarda mildew-free hybrids:	BEE BALM

'Blue Stocking', 'Blue Wreath', 'Colrain Red', 'Dark Ponticum',
'Gardenview Scarlet', 'Grand Marshall', 'Marshall's Delight', 'Purple Rooster',
'Raspberry Wine', 'Violet Queen'

Monarda 'Lambada'	LAMBADA BEE BALM
Monardella odoratissima	MOUNTAIN MINT, COYOTE MINT ❖
Nepeta x faassenii	CATMINT
Nepeta racemosa 'Walker's Low'	WALKER'S LOW CATMINT
Nepeta 'Six Hills Giant'	CATMINT
Origanum dictamnus	DITTANY OF CRETE
Origanum majorana (summer seasonal)	SWEET MARJORAM
Origanum x majoricum	ITALIAN/SICILIAN MARJORAM, HARDY MARJORAM
Pelargonium (hundreds of tender species and cultivars)	SCENTED GERANIUMS
Phlomis russeliana	TURKISH-SAGE
Phlomis tuberosa	SAGE-LEAF MULLEIN
Pycnanthemum pilosum	MOUNTAIN MINT
Salvia cohuilensis 'Nuevo Leon'	NUEVO LEON SAGE
Salvia dorrii	GRAY BALL SAGE, PURPLE SAGE ❖

Salvia (Perovskia) 'Filigran'	CUT-LEAF RUSSIAN SAGE
Salvia melissodora	GRAPE-SCENTED SAGE
Salvia sclarea (biennial)	CLARY SAGE
Salvia spathacea	HUMMINGBIRD SAGE
Salvia yangii (Perovskia atriplicifolia) and hybrids	RUSSIAN SAGE
Santolina chamaecyparissus	LAVENDER COTTON
Santolina virens	GREEN SANTOLINA
Saponaria officinalis	SOAPWORT, BOUNCING BET
Stachys albotomentosa	SEVEN-UP SAGE
Stachys chamissonis var. *cooleyae*	HEDGE-NETTLE ❖
Stachys coccinea	SCARLET BETONY
Tanacetum (Chrysanthemum) balsamita	COSTMARY
Tanacetum parthenium	FEVERFEW
Teucrium canadense	AMERICAN GERMANDER, WOOD SAGE ❖
Thymus many ornamental forms	THYME

"It is a golden maxim to cultivate the garden for the nose, and the eyes will take care of themselves."
~~ Robert Louis Stevenson

FUZZY, FURRY, WOOLLY,
TOUCHY-FEELY FOLIAGE

In addition to inviting touch, these plants provide a background foil to rich, dark, and/or bright colors. Rule of thumb: almost all of these would prefer to be in a lean dry soil. Includes a few annuals/tender perennials.

Achillea ageratifolia	GREEK YARROW
Achillea clavennae	SILVER YARROW
Achillea serbica	SERBIAN YARROW
Amicia zygomeris	YOKE-LEAVED AMICIA
Artemisia ludoviciana 'Silver Queen'	SILVER QUEEN SAGE
Brachyglottis 'Sunshine'	DAISY BUSH
Buddleja crispa	HIMALAYAN BUTTERFLY BUSH
Buddleja curviflora	LAVENDER BUTTERFLY BUSH
Buddleja knappii	LILAC BUTTERFLY BUSH
Buddleja loricata	MOUNTAIN SAGEWOOD
Buddleja marrubiifolia	WOOLLY BUTTERFLY BUSH
Buddleja 'Morning Mist' ('Silver Anniversary')	MORNING MIST BUTTERFLY BUSH
Buddleja nivea	WOOLLY BUTTERFLY BUSH
Buddleja x pikei 'Hever'	CASTLE BUTTERFLY BUSH
Buddleja salviifolia	SAGE WOOD
Calceolaria arachnoidea	CAPACHITO MORADO, SILVER SLIPPERWORT
Celmisia semicordata	LARGE MOUNTAIN DAISY
Centaurea cineraria	VELVET CINERARIA, DUSTY MILLER
Centaurea gymnocarpa	DUSTY MILLER
Centaurea ragusina	SILVER KNAPWEED, DUSTY MILLER
Cerastium tomentosum	SNOW-IN-SUMMER
Coleus (Plectranthus) argentatus	SILVER SPURFLOWER
Epilobium canum (Zauschneria californica)	CALIFORNIA FUCHSIA
Epilobium (Zauschneria) septentrionalis 'Select Mattole'	CALIFORNIA FUCHSIA
Eriogonum latifolium	SEASIDE BUCKWHEAT ❖
Eriogonum niveum	SNOW BUCKWHEAT ❖
Eriogonum ovalifolium var. *nivale*	CUSHION BUCKWHEAT ❖
Eriophyllum lanatum var. *integrifolium*	OREGON SUNSHINE ❖
Helichrysum argyrophyllum	GOLDEN GUINEA EVERLASTING
Helichrysum italicum	CURRY PLANT
Helichrysum petiolare	LICORICE PLANT
Jacobaea maritima	DUSTY MILLER
Lavandula x chaytoriae 'Richard Gray'	RICHARD GRAY LAVENDER
Lavandula lanata	WOOLLY LAVENDER
Leptospermum lanigerum	WOOLLY TEA TREE
Lotus (Dorycnium) hirsutus	HAIRY CANARY-FLOWER
Marrubium rotundifolium	SILVER EDGED HOREHOUND
Origanum dictamnus	DITTANY OF CRETE, DITTANY
Phlomis anatolica 'Lloyd's Variety'	ANATOLIAN-SAGE
Phlomis angustissima	DWARF GOLDEN TURKISH-SAGE
Phlomis fruticosa	JERUSALEM-SAGE

Phlomis italica	BALEARIC ISLAND-SAGE
Phlomis purpurea	PURPLE-SAGE
Phlomis russeliana	TURKISH-SAGE
Rhodanthemum (Chrysanthemum) hosmariense	MOROCCAN DAISY
Salix helvetica	SWISS WILLOW
Salix lanata	WOOLLY WILLOW
Salix lapponum	DOWNY WILLOW
Salix repens ssp. *argentea*	CREEPING WILLOW
Salix salicola 'Polar Bear'	POLAR BEAR WILLOW
Salvia argentea	SILVER SAGE
Salvia discolor	ANDEAN SILVER-LEAF SAGE
Salvia dorrii var. *incana*	PURPLE SAGE
Salvia canescens var. *daghestanica*	DWARF SILVERLEAF SAGE
Santolina chamaecyparissus	LAVENDER COTTON
Senecio candicans 'Angel Wings'	DUSTY MILLER
Senecio niveoaureus	SILVER FEATHERS
Senecio vira-vira	DUSTY MILLER
Silene (Lychnis) coronaria	ROSE CAMPION
Sphaeralcea ambigua	DESERT GLOVE MALLOW
Stachys byzantina (S. lanata)	LAMB'S-EARS
Tanacetum haradjanii (T. densum amanii)	SILVER LACE TANSY
Tanacetum ptarmiciflorum	SILVER LACE PLANT
Teucrium aroanium	GRAY CREEPING GERMANDER
Thymus praecox 'Pseudolanuginosus'	WOOLLY THYME
Verbascum bombyciferum 'Arctic Summer' (biennial)	GIANT SILVER MULLEIN
Verbascum densiflorum	DENSE-FLOWERED MULLEIN
Verbascum eriophorum	COTTON MULLEIN
Verbascum epixanthinum	YELLOW MULLEIN
Verbascum x splendidum	SPLENDID MULLEIN
Veronica pectinata	WOOLLY SPEEDWELL
Vitis vinifera 'Incana'	DUSTY MILLER GRAPE VINE

STYLES & THEMES

There is the very common practice of collecting one's favorite plants and growing them well. There is then putting all the plants together using the principles of "design." And ultimately there is choosing particular plants for the design and using them all in a way which gives a particular "feel" to the whole and sends a "message." This is called "style."

Look for the symbol ❖ which indicates a native plant.

AN OLD-FASHIONED GARDEN

It's all about memories. In plant names, in fragrances, and mostly in what our mom or dad or grandmother, etc. grew in their gardens. Some plants may simply have that casual "feel" of olden days. I've put "introduction" dates to many of these plants; a history lesson if nothing else.

TREES

Abies concolor	WHITE FIR
Betula pendula	EUROPEAN WHITE BIRCH
Crataegus crus-galli	COCKSPUR HAWTHORNE
Cedrus deodara	DEODAR CEDAR
Erica arborea	TREE HEATH
Fagus sylvatica	EUROPEAN BEECH
Magnolia kobus	KOBUSHI
Magnolia x *soulangeana* (<1825)	SAUCER MAGNOLIA
'Rustica Rubra' (<1893), 'Lennei Alba' (ca 1900), 'Norbertii' (<1935)	
Malus pumila	WILD APPLE, CRABAPPLE
Especially 'Dolgo' (1897), 'Hewes Virginia' (<1817), 'Transcendent' (<1844), 'Whitney' (1869)	
Malus floribunda	JAPANESE FLOWERING CRAB
Picea abies	NORWAY SPRUCE
Picea glauca	WHITE SPRUCE
Picea orientalis	ORIENTAL SPRUCE
Pinus densiflora	JAPANESE RED PINE
Pinus nigra	AUSTRIAN PINE
Platanus x *acerifolia*	LONDON PLANE
Quercus robur	ENGLISH OAK
Syringa reticulata	JAPANESE TREE LILAC
Vitex agnus-castus (standard)	CHASTE TREE

SHRUBS

Aucuba japonica	JAPANESE LAUREL
Buxus sempervirens [especially 'Suffruticosa']	EUROPEAN BOXWOOD
Callicarpa japonica	JAPANESE BEAUTYBERRY
Calluna vulgaris	SCOTCH HEATHER
Camellia (see separate list)	CAMELLIA
Chaenomeles japonica	JAPANESE QUINCE, JAPONICA
Chaenomeles x *superba* (ca 1913)	FLOWERING QUINCE
Dasiphora (*Potentilla*) *fruticosa*	SHRUBBY CINQUEFOIL
Deutzia crenata 'Pride-of-Rochester'	DOUBLE-FLOWERED DEUTZIA
Deutzia scabra 'Flore-pleno'	DOUBLE-FLOWERED FUZZY DEUTZIA
Forsythia x *intermedia*	FORSYTHIA
Hibiscus syriacus	ROSE-OF-SHARON
Hydrangea arborescens	WILD HYDRANGEA
Hydrangea macrophylla (1788)	HYDRANGEA

'Nigra' (1853), 'Otaska' (1862), 'Mariesii' (1879), 'Curtis Legacy' (1885),
'Blue Wave' (ca 1900), 'Lilacina' (ca 1900), 'Veitchii' (1881/1903),
'General Vicomtesse de Vibraye' (1909)

Hydrangea paniculata	PANICLE HYDRANGEA
Hydrangea quercifolia	OAK-LEAF HYDRANGEA
Hydrangea serrata	MOUNTAIN HYDRANGEA
Kerria japonica 'Pleniflora' (1805)	JAPANESE ROSE
Linnaea (Abelia) x grandiflora	ABELIA
Philadelphus coronarius	MOCK ORANGE
Pieris japonica	LILY-OF-THE-VALLEY SHRUB, ANDROMEDA
Prunus triloba var. *plena*	FLOWERING ALMOND
Rhododendron Ghent hybrids	AZALEAS
Rosa (see separate section)	ROSES
Sambucus nigra f. *laciniata*	FERN-LEAF ELDER
Sambucus nigra var. *canadensis* 'Aurea'	GOLDEN ELDER
Spiraea cantoniensis 'Flore Pleno' (1849)	BRIDAL WREATH
Spiraea prunifolia 'Plena' (ca 1800)	BRIDAL WREATH
Spiraea x vanhouttei	VANHOUTTE SPIREA
Syringa x chinensis 'Bicolor' (1853)	CHINESE HYBRID LILAC
Syringa villosa	LATE LILAC
Syringa vulgaris	LILAC

Especially 'Alba Grandiflora' (1831), 'Philémon' (1840), 'Azurea Plena' (1843),
'Clara Cochet' (1855), 'Marlyensis Pallida' (1864), 'Scipion Cochet' (<1872),
'Princess Alexandra' (1874), 'Lemoinei' (1878), 'Mathieu de Dombasle' (1882),
'Dr. von Regel' (1883), 'Frau Berta Dammann' (1883), 'Geheimrat Heyder' (1883),
'Le Gaulois' (1884), 'Alphonse Lavallée' (1885), 'Michel Buchner' (1885),
'Emil Liebig' (1887), 'Fürst Lichtenstein' (1887), 'Geheimrat Singelmann' (1887),
'Vergeismeinnicht' (1887), 'Léon Simon' (1888), 'Claude de Lorrain' (1889),
'Professor Sargent' (1889), 'Linné' (1890), 'Belle de Nancy' (1891),
'Mme F. Morel' (1892), 'Charles Baltet' (1893), 'Louis Henry' (1894),
'Abel Carrière' (1896), 'Boussingault' (1896), 'Maréchal de Bassompierre' (1897),
'Arthur William Paul' (1898), 'Marc Micheli' (1898), 'Colbert' (1899)

Syringa French hybrids	FRENCH LILAC

Especially 'Jacques Callot' (1876), 'Ludwig Späth' (1883),
'Michael Buckner' (1885), 'Congo' (1890s), 'Charles Joly' (1896)

Syringa x hyacinthiflora	HYBRID LILAC

Especially 'Hyacinthiflora Plena' (1874), 'Berryer', 'Catinat',
'Montesquieu', 'Necker', 'Turgot', 'Vauban'

Viburnum opulus "Sterile" (<1554)	SNOWBALL BUSH
Viburnum plicatum f. *tomentosum* 'Mariesii'	DOUBLEFILE VIBURNUM
Vitex agnus-castus	CHASTE TREE
Weigela florida	WEIGELA

CAMELLIAS

Camellia japonica   CAMELLIA

'Momoiro Wabisuke' (1600s)
'Hagoromo' ("Feathered Robe",
    'Cho No Hagasane') (1695);
    introduced to US as
    'Magnoliaeflora' in 1886
'Kumasaka' (1695)
'Tinsie' ('Bokuhan', 1719)
'Alba Plena' (1792)
'Elegans' ('Chandleri Elegans Pink')
    (<1806/1831)
'Candidissima' (1812)
'Alba Simplex' (1813)
'Althaeiflora' (1819)
'Nobilissima' (1834)
'Coquettii' (1840)
'Sarah Frost' (1841)
'Marguerite Gouillon' (1845)
'Dobrei' (1849)
'C. M. Hovey' (1850)
'Daikagura' ("Great Sacred Dance")
    (1851)
'Mme de Strekaloff' (1855)
'Carousel' (1858)
'Contessa Lavinia Maggi' (1858)
'Mathotiana Alba' (1858)
'Hikaru Genji' ("Brilliant Genji")
(1859)
'Margherita Coleoni Variegated' (1859)
'Mikenjaku' ('Nagasaki') (1859)
'Prince Eugene Napoleon' (1859)
'Christmas Beauty' (1859)
'Variegata' (1866)

'Apollo' (1874)
'Mathotiana Rosea' (1874)
'Herme' (1875)
'Francine' ('Chandleri Elegans Pink
    Variegated', "Pride of the
    Emperor's Garden") (1860)
'Pink Perfection' ('Usu-otome') (1875)
'Adolphe Audusson' (1877)
'Arejishi' (1877)
'Side Kakushi' ('Lotus') (1879)
'Elena Nobile' (1881)
'Beni-otome' (1884)
'Mathotiana' (1886)
'Lady Clare' (1887)
'Lady Vansittart' (1887)
'Purity' (1887) ('Shiragiku'?; 1695)
'Grandiflora Rosea' (1890)
'Gloire de Nantes' (1895)
'Yuki Botan' (1895)
'Kumasaka' (1896)
'Apollo' (1900)
'Jupiter' (1900)
'Kimberley' (ca 1900)
'Devonia' (1901)
'Debutante' (early 1900s)
'Imperator' (1908)
'Prof. Charles S. Sargent' (1925)
'Haku Rakuten' (1929)
'Apple Blossom' (1930)
'Kouron Jura' (1930)
'Furo an' (1939)

Camellia sasanqua var. *anemoniflora* (1850)   JAPANESE CAMELLIA
Camellia x williamsii   HYBRID CAMELLIA

'Bow Bells' (1925)
'Mary Christian' (1920s?)
'C. F. Coates' (1935)

'St. Ewe' (<1940)
'J. C. Williams' (1940)
'Philippa Forwood' (1940)

Other hybrids

'Salutation' (1936)

ROSES

VF indicates very fragrant
++ indicates repeat bloom

Species Roses and Earliest hybrids

Rosa x damascena bifera **VF**	ROSE OF CASTILE
Rosa foetida	AUSTRIAN BRIAR
Rosa foetida 'Bicolor' (<1590)	AUSTRIAN COPPER
Rosa foetida 'Persiana' (<1837)	PERSIAN DOUBLE YELLOW
Rosa 'Harison's Yellow' (Foetida hybrid) **VF** (1830)	HARISON'S YELLOW ROSE
Rosa 'Macrantha' **VF** (early Gallica hybrid)	MACRANTHA ROSE
Rosa x odorata 'Mutabilis' **VF** ++ (<1896)	BUTTERFLY CHINA ROSE
Rosa roxburghii (<1814)	CHESTNUT ROSE
Rosa rugosa **VF** ++	JAPANESE BEACH ROSE
Rosa rugosa alba **VF** ++	WHITE JAPANESE BEACH ROSE
Rosa rugosa rubra **VF** ++	RED JAPANESE BEACH ROSE
Rosa wichuraiana	MEMORIAL ROSE

Old Garden Roses

There are plenty more "old garden roses" (OGRs) available. The following are cultivars with minimal disease and other issues in our climate. In order of year discovered/bred.

Rosa x centifolia   PROVENCE ROSE

'Bullata' (1801) "LETTUCE ROSE"   'Village Maid' (1839)
'Spong' (1805)   'Panaché Double' (1839)
'Andrewsii' (1807)   'Variegata' (1845)
'Unique Panachée' (<1821)   'La Noblesse' (1856)
'Cristata' (1827)   'Petitie Orléannaise' (1900)
'Alain Blanchard' (1829)

Rosa x damascena   DAMASK ROSE

'Celsiana' (before 1817)   'Gloire des Mousseux' (1852; Moss)
'Petitie Lisette' (1817)   'René d'Anjou' (1853; Moss)
'The Bishop' (?1821)   'Maréchal Davoust (1853; Moss)
'Isaphan' (1827)   'Capitaine John Ingram' (1854; Moss)
'Leda' (1827)   'Salet' (1854; Autumn Damask Moss)
'Mme Zoetmans' (1830)   'Mousseline' (1855; Moss)
'Mme Hardy' (1832;   'Botzaris (1856)
   maybe a Damask x Alba)   'Mme Delaroche-Lambert' (1856;
'Quarte Saisons Blanc Mousseux'   Autumn Damask Moss)
   (1835)   'Duchesse de Verneuil' (1856; Moss;
'Blanchefleur' (1835)   or x ?China)
'La Ville de Bruxelles' (1836/1849?)   'James Mitchell' (1861; Moss)
'Ocillet Parfait' (1841)   'Henri Martin' (1863; Moss)
'Comtesse de Murinais' (1843; Moss)   'Soupert et Notting' (1874;
'Nuits de Young' (1845; Moss)   Autumn Damask Moss)

'Little Gem' (1880; Moss)   'Striped Moss' (1880; Moss)
'Blanch Moreau' (1880; Moss)   'Omar Khayyam' (1894)
'Rose de Resht' (Autumn Damask)

Rosa gallica   GALLICA ROSE

Rosa gallica var. *officinalis* APOTHECARY ROSE (traditional for making tea/tisane)
Rosa gallica var. *officinalis* 'Versicolor' (<1581) ROSA MUNDI

'Charles de Mills' ('Bizarre   'Cramoisi Picoté' (1834)
   Triomphant'?; ca 1786/1790)   'Duc de Guiche' (1835)
'Agathe' (<1815)   'Président de Sèze' (1836)
'Hippolyte' (early 1800s)   'Alain Blanchard' (1839)
'Duc de Guiche' (pre-1810)   'Néron' (1841)
'Marie Louise' (1813)   'Belle Isis' (1845)
'Gloire de France' (1819)   'Perle des Panachés' (1845)
'Ipsilante' (1821)   'Tricolor de Flandres' (1846)
'Beau Narcisse' (pre-1824)   'Duchesse de Buccleugh' (1846)
'Cristata' (1826; Moss)   'Cardinal de Richelieu' (pre-1847)
'Jenny Duval' (1837)   'Boule de Nanteuil' (1848)
'D'Agueseau' (1823)   'Belle de Crécy' (1848)
'Assemblage des Beautées' (1823)   'Tuscany Superb' (1848)
'Duchesse de Montebello' (1824)   'Georges Vibert' (1853)
'Camaieux' (1830)   'Marcel Bourgouin' (1889)
'Surpasse Tout' (1832)

Hybrid Perpetuals

'Baronne Prévost' (1842)   'Prince Camille de Rohan' (1861)
'Le Reine' (1842)   'John Hopper' (1862)
'Jules Margottin' (1853)   'Gloire de Ducher' (1865)
'Général Jacqueminot' (1853)   'Fisher Holmes' (1865)
'Triomphe de l'Exposition' (1855)   'Paul Neyron' (1869)
'Empéreur du Maroe' (1858)   'Le Havre' (1871)
'Reine des Violettes' (1860)   'Eugène Fürst' (1875)

Rosa rugosa hybrids

'Fimbriata' (1891)   'Hansa' (1905)
'Blanc Double de Coubert' (1892)   'Magnifica' (1905)
'Belle Poiterine' (1894)   'Gipsy Boy' (Bourbon x *R. rugosa*)
'Mrs. Anthony Waterer' (1898)   (1909)
'Delicata' (1898)   'Frau Dagmar Hastrup' (1914)
'Conrad Ferdinand Meyer' (1899)   'F. J. Grootendorst' (1918)
'Roseraie de l'Hay' (1901)

Rosa eglanteria (R. rubiginosa) Penzance hybrids (1894-1895)

'Anne de Geierstein'   'Lady Penzance'
'Brenda'   'Lord Penzance'
'Edith Bellenden'   'Lucy Ashton'
'Greenmantle'   'Meg Merrilees'
'Jeanie Deans'   'Minna'

VINES

Akebia quinata	CHOCOLATE VINE
Ampelopsis brevipedunculata	PORCELAIN BERRY
Clematis armandii	SWEET AUTUMN CLEMATIS
Clematis 'Beauty of Worcester' (1890)	CLEMATIS
Clematis cirrhosa	WINTER CLEMATIS
Clematis 'Fair Rosamond' (1881)	CLEMATIS
Clematis x jackmanii	JACKMAN'S CLEMATIS
Clematis lanuginosa especially 'Candida' (1862)	LANUGINOSA CLEMATIS
Clematis 'Madame Édouard André' (1892)	CLEMATIS
Clematis montana	MOUNTAIN CLEMATIS
Clematis 'Nellie Moser' (1895)	NELLIE MOSER CLEMATIS
Clematis paniculata	SWEET AUTUMN CLEMATIS
Clematis viticella (1569)	VIRGIN'S BOWER

    'Purpurea Plena Elegans' (1629), 'Venosa Violacea' (<1860), 'Kermesina' (1883),
    'Étoile Violette' (1885), 'Abundance' (ca 1900), 'Etoile Rose' (early 1900s),
    'Alba-Luxurians' (early 1900s)

Jasminum officinale f. *grandiflorum*	POET'S JASMINE
Lonicera fragrantissima	WINTER HONEYSUCKLE
Parthenocissus henryana	SILVER-VEIN CREEPER
Parthenocissus tricuspidata	BOSTON IVY
Rosa (see separate list)	CLIMBING ROSES

PERENNIALS

Acanthus mollis	BEAR'S BREECH
Achillea tomentosa	WOOLLY YARROW
Aconitum napellus	MONKSHOOD
Adonis vernalis	PHEASANT'S EYE
Anchusa azurea 'Dropmore' (1905)	ITALIAN BUGLOSS
Anthericum liliago 'Major'	ST. BERNARD'S LILY
Aquilegia vulgaris	COLUMBINE, GRANNY'S BONNET
Aruncus dioicus	GOAT'S-BEARD ❖
Aspidistra elatior (1822)	CAST IRON PLANT
Aster x frikartii (1918)	HYBRID ASTER
Campanula latifolia	CAMPANULA, BELLFLOWER
Centranthus ruber	JUPITER'S BEARD, RED VALERIAN
Chrysanthemum x morifolium (1798 to America)	MUM

Chrysanthemum x rubellum	HARDY CHRYSANTHEMUM
Delphinium x cultorum	DELPHINIUM
Dianthus Allwoodii hybrids	PINKS
Dianthus caryophyllus	CARNATION
'Souvenir de Malmaison' (1857), "Chabaud" strain (1870s)	
Dianthus 'Chomley Farran'	BIZARRE CARNATION
Dianthus 'Queen of Hearts'	PERPETUAL CARNATION
Dianthus 'Queen of Sheba' (17th century)	PERPETUAL CARNATION
Digitalis 'John Innes Tetra' (1920s)	COPPER FOXGLOVE
Erysimum cheiri	WALLFLOWER
Geum chiloense (*G. coccineum*) and *G. quellyon*	AVENS
Helianthus x multiflorus 'Flore-Pleno'	DOUBLE THIN-LEAFED SUNFLOWER
Helleborus argutifolius	CORSICAN HELLEBORE
Helleborus lividus	HELLEBORE
Helleborus viridis	GREEN HELLEBORE
Hemerocallis lilioasphodelus	LEMON-LILY
Hemerocallis middendorffii	AMUR DAYLILY
Hesperis matronalis 'Flore-Pleno'	DOUBLE DAME'S-ROCKET
Hosta plantaginea	HOSTA
Hosta sieboldiana	PLANTAIN LILY
Hosta undulata 'Albo-marginata'	WHITE-MARGINED HOSTA
Hosta ventricosa	HOSTA
Hylotelephium (Sedum) Autumn hybrids ('Autumn Charm', 'Autumn Delight',	
'Autumn Fire', 'Autumn Joy')	HYBRID AUTUMN SEDUM
Iris germanica	BEARDED IRIS
Especially 'Sambucina' ('Queen of Gypsies') (<1823), 'Aurea' (1830),	
'Flavescens' (1830), 'Plumeri' (1830), 'Honorable' ('Sans Souci') (1840),	
'Jacquesiana' (1840), 'Major' (1840), 'Mme. Chereau' (1844),	
'Innocenza' (1854), 'Queen of May' (1859), 'Gypsy Queen' (1859),	
'Mrs. Horace Darwin' (1873), 'Attraction' (1885), 'Caprice' (1904)	
Iris germanica var. *florentina* (<1500)	ORRIS ROOT
Iris pallida (<1600)	DALMATIAN IRIS
Iris siberica	SIBERIAN IRIS
Iris unguicularis	WINTER IRIS
Iris variegata 'Gracchus' (1884)	HUNGARIAN IRIS
Kniphofia uvaria	RED-HOT POKER, POKER PLANT
'Pfitzeri', 'Tower of Gold' (Burbank, 1923)	
Lamprocapnos (Dicentra) spectabilis	OLD-FASHIONED BLEEDING HEART
Lavandula angustifolia	"ENGLISH" LAVENDER
Leucanthemum x superbum 'Alaska' (Burbank, 1904)	SHASTA DAISY
Lychnis chalcedonica	MALTESE CROSS
Lychnis viscaria 'Splendens Plena'	GERMAN CATCHFLY
Mirabilis jalapa	FOUR O'CLOCK
Paeonia lactiflora hybrids	PEONY
Especially 'Queen Victoria' (Whitleyi) (1803), "Fragrans" (1805),	
'Humei' (1810), 'Edulis Superba' (1824), 'Francois Ortegat' (1850),	
'Festiva Maxima' (1851), 'Duchesse de Nemours' (1856),	
'Mons Paillet' (1857), 'L'Eclatante' (1860), 'Boule de Neige' (1867),	
'Mons Dupont' (1872), 'Felix Crousse' (1881), *more...*	

'Madame de Verneville' (1885), 'Avalanche' (1886), 'La Perle' (1886),
'Mons Jules Elie' (1888), 'Mikado' (1893), 'Mons Martin Cahuzac' (1899)

Paeonia officinalis	PEONY
Papaver orientale and hybrids	ORIENTAL POPPY
Phlox paniculata	SUMMER PHLOX
Polygonatum odoratum	SOLOMON'S SEAL
Polygonum (Persicaria) bistorta 'Superba'	EUROPEAN BISTORT
Primula veris	COWSLIPS
Primula vulgaris	PRIMROSE
Sedum sarmentosum	STONECROP, GRAVEYARD MOSS
Sempervivum arachnoideum ssp. *tomentosum*	WOOLLY COBWEB HOUSELEEK
Tanacetum coccineum	PAINTED DAISY, PERSIAN DAISY, PYRETHRUM
Viola cornuta	VIOLA
Viola odorata	SWEET VIOLET

'Princess of Wales' (late 1800s), 'Rosina' (late 1800s), 'Rawson's White' (1888),
'The Czar' (<1893), 'John Raddenbury' (1895), 'St. Helena' (1897),
'Lianne' (ca 1900), 'Governor Herrick' (1906), 'Luxonne', 'Perle Rose'

Viola alba ssp. *dehnhardtii*	PARMA VIOLET

'Parme de Toulouse' (1854), 'Maria Louise' (<1865), 'New York' (1869),
'Duchesse de Parme' (1870), 'Lady Hume Campbell' (1875),
'Comte de Brazza' ('Swanley White') (1883), 'Mrs. Arthur' (1902), 'd'Udine' (1903),
'Queen Mary' (1915)

BULBS

Acis (Leucojum) autumnale	AUTUMN SNOWFLAKE
Allium moly	GOLDEN LEEK
Allium neopolitanum	DAFFODIL GARLIC
Allium (Nectaroscordum) siculum	SICILIAN HONEY BELLS
Amaryllis belladonna	NAKED LADY
Canna x generalis	CANNA-LILY

Especially 'Konigen Charlotte' (1892), 'Cleopatra' (1895),
'Tarrytown' (= 'Florence Vaughan'; Burbank, 1895), 'Madame Caseneuve' (1902),
'Firebird' (1911), 'En Avant' (1914), 'City of Portland' (1915),
'Robert Kemp' (*C. compacta*?), 'Madame Angele Martin' (1915),
'Oiseau d'Or' (1918), 'Yellow King Humbert' (Burbank, 1918)

Colchicum autumnale	AUTUMN CROCUS
Crocus x luteus	YELLOW CROCUS
Crocus speciosus	BIEBERSTEIN'S CROCUS
Crocus tommasinianus (1847)	CROCUS
Crocus vernus	SPRING CROCUS
Dahlia hybrids	DAHLIA

Especially 'Atropurpurea' (1789), 'White Aster' (1879), 'Union Jack' (1882),
'Stolz von Berlin' (1884), 'Kaiser Wilhelm' (1892), 'Little Beeswings' (1909),
'York and Lancaster' (1915), 'Bishop of Llandaff' (1927), 'Thomas Edison' (1929)

Fritillaria imperialis lutea	CROWN IMPERIAL
Galanthus nivalis 'Flore Pleno' (1731)	DOUBLE SNOWDROPS
Gladiolus x colvillei	HYBRID GLADIOLA

Gladiolus communis ssp. *byzantinus* (1629)	MEDITERRANEAN GLADIOLA
Gladiolus italicus and *G. i. albus*	ITALIAN GLADIOLA
Gladiolus murielae (1888)	ABYSSINIAN GLADIOLA
Hesperantha (Schizostylis) coccinea	CRIMSON RIVER LILY
Hyacinthus orientalis	HYACINTH

    Especially 'Bismarck', 'Chestnut Flower', 'City of Haarlem', 'General Köhler',
    'L'Innocence', 'La Victoire', 'Lady Derby', 'Lord Balfour'

Iris florentina	FLORENTINE IRIS
Iris germanica	GERMAN IRIS, BEARDED IRIS

    Especially 'Caprice', 'Flavescens', 'Gracchus', 'Honorable', 'Mrs. Horace Darwin',
    'Plumeri', 'Queen of May'

Iris x *hollandica* (<1900)	DUTCH IRIS

    'Imperator', 'Wedgewood'

Ixiolirion tataricum ssp. *pallasii* (1821)	LAVENDER MOUNTAIN LILY, SIBERIAN LILY
Leucojum aestivum	SNOWFLAKES
Lilium auratum (described in 1862)	GOLD-BAND LILY
Lilium candidum	MADONNA LILY
Lilium x *elegans* (<1800)	ASIATIC HYBRID LILY
Lilium martagon (described in 1753)	MARTAGON LILY
Lilium regale	REGAL LILY
Lilium speciosum (described in 1794)	JAPANESE LILY
Lilium x *testaceum* (early 1800s)	NANKEEN LILY
Leopoldia (Muscari) comosum 'Plumosum' (1612)	FEATHERED HYACINTH
Muscari neglectum	GRAPE HYACINTH
Narcissus bulbocodium (1629)	HOOP PETTICOATS
Narcissus cantabricus	WHITE HOOP PETTICOAT DAFFODIL
Narcissus jonquilla	JONQUIL
Narcissus poeticus 'Actaea'	PHEASANT'S EYE
Narcissus pseudo-narcissus cultivars	DAFFODILS

    'Henry Irving' (1885), 'Mrs. R. O. Backhouse' (1921), 'Beersheba' (1923),
    'Fortune' (1924), 'Carlton' (1927), 'Irene Copeland' (1915)

Narcissus tazetta	TAZETTAS

    'Grand Soleil d'Or' (<1770), 'Grand Primo' (1780), 'Grand Monarque' (1798),
    'Early Pearl' (1899), 'Avalanche' (<1700?/1906), 'Cheerfulness' (<1923),
    'Geranium' (1930), 'Yellow Cheerfulness' (1937)

Narcissus tazetta var. *orientalis* (?*chinensis*)	CHINESE SACRED LILY
Narcissus triandrus hybrids	ANGEL'S TEARS

    'Orange Phoenix' (<1731), 'Butter and Eggs (<1777; "incomparabilis aurantius plenus"),
    'Sulphur Phoenix' (<1820; "Coddlins and Cream"), 'Princeps' (<1830), 'Elegans' (<1851),
    'Mrs. Langtry' (<1869), 'Stella' (1869), 'W. P. Milner' (1869), 'Silver Chimes' (1916)

Nerine sarniensis 'Fothergillii Major'	GUERNSEY LILY
Puschkinia scilloides (1808)	STRIPED SQUILL
Scilla siberica 'Spring Beauty' (1796)	SIBERIAN SQUILL
Tigridia pavonia	MEXICAN SHELL FLOWER
Ipheion uniflorum (1836)	SPRING STARFLOWER
Tulipa clusiana	LADY TULIP
Tulipa x *gesneriana*	TULIPS

    'Absalon', 'Blue Flag', 'Duchesse de Parma', 'Duc van Tol Rose', 'Keizerskroon' (1750),
    'Lac van Rijn', 'Zomerscroon', 'Couleur Cardinal" (1845)

Tulipa humilis var. *violacea* (ca 1860)	CROCUS TULIP
Tulipa saxatilis (T. bakeri) (1825)	CANDIA TULIP, ROCK TULIP
Tulipa sylvestris	WOODLAND TULIP

ANNUALS & BIENNIALS

Cool Season

Alcea rosea	HOLLYHOCK
Amberboa (Centaurea) moschata	SWEET SULTAN
Antirrhinum majus	SNAPDRAGON
Calendula officinalis	POT MARIGOLD
Campanula medium	CANTERBURY BELLS, CUP-AND-SAUCER
Campanula pyramidalis	CHIMNEY BELLFLOWER
Centaurea cyanus	CORNFLOWER, BACHELORS' BUTTONS
Cheiranthus cheiri	WALLFLOWER
Consolida ajacis (C. ambigua)	ROCKET LARKSPUR
Dianthus barbatus	SWEET WILLIAM
Dianthus chinensis	PINKS
Dianthus superbus	LACE PINK
Eryngium giganteum 'Miss Willmott's Ghost'	MISS WILLMOTT'S GHOST
Glebionis (Chrysanthemum) coronaria	CROWN DAISY
Glebionis (Chrysanthemum) segetum	CORN MARIGOLD
Iberis amara "Hyacinthiflora"	ROCKET CANDYTUFT
Iberis umbellata	CANDYTUFT
Ismelia (Chrysanthemum) carinata	TRICOLOR DAISY
Lathyrus odoratus	SWEET PEA

   'Cupani' (<1700), 'Painted Lady' (ca 1730), 'Violet Queen' (1877), 'Senator' (1891),
   "Cupid" types (1893), 'Pink Cupid' (1895), "Eckford's Mix" (late 1800s),
   'Purple Prince' (<1894), 'Lady Grisel Hamilton' (1895), 'America' (1896),
   'Prima Donna' (1896), 'Black Knight' (1898), 'Miss Wilmott' (1900),
   'Matucana' (1900s), 'Mrs. Walter Wright' (1902), 'King Henry VII' (1903),
   'Unique' (1904), 'Queen Alexandra' (1905), 'Lord Nelson' (1907)

Lavatera trimestris	BUSH MALLOW
Lobularia maritima	SWEET ALYSSUM
Lunaria annua	HONESTY
Malcomia maritima	VIRGINIA STOCK
Matthiola incana	STOCK
Matthiola longipetala bicornis	EVENING-SCENTED STOCK
Molucella laevis	BELLS-OF-IRELAND
Myosotis scorpioides	TRUE FORGET-ME-NOT
Myosotis sylvatica	WOOD FORGET-ME-NOT
Nigella damascena	LOVE-IN-A-MIST
Papaver commutatum	FLANDERS POPPY
Papaver rhoeas	CORN POPPY, SHIRLEY POPPY
Papaver somniferum	PEONY POPPY
Pericallis (Senecio) x *hybridus*	CINERARIA
Primula japonica (1870)	JAPANESE PRIMROSE

Primula malacoides	FAIRY PRIMROSE
Reseda odorata	MIGNONETTE
Scabiosa atropurpurea	PINCUSHION FLOWER
Schizanthus pinnatus	BUTTERFLY FLOWER
Tropaeolum majus, "Phoenix Mix" (1903), 'Vesuvius' (1923)	NASTURTIUM
Verbascum bombyciferum	GIANT SILVER MULLEIN
Viola cornuta	VIOLA
Viola tricolor	JOHNNY-JUMP-UP
Viola x wittrockiana	PANSY

Warm Season

Amaranthus caudatus	LOVE-LIES-BLEEDING
Amaranthus tricolor 'Molten Fire' (Burbank, 1922)	AMARANTH
Amaranthus tricolor 'Splendens'	JOSEPH'S COAT
Argemone mexicana	PRICKLY POPPY
Browallia speciosa	AMETHYST FLOWER
Callistephus chinensis	CHINA ASTER
Cardiospermum halicacabum (1800s)	LOVE-IN-A-PUFF
Cleome hasslerana (1800s)	SPIDER FLOWER
Cosmos bipinnatus	GARDEN COSMOS
Cosmos sulphureus	SULFUR COSMOS
Cuphea llavea	BAT-FACE
Cuphea micropetala	GIANT CIGAR PLANT
Euphorbia marginata	SNOW-ON-THE-MOUNTAIN
Gaillardia pulchella	BLANKET FLOWER
Helianthus annuus	SUNFLOWER
Heliotropium arborescens (1757)	CHERRY PIE, GARDEN HELIOTROPE
Impatiens balsamina "Camellia-Flowered Mix" (<1900)	BALSAM
Ipomoea nil	JAPANESE MORNING GLORY
Ipomoea tricolor	MORNING GLORY
Nicotiana alata	NIGHT-SCENTED FLOWERING TOBACCO
Persicaria (Polygonum) orientalis (1737)	KISS-ME-OVER-THE-GARDEN-GATE
Petunia axillaris	WHITE MOON PETUNIA
Petunia integrifolia	VIOLET FLOWER
Phaseolus coccineus	SCARLET RUNNER BEAN
Phlox drummondii 'Isabellina' (1889)	ANNUAL PHLOX
Ricinus communis	CASTOR BEAN
Salpiglossis sinuata	PAINTED TONGUE
Tagetes erecta	AFRICAN MARIGOLD
Tagetes tenuifolia	IRISH LACE
Zinnia elegans	ZINNIA

"Giants of California" (1919), "Giant Dahlia" strain (Burbank, 1925)

AN ENGLISH COTTAGE-STYLE GARDEN

A cottage garden is casually informal and generous in its plantings. It's lushness is what leads most gardeners to this style, especially those gardeners who call themselves plant addicts. Historically, it stated as an ornamental extension of the "kitchen garden," the plantings out the back door, the plantings which were composed of the edibles and medicinals for the home. Even today, planting ornamental edibles throughout a garden is appropriate (see the list "ORNAMEDIBLES").

A well-designed cottage garden may seem "cluttered" but it should actually complement the character of the house and fit within the confines of a tiny lot without overwhelming it with busy-ness. The plants within this list are lush and almost all are floriferous; many deserve planting to spill onto pathways a bit.

Tall vertical plants help provide the backbone yet some taller plants seem to fit even when interspersed among the shorter plants.

Hardscaping is minimal but a few elements are traditional: pathways, lattice-work including trellises and arbors, an obelisk (a tuteur, especially in the vegetable/fruit garden), and a gate. Many of the hardscape elements should be made of natural materials (sometimes quite rustic).

MEDIUM SHRUBS *(5 to 8 feet tall)*

Enkianthus campanulatus	ENKIANTHUS
Fothergilla gardenii	DWARF WITCH ALDER
Hydrangea macrophylla 'Mariesii'	LACE-CAP HYDRANGEA
Hydrangea quercifolia 'Snow Queen'	OAKLEAF HYDRANGEA
Hydrangea serrata 'Beni-gaku'	MOUNTAIN HYDRANGEA
Hydrangea serrata 'Preziosa'	MOP-HEAD HYDRANGEA
Philadelphus 'Belle Etoile'	MOCK ORANGE
Philadelphus lewisii	LEWIS' MOCK ORANGE ❖
Ribes aureum	GOLDEN CURRANT
Syringa pubescens ssp. *patula* 'Miss Kim'	DWARF KOREAN LILAC
Viburnum x *bodnantense* 'Dawn'	PINK DAWN VIBURNUM
Weigela florida	WEIGELA

SMALL SHRUBS *(1 to 5 feet tall)*

Calluna vulgaris	HEATHER
Caryopteris x clandonensis	BLUEBEARD
Corylopsis spicata	SPIKE WINTERHAZEL
Daphne odora 'Aureomarginata'	VARIEGATED WINTER DAPHNE
Erica x darleyensis	DARLEY DALE HEATH
Forsythia x intermedia 'Fiesta'	VARIEGATED FORSYTHIA
Hydrangea arborescens 'Annabelle'	SMOOTH HYDRANGEA
Hydrangea macrophylla	MOP-HEAD HYDRANGEA
Hydrangea serrata 'Little Geisha'	MOUNTAIN HYDRANGEA
Spiraea betulifolia 'Tor'	BIRCH-LEAF SPIREA ❖

Spiraea splendens (S. densiflora) SUBALPINE OR MOUNTAIN SPIREA ❖
Spiraea japonica JAPANESE SPIRAEA
Spiraea thunbergii THUNBERG'S SPIREA, BRIDALWREATH SPIREA

ROSES

English Shrubs

'Benjamin Britten'   'James Galway'
'Boscobel'   'Lady Emma Hamilton'
'Carding Mill'   'Munstead Wood'
'Charlotte'   'Princess Anne'
'Crown Princess Margareta' 'Queen of Sweden'
'Gentle Hermione'   'Susan Williams-Ellis'
'Golden Celebration'   'Sweet Juliet'
'Grace'   'The Mayflower'
'Harlow Carr'   'Wollerton Old Hall'
'Heritage'

Species and Old Hybrid Roses

Rosa gallica var. *officinalis*   APOTHECARY ROSE
Rosa gallica var. *officinalis* 'Versicolor'   ROSA MUNDI
Rosa glauca   RED-STEM ROSE
Rosa x *odorata* 'Mutabilis'   BUTTERFLY ROSE
Rose rugosa   BEACH ROSE

Rosa rugosa selections and hybrids

'Blanc Double de Coubert'   'Hansa'
'Buffalo Gal'   'Roseraie de l'Haÿ'
'Charles Albanel'   'Thérese Bugnet'
'Frau Dagmar Hastrup'   'Topaz Jewel'

Old Garden Rose hybrids (OGRs)

'Adélaide d'Orléans'   'Ghislaine de Feligonde'
'Ballerina'   'Marchesa Boccella'
'Complicata'   'Robusta'
'Félicité Perpétue'   'The Fairy'

»» *More* ...

VINES

Small (generally 8 to 12 feet)

Clematis alpina 'Pamela Jackman'	BLUE ALPINE CLEMATIS
Clematis x *cartmanii* 'Avalanche'	AVALANCHE EVERGREEN CLEMATIS
Clematis x *cartmanii* 'Joe'	JOE EVERGREEN CLEMATIS
Clematis 'Constance'	CONSTANCE ALPINE CLEMATIS
Clematis 'Etoile Violette'	VITICELLA CLEMATIS
Clematis 'Josephine'	JOSEPHINE LARGE-FLOWERED CLEMATIS
Clematis 'General Sikorski'	GENERAL SIKORSKI LARGE-FLOWERED CLEMATIS
Clematis 'Helsingborg'	HELSINGBORG ALPINE CLEMATIS
Clematis 'Pink Champagne'	PINK CHAMPAGNE LARGE-FLOWERED CLEMATIS
Clematis 'Madame Julia Correvon'	VITICELLA CLEMATIS
Clematis 'Mrs. George Jackman'	MRS. GEORGE JACKMAN CLEMATIS
Clematis 'Niobe'	NIOBE LARGE-FLOWERED CLEMATIS
Clematis 'Pink Flamingo'	PINK FLAMINGO ALPINE CLEMATIS
Clematis 'The President'	THE PRESIDENT LARGE-FLOWERED CLEMATIS
Clematis 'Princess Diana'	PRINCESS DIANA CLEMATIS
Clematis 'Silver Moon'	SILVER MOON LARGE-FLOWERED CLEMATIS
Clematis 'Warzawska Nike'	WARZAWSKA NIKE CLEMATIS
Clematis 'Westerplatte'	WESTERPLATTE LARGE-FLOWERED CLEMATIS
Codonopsis lanceolata	BONNET BELLFLOWER
Rosa 'Jeanne Lajoie'	CLIMBING MINIATURE ROSE
Rosa 'New Dawn'	NEW DAWN ROSE
Tropaeolum leptophyllum	CLIMBING NASTURTIUM
Tropaeolum speciosum	RED NASTURTIUM
Tropaeolum tricolor	THREE-COLORED NASTURTIUM
Tropaeolum tuberosum var. *lineomaculatum* 'Ken Aslet'	MASHUA

Medium (generally 12 to 24 feet)

Akebia quinata	CHOCOLATE VINE
Clematis 'Betty Corning'	VITICELLA CLEMATIS
Clematis cirrhosa	WINTER CLEMATIS
Clematis 'Polish Spirit'	POLISH SPIRIT LARGE-FLOWERED CLEMATIS
Jasminum x *stephanense*	STEPHAN'S JASMINE
Lonicera acuminata (*L. henryi*)	HENRY'S HONEYSUCKLE
Lonicera ciliosa	ORANGE HONEYSUCKLE ❖
Lonicera x *tellmanniana*	RED-GOLD HONEYSUCKLE

Large (generally 24 feet and upwards of 100 feet)

Campsis x tagliabuana 'Indian Summer', 'Madame Galen'	HYBRID TRUMPET CREEPER
Clematis montana	ANEMONE CLEMATIS
Parthenocissus henryana	SILVER-VEIN CREEPER
Parthenocissus quinquefolia	VIRGINIA CREEPER
Parthenocissus tricuspidata 'Veitchii'	BOSTON IVY
Vitis coignetiae	CRIMSON GLORY VINE
Vitis vinifera 'Purpurea'	PURPLE-LEAF GRAPE VINE

GROUNDCOVERS
* will tolerate various degrees of traffic; some are mowable (lawn substitute)

Clinopodium (Micromeria, Satureja) douglasii	YERBA BUENA ❖
Epimedium hybrids	HYBRID EPIMEDIUM
Helianthemum nummularium	SUN ROSE
Linnaea borealis	TWINFLOWER
Omphalodes verna	CREEPING FORGET-ME-NOT
Pachysandra procumbens	ALLEGHENY SPURGE
Petrosedum (Sedum) rupestre	BLUE SEDUM
Phedimus (Sedum) kamtschaticus	KAMSCHATKA SEDUM, ORANGE STONECROP
Phedimus (Sedum) spurius	CAUCASIAN STONECROP
Phlox adsurgens	WOODLAND PHLOX
Phlox caespitosa	TUFTED PHLOX ❖
Phlox diffusa	SPREADING PHLOX ❖
Phlox divaricata	WOODLAND PHLOX
Vancouveria hexandra	WHITE INSIDE-OUT FLOWER ❖
Waldsteinia ternata*	BARREN STRAWBERRY

PERENNIALS & BULBS

Tall (3 to 6 feet tall)

Campanula lactiflora	MILKY BELLFLOWER
Campanula latiloba	GREAT BELLFLOWER
Cardiocrinum giganteum	HIMALAYAN LILY
Delphinium elatum hybrids	DELPHINIUM
Digitalis ferruginea	RUSTY FOXGLOVE
Eriocapitella (Anemone) x *hybrida*	JAPANESE ANEMONE
Iris Spuria hybrids	SPURIA IRIS
Lupinus x regalis (*L.* x russellii)	RUSSELL LUPINE
Sidalcea hendersonii	HENDERSON'S CHECKER MALLOW ❖
Thalictrum delavayi 'Hewitt's Double'	DOUBLE-FLOWERED MEADOW RUE
Veronicastrum sibericum	JAPANESE CULVER'S ROOT

Medium (1 to 3 feet tall)

Achillea 'Moonshine'	MOONSHINE YARROW
Aconitum x cammarum 'Bicolor'	MONKSHOOD
Aconitum napellus	COMMON MONKSHOOD
Anemonopsis macrophylla	FALSE ANEMONE
Aquilegia vulgaris and hybrids	EUROPEAN COLUMBINE, GRANNY'S BONNET
Aster x frikartii	FRIKART'S ASTER
Astrantia major	GREAT MASTERWORT
Betonica (Stachys) macrantha 'Robusta'	BIG BETONY
Betonica (Stachys) officinalis	WOOD BETONY
Camassia quamash	CAMAS ❖
Campanula 'Sarastro'	SARASTRO BELLFLOWER
Chrysanthemum x rubellum	HARDY CHRYSANTHEMUM
Chrysanthemum zawadskii	MANCHURIAN CHRYSANTHEMUM
Clematis columbiana	ROCK CLEMATIS ❖
Clematis recta	GROUND VIRGIN'S BOWER
Dierama dracomontanum	DRAKENBERG WANDFLOWER
Digitalis grandiflora	LARGE YELLOW FOXGLOVE
Digitalis obscura	SUNSET FOXGLOVE
Filipendula purpurea 'Elegans'	JAPANESE MEADOWSWEET
Helenium autumnale and hybrids	MOUNTAIN SNEEZEWEED ❖
Helianthus angustifolius 'First Light'	FIRST LIGHT SWAMP SUNFLOWER
Helianthus angustifolius 'Low Down'	LOW DOWN SWAMP SUNFLOWER
Helianthus x multiflorus 'Happy Days'	DWARF PERENNIAL SUNFLOWER
Helianthus x multiflorus 'Meteor'	METEOR SUNFLOWER
Helianthus salicifolius 'Table Mountain'	T. M. WILLOW-LEAF SUNFLOWER
Heliopsis helianthoides	FALSE SUNFLOWER
Helleborus argutifolius	CORSICAN HELLEBORE
Helleborus hybrids such as Winter Plum', 'Great White', 'Searchlight', 'Fresco', 'Great White Double', 'Pink Frost Double', 'Winter Plum Double'	HELLEBORE
Incarvillea delavayi	GARDEN GLOXINIA
Iris siberica	SIBERIAN IRIS
Iris pallida	DALMATIAN IRIS
Leucanthemum x superbum	SHASTA DAISY
Meconopsis 'Lingholm' (*M.* x sheldonii; "Fertile Blue Group")	HIMALAYAN POPPY
Monarda mildew-free hybrids: 'Blue Stocking', 'Blue Wreath', 'Colrain Red', 'Dark Ponticum', 'Gardenview Scarlet', 'Grand Marshall', 'Marshall's Delight', 'Purple Rooster', 'Raspberry Wine', 'Violet Queen'	BEE BALM
Paeonia lactiflora hybrids	PEONY
Papaver orientale hybrids	ORIENTAL POPPY
Primula species and hybrids	PRIMROSE
Salvia nemorosa	PURPLE WOOD SAGE
Salvia x sylvestris	BLUE MEADOW SAGE, BLUE WOOD SAGE
Salvia verticillata	LILAC SAGE
Scabiosa caucasica	PINCUSHION FLOWER
Scutellaria incana	DOWNY SKULLCAP
Sidalcea malviflora	DWARF CHECKERBLOOM ❖

Short (1 inch to 12 inches tall)

Allium amplectens	SLIM-LEAF ONION ❖
Allium cernuum	NODDING ONION ❖
Anemonoides (Anemone) nemorosa	WOOD ANEMONE
Campanula rotundifolia	BLUEBELL BELLFLOWER ❖
Campanula portenschlagiana	DALMATIAN BELLFLOWER
Centaurea pulcherrima	TALL PINK BACHELOR'S BUTTON
Clematis hirsutissima var. *hirsutissima*	HAIRY CLEMATIS ❖
Codonopsis ovata	BONNET BELLFLOWER
Corydalis scouleri	SCOULER'S CORYDALIS ❖
Dicentra formosa	PACIFIC OR WESTERN BLEEDING-HEART ❖
Epimedium species and hybrids	BISHOP'S HAT
Erodium chrysanthum	HERONSBILL, STORKSBILL
Filipendula 'Kahome'	DWARF JAPANESE MEADOWSWEET
Geranium x *cantabrigiense*	HARDY GERANIUM
Geranium cinereum	HARDY GERANIUM
Geranium renardii	HARDY GERANIUM
Geranium x *riversleaianum*	HARDY GERANIUM
Geranium wlassovianum	HARDY GERANIUM
Geum hybrids	GEUM, AVENS
Helianthemum nummularium and hybrids	SUN ROSE
Iris chrysophylla	YELLOW-LEAF IRIS ❖
Iris purdyi	PURDY'S IRIS ❖
Lewisia cotyledon and hybrids	SISKIYOU LEWISIA ❖
Omphalodes verna	CREEPING FORGET-ME-NOT
Polemonium carneum	SALMON POLEMONIUM ❖
Saxifraga fortunei	FORTUNE SAXIFRAGE
Stachys coccinea	SCARLET BETONY
Symphyotrichum (Aster) ericoides	HEATH ASTER
Thalictrum (Anemonella) thalictroides	RUE-ANEMONE
Veronica liwanensis	TURKISH SPEEDWELL
Viola alba ssp. *dehnhardtii*	PARMA VIOLET

"SOFT"-GROWING PERENNIALS

Technically, these are "decumbent" (kind of trailing) or almost 'scandent' (kind of climbing) plants which scramble over the tops of other, larger perennials or woody shrubs, with a near free-form habit. A good tool for helping enhance the lusciousness of a cottage garden.

Aconitum columbianum	MONKSHOOD ❖
Ampelaster carolinianus	CLIMBING ASTER
Callirhoe involucrata	WINECUPS
Campanula poscharskyana	SERBIAN BELLFLOWER
Clematis 'Alionushka'	SCRAMBLING CLEMATIS
Clematis 'Arabella'	ARABELLA CLEMATIS
Clematis x *cartmanii* 'Pixie'	PIXIE CLEMATIS
Clematis columbiana	ROCK CLEMATIS

378

Clematis x durandii	DURAND'S CLEMATIS
Clematis integrifolia	SOLITARY CLEMATIS
Clematis × jouiniana	JOUIN CLEMATIS
Clematis 'Lunar Lass'	LUNAR LASS CLEMATIS
Clematis repens	TWINKLE BELL CLEMATIS
Clematis 'Rooguchi'	ROOGUCHI CLEMATIS
Clematis 'Sapphire Indigo'	SAPPHIRE INDIGO CLEMATIS
Codonopsis vinciflora	BLUE BONNET BELLFLOWER
Lathyrus vernus	VERNAL PEA
Tropaeolum polyphyllum	WREATH NASTURTIUM
Veronicastrum latifolium	CHINESE VEIL

ANNUALS & BIENNIALS

Alcea rosea	HOLLYHOCK
Antirrhinum majus	SNAPDRAGON
Calendula officinalis	POT MARIGOLD
Campanula medium	CANTERBURY BELLS, CUP-AND-SAUCER
Campanula pyramidalis	CHIMNEY BELLFLOWER
Cardiospermum halicacabum	BALLOON PLANT, LOVE-IN-A-PUFF
Centaurea cyanus	CORNFLOWER
Consolida ajacis (C. ambigua)	ROCKET LARKSPUR
Dianthus barbatus	SWEET WILLIAM
Ipomoea tricolor	MORNING GLORY
Lathyrus odoratus	SWEET PEA
Nigella damascena	LOVE-IN-A-MIST
Papaver rhoeas	CORN POPPY, SHIRLEY POPPY
Pelargonium hybrids	GERANIUM
Pericallis (Senecio) x hybridus 'Giovanna's Select'	TALL CINERARIA
Primula annual species	PRIMROSE
Tropaeolum majus	NASTURTIUM
Viola x wittrockiana	PANSY

"For most of us who are intimidated by theories of garden design, the cottage garden provides immediate appeal, since it is a horticultural rather than an architectural solution to a limited area."
~~ Patricia Thorpe

A MEDITERRANEAN-STYLE GARDEN

    Emphasis here is on evergreen plants and gray to silver plants ("evergray/eversilver"?). The overall look is not unlike the chaparral of California, the matorral scrub of Chile, the mallee of western Australia, the maquis around the Mediterranean, and the fynbos of the Western Cape of South Africa; these are the signature floral provinces of the five Mediterranean climate regions of the world. There's a predominance of winter-spring annuals, seasonal bulbs, both spring into summer bloomers and fall bloomers, along with succulents. Vines, too, play a big role in Mediterranean gardens.

LARGE TREES

Alnus cordata	ITALIAN ALDER
Arbutus x *reyorum* 'Marina'	MARINA MADRONE
Calocedrus decurrens	INCENSE-CEDAR ❖
Cedrus atlantica 'Glauca'	BLUE ATLANTIC CEDAR
Chrysolepis chrysophylla	GOLDEN CHINQUAPIN ❖
Eucryphia x *nymansensis* 'Nymansay'	NYMAN'S EUCRYPHIA
Fitzroya cupressoides	PATAGONIAN CYPRESS
Fraxinus ornus	BOUQUET ASH
Hesperocyparis (Cupressus) bakeri	BAKER CYPRESS
Nothofagus antarctica	ANTARCTIC BEECH
Notholithocarpus densiflorus	TANBARK OAK ❖
Pinus pinea	ITALIAN STONE PINE
Pinus wallichiana	HIMALAYAN PINE
Quercus chrysolepis	CANYON LIVE OAK ❖
Quercus frainetto	HUNGARIAN OAK
Quercus garryana	GARRY OAK, OREGON WHITE OAK ❖
Quercus hypoleucoides	SILVERLEAF OAK
Sequoiadendron giganteum	BIG TREE, INTERIOR REDWOOD

SMALL TO MEDIUM TREES

Catalpa ovata	CHINESE CATALPA
Cercis siliquastrum	LOVE TREE
Cornus mas	CORNELIAN CHERRY
Crinodendron patagua	CHILEAN LILY-OF-THE-VALLEY TREE
Cupressus sempervirens	ITALIAN CYPRESS
Cupressus torulosa	HIMALAYAN CYPRESS
Dendropanax trifidus	IVY TREE
Diospyros kaki	JAPANESE PERSIMMON
Embothrium coccineum	CHILEAN FIRE TREE
Emmenopterys henryi	EMMENOPTERYS
Eucryphia glutinosa	NIRRHE
Ficus johannis ssp. *afghanistanica*	AFGHAN FIG
Hesperocyparis (Cupressus) arizonica var. *glabra*	SMOOTH ARIZONA CYPRESS
Hesperocyparis (Cupressus) pygmaea	PIGMY CYPRESS
Juniperus chinensis 'Kaizuka'	HOLLYWOOD JUNIPER

Lyonothamnus floribundus ssp. *asplenifolius*	ISLAND IRONWOOD
Magnolia grandiflora 'Teddy Bear'	TEDDY BEAR MAGNOLIA
Magnolia laevifolia (Michelia yunnanensis)	YUNNAN MAGNOLIA
Olea europaea (marginally hardy in most areas)	OLIVE
Pinus densiflora 'Umbraculifera'	TANYOSHO PINE
Quercus myrsinifolia	CHINESE EVERGREEN OAK
Tetradium (Evodia) daniellii	KOREAN EVODIA
Trachycarpus fortunei	CHINESE WINDMILL PALM
Trochodendron aralioides	WHEEL TREE

VERY SMALL TREES
Shrubs which can be pruned up.

Arbutus unedo	STRAWBERRY TREE
Arctostaphylos columbiana	HAIRY MANZANITA ❖
Arctostaphylos manzanita 'St. Helen'	ST. HELENS MANZANITA ❖
Argyrocytisus battandieri	MOROCCAN PINEAPPLE BROOM
Azara microphylla	SMALL-LEAVED AZARA
Azara serrata	TOOTHED LEAVED AZARA
Ceanothus thyrsiflorus 'Rogue Sky'	COAST BLUE BLOSSOM
Chamaerops humilis	MEDITERRANEAN FAN PALM
Chrysolepis sempervirens	BUSH CHINQUAPIN ❖
Cinnamomum checkiangense	HARDY CINNAMON LAUREL
Clerodendrum trichotomum	HARLEQUIN GLORYBOWER
Cotinus coggygria cultivars including purple forms	SMOKEBUSH
Cotinus 'Grace'	HYBRID SMOKEBUSH
Drimys winteri	WINTER'S BARK
Eucryphia x intermedia 'Rostrevor'	BRUSHBUSH
Feijoa (Acca) sellowiana	PINEAPPLE GUAVA
Ficus carica	FIG
Grevillea victoriae	ROYAL GREVILLEA
Heptapleurum (Schefflera) taiwanianum	HARDY SCHEFFLERA
Leptospermum lanigerum	WOOLLY TEA TREE
Leptospermum namadgiensis	ALPINE TEA TREE
Luma apiculata (hardy form)	CHILEAN GUAVA
Metapanax (Nothopanax) delavayi	DELAVAY FALSE GINSENG
Osmanthus x fortunei 'San Jose'	FORTUNE'S TREE OLIVE
Osmanthus fragrans	FRAGRANT TEA-OLIVE
Pittosporum tenuifolium	KOHUHU, TAWHIWI
Viburnum suspensum	SANDANKWA
Vitex agnus-castus	CHASTE TREE

»» More ...

LARGE SHRUBS *(8 to 16 feet tall)*

Arbutus unedo	STRAWBERRY TREE
Arctostaphylos densiflora 'Howard McMinn'	MANZANITA
Chrysolepis sempervirens	BUSH CHINQUAPIN ❖
Cotinus coggygria cultivars	SMOKEBUSH
Elaeagnus pungens cultivars	ELAEAGNUS
Garrya elliptica	SILK-TASSEL
Grevillea 'Audrey' (sold as 'Poorinda Constance')	AUDREY GREVILLEA
Grevillea 'Canberra Gem'	SPIDER FLOWER
Grevillea miqueliana var. *moroka*	ROUND-LEAF GREVILLEA
Grevillea victoriae	ROYAL GREVILLEA
Lomatia myricoides	RIVER LOMATIA
Morella (Myrica) californica	PACIFIC WAX MYRTLE ❖
Notholithocarpus densiflorus var. *echinoides*	SHRUB TANOAK ❖
Osmanthus heterophyllus	PURPLE-LEAF FALSE HOLLY
Pyracantha 'Mohave'	FIRETHORN

MEDIUM SHRUBS *(5 to 8 feet tall)*

Arctostaphylos canescens var. *sonomensis*	SONOMA MANZANITA
Arctostaphylos columbiana	BRISTLY OR HAIRY MANZANITA ❖
Arctostaphylos glandulosa ssp. *glandulosa* 'Demeter'	DEMETER OREGON MANZANITA
Berberis darwinii	DARWIN'S BARBERRY
Ceanothus × *delileanus* 'Gloire de Versailles'	HARDY HYBRID CEANOTHUS
Ceanothus 'Skylark' ('Victoria')	VICTORIA CALIFORNIA LILAC
Ceanothus thyrsiflorus 'Dark Star'	DARK STAR CALIFORNIA LILAC
Ceanothus thyrsiflorus 'Julia Phelps'	JULIA PHELPS CALIFORNIA LILAC
Chrysolepis chrysophylla var. *minor*	BUSH CHINQUAPIN ❖
Cistus x ladanifer 'Blanche'	LARGE WHITE ROCKROSE
Cistus x pagei	FRAGRANT ROCKROSE
Erica terminalis	CORSICAN HEATH, UPRIGHT HEATH
Fabiana imbricata 'Violacea'	CHILEAN HEATHER
Frangula (Rhamnus) californica	COFFEEBERRY ❖
Grevillea australis	SOUTHERN GREVILLEA
Grevillea 'Poorinda Leanne' ('Poorinda Queen')	LEANNE GREVILLEA
Grevillea rivularis	CARRINGTON FALLS GREVILLEA
Leptospermum minutifolium	SMALL-LEAVED TEA TREE
Leptospermum sericeum	SILVER TEA TREE
Mahonia x media cultivars	HYBRID MAHONIA
Osmanthus delavayi	SWEET OLIVE
Rosa laevigata	CHEROKEE ROSE
Salvia rosmarinus (Rosmarinus officinalis)	ROSEMARY
Vaccinium ovatum	EVERGREEN HUCKLEBERRY ❖
Viburnum tinus	LAURUSTINUS

SMALL SHRUBS *(1 to 5 feet tall)*

Arctostaphylos x media	HYBRID MANZANITA ❖
Artemisia abrotanum	SOUTHERNWOOD
Baeckea gunniana	HEATHMYRTLE
Berberis wilsoniae	WILSON'S BARBERRY
Brachyglottis monroi	MONRO'S DAISY BUSH
Brachyglottis 'Otari Cloud'	OTARI CLOUD DAISY BUSH
Calluna vulgaris	HEATHER
Choisya ternata	MEXICAN MOCK ORANGE
Cistus x bornetianus 'Jester'	JESTER ROCKROSE
Cistus x canescens 'Albus'	WHITE ROCKROSE
Cistus x crispatus 'Warley Rose'	WARLEY ROSE ROCKROSE
Cistus x dansereaui 'Jenkyn Place'	JENKYN PLACE ROCKROSE
Cistus x heterocalyx 'Chelsea Bonnet'	CHELSEA BONNET ROCKROSE
Cistus x obtusifolius	COMPACT WHITE ROCKROSE
Cistus 'Snowfire'	SNOWFIRE ROCKROSE
Erica x darleyensis cultivars	DARLEY DALE HEATH
Grevillea juniperina cultivars	JUNIPER-LEAF GREVILLEA
Hebe 'Blue Mist'	BLUE MIST HEBE
Hebe 'Emerald Gem'	HEBE
Hebe 'Hinerua'	HEBE
Hebe cupressoides	HEBE
Hebe pinguifolia 'Sutherlandii'	BLUE-LEAF HEBE
Hebe topiaria	HEBE
Helichrysum splendidum	CAPE GOLD
Lavandula x chaytoriae 'Richard Grey', 'Silver Frost'	ENGLISH LAVENDER HYBRIDS
Lavandula x intermedia	LAVANDIN
Lavatera x clementii	TREE MALLOW
Leptospermum namadgiensis	ALPINE TEA TREE
Leptospermum rupestre 'Highland Pink'	HIGHLAND PINK TEA TREE
Leucothoe fontanesiana 'Zeblid'	DROOPING LAUREL
Linnaea (Abelia) x grandiflora	GLOSSY ABELIA
Melicytus crassifolius	THICK-LEAVED MAHOE
Myrteola nummularia	CRANBERRY-MYRTLE
Olearia moschata	INCENSE PLANT
Olearia x oleifolia 'Waikariensis'	HARDY DAISY-ON-A-STICK
Prostanthera cuneata	ALPINE MINT BUSH
Rhodanthemum (Chrysanthemum) hosmariense	MOROCCAN DAISY
Ribes laurifolium	EVERGREEN CURRANT
Rosa glauca	RED-STEM ROSE
Ruscus hypoglossum	ITALIAN BUTCHER'S BROOM
Santolina chamaecyparissus	LAVENDER-COTTON
Sarcococca confusa	SWEETBOX
Sarcococca hookeriana	SWEETBOX
Viburnum davidii	DAVID'S VIBURNUM
Vitex agnus-castus 'Blue Puffball'	CHASTE TREE

VINES

C = climbs by clinging; **S** = "climbs" by scrambling; **Te** = climbs by tendrils;
Tw = climbs by twining

Small

Billardiera longiflora	TASMANIAN BLUEBERRY VINE Tw
Clematis x cartmanii 'Joe'	JOE EVERGREEN CLEMATIS Te
Clematis chiisanensis 'Lemon Bells'	YELLOW BELL CLEMATIS Te
Clematis 'Etoile Violette'	VITICELLA CLEMATIS Te
Clematis occidentalis	WESTERN BLUE VIRGINS' BOWER ❖ Te
Clematis tangutica	GOLDEN-BELL CLEMATIS Te
Codonopsis convolvulacea ssp. *grey-wilsonii*	CLIMBING BELLFLOWER Tw
Codonopsis lanceolata	BONNET BELLFLOWER Tw
Ercilla spicata (E. volubilis)	CHILEAN CLIMBER C
X *Fatshedera lizei*	FATSHEDERA S
Lapageria rosea	CHILEAN BELLFLOWER Tw
Mitraria coccinea	CHILEAN MITRE FLOWER S
Rosa 'Jeanne Lajoie'	CLIMBING MINIATURE ROSE S
Rosa 'New Dawn'	NEW DAWN ROSE S
Trachelospermum asiaticum 'Theta'	BIRD-FOOT STAR JASMINE S
Tropaeolum species	PERENNIAL NASTURTIUM S, Tw

Medium

Clematis cirrhosa	WINTER CLEMATIS Te
Clematis 'Polish Spirit'	POLISH SPIRIT CLEMATIS Te
Chrysojasminum (Jasminum) humile f. *wallichianum*	NEPAL JASMINE Tw/S
Jasminum x stephanense	STEPHAN'S JASMINE Tw/S
Passiflora x belotii (*P.* x alato-caerulea)	BLUE PASSION FLOWER Te/Tw
Solanum crispum 'Glasnevin'	CHILEAN POTATO VINE S
Stauntonia purpurea	STAUNTONIA VINE Tw

Large

Clematis armandii	EVERGREEN CLEMATIS Te
Clematis paniculata	SWEET AUTUMN CLEMATIS Te
Hedera algeriensis 'Glorie de Marengo'	VARIEGATED ALGERIAN IVY C
Hedera colchica 'Dentata Variegata'	VARIEGATED PERSIAN IVY C
Holboellia coriacea	SAUSAGE VINE Tw
Parthenocissus henryana	SILVER-VEIN CREEPER C
Vitis californica	PACIFIC GRAPE ❖ Te
Vitis riparia	RIVERBANK GRAPE ❖ Te
Vitis 'Roger's Red'	ROGER'S RED GRAPE Te
Vitis vinifera 'Incana'	DUSTY MILLER GRAPE VINE Te
Vitis vinifera 'Purpurea'	PURPLE-LEAF GRAPE VINE Te

GROUNDCOVERS
* Can be walked on, some even mowed

Arctostaphylos 'Pacific Mist'	PACIFIC MIST MANZANITA
Arctostaphylos uva-ursi	KINNIKINNICK, BEARBERRY ❖
Bergenia species and hybrids	BERGENIA
Campanula poscharskyana	SERBIAN BELLFLOWER
Carex pansa*	DUNE SEDGE, MEADOW SEDGE ❖
Carex praegracilis*	FIELD SEDGE ❖
Carex tenuiculmis 'Cappuccino'	COFFEE SEDGE
Carex tumulicola	FOOTHILL SEDGE ❖
Ceanothus 'Centennial'	CENTENNIAL CALIFORNIA LILAC
Ceanothus gloriosus 'Anchor Bay'	ANCHOR BAY CALIFORNIA LILAC
Festuca rubra var. *juncea* 'Patrick's Point'*	BLUE CREEPING FESCUE ❖
Fragaria chiloensis*	BEACH STRAWBERRY❖
Gazania linearis	TREASURE FLOWER
Grevillea australis "Prostrate"	TASMANIAN ALPINE GREVILLEA
Hebe 'Wingletye'	WINGLETYE HEBE
Hebe decumbens	CREEPING HEBE
Helianthemum nummularium	SUN ROSE
Juniperus communis selections	COMMON JUNIPER ❖
Leptinella gruveri*	MINIATURE BRASS BUTTONS
Leptinella squalida*	NEW ZEALAND BRASS BUTTONS
Leptospermum humifusum 'Horizontalis' ("Prostrate Form")	
	PROSTRATE TASMANIAN MANUKA
Leptospermum rupestre "Low Form"	CREEPING TEA TREE
Muehlenbeckia axillaris 'Nana'*	CREEPING WIRE VINE
Myrteola nummularia	CRANBERRY-MYRTLE
Oxalis oregana Evergreen types*	EVERGREEN REDWOOD SORREL ❖
Petrosedum (Sedum) rupestre	BLUE SEDUM
Phedimus (Sedum) kamtschaticus	KAMSCHATKA SEDUM, ORANGE STONECROP
Phedimus (Sedum) spurius	CAUCASIAN STONECROP
Pimelea prostrata	NEW ZEALAND DAPHNE
Podocarpus lawrencei 'Purple King'	PURPLE KING MOUNTAIN PLUM-PINE
Pratia (Lobelia) pedunculata 'County Park'	SUPER STAR CREEPER
Saxifraga stolonifera	STRAWBERRY BEGONIA
Sedum many species	SEDUM, STONECROP
Thymus cherierioides	SILVER NEEDLE THYME
Thymus x *citriodorus*	LEMON THYME
Thymus herba-barona	CARAWAY-SCENTED THYME
Thymus polytrichus ssp. *brittanicus* (*T. praecox* ssp. *arcticus*)	CREEPING THYME
Thymus serpyllum	WOOLLY THYME

PERENNIALS & BULBS

Tall (3 to 6 feet tall)

Acanthus spinosus	BEAR'S BREECH
Artemisia lactiflora	WHITE MUGWORT
Dierama dracomontanum	DRAKENBERG WANDFLOWER
Dierama grandiflorum	ANGEL'S FISHING ROD
Digitalis ferruginea	RUSTY FOXGLOVE
Eremurus himalaicus	HIMALAYAN FOXTAIL LILY
Eremurus hybrids	FOXTAIL LILY
Eremurus stenophyllus	DESERT CANDLE
Gunnera tinctoria	GIANT RHUBARB, CHILEAN RHUBARB
Iris Spuria hybrids	SPURIA IRIS
Kniphofia northiae	GIANT POKER
Lilium taliense	FRAGRANT TURK'S-CAP LILY
Lilium x *testaceum*	NANKEEN LILY
Lobelia tupa	DEVIL'S TOBACCO
Miscanthus sinensis	CHINESE SILVER-GRASS
Salvia barrelieri	NORTH AFRICAN SAGE
Stipa gigantea	GIANT FEATHER GRASS
Yucca species and hybrids	YUCCA

Medium (1 to 3 feet tall)

Achillea 'Moonshine'	MOONSHINE YARROW
Allium (Nectaroscordum) siculum	SICILIAN HONEY GARLIC
X *Amarine tubergenii*	VAN TUBERGEN'S AMARINE LILY
X *Amarygia parkeri*	HYBRID AMARYLLIS
Amaryllis belladonna	NAKED LADY
Artemisia versicolor 'Sea Foam'	CURLICUE SAGE
Aspidistra elatior	CAST-IRON PLANT
Aster x *frikartii*	FRIKART'S ASTER
Campanula 'Sarastro'	SARASTRO BELLFLOWER
Centranthus ruber	JUPITER'S BEARD, RED VALERIAN
Digitalis grandiflora	LARGE YELLOW FOXGLOVE
Echinops ritro	GLOBE THISTLE
Epipactis gigantea 'Serpentine Knight'	STREAM ORCHID
Epipactis 'Sabine'	HYBRID STREAM ORCHID
Eryngium agavifolium	AGAVE-LEAF SEA HOLLY
Eryngium alpinum	ALPINE SEA HOLLY
Eryngium amethystinum	BLUE SEA HOLLY
Eryngium bourgatii	MEDITERRANEAN SEA HOLLY
Eucomis autumnalis	AUTUMN PINEAPPLE LILY
Eucomis bicolor	VARIEGATED PINEAPPLE LILY
Eucomis comosa	WINE PINEAPPLE LILY
Eucomis pole-evansii	TALL PINEAPPLE LILY
Gladiolus (tubergenii) 'Charm'	SWORD LILY
Gladiolus communis var. byzantinus	BYZANTINE GLADIOLUS

Gladiolus oppositiflorus ssp. salmoneus	SALMON GLADIOLUS
Gladiolus (papilio hybrid*)* 'Ruby'	RUBY GLADIOLUS
Gladiolus saundersii	SAUNDER'S GLADIOLUS
Helleborus argutifolius	CORSICAN HELLEBORE
Hesperantha (Schizostylis) coccinea	CRIMSON FLAG
Iris douglasiana	DOUGLAS IRIS ❖
Iris PCH hybrids	PACIFIC COAST IRIS HYBRIDS
Linaria (*purpurea* Hybrid) 'Natalie'	NATALIE TOADFLAX
Ornithogalum (Galtonia) candicans	SUMMER HYACINTH
Ornithogalum (Galtonia) princeps	BERG LILY
Ornithogalum (Galtonia) viridiflora	GREEN SUMMER HYACINTH
Paeonia cambessedesii	MAJORCAN PEONY
Paeonia mascula	WILD PEONY
Penstemon azureus	AZURE PENSTEMON ❖
Phlomis cashmeriana	KASHMIR-SAGE
Phlomis fruticosa	JERUSALEM-SAGE
Phlomis viscosa	STICKY JERUSALEM-SAGE
Phlomoides (Phlomis) tuberosa	SAGE-LEAF MULLEIN
Psephellus (Centaurea) simplicicaulis	LILAC CORNFLOWER
Salvia yangii (Perovskia) including other species and hybrids	RUSSIAN SAGE
Salvia spathacea	HUMMINGBIRD SAGE
Sphaeralcea munroana	ORANGE GLOBE MALLOW ❖
Watsonia angusta	SCARLET BUGLE FLOWER

Short (1 inch to 12 inches tall)

Acis autumnalis	AUTUMN SNOWFLAKE
Allium acuminatum	HOOKER'S ONION ❖
Allium amplectens	SLIM-LEAF ONION ❖
Allium cernuum	NODDING ONION ❖
Anemonoides (Anemone) blanda	GRECIAN WINDFLOWER
Anthemis punctata ssp. *cupaniana*	SICILIAN CHAMOMILE
Barnardia (Scilla) japonica	JAPANESE SQUILL
Bergenia ciliata	FUZZY-LEAVED BERGENIA
Bergenia cordifolia	HEART-LEAVED BERGENIA
Bergenia hybrids	HYBRID BERGENIA
Bloomeria (Triteleia) crocea	GOLDEN STARS ❖
Brodiaea coronaria	HARVEST BRODIAEA ❖
Brodiaea elegans ssp. *hooveri*	HARVEST LILY ❖
Calochortus elegans var. *elegans*	ELEGANT CAT'S EAR ❖
Calylophus hartwegii	HARTWEG'S SUNDROPS
Campanula poscharskyana	SERBIAN BELLFLOWER
Carex flacca 'Blue Zinger'	BLUE SEDGE
Colchicum x agrippinum	AUTUMN CROCUS, MEADOW SAFFRON
Colchicum autumnale	AUTUMN CROCUS
Colchicum byzantinum	BYZANTINE MEADOW SAFFRON
Colchicum hybrids	AUTUMN CROCUS
Colchicum speciosum	AUTUMN CROCUS
Colchicum variegatum	SPOTTED AUTUMN CROCUS

Crocus goulimyi	PELOPONNESE CROCUS
Crocus imperati	ITALIAN CROCUS
Crocus laevigatus	LATE CROCUS
Crocus longiflorus	ITALIAN CROCUS
Crocus niveus	FALL CROCUS
Crocus ochroleucus	YELLOW CROCUS
Crocus pulchellus	TURKISH CROCUS
Crocus serotinus	LATE CROCUS
Crocus speciosus	BIEBERSTEIN'S CROCUS
Cyclamen coum	HARDY CYCLAMEN, EASTERN SOWBREAD
Cyclamen graecum	GREEK CYCLAMEN
Cyclamen hederifolium	IVY-LEAF CYCLAMEN
Dichelostemma capitatum ssp. *capitatum*	BLUEDICKS ❖
Dichelostemma congestum	OOKOW, FIELD CLUSTER LILY, HARVEST LILY ❖
Dichelostemma ida-maia	FIRECRACKER FLOWER ❖
Dichelostemma x *venustum*	SNAKE-LILY ❖
Eriogonum latifolium	COAST BUCKWHEAT ❖
Eriogonum ovalifolium	OVAL-LEAF BUCKWHEAT ❖
Eriogonum umbellatum	SULPHUR BUCKWHEAT ❖
Eriophyllum lanatum	OREGON SUNSHINE, WOOLLY SUNFLOWER ❖
Eucomis 'Nani'	DWARF PINEAPPLE LILY
Geranium renardii	HARDY GERANIUM
Geum hybrids	GEUM, AVENS
Helianthemum nummularium and hybrids	SUN ROSE
Helleborus foetidus	STINKING HELLEBORE
Hyacinthoides (Scilla) lingulata	AUTUMN BLUEBELL
Hylotelephium (Sedum) cauticola 'Lidakense'	LIDAKENSE CLIFF STONECROP
Hylotelephium (Sedum) sieboldii	OCTOBER DAPHNE SEDUM
Hylotelephium (Sedum) 'Vera Jameson'	PURPLE AUTUMN SEDUM
Iris unguicularis	WINTER IRIS, ALGERIAN IRIS
Moraea spathulata	YELLOW BUTTERFLY LILY
Nerine bowdenii and hybrids	SPIDER LILY
Nerine sarniensis and hybrids	GUERNSEY LILY
Oncostema (Scilla) peruviana	PORTUGUESE SQUILL
Opuntia fragilis	BRITTLE PRICKLY PEAR ❖
Oxalis fabaefolia	RABBIT'S EARS
Oxalis purpurea	PURPLE WOOD SORREL
Paeonia clusii	CLUSIUS'S PEONY
Penstemon newberryi var. *berryi*	BERRY'S MOUNTAIN PRIDE ❖
Phalocallis (Cypella) coelestis	GOBLET FLOWER
Phedimus (Sedum) kamtschaticus	KAMSCHATKA SEDUM, ORANGE STONECROP
Phedimus (Sedum) spurius	TWO-ROW STONECROP
Prospero (Scilla) autumnale	AUTUMN SQUILL
Rhodiola pachyclados	AFGHAN SEDUM
Rhodanthemum (Chrysanthemum) hosmariense	MOROCCAN DAISY
Scilla bifolia	TWO-LEAF SQUILL
Sedum spathulifolium	BROAD-LEAF STONECROP ❖
Sempervivum arachnoideum	HENS AND CHICKS, HOUSELEEK
Sisyrinchium bellum	WESTERN BLUE-EYED GRASS ❖

Sisyrinchium californicum	GOLDEN-EYED GRASS ❖
Stachys byzantina (S. lanata)	LAMB'S EARS
Sternbergia lutea	AUTUMN DAFFODIL
Triteleia (Brodiaea) hyacinthina	WHITE TRIPLET-LILY ❖
Triteleia grandiflora	LARGE-FLOWERED TRIPLET-LILY, WILD HYACINTH ❖
Triteleia ixioides	PRETTYFACE ❖
Veronica liwanensis	TURKISH SPEEDWELL
Viola alba ssp. *dehnhardtii*	PARMA VIOLET

GRASSES AND GRASS-LIKE PLANTS

Aciphylla glaucescens	BLUE SPEARGRASS
Austrostipa ramosissima	AUSTRALIAN PLUME GRASS
Cannomois grandis	BELL REED
Carex flacca 'Blue Zinger'	BLUE SEDGE
Carex phyllocephala 'Sparkler'	SPARKLER PALM SEDGE
Chondropetalum elephantinum	LARGE CAPE RUSH
Chondropetalum tectorum	SMALL CAPE RUSH
Chondropetalum tectorum "dwarf form"	DWARF CAPE RUSH
Dierama dracomontanum	DRAKENBERG WANDFLOWER
Dierama grandiflorum	ANGEL'S FISHING ROD
Dierama pendulum	FAIRY WAND, HAIR BELL
Dierama pulcherrimum	FAIRY WAND, ANGEL'S FISHING ROD
Elymus (Agropyron) magellanicum	CHILEAN BLUE WHEAT GRASS
Helictotrichon sempervirens	BLUE OAT GRASS
Iris typhifolia	CATTAIL IRIS
Juncus effusus 'Big Twister', 'Spiralis'	COMMON RUSH
Juncus patens 'Elk Blue', 'Occidental Blue'	SPREADING RUSH
Olsynium (Sisyrinchium) douglasii	DOUGLAS' BLUE-EYED-GRASS ❖
Restio (Ischyrolepis) subverticillata	DUNE RESTIO
Rhodocoma capensis	CAPE RESTIO
Rhodocoma gigantea	DEKRIET, GIANT RESTIO
Sisyrinchium bellum	WESTERN BLUE-EYED GRASS
Sisyrinchium californicum	GOLDEN-EYED GRASS ❖
Sisyrinchium hitchcockii	HITCHCOCK'S BLUE-EYED-GRASS
Sisyrinchium idahoense	BLUE-EYED GRASS ❖
Sisyrinchium macrocarpum	CHILEAN YELLOW-EYED GRASS
Sisyrinchium striatum	SATIN FLOWER
Thamnochortus rigidus	CAPE REED

SUCCULENTS

Agave asperrima	SCABROUS CENTURY PLANT
Agave bracteosa	CANDELABRUM AGAVE
Agave 'Desert Love'	DESERT LOVE HYBRID CENTURY PLANT
Agave harvardiana	HAVARD'S CENTURY PLANT

389

Agave multifilifera 'Basaseachic Falls'	BASASEACHIC FALLS CENTURY PLANT
Agave nickelsiae	KING FERDINAND CENTURY PLANT
Agave ovatifolia	WHALE'S TONGUE CENTURY PLANT
Agave x *ovatispina* 'Blue Rapture'	BLUE RAPTURE HYBRID CENTURY PLANT
Agave parryi ssp. *neomexicana*	NEW MEXICO AGAVE
Agave x *pseudoferox* 'Bellville'	BELLVILLE CENTURY PLANT
Agave victoriae-reginae	QUEEN VICTORIA CENTURY PLANT
Aloe polyphylla	SPIRAL ALOE
Aloiampelos (Aloe) striatula	HARDY ALOE
Aristaloe (Aloe) aristata	LACE ALOE
Dasylirion wheeleri	SPOON YUCCA, DESERT SPOON
Delosperma species (many)	HARDY ICE PLANT
Dudleya cymosa	LIVE-FOREVER
Dudleya farinosa	CHALKY LIVE-FOREVER
Hesperaloe parviflora	RED-FLOWERED YUCCA
Hylotelephium species and hybrids	BORDER SEDUM, AUTUMN STONECROP
Jovibarba species	HEN-AND-CHICKENS
Petrosedum (Sedum) species	STONECROP
Phedimus (Sedum) species	STONECROP
Rhodiola species	STONECROP
Sedum species	STONECROP
Sempervivum species and hybrids	HENS-AND-CHICKS
Yucca species	YUCCA

ANNUALS *for sowing direct in Fall for the "Wildflower" look*

Agrostemma gracilis (usually sold as A. githago)	CORNCOCKLE
Clarkia amoena	GODETIA ❖
Clarkia bottae	BOTTAE'S CLARKIA
Clarkia pulchella	PINK FAERIES ❖
Clarkia rubicunda	RUBY CHALICE CLARKIA
Clarkia unguiculata (C. elegans)	CLARKIA
Collinsia grandiflora	GIANT BLUE-EYED MARY ❖
Collinsia heterophylla	CHINESE HOUSES
Collomia grandiflora	LARGE-FLOWERED COLLOMIA ❖
Consolida ajacis (C. ambigua)	ROCKET LARKSPUR
Eschscholzia californica	CALIFORNIA POPPY
Gilia capitata	QUEEN ANNE'S THIMBLES ❖
Gilia tricolor	BIRD'S EYE GILIA
Iberis umbellata	CANDYTUFT
Lavatera trimestris	ROSE MALLOW
Layia platyglossa	COASTAL TIDY-TIPS ❖
Linum grandiflorum	SCARLET FLAX
Lupinus densiflorus	GOLDEN LUPINE
Lupinus succulentus	ARROYO LUPINE
Nemophila maculata	FIVE-SPOT ❖
Nemophila menziesii	BABY BLUE-EYES ❖
Papaver commutatum	FLANDERS POPPY

Papaver rhoeas	CORN POPPY, SHIRLEY POPPY
Phacelia campanularia	CALIFORNIA BLUEBELL
Phacelia tanacetifolia	TANSY-LEAF PHACELIA
Silene coeli-rosa	ROSE-OF-HEAVEN
Vaccaria hispanica (V. pyramidata)	COW-COCKLE
Valeriana (Plectritis) congesta	SEA BLUSH ❖

ANNUAL SUMMER VINES

Cardiospermum halicacabum	BALLOON VINE, LOVE-IN-A-PUFF
Cobaea scandens	CUP-AND-SAUCER VINE
Eccremocarpus scaber	CHILEAN GLORY VINE
Lablab purpureus	HYACINTH BEAN
Ipomoea alba (Calonyction aculeatum)	MOON VINE, MOON FLOWER
Ipomoea x *imperialis*	HYBRID MORNING GLORY
Ipomoea lobata	FIRECRACKER VINE
Ipomoea x *multifida*	CARDINAL CLIMBER
Ipomoea nil	JAPANESE MORNING GLORY
Ipomoea quamoclit	CYPRESS VINE
Ipomoea tricolor	MORNING GLORY
Lophospermum (Asarina) erubescens	MEXICAN TWIST, CREEPING GLOXINIA
Lophospermum (Asarina) scandens	CLIMBING SNAPDRAGON
Maurandella (Asarina) antirrhiniflora	VIOLET TWINING SNAPDRAGON
Phaseolus coccineus	SCARLET RUNNER BEAN
Rhodochiton atrosanguineus	PURPLE BELL VINE
Scyphanthus elegans (S. grandiflorus)	LITTLE NUN, MONJITA
Thunbergia alata	BLACK-EYED SUSAN VINE

AN ASIAN STYLE GARDEN

An Asian garden is as much about hardscape and symbolism as it is about the plants used therein. There is stone and things made of stone and bridges in the right places; there is the dwarfing of plants and the pruning that goes along with it; and most of all, there is a delicate touch, a restrained use of plants altogether, especially with flower color. This list is, then, an occidental view of this subject at best.

SMALL TO MEDIUM TREES
Many of these are pruned sternly yet meticulously to keep them at a critical size as well as to find an artistic shape within the natural tendencies of the specimen.

Acer buergerianum 'Goshiki Kaede'	GOSHIKI KAEDE TRIDENT MAPLE
Acer japonicum 'Green Cascade'	GREEN CASCADE FULLMOON MAPLE
Acer japonicum 'Junihitoye'	JUNIHITOYE FULLMOON MAPLE
Acer japonicum 'Meigetsu'	MEIGETSU FULLMOON MAPLE
Acer palmatum cultivars	JAPANESE MAPLE
Acer miyabei	MIYABEI MAPLE
Acer truncatum	SHANTUNG MAPLE
Cedrus deodara 'Descanso Dwarf'	DWARF DEODAR CEDAR
Cercidiphyllum japonicum 'Pendulum'	WEEPING KATSURA TREE
Cercis canadensis 'Forest Pansy'	FOREST PANSY REDBUD
Cryptomeria japonica 'Elegans'	ELEGANT PLUME CEDAR
Diospyros kaki 'Izu'	SEMI-DWARF JAPANESE PERSIMMON
Juniperus scopulorum 'Tolleson's Blue Weeping'	WEEPING JUNIPER
Magnolia stellata 'Royal Star'	ROYAL STAR MAGNOLIA
Pinus attenuata	KNOB-CONE PINE
Pinus densiflora 'Pendula'	WEEPING JAPANESE RED PINE
Pinus densiflora 'Umbraculifera'	TANYOSHO PINE
Pinus parviflora 'Glauca' (pruned)	BLUE JAPANESE WHITE PINE
Pinus thunbergii cultivars	JAPANESE BLACK PINE
Prunus campanulata	TAIWAN CHERRY
Prunus mume many cultivars	JAPANESE APRICOT
Prunus 'Okame'	OKAME CHERRY
Prunus serrulata 'Shirotae'	MOUNT FUJI FLOWERING CHERRY
Prunus serrulata 'Shogetsu'	SHOGETSU FLOWERING CHERRY
Prunus x *subhirtella* 'Pendula'	WEEPING HIGAN CHERRY
Prunus x *subhirtella* 'Yae-shidare-higan'	YAE SHIDARE HIGAN CHERRY
Prunus x *yedoensis* 'Akebono'	AKEBONO CHERRY
Prunus x *yedoensis* 'Somei-yoshino'	YOSHINO CHERRY
Quercus myrsinifolia	CHINESE EVERGREEN OAK
Quercus phillyraeoides	UBAME OAK
Sciadopitys verticillata	UMBRELLA PINE
Wisteria floribunda 'Longissima Alba' (as standard)	TREE WISTERIA
Wisteria 'Rosea Beni Fuji' (as standard)	TREE WISTERIA
Wisteria venusta 'Alba' (as standard)	TREE WISTERIA
Ziziphus jujuba 'So'	JUJUBE

SPECIAL DWARF OR SEMI-DWARF CITRUS FOR CONTAINERS
To be moved inside when temperatures are expected below 32°F.

Citrus Calamondin Variegated Dwarf
Citrus Citron, Japanese (Yuzu; *Citrus junos*)
Citrus Kumquat 'Fukushu' ('Fucushii'), 'Marumi', 'Meiwa', 'Nagami'
Citrus Mandarin 'Kara', 'Kinnow', 'Kishu Mini', 'Owari' (Satsuma)
Citrus Mandarin, Sour-acid 'Otaheite'
Citrus Orangequat 'Nippon'
Citrus Trifoliate Orange 'Flying Dragon'

SHRUBS

Aucuba japonica	JAPANESE AUCUBA
Azara microphylla	SMALL-LEAF AZARA
Camellia x 'Elina Cascade'	HYBRID CAMELLIA
Camelia japonica	JAPANESE CAMELLIA
Camellia reticulata	FOREST CAMELLIA
Camellia sasanqua	SASANQUA CAMELLIA
Camellia x *williamsii*	HYBRID CAMELLIA
Cedrus deodara 'Cream Puff'	CREAM PUFF DEODAR CEDAR
Chaenomeles speciosa 'Contorta'	CONTORTED FLOWERING QUINCE
Chaenomeles speciosa 'Toyo Nishiki'	T.N. FLOWERING QUINCE
Choisya ternata 'Sundance'	VARIEGATED MEXICAN MOCK ORANGE
Corokia cotoneaster 'Little Prince'	SMALL-LEAFED COROKIA
Cotinus coggygria 'Golden Spirit'	GOLDEN SMOKE TREE
Cotinus coggygria 'Purple Robe', 'Royal Purple', 'Velvet Cloak'	PURPLE SMOKE TREE
Cotoneaster microphyllus	LITTLELEAF COTONEASTER
Cryptomeria japonica 'Globosa Nana'	GLOBE PLUME CEDAR
Danae racemosa	POET'S LAUREL
Fatsia japonica	JAPANESE ARALIA
Hydrangea macrophylla many cultivars	HYDRANGEA
Hydrangea quercifolia	OAKLEAF HYDRANGEA
Hydrangea serrata 'O-amacha Nishiki'	GOLD DUST MOUNTAIN HYDRANGEA
Osmanthus fragrans	FRAGRANT TEA-OLIVE
Osmanthus heterophyllus 'Rotundifolius'	ROUNDLEAF HOLLY OSMANTHUS
Paeonia x *suffruticosa* hybrids	TREE PEONY
Pieris japonica	LILY-OF-THE-VALLEY SHRUB, ANDROMEDA
Pinus mugo especially dwarf cultivars	COMPACT MUGO PINE
Pinus densiflora 'Alice Verkade'	DWARF JAPANESE RED PINE
Pinus densiflora 'Tanyosho Compacta'	COMPACT TANYOSHO PINE
Pinus koraiensis 'Winton'	SPREADING BLUE KOREAN PINE
Pinus thunbergii 'Thunderhead'	THUNDERHEAD JAPANESE BLACK PINE
Pittosporum tobira 'Shima'	SHIMA MOCK ORANGE
Pittosporum tenuifolium 'Marjorie Channon', 'Silver Sheen'	KOHUHU
Platycrater arguta	TEA OF HEAVEN, COBWEB FLOWER
Podocarpus lawrencei 'Purple King'	PURPLE KING MOUNTAIN PLUM-PINE
Podocarpus totara	TOTARA

Prunus 'Hally Jolivette'	H. J. FLOWERING CHERRY
Rhododendron (Azalea) both evergreen and deciduous	AZALEA
Rosa wichuraiana 'Gardenia'	GARDENIA ROSE
Rosa pretty much any and all	ROSE
Sarcococca hookeriana var. *humilis*	DWARF SWEETBOX
Spiraea cantoniensis 'Flore-Pleno'	DOUBLE BRIDAL WREATH
Spiraea japonica bulmada 'Shirobana'	SHIROBANA SPIREA
Spiraea nipponica 'Snowmound'	SNOWMOUND SPIREA
Spiraea thunbergii	BABY'S-BREATH SPIREA
Vaccinium ovatum	EVERGREEN HUCKLEBERRY
Viburnum davidii	DAVID'S VIBURNUM
Vitex agnus-castus 'Silver Spire'	VARIEGATED CHASTE TREE

AUTUMN COLOR

Acer buergerianum	TRIDENT MAPLE
Acer circinatum 'Del's Dwarf', 'Little Gem', 'Pacific Sprite'	DWARF VINE MAPLE
Acer circinatum especially 'Pacific Fire', 'Pacific Purple'	VINE MAPLE
Acer griseum	PAPER-BARK MAPLE
Acer japonicum	AMUR MAPLE
Acer palmatum var. *dissectum* 'Viridis', 'Seiryu'	CUT-LEAF JAPANESE MAPLE
Acer palmatum 'Bloodgood', 'Higasayama', 'Kihachijo', 'Osakazuki', 'Orido nishiki', 'Sango Kaku'	JAPANESE MAPLE
Acer palmatum 'Aka Kawa', 'Asagi Nichiki', 'Bonfire', 'Cornara Pygmy', 'Killarney', 'Koto Maru', 'Sharp's Pygmy', 'Winter Gold', 'Yellowbird')	DWARF JAPANESE MAPLE
Acer pseudosieboldianum	KOREAN MAPLE
Acer shirasawanum	FULL-MOON MAPLE
Aronia melanocarpa 'Autumn Magic'	AUTUMN MAGIC BLACK CHOKEBERRY
Berberis koreana	KOREAN BARBERRY
Berberis jamesiana 'Exuberant'	JAMES' BARBERRY
Cercidiphyllum japonicum	KATSURA
Cornus kousa and hybrids	KOREAN DOGWOOD
Cotinus 'Grace'	HYBRID SMOKETREE
Cotinus obovatus	AMERICAN SMOKETREE
Diospyros kaki 'Ichi-Ki-Kei-Jiro', 'Izu'	DWARF PERSIMMON
Diospyros kaki many cultivars	JAPANESE PERSIMMON
Disanthus cercidifolius	REDBUD HAZEL
Fothergilla gardenii	DWARF WITCH ALDER
Ginkgo biloba 'Saratoga,' 'Tremonia'	GINKGO
Ginkgo biloba 'Jade Butterflies', 'Spring Grove', 'Troll'	DWARF GINKGO
Hamamelis x *intermedia*	HYBRID WITCH-HAZEL
Hydrangea quercifolia	OAK-LEAF HYDRANGEA
Lindera benzoin	SPICEBUSH
Oxydendrum arboreum	SOURWOOD
Parrotia persica	PERSIAN IRONWOOD
Parrotiopsis jacquemontiana	HATAB
Parthenocissus henryana	SILVER-VEIN CREEPER

Parthenocissus tricuspidata	BOSTON IVY
Pistacia chinensis	CHINESE PISTACHE
Rhus trilobata	SKUNKBUSH SUMAC
Rhus typhina 'Tiger Eyes'	DWARF SUMAC
Sorbus hupehensis 'Coral Cascade'	CHINESE ROWAN
Stachyurus praecox	STACHYURUS
Stewartia pseudocamellia	JAPANESE STEWARTIA
Styrax japonicus	JAPANESE SNOWBELL
Viburnum carlesii	KOREAN SPICE
Viburnum trilobum (V. opulus var. *americanum)*	AMERICAN CRANBERRYBUSH ❖
Vitis coignetiae	CRIMSON GLORY VINE

SMALL VINES

Billardiera longiflora	TASMANIAN BLUEBERRY VINE
Clematis many species and hybrids	CLEMATIS
Codonopsis lanceolata	BONNET BELLFLOWER
Codonopsis pilosula	POOR-MAN'S GINSENG
Ercilla spicata (E. volubilis)	CHILEAN CLIMBER
X *Fatshedera lizei*	FATSHEDERA
Lapageria rosea	CHILEAN BELLFLOWER
Rosa 'Jeanne Lajoie'	CLIMBING MINIATURE ROSE
Rosa 'New Dawn'	NEW DAWN ROSE

BULBS

Arisaema species	COBRA LILIES
Begonia (many)	BEGONIA
Dahlia Shogun Series	DAHLIA
Ipheion uniflorum	STARFLOWER
Lycoris radiata	JAPANESE SPIDER LILY
Narcissus jonquilla 'Kinglet', 'Suzy', 'Sweetness', 'Trevithian', 'Vireo'	JONQUILS
Narcissus tazetta 'Cheerfulness', 'Geranium', 'Matador', 'Martha Washington', 'Silver Chimes', 'Yellow Cheerfulness'	TAZETTAS
Narcissus triandrus 'Hawera', 'Thalia'	TRIANDRUS DAFFODIL
Nerine bowdenii	GUERNSEY LILY
Sternbergia lutea	WINTER DAFFODIL

PERENNIALS

Adiantum aleuticum	WESTERN MAIDENHAIR
Adiantum capillus-veneris	SOUTHERN MAIDENHAIR
Adiantum pedatum	FIVE-FINGER MAIDENHAIR
Aspidistra elatior	CAST IRON PLANT
Asplenium scolopendrium	HART'S TONGUE FERN
Blechnum (Struthiopteris) spicant	DEER FERN

Chrysanthemum x *morifolium*	MUMS
Corydalis species and hybrids	CORYDALIS
Dierama pulcherrimum	FAIRY WAND
Helianthus species and hybrids	PERENNIAL SUNFLOWERS
Helleborus species and hybrids	HELLEBORE
Hemerocallis (especially smaller cultivars)	DAYLILIES
Heuchera cultivars	CORAL BELLS
Iris confusa	BAMBOO IRIS
Iris ensata/kaempferi	JAPANESE IRIS
Iris japonica	CRESTED JAPANESE IRIS
Iris koreana 'Firefly Shuffle'	KOREAN WOODLAND IRIS
Iris laevigata	JAPANESE WATER IRIS
Iris Spuria hybrids	SPURIA IRIS
Lavandula species and hybrids	LAVENDER
Ophiopogon jaburan	GIANT LILY TURF
Ophiopogon japonicus	MONDO GRASS
Ophiopogon planiscapus	BIG MONDO GRASS
Paeonia lactiflora hybrids	PEONY
Pyrrosia lingua	JAPANESE FELT FERN
Pyrrosia polydactyla	PALM-LEAF FERN
Rohdea japonica	CHINESE SACRED LILY
Tricyrtis species and hybrids	TOAD LILY
Viola (perennial forms)	VIOLET
Zantedeschia aethiopica especially dwarf cultivars	DWARF CALLA-LILY

GRASSES AND GRASS-LIKE PLANTS

Carex albula	BLONDE SEDGE
Carex dolichostachya 'Kaga-nishiki'	GOLD FOUNTAIN SEDGE
Carex elegantissima 'Variegata'	GOLDEN-EDGED SEDGE
Carex flacca (*C. glauca*)	BLUE SEDGE
Carex morrowii expallida ('Variegata')	VARIEGATED JAPANESE SEDGE
Carex morrowii 'Fisher's Form', 'Ice Dance', 'Silver Sceptre'	JAPANESE SEDGE
Carex phyllocephala 'Sparkler'	SPARKLER SEDGE
Hakonechloa macra cultivars	JAPANESE FOREST GRASS
Juncus effusus 'Spiralis'	SPIRAL SOFT RUSH
Miscanthus transmorrisonensis	TAIWAN EVERGREEN MISCANTHUS

HARDIEST CLUMPING BAMBOOS

Bambusa multiplex 'Riviereorum'	CHINESE GODDESS BAMBOO
Borinda (Fargesia) fungosa	CHOCOLATE BAMBOO
Borinda (Fargesia) lushiensis	RED-STEM BAMBOO
Borinda (Fargesia) papyrifera	WHITE WAX BORINDA
Borinda (Fargesia) yunnanensis	YUNNAN FOUNTAIN BAMBOO
Chusquea culeou	CHILEAN BAMBOO
Fargesia denudata	DENUDATA BAMBOO

Fargesia dracocephala	DRAGON'S HEAD BAMBOO
Fargesia murielae	UMBRELLA BAMBOO
Fargesia nitida	BLUE FOUNTAIN
Fargesia robusta	ROBUST BAMBOO
Fargesia scabrida	ORANGE-STEM BAMBOO
X Hibanobambusa tranquillans 'Shiroshima'	SHIROSHIMA BAMBOO
Himalayacalamus planatus (H. asper)	MALINGE NAGALO BAMBOO
Thamnocalamus crassinodus	TIBETAN BAMBOO
Yushania confusa	GUADUA BAMBOO

DISTINCTIVE GROUNDCOVERS

Carex siderosticha var. *ciliatomarginata* 'Treasure Island'	
	CREEPING BROAD-LEAF SEDGE
Cedrus deodara 'Feelin' Blue'	BLUE CREEPING DEODAR CEDAR
Cedrus deodara 'Prostrate Beauty'	CREEPING DEODAR CEDAR
Juniperus conferta	SHORE JUNIPER
Juniperus horizontalis 'Wiltonii'	WILTON JUNIPER
Juniperus procumbens 'Green Mound'	JAPANESE GARDEN JUNIPER
Prunus serrulata 'Snow Fountains' (without trunk)	CREEPING FLOWERING CHERRY
Hydrocotyle sibthorpioides 'Crystal Snowflake'	CONFETTI PENNYWORT
Ophiopogon planiscapus 'Nigrescens'	BLACK MONDO GRASS
Sedum makinoi 'Ogon'	GOLDEN JAPANESE SEDUM
Sedum makinoi 'Variegatum'	VARIEGATED JAPANESE SEDUM
Viola 'Dancing Geisha', 'Silver Samurai'	HYBRID VIOLET

"In a traditional Japanese or Chinese garden, it's not only about the building or temple but about the whole setup — the structure, the landscape, the light, the plants, the water. The whole experience that makes your life there so beautiful." ~~ Ma Yansong

A "TROPICALESQUE" GARDEN

For those who love tropical-LOOKING plants and gardens but live where it's too cold to grow true tropical plants (plants that will take little or no frost and certainly no freeze), this is a list of plants hardy in USDA Zone 8 (Sunset Zones 5, 6) that will give you that "feel."

These are flamboyantly flowering, lusciously foliaged and/or otherwise "tropical" or "exotic" looking. Almost all of these plants are uncommon, as well, giving them an even more interesting and mysterious feeling. Many are evergreen. A few of these plants are quite familiar with PNW gardeners and it may take a shift in gears to see the "tropicalness" in such common plants.

Of course, you can always grow true tropical plants indoors (or in a greenhouse) during the winter and parade them outdoors when the days warm up and the nights don't drop frosty air upon your beauties. But if you want a full garden of such extravagance, a garden that doesn't need protection in the winter, here are the plants that will create your dream bit of "tropical" paradise. Most of these plants rival the distinctive beauty of true tropicalia. "Tropical" is as much in your mind as it is in a climate.

SMALLISH TREES

Aesculus x carnea	HYBRID HORSE CHESTNUT
Aesculus pavia	RED BUCKEYE
Asimina triloba	PAW-PAW
Catalpa erubescens especially 'Purpurea'	PURPLE-LEAF CHINESE CATALPA
Citrus cavaleriei hybrids 'Shangjuan', 'Yuzu'	ICHANG LEMON and YUZU
Clerodendrum trichotomum, especially variegated forms	HARLEQUIN GLORYBOWER
Crinodendron patagua	CHILEAN LILY-OF-THE-VALLEY TREE
Embothrium coccineum	CHILEAN FIRETREE
Eucryphia glutinosa	BRUSH BUSH, NIRRHE
Eucryphia x *nymansensis* 'Nymansay'	HYBRID BRUSH BUSH
Hoheria angustifolia	NARROW-LEAVED LACEBARK
Hoheria lyallii	MOUNTAIN LACEBARK
Kalopanax septemlobus	CASTOR ARALIA
Magnolia laevifolia (Michelia yunnanensis)	YUNNAN MAGNOLIA
Magnolia macrophylla	LARGE-LEAVED MAGNOLIA
Magnolia tripetala	UMBRELLA MAGNOLIA
Rehderodendron macrocarpum	RED PAPAYA
Sinopanax formosanus	HUASSENG

BAMBOOS, CYCADS, PALMS *(which many are marginally hardy here, requiring a protected microclimate; often they tolerate the winter cold but dwindle in the lack of heat)*

Bambusa multiplex 'Riviereorum'	CHINESE GODDESS BAMBOO
Borinda (Fargesia) fungosa	CHOCOLATE BAMBOO
Borinda (Fargesia) lushiensis	RED-STEM BAMBOO
Borinda (Fargesia) papyrifera	WHITE WAX BORINDA

398

Borinda (Fargesia) yunnanensis	YUNNAN FOUNTAIN BAMBOO
Butia eriospatha	WOOLLY JELLY PALM
Butia odorata (B. capitata)	JELLY PALM, PINDO PALM
Chamaerops humilis especially blue form	MEDITERRANEAN FAN PALM
Chusquea culeou	CHILEAN BAMBOO
Cycas revoluta	SAGO PALM
Fargesia denudata	NAKED CLUMPING BAMBOO
Fargesia dracocephala	DRAGON'S HEAD BAMBOO
Fargesia murielae	UMBRELLA BAMBOO
Fargesia nitida	OBEDIENT BLUE FOUNTAIN BAMBOO
Fargesia robusta	ROBUST BAMBOO
Fargesia scabrida	FOUNTAIN BAMBOO
X *Hibanobambusa tranquillans* 'Shiroshima'	SHIROSHIMA BAMBOO
Himalayacalamus planatus (H. asper)	MALINGE NAGALO
Jubaea chilensis	CHILEAN WINE PALM
Nannorrhops ritchiana	MAZARI PALM
Rhapidophyllum hystrix	NEEDLE PALM
Trachycarpus fortunei (including *T. f. wagnerianus*)	CHINESE WINDMILL PALM
Trachycarpus takil	HIMALAYAN WINDMILL PALM
Trithrinax campestris	CARANDAY PALM
Yushania confusa	GUADUA BAMBOO

SHRUBS

Acnistus (Iochroma) australis	MINI BLUE ANGEL'S TRUMPET
Aralia elata, especially 'Silver Umbrellas'	JAPANESE ANGELICA TREE
Aucuba japonica	JAPANESE LAUREL
Brassaiopsis dumicola	BUSHY ARALIAD
Callianthe (Abutilon) megapotamica and hybrids	BRAZILIAN BELLFLOWER
Chondropetalum elephantinum	LARGE CAPE RUSH
Clerodendrum bungei	ROSE GLORYBOWER
Crinodendron hookerianum	CHINESE LANTERN TREE
Daphniphyllum macropodum and its var. *humile*	FALSE DAPHNE
Desfontainia spinosa	ANDEAN HOLLY
Dichroa (Hydrangea) febrifuga	CHINESE QUININE
X *Didrangea versicolor*	BIGENERIC HYDRANGEA
Eleutherococcus sieboldianus, especially 'Variegatus'	FIVE-FINGERED ARALIAD
Eucryphia glutinosa 'Snowball'	COMPACT BRUSH BUSH
Eucryphia milliganii	DWARF LEATHERWOOD
Fatsia japonica cultivars, especially variegated types	JAPANESE ARALIA
Fatsia polycarpa	GREEN FINGERS
Fuchsia shrubby hardy species	HARDY FUCHSIA
Grevillea 'Canterbury Gold'	CANTERBURY GOLD GREVILLEA
Grevillea 'Marshall Olbrich'	MARSHALL OLBRICH GREVILLEA
Grevillea miqueliana var. *moroka*	ROUND-LEAF GREVILLEA
Grevillea 'Neil Bell'	NEIL BELL GREVILLEA
Grevillea 'The Precious'	THE PRECIOUS GREVILLEA
Grevillea victoriae	ROYAL GREVILLEA

Heptapleurum alpinum, H. delavayi, H. fengii, H. gracilis, *H. hoi, H. impressum, H. taiwanianum*	SCHEFFLERAS, ARALIADS
Indigofera pendula	WEEPING INDIGO
Paeonia ludlowii	TIBETAN YELLOW TREE PEONY
Raukaua (Pseudopanax) laetevirens	DEVIL'S ELDER
Rhodocoma capensis	CAPE RESTIO
Rhododendron ambiguum	RHODODENDRON
Rhododendron brachycarpum	RHODODENDRON
Rhododendron caucasicum	RHODODENDRON
Rhododendron dauricum	RHODODENDRON
Rhododendron oreodoxa	RHODODENDRON
Rhododendron sutchuenense	RHODODENDRON
Telopea truncata	TASMANIAN WARATAH

VINES

Actinidia arguta	HARDY KIWI
Actinidia kolomikta 'Arctic Beauty'	KOLOMIKTA VINE
Akebia quinata	CHOCOLATE VINE
Ampelopsis glandulosa var. *brevipedunculata* 'Elegans'	PORCELAINBERRY
Aristolochia durior	DUTCHMAN'S PIPE
Boquila trifoliolata	VOQUICILLO, PILPIL, VOQUI
Campsis x tagliabuana 'Indian Summer', 'Madame Galen'	HYBRID TRUMPET CREEPER
Clematis x cartmanii 'Joe'	JOE CLEMATIS
Clematis chiisanensis 'Koreana Amber'	KOREAN CLEMATIS
Clematis serratifolia	YELLOW KOREAN CLEMATIS
Clematis tangutica	GOLDEN CLEMATIS
Clematis texensis	SCARLET LEATHER FLOWER
Clematis tibetana	TIBETAN CLEMATIS
Codonopsis pilosula	DANG SHEN
X *Fatshedera lizei*, especially variegated forms	BOTANICAL WONDER
Hedera algeriensis 'Glorie de Marengo'	VARIEGATED ALGERIAN IVY
Hydrangea anomala	CLIMBING HYDRANGEA
Hydrangea petiolaris	CLIMBING HYDRANGEA
Hydrangea (Schizophragma) hydrangeoides	JAPANESE HYDRANGEA VINE
Hydrangea integrifolia	EVERGREEN CLIMBING HYDRANGEA
Hydrangea serratifolia	SAW-LEAF CLIMBING HYDRANGEA
Mitraria coccinea	CHILEAN MITRE FLOWER
Mutisia decurrens	CLAVEL DEL CAMPO ANARANJADO
Passiflora x belotii (x alatocaerulea)	BLUE PASSION FLOWER
Passiflora 'Blue Bouquet'	BLUE BOUQUET PASSION FLOWER
Passiflora 'Purple Haze'	PURPLE HAZE PASSION FLOWER
Periploca graeca	SILK VINE
Pileostegia viburnoides	CLIMBING HYDRANGEA
Schisandra arisanensis	SOUTHERN CHINA MAGNOLIA-VINE
Schisandra elliptifolia	MAGNOLIA VINE
Schisandra incarnata	RED MAGNOLIA-VINE

PERENNIALS

Acanthus species and hybrids	BEAR'S BREECH
Achimenes 'Harry Williams'	HARRY WILLIAMS ORCHID PANSY
Aplectrum hyemale	ADAM AND EVE
Alpinia pumila	DWARF GINGER
Alstroemeria hybrids	PERUVIAN LILY, LILY OF THE INCAS
Alstroemeria isabellana	ISABELL'S PERUVIAN LILY
X *Amarcrinum* hybrids	CRINODONNA
Anacamptis pyramidalis	PYRAMIDAL ORCHID
Aralia cordata	JAPANESE SPIKENARD
Asarum species and cultivars	WILD GINGER
Aspidistra species	CAST IRON PLANT
Astilboides tabularis	SHIELD LEAF
Begonia 'Eruption'	SPLIT-LEAF BEGONIA
Begonia grandis	HARDY BEGONIA
Begonia omeiana	SICHUAN BEGONIA
Begonia pedatifida	HARDY BEGONIA
Begonia sutherlandii	TRAILING BEGONIA
Boehmeria platanifolia	SYCAMORE-LEAFED FALSE NETTLE
Cardiocrinum cathayanum	HIMALAYAN GIANT LILY
Cardiocrinum cordatum	HEART-LEAF GIANT LILY
Cardiocrinum giganteum	GIANT LILY
Carex hachijoensis cultivars	JAPANESE SEDGE
Carex oshimensis cultivars	OSHIMA KAN SUGE
Carex phyllocephala 'Sparkler'	SPARKLER SEDGE
Carex scaposa	PINK FAIRY SEDGE
Carex siderosticha cultivars	BROAD-LEAF SEDGE
Cremanthodium reniforme	TRACTOR SEAT PLANT
Clematis fruticosa	MONGOLIAN GOLD BUSH CLEMATIS
Cautleya cathcartii, *C. gracilis*, *C. spicata*	HIMALAYAN GINGERS
Cheilocostus lacerus	CREPE GINGER
Crinum bulbispermum	ORANGE RIVER GINGER
Crinum x *powellii*	POWELL'S SWAMP LILY, CAPE LILY
Dactylorhiza species	MARSH ORCHIDS
Darmera peltata	UMBRELLA PLANT
Diphylleia cymosa	AMERICAN UMBRELLALEAF
Disporum longistylum, especially 'Green Giant', 'Night Heron'	FAIRY BELLS
Dysosma (*Podophyllum*) *delavayi*, many cultivars	MARBLED MAYAPPLE
Dysosma (*Podophyllum*) *pleianthum*	CHINESE MAYAPPLE
Epimedium wushanense	EVERGREEN EPIMEDIUM
Eucomis comosum 'Sparkling Burgundy'	SPARKLING BURGUNDY PINEAPPLE LILY
Farfugium japonicum, especially 'Giganteum'	LEOPARD PLANT
Fascicularia bicolor, including *F. b.* ssp. *canaliculata* (*F. pitcairnifolia*)	BROMELIAD
Gunnera magellanica	CREEPING GUNNERA
Gunnera manicata	GIANT RHUBARB
Gunnera tinctoria	CHILEAN RHUBARB
Hakonechloa macra	JAPANESE FOREST GRASS
Hedychium coccineum	GINGER LILY

Hedychium densiflorum	HARDY GINGER LILY
Hedychium greenei	RED BUTTERFLY GINGER
Hedychium 'Kin Ôgi'	KIN ÔGI GINGER LILY
Hedychium spicatum	PERFUME GINGER
Hedychium 'Tahitian Flame'	TAHITIAN FLAME GINGER
Hedychium 'Tara'	TARA GINGER
Helleborus foetidus	BEAR'S-FOOT HELLEBORE
Hemiboea subcapitata	GLOSSY FALSE SINNINGIA
Hibiscus laevis (H. militaris)	SMOOTH ROSE-MALLOW
Hibiscus 'Midnight Marvel'	MIDNIGHT MARVEL HIBISCUS
Hibiscus moscheutos and hybrids	CRIMSON-EYED ROSE-MALLOW
Hibiscus mutabilis	COTTON ROSE-MALLOW
Hosta, especially 'Blue Mammoth', 'Blue Wu', 'Empress Wu',	GIANT HOSTAS
'Eola Sapphire', 'Jurassic Park', 'Komodo Dragon', 'Mikado',	
'Sum and Substance, 'Sum of All', 'T Rex'	
Impatiens arguta	EAST HIMALAYAN BALSAM
Impatiens flanaganae	MRS FLANAGAN'S IMPATIENS
Impatiens omeiana	HARDY IMPATIENS
Impatiens pritzelii, including 'Sichuan Gold'	PERENNIAL IMPATIENS
Impatiens tinctoria	DYERS' BUSY-LIZZIE
Incarvillea delavayi	DELAVAY'S HARDY GLOXINIA
Incarvillea mairei var. *grandiflora*	LARGE-FLOWERED HARDY GLOXINIA
Incarvillea zhongdianensis	YUNNAN TRUMPET FLOWER
Iris Spuria hybrids	SPURIA IRIS
Ischyrolepis subverticillata	BROOM RESTIO
Kniphofia northiae	GIANT POKER
Ligularia dentata 'Britt-Marie Crawford'	BRONZE BIG-LEAF LIGULARIA
Ligularia przewalskii 'Dragon Wings'	DRAGON WINGS LIGULARIA
Ligularia stenocephala 'Osiris Cafe Noir', 'Osiris Fantasie'	BLACK LIGULARIA
Lobelia bridgesii	TUPA ROSADA
Lobelia tupa	TUPA, DEVIL'S TOBACCO
Lysimachia paridiformis var. *stenophylla*	CHINESE LOOSESTRIFE
Lysionotus pauciflorus	PURPLE-LIP LYSIONOTUS
Manihot grahamii	HARDY TAPIOCA
Melianthus major including 'Antonow's Blue', 'Purple Haze'	HONEYBUSH
Musa basjoo	HARDY BANANA
Musella lasiocarpa	CHINESE YELLOW BANANA
Petasites japonicus ssp. *giganteus*	GIANT JAPANESE SWEET COLTSFOOT
Phormium colensoi	COOK'S MOUNTAIN FLAX
Polygonatum biflorum (including var. *commutatum*)	GREAT SOLOMON'S SEAL
Polygonatum cyrtonema	HUSKY SOLOMON'S SEAL
Polygonatum huanum (P. kingianum)	
SIBERIAN SOLOMON'S SEAL, ORANGE-FLOWERING SOLOMON' SEAL	
Polygonatum x hybridum 'Betberg'	BETBERG'S SOLOMON'S SEAL
Polygonatum odoratum 'Byakko'	WHITE TIGER FRAGRANT SOLOMON'S SEAL
Ponerorchis graminifolia	SATSUMA PLOVER ORCHID
Rheum palmatum	GIANT ORNAMENTAL RHUBARB
Rodgersia aesculifolia	FINGER-LEAF RODGERSIA
Rodgersia pinnata, especially 'Chocolate Wings'	PINNATE RODGER'S FLOWER

Rodgersia podophylla	BRONZE-LEAF RODGERSIA
Roscoea species (many)	GINGER LILY, ROSCOE LILY
Seemannia 'Little Red'	LITTLE RED GLOXINIA
Seemannia sylvatica 'Bolivian Sunset'	BOLIVIAN SUNSET GLOXINIA
Sinningia 'Carolyn'	CAROLYN'S HARDY SINNINGIA
Sinningia tubiflora	TUBE-FLOWERED HARDY WHITE GLOXINIA
Sinopodophyllum (Podophyllum) hexandrum var. *chinense*	HIMALAYAN MAYAPPLE
Syneilesis aconitifolia	SHREDDED UMBRELLA PLANT
Syneilesis palmata	PALM-LEAF MAYAPPLE
Tricyrtis hirta, T. latifolia, T. macropoda	TOAD LILY
Zantedeschia aethiopica 'Swartberg Giant'	SWARTBERG GIANT CALLA LILY
Zantedeschia aethiopica 'White Giant'	WHITE GIANT CALLA LILY
Zingiber mioga, especially 'Dancing Crane'	MIOGA GINGER

FERNS

Adiantum venustum	HIMALAYAN MAINDENHAIR FERN
Arachniodes standishii	UPSIDE-DOWN FERN
Asplenium scolopendrium	HART'S-TONGUE FERN
Athyrium filix-femina (many cultivars)	LADY FERN
Athyrium niponicum (many cultivars)	JAPANESE PAINTED FERN
Coniogramme emeiensis 'Golden Zebra'	STRIPED MT. EMEI BAMBOO FERN
Coniogramme intermedia	BAMBOO FERN
Coniogramme japonica	JAPANESE BAMBOO FERN
Coniogramme intermedia	BAMBOO FERN
Cyrtomium caryotideum	DWARF NET-VEIN HOLLYFERN
Cyrtomium falcatum, especially 'Rochfordianum'	HOLLYFERN
Cyrtomium fortunei	ASIAN NET-VIEW HOLLYFERN
Dryopteris australis	DIXIE WOOD FERN
Dryopteris x celsa	LOG FERN
Dryopteris clintoniana	CLINTON'S WOOD FERN
Dryopteris goldiana	GIANT WOOD FERN
Myriopteris (Cheilanthes) lanosa	HAIRY LIP FERN
Phlebodium pseudoaureum (Polypodium areolatum)	BLUE RABBIT'S FOOT FERN
Polystichum braunii	BRAUN'S HOLLYFERN
Pteris wallichiana 'Taoshan Trail'	WALLICH'S GIANT TABLE FERN
Pyrrosia polydactyla	FIVE-FINGER TONGUE FERN
Selaginella apoda	MEADOW SPIKEMOSS
Thelypteris kunthii	ABUNDANT MAIDEN FERN
Woodwardia orientalis	ORIENTAL CHAIN FERN

BULBS

Arisaema species	COBRA LILY, JACK-IN-THE-PULPIT
Arum korolkowii	WEST ASIAN ARUM
Arum maculatum	CUCKOO-PINT

403

Arum nigrum	BALKAN BLACK ARUM
Canna glauca 'Panache'	PANACHE CANNA LILY
Dracunculus vulgaris	VOODOO LILY
Eremurus species and hybrids	FOXTAIL LILY, DESERT CANDLE
Eucomis species and hybrids	PINEAPPLE LILY
X Hippeastrelia 'Red Rover'	RED ROVER HIPPEASTRELIA
Hippeastrum x johnsonii	ST. JOSEPH'S LILY
Lilium auratum	GOLD-BAND LILY
Lilium duchartrei	DUCHARTRE LILY
Lilium formosanum	FORMOSA LILY
Lilium regale	REGAL LILY
Lilium "Rose Lily Series"	DOUBLE-FLOWERED LILY
Lilium speciosum	RUBRUM LILY
Lycoris chinensis	GOLDEN SURPRISE LILY
Lycoris incarnata	PEPPERMINT SPIDER LILY
Lycoris sanguinea	RED HEART LILY
Lycoris sprengeri	BLUE SPIDER LILY
Lycoris straminea (may be the same as *L. longituba*)	SURPRISE LILY
Lycoris x squamigera	RESURRECTION LILY
Nerine bowdenii	GUERNSEY LILY
Phalocallis (Cypella) coelestis	GOBLET FLOWER
Sauromatum venosum, especially 'Indian Giant'	VOODOO LILY

In addition to the bulbs listed above, there are hundreds of other exotic-looking bulbs (e.g., *Eucomis, Canna, Zantedeschia*) that are suitable for planting out in the garden in late spring for summer color and then digging up in the fall for storing dryish through winter. One popular summer bulb, *Caladium*, doesn't like our short, cool summers.

"Plant a garden in which strange plants grow and mysteries bloom." ~~ Ken Kesey

"ORNAMEDIBLES"

Ornamental plants with edible fruits or other parts. Or maybe these are best described as edible plants which are good looking enough for general landscaping.

TREES

APRICOT (*Prunus armeniaca*) [Puget Gold] – spring flowers, fall color
CHESTNUT (*Castanea sativa*) takes two to pollinate [Colossal, Dunstan, Eurobella]
CRABAPPLE (*Malus* hybrids) [such as 'Strawberry Parfait'] – spring flowers
DAMSON* (*Prunus domestica* ssp. *insititia*) – spring flowers
ELDERBERRY, BLACK/BLUE (*Sambucus nigra/S. nigra caerulea*) – late spring flowers
FIG (*Ficus carica*) [Brown Turkey, Chicago Hardy, Genoa, Lattarula (Italian Honey),
    Osborn Prolific, Peter's Honey, Violette de Bordeaux (Negronne)] — great structure,
    accent plant
FILBERT, HAZELNUT (*Corylus avellana* hybrids) takes two to pollinate [Gamma,
    Jefferson, Santiam, Yamhill] — autumn color; prune to show off structure
GUAVA, CHILEAN (*Luma apiculata* "hardy form") — evergreen foliage, beautiful bark
LAUREL, BAY/GRECIAN (*Laurus nobilis*) —shade tree, hedging, espalier, containers
MULBERRY, BLACK (*Morus nigra*) [Black Beauty, Kaester, Pakistan King,
    Persian, Sullivan, Thompson] — small accent tree; good fall color
MULBERRY, WHITE (*Morus alba*) [Beautiful Day, Oscars, Riviera, Shangri La]
MULBERRY HYBRIDS ['Collier' (*Morus alba* x *M. rubra*) ['Illinois Everbearing'
    (*M. alba* x *M. rubra*), 'Tehama' ("Giant White"), 'Wellington' ('New American')]
PAWPAW (*Asimina triloba*) [one self-fertile, otherwise hand pollinated:
    'Mary Foos Johnson', 'Mitchell', 'Overleese', 'Potomac', 'Prolific', 'Rebecca's Gold',
    'Shenandoah', 'Sunflower' (sf), 'Taylor', 'Taytoo', 'Wells'] — for shady gardens
PERSIMMON, AMERICAN (*Diospyros virginiana*) [especially 'Meader']
PERSIMMON HYBRIDS ['Keener', 'Nikita's Gift', 'Rossiyanka']
PLUM, EUROPEAN* (*Prunus domestica* ssp. *domestica*; includes prunes)
    ['Blue's Jam', 'Brooks', 'Coe's Golden Drops', 'Early Laxton', 'French Prune',
    'Imperial Epineuse' ('Imperial'), 'Italian Prune', 'Jam Session', 'Mt. Royal',
    'Sehome Italian Prune', 'Seneca', 'Stanley', 'Sugar', 'Valor', 'Yellow Egg']
PLUM, GREENGAGE* (not all "green"; *Prunus domestica* ssp. *italica*)
    ['Denniston's Superb', 'Green Gage', 'Imperial Gage', 'Reine Claude', 'Washington']
PLUM, MIRABELLE* (*Prunus domestica* ssp. *syriaca*) 'Mirabelle', 'Geneva Mirabelle',
    'Lorraine Mirabelle'
QUINCE (*Cydonia oblonga*)
QUINCE, CHINESE (*Pseudocydonia sinensis*) takes two to fruit
SERVICEBERRY (*Amelanchier alnifolia*) ['Martin,' 'Northline,' 'Smokey, 'Thiessen']
WALNUT, ENGLISH (*Juglans regia*) ['Belle Epine', 'Chambers No. 9', 'Colossal',
    'Dunstan', 'Eurobella', 'Franquette', 'Howard, Marigoule', 'Nevada', 'Precoce Migoule',
    'Regina Montis', 'Spurgeon', 'Wepster No. 2']

I have not included apples, pears, nor cherries. These, among all fruits grown in the western PNW, are the most seriously prone to pests and diseases. Although I have included some *Prunus* species (those marked * above), these, too, must be watched for issues.

SHRUBS

BLUEBERRY, ALASKAN (*Vaccinium alaskaense*)
BLUEBERRY, DWARF (*Vaccinium caespitosum*)
BLUEBERRY, LOW (*Vaccinium deliciosum*)
BLUEBERRY, OVAL-LEAF (*Vaccinium ovalifolium*)
BLUEBERRY, VELVETLEAF (*Vaccinium myrtilloides*)
"BLUEBERRY," MEXICAN (*Fuchsia arborescens* hybrid 'Blutini')
CHOKECHERRY, BLACK (*Aronia melanocarpa*)
CURRANT, BUFFALO (*Ribes aureum*)
CURRANT, BLACK (*Ribes nigrum*) 'Noir de Bourgogne' is historically used for making crème de cassis.
CURRANT, PINK (*Ribes vulgare*)
CURRANT, RED AND WHITE (*Ribes rubrum*)
GOJI, BOX THORN (*Lycium barbarum*)
GUAVA, CHILEAN (*Ugni molinae*)
GOOSEBERRY, EUROPEAN (*Ribes uva-crispa*)
HASKAP (*Lonicera caerulea var. emphyllocalyx*)
HONEYBERRY (*Lonicera caerulea var. kamtschatica*)
HUCKLEBERRY, EVERGREEN (*Vaccinium ovatum*)
HUCKLEBERRY, RED (*Vaccinium parvifolium*)
HUCKLEBERRY, THINLEAF (*Vaccinium membranaceum*)
LAUREL, GOLDEN BAY (*Laurus nobilis* 'Sicilian Sunshine')
LINGONBERRY (*Vaccinium vitis-idaea*)
JOSTABERRY (*Ribes* x nidigrolaria)
QUINCE, JAPANESE (*Chaenomeles speciosa*)
ROSEMARY (*Salvia rosmarinus* [*Rosmarinus officinalis*]) [choose hardiest cultivars]
SICHUAN PEPPERCORN, BLACK (*Zanthoxylum bungeanum*)
SICHUAN PEPPERCORN, RED (*Zanthoxylum armatum*)
WHORTLEBERRY, GROUSE (*Vaccinium scoparium*)
WINTER SAVORY (*Satureja montana*)

GROUNDCOVERS

CHAMOMILE, ROMAN (*Chamaemelum nobile*)
MINER'S LETTUCE (*Claytonia perfoliata*)
NEW ZEALAND SPINACH (*Tetragonia tetragonoides,* annual)
OCA (*Oxalis tuberosa*)
SICILIAN OREGANO, HARDY MARJORAM (*Origanum* x majoricum)
STRAWBERRY (*Fragaria* x ananassa)
STRAWBERRY, ALPINE (*Fragaria alpina, F. vesca*)
SWEET WOODRUFF (*Galium odoratum*)
THYMES (*Thymus*; many)

VINES

GRAPES (all American or American hybrids) ['Bluebell', 'Buffalo', 'Campbell Early', 'Canadice', 'Edelweiss', 'Himrod', 'Interlakken', 'Mars', 'Price', 'Reliance', 'Swenson Red', 'Valiant', 'Vanessa', 'Venus']

KIWI, HARDY (*Actinidia arguta;* tara vine, grape kiwi, baby kiwi)

KIWI, CHINESE (*Actinidia chinensis*; yang tao, sunny peach, strawberry peach)

KIWI, KOLOMIKTA (*Actinidia kolomikta*; Arctic Beauty)

KIWI (*Actinidia deliciosa*) need a male plant to pollinate several females

MASHUA (*Tropaeolum tuberosum*)

SCARLET RUNNER BEAN (*Phaseolus coccineus*)

PERENNIALS

ANISE HYSSOP (*Agastache foeniculum*)

CARDOON (*Cynara cardunculus*) (technically a biennial)

CHINESE ARTICHOKE (*Stachys affinis*)

CHINESE CHIVES (*Allium tuberosum*)

CHIVES (*Allium schoenoprasm*)

DAYLILIES, GOLDEN NEEDLES (primarily *Hemerocallis citrina, H. fulva, H. lilioasphodelus*)

FENNEL (*Foeniculum vulgare neopolitanum)*

GLOBE ARTICHOKE (*Cynara scolymus*)

SEA BEET (*Beta vulgaris* var. *maritima*)

HORSERADISH (*Amoracia rusticana*) especially the variegated form

JAPANESE PARSLEY (*Cryptotaenia japonica,* especially f. *atropurpurea*)

JERUSALEM ARTICHOKE, SUNCHOKE (*Helianthus tuberosum*)

LICORICE, WILD *(Glycyrrhiza lepidota)*

LOVAGE (*Levisticum officinale*)

MARSH WOUNDWORT (*Stachys palustris*)

OCA (*Oxalis tuberosa*)

OYSTERLEAF (*Mertensia maritima*)

PERENNIAL SWEET LEEK (*Allium ampeloprasum*)

PERPETUAL SPINACH (*Beta vulgaris* var. *cicla*)

POT MARJORAM (especially *Origanum onites* 'Aureum')

POTATO ONION (*Allium cepa* Aggregatum Group)

RHUBARB (*Rheum* x cultorum)

SAFFRON CROCUS (*Crocus sativus*)

SAGE (*Salvia officinalis*)

SEA KALE (*Crambe maritima*)

SHALLOTS (*Allium cepa* Aggregatum Group)

SICILIAN OREGANO, HARDY MARJORAM (*Origanum* x majoricum)

WALKING ONION, TREE ONION (*Allium* x proliferum)

WELSH ONION, JAPANESE BUNCHING ONION (*Allium fistulosum*)

YACÓN (*Smallanthus sonchifolius*)

EDIBLE ANNUAL FLOWERS

CALENDULA *(Calendula officinalis)*
IRISH MARIGOLD (*Tagetes tenuifolia*)
JOHNNY-JUMP-UPS *(Viola tricolor)*
NASTURTIUMS *(Tropaeolum majus)*
PANSIES *(Viola* x wittrockiana*)*

COLORFUL/TEXTURAL ANNUALS (and those treated as annuals)

BASILS, 'Purple Ruffles', 'Dark Opal'
BEET 'Macgregor's Favourite'
BRUSSELS SPROUTS 'Rubine'
CABBAGE Purple and Savoy Types
CARDOON
CHERVIL
CHINESE CHIVES
ENDIVE/CHICORY Red-Leafed Types
KALES: 'Blue Russian', 'Frosty', 'Russian Red', "Lacinato", 'Ragged Jack', 'Tuscan',
    'Palm Tree' ('Chou Palmier')
KOHLRABI 'Purple Vienna'
LETTUCE, Red-Leafed Types
NEW ZEALAND SPINACH
ORACHE (*Atriplex*, "Red Mountain Spinach")
PARSLEY, Curly Types
PERILLA
RHUBARB CHARD, Red-Stemmed Beet Leaf
SMALLAGE (Leaf Celery, Soup Celery)
SUMMER SAVORY
SWISS CHARD

SOURCES

Probably the final deciding factor as to what actually gets planted in your landscape: availability.

We have plenty of really good plant-oriented independent garden centers in the Pacific Northwest. Add to that the many big-box centers who regularly bring in some fun plants, and there is a wealth of good plant material available to home gardeners. If you trust a nearby brick-and-mortar store, then by all means, take your now-developed "short list" to them to see what they have and/or what they can order.

If your local plant sellers don't have it, review the catalog inventory of the mail-order specialists listed within the following pages. Specialty mail-order nurseries (some with a retail store, as well), often just mom-and-pop scale, offer choice plants that aren't available elsewhere.

I've emphasized Pacific Northwest operations. Not all of them actually breed or grow plants here in the PNW (especially the seed companies); but it does mean they are more in tune with what will actually grow here. Keep in mind that many of the plants in the multitude of lists here are available only in seed form. If you have zeroed in on a particular preferred plant and you can't find it from a "plant" company, do check the specialty seed companies before giving up. Don't be hesitant to call or e-mail with questions to determine just what you'll be getting, and when.

PLANTS

ADELMAN PEONY GARDENS
www.peonyparadise.com
Salem, OR
503.393.6185

A & D PEONIES
adpeonies.com
P.O. Box 2338
Snohomish, WA
360.668.9690
adpeonies@frontier.com

ANNIE'S ANNUALS & PERENNIALS
www.anniesannuals.com
Richmond, CA (not PNW)
888.266.4370

BAMBOO GARDENER LLC
www.bamboogardener.com
Seattle, WA
206.371.1072

BAMBOO GARDEN NURSERY
www.bamboogarden.com
North Plains, OR
503.647.2700

BLOOM RIVER GARDENS
www.bloomriver.com
39744 Deerhorn Road
Springfield, OR
541.726.8997

BROOKS GARDENS PEONIES
www.brooksgardens.com
6219 Topaz Street, NE
Brooks, OR
503.393.7999
brooksgardens@gmail.com

BURNT RIDGE NURSERY
www.burntridgenursery.com
432 Burnt Ridge Road
Onalaska, WA
360.985.2873
mail@burntridgenursery.com

CASCADIA IRIS GARDENS
www.cascadiairisgardens.com
3011 134th Ave NE
Lake Stevens, WA
425.770.5984

CHALK HILL CLEMATIS
chcfarm.com
Healdsburg, CA
707.433.8416
farmmgr@chalkhillclematis.com

CISTUS NURSERY LLC
www.cistus.com
Portland, OR
503.621.2233

CLINTON INC. BAMBOO GROWERS
www.clintonbamboo.com
Seattle, WA
206.242.8848
clintonbamboo@q.com

CONIFER KINGDOM
Silverton, OR
503.894.6123
www.coniferkingdom.com

DANCING OAKS NURSERY
www.dancingoaks.com
Monmouth, OR
503.838.6058

EDELWEISS PERENNIALS, INC.
www.edelweissperennials.com
29800 S Barlow Rd.
Canby, OR

FANCY FRONDS
www.fancyfrondsnursery.com
PO Box 1090
40830 172nd Street SE
Gold Bar, WA
360.793.1472; 206.707.4807

FAR REACHES FARM
www.farreachesfarm.com
Port Townsend, WA
360.385.5114

FOREST FARM
www.forestfarm.com
Pacifica, WA
541.846.7269

FRASER'S THIMBLE FARM
www.thimblefarms.com
Salt Spring Island, BC
250.537.5788
thimfarm@telus.net

GOODWIN CREEK GARDENS
www.goodwincreekgardens.com
Williams, OR
800.846.7359
goodwincreekgardens@gmail.com

GOSSLER FARMS NURSERY
gosslerfarms.com
Springfield, OR
541.746.3922
marj@gosslerfarms.com

HEATHS AND HEATHERS
http://www.heathsandheathers.com
631 E Pickering Road
Shelton, WA
360.427.5318
handh@heathsandheathers.com

HIGHLAND HEATHER
www.highlandheather.com
8268 S Gribble Rd
Canby, OR
503.263.2428

HYDRANGEAS PLUS
www.hydrangeasplus.com
Aurora, OR
503.651.2887

LEONINE IRIS
www.leonineiris.com
7051 S 126th St
Seattle, WA

MENDOCINO MAPLES
mendocinomaples.com
41569 Little Lake Rd.
Mendocino, CA
707.397.5731

MID-AMERICA GARDEN, LLC
www.beardedirisflowers.com
Salem, OR
503.390.6072
thomasjohnson@mid-americagarden.com

MOUNTAIN CREST GARDENS
mountaincrestgardens.com
402 Bridge St.
Fort Jones, CA
877.656.4035

PLANT DELIGHTS NURSERY
www.plantdelights.com
Plant Delights Nursery, Inc.
9241 Sauls Road
Raleigh, NC 27603 (not PNW)
919.772.4794
sales@plantdelights.com

RAINTREE NURSERY
raintreenursery.com
408 Butts Rd,
Morton, WA
800.391.8892
customerservice@raintreenursery.com

RIVER ROCK NURSERY
www2.rdrop.com/users/green/plantit/
19251 SE Hwy 224
Clackamas, OR
503.658.4047
Gretchenriverrock@gmail.com

SCHREINER'S IRIS GARDENS
www.schreinersgardens.com
3625 Quinaby Rd NE
Salem, OR
503.393.3232

SEBRIGHT GARDENS
www.sebrightgardens.com
7185 Lakeside Drive NE
Salem, OR
503.463.9615

SECRET GARDEN GROWERS
www.secretgardengrowers.com
29100 S. Needy Rd
Canby, OR
503.651.2006
Secretgrwr@aol.com

WHITMAN FARMS
www.whitmanfarms.com
3995 Gibson Rd NW
Salem, OR
503.585.8728

WILD GINGER FARM
wildgingerfarm.com
24000 S Schuebel School Rd
Beavercreek, OR
503.632.2338

ROSES

DAVID AUSTIN
www.davidaustinroses.com/us/
English roses, old garden roses, shrub, species, climbers, and modern roses.
800.328.8893
us@davidaustiroses.com

GREENMANTLE NURSERY
www.greenmantlenursery.com
Heritage/Old garden roses organically grown on their own roots in 2-gallon containers.
707.986.7504

HEIRLOOM ROSES
www.heirloomroses.com
St. Paul, OR
Own-root, container-grown English Legend, hybrid teas, floribundas, landscape roses, miniatures, climbers, David Austin, old garden roses, Buck roses, and Heirloom's own varieties.
503.538.1576, 800.820.0465

NORTHLAND ROSARIUM
northlandrosarium.com/
9405 S. Williams Lane
Spokane, WA
509.448.4968
Own root roses.
360.382.2055

PALATINE ROSES
palatineroses.com
2108 Four Mile Creek Road, RR# 3
Niagara-On-The-Lake, ON
Bare-root and potted roses.
905.468.8627

REGAN NURSERY
www.regannursery.com/
Grade #1 bare root roses.
510.797.3222

ROSES OF YESTERDAY AND TODAY
www.rosesofyesterday.com
Bare root old garden roses and selected modern roses; own root in one gallon pots shipped year-round.
831.728.1901

SELECT ROSES
www.selectroses.ca
22771 38 Avenue
Langley, BC
Own breeding and selected roses for the PNW.
604.530.5786
selectroses@shaw.ca

BULBS

B & D LILIES
www.bdlilies.com
PO Box 2007
Port Townsend, WA 98368
360.765.4341
dianna@bdlilies.com

BRENT AND BECKY'S
www.brentandbeckysbulbs.com
7900 Daffodil Lane
Gloucester, VA 23061
804.693.3966

CLACK'S DAHLIA PATCH
www.clacksdahliapatch.com
5585 North Myrtle Rd
Myrtle Creek, OR 97457
541.863.4501
info@claksdahliapatch.com

CLEARVIEW DAHLIAS
www.clearviewdahlias.com
20212 65th Ave. SE
Snohomish, WA 98296
425.486.6163
clearviewdahlias@gmail.com

DAHLIA BARN
www.dahliabarn.com
13110 446th Ave SE
North Bend, WA 98045
425.888.2155
info@dahliabarn.com

FLORET FLOWERS
shop.floretflowers.com
P.O. Box 281
Mount Vernon, WA
98273shipping@floretflowers.com
Dahlia varieties for cutting

JOHN SCHEEPERS, INC.
www.johnscheepers.com
23 Tulip Drive P.O. Box 638
Bantam, CT 06750
860.567.0838
customerservice@johnscheepers.com

THE LILY GARDEN
www.thelilygarden.com
35306 Northwest Toenjes Road
Woodland, WA 98674
360.253.6273
thelilygarden@aol.com

ODYSSEY BULBS
odysseybulbs.com
P.O. Box 382
South Lancaster, MA 01561
800.517.5152
mail@odysseyplants.com

OLD HOUSE GARDENS
www.oldhousegardens.com
4175 Whitmore Lake Rd., Ann Arbor, MI 48105
734.995.1486
help@oldhousegardens.com
Heirloom bulbs

SWAN ISLAND DAHLIAS
www.dahlias.com/index.aspx
995 NW 22nd Ave.
Canby, OR 97013
503.266.7711, 800.410.6540
info@dahlias.com

TELOS RARE BULBS
telosrarebulbs.com
P. O. Box 1067
Ferndale, CA 95536
telosrarebulbs@suddenlink.net

VAN ENGELEN, INC.
www.vanengelen.com
23 Tulip Drive P.O. Box 638
Bantam, CT 06750
860.567.8734
customerservice@vanengelen.com
Large quantity (wholesale/landscaper)

SEEDS

ADAPTIVE SEEDS
www.adaptiveseeds.com
25079 Brush Creek Rd
Sweet Home, OR 97386
541.367.1105
seed@adaptiveseeds.com

ALPLAINS
www.alplains.com
P.O. Box 489
Kiowa, CO 80117-0489
alandean7@msn.com

ANTONIO VALENTE FLOWERS
antoniovalenteflowers.ca
ON, Canada
antoniovalente@rogers.com
Specializing in flowers for cutting.

B & T WORLD SEEDS
www.b-and-t-world-seeds.com
Paguignan
34210 Aigues-Vives, France
00 33 (0) 4 68 91 29 63
Offering 35,000 listings

CHILEFLORA
www.chileflora.com
56 (9) 78597067
2 Sur 665, Dpto. 208
Talca, Chile
michail@chileflora.com

CHILTERN SEEDS
www.chilternseeds.co.uk
Bortree Stile, Ulverston
Cumbria LA12 7PB
England

FLORET
www.floretflowers.com
Mount Vernon, WA 98273
support@floretflowers.com
Specializing in flowers for cutting.

HIGH MOWING ORGANIC SEEDS
www.highmowingseeds.com
76 Quarry Road
Wolcott, VT 05680
802.472.6174
Emphasis on vegetable seeds.

J. L. HUDSON
www.jlhudsonseeds.net
Star Route 2, Box 337
La Honda, CA 94020

JELITTO SEEDS
www.jelitto.com
Specializing in seeds for perennials.

JOHNNY'S SELECTED SEEDS
www.johnnyseeds.com
955 Benton Avenue
Winslow, ME 04901
877.JOHNNYS (877.564.6697)
Organic vegetables, flowers, and herbs.

NARGS SEED EXCHANGE
North American Rock Garden Society
membership program
www.nargs.org/seed-exchange
537 Taugwonk Road
Stonington, CT 06378-1805

NZ SEEDS
nzseeds.com.nz
P. O. Box 435
Rangiora, South Island 7440
New Zealand
+64 3 3121635
sales@nzseeds.co.nz

PLANT WORD SEEDS
www.plant-world-seeds.com
St. Marychurch Rd, UK, TQ12 4SE
+44 1803 872939
info@plant-world-seeds.com

RENEE'S GARDEN SEEDS
www.reneesgarden.com
6060 Graham Hill Rd.
Felton, CA 95018
888.880.7228
Including certified organic.

SEEDHUNT
www.seedhunt.com
Seeds of Western native plants and more.

SEEDS OF CHANGE
www.seedsofchange.com
3209 Richards Lane
Santa Fe, NM 87507
888.762.7333
Organic seeds.

SILVERHILL SEEDS AND BOOKS
www.silverhillseeds.co.za
Suite 18, Bergvliet, 7864
Cape Town, South Africa
+27 21 705 4226
info@silverhillseeds.co.za

STEMS FLOWER FARM
edgebrookfarm.ca
Cookstown, ON, Canada
Specializing in flowers for cutting.

SUMMER HILL SEEDS
summerhillseeds.com
13505 Hamilton Pike Road
Whittington, IL 62897
618.248.2010
robin@summerhillseeds.com

TERRITORIAL SEED COMPANY
www.territorialseed.com
PO Box 158
Cottage Grove, OR 97424
800.626.0866
Emphasis on vegetable seeds.

UPRISING SEEDS
uprisingorganics.com
2208 Iron St.
Bellingham, WA 98225
360.778.3749
uprisingseeds@riseup.net
Certified organic.

VICTORY SEEDS
www.victoryseeds.com
P.O. Box 192
Molalla, OR 97038
503.829.3126
Open-pollinated and heirloom garden seeds.

WEST COAST SEEDS
www.westcoastseeds.com
3925 64th Street
Delta, BC V4K 3N2, Canada
customerservice@westcoastseeds.com

WILLIAM DAM SEEDS
www.damseeds.ca
279 Hwy 8 Dundas, ON L9H 5E1, Canada
905.628.6641
www.damseeds.com

Also check "Native Plants & Seeds," next section

NATIVE PLANTS & SEEDS

BRITISH COLUMBIA

B.C.'S WILD HERITAGE PLANTS
www.bcwildheritage.com
47330 Extrom Rd
Sardis, BC V2R 4V1, Canada
604.858.5141
bcwildplants@uniserve.com
Plants and seeds.

FRASER'S THIMBLE FARMS
www.thimblefarms.com
175 Arbutus Rd
Salt Spring Island, BC, V8K-1A3, Canada
250.537.5788
thimfarm@telus.net
Plants and seeds.

PACIFIC RIM NATIVE PLANT NURSERY
www.hillkeep.caplants@hillkeep.ca
44305 Old Orchard Rd
Chilliwack, BC V2R 1A9 Canada
604.792.9279
Plants and seeds.

WASHINGTON

CLASSIC NURSERY & LANDSCAPE
www.classicnursery.com
12526 Avondale Rd NE
Redmond, WA 98052
425.885.5678
classicnursery@msn.com
Plants and seeds.

ELEMENTAL PLANTS
www.treeslivehere.com/elemental-plants.html
13008 37th Ave NE
Seattle, WA 98125
206.518.1855
elemental@clearwire.net
Plants and seeds.

FANCY FRONDS
www.fancyfronds.com
40830 172nd St SE
PO Box 1090, Gold Bar, WA 98251
360.793.1472
fancyfronds@gmail.com
Plants, especially temperate ferns.

FRIENDLY NATIVES PLANTS AND DESIGN
www.friendlynatives.net
2464 Happy Valley Rd
Sequim WA
206.387.5943
lissa@friendlynatives.net
Plants and design. By appointment.

FRINGE NURSERY
www.fringenursery.com
Seattle, WA
206.495.5585
fringenursery@gmail.com
Plants and seeds.

GO NATIVES! NURSERY
www.gonativesnursery.com
2112 NW 199th
Shoreline, WA 98177
206.542.1275
gonatives@gmail.com
Plants and seeds.

**INSIDE PASSAGE NATIVE SEEDS &
PLANT SERVICES**
www.insidepassageseeds.com
P.O. Box 639
Port Townsend, WA 98368
800.361.9657
forest@insidepassageseeds.com
*Native seeds of the Salish Sea bioregion (Puget
Sound), coastal areas north and south.*

**MSK RARE & NATIVE PLANT
NURSERY AT THE KRUCKEBERG
BOTANIC GARDEN**
www.kruckeberg.org/msk-nursery/
20312 15th Ave NW
Seattle, WA 98177-2166
206.546.1281
kbgf@kruckeberg.org
Plants and seeds.

NORTHWEST MEADOWSCAPES
northwestmeadowscapes.com
1240 W. Sims Way, #218
Port Townsend, WA 98368
503.705.1357
info@northwestmeadowscapes.com

PLANTS OF THE WILD
www.plantsofthewild.com
PO Box 866
Tekoa, WA 99033-0866
509.284.2848
Kathy@plantsofthewild.com
Plants and seeds.

SHORE ROAD NURSERY
www.shoreroadnursery.com
Port Angeles, WA
360.775.8984
shoreroadnursery@gmail.com
Wholesale and retail (by appointment only).

SOUND NATIVE PLANTS
www.soundnativeplants.com
PO Box 7505
Olympia, WA 98507
360.352.4122
cathy@soundnativeplants.com
Plants and seeds.

TADPOLE HAVEN NATIVE PLANTS
www.tadpolehaven.com
20322 197th Ave NE
Woodinville, WA 98077
425.788.6100
growing@tadpolehaven.com
Plants and seeds.

**WASHINGTON ASSOCIATION OF
CONSERVATION DISTRICTS (WACD)
PLANT MATERIALS CENTER**
www.wadistricts.org/plant-materials-
center.html
16564 Bradley Rd
Bow, WA 98232
360.757.1094
wacd@ncia.com
pmcsales@clearwire.net
Plants and seeds.

WATERSHED GARDEN WORKS
www.watershedgardenworks.com/
2039 44th Ave
Longview, Washington 98632
360.423.6456

**WOODBROOK NATIVE PLANT
NURSERY**
woodbrooknativeplantnursery.com
5919 78th Ave NW
Mail: 1620 59th Ave NW
Gig Harbor, WA 98335-7568
253.857.6808 or 253.225.1900
woodbrk@harbornet.com
Plants and seeds.

OREGON

ALDER VIEW NATIVES
28315 SW Grahams Ferry Rd
Wilsonville, OR 97070
503.570.2894
natives1@gte.net

ALTHOUSE NURSERY
www.althousenursery.com/Welcome.html
5410 Dick George Rd
Cave Junction, OR 97523
541.592.2395
althousenursery@frontiernet.net
One and two year old native seedlings.

BOSKY DELL NATIVES
www.boskydellnatives.com
23311 SW Bosky Dell Ln
West Linn, OR 97068
503.638.5945
boskydellnatives@aol.com

CHAMPOEG NURSERY INC
www.champoegnursery.com
9661 Yergen Rd N
Aurora, OR 97002
503.678.6348
info@champoegnursery.com
Plants and seeds.

DOAK CREEK NATIVE PLANT NURSERY
www.doakcreeknursery.com
83331 Jackson Marlow Rd
Eugene, OR 97405
541.484.9206
doakcreeknursery@gmail.com
Container plants.

ECHO VALLEY NATIVES
www.echovalleynatives.com
18883 S Ferguson Rd
Oregon City, OR 97045
503.631.2451
info@echovalleynatives.com

FORESTFARM AT PACIFICA
www.forestfarm.com
14643 Watergap Rd
Williams, OR 97544
541.846.7269
plants@forestfarm.com
Plants.

HUMBLE ROOTS FARM & NURSERY
www.humblerootsnursery.com
Mosier, OR 97040
503.449.3694
humbleroots@gorge.net

KLAMATH-SISKIYOU NATIVE SEEDS
klamathsiskiyouseeds.com
klamathsiskiyou@gmail.com

KRUEGER'S TREE FARMS
www.kruegertree.com
PO Box 32
North Plains, OR 97133
503.647.1000
sales@kruegertree.com

OAK POINT NURSERY
www.oakpointnursery.com
2300 Independence Wy
Independence, OR 97351
503.399.7813
tim@oakpointnursery.com
Containers and plugs available.

PLANT OREGON
www.plantoregon.com
8677 Wagner Creek Rd
Talent, OR 97540
541.535.3531
dan@plantoregon.com
Specimen sized B and B native trees and shrubs a specialty.

SCHOLLS VALLEY NATIVE NURSERY
www.schollsvalley.com
4036 NW Half Mile Ln
Forest Grove, OR
503.624.1766
info@schollsvalley.com
Container and bare-root plants.

SISKIYOU RARE PLANT NURSERY
www.siskiyourareplantnursery.com
2825 Cummings Rd
Medford, OR 97501
541.772.6846
customerservice@srpn.net

VALLEY GROWERS NURSERY & LANDSCAPE
valleygrowers.com
30570 S Barlow Rd
PO Box 610
Hubbard, OR 97032
503.651.3535
vlygrwrs@web-ster.com
Plants and seeds.

WILLAMETTE GARDENS
www.willamettegardens.com
3290 SW Willamette Ave
Corvallis, OR 97333
541.990.0948
natives@willamettegardens.com

WHITMAN FARMS
www.whitmanfarms.com
3995 Gibson Rd NW
Salem, OR 97304
lucile@whitmanfarms.com

"Always try to grow in your garden some plant or plants out of the ordinary, something your neighbors never attempted. For you can receive no greater flattery than to have a gardener of equal intelligence stand before your plant and ask, 'What is that?'" ~~ Richardson Wright

PUBLIC GARDENS WITH PLANT SALES

BRITISH COLUMBIA

BUTCHART GARDENS
www.butchartgardens.com
800 Benvenuto Avenue
Brentwood Bay, BC V8M 1J8
250.652.4422

UBC BOTANICAL GARDEN
botanicalgarden.ubc.ca
https://www.ubc.ca/about/
2329 West Mall
Vancouver, BC V6T 1Z4
604.822.2211

WASHINGTON

BELLEVUE BOTANICAL GARDEN
bellevuebotanical.org
12001 Main Street
Bellevue, WA 98005
425.452.2750

BLOEDEL RESERVE
bloedelreserve.org
7571 NE Dolphin Drive
Bainbridge Island, WA 98110
206.842.7631

HERONSWOOD GARDEN
heronswoodgarden.org
31912 Little Boston Rd NE
Kingston, WA 98346
360.297.9620

**HIGHLINE SEATAC BOTANICAL
GARDENS**
highlinegarden.org
13735 24th Ave S
SeaTac, WA 98168
206.391.4003

KRUKEBERG BOTANIC GARDEN
www.kruckeberg.org
20312 15th Ave NW
Shoreline, WA 98177
206.546.1281
kbgf@kruckeberg.org

**RHODODENDRON SPECIES
BOTANICAL GARDEN**
rhodygarden.org
PO Box 3798
Federal Way, WA 98063
253.838.4646
info@rhodygarden.org

**UW BOTANIC GARDENS,
WASHINGTON PARK ARBORETUM,
CENTER
FOR URBAN HORTICULTURE**
botanicgardens.uw.edu/center-for-urban-
horticulture/
botanicgardens.uw.edu/washington-park-
arboretum/
2300 Arboretum Drive E
Seattle, WA 98112
206.543.8800
uwbg@uw.edu

VOLUNTEER PARK CONSERVATORY
www.volunteerparkconservatory.org
1400 East Galer Street
Seattle, Washington, USA 98112
206.684.4743
foc@volunteerparkconservatory.org

OREGON

LEACH BOTANICAL GARDEN
leachgarden.org
704 SE 122nd Ave.
Portland, OR 97236
503.823.9503
info@leachgarden.org

HOW TO FIND
MORE INFORMATION
ALONG WITH PLANT PHOTOS
ON THE INTERNET

There is no one good book with photos to illustrate every plant mentioned in these many lists. There is, however, a way to look at everything. And it's better than any book.

1. Go to **www.google.com** (other search engines, such as Bing, work similarly, although not exactly the same).

2. In the Search field, type in the *botanical name* (NOT common name) and any cultivar name of the plant (no need for capital letters; no need for single quotes around the cultivar name).

3. Enclose the botanical name in quotation marks ("xxx").

4. Hit the "Enter/Return" key or click on the "Search" button. You will get a listing of "web pages."

5. Click on the hypertext "Images" tab that is above or below the search field box. A selection of "thumbnail" photos will appear. Sometimes you'll get MANY thumbnails, sometimes but a few, depending on the popularity of the plant. Unfortunately in many cases, if there aren't a good amount of photos of your exact plant, Google will flesh it out with photos of related or look-alike plants; in which case, be wary.

6. You can expand each photo with a click on the photo itself or you can open up the webpage from which the photo was taken, for more information.

"When I'm writing, I think about the garden, and when I'm in the garden I think about writing. I do a lot of writing by putting something in the ground." ~~ Jamaica Kincaid

INDEX TO PLANT LISTS

About the Author

Mr. Seals has spent fifty years in the horticulture/gardening industry. And longer as a passionate hobby gardener.

He earned his degree in Environmental Horticulture and took that into landscape design and retail and wholesale nursery management. A slight curve in his career later led him into the publishing business with time spent at *Sunset Books* and *Sunset Magazine.* Another bend in the path took him through the large-scale commercial end of the seed industry, with time at the largest seed companies in the US — the biggest wholesale horticultural company, a wildflower seed company, the biggest mail-order seed company, and the biggest packet seed company.

The last many years included teaching at four colleges, training Master Gardeners in three states, and consulting to home gardeners and professional growers. This is when he made lists, many of which ended up in this book.

Now he spends time doing a little teaching, a little consulting, and as much gardening as possible. With just enough writing to fill the spare time.

The author is solely responsible for the accuracy of the plants in this list, their spelling, their current botanical name, and their appropriateness to the lists wherein they may be contained (the latter allowing for subjective judgment in some cases).

Made in United States
Orlando, FL
20 September 2022

22620133R00243